TAKING THE HIGH ROAD

TAKING THE HIGH ROAD

COMMUNITIES ORGANIZE FOR ECONOMIC CHANGE

DAVID B. REYNOLDS

M.E.Sharpe
Armonk, New York
London, England

Cover photo by Rick Reinhard, Photographer.

Library of Congress Cataloging-in-Publication Data

Reynolds, David B., 1963-
Taking the high road : communities organize for economic change / David B. Reynolds.
    p. cm.
Includes bibliographical references and index.
ISBN 0-7656-0744-1 (alk. paper) ISBN 0-7656-0745-X (pbk. : alk. paper)
    1. Social justice—United States. 2. Social justice—Europe. 3. Capitalism—United States.
4. Capitalism—Europe. 5. United States—Economic policy—1993- 6. United States—Economic
policy—Citizen participation. 7. Political participation—United States.
    I. Title.

HN65 .R47 2002   2001049164
303.3′72′0973—dc21   CIP

Printed in the United States of America

Contents

List of Tables

Acknowledgments

As this book has been many years in the making, the contributions of many have helped to make it a reality. Much of the inspiration has come from the many informal discussions, debates, and real-life activism in which I have been fortunate to participate in over the years. I would especially like to acknowledge all the wonderful activists involved in the mushrooming living wage movement. I have spoken to many at conferences and over the phone. With living wage laws passed in nine municipalities, our own Michigan movement has been an inspiration from dedicated activists. I have been continuously surprised by the number of people who have "come out of the woodwork" at the crucial times in our living wage organizing. Also special thanks to Jen Kern at ACORN's Living Wage Resource Center for our productive partnership on producing our living wage campaign organizer handbook and for many informative phone conversations and e-mails.

Hal Stack, director of the Labor Studies Center at Wayne State University, allowed me the time and encouraged me to research and write this book. His continued faith in my interests and abilities has allowed me to pursue labor-community coalitions both in my writing and as an on-the-ground organizer. Hal's able and caring direction of the center and the dedication and friendship of all the staff—including Steve Babson, Michelle Fecteau, and Geri Hill— have made the past five years at the center a wonderful experience.

In 1999, the Blue Mountain Center generously provided an all-expense-paid month at their facility in New York State's beautiful Adirondack Mountains. This artist's retreat allowed me the time and energy to complete drafts of Part I. Thanks to the staff and other participants for your warmth and inspiration. Also for Part I, Jonas Pontusson at Cornell University provided helpful feedback and encouragement on drafts of several chapters.

My wife, Susan Santone, patiently endured my many hours of singular concentration on producing this manuscript while other matters were allowed to fall by the wayside. Thanks for your feedback, encouragement, and warm, sustaining friendship.

Thanks to the staff at M.E. Sharpe who made the production of this book a smooth process.

Finally, I cannot thank enough the activists with whom I interacted and interviewed in preparing the book. They provided more than simple research data. They took time out of their busy schedules to meet with a stranger and to share ideas and often pages of materials. Their friendship, reflections on politics, and outright enthusiasm for what they are doing animate this book.

1

Introduction

Paving the High Road; Closing the Low Road

Dear David Reynolds,

It is a great time to be an American. Our nation is experiencing the longest economic upturn in its history. Unemployment is at record lows. Wages are up, inflation is down. Companies are investing in the future. . . .

So were the words of President Bill Clinton in a mass mailing fund-raising letter sent on behalf of the Democratic Party. For years the nation's media has informed the American public that they have never done better. Even in the face of an economic downturn by 2001, the pundits continued to predict recovery as the "fundamentals" remained solid. Yet, a deep secret exists at the heart of our nation's political and economic debates. It is the reality faced by millions of Americans for whom the "miracle economic boom" meant mounting insecurity and stress. Despite nearly a decade of steady economic growth, one out of six Americans, and one out of four children, still lived below the federal poverty line in 2000—the same portion as a decade ago. While real wages made modest gains at the end of the 1990s, their buying power had not come near to the highs of the 1970s. Nearly one out of three Americans no longer works at a traditional full-time job. While many seek alternative work arrangements, a growing number of workers are involuntarily part time and contingent. By 2000, the personal savings rate was at an all-time low, while personal debt hit record

high. Today Americans work at their jobs 165 more hours per year than they did in 1972. Most telling, recent polls reveal the vast majority of Americans saying that corporations, the engines of our nation's official prosperity, have "too much power."

While official media coverage and political debates attempt to maintain this reality, across the country coalitions of labor, religious, and community groups are beginning to raise questions and to demand change. Each year they win concrete local and state victories. Most important, as they develop, these groups lay the seeds of an emerging grassroots movement for fundamental economic change. This book examines that movement.

Our work is rooted in the belief that the basic problems confronting our society originate in an economic system that increasingly produces greater wealth and power for the few while dismantling the standard of living and quality of life for the many. It is a system that steadily mortgages our society's social and environmental future. It is a system that a growing number of people of this country are organizing to change.

Many books have outlined an alternative economic path through intellectual models and specific policy proposals. However, *Taking the High Road* explores a new economic agenda not as an abstraction, but as lived experience. In Part I, we examine the possibilities for change drawn from Europe's daily realities. By comparing existing European policy and debates to the dominant agenda found in the United States, we demonstrate that much of the "common sense" wisdom about how our economy "must" operate in an age of "globalization" is simply nonsense. While Europe hardly presents a utopia, its differences to the United States demonstrate how mass social movements and deliberate public policy can shape capitalism.

In Part II, we show how a movement for economic change is developing within the United States today. We tell the story of grassroots coalitions of labor, community, and religious groups who have not only begun to organize for progressive alternatives, but have also won concrete victories. The details in Part II offer a kind of activists' guide toward organizing for economic change in one's own community. Be it living wages, community-driven regional development plans, corporate responsibility legislation, battling Wal-Mart and suburban sprawl, or organizing contingent workers, grassroots activists are coming together in broad coalitions to fight for a better future. Our focus will move from the local to state to national levels as we identify the basic agenda and grassroots building blocks for what promises to become the great movement for economic democracy in the early twenty-first century. It is with the goal of helping to foster such a movement that our work is written. In this introduction, we summarize the basic ideas that undergird what follows.

High-Road Economics 101

The current economic path is not the only possibility. Even within the world of capitalism, our society's current direction marks only one option. Throughout the book we distinguish between "low road" and "high road" versions of the seemingly monolithic capitalist system. The difference between these two business paths opens possibilities for progressive alternatives to push American capitalism in a far more socially and environmentally friendly direction. Such a move can also steer our economy toward greater economic democracy.

In our work as labor educators, we use the following exercise to open discussions of the differences between high- and low-road management strategies. Listed below are twelve ways that major American companies can and do use to increase their bottom line.

Twelve Ways to Make a Profit

New Products
Expand Overseas Production
Worker Training
New Ad Promotions
Outsource to Low-Cost Suppliers
New Work Methods
Wage Concessions
Acquisitions and Mergers
Increase Prices
New Technology
Sell Assets
Seek Government Assistance

Any good-size firm will likely have all of these elements active. However, management clearly sets priorities—emphasizing some strategies over others. In our exercise, we ask workers to go through the list twice. The first time they choose the priorities that maximize job security for all workplace-level employees. The second time, they brainstorm which strategies top management actually prioritizes. While specific results vary, typically the two lists end up as follows.

Best for Workers

New Products
New Technology
Worker Training
New Work Methods

CEOs Actually Favor

Expand Overseas Production
Outsource to Low-Cost Suppliers
Wage Concessions

Acquisitions and Mergers
Increase Prices
Sell Assets
Seek Government Assistance

While pursuing either sublist will deliver clear profits, the two strategy groups have a clearly different impact on workers and the community. The first list potentially melds the health of the firm to the well-being of the workforce and society. By contrast, the second list treats workers as a cost to be reduced and the community as something from which to seek independence. To pursue the first list requires companies to make significant investments in order to enjoy a payoff down the road. By contrast, actual CEOs often push strategies that require few up-front expenditures and that promise fast returns. While such actions can deliver quick paper profits in the short run, they often mortgage the future of both the company and the community in the long run. The first list exemplifies what we call the high road; the second represents a contrasting low road.

For reasons that we will explain during the course of this book, American capitalism is increasingly traveling down the low road. Both current governmental policies and the financial framework within which U.S. firms operate push and reward corporate strategies that seek an ever-increasing immediate bottom line. Even worse, the efforts of U.S. business and political leaders today to spread the "gospel of free trade" only serve to further institutionalize low-road priorities at a global level.

Companies following the low road focus on reducing costs. That ultimately means cutting labor costs through some combination of wage concessions, increased overtime, outsourcing to low-wage suppliers, overseas plants, temporary and part-time work, downsizing, and union busting. Since such actions produce an increasingly demoralized and unmotivated workforce, low-road companies have to further centralize skill and brain work into the hands of the trusted few. When directed by a management with low-road priorities, even strategies such as new work methods and new technology can simply serve as mechanisms to deskill work, gain further control over workers, speed up the work pace, and manage by stress. Low-road firms prioritize quantity over quality. Their competitive edge comes from the relatively cheap sticker price of their products or services sold in mass quantities.

However, while a product's actual price tag may be relatively low, the true costs of the low road typically prove far greater than the "savings." Low-road strategies cut immediate, surface expenditures by transferring the costs of business operations onto workers, the community, and often the future of the firm. The low road celebrates increasing inequality as firms split the labor market into a privileged few and a highly exploited many. Companies pursuing actions designed around short-term horizons and paper profits do not consider the long-term impact on either society or the environment. When such "externalities" hit home as financial crises or environmental disaster, the public pays the costs of mass layoffs, closures, and cleanups. Yet, no firm can ultimately escape its link to the society within which it operates. Any economic historian knows that the Great Depression of the 1930s was a demand-side crisis. The stock market bonanza and high corporate living of the 1920s had so skewed the distribution of wealth in this country that American workers could not buy the products they produced. Once consumer demand fell behind production, companies reacted with a classic low-road approach: They cut immediate costs by laying people off. Yet, with a growing number of workers out of a job, demand shrank even more—leading to a steady cycle of more layoffs and ever-decreasing demand.

Just in terms of a company's individual future, get-rich-quick strategies often do not pay off in the long run. The U.S. auto industry, for example, was caught savagely in the 1970s and 1980s when Japanese competition flooded into U.S. markets. The origins of the crisis date back to the 1940s and 1950s when the Big Three auto makers, ignoring advice from United Auto Workers leaders, canceled their four-cylinder product lines to focus entirely on bigger, poorly made cars that delivered higher profit margins. U.S. firms continued with these exclusive priorities even after products such as the Volkswagen Bug pointed to warning signs. The Japanese successfully entered the U.S. market precisely by using longer-term strategies. They offered cheap, fuel-efficient, low-profit cars as a way of entering the market. Once they had established a loyal customer base, the Japanese then gradually moved up the product line to more expensive, and hence more profitable, cars. In a similar way, foreign producers have acquired many segments of the U.S. electronics mass market from American firms that prioritized high-profit military technology at the expense of consumer products.

The choice between the low and high road is not simply a question of business competition, but the very fundamental direction of society. America's increasing pursuit of the low road lies behind a wide range of social malaise—be it the growing gap between rich and poor, the shrinking middle, increased ecological damage, or simply the ever more stressful and unfulfilling lives experienced by more and more Americans.

Fortunately, another economic path exists. Firms can compete over the superior quality of their product and services rather than surface price. Managers who pursue such a high road seek to increase the value of their investments, rather than cut short-term costs. Thus, workers become assets to be cultivated and developed, rather than costs to be minimized. By investing in workers and empowering them as partners in running the business, high-road firms benefit from employees who can contribute far more than simply a pair of hands. Companies ultimately make money by the far greater value that skilled and empowered workers add to the inputs they are given.

Well-paid, motivated workers also have the skills and input that allow companies to incrementally adjust to a changing economic environment. A high-road firm is far more flexible and adaptable than one locked into an "us versus them" relationship with its employees. Since firms on the high road partner with

their workforce, unions become assets. Study after study has made clear that unionized workplaces are more productive because workers have a greater voice in the workplace and a greater sense of basic security. High-road firms also draw benefits from the collective resources found in a prosperous and organized community. By seeking long-term, sustainable business practices, high-road firms can also prove far more environmentally friendly since more of the full costs of company actions are factored into the decision-making process.

A clear case can be made that the high road benefits not only society, but, in the long run, the firm as well. Indeed, as we will show in Part I, comparison of the long-term economic health between the United States and Western Europe suggests that even by capitalist criteria the high road pays off better over the long haul. Even within the United States, the high road can win awards. For example, *Fortune* magazine awarded its 2000 top employer of the year to the Container Store—a retail firm with a decidedly different business strategy from the low-road norms pursued by Wal-Mart and other superstores. To attract and retain the best-quality employees, the Container Store pays wages 50 to 100 percent above the industry average. By valuing its employees, the company cut annual worker turnover to 28 percent in an industry that averages three-quarters of all employees a year. With workers staying on the job, the firm is able to invest in training and skill development. With more capable workers, the store chain has relaxed the traditional management hierarchy so that frontline workers can interact with customers with the knowledge and skills normally associated with management. The Container Store shares all sales and other firm financial information with its employees. It also routinely gathers store managers together to discuss business plans. A summary of these meetings is sent to all employees. The end result of these high-road practices is stores that are able to attract customers by offering quality customer service well beyond the poor industry norms.

While the U.S. economy offers many individual

firm examples of high-road practices, our economic structures, business culture, and public policies do not support such strategies. When left to their own devices, few firms will take the high road since the low road is far more readily available. The high road may deliver a larger economic pie, but the low road provides management exclusive control over how the existing pie is distributed. Furthermore, the high road is a collective, not individual, strategy. For example, extensive worker training is very difficult for most individual firms to pursue. The infrastructure can be expensive, and trained workers can always leave. As we will see in Europe, the most effective worker-training programs are organized at the societal level. Similarly, small- to medium-sized firms face cost and other hurdles in adopting new worker-friendly technology. The best modernization solutions network firms and build alliances with community groups and institutions. And experience shows that the best technology is only as good as the training levels of the workers who use it. In short, high-road companies do not go it alone. They cross-fertilize with related firms. They work in partnership with an organized workforce and community. And they rely on quality services provided by active government policies around physical infrastructure, training and education, economic planning, resources and land-use planning, and an overall high quality of life.

Based on private ownership of the economic means, capitalism holds an inherent bias toward the low road. Those who own property have the power to determine how that property is used. The low road reinforces management's unilateral authority, while the high road can be traveled only by ultimately sharing power. However, even among the capitalist nations, America stands out for its lack of collective thinking. Our nation's official entrepreneurial mythos celebrates the "rugged individualist." The low road also flows as the natural outcome of our society's distinctive worship of the "free market." When business and policy makers blindly follow the lead of the market's "invisible hand," they leave opportunities for collective high-road practices fall by the wayside.

Two decades of supply-side economics have left our nation only further stuck in a low-road spiral.

Thus, setting our economy toward a high-road future requires grassroots organizing. While activists can build ties of cooperation to firms already oriented toward a high road, it is up to unions, community organizations, religious leaders, and governments to establish the institutional framework that makes the high road the rule, not the exception. Ultimately, most companies will discover more socially and ecologically responsible business practices only to the degree that society closes low-road options and provides collective opportunities for the high road. In other words, it is up to grassroots movements and government policy to push and pull our economy toward a more sustainable future.

It is this opportunity for mobilizing community action that is most attractive about the concept of the high road. High-road capitalism is still capitalism—with all the inherent contradictions between those who own the wealth and those who create it. Steering our economy down the high road, however, requires building progressive social and political power. Not only does the high road require firms to share a far greater piece of the economic pie, but also it asserts a greater popular voice in how the pie is made. By organizing for the high road, people can establish the community's basic right to participate in deciding its economic destiny. When placed in progressive hands, the high road is the path toward ever-increasing economic democracy.

Organizing for the High Road Is Happening Now: A Summary of the Book

The struggle for the high road is not simply an abstraction, but an emerging reality. This book breaks into two parts to examine concrete, on-the-ground practices emerging in the United States today and those already practiced in Europe. We will summarize the two parts in reverse order.

The basis of our hope for a high-road future in

the United States lies in the activism emerging across the country today. This nascent grassroots movement for economic democracy is the focus of the second part of this book. We begin Part II with chapter 7's examination of one of the most promising signs of grassroots change—the mushrooming living wage movement. More than any other recent local policy reform effort, living wage activism points to the coalition seeds of a broad movement for economic democracy. Chapter 8 offers an example of how activists in two Wisconsin communities connected single-issue campaigns into more long-term and comprehensive visions and institutions for their region's economic future. In chapter 9, we move to the state level to examine how grassroots coalitions are fighting for corporate subsidy accountability, fairness in contingent work, and increases in the minimum wage.

Organized labor has historically been one of the great social forces for progressive economic change and economic justice. In chapter 10, we explore how the American labor movement is reorganizing to re-establish its central role as a force for economic democracy. While the goals of social justice motivated the great social awakenings of the past, in the twenty-first century ecological survival adds an equally powerful necessity prompting grassroots change. Unfortunately, social justice organizing and the environmental movement do not always connect. Chapter 11 explores how the emerging battles over our nation's unsustainable land-use practices offer a promising avenue for uniting these two great prongs of progressive activism.

Chapter 12 brings together the policy ideas raised throughout the book by offering a sample of what a national agenda for high-road economic change might look like. We also explore some of the signs as to why such a national movement for fundamental economic change is by no means an empty pipe dream, but a possibility to organize for. Finally, economic change can only happen with political change. In chapter 13, we explore how the American political system is structured to undermine progressive change and how

activists today are organizing to overcome these obstacles and establish progressive political power.

Part II ends by pointing to bold possibilities. Most Americans, however, even those on the left, rarely consider the United States suitable terrain for fostering wholesale societal change. Part I sets the stage for seeing such potential within current U.S. activism by prying open the possibilities for large-scale economic change suggested by already existing contemporary capitalism. While not utopia, European capitalism nevertheless differs in important ways from American practices—ways that point to high-road directions. Not only, for example, do German workers elect half their companies' board of supervisors and Swedes enjoy access to a wide range of public wealth, but these countries have been socially and economically successful precisely by violating the holy "truths" of U.S. capitalism. This reality raises important possibilities of what other capitalist sacred cows might be placed into question. Indeed, as we will see, debates within the European left point to bold possibilities for pursuing economic democracy. The strength of the European experience comes from the fact that, while the details may have to differ, the general principles behind European practices are perfectly applicable to the United States. Current American policies come from political decisions, not economic imperatives. Indeed, as we will argue in chapter 6, in certain respects, the United States is uniquely qualified to carry forward an agenda of progressive economic reform. Part I prepares the reader to approach the activism covered in Part II ready to consider the bold possibilities of what may come.

A Tale of Two Railway Stations: An Introduction to Part I

One summer evening in inner-city Detroit, we took a visiting German family to a local Tigers baseball game. To reach the old stadium, we had to drive through an underpass connected to the former Detroit railway station. Our German guests seemed quite confused by the sight of this long-abandoned relic from the city's heyday. There sat a once-mag-nificent twenty-story building, with crumbling hand-carved stone masonry and broken Victorian windows. "Why doesn't anyone use that building?" one of our guests innocently asked. "Aren't there a lot of home-less people in this city?" We had to explain that in America, not only buildings are abandoned, but en-tire cities. The decaying shell of the railway station stood as a monument to the crumbling city that sur-rounded it—a victim of years of corporate disinvest-ment. Detroit, home of the auto industry, had only two remaining assembly plants within city limits. The rest, along with most of the white population, had moved to the suburbs. And the process of disin-vestment continues as developers' bulldozers tear up more fertile farmland—pushing suburban flight far-ther and farther from the urban core.

Several years before this incident, I visited the main rail station in Frankfurt, one of Germany's major cities. While General Motors' war against public transportation had shut down the Detroit sta-tion long ago, in Frankfurt the commuter rail lines were bustling with traffic. Emerging from the busy rail station, I strolled through modest, yet well-kept, blocks of buildings and neighborhood stores. Later, I was shocked to be told by some German students that they considered this neighborhood the "poor and seedy part of town." There were none of the usual American signs of social devastation—abandoned buildings, homeless people, crumbling streets. In-deed, in my travels throughout Europe, I never found the American equivalent of a vast urban slum. While Europe certainly has its inequalities and poor people, the ability to abandon entire neighborhoods and cit-ies seems distinctly American. A journey into the German countryside proved an equal culture shock. Despite the higher population density, German cit-ies are surrounded by open vistas of farmland dot-ted with tightly defined villages and towns. The vast sprawl of shopping malls and housing developments that congests life in the United States is simply not a common feature of much of Europe.

The United States and Germany are two of the world's leading capitalist countries. However, as the aforementioned images suggest, U.S. capitalism and German capitalism are clearly not identical. In the United States, a less-fettered capitalism has been allowed to pursue the low road with abandon, rela-tive to Germany's more high-road-oriented "social market." Clearly politics makes a difference. The often stark contrast between American and European cities reflects, in part, the difference in influence between our New Deal liberalism and full-blown social democracy.

European social democracy, the dominant politi-cal agenda put forward by Europe's labor movements, is one of the best-kept secrets in American politics. Generally speaking, the media establishment only mentions Europe in the context of how supposed American economic success contrasts with European troubles. "See, they must become more like us," the message goes. Unfortunately, progressive writers have generally not offered a countervision. Currently, only two works are available in English specifically summarizing the history of European social democ-racy: one has to be imported from England; the other, while excellent, is one thousand pages long.[1] The last American book that set out explicitly to use Eu-ropean reality to critique American policies for a general audience was Robert Kuttner's work pub-lished in 1984.[2] The dearth of popular information about Europe reflects, in part, our nation's general self-centeredness promoted by our media and offi-cial culture. However, it also reflects traditions within the American left that have tended to view Euro-pean social democracy as a sellout to the original dreams for fundamental social change. At their worst, the major social democratic parties have indeed be-come part of the establishment that they were origi-nally organized to overthrow. However, as we will explore in Part I, where its roots are the deepest, so-cial democracy advanced agendas so different from U.S. practices that they can hardly be written off as just another variation on the capitalist theme. Rather, they provide critical tools for conceiving of funda-mental progressive change.

Information on Europe does exist in English. It simply is not available to a general audience. Within academia, the study of international political economy has been particularly fruitful in producing an entire literature for examining European economic and social policies. The bulk of these researchers are sympathetic to social democratic aims and generally see European experiences as having lessons for Americans. Unfortunately, this rich literature remains largely locked away in our nation's research libraries. In the unlikely event that the average progressive activist or general reader even encounters these works, titles such as *The Limits of Social Democracy: Investment Politics in Sweden* are hardly likely to get a second glance. Yet, this excellent academic work details decades of Swedish policy debates that took seemingly unquestionable management and market prerogatives and turned them into topics of public debate and action.[3] Our task is thus to make the lessons of this valuable literature available to a general audience.

In the first three chapters, we use Sweden, Germany, and Austria to illustrate the degree to which capitalism has been shaped by the political forces of strong labor movements and a people-oriented politics. Although the U.S. economy did well during the postwar boom years, these countries displayed equal or superior economic performances with decidedly better social results. Their examples demonstrate that even within capitalism, society faces choices in how to organize basic welfare and economic activity. In each chapter, we will draw out the principles relevant for application to an American context.

We undertake our overview with the realization that today, European social democracy faces major challenges for its future. Indeed, no small number of American observers pointed to current European troubles to gleefully pronounce how the American model marks Europe's future. In chapters 5 and 6, however, we draw the opposite conclusion. It is true that the old ways alone are no longer adequate. However, rather than narrowing the terrain for economic reform, the current economic impasse actually points to broad possibilities for widening reforms into realms that include basic capitalist prerogatives. Economic democracy must become the rallying cry of a progressive resurgence—whether in the United States or Europe.

We end Part I by considering the obstacles and possibilities for pursuing such an agenda in the United States. The relative lack of social democratic policies and institutions in this country comes not from some kind of fixed American exceptionalism. Rather, the twentieth century witnessed a series of specific compromises in which a liberal agenda displaced more profound calls for economic reform. These results, however, came from historical constellations of forces that only partially carry into the present day. They also left behind a series of economic and social stresses and strains that today are increasingly visible in the lives of most Americans. The battle is political, not economic. Indeed, we will end chapter six by identifying several ways in which, from a strictly economic standpoint, the United States is in a unique position to lead the world to a progressive economic future.

Part I

European Social Democracy Points Toward the High Road

1

Social Citizenship:
Lessons from Sweden

For over two decades, progressives have had to withstand an antigovernment crusade that has spread throughout American politics. While politicians and businesspeople decry the excesses of government and its "burdensome" taxation, average Americans are bombarded with antigovernment propaganda—witness such nightly news specials as "The Fleecing of America," which focused on government, not corporate, waste. The onslaught has been so continuous that many activists have become shy about defending so-called big government. Yet, as the ongoing reality of social democratic politics in Scandinavia makes clear, it is precisely by championing more extensive and universal public programs that progressives can effectively roll back the right wing's social budget cuts and tax-breaks-for-the-rich agenda.

The Scandinavian countries of Sweden, Norway, and Denmark form the classic examples of social democracy. All three are characterized by strong labor movements, large and developed welfare states, and high living standards. Among the three countries, Sweden provides the most famous example of social democratic dominance. The Swedish labor movement is the strongest in the world. Today, nine out of ten Swedish workers are union members. The union movement is centralized into three major union federations, which tend to complement, rather than compete with, each other. The political party formed by the labor movement, the Social Democratic Labor Party (SAP), has governed Sweden for roughly 80 percent of the time period since Sweden introduced universal suffrage in 1909. Between 1936 and 1976, the party enjoyed forty unbroken years with a social democrat as prime minister. Sweden offers the best living image of what happens to a country when working people and their social movements set the budget priorities of government. Before delving into the details of current policies, we should first review the historical context in which social citizenship arose in the first place.

Social Democracy's Rise to Power

The Swedish labor movement began in conditions that, on the surface, hardly seemed conducive to social democracy. In the mid-nineteenth century, Sweden was an underdeveloped and peripheral nation of farmers. An impoverished peasantry and emerging working class confronted a centralized state that banned them from politics through laws requiring property to vote.

Backwardness, however, gave way to world leadership. The country's rapid industrialization produced a society of classic class divisions. As a displaced rural population swelled the ranks of a rapidly growing working class, the Swedish labor movement overcame early defeats to become one of Europe's strongest. Unlike in the United States, where the legacy of decentralized craft-unionism competed with industry throughout the first half of the twentieth century, the Swedish labor movement built strong industry-based unions centralized into a single federation, the Trade Union Confederation (LO). For decades this federation conducted collective bargaining at a national level, which set the basic terms of wages and work conditions for most of the nation.

The twin battles for union organizing and the right to vote (given a century later than to white men in the United States) fostered a powerful, class-conscious political movement. After World War I, the SAP emerged as the nation's largest party, with "Labor Communes" (local social democratic clubs) active in communities across the country. Unlike the Socialist Party in the United States, it had no rivals for working-class loyalty. With no universal suffrage until 1909, none of the elite parties had developed a mass base similar to the Republican and Democratic machines. The centralized Swedish state also did not provide the kind of patronage spoils that the two main U.S. parties used to build grassroots armies. Within the Swedish working class wage differentials were not as pronounced as elsewhere. At the same time, the nation's middle class was weak and fragmented. With the state church as part of officialdom, religion did not present the same political force as it did in other parts of Europe or in the United States. No rival Christian democratic labor movement emerged in Sweden. Mechanisms that the wealthy used to divide and conquer the working class in the United States, such as nationalism and racism, were also not as potent in Sweden.

Key to social democratic dominance, however, was its ability to build coalitions. Internally, the movement produced a high level of unity. The labor federation and SAP developed strong ties of mutual support. The party itself avoided a great deal of the factionalism between reform and revolutionary camps that characterized much of the European labor movement. Early on, the reform voice held sway. However, the party's leadership avoided a polarizing course of action and maintained appeals to its left.

The key to political power came from the party's ability to build coalitions outside its own ranks. Although the largest party in Sweden, the social democrats did not originally have the political strength to govern alone. The breakthrough came in the 1930s when the social democrats were able to form a coalition government with the Agrarian Party. Unlike many other parts of Europe, Sweden's peasant class had developed a high degree of autonomy and political independence. The social democrats in Sweden were able to ally with this homegrown farmer populism. At the base level, Sweden's working class often came directly from agrarian backgrounds. At the governmental level, the social democrats traded away socialist calls to nationalize private property in return for Agrarian support for crisis measures intended to lift the nation out of the global Great Depression. By contrast, elsewhere in Europe, elite parties absorbed peasant politics under their own direction. Indeed, small farmers provided one of the recruiting grounds for fascism. In Sweden, social democratic-agrarian cooperation lasted well into the 1950s, allowing the social democrats to become the nation's dominant political force.

When economic changes steadily decreased the agrarian population, social democracy was able to remain the dominant force by building new alliances with the emerging groups of white-collar workers. Through universal social policies that appealed to professional lifestyles, the Swedish social democrats wedded the new middle class to the Swedish welfare state. Extensive investments in public-based human services also meant that many who worked in the growing service sector became literally dependent on the welfare state for their jobs.

Social democracy also benefited from a strong, yet politically divided, capitalist class. The nation with the strongest labor movement also has the most organized capitalist class. To counter the organizational unity of the growing unions, Swedish employers established the Swedish Employers Federation (SAF) as a centralized body capable of negotiating on behalf of Swedish business. This organization is backed by close to one thousand employer political bodies, which try to influence public opinion and politicians.[1] During the early part of the twentieth century, employers engaged in a vicious battle against the growing labor movement. According to historian Klas Åmark, "from 1890 and mid-1930, more than any other country Sweden was a nation of lock outs and strikes."[2] That ended with the Saltsjöbaden Accords of 1938. Swedish employers struck a peace with organized labor. Employers recognized Swedish unions and agreed to a system of collective bargaining in return for union acceptance of employers' right to manage the company, dropping socialist aims to eliminate or control capitalism. Following the organization of the Congress of Industrial Organizations (CIO), a similar peace emerged in the United States. However, the Swedish deal kept the state out of collective bargaining, while also laying the groundwork for a far more extensive welfare state and social democratic influence over the economy.

Several factors helped encourage Swedish employers' overall acceptance of social democracy. Industry has always played a dominant role in the business community, leaving trade and finance in a secondary position. Large export-producing firms came to dominate both the Swedish economy and the SAF. These firms rely on a highly efficient and highly skilled workforce for their competitive edge. As we will see below, social democracy was able to gain the cooperation of these capitalists by developing a high-wage economy and welfare state that explicitly favored large, efficient firms. Within this deal social democratic political dominance was aided by the business community's political fragmentation. Although Swedish employers are well organized, their political power is divided among several bourgeois parties. Social democracy rose to dominance through selective coalitions that kept these parties divided. Thus, while workers and corporations came to the United States New Deal through the political direction of a corporate party, the Democrats, in Sweden the deal came under the dominance of a party built by the labor movement.

The Social Democratic Welfare State

By accepting capitalism, Swedish social democracy was able to take a significant portion of the wealth created by the postwar capitalist boom and convert it into a welfare state that has been the envy of many progressives worldwide. This accomplishment did not come all at once. Indeed, in the 1950s, the Swedish welfare state looked quite modest. Comparisons to the United States New Deal would not have revealed large disparities. Today, however, Sweden may look to many American observers as an entirely different world.

A Tale of Two Children

Consider two people growing up—one in the United States; the other in Sweden. The quality of the American's childhood will largely revolve around the job market luck and skill of his or her parent(s). The parents' jobs will determine whether or not the family has access to health care, where they live, the quality of the schools, and the child's overall standard of living. The pay level and leave policies of the parents' employers will also play a large role in determining who raises the child—will a parent stay home, can either use flexible schedules, can they afford high-priced child care providers, or must they arrange makeshift supervision? Access to recreation facilities will also depend on the ability of the parents to pay. When the child graduates from high school, his or her parents' income will play a big role in determining the possibilities of college and whether the child will have to work her or his way through higher education. A young adult who cannot or does not want to go to college will find only modest alternative training opportunities and most will be based on ability to pay. Once the American has completed his or her working life, the quality of his or her retirement will depend on the presence or absence of an employer-provided pension and/or personal savings to supplement a social security pension that has not kept pace with the rise in the cost of living. At any point in this child's life a turn of bad luck through sickness, disability, divorce, or unemployment could shatter his or her standard of living and make him or her dependent on degrading charity-type state aid.

By contrast, the Swedish child will experience a more secure life far less dependent on the job market and the parents' employers. The family will receive access to full public health care and quality schools regardless of the parents' job or even employment status. Rent subsidies and cooperative housing will add choices to where the family can live. Meanwhile, the family's ability to maintain its standard of living will be aided automatically by a universal child allowance paid by the government for each child. Few children who have a parent who works full time will live in poverty, because wage levels in Sweden have far less room for poverty-level jobs. Because both parents have access to universal paid parental leave and child sickness leave, and because they are guaranteed at least five weeks of paid vacation by law, the child, especially as an infant, will likely see more of his or her parents than his or her U.S. counterpart will. When the parents cannot be at home, the child will be cared for at an affordable quality public day care center or in the home of a child minder employed by the municipal government. When the child graduates from high school, he or she will have the option of attending a university or enrolling in a workforce skills training program—both of which are free to all citizens. When the Swede retires, his or her entire pension will come through a generous public system paid for by employer payroll taxes. Any tragedy that strikes during the Swede's life will prove less likely to lower his or her standard of living. In the event of illness, disability, divorce, or unemployment, he or she will receive some form of income support from the state nearly equal to his or her prior wages. And this aid will come with far less of the social stigma that is found in the United States, because it comes as a basic right of citizenship.

Social Spending: Sweden and the United States

The above sketches reveal a range of noticeable differences between the U.S. and Swedish welfare states. Table 1.1 further illustrates the contrast in summary form.[3]

The first noticeable difference lies in the levels of support. Sweden simply has more. For example, retirement pensions constitute the single greatest financial outlay of any welfare state. While the Swedish public pension system ranks as one of the most extensive in the world, U.S. social security ranks among the lowest of industrialized countries. In 1980, for example, U.S. social security retirement benefits amounted to 5 percent of the gross domestic product (GDP). Private pensions accounted for 1.4 percent, while government employee pensions were another 1.5 percent. By contrast, that same year, 9.7 percent of Sweden's GDP went into public pensions—another 1 percent into government employees and a mere half a percent into private employer plans.[4] The public expenditures are higher in Sweden because in the 1950s the social democrats created a supplement to the basic and inadequate flat-rate retirement scheme. The Supplementary Pension Fund (ATP) pension plan was mandatory for all employees in the private and public sector. As the long-term trend in the United States is for less employers to provide pension benefits, a growing number of future retired U.S. workers will likely have to depend on social security. By contrast, most Swedish workers are still covered by the supplementary system. Unlike private employer plans whose funds support private investment logics, the ATP system was established as public funds. Originally, these funds were directed away from investment in the stock market and toward public projects such as housing construction.

Similar differences in generosity and use apply to the unemployment insurance system. In the United States, the actual terms vary by state. However, generally speaking, the benefits will be well

Table 1.1

Social Spending—United States versus Sweden

	United States	Sweden
Pensions	Social Security 5% GDP 1 out of 4 live in poverty Based on work or marriage	Public System 10% GDP Poverty among elderly unknown House parent & education qualify
Unemployment	1991 recession 42% covered Much lower than wages 26 weeks' duration	75% qualify (includes students) At least 80% of original pay Well over 1 year Public training program Relocation assistance Constitutional right to a job
Housing	Mortgage tax credit "Ghetto" high-rise	90% rental housing public funded Pensions fund low-cost housing Constitutional right to housing
Work life	No vacation or sick-day laws	5 weeks paid vacation (up to 8) 14 days/year paid sick days
Family policy	12 weeks unpaid leave Parents primary care for 55% infants	15 months paid leave either parent Paid leave for sick child/relative up to 60 days/year 95% infants have parents for primary care
	AFDC—now forced work 50% solo parents in poverty Child tax credit	Child allowance (min. $916/year per child) 5% solo parents in poverty Public supported child care centers and home care
Health care	Private with state money for poor and seniors 40 million no coverage 12% of GDP = health industry	Full public system Automatic coverage 6% of GDP
Higher education	Student loans	Free accesses plus stipend
Total spending (1980)	22% GNP (one of lowest) 1/6 work for state 1/6 work for private service comp. 25%+ budget military	40% GNP (one of highest) 1/3 work for state 12% budget military
Principles	Depend on market Charity Band-Aids	Independence from market Universal right Preventative—full employment, low social ills
Taxes	Personal up to 38% Corporate taxes low	Personal up to 50% Corporate taxes low
Politics	Tax revolt	Support for spending remains high

Sources: Data derived from Gøsta Esping-Andersen, *The Three Worlds of Welfare Capitalism* (Princeton: Princeton University Press, 1990); National Social Insurance Board of Sweden, *Social Insurance in Sweden 1999* (Stockholm).

below people's prior salary, roughly 30 to 40 percent of the original, and will last a relatively short time (twenty-six weeks). Furthermore, fewer and fewer people qualify. During the 1991 recession, only 42 percent of the unemployed received benefits. That proportion went as low as one-quarter in some states. By contrast, in Sweden, by 1980 the number qualifying had risen to at least 65 percent—only a quarter of the unemployed received no benefits. Furthermore, the amount of the compensation was much closer to a person's prior wages—80 percent as of 1998.[5] The payments can last up to 300 days, 450 for workers fifty-seven years or older. Also noteworthy, the unemployment insurance funds are not administered by the government, but by forty "societies" organized by the labor movement. Unlike in the United States, the jobless person who no longer qualifies for unemployment can tap into other income programs. Sweden's labor market cash allowance not only picks up the jobless not covered through unemployment insurance, but is also available to people entering or reentering the labor market. Thus, a person who graduates from school or a training program and cannot find work immediately will receive public aid until a job is available.

The same kind of social programs can take on a different meaning in Sweden compared to the United States. In America, the term "public housing" paints a picture of dilapidated buildings in sinister-looking urban conditions. Indeed, the stereotypical public housing high-rises were built as much to warehouse and ghettoize the poor as to provide a solution to the nation's shortage in affordable housing. By contrast, a significant section of Sweden's population live in "public housing." Almost all pensioners and about half of all renters live in cooperative rental units—most of which were built by the government.[6] In response to Sweden's housing shortage, the social democrats pledged in 1964 to build 1 million dwellings in the next decade. They largely succeeded. Although critics pointed to their often drab uniformity and subur-

ban isolation (the same can be said of American private suburban developments), this housing stock was of generally high quality and available to everyone, unlike in the United States. Instead of creating marginalizing ghettos, Swedish policy made public housing a common fact of life. Those who own their own home have also been linked to governmental housing policy. Between 1946 and 1985, 90 percent of all housing produced in Sweden involved state loans. Such a commitment reflects an awareness that having a place to live is a basic human right. Indeed, in 1974, the new Swedish constitution guaranteed all citizens the right to housing, as well as a job and an education.

The contrast between poor-quality charity in America and common-place basic rights in Sweden applies to many other areas as well. The United States has no laws mandating or regulating sick leave from work. An individual has to rely on the policy of his or her employer. Only in the case of catastrophic illness will a person receive public assistance, and the low levels of support will likely drop the person into poverty. Swedish law guarantees paid sick leave. No medical certificate is needed until after the first week. Not surprisingly, in Sweden, workers average twenty sick days a year; in the United States, only five days.[7] Swedish workers can also qualify for leave not related to illness, such as for pursuing education or trade union work.

Sweden has a range of state programs that simply do not exist in the United States. Most notably, the United States is the only industrialized country that does not have a national health care system. In Sweden, the bulk of health care comes through county council–run health care institutions paid for by local tax levies. The national insurance system provides dental coverage and pays for prescription drug costs beyond modest levels.[8]

The United States also does not have a fully public system of higher education. By contrast, all Swedish universities are free public institutions. Sweden's state-run worker-training system contrasts sharply to the absence of any governmental provisions for systematic worker training in the United States. With no governmental leadership, American companies are often notoriously reluctant to invest in worker training since workers may simply leave the firm. Swedish employers and unions participate in a government-led training network that has been established systematically across the country.

On behalf of workers, Swedish law places other restrictions and requirements on employers that simply do not exist in the United States. The United States has no laws requiring paid vacation time. Sweden mandates five weeks, and unions often negotiate additional time. In the United States, lawmakers only just recently established a limited right to family-related leave from work. Under our Family Medical Leave Act, workers at firms with at least fifty employees are guaranteed up to twelve weeks of *unpaid* leave from work to tend to their families. Many employers have not respected the law. A governmental commission also found that many people cannot afford to take an unpaid leave. Only 1.2 percent of workers went on family leave during the eighteen months studied by the commission. Sixty-four percent of those who said they wanted to go on leave but did not, cited financial limitations. Almost half of all workers are not covered, either because they have worked at their current work site for under a year or because their place of employment has fewer than fifty workers.

Sweden recognizes not only a parent's right to care for his or her sick child, but also the right to be home when the child is young. Mothers and fathers are eligible for *paid* parental leave of 450 days per child, which can be drawn on up through that child's eighth year. The first 360 days, the parent is paid at 80 percent of his or her wages. If a parent did not work previously, he or she still can qualify for leave at a flat rate of pay. For more short-term occasions, the state will pay a parent, relative, or other person to care for a sick child. This temporary parental benefit provides sixty paid days annually per child under twelve. While American parents face high day care costs, Swedish parents have access to public day care centers and publicly funded home day care providers. Fees are set on a sliding scale based on a parent's ability to pay. On average, parents' fees are approximately 5 percent of a family's income for both lone parents and two-parent families. Already by the 1980s, three-quarters of Swedish preschool children were supported with the help of public measure. Almost half of all families used public day care, including 70 percent of solo parent families. Only 10 percent of Swedish families relied on private care. While U.S. conservatives would decry such governmental "intrusion" into family life, Sweden's combination of genuine family leave rights and public-supported child care options has actually resulted in more parental care. In 1991, roughly 95 percent of Swedish infants were cared for exclusively by their parents, compared to only 55 percent in the United States. For 20 percent of U.S. infants, their primary care came from child care centers or family day care. The average time these infants spent outside the home in these arrangements averaged more than forty hours per week.[9]

What Makes Sweden's Welfare State Distinct?

Scale

Obviously, with a much more extensive range of services and more generous benefits, Sweden's welfare state is much larger than in the United States. In 1980, before the Reagan cuts, the United States spent roughly 22 percent of its GDP on social spending. By contrast, the Swedish proportion in 1981 was almost double that—40 percent.[10] Figures for 1985 show one out of every three Swedish workers employed by the government. This contrasts to one out of six in the United States. Roughly two-fifths of these American government workers were employed in the military.[11]

Universalism

Contrasting the overall size, however, highlights only one distinguishing characteristic. Most European countries spend far more on their welfare states than the United States does, yet they can differ in important ways from the Swedish social democratic model. Indeed, the principles behind Sweden's welfare state are as important as the level of financing.

First, and most important, Sweden built its social democratic welfare state around the principle of universalism. Swedes qualify for government services as a basic right of citizenship. This contrasts to the liberal model found in the United States, which emphasizes targeting and means-testing. Typically, U.S. public assistance goes only to those who can meet certain financial requirements. Contrasting government child supports in the United States and Sweden illustrates the difference. In the United States, the now-defunct Aid to Families with Dependent Children (AFDC) program focused solely on poverty-stricken families—typically with single parents. This meager aid came with the stigma of receiving a "government handout" and was administered by a system that reinforced the "charity" character of the welfare. Sweden, by contrast, provides a universal child allowance and housing allowance to all families on having a new child.[12] Single parents who face particular financial difficulties are then eligible for additional maintenance allowances. Since all families receive the basic allowance, there is no stigma—financial support to help raise a family is an expected basic human right.

The difference between universal versus targeted, means-tested programs has important political consequences. It is ironic that Americans, who experience the lowest tax burden in the industrial world, are, at least in terms of the official political debates, the most upset about paying taxes and government spending. However, the contrasting principles behind Swedish and American social spending help explain this seeming contradiction. In the United States, right-wing politicians have led the charge against social spending by scapegoating so-called welfare dependency. It has been easy to attack AFDC since only a minority of the population received it. And since the majority of the white recipients re-

mained invisible in the eyes of many politicians and the media, "welfare reform" has involved no small use of racism. Thus, in the United States, the conservatives in both parties try to pit "taxpayers" against "those people." Yet, in Sweden, such right-wing dynamics are not possible. Since all taxpayers qualify for the universal programs, they all have a vested interest in them. In Sweden, when the social democrats lost power in the late 1970s, the ruling coalition of bourgeois parties simply could not generate a serious budget-cutting momentum.

Indeed, among the industrialized countries, the strongest right-wing antigovernment movements come from the two countries with the most modest and least social-democratic welfare states: the United States and Britain. By contrast, in the most social-democratic countries, in those with the greatest "big government," the equivalents of Reaganism and Thatcherism have made the fewest inroads. In the United States, this same political dynamic of universalism has similarly made Social Security, our one major universal American social program, a sacred cow. Right-wing efforts to undermine it have been unable to attack it frontally. Instead, conservatives have sought to foster public cynicism about the system's future through largely exaggerated claims about its impending insolvency.

Social democratic universalism also contrasts with the social conservative influences found in continental Europe. In this case we use the word "conservative" to refer to the classic, feudal notions, not the politics of the Republican Party. Such classical conservatism views society as inherently divided into different classes and status groups—often established this way by divine ordinance. In the face of growing working-class organizing, European conservatives sought to coopt working people into social provisions that would reinforce class and status divisions.

Bismarck's social-insurance system in turn-of-the-century Germany offered a pioneering example of conservative welfare policies. Bismarck's system divided wage earners by legislating distinct programs for different status groups and classes. The system accentuated an individual's position in life. It also attempted to bind his or her loyalty to the central state. By contrast, social democratic universalism moves in an opposite direction by providing equal access as a common right of citizenship.

High Standards

Sweden's welfare state has also been built around high standards. Universal education training, housing supports, child care, and so forth, offer more than simply minimal survival needs. They establish basic services, protections, and opportunities integral to Swedish society. What Americans would call a middle-class lifestyle is available to all Swedes through their universal welfare state. These high standards have the political impact of helping to ally new sectors of white-collar and salaried workers to the welfare state.

By contrast, the U. S. welfare state offers largely minimal payments and modest services. It aims to provide only a most basic safety net that avoids social catastrophe. AFDC, for example, even when coupled with food stamps and other programs, still left recipient families in poverty. Because of inadequate welfare support and low-wage jobs, almost half of all female householders with children under eighteen lived in poverty in 1992.[13] By contrast, the disposable income of single-parent households in Sweden was only slightly less than that of comparable two-parent households—about 90 percent for families with one or two children.[14] This relative equality comes from Sweden's greater cash transfers as well as higher wages and greater employment opportunities.

Universal programs can create problems. If the funds allocated to programs prove too modest, then the individual benefits may prove too low to maintain popular support. Indeed, in the United States, conservatives typically attempt to privatize popular government programs such as Social Security and public education by first cutting funds so that the quality of the programs erodes over time. In Swe-

den, the original basic flat-rate universal pension proved insufficient for people to live on. In such a situation, those with the individual resources would have secured private pension supplements. Such actions would have created a two-tiered system of those dependent on the state pensions and those relying on private employer-provided resources. Politically, such a dynamic could have split the social democrats' voting base between those who wanted to pay for public pensions and those who did not.

In response to this kind of dilemma, parts of Sweden's universal system do graduate benefits based on income. This solution can be seen at two levels in the Swedish pension system. The supplemental ATP system retains the public character of the pension system. However, the benefit levels vary, based on past income earnings (and, today, also past parental and household work). To offset the danger that those at the bottom of the income ladder will not have a sufficient retirement income, the state provides a retirement supplement to those with low incomes. This dual supplemental system guarantees that most Swedes rely on the public system as their main source of retirement while ensuring a basic standard. The system does, however, partially offset the egalitarian norms of a flat-rate pension as differences in job income carry over into retirement.

Proactive Spending

In addressing social problems, the Swedish welfare state notably focuses on preventative measures. Income transfers and public services represent social investments. Individuals receive the opportunity to develop themselves and thus become fully contributing members of society. Money invested in child care, health care, training, and income support avoids the costs of high crime rates, low skill levels, emergency care, and unemployment later. Indeed, well-known authority Gøsta Esping-Andersen notes the distinct bias toward meaningful work in Sweden's welfare state:

Some equally expensive welfare states target most of their spending on compensating for social ills. The Swedish model is unique in its bias toward a "productivistic" and preventative social policy; it spends relatively little on unemployment benefits but invests heavily in employment, training, job mobility, adult education, the prevention of illness and accidents, and family services. It is a welfare state both designed for and dependent upon the minimization of social need and the maximization of employment. . . . In the Swedish welfare state, therefore, a large share of welfare costs might well be regarded as investments in economic growth.[15]

In stark contrast, U.S. welfare spending provides mostly a kind of Band-Aid—offering minimal survival. Indeed, the structure of programs like AFDC actually helped worsen a person's work situation and narrowed their job options. AFDC and Medicaid benefits were typically lowered or withdrawn if a parent worked, for example. Furthermore, supports for child care for working parents are often minimal. Thus, for example, a parent receiving public assistance who took a near-minimum-wage full-time job with no benefits would not seriously increase their income and would jeopardize the family's health care and risk leaving the children unsupervised. When it does support work, the American welfare state often simply subsidizes poverty-wage employers by providing public funds to offset low wages.

A Public Service Economy

A final notable characteristic of Sweden's welfare system is the emphasis it places on services. While other countries focus on income transfers that allow individuals to purchase services, Sweden has invested heavily in the public provision of such items. This includes public day care, universal health care, public higher education, worker-training schools, and so forth. According to 1985 figures, 93 percent of all employment in the fields of health, education,

and welfare services came from state employers. Indeed, public workers in these areas accounted for a quarter of the entire workforce.[16]

Right-wing politicians in our country would label such a reality "big government" and attempt to conjure up images of bloated, inefficient bureaucracy. However, both the United States and Sweden have large, developed service sectors. While in 1985 total health, education, and welfare services accounted for 26 percent of employment in Sweden, these services also employed 17 percent of the U.S. workforce. This figure put the United States ahead of many European counties, including Austria, Germany, Italy, and France. In the United States, however, most of these services come from private bureaucracies, not from public agencies.[17] The difference has important consequences. Private services go to those who can afford them; public services are available to everyone. In the United States, many private-sector service jobs pay low wages and offer insecure terms of employment. In Sweden, public salaries are much higher and stable. German scholar and researcher Fritz Scharpf paints a vivid contrast:

> In America, low levels of taxation, weak or nonexistent unions, and low or nonexistent social assistance allows large numbers of rich consumers to buy in the private market the services of large numbers of poor workers who must offer their services at very low wages. The unsolved problem . . . is poverty.
>
> In Scandinavia, by contrast, very high levels of taxation, strong unions, and generous social assistance have prevented the expansion of private services. High levels of employment are nevertheless achieved because Scandinavian-type welfare states are service-intensive, providing large numbers of public-service jobs in child care, education, health care, care for the elderly, and other social services—including jobs that do not require very high levels of formal training.[18]

A person who, for example, works in an underpaid and overworked position in a private nursing home in the United States would likely find themselves as a better-paid public servant delivering home care in Sweden.

U.S. conservatives have tarred the notion of state services with images of bureaucracy and inefficiency. And in the 1980s and 1990s, Swedish public debates have pointed to some problems of bureaucracy and inefficiency. From a progressive standpoint, the solution, however, is more innovative public management and organization. Indeed, public employers should provide leading examples of effective worker empowerment and effective collective decision making. By contrast, market-provided services can be delivered by private bureaucracies capable of even grosser errors in bad management, especially when their goal is profit, not quality services. Indeed, conservatives who are willing to root out any example of public bureaucratic incompetence, no matter how unrepresentative, are utterly blind to the daily irrationalities found in corporate America. As economist David Gordon recently documented, management-heavy U.S. corporations are hardly lean, mean, competitive machines.[19]

The huge area of health care clearly shows the superiority and efficiency of universal, public services over private business. The United States spends over 12 percent of its GDP on health—more than any other country—yet has inferior care. Roughly one out of every six of these dollars is wasted through the bureaucratic overhead of the private insurance industry as insurance companies micromanage health care. For-profit medicine prioritizes expensive treatments and services. In the past few years, specialists in surgery, radiology, and obstetrics have seen their income significantly increase, while general practitioners have seen their net income decline. The United States has an abundance of specialists and facilities for high-cost treatments for those who can pay, yet a growing shortage of family physicians and routine care. Drug companies push ever-expensive chemical treatments, while preventative medicine and natural remedies are neglected. In 1992, 14 percent of Americans under sixty-five had no insurance.[20] Meanwhile, the government-funded Medicaid and Medicare programs have to absorb the strain of rising medical costs caused by the inefficiencies and greed of the private health care industry.

By contrast, national health care systems guarantee care to all citizens. They also provide an institutional framework for publicly determining the direction of health care development. Even where private manufactures and providers are involved, the state system negotiates costs and regulates profits. Research shows that public health care simply provides better care. A 1990 survey of health care in ten countries found, for example, that half of Canadians expressed satisfaction with their "single payer" public health care system, while only 10 percent of Americans held similar feelings for the U.S. private system.[21]

While providing greater social services can mean a greater tax burden, the overall costs of public services can prove far less. In 1992, Swedish government figures for the various social insurance programs showed an administrative cost of under 2 percent for the payments made through the public programs. By contrast, private insurance companies showed administrative costs of 15 percent or higher. A personal tax rate of up to 38 percent in this country may compare with up to 50 percent in Sweden. Yet, when an American family adds in the costs of private child care, private education, health insurance or insurance co-pays, personal retirement savings, private mortgages, and so forth, their actual expenses may well exceed those of a family enjoying full social citizenship. Social citizenship can also benefit employers. The notoriously low skill development among the American workforce as compared to its European counterparts suggests that public supports for training and education are simply more effective and less costly than the efforts of isolated private employers. Furthermore, in the United States, private services can pit employers that pay for employee benefits against those that do not. While American business leaders might denounce Swedish levels of payroll taxes, employee benefits can easily run in costs equal to 25 percent or more of a worker's salary. For health insurance, for example, U.S. employers have to either pass on the burden to employees or face having to help fund the most inefficient health care system in the industrial world.

The Impact of the Social Democratic Welfare State

Living Standards and Equality

The most obvious effect of welfare spending comes in reducing inequality and raising the standard of living of those least well-off. Indeed, welfare policies are often deliberately enacted with such goals in mind. A solid literature of scholarship on the welfare state has measured the impact of welfare policies on income distribution. Generally, the research has revealed a noticeable impact, although the degree of results varies considerably by country.

Comparisons between the United States and Sweden do show very clear differences. For example, Deborah Mitchell calculates that income inequality in Sweden for 1980 was reduced by half when the impact of taxation and welfare spending was calculated.[22] By contrast, the more modest U.S. welfare state produced only a one-quarter reduction. While Swedish progressive taxes played a role, the main impact came from the country's generous transfer payments and services. Indeed, Esping-Andersen notes that as tax levels increase, eventually the entire population is so heavily taxed that the redistributive effect of taxes alone decreases.[23]

Another classic way of measuring the impact of social spending is to compare poverty rates for the most economically vulnerable: women and children. In 1980, 53 percent of solo parents in the United States qualified as living in poverty based on their income earnings alone. After welfare payments were added, 46 percent still lived below the poverty line. By contrast, a third of Swedish solo parents would have been in poverty without welfare spending. However, after public transfers were added on, only

5 percent actually lived in poverty.[24] Similar shocking comparisons emerge by comparing poverty among the elderly. In the United States, roughly one-quarter of the aged live in poverty. Before the increases in Social Security payments in the 1970s, the rate was far higher. However, in Sweden, less than 1 percent of the aged live in poverty![25] In the United States, with roughly one out of every six Americans living in poverty, official "common sense" cynically proclaims that there is nothing the country can do. In Sweden, deliberate state policy has virtually eliminated this social ill.

Some scholarly studies have looked beyond income distribution to include health, housing, working life, education, and other areas vital to human life. As such, they measure overall living standards. Through national surveys conducted in Scandinavia over several decades, researchers found that the high level of public services contributed to an overall high level of living. Indeed, they found that this quality of life continued to improve despite worsening economic conditions.[26]

Decommodification

Contrasting levels of equality in living standards, however, offers only one way of measuring the impact of the welfare state on people's lives. Researcher Gøsta Esping-Andersen sees the ability of welfare states to insulate people from their life in the capitalist market as a goal in and of itself. Prior to the advent of capitalism, people generally had greater access to economic resources. In medieval Europe, for example, the system of feudal obligations provided peasants basic rights to farm land. The friction point came over the reciprocal obligation of the peasants to pay substantial taxes to support the aristocracy—an obligation that often grew to a crushing burden by the end of the period. Generally, however, a person's ties to family and community ensured a minimal survival and control over their own labor. Capitalism, however, separated workers from economic resources. Most people's survival came to depend on their relative ability to enter the marketplace and sell their labor for a wage. That wage was then taken back into the market to purchase the necessary means of life. Capitalism converted both worker's labor and the means of life into commodities that are bought and sold.

For well over a century and a half, critics of capitalism have detailed the horrors that this commodification produces. Under pure capitalism, talented, hard-working people can literally starve to death because no owner of capital will hire them. The never-ending battles of the labor movement testify to the disadvantages workers suffer when they are forced to compete in the marketplace to sell their labor. The buyers of labor clearly have the upper hand.

At the consumption end, capitalist commodity production is driven by what can be sold for a profit, not society's direct needs. Thus, our health care industry prioritizes expensive treatment for those with health insurance while neglecting primary care. Similarly, in the 1950s General Motors bought up streetcar lines in major cities like Detroit and Los Angeles for the sole purpose of destroying them. Public transportation makes more sense from the perspective of societal costs and people's and the environment's well-being. However, from the viewpoint of making money, automobiles bring in more company profits than building trains and streetcars. Since it does not generate profits, the capitalist market places little value on a wide range of important human activity. For example, a single woman who stays home to raise her children in the United States is stigmatized as a "welfare queen." However, the market would pay her well if she instead abandoned her infant to the care of relative strangers and went to work at a strip club. Clearly, what the market values is not always what a democratic society would prioritize.

The exploitation and irrationality found in the market have motivated never-ending calls to abolish capitalism outright. Within a society that is still capitalist, however, the welfare state can free significant parts of people's lives from dependence on the market. Esping-Andersen argues that the social democratic welfare state does just this. Because of social citizenship, a Swede's access to health care, education, child care, vacation time, retirement, housing, and minimal income is guaranteed regardless of his or her experience in the market. Overall, in 1997, government estimates placed women averaging 39 percent and men 30 percent of their income through public transfers. Indeed, under certain conditions such as raising an infant, people can outright withdraw from the labor market and still maintain a basic standard of living. By contrast, an American parent who decides to practice good "family values" and quit his or her job to focus on raising his or her children would face a drastic income reduction as well as possible loss of health care, retirement, and other benefits. In comparison to most Americans, Swedes can live a substantial part of their lives independent of the capitalist market. And their ability to do so strengthens the relative power of workers when they do sell their labor for a wage.

Publicly run services can also potentially respond much more directly to society by shaping their products directly around human need. For example, far greater emphasis can be found on preventative health care and alternative medical practices in countries with national health care systems than in our profit-dominated system. In the United States, the dominant for-profit nursing-home industry is known for the horrors of understaffing, inadequate care, and the general "warehousing" of our nation's more disabled elderly.[27] It has also led to an emphasis on nursing-home care rather than more home-based alternatives. By contrast, both Sweden and Denmark have decisively shifted national priorities by no longer building nursing homes. They instead make new investments in alternative options for elderly care. Overall, in Sweden, public social expenditures represent over 40 percent of Sweden's GDP (and nearly 60 percent of all state spending). Thus, entire areas of health, housing, education, and so forth, are organized outside the formal logic of the profit-seeking marketplace.

This picture contrasts sharply with that of the

United States. Liberal welfare polices have aimed not to decommodify people's lives, but to actually enhance the market's power over them. The state provides a minimal social protection so that only the worst excesses of capitalism do not outright tear society apart—as it did in producing the Great Depression. Beyond this safety mechanism, one's access to welfare provisions and the quality of support revolves around the marketplace. Thus, for example, the amount of a person's Social Security pension is determined by his or her work history. Eligibility for unemployment compensation is based on work prior to unemployment. Means-tests force the poor to prove that they are not otherwise able to survive through work in the labor market. And the welfare aid that is provided is usually set low to compel people back into the market.

Most important, in the United States, access to most basic services is controlled by employers. Thus, a person's eligibility for health insurance, sick leave, vacation time, disability pay, training, and private pensions is entirely dependent on the policies of an employer. Indeed, state policy has enhanced market dominance. The government invests heavily in tax write-offs to middle- and upper-class homeowners, rather than public investments in housing. Similarly, tax breaks encourage private retirement plans rather than expansions in Social Security payments. Congress debates child tax credits, while public day care is largely nonexistent. The dominant U.S. policy solutions to unemployment revolve around tax breaks and public subsidies to private business, not the expansion of public employment and state-funded jobs training as in Sweden. Contrary to popular images, far more taxpayer money goes to support mortgage write-offs to homeowners than to any poverty program. Tax breaks and subsidies for corporate welfare, along with the huge military budget, are the principle cause of the federal budget deficit.

Overall, using calculations based on public expenditures for old-age pensions, sickness benefits, and unemployment insurance in eighteen countries, Esping-Andersen rates Sweden's welfare state as the most decommodifying in the world. The key elements are universal access, generous benefits, and ample public services. Next in line are Norway and Denmark. Esping-Andersen notes that for all three, the significant decommodifying impact came after World War II when social democratic governments were driving policy. Britain's high scores in the 1950s but low ranking by 1980 demonstrates the weakness of policies begun during the Labour Party's electoral breakthrough after the war but not sustained and expanded over time. Not surprisingly, the United States is down at the bottom of the list, just above Australia with the lowest decommodifying effect.

Decommodification can have an important impact on class politics. Life in the capitalist market divides working people by differing levels of income, status, and so forth. Capitalist politics then attempts to use these differences to mobilize one segment of workers against another. Social democracy aims to unify working people under a common solidarity. The Swedish welfare state aids social democratic politics by reducing the fragmenting influence of the market. At the same time, its universal programs provide a material basis for broad solidarity by bringing the entire population within the "People's Home." Thus, rather than the passive recipients of a nation's class structure, Swedish social democracy has played an instrumental role in shaping it.

Ironically, a pro-worker, universal-style welfare state that employers bitterly oppose when left to their own devices, can also foster areas of greater cooperation between workers and owners. It can lower employer resistance to unions, since issues such as health care, base vacation time, parental leave, and so forth, are taken out of the contract negotiations and into the hands of public services and laws. Employers cannot compete on the basis of cost cutting in such areas, as social citizenship requires them all to pay equally through payroll taxes. By contrast, American employers can gain significant competitive cost advantages by keeping themselves union and benefit free. On the union side, the welfare state also provides a kind of social wage. Since workers are not entirely dependent on their paycheck for their well-being and economic security, unions have greater flexibility in moderating wage demands when such action is in the interest of economic health as a whole. Indeed, European governments can offer expansions in the social wage as a trade for union wage moderation.

Gender Equality

Feminist researchers have drawn attention to the male bias found among both welfare states and those who study them. As we will see, even reforms that are officially gender neutral can merely reinforce society's gender inequalities. Such policies take the man as the norm and often directly or indirectly reinforce women's subordinate position. Comparative feminist research, however, has revealed important differences among countries. Welfare policies can reinforce male domination, but they can also help liberate women. The impact of a welfare program depends on the rules governing who has access to it and the type and level of benefits. Diane Sainsbury offers a parallel to Esping-Andersen's concept of decommodification. She examined welfare policies in terms of the independence that they provide women from family and dependence on men—what could be called "defamilization."

Many welfare policies actively reinforce women's dependence by implicitly assuming the presence of a dominant male breadwinner. For example, the U.S. Social Security system is based on a person's past record of contribution into the system. However, this system does not cover women whose work involves raising a family instead of wage labor. In 1991, the requirement for forty years of employment in order to receive benefits discriminates against those who interrupt their paid work life to raise children. The formula also counts the best thirty-five years, with years of zero earnings averaged in. Add to this the fact that, even today, women's wages average only seventy-two cents to a man's dollar. Together, these policies help ensure that most women retiring today will receive better benefits if they apply for Social Security based on their husband's income, rather than their own employment record. Originally, Social Security penalized divorced women by excluding them from any benefits based on their previous husband's contribution. The U.S. tax code also shows a breadwinner bias. Although some changes have been made, the tax code still favors marriage with one-earner families.

The male breadwinner ideology has also been apparent in aid to the poor. For AFDC, the state essentially assumed the role of the absent man. Women who tried to work found their benefits reduced, while state laws often discriminated against children born out of wedlock. Current "welfare reform" efforts also show a clear male bias by equating paid work with socially meaningful activity. By contrast, a woman who stays in the home to raise infant children is presumed not to be contributing to society or "carrying her fair share." Public policy simply does not attach value to the people-care roles that society traditionally assigns to women. Furthermore, the market either does not provide these functions a wage value or, in the case of institutional care, typically pays low wages. In a welfare state that reinforces the market, patriarchy and capitalism combine to penalize women.

By contrast the universal norms of the Swedish system have combined with deliberate efforts since the 1960s to promote greater gender equality and to value people-care activities. The decommodifying impact of universal programs has aided women by providing equal access to benefits and services regardless of their experience in the labor market. Thus, Swedish women receive more benefits in their own right than in terms of their status as the wives of wage-earning breadwinners. For example, the basic pension system is available to all citizens regardless of a person's marital status or work history. Therefore, a full-time parent can earn credit toward retirement, just as a full-time wage earner does. (In the ATP system, inequality between men and women persists—although a majority of women now claim on their own basis rather than on their status as wives.) Today, any woman (or man) with children can qualify for the universal family allowance regardless of the presence or absence of a spouse or whether they work in the labor market. Less-well-off families can also qualify for an advanced maintenance allowance, also regardless of marital status. Since the Swedish welfare state will bring a single woman with children up to almost the level of disposable income of a similar two-parent household, Swedish women do not face the tough economic choices between their standard of living and independence as they do in the United States. An American woman with children, for example, who lives with a violent, battering spouse will find her efforts to escape often a quick path into poverty. Swedish women simply have more options. Indeed, in stark contrast to the so-called feminization of poverty in the United States, more Swedish men than women fall below the poverty line.[28]

Far more than the United States, Sweden has recognized the principle of care—that a person who raises children or aids the sick or elderly is engaged in meaningful activity just as valuable as paid work. Thus, as mentioned above, Sweden guarantees the universal right to paid parental leave of up to 450 days. Originally designed for mothers, this benefit was extended in 1974 to fathers, in recognition that family care is a joint responsibility (the parents decide how to split the time between them). Either spouse can qualify for parental benefits regardless of prior work in the labor market. Parenthood, not having a prior paid job, is the sole qualifier. Since 1979, parental leave has also been broadened to allow parents to shorten their daily hours (and corresponding pay) until a child is ten to twelve years old. Widespread public day care and home care programs run by workers paid decent wages places further value on care functions and provides women greater options. Swedish laws supporting leave from work for care of sick children or infirm elderly also do the same. By placing a public value on the principle of care and establishing public services and

support, Sweden has also helped move care functions from private responsibilities isolated in an assumed nuclear family to societal roles. The Swedes have backed up the famous slogan "it takes a village to raise a child" with concrete policies.

Sweden's universal access and recognition of the principle of care has produce several concrete results. First, by allowing flexibility and support for family caregiving, Sweden has encouraged a record proportion of women to enter the labor market. By 1990, 81 percent of Swedish women worked outside the home, while 68 percent of American women did the same.[29] The different context is also important. In the United States, more families are pushed to send both parents to work because of declining single-earner incomes. In Sweden, women are pulled into the labor market by greater options and support. Unlike in the United States, social services complement paid work, rather than being sacrificed once paid earnings have reached a minimal level. Swedish parents do not have to sacrifice care functions to enter the labor market. While in 1985 the percentage of Swedish mothers with infants one to two years old in the labor market was almost as high as the average for all women, close to half of these were absent from work on any given day thanks to profamily job regulations and services.[30]

Ironically, while Sweden has a record proportion of women who work outside the home, far more Swedish children are cared for directly by their parents than in the United States. Sweden has not only the highest female labor participation rate in Europe, but also shares with Ireland the highest fertility rate as well.[31] Men's roles have also begun to change. By the 1990s, one-third of short-term paid-leave days (e.g., for a sick child) were taken by fathers. A quarter of the claimants for longer-term parental leave were men, although 90 percent of the total amount of time was taken by women.[32] To foster further male child care activity, the Swedish government introduced a "daddy month" in 1995, assigning one month of leave directly to the father.

These family policies, while a clear aid to women,

also can have the less desirable effect of making it easier for women to balance society's traditional gender division of labor. Indeed, allowing greater leave and reduced job time may simply reinforce, in a new form, women's primary role as homemaker and child rearer. Women remain the chief users of family policies, with men drawing on them only selectively. Thus, men continue to develop full careers with higher pay and breadwinner capacity, while women balance child rearing with interrupted careers, part-time work, and lower rates of pay. Employment segregation is quite noticeable in Sweden, with the bulk of women's increased employment coming almost entirely in public service jobs.[33] Leave policies can simply reinforce women's dependence on part-time, flexible, and female-dominated jobs. Reflecting these limitations, in the 1970s, the women's division of both the trade union federation and the SAP raised an alternative profamily policy—a six-day, thirty-hour workweek—explicitly as a way of achieving gender equity.[34] Only by having everyone work less at their jobs could everyone also work equally at maintaining a home and raising a family. Instead of the modified workweek, however, successive governments provided the expanded parental leave. The issue of work time remains. In 1992, for example, Frank Boddendijk of the Dutch Emancipation Council echoed similar arguments from Sweden when he claimed, "As long as men still have full-time jobs and women only part-time jobs, there will be no real equality, since in that case women have the full responsibility for domestic labor, including child care."[35]

While more needs to be done, Sweden is clearly much farther down the road toward policy support for rethinking gender roles and supporting child rearing than the United States. Social citizenship has complemented other gender equality efforts. Through legislation, labor market policies, and collective bargaining, women's wages have been brought to 80 percent of men's wages in Sweden, compared to 72 percent in the United States. By 1998, 50 percent of all government ministerial positions and 44 percent of the seats in the Swedish legislature were filled by women. That same year, less than 10 percent of the members of the U.S. Congress were women. Economically, the American "free market" system still relegates four out of five women to female-dominated sectors of the economy where wage and benefits are generally lower and public family supports are virtually nonexistent. As with poverty, issues that official U.S. political wisdom deems not solvable or beyond the scope of public intervention, have been addressed by Sweden's social democratic state with noticeable effect.

The Full Employment Economy

Sweden's welfare state does not exist in a vacuum. Indeed, public social programs come as only one part of social citizenship. Economic policies that promote full employment around high standards are critical to maintain the country's generous welfare state. By steering the economy to use the full productive talent of all citizens, Swedish policies help produce the tax base needed to support social spending. By contrast, rising unemployment threatens the welfare state by cutting tax revenues and increasing state spending on unemployment compensation and other safety net programs. More generally, an economy that marginalizes individuals or that forces them into the ranks of working poor drives up both welfare spending and the social costs of crime, drug use, and other symptoms of social crisis.

Sweden has traditionally avoided these costs and established a healthy tax base by maintaining very high rates of employment at overall high wage levels. During the 1980s, when official unemployment in the United States threatened to go into double digits, Sweden's rate never exceeded 3.5 percent.[36] Part of this achievement came from the Swedish welfare state's heavy investment in developing people's talents and opportunities. However, full employment also came from deliberate macroeconomic policies. The basic Keynesian formula behind these measures is not unique to Sweden. These measures have been used to greater and lesser degrees by all of the industrially developed countries, including the United States. However, Sweden's social democrats took their policies in several innovative directions, which produced a distinct Swedish model of economic development.

Keynesian Economics 101

Keynesian economics, named after British economic theorist John Maynard Keynes, grew out of the crisis of the Great Depression.[37] Before that time, classical economic thought dominated business and governmental policy, while Marxism and other radical doctrines held official preeminence within the European labor movement.

Classical economics, the doctrine that has now made a comeback both in the United States and abroad as "neoliberalism," and "supply-side economics" centered around the supposed superiority of the capitalist market. According to classical economics, the "laws" of supply and demand and the "entrepreneurial drive" of private capitalists delivered efficiency and prosperity. Government and other "outsider" intervention could only disrupt the market's natural magic. Under classical economic direction, government policies refrained from "interfering" with business decisions. Instead, government restricted itself to ensuring market conditions. Governments could break up the worst cases of monopolies and provide basic and costly infrastructure. Ultimately, however, the market's "invisible hand," not collective public decisions, was best suited for guiding economic behavior. When capitalist economies showed signs of difficulties and slowdowns, classical economics looked for the source of the problems in excessive government policy, union organizing by workers, or some other outside forces that must have interfered with the self-correcting market mechanism. The economic solutions to difficult times were simple: free the market to do its wonders.

Marxism and other radical doctrines pointed to the obvious shortfalls of such capitalist reasoning.

The owners of capital competed with each other by exploiting workers, their communities, and the environment. The much-vaunted free-market competition over time produced less heroic entrepreneurial innovation and more crude power politics and gradual concentrations in wealth. This rise of the great "captains of industry" did not produce a stable, "self-correcting" system, but ever more serious cycles of boom and bust. Indeed, some brands of European Marxism looked for capitalism to collapse under the weight of its own economic irrationality.

When the great crisis did finally come in the 1930s, it thoroughly discredited classical ways of thinking and left capitalism with a big black eye. However, the revolution anticipated by many radicals did not, with important exceptions, materialize in Western Europe. Instead, the bulk of the mass movements of the 1930s sought to reform capitalism, rather than abolish it. Enter John Maynard Keynes. Hardly a working-class radical, Keynes was born into a comfortable middle-class family. His career combined various stints as an economic policy–making technocrat in British government with successful private business endeavors. Despite his personal wealth, Keynes held many classical economic notions in scorn. Indeed, his liberal politics leaned toward the pro-Labour side of the nation's political spectrum.

Keynes's great achievement lay in developing an approach to the Great Depression, and the economic ups and downs of capitalism generally, that married two seemingly irreconcilable goals: social justice and business profits. For Keynes, the Great Depression grew out of a crisis of demand. The economy had simply outstripped the capacity of the population to buy all of the products that workers produced. The growing inequality that seemed inherent to unfettered capitalism had produced the system's undoing. In the United States, for example, two out of five Americans lived below a level of minimum subsistence, as defined by the federal government, on the eve of the stock market crash of 1929. When the boom of the 1920s hit the slack demand of harsh inequality, business responded to overcapacity by laying off workers. The Ford Motor Company, for example, shrank from a workforce of 128,000 in 1929 to a mere 37,000 three years later. By 1932, U.S. unemployment had reached 25 percent. In many of the nation's industrial cities, half or more of the working population could not find work.

For Keynes, rising unemployment further lowered demand for goods, leading to a spiral of more lay-offs, lower demand, and so forth. Classical economic formulas, which simply put more power and wealth into the hands of the few, could not solve the crisis, but only make it worse. The Keynesian solution required government to help manage the economy. To put people back to work, and thereby increase demand, governments had to increase social spending. Hence, for example, the famous federal jobs programs of the U.S. New Deal could be justified on solid Keynesian grounds. The more people at work and the more money in their pockets, the more goods they would consume and the more selling opportunities for business.

Keynesian economics gave governments a new role. They were to oversee the ups and downs of capitalism. The primary goal was to maintain high levels of employment. Thus, when the signs of an economic downturn appeared, governments would respond by raising demand and preventing further collapse. Over the long haul, a thriving economy could be built on the buying power of an ever-growing "middle class" workforce. Full employment avoided wasting talent and resources, while decent wages allowed workers to buy what they produced.

Governments that practiced Keynesian policies had a number of mechanisms at their disposal.[38] Through their direct spending on social programs, they could put money into the hands of consumers while also providing jobs through public employment. Deficit spending during downturns would be paid off when economic expansion returned. Interest rate policies of central banks could complement expansionary fiscal policies. Low interest rates and easier money increased demand and provided fur-

ther support for business investment. "Responsible" labor unions, those that stuck to collective bargaining and did not challenge the right of management to run the company, were a friend of this economic logic as their wage and benefit gains provided growing consumer demand.

Keynesian policies could grow in popularity because they had something to offer to both sides of the class divide. For workers, they promised a rising standard of living, a social safety net, and basic economic security. For business, Keynesianism offered to achieve greater economic stability in ways that did not threaten basic management prerogatives. Keynesian policies aimed to influence the broader economic environment by manipulating mechanisms outside of a company's internal lines of authority. This contrasted sharply with traditional socialist demands for direct state and worker participation in, and outright control of, the enterprise. In short, Keynesianism aimed to help capitalism expand the economic pie by distributing the fruits of that pie relatively more equally.

Indeed, Keynesianism held special attraction for social democrats. Having abandoned in practice (if not always in rhetoric) the goal of abolishing capitalism, social democrats faced a major dilemma in trying to provide capitalism a human face. Union organizing and the welfare state could provide workers a more prosperous living by redistributing the wealth created within the capitalist economy. However, these gains remained insecure and contingent as long as capitalism retained its distinct propensity for boom and bust. The gains made during a period of upswing could simply be wiped out by the next depression. By managing the business cycle to maintain full employment, Keynesianism provided a way to replace great collapses with a sustained economic boom.

The Achilles Heel—Inflation

Most of the industrially developed countries emerged from the Great Depression and World War II with

Keynesianism in ascendance. To a greater or lesser degree, it guided the policies of most western nations throughout the postwar boom. The logic of full employment, however, did have a weakness: inflation. While avoiding a direct challenge to capitalist decision making, full employment altered the balance of power between worker and management. Unless they win rights through union organizing, the only inherent right that a worker has under capitalism is the right to quit. The higher the rate of unemployment, the more difficulty workers face in finding new jobs, and the less willing they will be to challenge management's decisions. Indeed, during the Great Depression, employers frequently developed elaborate spy networks to use the threat of firing to root out pro-union workers. Similarly, in U.S. industries like auto and steel manufacturing, employers used threats of plant closings during the insecurity of the high unemployment years of the 1980s to demand concessions from their unionized workforce.

When the economy nears full employment, however, the bargaining power of workers increases. Those not happy with their work situation can more easily quit and find jobs elsewhere. When union contract negotiations come around, the workforce has greater confidence in pushing for a greater share of the pie. With the supply of workers restricted, employers may find themselves competing with each other to attract ideal employees.

These dynamics can produce a wage-price spiral.[39] Under conditions of an expanding full-employment economy and growing business profits, workers can seek a greater share of the economic pie. Especially when they are highly unionized, workers can win major gains in wages and benefits. Businesses can pay for these increased labor costs in two ways: They can divert a portion of their profits or they can pass on the costs to the consumer through price increases. Within the logic of a capitalist economy, "squeezed" profits can mean lower investment and hence an economic downturn—something that Keynesian economics seeks to avoid. Increased prices, however, means inflation. Inflation lowers the buying power of workers' wages, which, in turn, can lead them to demand even higher compensation. Within the confines of this scenario, workers can choose either to moderate their wage demands or to face rising inflation.

This dilemma was partially offset in both the United States and Europe by the postwar boom's unprecedented period of exceptionally high growth. A fast-growing pie fed both expanding profits and wage increases. Profits, however, still had to grow faster than wage increases for inflation to be avoided. Even in boom years, the business cycle's moderate ups and downs could threaten to put rising inflation on the bargaining table. Social democrats who wished to use Keynesian methods to steer their capitalist economies, thus needed viable income policies that could allow their labor movement to consent to reduced wage demands in the face of inflationary pressures.

Rehn–Meidner to the Rescue

Sweden entered the postwar era facing just such serious inflationary pressures. Under government requests, the LO unions agreed to a voluntary wage freeze in 1948 and 1949. This action, however, strained relations between the ruling Social Democrats and the unions. Business profits increased while workers were told they had to hold their wages steady for the good of the economy. The LO faced the twin dangers of a revolt among its membership and the mutiny of individual unions from collective wage negotiations by signing their own independent wage contracts. Tensions between employers, the Social Democratic government, and the unions increased in the 1950s. As business expanded and profits increased, workers continued to be asked to contain their wage demands as the price for full employment. The Social Democrats found themselves in the rather uncomfortable position of having to hold back their labor movement. As Finance Minister Sköld commented in 1955, "we are facing one of the most difficult problems of full employment: a strong trade union movement and weak employers."[40]

The LO saved itself and the social democratic agenda by providing a solution. Formulated by two of their economists, Gösta Rehn and Rudolph Meidner, the model took advantage of Sweden's powerful unions and their centralized bargaining with Swedish employers. Rehn and Meidner's achievement lay in taking the logic of the business community's dire predictions that greater wage demands would ruin weaker companies and turning the argument on its head. They proposed a system of solidaristic wages. This could be done because the focus of collective bargaining was not the individual firm, as in the United States, but the national economy as a whole. For decades the LO and the two white-collar labor federations operated not simply as umbrella organizations, such as with our AFL-CIO, but as actual bargaining agents who established with employers national frame agreements that laid out the basic terms of all wage and working conditions in the country. The Rehn–Meidner plan held that the labor federations would use national bargaining to collapse the differences in the nation's wage levels. Wages would tend to move up toward the higher end, but not toward the highest possible for those workers placed in especially strong economic sectors. These solidaristic wages would indeed push less productive firms out of business. However, it rewarded especially efficient firms by placing a limit on the wage demands of their workforce. Companies that competed well on the basis of product design, worker productivity, quality, and so forth, could look forward to quite healthy profit margins, while companies that looked for a bottom line built around minimal labor costs would not survive.

In the short run, the model meant company closings. However, in the long run, it would produce an economy organized around efficient, productive firms. To avoid significant increases in unemployment, Rehn and Meidner required government action to ensure that workers laid off in one part of the economy would quickly move to the expanding sectors rewarded by the model. Thus developed Sweden's active labor market policy in 1956. It aimed to transfer the cost of unemployment and retraining off the backs of individuals and onto collective public policy. The Swedish Labor Market Board, originally established in 1939, was given increased resources to promote employment. By 1979, the active labor market policy consumed 2.24 percent of the GDP.[41] In the high unemployment years of the early 1990s, labor market and unemployment expenditures consumed roughly 10 percent of national government spending and 4 percent of the GDP. Until recently, the labor movement enjoyed a formal majority on the national board with three seats for the LO and three for the white-collar worker unions. Three other seats went to the SAF and two were appointed by the government to represent the special concerns of women and the rural population. Similar balances of power appear at the county and district levels. The basic logic of the labor market policies, however, depends on cooperation from Swedish employers.

Under the active labor market policies, an unemployed worker would receive, in the short run, generous unemployment compensation from the country's welfare state. However, public employment boards would direct the worker to new job opportunities. The government would provide financial assistance if the worker had to relocate. Furthermore, with the cooperation of business and unions, extensive government-sponsored training programs aimed to provide workers the skills relevant to the expanding sectors of the economy.

Over time, the Labor Market Board's scope expanded to meet new needs. When business behavior under the policies of solidaristic wages and active labor market policy fostered economic concentration in the large cities with stagnation elsewhere, the board acquired a greater role in regional development policies. Since the availability of housing played a major role in labor mobility, the Labor Market Board also played an important role in housing construction.

To help regulate the ups and downs of the business cycle, the Social Democrats also expanded a prewar investment reserve system. Under the expanded system, companies could lessen their tax burden by placing up to 40 percent of their before-tax profits into a public account. Once in the system, the funds were frozen until released by the state authorities. During periods of declining business investment, the state would release the investment reserves—hoping to counterbalance the economic downturn. Authorities could restrict the release of the fund to particular areas, such as building or machinery investment, and it could confine the releases to specific firms or sectors.

The system had its strength and weaknesses. The 1958 release was mistimed, whereas the releases of 1962–63 and 1967–68 provided significant stimulus.[42] Although authorities tried to use the fund to promote regional development, only about 15 percent of company investment financed with released funds in the 1960s actually went to the areas targeted for government assistance.[43] The entire system depended on voluntary business contributions and use.

The ATP pension plan also included an economic rationale. While the labor movement clearly aimed to address people's retirement needs, the funds also created a huge pool of savings not dependent on the private marketplace. Because it was publicly controlled, the ATP system complemented the active labor market policy with a large surplus fund that could be steered toward public priorities. The business community opposed the plan precisely over this aspect. Employers agreed with the need for better retirement pensions and were prepared to shoulder part of the bill. However, they saw the collectively controlled public funds as extending state power over investment, reducing privately controlled savings, and violating the principles of the free market. The business community preferred voluntary private pension plans of the sort that dominate in the United States.

The Social Democrats decided to fight it out with employers in a very public and very close battle. In the end, the second chamber of the legislature passed the ATP measure by a one-vote majority in 1959. The struggle proved a turning point for Swedish so-

cial democracy. The victory organized the single largest financial part of the welfare state, the retirement system, firmly around social democratic lines. Furthermore, the ATP funds succeeded in establishing a large pool of public savings. The victory reinforced the social democratic vision of an active state role in the economy. The social democrats also gained lasting political dividends from their fight. In defending basic principles over employer resistance, the party reasserted its left credentials and revitalized its base. During the pension struggle, the social democrats won over the white-collar unions to the ATP plan. This established a lasting blue-collar/white-collar alliance. Once again economic and welfare policies reinforced class politics.

We should note the potential economic importance of a publicly directed pension system for the United States. By 1991, total corporate, state, and local employee benefit funds amounted to over $3 trillion. According to one estimate, as much as 40 percent of all corporate stock and 50 percent of bonds were held by pension funds.[44] Yet, the United States' private, market-oriented system has placed this tremendous wealth in the hands of private finance and Wall Street. As we will detail in Chapter 6, these funds are used to encourage particularly shortsighted and destructive forms of corporate activity that often jeopardize the lives of the workers from whom the investments are supposedly made. By contrast, by placing workers' pension wealth in a public system, Swedish social democracy established the institutional basic for public use of the funds. Indeed, in the 1960s and 1970s, pension fund wealth was used to finance large-scale housing construction. Thus, a worker's pension provided not only a decent retirement income, but also a place to live as well. Classical economists and business leaders often argue that income inequality is a necessary evil in order to promote savings and investment. Only by supporting large pots of personal wealth not used for consumption can an economy accumulate the financial resources needed to support new firms and company expansion. However, Sweden's public pension system demonstrates how significant national savings can be accumulated by programs that further equality and the rights of social citizenship. Indeed, the ATP funds pushed out not only private pension schemes, but also private housing finance—a possibility that any U.S. home buyer who has looked at the cumulative interests extracted through their private mortgage might appreciate.

Overall, Rehn and Meidner's model did not come without costs. Individual workers still had to face job and career changes. And, in practice, the policies favored large firms and thus a greater concentration of business wealth. The policies also worked particularly well for the nation's export industries, thus increasing these sectors' influence on the economic and political life of the nation. We will return to these aspects and the strains in Chapter 4.

The model did, however, help save Sweden's Keynesian social democracy. While business protested specific mechanisms, the overall system worked for both workers and management. Despite high wage levels, Swedish industry remained internationally competitive because the system promoted streamlined production and efficiency. For Swedish employers, the Rehn–Meidner model regulated the environment surrounding business while leaving their basic decision-making power as capitalists unchallenged. It avoided the calls for large-scale nationalization that had been the rallying cry of the early labor movement.

The Swedish labor movement was made stronger by wage solidarity and union involvement in labor market programs. Under the system, workers could look forward to a gradually increasing and more equal standard of living. While the welfare state provided basic social needs separate from the market, the active labor market policies sharply reduced economic insecurity, and overall social democratic management of the economy delivered some of the lowest unemployment rates in the world. Capitalist prosperity, under social democratic guidance, provided the resources to build the nation's model welfare state and prosperous society.

The half-century tradition of active government involvement in the labor market has also set the stage for public policy to enter new economic areas. Women's equality provides a telling case. The mere fact that the national government today has a Minister for Gender Equality Affairs and a Division for Gender Equality suggests that official Swedish public policy in this area is far ahead of our country's. In the 1970s and 1980s, new governmental programs aimed to reduce gender segregation in the labor market—in particular, opening more higher paid, higher status male-dominated professions to women. By the 1990s, however, research findings showed that these efforts had delivered only modest results. In response, government policy shifted toward upgrading women's experiences within female-dominated sectors. Labor market policies have developed skill training, mentoring, and networking efforts specially designed to enhance women's opportunities for personal development. Public policy has also offered extra support for women who have to move in and out of the labor market. Health and safety efforts have targeted the high rates of chronic stress-related injuries among women workers. Other programs have developed and promoted models of work reorganization. New workplace structures aim not only to address gender imbalances in influence and responsibility, but also to implement cooperative group-oriented work norms that reflected women's skills and experiences. Sweden's Equal Opportunities Act now opens private employers to public scrutiny by requiring them to annually publish their wage data broken down by gender. The Working Life Institute developed a gender-neutral job evaluation system for promoting equal pay for equal work. Furthermore, in 1994, government funding established regional resource centers run by and for women based on their local needs.

The Scandinavian Model

While the best-known example of social democracy, Sweden shares its general social democratic preeminence with the rest of Scandinavia. Norway and Denmark have enjoyed many of the same broad characteristics of their larger neighbor. Both countries have strong labor movements. Today the majority of Danes and Norwegians belong to unions. Like Sweden, their labor movements are organized into centralized and national peak organizations. Late industrialization throughout Scandinavia produced a well-organized and much more independent class of small farmers, which provided the key ally in achieving Social Democratic power.

Social democratic policies are also readily evident throughout the region. Norway and Denmark have welfare states that rival Sweden's. These were all built on national commitments to full employment and basic Keynesian management of the economy to ensure sustained growth. A key sign of social democracy's dominance is also evident in Norway and Denmark—social citizenship policies have continued, indeed at times have even been furthered, during periods when the opposition parties have controlled the government.

The achievements of these other social democratic powerhouses occasionally win mention here in the United States. For example, in late 1996, the *New York Times* acknowledged Norway's accomplishments through an article entitled "Welfare's Snug Coat Cuts Norwegian Cold." The reporter tells the story of Dr. Sidsel Kreyberg, a forty-two-year-old pathologist. In 1987, Norway's social citizenship stepped in when Kreyberg's husband left her and her two children. For nearly eight years the state paid her a pension to raise her two children. Free day care, subsidized housing and vacations, and free medical and dental care all helped to maintain the family's standard of living. Kreyberg took advantage of a free university education to complete a Ph.D. and obtain a better-paying job than she had had before. The article cites other noteworthy details of profamily social democracy. The base family stipend for every child under seventeen worked out to $1,620 a year, while parents who stayed home to raise their children build up

retirement pay at rates equivalent to industrial workers. Maternity leave provided forty-two weeks at full pay. At the time of the reporting, the Norwegian legislature was debating a "Lifelong Learning" program, which would provide all citizens a year off their jobs at full pay every decade or so to hone their work skills. As in Sweden, this commitment to investing in people has gained the support of businesspeople. While they may criticize individual details, businesses enjoy access to a highly educated and productive workforce.[45]

Just before his death in 1996, historian Andreas Jørgensen sent to the U.S. publication *Monthly Review* a short article in which he countered celebrations of the American economic model with a pointed description of life as a citizen of Denmark. Among other items, Jørgensen pointed to a universal public health system that spent half the relative costs in GNP as the U.S. system. Denmark's minimum wage at that time worked out to $14 an hour, with average wages of unskilled workers running between $18 and $20 an hour. Students received not only free enrollment at universities but an annual stipend of about $6,000 a year for up to five years. When the social democrats formed a government in 1993, for the first time in twelve years, they passed legislation granting all working adults the right to one year of paid leave from the labor market to care for young children, pursue adult education, or simply take a sabbatical. Horrified by the low reach of our wage structure, Jørgensen pointed out that even the worst-off Dane on public assistance would receive a yearly income higher than an American who works full time for minimum wage. Contrary to American business claims of economic ruin, Jørgensen argued that his country had been able to sustain this social citizenship with rates of GNP and productivity growth that have far exceeded those of the United States.[46]

While Denmark and Norway share in many of Sweden's accomplishments, important differences among these countries further highlight the politics behind social citizenship.[47]

Denmark's Qualified Social Democracy

In Denmark, social democracy never achieved the unqualified dominance that it did in Sweden and Norway. Relative to the other two countries, Denmark's working class was more divided between craft- and industry-based unions. Postwar policies took place in a country dominated both by small firms and by a large class of small producers. Social democracy never achieved the electoral strength that it did in Sweden and Norway. While in the other two nations the main Social Democratic Party enjoyed years of majority rule, Denmark's Social Democrats governed without majority votes in parliament. In social democracy's necessary coalition governments with agrarian politics, the farmers held much greater weight. The opposition parties, when acting in concert, held the parliamentary strength to block the Social Democrats' agenda. At the same time, compromises with more conservative forces produced revolts within social democracy's own ranks. Beginning in 1960, the new Socialist People's Party challenged the Social Democrats from the left.[48] Their initial hostility to this challenge further drove social democracy into compromise to its right.

As a result of its weaker position, Danish social democracy had to resort to much greater compromise. These limits can be seen in the nation's welfare state. Although the level of spending is roughly similar to Sweden, Danish programs incorporate far greater liberal influences. For example, to establish the basic pension system, the Social Democrats had to compromise by agreeing to tax incentives for private pension plans. These incentives went mainly to company plans benefiting mostly white-collar workers. Such a duel public-private system undermined further attempts at reform. When the Social Democrats attempted to enact a Swedish-style ATP pension system, they were not able to win the support of salaried workers who, unlike their Swedish counterparts, now already had well-established, tax-supported private alternatives. The final ATP system had quite low contributions, and hence meager benefits,

and was paid for mostly by the workers themselves.

Other reforms took far longer to win. The health care system became fully universal and under state control only in 1971. The bourgeois parties have successfully pushed market-oriented approaches to housing. In marked contrast to Sweden, a 1958 compromise with the social democrats withdrew the state from the credit market, leaving only private financial institutions to fund housing. Rent controls were gradually reduced and subsequent legislation prioritized tax deductions for home ownership rather than collective and affordable rental options.

Compromises also had to be made on questions of funding the welfare state. Denmark's tax structure is less progressive relative to Sweden and relies much more heavily on visible, direct taxation. The compromises on universal public programs, combined with the tax structure, produced a major tax revolt in the 1970s, the likes of which were not seen in either Sweden or Norway.

The Danish Social Democrats' weaker position, relative to their northern counterparts', also held back economic policy innovations. Despite efforts to forge such mechanisms, the Social Democrats were unable to secure policies for influencing structural change. There was no Swedish-style active labor market policy nor Norwegian-style state planning. As a result, the Social Democrats have had to rely on conventional mechanisms of Keynesian fiscal and monetary policy. With no creative alternative, economic crises could force the Social Democrats to resort to mandatory state income policies in which wages were frozen in return for promised price stability and improved social benefits. Demands by unions and left-socialists for greater public control of credit and structural change were repeatedly blocked.

Norway's Complementary Path

Charting its own policies was much less a problem for the Norwegian Labor Party than its Danish counterpart. From the end of World War II and stretching well into the 1960s, the Social Democrats held an absolute majority in the national legislature. The Labor Party built its majority by successfully incorporating many of the nation's small farmers, fishers, and forestry workers alongside industrial workers into its ranks. Social democracy's dominance was so strong that the bourgeois parties chose not to engage in direct confrontation with the Labor Party, but instead followed the general consensus. Indeed, although the Labor Party first articulated a Swedish-style ATP pension system, a bourgeois government actually enacted the legislation.

While many Norwegian policies run parallel to Sweden's, on economic policies the two nations have important differences. Sweden's Rehn–Meidner model focused on state intervention in the labor market. By contrast, Norway's Social Democrats focused on credit and direct investment.

Many factors contributed to the difference. While Danish Social Democrats abandoned revolutionary ambitions early and the Swedes held reform and revolution in a delicate balance, the Norwegian party carried its revolutionary convictions right into the 1920s. During the years of the Bolshevik triumph in Russia, 1918 to 1920, the Labor Party pushed for worker and peasant soviets in Norway. In 1927, the party formed a minority government calling for the outright socialization of the economy. In response, the business community threatened massive capital flight and general financial collapse. After only a few weeks, a no-confidence vote by the bourgeois parties brought down the government. Only after its defeat in the 1930 elections did the Labor Party move toward reform rather than revolution. When the party came to power after the destruction of World War II, it enjoyed widespread support from all segments of society for a specifically active state role in rebuilding the nation's economy.

The Social Democrats used state action to meet a broad spectrum of interests. While the unions and employers worked out formal wage agreements, both sides agreed to abide by the guidelines set by the government's Public Wage Board. For business, this arrangement delivered union wage restraint that limited labor costs to the parameters set by the world-market prices and productivity growth. Active state economic intervention, however, promised workers both full employment and the security of price and profit controls. Meanwhile, state income and price subsidies aided farmers and fishers.

A number of policies enhanced the state's ability to engage in economic planning. Through nationalization, the state assumed control of important industries, particularly in the valuable energy sector. This sector not only included the extensive hydroelectric industry, but also brought the now multibillion-dollar-a-year North Sea oil industry under public ownership. The oil riches have helped Norway maintain both an extensive welfare state and impressive budget surpluses. The Social Democrats also engaged in active policies of decentralized regional development that spread the benefits of growth throughout the country. These policies included direct state investment as well as generous subsidies for local industrial development and reorganization.

Early during the postwar period, the Social Democrats committed the nation to the financial goals of credit centered around low interest rates. Such priorities aimed to help modest families while also directing funds toward productive investment rather than financial speculation. To this end, the state determined both the volume of credit and the rate of interest. The Social Democrats capitalized on the nation's unique and long history of state banks. They consolidated the existing institutions and also established banks for housing, education, agriculture, and regional development. By 1958 through 1961, these public institutions had assumed the dominant role in Norwegian credit—issuing over half of all loans. New legislation also further increased the state's ability to regulate private financial institutions. The efforts during the 1980s by a right-wing government to dismantle the system had ironic results. Greater deregulation and a turn to market mechanisms led not to higher efficiency, but to a more unstable economy. The state had to step in to prevent a wholesale collapse of the financial sector. In the end, the dismantling of "credit socialism" led to an increased government role in finance with the state becoming the majority shareholder in the three largest commercial banks.[49]

Life Under Different Rules: Lessons for Americans

While the different Scandinavian countries show variations, their basic experience remains similar. Citizens in these countries collectively enjoy one of the highest standards of living in the world. The gaping economic inequalities endemic to the United States are simply not part of the Scandinavian landscape. Furthermore, this social citizenship was achieved during the postwar boom with capitalist economic performances equal to or better than those of the United States. Social justice and economic health seem not mutually exclusive. Indeed, the Scandinavian countries have established a framework of strong public institutions so necessary for pursing high-road economics.

Most important, social citizenship provides reasons for U.S. progressives who battle for more collective notions of success and well-being to hold their heads high. Both government policies and American corporate and media culture encourage people to look toward individualized paths to success. Private wealth is seen as the sole means to access a higher quality of life. However, notions of private success provide a mechanism for maintaining class privilege. Half of all the wealth of Americans under the age of fifty was inherited. Today, the top 10 percent of Americans own three-quarters of all household wealth.[50] Thus, the private path to happiness is in fact closed to the vast majority of all Americans. By contrast, social citizenship opens opportunities for collective gain. As society as a whole prospers, universal programs mean that everyone gains more opportunities for education, family time, and an overall high quality of life. Government spending, so much reviled by American conservatives, becomes a collective asset to rally people around, rather than a source of manipulated resentment.

Social citizenship is hardly alien to the U.S. experience. At the time, the New Deal provided a pioneering example of new governmental economic and social policies. The differences between the United States and Europe came in the American failure to build on this foundation. Even with an underdeveloped public sphere, those elements of social citizenship that do exist within our society have proven quite enduring in their popularity. Few conservatives frontally attack such institutions as Social Security, public education, or the forty-hour workweek. Rather, they resort to secretive or misleading attempts to undermine public funding or quietly change the rules—thus eroding the public's collective assets over time. And even in today's officially conservative political climate, advances are made. As weak as it is, the Family Medical Leave Act asserted a government role in tackling one of the basic strains facing American families. More recent discussions of allowing states to use the unemployment system to cover family leave point to further possibilities.

Even the seeming public resentment against taxes and government spending can be turned on its head. In light of what Swedes get for their taxes, Americans may be justifiably outraged that they do not get their money's worth. Their disaffection does not come from an innate hostility to government, but from their desire to see real results. The reservoir of hope for effective government runs deep. Despite two decades of conservative propaganda the public still largely believes in the basic ideas of Social Security, public education, and even government's responsibility to address social problems. The key is to battle for tax and budget policies that use tax resources to fund genuine collective public gains. For the average American, shared public wealth ultimately offers the best promise for a higher quality of life—far more so than any dream of hoarded private gains. American progressives should not apologize for defending the public sphere. They should boldly assert a vision of a better future.

2

Associative Democracy: Lessons from Europe's German Powerhouse

Between State and Market

In the United States, mainstream political debates over economic policy present two narrow choices between government regulation and the so-called free market. Conservatives, in turn, try to frame the choice as one between the controlling machinations of a bloated government bureaucracy and the wonders of an efficient and spontaneous market. U.S. progressives have strong critiques of the capitalist market and the social, economic, and environmental damages it causes when unrestrained. However, they are much weaker in expressing an alternative. As we saw in the last chapter, progressives can and should unapologetically advocate strong government institutions that pursue collective goods. While direct government regulation of business must be part of a progressive agenda, progressives also have additional options.

In actuality, many of our nation's government regulatory mechanisms are top-down and less than effective. For example, our workplace health and safety laws rely on a staff of full-time inspectors to document employer violations and enforce the laws. However, with literally millions of workplaces in this country, this mechanism is not up to the task. Even without conservatives continuously attempting to cut the Occupational Safety and Health Administration's (OSHA) budget, the agency would need a veritable army of inspectors to truly enforce the nation's health and safety laws. Similar prob-

lems plague our environmental laws. In addition, regulations developed at a centralized level may not make sense when applied to diverse conditions at the local level.[1]

The difficulties found within our existing regulatory framework provide ample room for business to denounce progressive notions of establishing even greater public control. If government cannot effectively administer health and safety, how could it possibly consider intervening in corporate investment, product, and financial decisions? Business leaders and their supporters would certainly raise the specter of the old Soviet-style planned economy to counter any suggestions of public involvement in firm decision making. While conservative attacks on "bloated bureaucracy" overstate the problems found within such programs as OSHA or the Environmental Protection Agency (EPA) and ignore these agencies' accomplishments, progressives should not simply be left to defend state administration.

In recent years, a series of scholarly works has pointed to the possibilities for a choice between direct state administration and market rule. This option can be called associative democracy.[2] This path focuses on using governmental resources and authority to build up a third force of voluntary associations that over time assumes a greater and greater role in economic and social decisions. In a sense, associative democracy aims to build up what could be called a strong civil society. However, it differs from liberal and conservative ideas of a "thousand points of light." In these mainstream conceptions, voluntary organizations spontaneously grow out of civil society. The goal of government is to step out of spheres in order to let this self-organized society have the freedom to administer itself. Under capitalist reality, however, not all groups are equal. Thus, mainstream notions of a spontaneously self-organized society of self-help mean, in actuality, rule by those with the wealth and power.

By contrast, associative democracy uses active government involvement to promote voluntary associations that accurately reflect the diversity of the society. Legislation establishes a legal framework that prompts and protects the development of various forms of association. State coffers offer public funds to support the operation and growth of such groups. Furthermore, the centralized organs of government do not leave the scene. Rather their role is redefined from the administration of a centralized bureaucracy to the coordination of a dense network of institutions. Centralized public authorities provide guidelines, standards, and goals to guide and hold public-private institutions accountable. Associative democracy aims to combine the strengths of centralized coordination with the rich opportunities for experimentation and on-the-ground administration.

Associative democracy aims to devolve central state authority and administrative functions to the diverse networks of voluntary associations. Thus, a welfare state organized on associative lines could maintain the goals and resources of social citizenship, yet place the responsibilities for day-to-day administration in the hands of a diverse array of institutions rooted at the local level. Associative democracy would also embed the capitalist market in a dense network of associations with extensive coordinative and regulatory powers over what are now considered "management decisions."

Paul Hirst summarized the difference between associative democracy and mainstream notions of voluntarism in the following terms. He writes:

Associationalism does not aim to reduce either social provision or economic governance, but to change their form of organization. It devolves the performance and administration of public functions to voluntary bodies that are accountable to their members and to the public power. . . . The administration of such voluntary bodies is doubly answerable: directly to their membership through their members' rights to participate in, and exit from, associations and, for the performance of publicly-funded activities, to common political institutions composed of elected representatives and appointed officials like judges or inspectors. Associative democracy aims at a manageable and accountable state, but not an under-governed society. Associationalism does not strip down and diminish the public sphere as economic liberalism does, but actually revitalizes it and extends it.[3]

One of the strengths of the associative vision is its ability to point toward the possibilities for fundamentally altering our social and economic order in a way that also offers doable incremental steps. It suggests a kind of revolution in slow motion. Yet, even gradual change requires major breaks with current policies. In an age in which cynicism is a major form of social control, advocates of associative democracy run the risk of being told that their ideas sound great in principle but are impractical in reality.

Fortunately, suggestive examples of associative democracy exist. Indeed, elements can be found at the heart of Europe's economic powerhouse: Germany. While a firmly capitalist country, Germany has a social market economy that differs in important ways from American-style capitalism. As we will see, to avoid extensive direct state intervention in economic decisions, German policy makers fostered a dense network of institutions that are neither fully private nor governmental. Some of these institutions, which would be denounced by American businesses as wild forms of "creeping socialism," are simply part of an everyday reality from which U.S. corporations operating in Germany draw great benefit.

The German example also holds added weight

since Germany, Japan, and the United States are the world's three major economies. The German economy has been the central player in Europe for much of the twentieth century. Even before the 1991 reunification, West Germany provided the dominant voice in discussion of European integration. The strength of West Germany's economy was shown by the 60-million-citizen nation's ability to absorb the strains of the outright annexation of the 20 million people living in the former German Democratic Republic.[4] The importance of Germany's economic strength comes from its foundation in a series of institutions and practices that organizes business activity and community life in ways fundamentally different to those of the United States. Before detailing these arrangements, some background is necessary to trace the "social markets'" origins in a distinct mixture of rival traditions and the ironic role played by the U.S. government.

The Origins of the Social Market

The origins of Germany's social market merit some attention because it was produced by an amalgamation of influences that on the surface appear mutually exclusive. Since influences of the Christian right are such a part of the American political scene, the interplay between German social democracy and Christian democracy are particularly relevant. Their example suggests the possibility that at the grassroots level, "conservative America" may not be a one-sided, antiprogressive monolith.

Social Democracy, Christian Democracy, and Reform Politics

Throughout the early years of socialism, the German Social Democratic Party (SPD) provided the flagship for the European movement. Birthplace of Karl Marx, the emerging Germany was well on its way to becoming Europe's dominant economic power. For European radicals, Germany provided the greatest hope for revolution. With Marxist socialism its official ideology, the German labor movement promised to lead all of Europe into a new society. Indeed, when Lenin returned to his homeland in 1917, he did so hopeful that a successful revolution in central Europe would come to the aid of a soon-beleaguered workers' state in Russia.

Ultimately, however, German socialism became more famous for its reformism than revolution. While the home of the young Karl Marx, Germany also produced the great intellectual spokesperson for reformist politics, Eduard Bernstein. A personal friend of Friedrich Engels, Bernstein was among the generation of socialist leaders who linked the founders of Marxism with the next century. At the turn of the century, Bernstein published a series of articles in which he rejected expectations for a great economic crisis of capitalism and its destruction at the hands of working-class insurrection. In its place, he embraced the emerging parliamentary democracy and a politics of gradual reforms as the best path toward a socialist society. The SPD's left wing immediately denounced Bernstein's ideas for losing sight of the final socialist goals.

While successive party congresses condemned Bernstein's views, actual party practice came more and more to resemble a reformist path. The rightward direction showed clearly during World War I when the majority of social democratic legislators cast successive votes to fund the German war effort.[5] This war support sparked an open party split in which the more revolutionary leaders left. Throughout the 1920s and early 1930s, the majority of social democrats repeatedly demonstrated their willingness to compromise official socialist aims in order to defend the formal structures of parliamentary democracy. Put briefly, the record of social democrat–led governments during these years was one of low expectations, mild reforms, and working-class demobilization in the face of rising Nazism.[6]

The SPD reemerged in 1945 from a twelve-year fascist nightmare as potentially the strongest political force in the country. Indeed, in the western-occupied zones, the SPD not only rebuilt its organization but also quickly moved beyond its 1931 strength. Under the leadership of Kurt Schumacher, the party called for large-scale socialization of major German industries. Such demands not only reflected traditional socialist thinking, but also addressed the open participation of German industrialists in Nazism. Indeed, for many on the left, liberal democracy would rest on a firm foundation only once the economic and political power of Germany's great monopolies was broken. Social democratic hopes for political power, however, went unfulfilled. Instead, social democratic reforms would come only through cooperation with a rival political force: Christian democracy.

While the Christian Democratic Party of Germany (CDU) was founded after World War II, its traditions stretch back much further. Indeed, elements can be found in medieval Christianity and the classic conservative ideology that buttressed feudal society. At the level of official power, Christianity justified medieval class divisions as the will of God and nature. Individuals were born into a fixed station in life. Peasants were peasants and lords were lords. Social classes, however, had reciprocal duties toward each other. A person's status in life provided not just a living, but also a source of respect, skill, and dignity.

In the hands of the powerful, such an organic view of society justified exploitation and enormous disparities of wealth. However, it also provided intellectual tools for moral opposition to capitalism. Private property and wage labor shattered feudal notions of mutual obligation and ethical codes. To conservative thinking, the capitalist free market dismantled the interconnected organic fabric of society and the status distinctions on which it lay. Various strands of Christian thinkers critiqued the inequalities, poverty, and social breakdown generated by capitalism.

A conservative critique of capitalism could serve many political purposes. In the hands of elite politicians, such as Bismarck, it aided a centralized, authoritarian state. The imperial government steered an emerging capitalism and controlled the growing workers' movement by enmeshing both in centralized state institutions that fostered industrialization and basic social protections. Conservative notions

of an organic natural society also ran throughout Nazi thinking, including its philosophy of a divine German nation, centralized leadership principles, racism, and anti-Semitism.

However, classic conservatism also fed more progressive Christian traditions. In 1864, for example, the Catholic bishop of Mainz, Wilhelm Emmanuel von Kettler, attacked the principle of private property for dismantling the welfare mechanisms inherent in the old status society. Those forced to sell their labor power did not enter into the realm of voluntary agreements, as liberals professed, but one of compulsion and manipulation. Capitalism produced "unnecessary suffering" by transforming people's labor power from a source of individual pride and identity into a mere commodity. As Kettler argued:

> Labour is the man himself, an essential part of his personality. In a civilized land, therefore, labour must be protected by laws. Where this does not obtain, where labour is considered a mere commodity and the capitalist can exploit the worker and slowly destroy his ability to work, there exists in that land, despite all its allegations of civilization, a good beginning toward the most despicable barbarism.[7]

Since the inherent structure of society no longer protected people's basic self-worth, people had to protect themselves through trade unions and artisan associations. In formulating his critique, Kettler could draw on lines of thinking that often reached into quite high places. Pope Gregory XVI, for example, had already condemned liberalism's notion of private property as "false, calumnious, rash, anarchic, contrary to the word of God, impious, scandalous and erroneous."[8]

In Protestant Germany, such prolabor social teaching helped place the Catholic Church alongside social democracy as enemies of the nation in the eyes of those in power. Both socialist and Christian radicals organized grassroots networks opposed to the central state and the corporate power. Such activities could literally place socialist and Christian activists in the same jail cells.

Christian democracy thus emerged in Germany with a dual face. While it challenged the actions of corporations and defended the rights of workers to assert their humanity, it did not challenge capitalism itself. Rich and poor could be reconciled if the needs of both were respected. Christian democracy sought to humanize capitalism by subjecting it to social standards. Having faced the authoritarianism of both the old empire and fascism, German Christian democracy developed a strong distrust of centralized power. For disciplining capitalism it looked less to direct state controls and more to activity within civil society. Christian democracy envisioned a complex web of autonomous organizations through which civil society would enforce its ethical standards and provide the individual a basic sense of self-worth. Government policy would steer state resources to support and encourage these societal institutions. The Christian principle of subsidiary taught that authority should be placed at the lowest level that still allowed for effective action.

With corporate power discredited by its Nazi ties, Christian democracy offered a clear "lesser evil" to social democracy for those who wished to save German capitalism. A simple reemergence of the center and right parties of the Weimar Era had been rendered impossible by their compromises and even outright participation in fascism. For German business and professional classes, the CDU provided a Nazi-free mechanism for preventing Social Democratic dominance. Unlike socialist voices on the left, Christian Democratic labor traditions did not aim to socialize large industry or impose state-led industrial planning. Yet, the new CDU represented a complex mixture of influences. Within it lay tendencies compatible with social democracy—currents that supported workers' rights to form unions and to develop greater say in decision-making at work. More generally, Christian Democratic notions of democratic self-organization held parallels within social democratic thinking. And the party included a genu-

ine radical Catholic wing whose resistance under fascism provided the CDU with much credibility.

The Ironic Role of the United States

The political dominance of a Christian democracy with probusiness tendencies at the forefront was aided by American authorities who oversaw the German occupation and reconstruction. U.S. policy makers looked toward a postwar world of global free-market capitalism where American corporations roamed the world in search of profitable investment and trade. German, Italian, and Japanese fascism, with its direct military control of colonies, had challenged this imperialism of free trade. After the war, U.S. policy makers saw two new threats to a free-market Europe. The first, Soviet Communism, provided the official justification for U.S. policy. However, as progressive historians have well documented, Cold War visions of Soviet armies sweeping into western Europe, while useful for propaganda, were not taken seriously by government officials.[9]

The main threat to American plans in Europe came not from the east, but from the various indigenous stands of western socialism. Throughout Europe, the left emerged from the war on the march. A labour government was elected in Britain, and Social Democratic governments quickly came to power in Scandinavia. U.S. intelligence agents became embroiled in a fierce struggle to prevent resurgent French and Italian Communist parties from being similarly elected to national power. And in Germany, the Social Democrats had quickly become a powerful political force with few legitimate rivals.

This last threat was particularly serious since Germany was seen as the key to the future of Europe. Despite the surface devastation, the nation's underlying economic power and industrial structure had not been lessened by the war. Indeed, Nazi planning had modernized and expanded Germany's economic capacity. Having the largest and most dominant economy in Europe, a free-market Germany was needed to lead a Europe reconstructed along free-market lines. The social democrats' calls to denazify Germany by nationalizing major monopolies threatened to turn this wealth into a tool for a socialist-leaning Europe. Even worse, as the allied forces moved into Germany, they were greeted by workers who had spontaneously taken matters into their own hands by seizing plants and operating them along democratic lines. In the words of W. Friedmann's detailed study on the German occupation:

> The first wave of socialization was not the result of any planned Russian actions. As observed earlier, the Russians interfered far less than the Western allies with the spontaneous actions of communists, work councils, and other left wing organizations. . . . Work councils, trade unions, action committees sprung up everywhere. In thousands of cases they took direct action against specific industrialists or managers and ensured, to start with, that factual control passed into the hands of workers committees.[10]

U.S. policy makers needed to prop up procapitalist forces to block this emerging left.[11] While the Christian Democrats would provide the political counterforce, they needed time to organize. To provide such an opportunity, American officials hampered the social democrats by restricting political activity and prohibiting newspapers with ties to political parties from operating in the U.S. zone of occupation. The Americans banned all workers councils until April 1946 and then allowed them only within narrow restrictions. United States efforts to denazify Germany also protected corporate power. In stark contrast to Soviet actions, which moved against top business and governmental officials, U.S. criminal prosecutions spanned the entire population. As a result, while Nazi prison guards found themselves targets of detailed investigations, key industrialists and financiers slipped through the cracks.[12]

In the end, U.S. policy makers achieved their ambitions of staving off a socialized Germany.[13] When the first elections for the West German Bundestag were finally held in 1949, the Social Democrats lost by the narrow margin of 29.2 percent to 31 percent for the CDU. While the Communist Party gained 5.6 percent of the vote, the liberal Free Democratic Party's (FDP) 11.9 percent provided enough of a margin for the Christian Democrats to form a coalition government without the Social Democrats. The Social Democrats would remain out of national power until 1966 when they formed the controversial "Great Coalition" with the Christian democrats. This final cooperation came only after the Social Democrats had dropped calls for economic planning and socialization in favor of vague definitions of "socialism" as a set of ethical values. By moving from a class party to a "people's party," the Social Democrats eventually won a chance to govern without the CDU in 1969 through an alliance with the FDP. The Social Democratic-Liberal coalition remained in power throughout the 1970s. Many of the institutions of Germany's social market were strengthened and expanded during this period.

Germany's Social Market

This complex history produced a series of institutions that are highly suggestive of the possibilities for associative democracy. The twin legacies of a powerful socialist movement and state-led industrialization predisposed many postwar German authorities toward strong political guidance of the nation's reconstruction. Yet, the country's internal balance of power coupled with pressures from American officials to rule out extensive direct state intervention in the nation's economy. What emerged instead is what Linda Weiss has called a "submerged developmental state."[14] Instead of direct state administration, government policy encouraged the development of a range of nongovernmental institutions that have guided the German economy.

Konrad Adenauer, West Germany's first Christian Democratic chancellor coined the phrase "social market" to describe the nation's distinct economy. The "market" half of the term pointed to the limited direct government intervention in corpo-

making. Germany does not have the extensive nationalized firms or strong state planning along the scales of Austria, France, or Japan. However, the "social" half refers to a series of institutions that upholds minimal societal standards and enhances social participation in economic decision making. The social market's logic can be seen both in several layers of Germany's distinct system of labor relations and in its welfare state.

Codetermination

Germany's unique system of industrial relations merits some detail because, while it parallels the ideals of associative democracy, it is virtually unknown in the United States. Anyone who walks into a supervisory board meeting of a significant German firm would immediately encounter what, in the American experience, would seem a startling picture. Sitting around the table the observer would find not only the "usual suspects"—the shareholder representatives—but also trade union officials and other representatives elected by the workforce. Venture into any major workplace and a person would find personnel management sitting down for routine meetings with elected worker representatives. Every four years, Germany holds national elections so that workers can select these representatives. Election turnout averages around 90 percent.[15] Germany, it seems, has discovered a way to combine capitalist economic health with a certain level of economic democracy. Indeed, codetermination has been heralded as one of the keys to the nation's economic success.

The Legal Framework

Codetermination operates at two levels. At the top layer, all German corporations have a two-tiered board structure. A managerial board oversees the day-to-day operation of the firm. They are selected, however, by a supervisory board that reviews the general direction of the company, including planning, new product programs, factory location decisions, and overall finances. By law, half the supervisory board for companies with two thousand or more employees must be elected by the workforce. One employee representative is elected by middle management; the rest by all workers. This system provides near, but not equal, parity between worker and stockholder representatives. In the case of a deadlock, the chairman, who is appointed by the shareholder representatives, casts the deciding vote. This firm-level codetermination covers roughly 4 million of western Germany's 30 million workers.[16] In addition, just over half a million workers in smaller incorporated firms receive one-third representation, while another half-million workers in the coal and steel industries enjoy complete parity.

At the enterprise level, elected works councils represent over 9 million workers in private industry and almost 4 million in a related public sector system. Under the Works Constitution Act, workers in any establishment with five or more employees have the right to elect a works council. The law sets the size of the council based on the number of employees. Employers are legally required to provide the works council resources necessary for its operation, including release from work duties and access to all relevant company records.[17] Companies with more than one establishment may have several councils coordinated through a central works council of delegates from each local body.

The teeth of the German system lies in the legal powers granted to the works councils. Management is legally required to negotiate with the council over such matters as reductions or increases in work times, shift scheduling, employee transfers, health and safety measures, hiring, training, bonuses, work rules, and employee leave arrangements. In these areas, management cannot implement policy unilaterally but must secure council approval. If management and the council do not agree, the issue goes to a conciliation committee selected equally by both sides.

German law restricts the ability of employers to lay off or fire employees. A works council may reject a dismissal on several grounds including management's failure to adequately consider "social considerations," particular cases of hardship, or opportunities to reassign the worker to another job or retain him or her through retraining. Management can implement dismissals even if the council objects, but the council can take the employer before a labor court.

In the event of a plant closure, or mass dismissals of more than forty-nine workers a month, management must provide six months' notice and secure approval of its plan from a local governmental labor administration. The company must demonstrate that its actions are necessary to protect the economic viability of the enterprise and the rest of the workforce. If management's plan receives approval, it must still negotiate a "social plan" with its works council for providing retraining, transfers, and relocation to affected workers, if possible, or adequate compensation to those laid off. By contrast, the first time many American workers find out about their plant's closure is the day the facility is closed! Furthermore, unless they have union representation, an American worker can be fired for any reason, with no right to appeal.

German law similarly regulates short-term layoffs. Employers must go before the labor administration and works council. The council has binding codetermination rights over how the temporary layoffs are implemented, but not over whether or not they happen. The works council may review all hiring decisions and reject them if, among other things, the "action is likely to result in dismissals or will in some other way prejudice the rights of employees of the establishment not warranted by operational or personnel reasons."[18]

The law also requires management to consult, but not secure the approval of, the works council over matters related to the introductions of new technology and new work methods. Management also does not have to negotiate with the council over wages and benefits. Indeed, where employees are covered by a union contract the management and the council are explicitly prohibited from superseding collective bargaining. In practice, however, unions do cede some fine-tuning of wages and benefits to council-based negotiations.

Since work councils are voluntary, not all eligible workplaces have them. According to 1990 data, 35 percent of eligible establishments have councils. Most of the workplaces that do not have councils, however, are small enterprises of less than one hundred workers. Since the large firms that have them constitute the bulk of employment, roughly 70 percent of German workers are covered by the council system.[19]

Historical Origins

Ironically, while to an American audience the current system may seem like a militant expression of worker empowerment, codetermination actually came over the direct resistance of radical currents within the German labor movement. The first works council system was enacted during the Weimar Republic as a less radical alternative to worker plant seizures and threatened socialist revolution. The day the Works Council Act was passed, machine-gun fire killed forty-two people in a demonstration of revolutionary workers in Berlin.[20] During the 1920s, however, employer resistance prevented the system from ever fully developing and the Nazis abolished it soon after seizing power.

Codetermination reemerged after World War II again in a context of social unrest including spontaneous worker seizure of workplaces and Social Democratic calls for significant socialization. The Christian Democrats enacted the 1951 Co-determination Act and the 1952 Works Constitution Act over the objections of both employers and unions. While employers saw the laws as threats to their "right" to manage, the legislation also marked a major political defeat for a labor movement that sought a broader economic transformation. Codetermination was designed to promote cooperation and negotiation in the workplace. Indeed, the law explicitly states that "the employer and the works council shall refrain from activities that interfere with operations or imperil the tranquillity of the establishment."[21] Councils, for example, cannot legally call strikes or disrupt production. Nor can either side engage in acts of "industrial warfare." The law aims to foster productive companies by encouraging a workplace culture of negotiations and mutual input. To achieve this end, the works councils were granted the legal status and powers necessary for management to take them seriously. The law provides for formal agreements between management and the works councils through written documents. Worker participation rights, however, were notably steered away from the core management controls over finances and investment.

While German unions originally feared that the works councils would be manipulated by management against unions, over time they developed close ties to the council system and now view codetermination as a central part of labor relations. At the same time, German companies learned to live with the system and many managers even came to view it as an asset. Within this evolving context, the Social Democrats, with union support, extended the system after coming to power in the 1970s. Laws passed in 1972 and 1976 expanded the scope and powers of codetermination both at the supervisory board and works council levels to the system described above.

The strength of an idea is often reflected in the frequency of its emulation. In various forms codetermination mechanisms have developed throughout much of Europe. Works-council-like bodies have been tried in Sweden, France, Spain, Italy, and the Netherlands, to name a few. In negotiations over European economic integration, unions have advanced works councils and codetermination rights as an important step toward institutionalizing high economic and social standards. In North America, Canada has experimented with joint committees on occupation health and safety that display council-like aspects.[22]

The German system, however, displays several characteristics that make it distinct. Its codetermination mechanism is formally independent of unions. By contrast, Sweden's system, for example, is rooted in the unions themselves. German codetermination also provides strong legal rights, while other countries have tended toward greater voluntarism. Businesspeople clearly favor voluntary systems that leave them an option for exit. German employers have no such choice. Works-council-like systems in other countries often focus more on fostering consultation. As any American worker who routinely feels left in the dark by management can testify, obtaining the right to basic information concerning a company's performance and plans is no small achievement. However, the German system stands out for the binding rights workers have to codetermine key areas of company policy.

The details are important. Critics of the business-oriented thrust of European integration have criticized the European Union's (EU) Works Council Directive. The measure required all firms with 1,000 or more staff in the EU or at least 150 in at least two member states to set up works councils in order to facilitate employee consultation. Critics charge, however, that this mechanism has been motivated and developed around the goals of improving competitiveness and productivity. Thus, the councils that have, in practice have operated more as a tool of human resource management than a mechanism for fostering cross-border worker solidarity.[23]

Codetermination in Action: The Auto Industry

As a leading economic sector, the auto industry has received ample research attention on both sides of the Atlantic. In his detailed introduction to German industrial relations, Wolfgang Streeck provides several illustrative examples of codetermination during the 1970s when the Social Democrats gradually strengthened the system.[24] The Volkswagen (VW) case is particularly instructive.

By 1974, mismanagement and the 1973 oil crunch had produced such losses that all observers agreed that the company had to shed workers. To make matters worse, VW's managing director, Herman Leiding, had alienated the stockholder and worker representatives on the company's supervisory board; the central works council; and the union, I.G. Metall, by his efforts to limit consultation with them to the legal minimum. When the board compelled Leiding to resign, worker representatives, backed by the Social Democrats, secured a new managing director with extensive experience using codetermination in the steel industry.

On the new director's request, the personnel department formulated several alternative workforce reduction plans. One of these, the "K1" scheme, called for eliminating thirty thousand jobs out of a workforce of eighty-one thousand. Both the union and the works council successfully campaigned against the plan, persuading management eventually to disown it. Instead, the company proposed a new plan that would reduce the workforce by twenty-five thousand. While legally he could have implemented the design on his own, Schmücker, the new managing director, had made clear that he would not act without supervisory board approval. Using a more optimistic and, in retrospect, more accurate calculation of future performance, I.G. Metall and the worker board representatives proposed a scheme that reduced the workforce by only twenty thousand. Despite a campaign by the union and the works council in favor of this alternative plan, the supervisory board voted 14 to 7 in favor of management's proposal. Only the seven worker representatives voted against it.[25]

From this case we can see several strengths and limitations. The rules of capitalism and past management policies set the basic terms of debate. However, within this context, the workforce had influence. It blocked the most drastic reduction plans. And, although the stockholders had the final say, the very fact that the decision making involved a process of negotiation rather than unilateral action set a good precedent for the future. Because of codetermination, the union and workforce knew about the

manpower decisions before the policies were actually set. The case also shows that the influence of the supervisory board can vary. In Germany, the board's role has been criticized as having more symbolic influence than real control at many firms. Actual practice depends on the balance of power and perspectives among the key players.[26]

The process of negotiated solutions that started with the 1974 layoffs continued to grow. VW had begun to consider building an assembly plant in the United States. When U.S. autoworkers hear of new plants in places such as Mexico, their reaction, born of experience, is one of "jobs will be lost." However, U.S. workers will have no say in the decision. The situation was different at VW. Because they had access to the company's records, the worker representatives could trust management's claim that the new plant was needed to save the company's disappearing U.S. market share. The worker representatives, however, secured significant changes to management's plan. The company agreed to limit initial production to final assembly, to produce only one model, and to ban the importation of the U.S.-built cars into Europe. Furthermore, management did not pursue closure of a German North American producing plant, but instead redistributed work so any employment loss would come through companywide attrition. Finally, management gave to the supervisory board—and thus to the union and the council—a detailed assessment of the prospects of the domestic employment in its German plants well into the 1980s. The role of the supervisory board was also extended so that all future decisions concerning the U.S. plant and its impact would require the board's formal approval.

The situation during the VW crisis contrasts starkly to the experience of U.S. autoworkers. Two oil shocks and decades of bad strategic planning hit the Big Three automakers hard in the late 1970s. Management's response was direct and unilateral: mass layoffs. Total employment in the U.S. auto industry dropped from 802,800 in December 1978 to 487,700 in January 1983.[27] Not only did the United Auto Workers (UAW) have few channels to influence layoff decisions, but also it soon confronted and gave in to major concession demands from all three automakers.[28] The mass layoffs hit deep into UAW membership, which dropped from a 1979 peak of 1.5 million to 974,000 by 1985. Today the union's membership is under 750,000. By contrast, the German auto industry went through similar crisis years without mass layoffs. German automakers made an impressive recovery and I.G. Metall preserved its membership. According to Wolfgang Streeck, the industry's remarkable competitive success lay in Germany's distinct system of industrial relations. Because union strength and codetermination rights sharply restricted layoffs, management had to seek alternative cooperative solutions that in the long term proved quite successful.[29]

The auto industry also provides illustrative examples of the works council system. American autoworkers face the twin strains of mass layoffs during industry downturns followed by massive overtime during good times. The U.S. auto industry's workforce has actually shrunk while workloads increase. Management sees large-scale overtime as cheaper and more flexible than hiring more workers. The result is routine workweeks of fifty to sixty hours or more.[30] By contrast, overtime issues in the German auto industry are the subject of intense codetermination bargaining. German car factories are restricted to overtime only in the form of eight-hour shifts on Saturdays. To schedule an additional shift, management legally must seek the works council's approval. While management can appeal a council's veto, the time involved in such a process means that even a favorable ruling may come too late.

Works councils have used their power to block overtime as a negotiating tool to secure agreements in areas not covered by legal codetermination rights. Council demands might include shift bonuses and higher overtime rates, additional holidays or breaks, changes in piece rates, profit sharing, and even discounts on cars produced during overtime shifts.[31] At VW in the late 1970s, the works councils traded consent for overtime in return for management agree-

ments for increased hiring and income security. An effort to require per shift contributions to an income maintenance fund for laid-off workers failed due to worker disagreements and management opposition.

Responding to Workplace Change

As the auto industry cases suggest, actual codetermination practice can vary considerably. In her case studies of workplace change in several German firms, Kirsten Wever found the results of codetermination varied by the types of employment and union presence.[32]

For example, during the 1980s, Bayer—a major global pharmaceutical company employing forty thousand people in Germany—undertook extensive automation and work rationalization. In an American context such efforts often result in workforce downsizing and either the replacement of less skilled workers or the deskilling of jobs. At Bayer, however, there were no layoffs. For example, management dropped its plans to reorganize a group of engineers after the works council objected on the grounds that it would narrow workers' skill base and reduce the company's ability to deploy people flexibly.[33] This action reflected a relationship between the central works council and management that both described as friendly. Indeed, a representative from the central personnel department described the interaction as follows:

> We inform the council in a . . . timely fashion regarding all issues concerned with new technology introduction. Two or three times a year we sit down and discuss broader developmental trends and decide how to work together in the medium and long term to change workplaces and look at what else needs to be done. We work not against, but with, the council and the employees, and that way we reach acceptance [of the new technologies].[34]

Councils can push worker interests successfully even when they conflict with management's plans.

For example, at Betrix Cosmetics, an employer of about one thousand mostly low-skilled female workers, the works council responded to management's adjustments to the filling and packaging assembly line with a proposed job rotation and cross-training system that would enhance, rather than degrade, the work. While the union, I.G. Chemie, had traditionally adopted an accommodationist stance toward management, the council, led by a forceful feminist, was proactive and, at times, confrontational. Management at first rejected the council plan out of hand. However, when an American buyout directly threatened to close the plant unless productivity improved, the council's persistence paid off and a jointly designed rotation schedule was developed.

At the Cologne branch of Commerzbank, however, the works council failed to steer in a more positive direction management's plans to introduce a new computer system that decreased the skill levels required of many employees. With the help of the national union, HBV, and contacts with other local councils, the Cologne council developed an alternative plan for reorganizing work that would meet management's desire for increased productivity while increasing skill levels. However, the central works council, covering all of Commerzbank's branches, decided that the plan required too much leverage on the part of local works councils to be effectively implemented at most branches. Because management's plans involved comprehensive change throughout the company, the Cologne council could not simply act on its own. Without the central council's support, the plan died.

Codetermination and German Unions

German codetermination is not a magic wand guaranteeing effective worker participation in company decisions. Since the law provides councils with only limited resources, the councils can easily become overworked. While councils can react to management initiatives for workplace change, proactive, worker-initiated policies typically require greater resources than many councils possess. Many German researchers have concluded that the legal rights of the works council do not provide sufficient clout for true codetermination in which the firm is jointly run by management and workers.[35] Specifically, works council legal participation rights are strong in social matters, less strong in personnel questions, and weak in financial and economic matters.[36]

Codetermination does not exist in a vacuum, however. Over time, it has become intimately intertwined with German unions. Initial fears that employers would manipulate councils to absorb workers into company agendas and undermine union organization have not been borne out. Today, union slates are the people elected to council office. According to the German national union federation (DGB) roughly three-quarters of all works councilors are union members; employer figures put the number at two-thirds.[37] Sympathetic councilors also provide unions key allies in attempting to recruit membership in mostly nonunion workplaces.

The works councils have become an instrumental part of a dual system of worker representation within the German labor movement. The councils represent the local workplace- and firm-specific worker concerns, while the unions focus on industry- and nationwide issues. This dual system reflects a structure of German industrial relations quite different from that found in the United States. Since the contrast opens possibilities for rethinking our own system, it is worth exploring.

The U.S. system, founded with the 1935 Wagner Act, is based on a system of exclusive representation. Under the law, workers achieve legal union recognition when 50 percent plus one of eligible employees vote in favor of a union. That union then legally becomes the workers' sole representative in the workplace. U.S. unions typically secure themselves from management counterattacks by negotiating contract requirements that all new employees must join the union.[38] U.S. law emphasizes formal collective bargaining contracts whose legal complexity can become quite impressive. American labor relations are based on an adversarial "arms-length" relationship. Unions and workers do not seek a voice in running the firm. Rather, negotiations between the workers and company occur every few years across the contract bargaining table. The U.S. labor movement is fragmented among over 150 unions. While many are broad industrial unions, some are more narrow craft unions. The national federation of unions, the American Federation of Labor-Congress of Industrial Organizations (AFL-CIO) is weak by European standards. It does not, for example, participate in bargaining with employers. Indeed, even among national unions, few industrywide collective bargaining practices exist.[39]

From the viewpoint of workers, the U.S. system has become quite obsolete. Legal protections for workers have eroded to the point where many union activists argue that the legal right to join a union does not exist in actual practice. Today, companies routinely and illegally fire selected workers during union organizing campaigns. By 2000, only 14 percent of U.S. workers belonged to unions—down from a peak of over one-third during the early 1950s.[40]

While the U.S. system encourages fragmentation, the German system promotes centralization. The German labor movement is concentrated into just sixteen major unions—all organized on an industrial basis. All belong to the DGB. As in Sweden, centralization within the labor movement has fostered a similar concentration among employers. Unlike their much weaker U.S. business counterparts, these employer and industry bodies have authority to negotiate with the unions. Collective bargaining in Germany occurs at a regional level by industry or group of industries.

Unlike in the U.S. system, German law does not base unionization around exclusive representation. Different workers in the same workplace can belong to different unions or none at all. To American eyes, these laws may seem like the antiworker "right to work" statutes, passed in close to twenty U.S. states, which ban negotiated requirements for new workers to join the union. In countries such as France and Italy, similar open union membership laws have allowed workers to become divided into rival unions aligned with different political parties. Such dangers have been offset in Germany, however, by the centralized nature of bargaining. Once an employer joins the appropriate employer association, it is bound by the agreement negotiated between that association and the union. Thus, all of a firm's workers are covered by the contract regardless of union membership. Not only the union, but also employers already covered by the contract have a vested interest in compelling all companies to join the employer association. Furthermore, German law permits the government to extend collective agreements to employers who have not participated in bargaining. Thus, union contracts can determine the labor standards for entire industries. While roughly two out of five German workers choose to join a union, the actual collective bargaining agreements cover 80 to 90 percent of the workforce.[41]

The German collective bargaining system has important implications. Since German unions do not need to cross a 50-percent-plus-one vote threshold to exist, they can operate in workplaces regardless of how many or how few workers join. Since an employer is likely to be covered by the regional industry bargaining agreement regardless of the specific level of union membership at their workplaces, they have less incentive to engage in the union avoidance strategies favored by their American counterparts. By contrast, an American employer's ability to terrorize a majority of workers to vote against union recognition is decisive in determining whether or not a union will legally exist. Similarly, in Germany, outsourcing to nearby nonunion supplier companies or contractors makes less sense since these companies are likely also covered by the same master labor agreement.

The more centralized bargaining allows German unions to emphasize regional, rather than workplace-specific, organization. For example, I.G. Metall's workplace structure does not participate in collective bargaining. Collective bargaining representatives are selected based on residence, not workplace.[42] With the exception of steel industry and metal artisan enterprises, I.G. Metall recognizes no industry-specific structure in its own organization. By contrast, the national UAW, for example, operates with specific departments dedicated to each of the three main U.S. auto companies.

On the positive side, the German system encourages unions to focus on broad concerns of a national scope. This larger context can foster forward-looking, proactive agendas. In this sense, German unions are much more directly political organizations than their U.S. counterparts. A potential weakness, however, is that the system can neglect localized worker concerns. Centralized unions that try to take up local issues risk dividing their membership between parochial concerns. I.G. Metall, for example, has faced potential conflicts over wage levels between its general membership and those who work at particularly profitable firms.

The works councils ease this dilemma through their ability to represent local concerns in separate, but legally protected, forums. I.G. Metall, for example, has negotiated contracts that allow works councils to negotiate supplements to the official wage scales. The local councils thus provide a critical second tier for worker representation. For German unions, the councils take care of many localized issues that in the United States are performed by the union locals. Furthermore, German unions can focus their regional collective bargaining on broad policy questions and general standards —leaving it to the councils to work out the details most relevant to specific workplaces and firms. Because the councils have ongoing powers to participate in company decisions between periods of contract negotiations, German unions can also avoid negotiating the level of highly detailed and legalistic contracts typical in the United States.

The unions support councils by providing resources and bargaining leverage crucial for extending the limited codetermination rights in more independent and proactive directions. A national union, for example, has the resources to conduct detailed research on a specific aspect of technological change faced in a given industry. The works councils can then take that information and use it to bargain over the reality of that change.

The dual system of worker representation has allowed the German labor movement to display a noticeable level of flexibility and forward-looking strategy. The pioneering efforts of I.G. Metall Workers union to lower work time well illustrate this interaction.

The Thirty-five-Hour Workweek

As we will detail in Chapter 4, Europe as a whole faces serious unemployment. While they are lower than some of its neighbors, West Germany's unemployment rates rose steadily in the 1980s and were still over 6 percent on the eve of the reunification. Following unsuccessful attempts to secure a political solution to this problem, I.G. Metall turned to innovative industrial action.[43]

The centerpiece of the union's bargaining agenda focused on reducing work hours. While generations have worked under the forty-hour workweek, there is nothing natural about this standard. It came as the fruit of decades of worker organizing both in the United States and Europe. Among developed nations, worker productivity, especially in manufacturing, has risen dramatically since the end of World War II. Much of this postwar productivity boom, however, was not channeled into easing people's workloads, but into increasing dramatically personal consumption. Companies also use productivity gains to do more work with fewer people. With the long-term slowing of overall economic growth, I.G. Metall sought to redirect the productivity boom by reducing official work hours in ways that would compel employers to hire more workers.

The showdown came in 1984 when I.G. Metall struck for reduced worktime in its stronghold of Nord-Wüttemberg/Nord-Baden. The strike quickly began the largest and most intense industrial conflict in the history of the Federal Republic of Germany. Employers responded by locking out workers in unprecedented numbers. Soon, over half a million workers were affected by the strike. In the end, Germany's codetermination system provided a vehicle for I.G. Metall to win a settlement. Employers agreed to lower the workweek by 1.5 hours. However, the union met employer demands for flexibility in implementation by allowing the reduction to take different possible forms: daily, weekly, or accumulated over longer periods. Negotiations between management and works council at each plant would decide on the version best suited for local conditions.

In a U.S. context, such union concessions to workplace "flexibility" would have opened the door for management to unilaterally manipulate the agreement to its own advantage. However, I.G. Metall could use the well-established works council system to ensure a process of genuine negotiation between workers and managers. Indeed, subsequent research found that management–council negotiations produced considerable diversity over how hours were apportioned over time, but few variations among individual workers.

This pattern, of using centralized union strength to win overall standards and then relying on the works council negotiations for flexibility of implementation, set the framework for I.G. Metall's ongoing work-time campaign. In 1987, the union secured a two-stage plan reducing the workweek to thirty-seven hours. Two further stages, lowering it to thirty-five hours, were won in 1990. As a result of the union's efforts, German metal workers, who already enjoyed some of the longest vacations in Europe (up to six weeks paid time), now had the shortest workweek as well. The flexibility provided by codetermination continued to provide a mechanism for employer acceptance of the union's demands. For example, plant managers feared that across-the-board cuts in work hours would create bottlenecks around key indispensable employees. The 1990 agreement met this concern by allowing up to 18 percent of a plant's workforce to voluntarily work a forty-hour week for either extra pay or accumulated time. Again,

the union demonstrated its reliance on the works councils to negotiate and monitor such flexible details to ensure that the system remained truly voluntary and that the 18 percent limit was not exceeded.

Today, reduced work time has become a European-wide debate. In 2000, the French Socialist–led government implemented a nationwide thirty-five-hour workweek with no cut in overall pay.

What's in Codetermination for Management?

From workers' standpoint, the attraction of legally mandated worker participation in company decisions backed by strong unions seems obvious. However, the noticeable support for the system among German managers requires some explanation. Indeed, although business fought the original implementation of codetermination in the 1950s and its expansion in the 1970s, employer attitudes have clearly changed over time. For example, a 1990 study of 111 senior managers found that no fewer than 96 percent held a positive attitude toward the works council. Some even commented that "if the works council did not exist, it would have to be invented."[44] Few employers openly challenge the system. Why the change of heart? German companies have gained a range of benefits by working with the system.

Be it through a works council or a union, greater worker input increases workplace effectiveness.[45] Not only does codetermination provide a channel for workers to voice ideas, but the process of negotiated management also helps produce better decisions. Having to fully explain changes to its workforce compels management to fully think through decisions and justify them to an outside audience. While the negotiations can slow the process of making decisions, such discussion makes implementation far smoother. A workforce that has been involved will be less resistant to changes and better able to understand how to put the decisions into action.

While in the eyes of an American manager codetermination may seem like a source of tension, in Germany it has actually helped avoid escalated labor–management conflict. Indeed, for a long time, Germany boasted some of the lowest strike rates in Europe. This comes not as a result of union weakness, but strength. Through codetermination, German workers have far greater access to company information than their counterparts in the United States. Since codetermination rights are protected by law, and since they generally strengthen the position of unions, worker representatives operate from a position of basic security. Unlike their U.S. counterparts, German unions do not fear for their future. The stronger and more secure a union, the greater room it has to meet management's agenda halfway. Indeed, mutual trust born from basic security is key for workers' willingness to consider trading short-term concessions for long-term goals.

Similarly, studies of various worker participation and work reorganization schemes have shown that programs gain more worker commitment the more they are institutionally independent of management's will.[46] In the United States, company-driven employee involvement programs always face the weakness that workers may not fully buy into them since management ultimately has the power to unilaterally pull out. This is especially the case in nonunion settings. By contrast, German workers know that the works councils are permanent. Rather than simply trying to block threatening management decisions, German unions and works councils have the ability to push those decisions in more work-friendly directions. Thus, the company gets a higher level of cooperation, and workers get better decisions.

The power sharing within the firm also opens the door for greater common ground. For example, reflecting real economic changes, the word "flexibility" became a popular catchword in management's lexicon during the 1990s. In the United States, management's "flexibility" can threaten time-honored union protections such as job classifications and seniority rights. These provisions protected workers from having their skills eroded and their wage levels undermined. Without detailed job boundaries,

management can threaten worker safety by having workers perform tasks they were not trained to do. By blurring job distinctions, companies can shed workers and force the remainder to take on more work. At the same time, however, the existing system of rigid work rules and job control unionism both prevents companies from meeting competitive challenges and holds back innovations that could genuinely increase workers' skills and job satisfaction. The dilemma comes because workers have no institutionalized voice in company decisions. As a result, when U.S. unions give in to company demands for greater flexibility in job assignments, they have no guarantee that management will not simply use the opening to undermine job security, skill levels, safety, wages, and so forth.

German companies, by contrast, face a different situation. While codetermination restricts management's ability to hire and fire, it also permits greater flexibility within the firm. German unions have not needed to defend rigid classifications and job rights because internal personnel decisions are not made unilaterally by management. Instead, works councils review personnel decisions and have the legal right to block those hostile to the overall workforce. In the end, German managers enjoy far greater potential flexibility, while workers have basic standards protected.

Both managers and workers also gain through codetermination's impact on the conduct of government regulation. U.S. companies typically view government regulations as unnecessary burdens. This stems in no small part from capitalism's tendency to subordinate community, worker, and environmental health to the needs of the bottom line. However, as we suggested at the beginning of this chapter, the United States also relies on a highly ineffective system of centralized regulation. Government health and safety enforcement is very legalistic. It relies on detailed, formal rules and government bureaucracies to enforce them. From management's standpoint, regulation is very intrusive. Government authorities come from outside the workplace and tell the company what to do. The system does not work well for workers either. With millions of workplaces in the United States, even an army of government inspectors can check at best only a minority of firms. And during an inspection, government agents may not be able to discover all health, environmental, and civil rights law violations.

By contrast, German law sets basic rules and then uses codetermination to empower those workers to enforce the law. Work councils have codetermination rights to fully review company compliance with all laws. From management's standpoint, this means less outsiders intruding into the workplace. Workers, however, have the ability not only to have violations addressed, but to block illegal management actions before they happen.

Codetermination does not mean conflicts go away. As I.G. Metall's battle for the thirty-five-hour workweek illustrates, strong institutions of worker representation allow workers to develop agendas independent of management, and provide them leverage to make their ideas reality. Ironically, however, those same institutions that can enhance worker capacity for conflict, also increase the ground for cooperation. By institutionalizing a process of management through negotiations, codetermination has fostered a level of mutual strength and security that undergirds a relative level of trust between labor and management missing in most American firms.

Nongovernmental Institutions for Competing on the High Road

We have explored codetermination in such lengths because it both offers an example consistent with associative democracy and points to ways of thinking about business that are decidedly different than American practices. Germany's social market suggests that even within capitalism there are different ways of competing. Worker and community health are not intrinsically set in a trade-off with firm performance. Rather than competing through low wages and low short-term costs, German firms tap into a workforce that can contribute more than simply a pair of hands. Well-paid, unionized workers have the skills and channels of input that allow German companies to incrementally adjust to a changing global environment. Indeed, the German competitive edge looks toward producing well-designed and top-quality products built in highly efficient, flexible, and productive workplaces.

Both American low-road and German high-road paths will deliver business profits and competitive edges. They contrast starkly, however, in their social impact. Comparing Germany to the United States also makes clear that left to their own devices, capitalist firms will head down the low road. Indeed, when German firms have located plants in the United States, they have not always rushed out to replicate German conditions. Instead, they often have used their greater freedom to experiment with new ways of conducting business. BMW and Mercedes, for example, located their new U.S. assembly plants in the less-unionized, lower-wage American South rather than in the auto industry's unionized heartland of the Midwest.

Low-road strategies can be pursued unilaterally by a firm. The high road, however, requires a collective framework. German managers have learned to use worker input to their advantage because they had few options to do otherwise. By writing codetermination into law, the German government ensured that worker input was legally protected and that all major German firms would be subject to the same system. The same dynamic holds true for German collective bargaining. Individual firms have little to gain by undercutting union wages since the union contracts apply across industries. Germany's social marker includes other elements that guide companies along a higher road.

Worker Training

The German economy benefits from an extensive system of worker training that produces the highly skilled workforce on which high-road strategies are built. Work councils, unions, management, and government authorities jointly administer the nation's famous apprenticeship system that ensures that young Germans who do not go to college, nevertheless pick up valuable skills. Between two-thirds to three-quarters of all German workers receive two to three years of vocational training. Typically, the student spends three to four days a week on the job and one to two days in the classroom. Such apprenticeships are available for over four hundred occupations from hairdressers to metal workers to bank tellers. To qualify for certification, students must pass an exam that demonstrates that they meet national standards. These standards are established by representatives of labor, management, and the state at the national level and are enforced by a similar partnership locally. Most apprentices receive jobs in the companies in which they were trained. Their training, however, emphasizes general skills, allowing them to move from firm to firm or to different positions within the same firm. Once employed, German workers benefit from the commitment of firms to an ongoing process of further training and skill development administered through codetermination.[47]

While Germany has one of the most skilled workforces in the world, the United States has an acute shortage of properly skilled workers, especially in manufacturing. Initial vocational education in the United States is based far more in isolated primary school programs. There are no national standards, nor a certification system. At best, American companies and unions are involved on an ad hoc, local basis. Enrollment in postsecondary vocational training has declined steadily since 1982, because it often fails to lead to better employment. Apprenticeships in the United States are extremely rare as companies are reluctant to invest in them. The training priorities of most American firms do not improve the picture. From an individual employer's standpoint, money spent in worker training can be easily lost if that individual leaves the firm. Thus, U.S. companies typically do not prioritize training. When they do train, they typically focus on narrow, job-specific skills not easily

transferred to other firms. The vast bulk of firm training goes to management, not frontline workers.

Studies have shown that worker training produces noticeable increases in firm productivity, as well as workers' wages.[48] Furthermore, to best adapt to new technology and changing work organization, U.S. companies need a workforce trained in the kinds of broad skills that the German system provides. However, even if they wanted to, most U.S. firms could not solve the training problem individually. Worker education requires a comprehensive solution that brings together business, union, and state resources. Yet, the never-ending attacks on "big government" and the millions of dollars spent by U.S. companies on antiunion law firms do not bode well for establishing institutions necessary to develop an adequately skilled workforce.

Supporting Craft Work

Tied into German apprenticeship education is a second high-road mechanism: the country's institutionally protected artisan economy. This so-called Handwerk sector produces customized quality goods in small workplaces organized around artisan lines. Handwerk contains two legally supported institutions. Chambers enforce apprenticeship laws, administer vocational training, and distribute master licenses. Any firm that practices recognized artisan trades without the appropriate accreditation is liable to prosecution by the chambers. Unlike the chambers that are organized by geography, guilds represent specific trades. Handwerk justifies itself by providing not only specialized tools, machinery, and parts to German industry, but also by providing skilled workers through its central role in administering vocational training.

Artisan work in Germany has not only survived but grown in recent years. In 1983, Handwerk represented 496,000 small firms, employing 3.9 million employees and involving over 10 percent of the nation's gross national product (GNP).[49] Handwerk has prospered as a result of deliberate government policy. At times this support came from quite conservative sources. The Nazis actively promoted Handwerk. The system also fits well with the "small business" image of capitalism promoted by the Christian Democrats.

Strong Community Standards

German laws uphold high-road community standards and further establish the social market. German towns and cities have, in comparison to the United States, done a much better job of maintaining a tighter distinction between the urban built environment and countryside. Clearly a different set of land-use policies has helped contain suburban sprawl. Germany also has held on to laws restricting business hours that have passed away in the United States. Thus, on Sundays, American malls are bustling with activity, and weekend jobs are common. By contrast, German downtowns are generally closed for business on Sunday while the hills are filled with families out for an afternoon stroll. Other laws prohibit retailers from holding sales on most merchandise except at specific times of the year.[50] In short, the country has a legal framework that prevents the capitalist marketplace from unilaterally dictating the basic quality of life.

High-Road Financing

The high road requires companies to operate with a long-term time horizon. While German financial structures encourage such a perspective, the U.S. system actually drives very short-term thinking. To expand and evolve, all companies need to secure sources of additional capital. While the accumulation of profits can provide an internal source of financing, most firms also seek new capital from the outside. In the United States, the stock market plays a central financial role. As we will detail in chapter 6, Wall Street today pushes firms down low-road, short-term business strategies.

By contrast, banks, not the stock market, play the central role in German financing. Bank dominance comes as the result of over a century of deliberate government policy. According to figures provided by Michel Albert, president of France's largest insurance company, the Frankfurt stock exchange's total capitalization is nine times smaller than Wall Street's.[51] Because German financial regulations give banks a high degree of freedom in the types of business they can pursue, they deal in stocks and bonds, manage company treasuries, operate commercial banks, provide investment advice, and carry out acquisitions and mergers. As a result of government policies, German banks and industry groups have developed a close and special relationship. They often hold ownership in each other and sit on each other's board of directors. Each partner is invested for the long haul because the welfare of each depends on the health of the others.

The concentration of economic power in Germany's "bank capitalism" is by itself no more democratic than America's Wall Street. However, together with the other institutions we have described, it helps establish an economy whose institutions support long-term, high-road paths to competition. Furthermore, as we will examine in the next chapter with Austria's example of nationalized economic sectors, bank-centered finance can also become publicly controlled finance.

Associative Social Citizenship— Possibilities from Germany's Welfare State

With the "social budget" encompassing roughly 30 percent of the nation's GNP in 1990, Germany comes far closer to Sweden than to the United States.[52] Indeed, the nation's social market requires an extensive welfare state. The German system not only provides basic security, but also shapes the German labor movement's ability to negotiate with employers. Unions can compromise on wage moderation and other employment conditions because, in return, workers have received a greater "social wage" from the welfare state.[53]

As we will detail below, the influences on

Germany's social spending are mixed and the outcomes not always the most desirable. However, the German system's use of institutions that are neither governmental nor private for-profit firms is suggestive of the possibilities for a social citizenship that combines governmental and associative mechanisms.

The German system differs from its Scandinavian counterparts. Social democratic values of solidarity are reflected in the universal nature of many programs. However, conservative influences are also quite clear. The basis of German policy comes from social insurance programs covering the key areas of health care, pensions, sickness, accident, unemployment, and long-term care. While each area has its own system, all are organized around principles dating back to the conservative nineteenth-century policies of Bismarck. Contributions to the insurance funds are paid half by employer and half by workers (employers pay all of the accident fund). Taxes come into play only to back up the security of the funds. When workers become eligible for insurance benefits, the amount they receive comes from the level of past contributions made.

Unlike American practices, German law requires mandatory enrollment in all of these insurance systems, with very few exceptions. Thus, most of the population is covered either through wage labor or by extended family coverage. Following conservative policy norms, the state generally does not directly run most of the system, but relies on semiautonomous, nongovernmental, nonprofit organizations to administer the funds. Health insurance, for example, is divided into over one thousand separate funds organized either on a geographical, workplace, or job-type basis. The sickness, pension, and disability funds similarly operate on a decentralized basis often through joint supervision by employers and unions. The single body that runs the unemployment system is also jointly administered by representatives of government, business, and unions. The system's reliance on nongovernmental institutions can be seen in sample figures. Of hospital beds, 35 percent are run by voluntary organizations, as are

70 percent of institutions caring for children and 65 percent of elderly care.[54] These organizations come in a wide variety of forms ranging from religious to union to private charity and nonprofits. This focus on nongovernmental institutions contrasts with the Scandinavian reliance on public and governmental bodies as well as the U.S. devotion to private, for-profit companies.

Conservative influences in the German system produce other important differences to the Scandinavian model. The German system focuses on income maintenance, not redistributing wealth or eliminating poverty. Indeed, by basing benefits on earning contributions, German social insurance replicates the economy's class and status divisions. Since the German system revolves around employment, rather than citizenship, people can fall through cracks either by not being employed for a long-time period or by having very low earnings. People in such cases are picked up by the tax-supported welfare programs. As means-tested support, they carry with them many of the same stigmas and drawbacks found in the U.S. system.

In the German system, benefits come largely through cash transfers rather than the Scandinavian-type provision of public services. Indeed, cash transfers comprise two-thirds of Germany's "social budget."[55] This distinct focus has contributed to the comparatively underdeveloped level of Germany's service sector. In the United States, the private wealth concentrated among a small segment of the population helps to sustain a large service sector oriented toward upscale needs. In Sweden, large publicly run universal services focus on general public needs. In contrast to both, Germany's service economy employs almost half the proportion of the workforce found in the United States and Sweden.[56]

By relying on a complex mixture of private and public providers, the German system fragments social policy. This decentralization is also enhanced by the country's federal system, which further divides government policies between national, state, and local governments. Such fragmentation makes rapid policy changes difficult.

Conservative influences are also visible in the way in which the system impacts women. Employment-based insurance ties to a traditional family vision of a male breadwinner and a dependent female. Indeed, not until the 1970s and 1980s did German law recognize key measures of equal status within the family. Even so, many women face a tough choice between employment and child rearing, despite newer laws providing parental leave. Without employment, a woman is dependent on a man's income since she must draw on insurance as a spouse. Alternatively, if she qualifies based on her own employment history, she will generally face lower levels of benefits since time taken for child rearing and the lower pay levels associated with interrupted careers and gender discrimination are reflected in the benefit calculus. Indeed, as Prue Chamberlayne argues, the German system promotes marriage, not child rearing, as women are forced to choose between a childless career and traditional homemaking. As with most of Europe, female employment has risen, especially among married women. Yet, in Germany, women's labor market participation levels are still lower than in either the United States or Sweden. Furthermore, only 20 percent of female German employees worked at full-time jobs.[57]

Despite its limitations, the German welfare state provides further evidence that stronger social policy benefits the community. Even with its fragmentation, the German health insurance system provides high-quality care that reaches the entire population while using less of the wealth of the nation than the United States. While more limited in its wealth redistribution and its provision of public services than the Scandinavian systems, the German welfare state is a key part of a social market that provides less of the social insecurity, glaring inequalities, and social decay found in the United States. Most important, it is suggestive of the possibilities for realizing associative principles. German welfare institutions reveal the ample ground for public policy that lies between direct state administration and the capitalist marketplace.

The German Economy Outperforms the United States'

Germany's social market economy is not without its problems. For example, according to Kirsten Wever, some businesses view the regulations that come as part of the social market as onerous and restrictive. The conservative German financial system makes finding startup funds for new businesses difficult. Internally, German management structures can seem overly hierarchical and bureaucratic when contrasted with U.S. counterparts.[58] Furthermore, as we will detail in chapter 4, Germany joins with the rest of Europe in facing severe economic strains.

None of these limitations, however, invalidates the strengths of the social market and its base in institutions suggestive of associative democracy. Quite the opposite. Measures of overall, long-term economic performance show the superiority of the social market over the American economy. Table 2.1 provides the conventional indicators of capitalist economic success.

The data contained in Table 2.1, taken from three different sources, show an overall pattern of superior German economic performance. Growth and unemployment rates in the United States momentarily were better than those of Germany during the mid-1980s' recovery. However, by the 1990s, the German economy had returned to the relative superiority it had demonstrated throughout the postwar boom. Furthermore, the so-called American Reagan recovery was bought by lowering the living standards of most Americans. Low official unemployment rates, for example, conceal a significant number of workers who are long-term unemployed or trapped in part-time, dead end, and low-paying jobs. Also in contrast to that of the United States, the German economy has maintained its industrial strength. While manufacturing is still a key sector in the U.S. economy, deindustrialization has hit many American communities hard. The German experience suggests that such a pattern is not inevitable. Because the social market has undergirded

Table 2.1

United States and German Economic Performance

	Federal Republic of Germany (%)	United States (%)
Average annual growth rate 1963–73		
	4.4	4.1
Real GDP growth average 1960–89	3.7	3.2
Rates of growth of real GDP		
1979	4.2	2.5
1982	–0.9	–2.2
1985	2.0	3.2
1988	3.7	3.9
1990	5.7	1.2
Fixed capital formation as age of GDP average 1960–89	22.5	18.1
Trade balance as age of GDP average 1960–89	2.7	–0.6
Average annual consumer price increases 1960–90	3.5	5.1
Annual inflation rate 1983–92	2.2	3.8
Unemployment rates		
1971	0.7	5.8
1976	4	7.6
1981	4.5	7.5
1986	7.6	6.9
1989	6.8	5.2
1992	6.3*	7.3

Sources: The first rows are derived from from Fritz Scharpf, *Crisis and Choice in European Social Democracy* (Ithaca, NY: Cornell University Press, 1987), p. 8; the yearly rates of growth in real GDP is taken from Anthony Atkinson, *Income Distribution in OECD Countries* (Organisation for Economic Co-Operation and Development, 1995), p. 28; the rest of the figures are from Kirsten Wever, *Negotiating Competitiveness: Employment Relations and Organizational Innovation in Germany and the United States* (Cambridge, MA: Harvard University Press, 1995), pp. 41–49.

*Figure for the former West Germany; unemployment in the former East Germany was considerably higher.

high performance workplaces, Germany has been able to maintain its role as an exporter of high-quality manufactured goods.

The German economy's underlying strengths were also demonstrated during the nation's reunification. In 1990, West Germany essentially annexed East Germany. As the West German economic institutions that we have described were transplanted in the east, the eastern economy collapsed. While opinions differ as to the exact challenges faced by German institutions in a united future, the basic structures that we have described here so far have displayed remarkable staying power.[59] After the fall of the Berlin Wall, German government, labor, and business authorities embarked on a unification pro-

cess driven by negotiations among the social partners. While success in transplanting West German institutions in eastern soil has varied, the overall process of negotiated cooperation and conflict continues. Faced with mass unemployment in the east, for example, the German government went more in the direction of Sweden than American free-market prescriptions. Through new forays into an active labor market policy, the government aggressively promoted employment through direct job creation and training programs negotiated among business, labor, and state administrators. Indeed, one of the centerpieces of this strategy, the employment and training companies, was developed by the union I.G. Metall. Reunification also displayed the simultaneous mixture of cooperation and conflict found in the social market. In 1993, I.G. Metall won a trendsetting strike to force employers to maintain their commitments to gradually raise East German wages to Western norms. While reunification and other economic strains have compelled German institutions to evolve, the social market as a whole continues to display remarkable resilience.

Lessons for Associative Democracy

Germany's social market is not some kind of worker utopia, but a more qualified and human version of capitalism. It is suggestive of associative principles, not their full realization. However, the successful performance of institutions that mirror associative ideals within one of the world's leading economies bolsters the case for progressive economic reforms. These real-life examples demonstrate the ability of government policy to establish institutions that empower social groups to participate in supposedly private decisions. Greater economic democracy is not a handicap lowering economic health, as American business would have us believe, but rather social participation in economic decisions can be the precondition for a robust economy.

Germany's example raises a host of intriguing questions. If Germany can successfully require works councils and codetermination in the boardrooms, how else might public policy share decisions within the firm? In what other areas, such as environmental regulations, might government action establish independent, democratically controlled institutions? How might state action foster and support the activity of organized labor and other social movements to pursue broad social goals? How might government resources be used to undergird experiments in new and democratic ways of organizing life activity? The idea of associative democracy opens up entirely new dimensions for progressive reform in the United States, which we will revisit in Part II.

The United States is not entirely unconnected to experiences of associative democracy. While we do not have works councils, U.S. labor law does provide a legal process for workers to establish a representative body, a labor union, in their workplace. For all its limitations, the National Labor Relations Act extends government authority into management's home terrain, the workplace, mandating that employers recognize the existence of legally created unions. In reorganizing federal training funds, Congress used a business-biased version of associative democracy when it recently passed the Workforce Investment Act (WIA). The new law channels federal funds through local WIA boards whose members come from the community, not government. As we will detail in chapter 10, while the law mandates business domination of these bodies, a more effective system would have followed a German-style partnership of labor and management.

American companies have had experiences in codetermination. General Motors and Ford, for example, have owned German operations for many decades. These plants have consistently received top ratings in the companies' own internal evaluations of their operations internationally. Individual firms have flirted with features of codetermination in the United States. For example, before its destruction at the hands of Frank Lorenzo, Eastern Airlines offered a model case of union-initiated power sharing. Faced with record losses from deregulation and bad management decisions, Eastern Airlines was heading for bankruptcy by the early 1980s. Faced with demands for further sweeping wage and benefit cuts, the machinists offered a creative alternative. In return for some wage cuts and work rule concessions, the union compelled a reluctant management to agree to a 25 percent worker ownership of stock, union seats on the company's board of directors, access to the company's financial records, and real worker say on the work floor. At some facilities, the union got the company to eliminate all of its frontline supervisors and let the machinists run their workplaces. For two years, the creativity and input of empowered workers drove the company toward record profits.

However, a renewed financial crisis from past loans and cutthroat nonunion competition shattered the fragile labor–management accord. In the end, the board majority voted to sell the company to Frank Lorenzo—providing investors a short-term windfall while sacrificing the firm's future. The Eastern experience further underlines the need to establish high-road practices on a societal level. If individual firms are not embedded in a larger social economy, the strains and pressures of capitalist competition will constantly pull toward the low road.

3

Social Partnership and Social Ownership: Lessons from Austria

Two fundamental assumptions undergird American economic policy debates. First, formal state policy making is the terrain of elected officials and government administrators. People influence the governing process by electing representatives. Of course, behind the scenes, lobbyists push legislation. While labor and other activist groups have some access, this informal system is clearly dominated by corporate interests. The notion, however, that state authorities might formally involve organized social interest in the process of governing seems beyond realistic consideration. Second, with very rare exceptions, government should not own productive businesses. The post office and scattered public utilities are the limit. The downfall of Soviet-style communism has only strengthened the belief—among right and left—that nationalization is a recipe for disaster.

Resting between rival blocks in the Cold War with a population of roughly 8 million, Austria built up a rather consistent record of strong, top-rated economic performance precisely by challenging these two assumptions. Austria's policy process includes a formal and significant role for unions in state policy making and a good portion of its economy was outright owned by the public. In this chapter, we detail the institutions that have allowed a small country, highly dependent on the global market, to outperform the United States.

Background: Socialist Party Dominance

While Sweden is upheld as the shining example of social democratic predominance, in fact, Austria's Socialist Party (SPÖ) has enjoyed even more spectacular political success. The Socialists have formed part of the governing coalition from 1945 to 2000. Austria has had a socialist or socialist-endorsed prime minister during all these years until Kurt Waldheim was elected in 1986. Between 1970 and 1983, the Socialists enjoyed rare success among the European left by governing outright without resort to a coalition with other parties. As in Sweden, Socialist predominance is also reflected by the degree to which the main opposition party, the conservative Peoples Party (ÖVP), has internalized the basic policies of social partnership.

Several factors contributed to Socialist success. While the official unionization rates are lower than in Sweden (48 percent in 1986), the labor movement enjoys considerable internal strengths. It is highly centralized. Unlike Sweden, just one peak federation, the Austria Federation of Trade Unions (ÖGB), encompasses both blue-collar and white-collar workers. Union members pay dues directly to this federation and ÖGB holds the strike funds—allowing it to decide which strikes to support. During the period of Grand Coalition from 1945 to 1966, in which a socialist-led coalition government included all the major parties, the socialists established a firm reputation for governing the economy effectively. The cogoverning parties were also substantially enmeshed in the social democratic policies. Adding to socialist strength has been the so-called *proporz* system whereby public-sector jobs are divided proportionately between the parties. This has meant that the Austrian administrative machinery is substantially staffed with experienced Socialist Party members. Thus, the elected governments have not faced resistance from administrative personnel not committed to social democratic reforms. As with the Swedish Social Democrats, the Socialist Party itself is well organized. In 1989, its membership stood at 617,000—with roughly a third of its voters also members. The party enjoys the support of a wide range of auxiliary mass organizations from the League of Socialist Freedom Fighters and Victims of Fascism to the Central Association of Austrian Small Gardeners, Homecrofters, and Pet Breeders.[1]

Social Partnership

Austria offers one of the most formalized expression of the European concepts of social partnership in which business, labor, and government officials jointly guide the economic health of the nation. Although such three-way cooperation is rare in official U.S. policy debates, Austria stands out in several ways: the degree to which social partnership has been formalized, the broad scope of its reach, and its enduring in the face of severe external and internal strains.

Origins

At first glance, Austrian history hardly seemed to indicate a potential for social partnership. To the contrary, growing class polarization broke out into outright civil war between 1920 and 1921. A failed revolution gave way to uneasy compromise between left and right. As in Germany, the left's inability to exercise working-class power or unity led to its opposite—a fascist regime in 1934 and German annexation in 1938.

However, Austrian history planted seeds for what came later. Starting in the mid-nineteenth century, the monarchy created the first chamber organizations as bodies to represent specific societal groups. Membership was compulsory and the chamber charters entitled each body to render an opinion on all government bills affecting their clientele. The original Chamber of Commerce, representing trade, industry, and business, was supplemented during the First Republic in 1918 with a Chamber of Labor and a Chamber of Agriculture. The First Republic also established many joint boards and joint committees to incorporate business and labor into the policy-making process. These arrangements aimed to balance off competing social interests. Such experiments were cut short, however, by the rise of fascism.

Emphasizing consensus over class confrontation, notions of centralized societal representation have long had a home in various Christian social teachings. When the Fascists took power, they took such traditions in a profoundly conservative direction. The existing interest organizations were eliminated and new *Bünde* installed in their place. The main purposes of these authoritarian organizations were to control their constituency by mobilizing support behind government policies.

After 1945, the Second Republic found itself in a position to turn the seeds of past social organization into full-blown social partnership. In contrast to the interwar period, both organized business and organized labor emerged from World War II with a greater degree of internal unity and sense of purpose. In contrast to the craft fragmentation and ideological disagreements of the interwar period, the Austrian labor movement emerged more centralized and capable of effective national action. A decade of fascism had also helped bring together opposition groups. Most generally, a wide range of Austrians shared a desire to end the Allied occupation as quickly as possible.

The Institutions of Social Partnership

The Second Republic restored and strengthened the chamber system.[2] While various professional chambers also exist, the three peak organizations of the Chamber of Commerce, Chamber of Labor, and Chamber of Agriculture form the foundations of social partnership. These bodies have the legal right to review and comment on all proposed legislation before it is taken up in parliament. Membership is compulsory and government policy has deliberately favored these three main chambers over smaller associations.

On the labor side, the Chamber of Labor has been monopolized by the already strong unions and their peak organization, the ÖGB. The ÖGB provides the national policy initiative within the labor movement—with the Chamber of Labor being composed of union leadership. The Austrian labor movement brought twin strengths crucial for establishing social partnership over the long term. In approaching employers, the unions were strong enough to compel business to view cooperation as a desirable alternative to other strategies. Indeed, the two major policy institutions of social partnership—the Parity Commission and the Council on Economic and Social Questions—were each established following a major strike wave.[3] At the same time, the ÖGB had enough internal strength to implement and internally enforce national agreements made with employers. Since World War II, Austria has been known for its low number of strikes. At the workplace level, Austrian law has established a system of works councils. As in Germany, the councils were explicitly established to encourage labor-management cooperation, not as tools for worker confrontation.

On the employer side, the Chamber of Commerce has provided an organizational and national leadership capacity far beyond anything seen among American business groups. Unlike the unions, Austrian business enjoyed a more modest level of independent self-organization. Thus, the Chamber of Commerce provided a necessary peak structure where none previously existed. In matters of collective bargaining, the employer chambers negotiate agreements in sectors where no encompassing entrepreneurs' association is available. The national-

ization of much of the nation's large industrial firms also weakened the organizational abilities of Austrian employers, thus increasing their willingness to seek more cooperative practices.

The Second Republic's party system also proved conducive to social partnership. As in Germany, collaboration with fascism had tarnished the image of business leaders and right-wing parties. Ties to national socialism discredited the Freedom Party, leaving the political arena to the socialists and the ÖVP. As the major business-affiliated party, the ÖVP emerged out of the war prepared to seek moderation. Similarly, the socialists dropped their revolutionary ambitions in policy, if not always in rhetoric. The basis for substantial cooperation was laid in 1945 when the ÖVP and SPÖ entered into the Grand Coalition. This joint government includes all of the major organized political and social groups. It lasted until 1966 and an SPÖ/ÖVP coalition was formed again in the 1980s. This prolonged political cooperation established substantial agreement on both employer and worker sides over the main contours of national economic policy. Particularly noteworthy, when the Socialist Party won the ability to govern outright without a coalition between 1970 and 1983, it stayed within boundaries of postwar policies in spite of calls for more radical actions.

The first attempt at institutionalized social partnership came between 1947 and 1951 when wage, price, and investment agreements were concluded between the three large chambers and the ÖGB, and officially announced by the government. In return for restrained wage demands by the unions, which amount to wage cuts in real terms, employers committed to rebuilding and modernizing the nation's economic structure. Labor leaders who supported the deal had concluded that substantial wage increases would not deliver long-term gains in a context of rapid national inflation. Nevertheless, this strategy proved controversial within the ranks of labor, especially among communist groups who saw the possibility for gains through militant confrontation. Following a wave of spontaneous strikes by the rank and file, the communists were expelled from the trade union movement and the position of the central leadership strengthened extensively. This first attempt at institutionalized social partnership was also undercut by employer resistance to the national deals.

Yet, institutions of social partnership got a second life when ongoing postwar inflation led the ÖGB and Chamber of Labor to propose what became a central tool of social partnership, the Joint Commission on Prices and Wages. Established in 1957, the commission was initially resisted by employers. The Joint Commission provides a meeting place for representatives of the three chambers and the ÖGB to develop agreements over national economic policy. Labor leaders wanted the commission in order to foster a social contract. They had established enough internal strength that they could enforce any wage agreements, including moderated wage demands. In return, they wanted influence over price setting and participation in general economic policy matters.

The wage and price controls introduced by the Joint Commission are flexible and, with some exceptions, voluntary. Although the federal chancellor acts as chairperson, government representatives have no formal vote. All decisions must be unanimous among the partners. The commission serves as the top-level bargaining institution within which labor and business reach agreements over wage and price policies. Although the individual unions carry out their own actual wage negotiations, the commission's Wage Subcommittee and the ÖGB authorize and coordinate the bargaining process. Because the commission includes both social partners and government officials, it also provides a forum for cooperatively approaching general economic policy. In 1963, the commission established a third subcommittee. The Advisory Council for Social and Economic Affairs is composed of experts from the social partners who analyze and make recommendations around important economic questions. Representatives of labor endorsed the council only after their primary choice, a top-level forum of government ministers and social partner leaders, was not realized.

In addition to the Parity Commission, individual government ministries establish advisory councils that solicit information and opinions from the social partners. In many cases, no governmental decision is made before an agreement is reached within these advisory councils. While the institutions connecting social partnership to government policy are important, ultimately their degree of influence resides not in their formal legal powers, but in the willingness of all involved to respect the tradition of cooperation. Indeed, social partnership is as much a cultural as a legal institution. While the social partners may disagree on specific issues and may not like individual policy agreements, they do agree to support the overall process and the overall economic goals that have maintained cooperation for half a century.

Social Partnership in Action

The practice of social partnership can be seen in its famous wage deals—the so-called incomes policy. One of the most powerful tools available to Austrian decision makers has been the ability of the union federation to subordinate wage demands to overall economic goals. Business typically argues that wage increases cause inflation by pushing up prices. They also lower investment by squeezing profits. Thus, government needs to place limits on wages and shift wealth to the people who do the investing. Unions need to accept such measures as economic necessities.

However, under this supply-side reasoning, workers who make the financial sacrifices have no guarantee that owners and managers will actually use the increased resource pool to invest in the long-term future. As many American workers who gave in to company concession demands can testify, management and investors can use profit windfalls to relocate overseas, introduce job-destroying technology, or pursue a wide range of speculative undertakings that have nothing to do with productive investment. Austrian unions, however, were able to concede to wage moderation because the process of social partnership delivered believable employer commitments on prices and investment. Thus, social partnership takes the promise of supply-side economics and makes it real by enmeshing business decisions in broader social goals, rather than relying on a trickle down from the "free market."

Through social partnership, Austrian unions sacrificed wage gains to further long-term economic security. In return for wage moderation, Austrian employers and their government representatives agreed to a national commitment for full employment. Normally, corporate leaders view low rates of unemployment as a threat. Workers who can easily find jobs elsewhere have increased bargaining leverage. In management's eyes, that means demands for higher wages. Yet, because of the process of social partnership, employers were willing to agree to full employment goals since unions were committed to moderating wage demands.

This full-employment "Austro-Keynesianism" included other components. In return for union wage moderation, business committed to high levels of domestic investment. In this way, workers traded immediate wages for actions that provided for long-term, multigeneration job security. This deal was backed up by government tax and economic policies that strongly encouraged investment rather than savings and consumption. Throughout the postwar boom, the Austrian economy showed significantly high investment levels. Wage moderation, however, limited the ability of collective bargaining to pursue the labor movement's goals for redistribution of wealth and greater income equality. This task has fallen onto the government's shoulders as a progressive tax structure combines with generous social programs and social insurance. In 1987, state expenditures rose to 56.3 percent of Austria's GDP.[4] Social citizenship provides a collective social wage that compensates for moderated personal wages.

The overall postwar Austrian experience suggests that social partnership works. The nation started the period with a level of productivity lower than the industrialized world as a whole. Thus, Austria had to engage in a continuous process of catch-up. During the 1960s, in terms of unemployment levels and increases in the GDP, the Austrian economy performed at or slightly above European averages and markedly better than the United States' did.[5]

Austria's real distinction, however, came at the end of the postwar boom when increasing economic difficulties hit all the industrialized countries. Austrian policy makers bucked the trend toward supply-side economics by continuing to pursue an Austro-Keynesian response to the crisis. The nation continued its commitment to full employment, maintained high levels of social spending, and built on the tradition of wage moderation in return for high investments. By the end of the 1970s, economic commentators began to notice a nation that seemed to be passing through the great capitalist slowdown relatively unscathed. Indeed, Austria largely escaped the malady suffered by most of the industrial world—stagflation—in which high inflation accompanied rising unemployment. Table 3.1 shows comparative economic figures for this period and beyond.

By the 1980s, the relative success of Austria and other small European countries began to attract growing scholarly interest. These nations seemed to offer a superior alternative to the supply-side policies personified by Ronald Reagan and Margaret Thatcher. Austrian economic performance seemed to demonstrate that traditional Keynesian full-employment goals could be pursued even in an economic crisis by using substantial cooperation among labor, business, and government.[6]

Austrian reality also became a counterweight to arguments that used supposed "globalization" to justify the pursuit of American-style supply-side economics. Austrian policies appeared to foster successful international competition in ways opposite to U.S. practices. Through social partnership and national ownership, Austrian public and private business reinvested in domestic production rather than spreading its operations abroad. Thus, Austrian firms entered world markets as competitive, nationally rooted firms, rather than as footloose multinational corporations.

Table 3.1

Comparative Economic Indicators (in percent)

	Average annual GDP increase 1973–1979	Average annual GDP increase 1974–1980	Average annual unemployment as percentage of total labor force 1974–1980	Unemployment 1986–1989	GNP growth 1986–1989
Austria	3.0	3.0	1.6	3.4	2.7
OEDC Europe	1.9			9.5	3.4
West Germany		2.3	3.5	7.5	2.8
United States		2.3	6.8	6.0	3.1

Sources: Peter Katzenstein, *Small States in World Markets* (Ithaca, NY: Cornell University Press, 1985), p. 195; Alois Guger, "Corporatism: Success or Failure? Austrian Experiences" in *Social Corporatism: A Superior Economic System?* Jukka Pekkarinen, Matti Pohjola, and Bob Rowthorn eds. (Oxford: Clarendon Press, 1992) p. 341; and Ferdinand Karlhofer, "The Present and Future State of Social Partnership" in *Austro-Corporatism*, Gunter Bischof and Anton Pelinka eds. (New Brunswick, NJ: Transaction Publishers, 1996), p. 137.

The pattern of continued high investment and low unemployment did come with a price, however. Measured between 1975 and 1986, Austria ranked with the United States, Canada, and Japan with high and increasing earning dispersion.[7] However, unlike the United States where greater wage inequality was accompanied by drastic social spending cuts and active union busting, in Austria workers enjoyed the benefits of a high social wage and strong labor unions.

Social partnership has its critics both inside and outside Austria. For many left-wing activists, partnership lowers the labor movement's ambitions to an acceptance not only of capitalism, but capitalist criteria of economic health. Centralized negotiations can coopt and/or discourage rank-and-file activism. Furthermore, while social partnership includes certain organized groups, it can exclude others. For example, for activists among the new left of the 1960s and 1970s, the practices of social partnership appeared as a stodgy establishment hostile to change. From the perspective of the women's movement, the Austrian economy has worked particularly badly for women's incomes. In 1987, women in Austria earned only 67 cents for every dollar a man earned, compared to 69 cents in the United States, 71 cents in Germany, 83 cents in Norway, and 90 cents in Sweden.[8] At the same time, the Economic and Social Advisory Board has served to suppress discussions of such crucial issues as environmental protection.[9] Seen from the perspective of a diverse U.S. progressive community, social partnership would have to include more societal interests than simply labor and business.

Finally, although it resisted the strains longer than most industrialized nations, Austria proved not immune to capitalism's global crisis. As Table 3.1 shows, while the nation was able to continue to maintain rates of unemployment much lower than either European or American averages, joblessness did increase. Equally serious, by the late 1980s, the growth rates on which social partnership rested were showing clear problems. Government spending had also accumulated a growing deficit.

Business-oriented critics blamed past policies for producing an overinvestment in industries that showed declining employment elsewhere in the capitalist world. They blamed regulations for "overpricing" wages in service industries. And they pointed to "distributional coalitions" in which workers and employers cooperated to produce high wages, high profits, and high prices in particular industry and agricultural sectors. The very institutions of social partnership and state ownership, critics charged, were slowing the economy's necessary restructuring for twenty-first-century global capitalism. Furthermore, the distinct national orientation of Austria's exporting firms could be seen as a liability. These companies had not built up the same level of global production and marketing assets as had more truly multinational enterprises.

While the public has maintained high levels of support for the concept of social partnership, the actual institutions have showed signs of weakening. While the Socialists retain the largest relative block of votes, both they and the ÖVP together have gone from a combined 93 percent support of the electorate in 1975 to 62.9 percent in 1994. Most alarmingly, extreme right-wing, neofascist political currents have grown into a significant political force, especially among the young. Despite their leader's penchant for expressing pro-Nazi sympathies, Austria's Freedom Party won 27 percent of the vote in recent national elections. In 2000, the People's Party made the controversial move of forming a coalition government with the Freedom Party—thus excluding the Socialists from office for the first time in forty-five years. Also noticeable, the overlap in membership between the parliamentary delegations and the union, business, and agrarian associations has also markedly declined. While still quite strong, the Austrian labor movement has seen a modest decline in its ranks. Union membership dropped from 47 percent of the workforce in 1985 to 42 percent in 1993.

Despite these pressures, scholars writing in the mid-1990s pointed to noticeable institutional continuity. Change occurred within and maintained the framework of the social partnership. For example, the unions have devoted increased attention to lowering wage inequality. The Advisory Board for Economic and Social Questions has also established a working group for environmental questions. In 1992, the Parity Commission expanded its institutional breadth by establishing a new Sub-Committee for International Issues. Since the 1980s, the government has tried to keep official unemployment down through additional measures to lower the workweek,

lift sharp restrictions on part-time work, and lower the retirement age. It has also restructured the nationalized industries, redesigned the tax system to favor technological improvement and an enlarged firm capital base, reduced subsidies, and introduced some deregulation. During the 1991–1993 recession, the Austrian economy once again showed a relatively superior economic performance with a higher GNP growth rate and a lower unemployment rate than both the European and U.S. averages.[10] Since 1994, the nation has experienced a strong economic recovery. Austria continued to be placed among the top performing economies in Europe.

Social Partnership Elsewhere in Europe

While Austria has the most institutionally formalized practices, the terminology and methods of social partnership are also features of politics and economics in Sweden and Germany. Indeed, an entire body of academic literature studies practices referred to as corporatism. While the term has different meaning for different researchers, it generally refers to practices in which organized social interests become part of the economic governing process. Corporatism can have a right-wing form, such as was the case under European fascism and Latin American authoritarian populism. These systems emphasized top-down control. Membership organizations, especially among ordinary people, served as instruments of government power. By contrast, the Austrian system is an example of democratic corporatism in which strong popular organizations become part of a system that includes liberal democratic institutions and rights.

Democratic corporatism has emerged notably in the small nations of Europe including Sweden, Austria, Switzerland, the Netherlands, Norway, Belgium, and Denmark. Germany provides the best example among the larger industrialized states. Indeed, codetermination can be seen as one institution part of a larger German social partnership. In his well-received work on these small countries, political scientist Peter Katzenstein argued that the development of democratic corporatism among these nations represents a common adaptation to the global economy.[11] Long before "globalization" became an official part of European and American policy debates, the small nations of Europe faced international vulnerability. They had no choice but to pursue policies of international economic integration. They both exported a large portion of their production abroad and imported a significant amount of consumer goods. As small players in a much larger world, these economically and financially open countries could not control their own destiny. Rather they needed the ability to adjust effectively to changes forced on them by international forces. Unlike the larger states, they could pursue neither long-term and state-led economic restructuring as in Japan nor the protectionism used by larger nations generally.

For Katzenstein, the institutions of democratic corporatism and social partnership have allowed these countries to adapt flexibly and relatively rapidly to changing international circumstances. The adjustments came incrementally as national export producers pursued niche markets for specialized, high-quality goods. Not all corporatism looks the same. Katzenstein distinguished between the two poles of social corporatism in Austria and liberal corporatism of Switzerland. Austria is distinguished by its stronger unions; nationally oriented companies; bargaining that covers wages, investment, and employment decisions; and relatively active state intervention in the economy. Swiss practice, by contrast, is far more market shaped. The organizational balance between labor and employers is more toward the latter. The policy networks are less centralized. Bargaining excludes questions of investment and employment. And large Swiss companies are more international in their operations. Swedish practices offer yet another combination. As in Austria, it is heavily labor-oriented. However, unlike Austria, Swedish income agreements prioritized wage solidarity during much of the postwar era. The Swedish state also does not exercise the same capacities for economic intervention as provided by Austria's large nationalized sectors.

As we have seen, Austrian social partnership has a broad scope that connects many aspects of social and economic policy. However, discussions of corporatism can lose sight of this broader context by focusing simply on narrow expression of incomes policy. Labor and management enter into wage negotiations that take the overall national economic health as their ultimate goal. Unions trade wage moderation for business commitments toward general economic prosperity. Without being linked to a broad long-term economic framework, however, incomes policy alone can become a short-term measure, often used in an emergency way to cope with inflation.

The British experience speaks to the difficulties of establishing corporatism when the broader context for cooperation is weaker. The Labour governments of 1945–1951, 1964–1970, and 1974–1979 all attempted to establish some form of incomes policy and corporatist bargaining. However, each attempt failed and income policy ended up becoming politically disastrous wage restraints imposed by a Labour government. Attempts to connect incomes policy to broader collective economic goals failed due to sharp disagreement between business and labor. Both British business and union organizations also did not posses the same centralization that their Austrian counterparts did. The British Trade Union Congress, for example, while supportive of entering into voluntary incomes policy, could not ensure collective support among its fragmented network of individual unions.[12]

Lessons for Americans

As the British experience suggests, social partnership cannot be imposed out of thin air. However, Austrian history also makes clear that conscious governmental policy and social organizing can establish the basis for partnership when pursued as a long-term, progressive goal. The Austrian experience also illustrates how conflict is not necessarily mutually exclusive to cooperation. Indeed, Austrian business leaders reluctantly agreed to many provisions of the social partnership only after they had come through protracted periods of class conflict with a strong and growing labor movement that threatened worse alternatives. The centralized power of Austrian unions also forced employers to raise their own level of organization. When taken alone, greater business unity and organizational purpose may seem like a threat to progressive politics. However, when done in a context of equally strong popular mobilization, it becomes a necessary ingredient for social partnership. Neither progressives' organizations nor government authorities can obtain concrete commitments from business unless they can negotiate with business leaders capable of delivering employer support for policy agreements.

The cooptive potential of social partnership notions should not be ignored. Indeed, business will attempt to steer government initiatives and collective projects toward their agenda or away from concerns deemed threatening to business. When pushed by the initiative of a powerful labor movement, as in postwar Austria and Sweden, social partnership delivered clear social gains. By contrast, in conditions of labor weakness, social partnership can prove a mechanism for business domination. This appears to be the case in the national bargaining deals struck between labor, business, and governments over European unification. The convergence criteria developed in the Maastricht Treaty for monetary union essentially forced European nations to slash social spending in order to limit their national debt. These cuts sparked a wave of protest throughout Europe. In EU-member countries the unions entered into social partner negotiations over the implementation of convergence. The unions attempted to trade concessions on social spending in return for business and governmental efforts to raise employment. In practice, however, the social cuts have far exceeded effective increases in employment. Overall, the process of social partnership over European unification seems to have served mainly to drawn unions in as a buffer between what is essentially a business agenda

and an angry population. Not surprisingly, such pacts have sparked protests within union ranks and led to national labor movements pulling out of the process altogether.

In short, the power relations and the economic context of social partnership is key to its positive or negative uses. While partnership in today's European context has become a moderating and cooptive force, within an American context, the concept could be quite radical. As we will see in chapter 10, unions that have pushed the most effective and genuine labor-management industry partnerships are typically those with the most progressive and mobilization-oriented leadership.

Indeed, when applied to the United States, the notion of social partnership can be used to advocate for public participation in economic decision areas that are currently seen as the exclusive domain of corporate managers and the "free market." Imagine the fundamental shift in public outlook if AFL-CIO leaders and other progressive organizations were to participate with business and governmental leaders in national forums for mutually deciding the country's overall economic policy goals. As we will see in Chapters 9, 10, and 11, popular groups that have first developed their own agenda can then use cooperation with business to tap industry knowledge and policies to transform the industry.

Austrian social partnership suggests that decentralization does not automatically lead to the most democratic outcome. Indeed, centralized agreements made by accountable peak organizations can offer a desirable counterforce to decisions that would otherwise be left in private hands. At the same time, the Austrian experience also provides a warning to the dangers of established organizations blocking the voice of less recognized groups. The composition and rules of active partnership are things that need to be continuously reexamined and adjusted to reflect current realities. Channels and supports have to be available to support new entering groups.

Social partnership widens the notion of representative democracy beyond electing candidates and political parties. Government policy can also recognize and even help establish the voice of important segments of society by developing a role for democratic and representative organizations to participate in the act of governing. Democracy thus becomes not simply a matter of casting votes each election season, but participating in a host of organizations and institutions that help society determine its own destiny.

This experience is not as foreign to American soil as our business and political leaders might have us think. As we will detail in Chapter 6, during World War II the federal government took over economic planning in a manner suggestive of social partnership. Wartime production was consciously planned out by overarching industry bodies that included not only government and business leaders, but organized labor as well. Indeed, union participation in wartime planning contributed to American production success and established a strong precedent for conscious economic direction that business campaigned hard against during the McCarthy era.

Nationalized Industry

In 1979, one out of five employed Austrians worked for firms owned and controlled by the Austrian government. The roughly two hundred public enterprises accounted for nearly half of the nation's domestic investments. Of the fifty largest Austrian firms, two-thirds were state owned. These public enterprises included the raw materials and utilities sectors commonly owned by the state in many parts of Europe. However, Austrian public firms also accounted for one-quarter of the nation's net manufacturing production and nearly three-quarters of its banks and financial institutions. The state-owned VOEST-Alpine was one of the largest steel and iron companies in the world.[13]

While this substantial public sector may have looked look like an incredible achievement in socialist ambitions, in reality it was born more in an act of nationalism, than revolution. Along with other industrialized countries, other than the United States, the Austrian state historically used public monopoly control over basic utility and raw material industries to aid the process of industrialization. The brief revolutionary upsurge experienced after World War I also helped to further this *Gemeinwirtshaft* ("common economy").

However, the current public enterprise sector had its main origins in the nationalization measures passed in 1946. Austria had only just regained its independence, having been annexed by Nazi Germany. As part of the losing side in World War II, the nation was occupied by the Allied powers and split between Western-controlled and Soviet-controlled zones. With their industrial heartland destroyed by Axis armies and pro-Nazi corporations having enjoyed substantial plunder of Soviet human and material wealth, Soviet authorities demanded substantial war reparations, including whole seizure of industrial facilities. Large sections of the Austrian industry were officially German owned, making them ripe targets for confiscation. To forestall mass loss of the nation's industrial and financial wealth, the Socialist-led Austrian government nationalized the firms. Although American authorities were ideologically opposed to such violations of the free market, and were actively battling nationalization elsewhere in Europe, they consented to Austrian actions as a necessary move to counter the Soviets. Socialist proposals for further nationalization, however, including those targeting French and American-owned firms, were dropped.

Control over the nationalized sector was organized to place it at "arm's length" from the legislature and the immediate political process. A state holding company, the Österreichische Industrieverwaltungs-Aktiengesellschaft (ÖeIAG), exercised overall administration of firms fully or partially owned by the public. Firm managers were given substantial decision-making autonomy and operated within market-based financial considerations. However, the overall direction of the nationalized sector followed the general economic and social objectives set by the nation's political consensus.[14]

The Social and Capitalist Uses of Nationalized Firms

While national protection motivated the original nationalization, it does not account for why these sectors remained largely under state ownership for half a century. Substantial support for maintaining the nationalized sector could be seen from the viewpoints of both Austrian labor and Austrian business.

The main goal of Austrian social democracy has been full employment. This priority enjoys substantial national consensus. The nationalized sectors proved a key tool for pursuing this aim in several ways. Most obviously, state-owned firms employed a fifth of the workforce. During times of economic downturn, public firms tended to behave differently than the private sector. Political scientist John Freeman summarized the Austrian experience of the 1970s economic crisis as follows. He writes:

> In the 1970s privately owned firms lowered production levels, disinvested from existing plants and left particular locations, diversified their private assets, laid off workers, and maintained financial returns. During the same period Austrian publicly owned firms maintained production levels, invested in existing plants and remained in particular locations, diversified the public's assets, maintained employment levels, and suffered a setback in financial earnings.[15]

When a private company lays off employees or shrinks its workforce, it can reap the benefits of reduced costs, while forcing the public and the individual workers to bear the price of unemployment. However, for a state-owned firm, especially in the context of an extensive system of unemployment compensation and social citizenship, the savings to the public purse of laying off workers is offset by the increased costs to maintain and support those same workers as unemployed. From a societal point of view, it can make more sense to operate a firm at a loss in order to maintain workers and invest in their training and productivity, rather than to suffer the social price of poverty, unemployment, and community disinvestment.

The nationalized sectors also aided full employment by supporting regional development. The state-owned Austrian steel industry maintained employment levels throughout the collapse of global steel and iron markets in the 1980s. This behavior contrasts sharply with the long-lasting community devastation experienced in the U.S. Mahonne Valley when private steel companies responded with mass layoffs and wholesale plant closures.

Since they encompass major industries and the better part of the nation's financial system, the public firms also helped promote productive investment. In international comparisons, the Austrian economy stood out for its high level of investment overall and for the distinct bias of this investment toward home national operations, rather than international ventures. The country had a quite small and underdeveloped stock market. Instead, firms sought outside financial resources from banks and other financial institutions that are largely publicly owned. When combined with other government policies, the priority of capital investment and stable prices, pursued by the public banks and industries, spilled over into the private sector. Private Austrian firms, relative to similar private employers in other countries, have shown relatively greater willingness to invest when faced with economic downturns.[16]

Finally, the nationalized sectors also helped the government maintain the incomes bargaining between labor and management. Workers and their unions could trade national wage moderation in return for promises of investment and job security more readily when a substantial block of the employers gaining from the wage concessions are public firms firmly committed to full employment. While not without limitations, the nationalized firms also aided union and socialist efforts to redistribute wealth and promote worker participation in the firm.

Even though the Socialist Party and the union movement represent a strong political force, the nationalized sector survived because it also worked for private business. In utilities, raw materials, and basic industries such as steel, efficiently run public firms delivered cheap inputs to private businesses that provide them a competitive advantage. Public ownership also permits the delivery of the cost benefits of large economies of scale without the dangers of private profit-seeking monopolies. Furthermore, nationalized firms continued to ensure domestic control by preventing foreign companies from acquiring ownership. Most important, the nationalized industries were used to support, not challenge, the private market.

Performance

Most American economists, businesspeople, and policy makers take as an article of faith that large-scale government economic ownership would prove nothing but trouble. Certainly, publicly owned firms could not perform as well as private companies. Such critics raise several lines of argument. They claim that public control is inherently inefficient. Since nationalized firm managers are not subject to market discipline, their decisions do not have to conform to the same tests of efficiency and ever-improving performance that guide private managerial decisions. Of course, the worst images come from Cold War descriptions of the Soviet economy in which a self-reinforcing network of bureaucrats created all manner of economic irrationalities. The Soviet experience, however, is only distantly relevant. Austrian nationalized firms operated in a market, rather than planned, economy. They were subject to capitalist financial criteria of loss and profits even while other factors also drove managerial decisions.

Critics of public ownership, however, also point to the dangers of "external interference" by workers, communities, and politicians who can pressure firm managers to maintain jobs, wages, and investments when the market clearly points in a different direction. Thus, public managers have their hands tied—preventing them from making the "tough decisions" that privately owned firms have to make in

order to retain a competitive edge over the long haul. Of course, seen from a social perspective, insulation from the one-dimensional needs of "competitiveness" can be a source of strength. As has been well documented in the U.S. economy, competition and private investor ownership often compel firms to maintain and increase profits at the expense of the workforce, community, and society.

The actual historical performance of Austria's public firms belied the critics. John Freeman summarized the experience as follows:

> Until the late 1970s the Austrian nationalized industries were considered among the most efficient publicly owned firms in the world. There has been relatively little controversy about whether or not they have promoted investment and growth. Throughout much of their history, Austrian publicly owned firms earned positive rates of return, and they managed to finance internally a large share of their investments and research and development. Thanks in part to the technological advantages they enjoyed, public firms also achieved a relatively high level of productivity. In addition, they employed and trained a large number of youths through the apprentice system.[17]

The nationalized sectors combined social and business success. They delivered low-cost goods to other Austrian businesses using modern and efficient plants. Between 1974 and 1981, years when the capitalist economic boom gave way to crisis, the Austrian state sector outperformed the comparably strong West German industries by higher rates of productivity growth. In the 1960s and 1970s, wages in the nationalized firms ran 10 to 15 percent higher than in the private sector. Polls conducted in 1964, 1979, and 1983 all showed that Austrian workers preferred the public sector to private employment. In 1983, 53 percent said, if given the option, they would choose a job in the nationalized industries.[18] Even critics of public ownership have had to admit to Austria's postwar success. In his analysis of privatization efforts,

Karl Aiginger wrote, "the first twenty years after the war were a period of remarkable recovery in Austria. And the efficient infrastructure provided by the [public-owned] national champions, as well as the inexpensive and high quality products produced by the state owned basic goods industry were two pillars of that process." This description comes from an author who repeatedly describes public ownership and government regulation as "state interference."[19]

By the 1980s, however, the public firms entered a period of difficulties. The business performance of some deteriorated seriously. When prices on the world steel market collapsed, VOEST-Alpine responded slowly—worsening the difficulties and ushering in unprecedented losses. Indeed, the nationalized industries as a whole suffered large financial losses in the 1980s. The consensus supporting the public sector showed signs of breaking down. As firms such as VOEST-Alpine continued to maintain high employment levels in an industry that was clearly downsizing internationally, public debate witnessed criticisms that collusion between workers, managers, and public officials sacrificed needed change to protect a "labor aristocracy" of privileged workers. The popularity of the state firms was further weakened by a series of scandals revealing corruption and patronage among state managers. In 1986, the holding company ÖeIAG was reorganized. All or parts of several state firms were sold off.

The crisis of the 1980s, however, has to be qualified. The public firms suffered financial losses, in part, because they absorbed the economic strains internally, by maintaining employment and investment, rather than passing the burden on to the rest of society through mass layoffs. By contrast, the U.S. steel industry, for example, returned to profitability only by inflicting the pain of restructuring on workers through massive layoffs, wage and benefit concessions, and deindustrialization. In Austria, while polls showed an increasing dissatisfaction with the particular way nationalized industries were being run, the public maintained a general commitment to the public sector for a long time.[20]

Public Ownership Is Far More Common Than Most Americans Might Think

While the extent and use of Austria's public companies made them distinct, public ownership as a government policy tool has been quite common. Indeed, every major industrialized country besides the United States has used nationalization as a significant policy tool. By the end of the 1970s, over fifty of the five hundred largest industrial corporations outside the United States were owned by governments. Over the course of the 1960s and 1970s, the annual average growth rate, in both sales and assets, of the top state-owned firms exceeded their private counterparts found in the same listings.[21] In 1979, among national workforces, one-quarter of Italians, one-tenth of Germans and French, and one out of twelve Britains worked for public enterprises. In each case, the public sector accounted for an even greater proportion of business investment. In total, 8 million Europeans worked for state enterprises. Even in North America, Canada has a significant history of state-run firms.[22]

Political scientists Jeanne Kirk Laux and Maureen Appel Molot have identified three major motivations driving public ownership. The earliest efforts tended to use stable government monopolies as a way of guaranteeing private business basic services and inputs from industries such as telecommunication, transportation, and energy. Especially during times of economic downturn, governments have also used public enterprises to make up for so-called market failures. When individual private firms that are of central importance to employment and economic activity experience a financial crisis, the government may take over these firms in order to save them when private investors have decided that their profit-making interests are best served elsewhere. Such action may simply cushion the social strains of a declining economic sector. However, public resources have been used to restructure firms and industries to return them to competitiveness when private investors have "jumped ship" by being unwilling to finance a bailout or reinvest for the future. This later action, Laux and Molot argue, provided a significant motivator behind the extension of public ownership in the 1970s and beyond. However, governments faced with a global economic slowdown and increasing competition also extended their control over domestic firms in order to keep them out of the hands of foreign companies. Redesigned nationalized firms can provide national champions successfully active in world markets. Indeed, by the mid-1970s, eight wholly or largely state-owned European firms had become multinational corporations.

The uses and performance of state-owned firms has varied considerably. The large Italian and British nationalized sectors have suffered from a lack of political agreement over their purpose and existence. While the Swedish government initially pursued modest national ownership in order to encourage proactive innovation and job growth, these priorities quickly gave way to defensive measures to save jobs in declining industries. The Austrian experience stood out by the degree to which the nationalized industries were part of an integrated economic policy.

The performance of state-owned firms varied from country to country. The overall record, however, hardly justified the conclusion that public control over industries is inherently inefficient and undesirable. As in Austria, European state-owned sectors have shared with private business the economic difficulties experienced by the world economy since the late 1960s. While in nations such as Britain, these strains led to successful calls for privatization in the 1980s, in other countries they led to the maintenance of the public sector through internal reforms and greater reliance on business profit-making criteria. According to Laux and Molot, the crisis-ridden years of the 1970s and early 1980s saw the relatively quiet extension of public ownership as nationalized firms were allowed to invest in other companies and subsidiaries.[23]

Ironically, the privatization-crazed Thatcher government actually validated the business skills of state ownership by its handling of British automaker Leyland. The company had been nationalized in order to prevent either its bankruptcy or acquisition by a foreign firm. When the Tories took power in 1979, they were committed to selling off nationalized industries—arguing that public companies were inherently bureaucratic and inefficient. However, the government could find no investors willing to buy the ailing Leyland company. Thatcher used government resources and management to restructure Leyland and return it to profitability. Having unintentionally demonstrated the achievements of state ownership, the government then proceeded to sell off the now moneymaking operation to private investors who enjoyed the private fruits of public efforts![24]

Reform, Not Revolution

While American businesspeople would view nationalization as a form of "creeping socialism," the European experience demonstrates how state ownership has been used to support, rather than threaten, capitalism. Such a purpose represents a significant retreat from the original desires expressed among the European working-class movements to use nationalization as the means for destroying capitalism. Indeed, publicly owned firms could offer a laboratory for experiments with alternatives to capitalist methods. However, this potential has not been seriously pursued. In country after country, even social democratic governments have conducted nationalization around clear commitments to run enterprises along capitalist lines. Thus, nationalized sectors have not experimented with replacing the managerial hierarchy or the strict division of labor with more cooperative forms of work and management. The Austrian public firms have displayed a set of priorities broader than simply capitalist profit making. And they have fostered practices of codetermination and a strong union presence. However, ultimately state managers direct the companies using traditional capitalist methods—neither the workers nor some other form of collective guidance hold sway.

The existent state-owned companies have also not

been used to compete directly with the legitimacy of the private sector. When successful, they may expand their operations and investments. However, their success is not used as a justification for further replacing private owners. Nationalized firms have operated firmly within capitalism. Despite their potential to do so, they have not been used to build a kind of socialism within capitalism that over time could demonstrate the viability and desirability of new ways of organizing human activity.

Privatization

By the 1990s, the ideology of free-market, supply-side economics had swept across the capitalist world. Its basic tenets have been written into the rules of the global economy and the European Union. Even the leadership of once–social democratic parties, such as Britain's Labour Party, has leaped into the new faith. The political triumph of free-market capitalism has hit public ownership particularly hard.

Austria's nationalized sectors did not prove immune to the massive privatization efforts in the former Soviet-bloc countries and more modest waves in the West. Between 1993 and 1995, the core of the nation's public-owned manufacturing sectors was sold off. Efforts to restructure the steel, aluminum, and oil and gas industries around criteria other than capitalist downsizing and cost cutting had failed to return the companies to financial success. Since privatization, these firms have followed the overall patterns in their industry by shedding workers. The country's second largest bank was sold off to its largest. While Bank Austria has substantial public connections, it has also played a major role in facilitating privatization. Indeed, by the end of the 1990s, the bank was advertising its privatization services for use in the former Soviet bloc.

Privatization of basic utilities moved slower in the 1990s and the state holding company continued to hold minority shares in once public-owned companies. Concerned with creeping foreign ownership, Socialist authorities preferred a slower route to privatization. Multinational corporations may not have the same priorities as a national firm. Indeed, in the worst cases such corporate giants may acquire firms simply to eliminate independent competitors. By contrast the People's Party has favored the full and complete sell-off of public firms. The recent formation of a People's Party–Freedom Party coalition government does not bode well for the future of the remaining nationalized sectors.

Lessons for Americans

Austrian and European experiences with nationalization offer twin lessons. Direct public ownership is not as far-fetched and unthinkable as American corporations, political leaders, and the corporate media would have us believe. The current privatization mania does not invalidate several decades of strong social and economic performance—especially when compared to some of the social disasters found within comparable private-owned industries. While public ownership is a valid policy tool, it is not necessarily a revolutionary act. Important choices must be made in how public ownership is used. Public ownership must be used as part of a broader agenda to transform basic social and economic relationships, not to simply achieve capitalist financial success.

As the existence of the U.S. Postal Service or the Tennessee Valley Authority demonstrates, large-scale public ownership is not entirely divorced from the American experience. The prospects of outright nationalization have also cropped up in American history. For example, faced with the prospect of a national steel strike that could have crippled the U.S. Korean War effort, President Truman issued an executive order in 1952 instructing the Secretary of Commerce to take possession of the nation's steel mills. With Congress taking no action either for or against, the U.S. Supreme Court, the great historical defender of private property interests, declared 6 to 3 that the president had exceeded his authority, and ruled the action unconstitutional.

Recent economic experiences in the United States

point to several cases in which public ownership could offer a straightforward solution. The most obvious are the cases in which the nature of a business sector leads to private monopolies. Deregulation of basic utilities has led not to the price and efficiency gains so predicted by its supporters, but to either cutthroat, low-road competition or private regulation through agreements among the major corporate players. In either case, the public has had to bear the burden of higher costs and layoffs. Yet, greater public ownership of the phone and cable systems, electricity and gas providers, and other basic utilities would place the United States into the mainstream of postwar national experiences.

Public ownership could also provide an effective tool to bolster the nation's antitrust laws. A century ago, the federal government broke up such conglomerates as Rockefeller's Standard Oil as illegal trusts. The solution, however, always aimed to restore the "free market" by establishing competition. Yet, the nature of an industry may favor monopolies. Imagine a solution to the controversy over Microsoft that led to outright public ownership. The nation's computer users could then have the benefits of common underlying software without risking the profit-seeking price and design priorities of a corporate monopoly.

The recurring mainstream debate over violence in the media rarely raises the question of why a handful of corporations are allowed to control most of the nation's media. Indeed, ongoing mergers in the industry place ownership of most of what the nation sees, hears, and reads in fewer and fewer hands. Even so-called public broadcasting depends on corporate money to operate. Yet, television and radio stations operate only because the federal government has granted them the right to broadcast over the public airwaves. Corporate electronic media depend on public permission for their very existence. The source of so much violence in the media, as well as so much simply bland programming, is obvious to anyone willing to question private ownership. For-profit corporations make money by offering a cheap prod-uct targeted to the largest audience of interest to advertisers. Since violence is cheap to make and offers a lowest common denominator to attract audiences, this is what corporations force the public to watch. Full public-owned and -funded, commercial-free media is not some wild notion, but a common reality. In both Europe and Canada, government-owned television and radio stations are typical. Indeed, the common use by the Public Broadcasting Service (PBS) and various cable stations of high-quality programming produced by the British Broadcasting Corporation (BBC) testifies to the strengths of public ownership. By contrast, Congress recently agreed to make a second broadcast frequency available to the major networks to allow their conversion to digital television. While the rights to these public assets were worth at least $70 billion, Congress gave away this public wealth for free.[25]

Public ownership is also a logical solution when private investors abandon firms and entire sectors. The prevalence of stock ownership and the central role played by Wall Street and financial markets over corporate America's operations, lead to frequent situations in which perfectly viable and socially useful companies are dismantled or closed simply because more money can be made elsewhere. In its work on plant closures in Chicago, the Midwest Center for Labor Research found that of eight hundred small inner-city companies with owners fifty-five or older, almost 40 percent were in danger of closing because of a lack of a successor.[26]

The United States already has experience with employee buyouts and stock-ownership plans. In many cases, these have led to viable companies.[27] Where they have not, they may have succeeded with access to greater resources and supports. Government policies could provide such supports and increase the ability of authorities to outright assume ownership of companies whose owners are not supporting their future viability.

As we will detail in Chapter 6, the record of Wall Street and our financial system in promoting productive, and socially useful, investment is not strong. Yet, in Europe and East Asia, publicly owned banks and financial institutions have formed a core part of many countries' financial structure. Imagine what communities would look like if a public-run mortgage system offered low rates to buyers and rebuilders in older urban neighborhoods while sharply penalizing new sprawl construction in rural areas.

Indeed, today American workers already own, through their private and public pension plans, as much as 40 percent of all corporate stock and 50 percent of bonds.[28] Yet, these vast resources are managed entirely along capitalist investor-oriented lines. Under law, pension funds are prohibited from using anything but "prudent financial" criteria. Thus, they are invested in order to seek the largest return over a relatively short period of time. That these funds exist at all on the present scale is due to federal law requiring that all pension plans be advance funded. Laws could easily require greater worker control over how the funds are used.

4

Confronting "Globalization" and the New Capitalist Agenda

Ten to fifteen years ago, American progressives could point to Europe for examples of the high road, without need for further qualifications. While business-oriented economists might have bad-mouthed European policies, the factual track record spoke for itself. European nations had combined superior economic performance with greater social justice and collective sensibilities.[1]

Today, however, those who seek to use Europe to open possibilities for alternative paths are likely to receive a litany on Europe's economic problems. In particular, double-digit European unemployment rates are far ahead of those in the United States. A growing collection of commentators now aggressively pronounces European "exceptionalism" over as twenty-first-century capitalism seemingly moves toward an American model. The problems for American activists are made worse by the rightward drift of Europe's major left parties. Rather than demonstrating the possibilities for sweeping economic reform, Europe appears to illustrate the unfolding triumph of unfettered capitalism.

Have the paths toward a high-road future indeed been closed? The supposed superiority of American-style capitalism rests on claims about today's economic environment that are encapsulated by the core concept of "globalization." According to the globalization enthusiasts, progressive economics is not possible today because all nations, great and small, must conform to an all-powerful worldwide transformation. In today's "global economy," indepen-

dent development strategies are no longer viable. In short, there is no alternative.

In this chapter, we will challenge the claim that so-called globalization has inevitably narrowed the boundaries of progressive reform. Indeed, we will argue that the opposite is true. Worldwide economic changes have actually opened opportunities for more aggressive and far-reaching progressive agendas.

Social Democracy in Retreat

The actions of Europe's main left parties seem, on the surface, to support the kind of "end of history" claims advanced by proponents of unfettered capitalism. For example, in 1981, hopes for radical change soared when French Socialists swept into power with calls for a "rupture with capitalism" and other revolutionary slogans. Yet, three years later, France had become a symbol for the impossibility of radical reforms. Under international economic pressure, the Mitterrand government made a vast U-turn, replacing calls for fundamental economic change with market-oriented austerity.

Throughout the 1980s, however, progressives could still take solace in the continued economic vigor among the strongholds of social democratic reform. Indeed, for most of the troubled recessionary years of the 1970s and 1980s, it looked as though both Sweden and Austria would survive capitalism's economic difficulties relatively unscathed. Yet, by the early 1990s, economic pressures hit home in these countries as well. Faced with mounting budget deficits, the Swedish Social Democrats cut social spending. At the same time, Swedish employers increasingly questioned centralized solidaristic wage bargaining. In 1991, the Social Democrats lost political power for the first time since 1984, receiving their lowest percentage of the vote since 1922. Unemployment, a nonissue in Swedish politics for decades, rose to an unprecedented postwar high of 7 percent in 1992. By this year, Austrian politics had also taken a turn to the right as questions of competitiveness, privatization, and tax reform dominated economic policy discussions.

The second half of the 1990s seemed to further confirm social democracy's retreat. In Britain, the Labour Party overcame nearly two decades of conservative rule in 1997 only after officially abandoning many of its traditional principles. Tony Blair's "New Labour" seemed more committed to pursuing merely a kinder, gentler version of Thatcher's right-wing agenda. A year later, the German Social Democrats took power with a similar "Clintonized" version of politics that seemed to accept the confines of the new world order as the basis for public policies.[2]

Today, Europe's economy faces severe difficulties. As left-wing British European Parliament member Ken Coates wrote in 1993:

> A spectre is haunting Europe. It is the shadow of unemployment. The present figures are quite dreadful, and have created desperate social tensions in many areas. But the situation today, even while we are caught in the depths of slump, is nothing like as bad as the forecast of what is to come.[3]

Indeed, the 1980s left Europe with 16 million to 17 million unemployed, roughly 9 percent of the workforce.[4] By 1998, unemployment in the EU countries remained at just under 10 percent. Six years of modest, but steady, economic growth, averaging 1.5 percent a year, had failed to increase employment.[5] Such unemployment strained Europe's welfare states as costs increased while tax revenues fell.

The problem, however, was not simply high unemployment levels. The economic restructuring of the 1980s and 1990s appears to have outright marginalized a sizable portion of Europe's population who face long-term unemployment.[6] The crisis is especially severe among a growing population of younger workers who simply find no jobs available. Unfortunately, frustrations over lack of economic opportunity all too readily translate into immigrant bashing and right-wing politics.[7] Indeed, parties and organizations of the far right have enjoyed notable success in nations such as France, Belgium, and Germany. The returns from the October 1999 Austrian elections left the Social Democrats and Greens unable to prevent an Austrian government in which the ÖVP included the far-right, neofascist Freedom Party in its coalition. The new government drew the condemnation from a good part of the rest of Europe.

Such problems seem to contrast starkly with the American "economic miracle." Our nation's official unemployment rate remained far below European levels, through most of the 1990s our stock markets boomed, and corporate profits appeared to have made a substantial recovery. For many political and business officials on both the left and the right, the conclusions were simple. European social democracy was a fair-weather experiment dependent on the unprecedented postwar economic boom. In today's tough global economy, however, extensive government social spending, strong wage bargaining, and strict regulatory standards impede national competitiveness. If social democracy is to survive, it must reshape itself in the American image. Only by encouraging the free market can Europe regain the economic growth that underpins social prosperity. The implications of this message for U.S. progressives are clear. Since the examples of alternative paths are being abandoned in the very countries where they seemed the strongest, then our nation's current path is the only viable option. Those who hope for economic change must confine themselves within the logic of the global market.

Fortunately, while such arguments may satisfy the

political needs of those ideologically committed to unrestricted private enterprise, they offer at best a superficial reading of Europe's current difficulties and America's seeming triumph. Indeed, the nature of the crisis is far different than what those who announce the "triumph of capitalism" describe. We will begin by questioning the core concept behind the "no-alternative" argument: globalization.

Globalization or Globaloney?

The term "globalization" encapsulates what has become the great ideological fig leaf of contemporary capitalism. Having failed to convince a substantial part of the world's population of the inherent superiority of unrestrained capitalism, the intellectual spokespeople of the free market have attempted to convince friend and foe alike that, as much as the current system may have its defects, there is simply no alternative. Today, we live in a global economy that has only one direction, so the argument goes. Any attempts to forge alternative economic paths are doomed to collapse before the all-powerful logic of the global free market.

Unfortunately, many progressives have bought into the globalization hype. While they may not join the celebrations of global capitalism, they nevertheless have conceded its triumph. The title of Gary Teemple's book *Globalization and the Decline of Social Reform* encapsulates this perspective. In his introduction, Teemple writes:

> The general trends of capitalist development in the industrialized nations are hindered less and less by national social and economic reforms. As a result, there is a progressive increase in economic inequality, with structural unemployment and poverty growing continuously; the trends in planetary pollution and environmental destruction continue to deepen; there is a decline in national sovereignty, with autocratic rule and coercive social control gradually becoming more common and alternations of the party in power

increasingly becoming meaningless; and there are widespread legislative assaults on wages, trade union rights, and labour standards. The victory of capital hastens its own very visible limitations. These consequences have not gone unchallenged, for at the same time counter movements, opposition, and challenges of all sorts have been expanding, both outside and inside the mainstream economic and political systems. While these alternatives and resistance are growing, the odds they face are enormous. The continuing legitimacy of the system, the persistent national "mind-set," hegemonic corporate control over the mass media, the conservatism of the trade unions, the concerted counter-attacks by the state and representatives of capital, the poverty of financial resources, the growing sense of disillusionment, cynicism, and impotence, and the inadequate analysis of the present situation have all conspired to limit the growth of resistance and alternatives.[8]

While Teemple goes on to suggest that the opposition "is far from moribund" and "much remains latent," the overall picture he paints is one of a global capitalist juggernaut swallowing up the possibilities of economic reform. Most important, he agrees with the globalization pundits that the nation-state is no longer capable of independent economic action.

Teemple is not alone in his assessment. While finding important variations in the ways in which Belgium, the Netherlands, Austria, and Sweden weathered the economic strains of the 1980s and 1990s, Paulette Kurzer finishes her survey seeing a common troubled future:

> Because the trend in the advanced industrialized world is toward ever-increasing financial integration and business internationalization, national accords between labor, government, and capital are unlikely to reemerge. The evidence in this book does not hold great promise for social democracy. Core ideas regarding Keynesian economic management and social democratic ideol-

ogy have ceased to be a source of alternative ideas and electoral appeal. This is not to say that social democratic parties will fade away. On the contrary, left-wing parties will continue to seek election and occasionally win power. However, these parties have little in common with their predecessors in terms of articulating progressive options and pursuing programs different from the conservative, or establishment, view.[9]

Kurzer suggests the only hope for social democracy lies in pursuing a united, social Europe able to rejuvenate a progressive economic agenda at the supranational level. Isolated national policy, however, is a strategy of the past; by implication local reforms represent a hopeless cause.

Fritz Scharpf, director of the Max Planck Institute in Germany, ended his comparative analysis of the dilemma facing social democracy with similar conclusions of a narrowing of traditional reform. Scharpf wrote:

> This concludes my survey of the options for social democratic full employment policy under the foreseeable conditions of the world economy. The vision is bleak. Unlike the situation in the first three postwar decades, there is now no economically plausible Keynesian strategy that would permit the full realization of social democratic goals within a national economic context without violating the functional imperatives of the capitalist economy. Full employment, rising real wages, larger welfare transfers, and more and better public services can no longer all be had simultaneously—because growth rates are inadequate and because the distributive claims that capital is able to realize have increased.[10]

Scharpf suggests that the social democracy must, therefore, choose between its traditional goals. Workers will have to accept high tax levels and shared work hours in order to support and include in economic activity those whom contemporary capitalism has increasingly marginalized. Unless such sacrifices are made, social democracy faces an internal war among its supporters between those who enjoy work and those who do not.

The assumption that the global economy simply narrows the options available for progressive reform prevails in much official social democratic thinking. It certainly guides the conservative policies of leaders such as England's Tony Blair. While the specifics of each particular analysis may differ, five interrelated propositions underlie most progressive arguments that see a narrowing of reform politics. First, they assume that we live in a new era qualitatively different from previous capitalist periods. Second, they view the power of global capital as hegemonic. National and local economic policy can do less and less in the face of global finance and global corporations. Third, in today's global economy, the growth on which social democracy built its policies cannot be sustained through traditional social democratic measures. Rather, growth can be revived only by adopting an economic framework exemplified by the American economy.

Fourth, social democracy was based on historical compromises between workers and the owners of capital that are no longer viable. Faced with a smaller economic pie, business is no longer interested in the old ideas. At the same time the global economy has fractured social democracy's political base. The employed are pitted against the unemployed and the working class is divided along dimensions of public and private, manual and professional, industrial and service, immigrant and native born. Finally, because of all of the above, social democracy is becoming less and less distinctive. As all nations face the same global pressures, they must adopt similar economic policies. America is Europe's future.

Such arguments are not entirely without merit. The world has changed and the aforementioned explanations do capture part of the new reality. However, the first three propositions overstate the nature and meaning of the changes, while the fourth and fifth draw the wrong conclusions. Most important, the above line of thinking does not consider the new progressive options that may grow out of recent changes.

Myths and Realities of International Economic Activity

While the celebrants of the new global economy speak in terms of a new and novel era for humanity, they do overstate their case and offer highly misleading conclusions. Among those critical of unfettered capitalism, the extent and meaning of current global changes have been a source of hot debate.[11] As a useful counterweight to the well-publicized positions of a new global epoch, we will first examine the evidence offered by those who argue that globalization is overstated.

The skeptics argue that much of what passes for globalization has indeed happened before. While today's level of trade and financial openness might be greater relative to prior postwar decades, it is not out of line with the levels seen in the late nineteenth and early twentieth centuries. In the 1990s, exports as a percentage of GDP only barely surpassed the levels of 1913 (17.9 percent in the Organization for Economic Cooperation and Development [OECD] countries, in 1992, compared to roughly 16 percent in 1913). Capital mobility, when measured as the ratio of capital flows relative to overall output, was much higher in the nineteenth-century era of the gold standard than it was even in the 1980s.[12]

When identifying changes that are novel, notions of globalization typically overstate their magnitude. It is true that world trade has grown in the past several decades. However, today most OECD nations have only two or three significant trading partners. And most trade and investment are regionally based, with Europe, North America (including Mexico), and Southeast Asia forming the major trade blocs. Furthermore, the growth in world trade has actually been slowing over the course of the 1980s and 1990s. Among the OECD countries, exports account for only 18 percent or less of their GDP. Thus, nearly 80 percent of what these regions consume is produced within their borders.[13]

The much-publicized movement of manufacturing jobs overseas to low-wage areas of the world does reflect a genuine reality. However, the magnitude of the "global assembly line" can be overstated. Most foreign direct investment does not go for manufacturing, but for speculative and other nonproductive assets (real estate, hotels, etc.). Furthermore, much of the money spent on industry has not been for new facilities, but to acquire and merge with existing assets. Most foreign investment takes the form of portfolio investments (bonds, stocks, mutual funds, etc.) rather than direct investment. Finally, most wealth is still invested domestically.[14] Foreign branches of multinational corporations account for about 15 percent of the world's industrial output, while 85 percent is produced by domestic corporations in single geographical locales.[15]

Obviously, the ability of corporations to use foreign direct investment as a weapon against workers varies by and within economic sectors. In the American auto industry, Big Three investments in Mexican production have been quite significant. Today, vehicles, especially smaller cars with tighter profit margins, are produced with dual United States and Mexican capacities in which plants on both sides of the border build the same product. The management of an independent automotive-parts plant in Michigan made the threat clear. During a unionization drive, it dismantled one of the assembly lines, packaged up the machinery, and attached a large sign reading "next stop Mexico." Cornell researcher Kate Bronfenbrenner found that employer threats to close if workers vote for a union increased from under 30 percent of union elections before the North American Free Trade Agreement (NAFTA) to 52 percent three years after. In manufacturing, the rate was nearly two-thirds. Before NAFTA, management actually closed operations in only 5 percent of cases; after, the rate increased to 12 percent.[16]

By contrast, the service industry generally cannot move the sites of its core activities abroad, although industries such as retail, restaurant, and hotel do use a significant number of immigrants driven to move to the United States by the ravages of "free trade." Overall, three out of four American workers are employed in the diverse service sector. According to one estimate, only about 10 percent of this sector's workforce holds jobs directly exposed to international competition.[17]

While the assets of international companies have grown, their ability to simply roam the world in search of the cheapest labor must be qualified. In terms of the share of assets, ownership, management, employment, and research and development, the national home base is still quite important. Several estimates have placed 70 to 75 percent of the value-added in the course of production as occurring within the home nation.[18] Even in such vulnerable industries such as automotive, while Mexican capacity increases, the bulk of North American production remains in the United States. If companies simply roamed the world exclusively in search of cheap labor, then far more company investment should be in low-wage nations. Yet, as of the early 1990s, at least 80 percent of the foreign direct investment went to high-wage and relatively high-tax countries.[19]

We should also keep in mind that the threat of job loss can occur mainly within national borders. In the United States, the chief outsourcing threat facing unionized autoworkers comes not from Mexico, but from a domestic parts industry that has grown largely nonunion.[20] An investigation of public subsidies in Minnesota found that in most cases, public loans, grants, and tax breaks had been used by firms that created "new jobs" mainly by relocating work within the state in ways that lowered pay levels.[21]

Globalization of production is part of a broader strategy of corporate restructuring known as lean production. Under this new way of thinking, large corporate conglomerates attempt to focus their operations around a stripped-down core workforce connected to a vast network of supplier chains and contingent workers. In this way, companies minimize their fixed full-time labor costs—organizing most production around "flexible" employment and contracting relationships. While quite threatening to workers in many ways, lean production can also increase the vulnerability of corporations to disruption. In extended supply chains that produce for "just in time" delivery, slowdowns in one part of the process can send ripples throughout the system. For example, in the past several years, strikes and industrial accidents at Big Three automotive plants in both the United States and Mexico have led to production halts in plants well on the other side of the border.

Of all the aspects typically described as evidence of "globalization," international finance provides the clearest cases of new changes that are indeed global and that do bode ill for effective government policy. Since the Nixon administration's formal removal of the gold standard in 1971, and the subsequent liberalization of exchange controls, international capital flows have grown to spectacular levels. Huge sums of money can rapidly flow around the globe, often on the basis of quite short-term calculations. In 1995, for example, the value of world trade in goods was $5 trillion. That same year the foreign exchange markets generated an annual turnover of $300 trillion.[22]

The world of international finance does undermine national and democratic controls. However, even here, the extent of globalization must be qualified. Globalization proponents claim that countries are inevitably converging around a single American-style model. Yet, even today clear financial differences remain among nations. Countries differ dramatically in terms of their interest rates, taxation policies, and rates of savings and investments. The United States continues to have low savings (0.5–2 percent of GDP) and low investment rates (15–19 percent of GDP). The Japanese savings rate is at least ten times greater than the United States'; their investment rate is twice ours.[23] Furthermore, despite increases in global financial flows, the bulk of domestic investment is still funded out of domestic savings—not from international lenders. Thus, in important ways, the increasingly global financial system is largely disconnected from actual activities that produce wealth. Despite the challenge posed by footloose finance, we should keep in mind that today's financial openness is nothing new—having reached an earlier high point before 1914.[24]

All of this is not to argue that new global conditions do not exist. While many current patterns may have parallels in the late nineteenth century, they do represent a significant change from the postwar boom conditions on which social democratic strategies were built. The ratio of exports to GDP roughly doubled from 1960 to 1990 among the OECD countries—from under 10 percent to over 20 percent. The stock of international bank lending rose from 4 percent of the OECD's GDP in 1980 to 44 percent by 1990. The trillion-dollar turnover in world currency markets seen daily today dwarfs the reserves of central bank regulators.[25] And while only 15 percent of world industrial output is produced by multinational corporations outside of their country of origin, this portion is double the ratios of the 1970s.[26]

The question remains, however, are global changes so sweeping that local and domestic economies have no choice but to conform to an all-powerful global logic? A case can be made, however, that today's world economy is hardly as one directional as the champions of unfettered capitalism would have us believe. Below we argue that national differences and the nation-state remain key economic forces. Rather than transcending nations and governments, the world economy has increased the interactions between them. Thus, we live in a world that has become more internationalized (increased interactions between nations), not globally transcendent. National and regional economies continue to provide the foundations for economic activity.

If "globalization" is not a single, all-powerful force, then it becomes more difficult to place economic strains—ranging from unemployment to increased inequality to growing poverty to environmental destruction—solely at the feet of some inevitable and monolithic "global economy." Instead, we have to look to specific state and corporate actions that drive the economic changes so often ascribed to anonymous global market forces.

Governments Are Not Powerless

The central claims of most procorporate globalization arguments focus on the state. If the globalization described by its enthusiasts is true, then national and local governments have much less ability to control their economic future. However, if our world has simply become more internationalized, with nation-states still the primary building blocks, then governments remain key players susceptible to pressures from below.

Globalization arguments do tap into a vein of truth. International changes have weakened the traditional Keynesian tools that predominated official macroeconomic policy debates throughout the postwar boom. Traditional Keynesianism tried to pull three major macroeconomic levers. Through monetary policy, governments regulated the supply and costs of money. By raising and lowering interest rates, authorities slowed and sped up economic activity. State spending through fiscal policy allowed governments to raise consumption in response to economic downturns. Finally, government currency policies allowed decision makers to manipulate the relative value of their nation's money. By devaluing their currency, they increased the costs of imports while lowering the price of exports. Although such an action risked inflation (if the nation depends on import), it raised demand for domestic goods and provided increased opportunities for exports. To this basic Keynesian toolbox, social democracy added a fourth mechanism, provided by corporatism. Fostered by governments, national wage deals between employers and unions aided national policy. To raise demand, governments and unions could push for steady wage gains. To help increase profitability and investment, unions could voluntarily constrain wages. Labor leaders could pursue such an option because national deals included commitments both by employers to invest and by government to provide a social wage through increased social spending.

The rise of global finance, however, has seriously compromised several of these mechanisms. The fixed exchange rates of the postwar Bretton Woods system ended with the Nixon administration's decision to move off the gold standard. In today's international currency trading, investors who lose confidence in a nation's economic policies can express their doubts collectively by selling off the currency in large volume. Thus, governments must compete against each other for buyers in an increasingly volatile world currency system. Similarly, governments no longer have exclusive control over their monetary policy. Global financial markets mean that interest rates in any given country are compared to other opportunities worldwide. Thus, in the 1980s, for example, many European governments found that they had to maintain high interest rates, even though that conflicted with their other policies for reducing unemployment, because investors could find more lucrative returns elsewhere due to high interest rates in the United States. Once their monetary and currency policy hands are tied, governments have to rely on fiscal mechanisms alone. Yet, in tackling rising unemployment in the 1980s, many European governments found that expanding government spending, especially when forced to follow interest rates and currency policies that pulled in the opposite direction, neither raised investment nor lowered unemployment. And without such gains, policy makers faced growing budget deficits. Finally, inasmuch as trade has increased, the classic Keynesian goal of raising domestic consumer demand can simply increase imports of foreign-made goods.[27]

In sum, as long as government policy must rely on private investors to foster domestic economic growth, it has to compete with other international investment opportunities. At its worst, international capital markets bring in investment wealth only in search of short-term gains that have little to do with productive investment in the long-term economic health of the nation. This grim picture, however, must be qualified. Researchers are unclear about how effective Keynesian demand management ever was and some nations, such as Germany, never relied on such mechanisms as their central strategies.[28] Most important, simply because one set of policies appears less effective does not mean that government policy in general has become less relevant.

Indeed, a growing body of research suggests that internationalization actually increases the economic role of government. While proponents often describe "globalization" as a spontaneous process, in actuality, government action lies behind every major facet. For example, the single greatest aspect of actual internationalization, the rise of global finance, has happened only because governments chose to weaken and remove controls over capital flows. Such decisions were not inevitable. Both the construction of capital controls earlier this century and their subsequent erosion fit into distinct government policy models. Emerging from the chaos of the Great Depression, Keynes and his followers concluded that international financial openness was not compatible with a free trade in goods. To promote liberal free trade policies, therefore, Keynesians enacted strict controls over capital movements. These restrictions provided the backdrop of growing international trade in the 1950s through 1970s. The leadership to strip away these controls came from the two countries, Britain and the United States, that were home to the conservative "revolution" against liberal, Keynesian thinking. In other words, Britain and the United States first abandoned Keynesian economics and then pushed for changes in national policies to free global finance.

Today's much-vaunted freedom of trade and investment continues to rely on active government support. According to political scientist Eric Helleiner, governments have had to consciously maintain the process of financial liberalization. On at least four different occasions in the 1970s and 1980s, individual governments could have taken steps that would have threatened continued global deregulation. As we will detail below, in Britain in

1976 and in France in 1981, left-wing parties came to power with official platforms calling for significant controls over capital movements. In the late 1970s, two crises with the United States' dollar similarly encouraged American policy makers to seriously consider imposing capital controls. In each case, governments chose domestic austerity (spending cuts and higher interest rates) and further liberalization rather than strategies to rein in footloose finance.[29]

On three other occasions, the entire system of global finance could have simply collapsed had national governments not intervened. In 1974, the U.S. Federal Reserve and close cooperation of central banks in the G-10 countries prevented the collapse of an American bank from sending ripples throughout the world financial system. Faced with a crushing burden of unpayable loans in 1982, Mexico threatened to default—an action that could have sparked a default wave throughout Latin America. To stave off such action, the United States and the International Monetary Fund (IMF) pressured private banks to commit further funds for Mexico as part of a stabilization package. When the stock markets crashed around the world in 1987, American, European, and Japanese policy makers again had to use government power to rescue the system. In each case, the international finance system avoided disaster only because governments stepped in with supervision and regulations to prevent the system from destroying itself through its own irrationalities.

The financial globalization that supposedly has taken place outside of governments has, in fact, required a redistribution of power within governments, as central banks (such as the U.S. Federal Reserve) play an important part in economic policy formulation. Policy makers have, in effect, insulated their monetary, currency, and even fiscal policy from legislatures vulnerable to popular influence by placing authority in the hands of those ideologically committed to "free trade."

The greatest evidence that economic patterns called globalization rely on governmental action comes from the so-called free trade agreements. If the evolution of the world economy was as spontaneous as its proponents claim, then international capitalism should not need treaties such as NAFTA, the General Agreement on Tariffs and Trade (GATT), the World Trade Organization (WTO), or the proposed Multilateral Agreement on Investment or Free Trade Agreement of the Americas. In each case, national governments have consciously agreed to limit their powers over economic decision making. These agreements essentially represent a list of what governments will not do, especially on behalf of their ordinary citizens or the environment. They aim not only to strip away existing government rules and regulations, but to prevent future action. Such provisions betray a fear that, unless certain governmental powers are restricted, they could serve as tools for popular pressures hostile to corporate activity. Indeed, as U.S. Trade Representative Charlene Barshefsky once commented, "the greatest threat to the global system came not from the difficulty of the negotiations, but from the failure of public trust and the public suspicion of the system, the public mistrust of secretive organizations."

Even in the case where governments have supposedly ceded their sovereignty to a global body, the WTO, the reality is far more complex. The WTO's critics have correctly raised alarms that non-elected secret tribunals can pronounce governmental actions in violation of free trade. The WTO's priorities clearly revolve around empowering corporations at the expense of labor, social, and environmental standards. However, the WTO is not all powerful. Indeed, it has no autonomous mechanisms for enforcing its rules and rulings. Instead, it must rely on two forms of state action. Ideally, targeted governments must voluntarily alter their behavior as directed by WTO actions. If not, the world's most powerful states must be willing to use their economic muscle to penalize noncompliance. While such mechanisms place people in smaller and less-developed countries in a vulnerable position, for activists in the United States and Europe's leading nations, "free trade" means ultimately questioning the policies of their own governments. The leaders of such dominant powers can essentially decide which WTO actions they care to vigorously support. Indeed, as we will detail in chapter 6, since Americans live in the most powerful actor in the world economy, we are in a unique position to unilaterally turn the WTO framework on its head.

Economist Ellen Meikins Woods summarized the importance of the state for global capitalism quite well when she wrote:

> But one thing is clear: in the global market, capital *needs* the state. It needs the state to maintain the conditions of accumulation, to preserve labor discipline, to enhance the mobility of capital while suppressing the mobility of labor. Behind every transnational corporation is a national base, which depends on its local state to sustain its viability and on other states to give it access to other markets and other labor forces. . . . As a consequence, the nation-state has acquired new functions as an instrument of competition. If anything, the nation-state is the *main agent* of globalization.[30]

Yet, even if governments play a key role in designing the global economy, they may still have no alternatives but to conform to a global logic. If international economic pressures are as strong as many proponents of globalization say they are, then governments may have no choice but to ultimately promote the current course. Later we will consider the debates over alternative paths that took place within Britian's Labour Party, Mitterrand's socialist government in France, and Swedish social democracy. In the next section, however, we outline two general arguments. First, the current model championed by proponents of globalization, namely the United States, is clearly not an answer. Second, unlike the United States, the ongoing business logics followed in the two other capitalist powerhouses, Japan and Germany, owe their success to active government economic intervention as a key tool to compete in the world economy.

The Low-Road United States Is Not the Answer

On close inspection, the supposed inevitable rules of the global economy closely resemble the neoliberal economic policies dominant in the United States. Indeed, one could argue that given the central role the United States has played in fostering the current international environment, "globalization" is really about reshaping the world in the American image.[31] And while globalization proponents often contrast a booming United States to a struggling Europe, the reality is actually far more complex. In terms of basic quality of life indicators—poverty, infant mortality, inequality in wealth and income, life expectancy, average wage levels—the United States is well behind Europe, with the distance growing, not shrinking. Indeed, the twin diseases of urban decay and suburban consumptive excess found in the United States far exceed anything in Europe.

The much-hailed American job growth of the late 1990s becomes, on closer inspection, hardly a source of superior performance. While the official unemployment rate in the United States is low, researchers have criticized government figures for significantly undercounting those without work.[32] Furthermore, while official unemployment was low, layoffs remained high. Thus, more and more workers traveled from one job to another. Yet, a large proportion of the new jobs—including half of the top twenty occupations with the fastest job growth—paid wages under $17,000 per year.[33] On average, displaced workers experience a 14 percent income cut when moving to their next job.[34] Indeed, a jobless person in Europe may simply translate into someone working at a poverty-paying job in the United States. What is worse, the unemployed European may have a higher standard of living from public assistance and social citizenship than the American who works full time at $6, $7, $8 an hour with no benefits.

Even in narrow business terms, it is not clear that, in the long run, corporate America embodies a promising future. The much-vaunted American freedom for entrepreneurial excellence has in reality seen the wholesale abandonment of entire industries, such as steel, when investors decided that they could make more money elsewhere. Indeed, as we will describe in chapter 6, the United States suffers from a free-market financial system that pushes firms to abandon long-term planning in favor of short-term gains.

The above picture does fly in the face of the, until recently, never-ending celebrations of "unprecedented prosperity" made by the U.S. media. Yet, even in strictly economic terms, there is ample room for caution. We must distinguish between routine cycles of economic upturn (and downturn) and the underlying, long-term patterns. While, at the time, the booming 1920s was held up as evidence of unbridled capitalist success, in retrospect, this period witnessed underlying long-term failures that led to the Great Depression. As then, so today, a booming stock market is at best only loosely connected to actual long-range economic performance. In the 1990s, stock market values increased much faster than actual gains in corporate earnings—thus the big downturn in 2000–2001. Indeed, the ratio of companies' stock market value to their net asset worth was higher than at any time since the 1920s.[35] Between 1991 and 1999 the real economy, in terms of GDP, averaged a 3.2 percent annual growth rate. During this same cycle, the Standard and Poor's 500 rose 15.9 percent per year.[36]

Having trailed the average for the G-7 countries throughout the postwar boom, the American GDP growth did move finally into the lead in the 1990s. However, this relative gain was the result of growth declining more slowly in the United States than elsewhere. At the same time, between 1990 and 1996, annual U.S. productivity gains remained below those of Japan and Germany. Real wage gains in the United States were half of that of Japan and one-third the German rate. And the growth of capital stock remained below Germany's and Japan's, the latter showing more than double the rate of the United States. These are comparisons of relative vitality between nations. Seen in terms of the world economy

as a whole, for all of these measures—productivity, wages, and capital stock—the 1990s remained the worst decade since the peak of the postwar boom.[37]

While neoliberal policies utterly failed to produce a superior economic turnaround in the United States throughout the 1980s and early 1990s, it is true that in the late 1990s, the American economy showed signs of a genuine economic boom. In 1996, corporate profitability decisively surpassed 1973 levels. Complemented by declining corporate debt and falling corporate taxes, rising rates of profit have led to clear jumps in private investment. In 1997, even wages showed real gains for the first time in five years. It may have taken time to get started, but the supply-side policies of the 1980s and 1990s had finally paid off—so the advocates of neoliberalism now exclaimed.

Even before the downturn of 2000, however, there was ample reason to doubt that the "U.S. economic miracle" could be sustained in the long run. Generally speaking, profits rose not because our economy was producing more wealth. Productivity gains remain modest, especially outside manufacturing. Rather, profit increases came mainly because the nation's wealth has become more unequally distributed as companies pursue low-road strategies. In other words, corporations have built their renewed economic vitality on the backs of working people. Recent wage gains were quite modest. Incomes remain, in real terms, below their postwar peaks. This reality is acknowledged in official debates by the continued surprise of mainstream commentators that inflation remained insignificant despite lower unemployment and a supposedly tight labor market. When such observers talk of "inflationary pressures," what they are really looking at are wage gains. Mainstream economic theory predicts price increases any time wage gains exceed productivity increases. Thus, the continued enthusiasm for low "inflationary pressures" is simply another way of acknowledging that wages remain stagnant despite a "booming economy." More detailed wage breakdowns continue to reveal the vast inequalities that separate a small prosperous minority from the growing ranks of working poor and a shrinking middle class.

Indeed, domestic consumer demand was supported only by extremely high rates of personal debt and low savings throughout the income ladder. Total household liabilities as a portion of disposable personal income increased from 65 percent over the 1960 to 1969 cycle to 92 percent between 1991 and 1999.[38] Indeed, consumer spending was maintained only by people's going into greater debt. By 2001, debt as a portion of household income had reached an all-time high of 97 percent while personal savings dropped to nearly zero. In part, this greater willingness to take on debt came from the false security provided by record growth in pension and investment portfolios dependent on Wall Street. Taken even at face value, the runaway consumption boom of the 1990s is simply unsustainable.

When seen in terms of a broader world economy, it remained questionable that the American boom can revive and sustain itself. Many progressive economists interpreted the stock market run between 1992 and 1999 as an artificial bubble bound to burst.[39] Even taking the 1990s boom at face value, the U.S. economy was hardly a capitalist miracle. Both real GDP and productivity growth for the 1991 through 1999 cycle were below the performances of the 1960s' and 1970s' cycles. Our nation's balance of trade swung negative in the 1970s and has remained that way ever since. The 1990s made no difference. No other country in the world, but one able to draw on its position as the sole economic and military superpower, could maintain such a negative balance for three decades.

Concerns over celebrating the "American miracle" have surfaced on the other side of the Atlantic. Michel Albert, president of France's largest insurance company, was so alarmed by the trend among fellow businesspeople to view the United States as the promised land that he wrote a book published in English as: *Capitalism vs. Capitalism: How America's Obsession with Individual Achievement and Short-term Profit Has Led It to the Brink of Collapse*.[40] In it, he paints a picture of a nation enjoying the present by sacrificing its future. In addition to the obvious signs of social decay and polarization, Albert points to major losses of American industry in areas such as consumer electronics, steel, and shipbuilding. Add to these abandoned industries a decaying infrastructure, a notoriously undertrained workforce, a bloated and inefficient health care system, and so forth, and one has to ask how long the United States can maintain its outward signs of economic success. Certainly, the American model of "less government, more corporate power" does not seem to be preparing us well for the future.

Active Governments Provide Advantages in Global Competition

Global capitalism needs active governments, if for no other reason than to keep domestic populations from resisting corporate power. However, even in strictly economic terms, active government policies can provide an attractive way to participate in world markets. Indeed, the global success of the two other leading capitalist powers, Germany and Japan, have been built on a foundation of such intervention. Both nations rose from the devastation of war and economic backwardness to preeminent world leadership precisely through extensive government involvement, which flies in the face of prevailing American practices.[41]

An Australian specialist on Japan and East Asia, Linda Weiss has identified several ways in which private business can benefit from an active partnership with government in the global economy. U.S. businesspeople continuously speak of the rapid change that characterizes today's economic reality. Yet, firms that partner with government, and through government with other firms, are arguably far better able to negotiate such change than those left to their own "entrepreneurial" skills. For example, adapting to change involves risk. Developing new technologies, new products, and finding new markets all involve expensive long-term investments typically beyond the capacity of an individual firm. Governments can help ensure such investments by socializing the risks through government-led programs that pool public and private resources. Furthermore, to respond to rapid change, firms need workers with skills that allow them to adjust quickly. Training such workers, however, is also expensive. Not surprisingly, the nations with the best records in workforce training are those that have systematic government-sponsored programs.

The higher the rate of national savings, the potentially greater the resources for productive investment. The United States has a notoriously low savings rate, due, in part, to business and government policies that prioritize consumption. By contrast, Japanese government policy deliberately encourages a high rate of savings. Thus, Japanese firms have gained access to resources needed to catch up to, and surpass, American-based corporations.

Finally, within each nation, global economic changes push certain industries into decline while others grow. Active government policy aids such transitions by helping restructure ongoing industries and by minimizing the social and economic disruption of those that continue to decline. By contrast, the U.S. market-oriented approach simply lets firms, and entire industries, collapse as investors prefer less risky, short-term ventures elsewhere. At the same time, potential new industries may sit dormant if the short-term startup costs outweigh the immediate benefits. Since, in reality, the U.S. government does not simply sit on the sidelines, Americans can experience the worst of both worlds. Policy makers let free markets and investor decisions chart the overall economic course. Authorities then intervene to correct "market failures." Thus, the public pays the costs when lobbying by industry representatives, unions, local governments, and citizen groups pressure authorities to use public resources to prop up the failing industries abandoned by private investors.

According to Weiss and other researchers, the key to Japanese, South Korean, and Taiwanese postwar global success has been their state-led capacity for economic transformation.[42] Government policy does not so much dictate to as partner with private business. Through extensive business umbrella organizations and public-private bodies, industry and government personnel interact to chart collective plans for the long-term future. Government powers over credit, trade, information, and direct spending then guide economic development along particular lines. In this way, for example, the Japanese put in place successful decade-long plans to enter and even dominate such global economic sectors as consumer electronics, automobiles, shipbuilding, steel, and so forth. By contrast, the American system of fragmented business and weak government planning leads to ad hoc policies that often respond to the short-term needs of individual industry lobbyists rather than consider long-term economic planning.

From a progressive standpoint, the main weakness of the Asian model is not the level of governmental participation, but the lack of a crucial third partner. While the system unites business and government, it excludes labor and other channels for popular input. These nations are not economic democracies. Indeed, in countries such as South Korea, state-sponsored industrialization has been accompanied with repressive authoritarian governments.

As the ongoing Asian economic crisis makes clear, such proactive states are not foolproof. Indeed, American commentators, steeped in the so-called virtues of the free market, are quick to ascribe every economic problem encountered by Japan or other East Asian countries to "excessive" governmental involvement. Not surprisingly, they prescribe solutions that essentially move these countries toward American lines. However, the causes for the difficulties are only indirectly related to state activity. Indeed, the nations hit hardest by the crisis were precisely those that had gone the furthest in embracing American-promoted financial openness and deregulation.[43]

As we will examine below, the underlying problem, ignored by American pundits, continues to be a lack of global demand—too few consumers with the resources to buy the goods that the world can produce. This is a problem that affects all nations, not just Asia. Most important, the Japanese and Taiwanese hardly seem to be listening to the American commentators by jettisoning their tradition of strong state involvement. Indeed, while individual aspects of state economic intervention may have faded, new policy mechanisms have come in their place. Arguably, the capacity of these states to participate in economic change will be restructured, rather than replaced.[44]

It is this lack of active state capacity to steer economic transformations that Weiss sees as the weakness of Keynesian social democracy. For example, Sweden's welfare state and centralized collective bargaining helped to redistribute wealth and establish an overall high standard of living. However, the direct decisions over how the actual wealth is created were left to private industry. The Rehn-Meidner model shaped the external environment. It did not establish extensive government policy or union intervention in firm decisions. This lack of influence has led to problems today. As an unintended consequence, the Rehn-Meidner model favored large, export-oriented firms. Over time, these firms have become less tied to Sweden. By the 1980s and 1990s, Swedish industry showed low rates of investment, a lack of new product development, technology investments that emphasized labor savings, and an overall lack of job creation in the industrial sector. Instead, public employment had to assume a greater share of providing new job opportunities. Without policies to foster direct industrial planning, government financial support to business has been primarily ad hoc and aimed at rescuing declining sectors.

For Weiss, the German economy remains relatively strong, in spite of the disruptions of reunification, because of its submerged capacity for state economic action. As another nation that, like Japan, industrialized relatively late, the German state historically played a major role in promoting industrial development. As we noted in chapter 2, the legacy of this period is the nation's strong banking sector

that aids long-term planning. Paralleling our analysis, Weiss argues that Cold War politics overseen by American authorities prevented the Germans from pursuing the kinds of overt governmental economic policies seen in Japan. Nevertheless, the German government has played an active role—working behind the scenes to build up the nongovernmental institutions that provide a source of German economic strength. The public-private institutions of the welfare state and codetermination have their business parallels in semipublic research, training, and credit institutions. As a result, German business enjoys a much higher level of organization than its American counterpart. This submerged transformative capacity provided the basis for Germany's postwar success and has worked well for gradual, incremental economic change.

While once again American free marketers are quick to ascribe any strain or problem experienced by the German economy to the supposed evils of too much government interference, excessive welfare spending, or high wages, Weiss points in the opposite direction. While the German system of state economic intervention-by-delegation worked well during the postwar boom, it has proven less suited for responding to the rapid economic shocks typical of today's unstable capitalism. Favoring behind-the-scenes intervention, the German state did not develop the kinds of centralized administrative capacity to plan out wholesale economic restructuring, undertaken in Japan. The question today is will German policy build on the traditions of social protection, social partnership, and the institutions of submerged industrial policy to add more overt government intervention in economic decisions or will policy makers embrace American free-market prescriptions?[45]

It's Not "Globalization"; It's Capitalism

The twin facts that significant aspects of today's world economy are not entirely new and that other industrialized countries have varied in their particular mechanisms for interacting with this economy shed serious doubt on the notion that today's changes must inevitably lead to one common American direction. Indeed, global economic pressures by themselves cannot account for the seeming inability of European social democracy to pursue new independent paths. In fact, the real issue is not economics but politics.

The real source of today's economic changes is not the various technological and other seemingly autonomous forces described under the rubric of globalization. Rather, so-called globalization represents the political response of capitalism to the worldwide crisis that it entered by the end of the 1960s. While different economists ascribe different reasons for the downturn, the facts of capitalism's global crisis are clear. By the 1970s, profit rates began to decline and economic growth slowed. In the United States, for example, annual growth rates of 3 to 4 percent in the 1950s and 1960s fell to 2.6 percent by 1979, 2.4 percent in the 1980s, and 2.1 percent between 1990 and 1996. The main engine of capitalism, the accumulation of more capital, as measured by growth in capital stock, also fell from highs of 4 percent annually between 1960 and 1973 to 2.1 by 1990 to 1996.[46] Similar declines hit the rest of the capitalist world. Economists on the political left ascribe this declining performance to a now-quarter-century fall in the rate of profit—one linked to stagnation in global demand and growing overcapacity.[47]

Since a capitalist economy maintains itself through growth and accumulation, slowdowns of this magnitude provided ample reasons for concern. Indeed, reduced growth and lower profits meant more layoffs and less investment, which translated into the higher unemployment that began to strain social democratic social spending policies. However, in the long term, the problem has not been just the actual economic difficulties, but the political agenda to which the slowdown gave birth. Seen in terms of the last two centuries, capitalism normally operates through cycles of boom and bust. During booms, a capitalist economy accumulates growing internal contradictions that eventually usher in a downturn

and crisis. It is through recessions and depressions that capitalism reorganizes itself by eliminating weaker firms, reducing the power of workers, and restructuring economic activity to clear the way for renewed growth. The dominant tendency, especially before the rise of social democratic and Keynesian redistribution efforts, was for the rich to gain the most during the booms and for the poor to pay during the busts. However, the outcome of each crisis ultimately involved political battles. Indeed, the collapse of the Great Depression, while paid for by the suffering of ordinary working people in the short run, did lead to the gains in government policy and union organizing that helped establish the postwar growth of middle-class living standards.

The current crisis, however, has given way to an agenda that directly threatens the lives of ordinary people. While this neoliberalism was embraced most fully in the United States and Britain, it also provides the framework for the policies of the IMF and World Bank as well as all of the major "free trade" agreements. It essentially involves institutionalizing the low road throughout the world. Keynesian economics focused on demand—thus combining economic health with a certain level of social justice. Neoliberalism, however, returns to the classical nineteenth-century capitalist focus on supply. The problem, so conclude the champions of the new faith, is not that people cannot buy what they produce, but that investors do not have the resources and freedom to invest. This conclusion has led to an entire package of policies dominant in the United States since the last years of the Carter administration and that our government today promotes worldwide.

Neoliberal economics aims to increase the power and resources among investors. Such actions are justified by the claims that the wealthy will use their windfall to invest and expand the overall economic pie. Neoliberalism's policy arsenal includes massive wage restraint through targeted recessions to raise unemployment, a war against labor unions, and reduced restrictions on the movement of capital. These policies redefine the balance of power between labor and management. They are complemented by "reverse Robin Hood" fiscal policies that cut social spending for the majority and give tax cuts skewed toward the wealthy. Corporate expenses are also reduced by gradually dismantling government regulations and forcing the public to pay the environmental and social costs of profitable business activity. Both ideologically and in concrete policy, the neoliberal agenda celebrates the private and chastises the collective. Thus, publicly owned firms are sold off and social services privatized as corporate forces attempt to colonize every aspect of human life.

Most important for our discussion, neoliberalism subordinates government policy to the needs of the market. Ideologically, government is portrayed as inherently controlling and inefficient. The popular aspects of government—social spending, business regulations, public education, and so forth—are attacked and privatized. Meanwhile, neoliberalism actually relies on active government efforts to support the market and guard it against popular resistance. The champions of so-called less government enthusiastically expand corporate welfare, military spending, the police and prison system, and state protections for property rights.

Since the bulk of the world's population, including, arguably, most Americans, continue to exercise a much greater belief in the positive role of government social spending and business regulation than neoliberalism can accept, the proponents of the new faith have had to couch their prescriptions within the mantle of inevitability. Thus, their enthusiasm for "globalization." The concept allows business and government to argue that they are not making deliberate policy choices to inflict harm on the population and the environment. Rather, they are simply conforming to an already established global reality. In other words, globalization arguments can be seen as much as an ideological weapon against notions of collective action as a fully accurate appreciation of worldwide economic conditions.

The progressive challenge is thus political. Activists face not so much a transcendent global economy but an aggressive, many-tentacled corporate agenda that operates from the local to the global levels. For example, while the threat of job loss can come in the form of a company relocating production abroad, it can equally come through the same firm outsourcing work to low-wage employers down the street. In the United States, plants move just as easily from one town to another and one state to another as across national borders. Indeed, the bidding wars between states to lure domestic investment run directly parallel to the prescriptions offered by globalization enthusiasts to national governments. While NAFTA added to the arsenal of union-busting employers, most of the techniques (including the illegal firing and terrorizing of workers) hardly require an ability to move out of the country. Globalization cannot be offered as the core explanation to account for the social budget cutting and "reverse Robin Hood" that began in the 1980s and continues in the United States today despite the much-trumpeted budget surpluses.

Neoliberal capitalism is the actual beast. "Globalization" is simply a mechanism for imposing new rules around a free-market agenda. These rules are written not just in the so-called free trade agreements, but in national, state, and local policies. Therefore, the main problem facing German social democracy, for example, is not the actual global pressures on what continues to be Europe's powerhouse, but the behavior of its own domestic capitalists increasingly eager to question the sacred cows of past German economic success. Faced with the same capitalist crisis as its American counterpart, German business has also begun to flirt with neoliberal freedoms. Thus, some employers complain that the system of codetermination hampers the rapid decisions needed to "compete in today's global market." They have begun to argue that German wage rates are too high, and have suggested that the nation needs to move back toward a forty-hour workweek with no increase in pay. German managers who hope to free themselves from the "burden" of social and economic regulations look longingly across the Atlantic. In 1996, employers fought a losing battle with the union

I.G. Metall to try to reduce continued payments of sickness benefits from 100 percent to 80 percent of workers' original pay. Even though the nation's apprenticeship system has been a key to German industrial competitiveness, employers have begun to reduce the number of training positions they offer. Centralized collective bargaining has also been threatened by the growing number of employers who either do not join or leave their respective industry's employers' federation. As German managers have tried to move in neoliberal directions, the results are quite familiar to Americans. Wage rates have fallen, the tax burden has been redirected onto the backs of working people, corporate profits have exploded, and few of the promised new jobs have materialized.[48]

Neoliberalism's social and environmental consequences have been well documented. Essentially, it raises capitalist profits by forcing the costs of corporate activity onto the public and nature itself. However, as our critique of the U.S. economy suggests, neoliberalism may prove a dead-end, even in narrow economic terms. It has utterly failed to solve the contradiction that gave it birth. Global overcapacity continues as neoliberal policies ignore demand-side questions of overcapacity and unequal consumption. To cite just one example, automobile manufacturers face such fierce competition because they have the collective capacity to produce over 70 million units per year, while the world's population is able to buy just over 50 million.[49] In fact, the neoliberal gospel has made things worse as even less people today can afford to buy the world's production, while more and more nations try to export their way to economic health. As a survey of global capacity by the *Economist* concluded in 1999, "Thanks to enormous over-investment, especially in Asia, the world is awash with excess capacity in computer chips, steel, cars, textiles, and chemicals. . . ." The bottom line, concluded the authors, is that the world output gap—between industrial capacity and use—is approaching its highest levels since the Great Depression era of the 1930s.[50]

The recent Asian economic crisis illustrates the dilemma. Since the end of the postwar boom, Southeast Asia has been the area to enjoy the largest investment boom. Lured by the prospects of cheap labor and supportive government policies, international investment flooded into Southeast Asian economies, fueling a building bonanza and a massive increase in manufacturing capacity. This investment boom, however, was premised around exporting to world markets. Asian workers were being mobilized not to produce for themselves, but for others, especially Western consumers. In 1996 and 1997, these export economies hit the global reality of stagnated consumer demand. In the financial panic that followed, international investors helped ensure an outright economic collapse as they fled from the region. The IMF, concerned mainly with protecting the interests of Western financiers, then forced the area to accept bitter neoliberal medicine: reduced wages, slashed social spending, and deregulation of business. Yet, the end goal of these draconian policies, increased exports, will simply worsen international competition as even more goods chase after fewer consumers. Championed by American officials, these policies will likely harm the U.S. domestic economy by further shrinking demand for U.S. exports and flooding American markets with low-priced goods.[51]

The same pattern of increasing economic volatility and massive economic contradictions has also been seen in Eastern Europe and parts of the former Soviet Union.[52] While American commentators are quick to ascribe the economic problems to lingering communist influence and state involvement, in fact the disease has been caused by the neoliberal cure. The same is true for Latin America, where two decades of American-inspired neoliberal prescriptions have produced massive inequality and economic instability.[53] Indeed, to see where the world is heading we need look no farther than our nation's own liberal economic past. During the nineteenth century, unfettered capitalism created increasingly more erratic cycles of boom and bust until the system very nearly destroyed itself during the Great Depression.

The neoliberal drive to become "leaner and meaner" might help individual companies or even national economies grab a greater share of world markets. However, they do not expand those markets. To the contrary, producing even more with fewer people simply adds to the world's overcapacity. Therefore, who is going to buy the products? The Japanese, the newly industrializing Asian countries, the Europeans, and the Latin Americans are all currently attempting to revive their economies by increasing exports. Their target is often the "miracle" U.S. economy with its huge consumer market. Yet, how long can the United States buy up the world's exports when the average American consumer is in debt up to his or her limit and American industry looks to increasing its own success by becoming leaner and meaner while selling and building more abroad?

In short, as Robert Brenner has pointed out, two decades of expanding neoliberal policies have utterly failed to solve the crisis they were intended to address. He explains:

> Ironically, there has been a very close correlation between the extent to which capital has got its way and the extent to which the performance of the advanced capitalist economies has deteriorated, cycle by cycle, since the 1960s. During the 1960s, when ostensibly over-strong labour movements, bloated welfare states, and hyper-regulating governments were at the height of their influence, the global economic boom reached historic peaks. Since then, as the neoclassical [neoliberal] medicine has been administered in ever stronger doses, the economy has performed steadily less well. The 1970s were worse than the 1960s, the 1980s worse than the 1970s, and the 1990s have been worse than the 1980s. Speaking only of results, and not for the moment of prospects, the long downturn has continued to defy capital's remedies.[54]

Our analysis has important implications. If the issue is framed as globalization and the power of a transnational capitalism, then progressives are confronted with only two possible responses. Society can lower its aspirations and conform to the logic of the global market. Government policy must strive to make domestically based firms the most competitive in their global arena. If particular national segments of global capitalism do well, benefits will hopefully be passed down to the broader society.

Alternatively, society can resist global forces by building networks of international solidarity. While certainly more attractive from a progressive point of view, this second approach also has its weaknesses. Certainly, global solidarity is a necessary part of progressive action today. However, it can potentially demobilize activism if it is seen as the sole hope for progressive change. Actions such as mass demonstrations when the WTO comes to town or pressuring local governments to not purchase goods produced in sweatshops are available to the average person. However, for other dimensions of struggle, international connections must be built at levels beyond the immediate access of many grassroots activists. Furthermore, establishing international solidarity strong enough to steer the world economy represents a long-term project that can appear simply overwhelming to many activists. If conferences and forums on globalization focus mainly on the ravages of global capitalism only to end with general calls for international solidarity, they risk leaving participants demoralized. What can the average person, union, or community do in the face of multinational corporations whose annual profits exceed the budgets of entire countries?

However, if the issue is reframed as neoliberalism capitalism, then the terrain for struggle significantly broadens. While international solidarity remains important, local, regional, and national actions and reforms also become key ingredients. In this way, progressive strategy aims to build popular power and control at every level that neoliberalism operates. And since capitalism takes form at local, regional, national, and international levels, a broad array of grassroots work can contribute to fostering economic democracy. Rather than offering empty dreams soon to be overwhelmed by global forces, grassroots domestic reforms provide possibilities for hitting core locations of capitalist power. Building worker-to-worker contacts at the nonunion plant down the street becomes just as important as fostering the same contacts across national borders. Enacting local measures to keep Wal-Mart out of the community and to revive downtown thus connects to battles to block transnational corporations from colonizing economic resources throughout the world.

This distinction between a transcendent global economy and a multilayered capitalism can be seen in the debates that have occurred within European social democracy. While the dominant leadership voices have chosen to narrow their strategies to fit within the logic of a "transcendent global economy," a vocal opposition called for a break from the global logic precisely by rethinking social democracy's domestic agenda.

The Paths Not Taken: Social Democracy in Crisis

The warning signs that the traditional social democratic agenda was in trouble began as early as the 1970s. The end of the postwar capitalist boom spelled the end of the goose that laid social democracy's golden egg: steady economic growth. An expanding welfare state and social partnership had been built on the unprecedented economic expansion of the 1950s–1970s era. Without such growth, a smaller economic pie meant sharper trade-offs between corporate profits, social spending, and social income.

While social democratic concessions to an "inevitable" global logic have received ample public attention, other paths were offered. Indeed, as we will see, several of the most famous examples of social democratic capitulation before all-powerful global forces were actually predated by the internal defeat of proposals to pursue more proactive and radical forms of change. Having some awareness of these alternative agendas can greatly aid American

activists by widening the boundaries of what is conceivable in today's "global economy."

Mitterrand's France

The Mitterrand government's dramatic U-turn in 1984 had as much to do with the internal politics of the Socialist Party as with outside economic pressures. While the official party platform and election slogans may have sounded quite revolutionary, in reality, the Socialist government that took power in 1981 was firmly rooted in more traditional reforms.[55]

Unlike most social democratic parties after World War II, the French Socialists had to compete with one of the two strongest communist parties in Europe (the other being in Italy). Initially, after the war, the French Communists exercised considerable influence—enjoying roughly a fifth of the national vote and substantial governmental power at the local level. By the 1970s, however, the repeated squandering of opportunities by an increasingly backward-looking Communist leadership provided the Socialists with a chance to seize the initiative on the left. However, continued Communist presence meant that to achieve national power, the Socialists either had to build a coalition with the Communists and/or lure away traditional Communist voters. Following repeated failures by the left to achieve power in the 1970s, Socialist leader Francois Mitterrand succeeded in positioning himself and the Socialists to reach for national power by the end of the decade. He did so by leaning left. More radical groups within the party were able to exercise considerable influence over official platforms and the party's public image. Thus, when the Socialists, in coalition with the Communists, won national power in 1981, it seemed as though France was poised for revolutionary change. A wide-ranging and bold common left platform was backed by a national constitution that gave considerable power to any president, such as Mitterrand, who held a majority in the Assembly. As the second largest country in Europe, France appeared ready to chart a new path.

The reality, however, proved far more brittle. The revolutionary slogans and bold calls for sweeping change reflected as much the need to win over Communists and other left voters as it did careful internal debate and consensus. Furthermore, most Socialist leaders had entered the 1981 elections not foreseeing the possibility that they might actually win outright power. Thus, while the Common Program had provided an effective mobilization tool, many of its specific proposals were neither widely understood nor supported. Indeed, many measures remained slogans rather than actual designs for effective policy. Furthermore, the Socialists took power after years of organizational weakening both within the party and of its connection to labor and other social movements. Thus, the grassroots upwelling needed to support the party's calls for bold change was not easily forthcoming.

The much-trumpeted concept of "autogestion" reflected the basic dilemma. Although a key element in defining a distinctly Socialist agenda, autogestion had different meanings for different parts of the left camp. For Marxists and other traditional left currents, autogestion pointed to a rupture with capitalism beginning with the large-scale nationalization of industry. Workers' organizing from below would be complemented by government action from above to progressively place the institutions of capitalist rule into popular hands. While sharing these revolutionary ambitions, the currents more associated with the new left of the 1960s gave autogestion a different spin. They focused less on nationalization and more on a withering of the state and central authority. This version of autogestion emphasized the autonomous nature of social groups and greater decentralization both within the state and within the party. A third interpretation of autogestion took up the cause of the various regions in France that saw the nation's tradition of strong, centralized government as exploitation of the regions by Paris. Autogestion meant greater devolution of power to the regional and local levels. While these different conceptions were not entirely incompatible, they meant that the Socialists took power without a clear consensus of what their ultimate goals were. Indeed, the beauty of autogestion as a mobilizing tool lay precisely in the ability of different groups to read into it their own hopes and desires. Such vagueness, however, left the Socialists less prepared to govern. Indeed, they found themselves thrust suddenly into national office with no coherent economic policy, but with a mixed collection of specific reforms unconnected to an overarching plan.[56]

Even in the best of circumstances, the lack of internal agreement and detailed designs would have caused the Socialists trouble. However, the economic situation that greeted them was hardly ideal. With the postwar boom clearly over, the Socialists took control of a nation headed for serious economic problems. They inherited from the previous government a serious trade deficit, spiraling inflation, and outdated industrial sectors clearly in need of the kind of overhaul likely to produce large-scale layoffs and displacement.

Nevertheless, the new government began by pursuing a relatively bold direction. Building on France's tradition of governmental economic planning and ownership, the Socialists embarked on a wave of sweeping nationalization. Nearly 90 percent of the banking sector and a third of industry were taken over by the state. Labor reforms increased trade-union control of working conditions, mandated annual wage bargaining, and protected worker "rights of expression" on the shop floor. To raise demand, the Mitterrand government pursued a major expansion of social spending, including a 40 to 50 percent increase in the per-child family allowance, a 50 percent increase in low-income housing benefits, and a 15 percent increase in the minimum wage. Added to these measures were a thirty-nine-hour workweek, paid vacation extended to five weeks, early retirement, and work sharing.[57] While seemingly sweeping in scope, all of these reforms were consistent with postwar social democracy. Depending on how it was used, even the massive nationalization was not out of line with the experiences of Britain or

Austria, or with the nation's own tradition of national planning.

These policies, however, were as far as the Socialist reforms went. Both domestically and internationally, business responded to Socialist actions by preparing for all-out war. Yet, the inherited economic problems were enough to spark a crisis. The Socialists underestimated the extent of the corporate sector's weakness. Many newly nationalized firms had already been closed due to insolvency. Even worse, due to domestic economic weakness, the Socialist stimulus package dramatically increased imports as French industry output failed to keep pace with people's rising incomes. The result was a massive balance-of-payments crisis. Inflation simply became worse and imports flooded local markets. It was within this context that global financial interests forced the issue by sending France's currency into a tailspin. The currency crisis presented the government with a clear choice. Either it could realign the franc within the European Monetary System (EMS), which meant implementing a major austerity program, or it could pull out of the EMS altogether and prepare to fight out the economic crisis with more radical reforms.

Evidence that the latter course was a possibility comes from both the sharp debates within the government as well as the clear fears of American and other Western officials that France would turn its back on the official international economic order. Mitterrand's government, however, progressively made decisions that took them down the other path. Reforms were halted and social spending cut dramatically. Government policy turned toward capturing greater international market share rather than resolving domestic social issues. The nationalized firms, once seen as the agents of social change and economic democracy, became engines for capitalist rationalization and lean international competition. The about-face in economic policy placed the burden of economic restructuring firmly on the backs of the very working people that the Socialists had been elected to protect. While the government made modest reform gains in areas such as women's rights, legal reform, and regional autonomy, its foreign policy reflected its neoliberal domestic economic policies. Indeed, Mitterrand proved to be one of Ronald Reagan's most dependable allies.

While seeming to conform to the notions of globalization, the details of the Socialist U-turn show as much internal influence as external influence. Breaking with the official international system and using more fundamental and radical reforms to drive an economic recovery required elements that the Socialists had not developed. For such a course of action, a substantial part of the population would have had to have been mobilized for an extended period of economic upheaval. Yet, not only had the Socialists not built a popular consensus for clear radical change, they did not even have clear agreement or capacity for mass mobilization within their own ranks. Mitterrand's lean to the left had covered over a substantial commitment within the party to quite traditional conceptions of social democratic action. Furthermore, the more radical currents within the party shared the general lack of detailed plans and popular consensus in how to administer power. In short, the Socialists took power completely unprepared to govern in an environment of economic crisis. Thus, governmental leaders, many of whom were never entirely committed to radical reforms, succumbed to pressures from business and other Western governments to toe the official neoliberal line. In doing so, however, the party further weakened its connections to social movements and contributed to a growing sense of cynicism and disillusionment among its supporters and the general population.

Writer and socialist Daniel Singer put the lessons of the Mitterrand years best when he wrote:

> Contrary to common wisdom, the Mitterrand experiment tells us directly nothing about the possibility, or impossibility, of building socialism—that is, about the search for a radically different society. . . . It has simply not been tried. The French events shatter the hopes or illusions that

the transformation can be carried out gradually, without a break, within existing institutions, by purely parliamentary means, without the active participation of the people in their factories and their offices, without the unconcealed vision of another world indispensable to produce such a mobilization.[58]

Britain's Alternative Economic Strategy

While the French Socialists were slowly making their electoral way to power, internal debates within the British Labour Party produced a plan for fundamental economic reform that the Socialists could have used in 1981. Of all the left opposition currents operating within the different European Social Democratic parties, Britain's Labour left produced one of the most comprehensive visions of an economic alternative. Its rejection by the Labour government that took power in 1974, despite support among party activists and the unions, proved a key stepping-stone toward the "new" Labour Party of Tony Blair and his open embrace of Thatcherism.[59]

Although the famous Clause IV of the party's constitution, which asserted the goal of public economic ownership, survived until Tony Blair's rise in the 1990s, the Labour Party emerged from World War II firmly committed to reformist, not revolutionary, aims. The triumphant 1945–1951 Labour government did nationalize a significant part of the British economy—amounting to the employment of 2.3 million people. However, the militancy of this action was offset by a reality in which nationalization was confined to the least-profitable industries and compensation to the former owners proved quite generous. Most important, nationalized firms maintained traditional capitalist forms of management. Little effort was made to use the nationalized sector either as an engine of democratic planning or as a counterweight to the logic of the capitalist market. The other major gain of the Labour administration, a growing welfare state—with its new national health care system as its shining achievement—fit firmly

into the postwar social democratic mainstream. Once forced out of power in 1951, the party used its years in opposition to formally reject traditional notions of socialism in favor of Keynesian-style social democracy. It was the frustrations with this agenda when the party returned to power from 1964 to 1970 that led to a strong left challenge within the party during the 1970s and early 1980s.

Harold Wilson led Labour to electoral victory in 1964, in part because of his ability to sound both radical and reformist at the same time. For the party's left wing, he appeared to call for fundamental change, while to the party's right and British business, he promised efficient capitalist management. Once in power, the government's actual policies clearly favored the latter course. The fate of Labour's famous incomes policy proved most telling in this respect. For the unions and the left, Labour's "planned growth of incomes" promised a reciprocal form of corporatism in which unions and business coordinated rising real incomes with growing investments and production. Despite measures to enact some form of industrial planning, the Wilson government remained committed to following the logic of the market. Thus, hit by financial crisis, the government found itself increasingly at odds with the unions. Labour's "planned growth of incomes" became one-sided wage restraint. Indeed, Wilson sought to restore economic health using classic neoliberal policies of sharp budget cuts coupled with a statutory wage freeze. In practice, the Labour government proved itself more effective at controlling and disciplining the unions than it did at empowering workers. While in capitalist terms these measures helped produce an economic recovery, the gains were bought with a real fall in income. The result was electoral disaster as the party lost some of its traditional base. The Labour vote among manual workers, for example, dropped from 69 percent in 1966 to 58 percent in 1970, when the party lost national power.

The electoral loss and growing internal discontent sparked by the Wilson government set into motion a process of debate that produced a strong left opposition inside the party. Several factors helped strengthen the Labour left. While the radical new left of the 1960s often rejected and critiqued parliamentary and electoral strategies, by the 1970s, significant currents within these movements began to look toward the possibilities of political power. The Labour Party provided the necessary tool. Eventually, these activists would help foster a vibrant period of municipal left-wing governments. The sixties also transformed the labor movement. The unions provided not only the party's core traditional constituency, but also, because of the party's internal organization, a strong leadership voice. Waves of militant strikes, often against the desires of the Wilson government, complemented internal union upheavals to produce a growing left-wing union leadership willing to challenge the policies promoted by the Labour Party's parliamentary leadership. At the same time, even less radicalized union leadership was forced leftward by the difficult dilemma posed by its commitment to supporting the party and its elected officials on the one hand, and the increasing antiworker policies pursued by Labour's governmental leaders on the other. If the government was going to ask the unions to support measures that meant significant sacrifice on the part of their membership, it had to offer some form of significant economic change in return.

By the early 1970s, internal changes had produced a militant party base able to pass Conference resolutions that proved far more militant than the positions taken by the parliamentary leaders. At the same time, the balance of power within the party's National Executive Council also leaned increasingly to the left. While comprising a rather heterogeneous collection of groups and individuals, this Labour left shared a willingness to question the postwar social democratic framework. Indeed, as one of its major leaders, Tony Benn, argued, if Labour did not offer ordinary working people a new vision, a right-wing counterrevolution would be the result. In a 1973 party Conference speech, Benn reminded delegates:

[If] we are only concerned to win votes we shall never mobilize the strength we need to implement policy. . . . We are offering much more than legislation. We are offering a perspective and a vision which will transform the political atmosphere of cynicism which has developed in recent years. Without a vision people will turn to their immediate and narrow self-interest. With some sense that they are part of a change in our society we shall be able to draw much more from them.[60]

As Benn's speech suggests, at issue was not simply the party's governmental agenda, but the internal life of the party as well. With half a million members in 1952, only the Swedish and Austrian Social Democratic parties exceeded Labour's strength in its ratio of membership to electoral votes. Yet, for several decades, the party leadership failed to use or even encourage this potential grassroots force. In fact, at times, it seemed that party leaders saw potential grassroots militancy as a threat to be controlled, rather than an opportunity to be harnessed. As a result, the internal life of the party had seriously declined by the 1970s. The Labour left aimed to revive party life by democratizing its internal structures and recapturing Labour's sense of itself as part of a social movement.

Economic issues were at the forefront of the Labour left's new agenda. Eventually, these ideas crystallized formally as the Alternative Economic Strategy (AES). A later version of the AES was put into book form by the London Working Group of the Conference of Socialist Economists in 1980.[61] This document synthesized the policy ideas and strategic perspective built over the course of the 1970s. Most of its major provisions were endorsed over time by Labour Party Conferences and/or officially supported by the trade union movement and the National Executive Council. The authors, however, stress the importance of seeing the strategy not just as separate policy proposals, but as an interrelated whole.

The London Working Group viewed the main economic problem facing the country not as the capitalist downturn itself, but rather the likely capitalist response to these difficulties. Accurately anticipating the rise of full-blown neoliberalism, the authors argued that mainstream capitalist solutions would try to return to economic health largely on the backs of working people.

In an analysis that is not entirely irrelevant to an American audience, the London Group also identified Britain's unique imperial history as a source of domestic economic weakness. The expanding British Empire established the City of London as a world financial center—one with an inordinate influence over both the economy and government policy. The colonial links also created a national economy that served as a major base for multinational companies more oriented to their global operations than Britian's domestic economic health. By 1977, the overseas production of these multinationals had become equal to 40 percent of Britain's total domestic output (by contrast, the U.S. ratio was only 17 percent). Inside the country, a mere thirty companies controlled 30 percent of all U.K. manufacturing output. The imperial legacy was exacerbated by the policies of both Tory and Labour governments as they tried to cling to colonies and world predominance well after the nation's capacity to do so had receded. The result was a particularly harsh long-term economic decline. Throughout the twentieth century, Britain's economic performance fell well below that of the other industrialized countries. By the 1970s, the country was experiencing major deindustrialization as an already weak industrial sector failed to invest in modernization and restructuring. Between 1965 and 1980, overseas investment by U.K. companies rose two and a half times as fast as investment in the United Kingdom. While personal consumption increased between 1955 and 1979, the rates fell below those of the United States and other parts of Europe.

Thus, the AES set out to address the postwar capitalist crisis in a nation particularly ruined by its international connections. The strategy sought to rebuild the economy in ways that restored economic vitality through worker-friendly measures. The strat-egy began with the very Keynesian mechanisms that emerging neoliberals were in the process of discrediting. By increasing public spending, the AES aimed to inject more money into the economy, raise employment through public-sector jobs, improve the quality of services, and challenge the market as the determiner of what activity is assigned economic value. Although mainstream policy makers were coming to see full employment goals as a relic of the past, the authors defended their public spending by arguing that placing more money into the hands of ordinary people would prove a much more effective way of putting resources into the domestic economy than neoliberal policies of enriching the wealthy. The authors also pointed to the increased bargaining power for workers and unions that would result from full employment. Indeed, the AES complemented its Keynesian job creation measures with calls for reductions in the workweek, training programs, and employment subsidies.

The AES, however, was not recycled Keynesianism. As the London Group readily acknowledged, the critics were partially right. Without other policy changes, reflation strategies alone were doomed to ineffectiveness. The AES, however, aimed to imbed reflation in a series of measures to use greater popular control over economic decisions to cancel out the global capitalist pressures that render traditional reflationary policies less viable. For example, to channel increased demand into domestic investment, rather than more imports, and to grapple with the nation's long-term industrial decline, the AES called for two major new mechanisms. First, the authors argued for targeted nationalization to place key firms within each industrial sector under public control. Unlike past uses, such nationalized firms would be used as laboratories for developing worker empowerment and democratic control. They would also foster examples of how firms could return to international competitiveness without resorting to wage cuts. Second, the government would require firm-level planning agreements—negotiated annually but for a five-year-period—which would cover each firm's strategic decisions on investment levels, location, employment, price policy, and so forth. These would be negotiated between the government and management, with unions also playing a clear role.

To foster greater democratic guidance of the larger economic picture, the government would also establish and strengthen sectoral working parties and a national planning agency. Such action would develop a public capacity for economic planning—one that could counterbalance the market mechanisms in which investment flowed toward the highest rate of return. Effective public planning also required increased control over finance. The AES proposed the establishment of several public investment alternatives. The authors called for the direct nationalization of several major banks and insurance companies. In addition, the establishment of a National Investment Bank would place pension fund resources, government contributions, and North Sea oil money under direct democratic control. The AES also pointed to alternative mechanisms such as price controls to battle inflation, rather than the classic neoliberal recession against wages. Within the firm, the AES advocated government policy to actively support, through resources and official recognition, worker efforts to design their own plans for the future of their workplace and firm. The government would work with the labor movement to develop a system of codetermination. The strategy also looked toward government action for extending collective bargaining and union rights.

As part of the imperial legacy, Britain was particularly dependent on international trade and especially vulnerable to financial destabilization from the outside. The London Group argued that for a left alternative to have any viability, the government must be prepared to break with the rules of the official global economy. Thus, the AES called for planned trade through short- and long-term controls over imports. Without such measures, raising demand would simply raise imports. Furthermore, some limits on foreign competition were needed to help re-

structuring domestic industries recover. The AES also pointed to the possibilities for developing targeted nation-to-nation trade measures that build special relationships with other countries pursuing progressive economic change as well as with poorer developing nations. To help rein in the multinationals, the AES suggested several additional measures to aid the labor movement including government efforts to compile information on multinational activities, the mandatory planning agreements, and direct support for international solidarity.

The AES also proposed to directly reverse global financial liberalization by enacting short- and long-term controls over capital movements. Without such controls, international investors could provoke a run on the sterling—reducing its value and creating havoc in the domestic economy. The authors sought to counter the possibilities of an international backlash through direct measures ranging from a total suspension of convertibility to essentially freezing foreign assets in the country. Such actions represented a full-scale confrontation with global capitalism. However, the authors believed that national governments had the power to fight back and win. Indeed, the London Group argued that since "globalization" was based on the cooperation of the major developed states, a single nation among this group could successfully buck the international system. Furthermore, the authors looked toward allies abroad since other nations had repeatedly considered and even used various elements found within the AES. The example of one nation calling global capitalism's bluff would inspire progressive forces elsewhere.

Key to understanding the AES is the realization that it provided not just an economic program, but a political agenda. The strategy started with the issues and policy ideas that British working people had already identified as central concerns. It then extended these desires in radical directions. The AES did not claim to solve all of Britain's economic problems, or to replace capitalism with socialism. It did hope to secure real gains for working people while decisively reorienting policy debates around new directions. By redefining the economic debate, the government would not have to retreat into neoliberalism measures when reforms hit up against capitalist resistance, as had past Labour governments. Rather, it could respond with newer and bolder ways of extending popular control over economic decisions. The AES relied on the ability of calls for genuine economic change to mobilize people to organize for change. Rather than demoralizing people through policy retreats, the AES sought to inspire action by asserting the primacy of popular control and collective action over the supposedly unquestionable logic of the market.

Whether or not the individual elements of the AES would have worked remain in a realm of speculation that we will not take up here. While such a debate was certainly relevant at the time, for progressive purposes today, the historical viability of each particular reform is less important. The main legacy of the AES lies in its overall direction. Even if individual measures might have failed in the short run, the AES was arguably Labour's only real option if it were to remain true to its founding principles. Subsequent events seem to validate such a conclusion. An AES that suffered significant opposition and setbacks would have at least drawn the battle lines in a manner far more favorable to progressive politics than the political disasters that actually followed.

In 1974, voters sent Labour back into office complete with party Conference and trade union resolutions supporting many elements of the AES, including planning agreements, nationalization, and capital controls. The parliamentary leadership and Labour cabinet, however, simply ignored this agenda. Benn and other left leaders within the cabinet were increasingly marginalized. The results were catastrophic. The outgoing Tories had left behind an economic bubble. They had renewed economic growth by expansionary fiscal and monetary policies that created a flood of imports, a growing budget deficit, a weakened currency, accelerating inflation, and rising unemployment. Once Labour took power, the situation only worsened. Attempts to pursue an incomes policy failed when government action to lift conservative wage controls produced a wave of wage militancy by a union rank and file skeptical of government promises of a "Social Contract."

Clearly the Labour government needed more than simply old policies. However, the predominant leadership actively fought efforts by the left to enact measures of industrial policy passed by the party membership. As Chancellor Dennis Healey argued in a 1974 debate with Tony Benn: "We have to maintain the confidence of business . . . because the whole of our future depends on the confidence of business." Speaking at the 1976 party Conference, Benn correctly predicted the results of such a logic in not only continued economic pain, but:

> As a party we are also paying a heavy political price for twenty years in which . . . we have played down our criticism of capitalism and our advocacy of socialism. . . . Comrades, the political vacuum we have left has been filled by many different voices . . . by the monetarists, by the nationalists, by the racialists and by all of those who seek each in their own way to divide working people from each other and to breed despair so we may be driven to lose faith in ourselves and our capacity to control our own destiny. Unless we speak more clearly now we shall be fighting the next election defensively, deep inside our own political territory, instead of being on the offensive on behalf of our own people.[62]

Despite a warm reception for its governmental leaders, this Conference approved calls for radical action. Delegates passed by healthy margins the National Executive Council's *Labour's Programme for Britain* and its *Banking and Finance*, both of which included many elements of the AES. The possibilities that the government might be pressured into implementing some of this agenda, especially the capital controls, sent shivers down spines on the other side of the Atlantic. As U.S. State Department official William Rodgers later told journalists:

We all had the feeling it could come apart in a quite serious way. . . . It was a choice between Britain remaining in the liberal financial system of the West as opposed to a radical change of course, because we were concerned about Tony Benn precipitating a policy decision by Britain to turn its back on the IMF. I think if that had happened the whole system would have begun to fall apart . . . so we tended to see it in cosmic terms.[63]

In retrospect, American officials had little to fear. A majority within the Labour government was committed to avoiding policies that would "lose the confidence of business." Ultimately, this meant traveling down the road to neoliberalism. Having bought into the dire predictions of the free-market-oriented Treasury department, governmental leaders concluded they had no choice but to desperately seek loans to bail out the nation's financial instability. They caved in to IMF demands for a major austerity package and made firm promises not to impose controls over international capital. Thus, a Labour government enacted policies that rivaled Thatcher's government's in their antiworker severity. While the move strained relations between the government and the unions, the labor movement as a whole chose not to fight for the left agenda, but supported the actions of their party's leadership.

The results were prolonged electoral defeat and a mass exodus of party activists and members. In its final push for an alternative path, the Labour left fought a valiant, but ultimately unsuccessful, battle to democratize the party so that the elected leadership actually followed the policy desires of the party's base. In defeating the left's efforts for internal reform, the right wing further centralized the party, encouraging the further erosion of its grassroots. The stage was set for the 1980s and beyond.

Benn's predictions proved accurate. With little to offer its supporters, Labour lost the 1979 election—ushering in nearly two decades of Tory rule. Margaret Thatcher would compete with Ronald Reagan as the global champion of right-wing neoliberalism. The defeat of the Labour left also established the path to Tony Blair's "New Labour." Repeated electoral defeat throughout the 1980s and 1990s forced the party's leadership to confront the reality that the old ways were not adequate. However, rather than heeding the surviving left's calls for a truly new direction that would distinguish Labour from the Tories, the dominant leadership ultimately chose the opposite path. The problem, for Blair and his followers, was not that Labour was not radical enough, but that it was too closely associated with the labor movement and crazy socialist ideas. If voters seemed to support conservative policies, then Labour needed to steal away this support by offering a similar agenda with a human face. This "Clintonization" of the Labour Party involved further centralization of leadership. Slick media campaigns have today become a substitute for serious grassroots activism.

Labour's 1997 electoral triumph arguably says more about popular disillusionment with conservative policies and a growing nation of rich and poor than it does Blair's New Labour alternative. Indeed, progressive critics have attacked the main economic policies of New Labour for being virtually indistinguishable from their Tory predecessors. The future is unclear. While the left remains fragmented, Blair's embarrassment at the party's connection to organized labor points to clear tensions with the party's founding constituency. And while nationally the party has converted to New Labour, individual parts remain unreconstructed.

A Socialist Sweden?

Debates within Swedish social democracy during the 1970s and early 1980s provide a final example of an alternative path not chosen—one in which economic pressures today associated with "globalization" were to be countered with an assault on the most fundamental of capitalist prerogatives: private ownership.[64]

With the postwar capitalist boom coming to an end, the Swedish labor movement realized that it was facing increased dangers. Labor's solidaristic wage policy faced the twin threats of growing wage militancy among white-collar unions and uneven corporate profits. By the 1970s, clear signs had emerged of a declining capacity among Swedish industry for self-financing. At the same time, the long-term effects of the Rehn-Meidner model had favored wealth concentrations among large and export-oriented firms. The labor movement needed to find proworker solutions that would increase domestic industrial investment and maintain the international competitive position of Swedish firms. Otherwise, a globally oriented Swedish capitalism was going to come up with its own, neoliberal, solutions.

Past efforts toward active industrial policy and union-based codetermination in the 1960s and 1970s, while achieving notable specific gains, had not established the basis for greater direct public control over investment decisions. Specifically, the state lacked the institutionalized capacity to intervene in capital markets—the hallmark of global finance. Without such a capacity, however, government policy had to rely on private investment. Increasingly this would come to mean neoliberal formulas for raising corporate profits in order to generate the surplus for investment. Such an action, however, would compel the unions to ask their membership to moderate wage demands so that their employers could have higher profits. It also would further weaken the LO's ability to maintain solidaristic wages.

Working on the LO's behalf and drawing on comparable Danish plans, Rudolph Meidner offered a new path through an innovative system of wage-earner funds. Over time, the funds were to make workers the collective owners of their own companies. Under the plan, corporations above a certain size were required to issue new shares corresponding to some portion of their annual profits. These shares would be placed in a central fund representing all wage earners. The Meidner committee suggested fifty or one hundred employees as the threshold and 20 percent of annual profits as the amount to be set aside. Except under special circum-

stances, these shares would remain part of the working capital in the company that generated them. Unlike traditional profit-sharing or stock-ownership programs common in the United States, the dividends from these collective shares would not go to individual workers. Instead, a portion would be used to purchase newly issued shares, so that new share issues would not dilute the workers' stake in a given firm. The rest would finance adult education, wage-earner consultants, and other programs aimed at helping workers, especially union activists, exercise their role as joint owners. Initially, voting rights and other prerogatives of stock ownership would be exercised solely by the local unions. However, once the wage-earner shares represented at least 20 percent of a firm's equity capital, control would be vested in sectorally based fund boards appointed mainly by the national unions, but including representatives of other social interests.

The Meidner plan aimed to achieve several goals. It would bolster solidaristic wages since any increased profits coming from wage restraint by workers would translate into greater collective ownership of the firm. Unions thus had a path for permitting companies to enjoy "super profits" while promoting support, rather than revolt, among their membership. The plan would also counteract the growing concentration of wealth resulting from past social democratic policies. Indeed, it would achieve increases in the supply side for investment in a way comparable with the labor movement's traditional goal of greater social equity. In addition, the wage-earner funds would further labor's long-standing desires to provide workers greater control over company decisions. Increased influence through collective ownership would complement the union codetermination and work humanization campaigns at the workplace level. While the plan did not establish worker influence over allocation of investment capital between firms, it did lay a foundation for democratizing corporate investment decisions. Indeed, since the funds were born out of and built around labor activism, their leadership would likely gravitate toward coordinated efforts for collective industrial policy. Assuming a rate of profit averaging 10 percent, Meidner estimated that in roughly thirty-five years, the wage-earner funds would acquire majority shares in their corporations. The more profitable the company, the sooner the wage-earner funds would achieve majority ownership.

Not surprisingly, Swedish employers did not embrace the new LO proposal, but instead denounced it as a form of creeping socialism. Business organizations across the country mobilized to win the battle for public opinion and to prevent the social democrats from adopting the LO plan in its full form. In the end, every single business organization refused invitations even to discuss the plan. Meanwhile, the bourgeois parties made clear their opposition to it. The major white-collar union federation, the Central Organization of Salaried Employees (TCO), decided to remain neutral. At the same time, the LO unions were unable able to mobilize grassroots support to offset the business counteroffensive. In the end, the social democrats pursued a strategy of watering down the proposal in order to both reassure business and to take the issue out of electoral politics. As a result, although wage-earner legislation was passed and funds established, these became inconsequential shadows of the original plan.

The social democrats similarly chose to forgo radical possibilities during a series of debates over the creation of a new pension fund and the reorganization of the existing system. With control over a huge pool of assets, the pension system, if invested in company stocks, could have provided a major mechanism for establishing public ownership and control over the economy. This potential, however, was repeatedly rejected. In 1991, for example, the government presented one of their most sweeping proposals to reorganize the five ATP funds and the small wage-earner funds into five entirely separate pension funds of equal size. The proposal allowed the new funds to freely invest 60 percent of their assets as they saw fit—including buying corporate stock. At the time, such a proportion added up to some 260 billion SEK—an amount equal to 47 percent of the Swedish stock market. Yet, the proposal made clear that the funds would not seek an active ownership role, but confine their efforts to "efficient portfolio management."[65]

While the failure to pursue an alternative path has not proven as disastrously dramatic in Sweden as the British experience, the rejection of attempts to establish greater public control over corporate decisions did signify a turning point. When in power, Social Democrats have been forced by economic strains to preside over austerity measures aimed at reestablishing growth along the lines of the neoliberal world order. Seen over the long term, social democratic budget cutting, however, has aimed to preserve the main contours of social citizenship while placing it within the boundaries of the country's restricted financial resources. By contrast, in recent years, the system of solidaristic wages has significantly broken under employer efforts to pursue more decentralized and fragmented bargaining. While many of the gains of postwar Swedish social democracy remain strong, by failing to open new, more radical, alternative paths for policy intervention, the Social Democrats find themselves today operating within an increasingly restricted set of options.

Social Democracy at the Crossroads

Whether the above alternative policies would have worked remains an issue of historical speculation. However, they ultimately died in political, not economic, battles. These debates pointed to the continuing dilemma faced by social democracy ever since the end of the postwar boom. Capitalism's main response to its internal crisis is the neoliberal project of increased corporate freedom and power. Although European corporate leaders are clearly mixed in their willingness to embrace this agenda wholesale, neoliberalism enjoys the support of the dominant power of the postwar era, the United States. Under U.S. leadership and with European and Japanese support, neoliberalism is clearly being institutionalized in the formal rules of the global economy. Furthermore, although the character of a united Europe remains an issue of hot debate, the dominant trajectory of European unification has leaned heavily in a neoliberal direction. Removing obstacles to trade and investment and establishing neoliberal principles of balanced budgets and modest debt levels has been more of a priority than raising social standards and establishing social citizenship and social partnership at a European level.

Confronted by the "new world order," social democracy has a choice. It can try to save as much of its postwar gains as possible by working within neoliberal prescriptions for renewed economic growth. This option enjoys the enormous advantage of allowing Social Democratic leaders to avoid a wholesale confrontation with the business class both domestically and internationally. It suffers, however, the catastrophic consequence of alienating and demobilizing social democracy's grassroots by accepting the claim of capitalist proponents that "there is no alternative" but to settle for increasingly lowered expectations.

As the examples of France, Britain, and Sweden illustrate, social democracy has been offered another path. Charting a vigorous high-road economic path in today's neoliberal capitalism involves challenging head-on the logic of free markets with programs to establish greater public control over corporate decisions. Such a course leads to a full-scale confrontation with global capitalism by seizing greater control over capitalist terrain domestically. While placing social democracy on an uncharted path of social and economic upheaval, it also provides grassroots supporters with something to fight for. In an age in which mass cynicism provides a major mechanism of social control, it unapologetically promotes clear alternatives. Later in the next chapter we will take up this agenda in greater detail and explore further why the dominant leadership within the social democratic parties have chosen to conform to, rather than confront, neoliberal capitalism. However, we will begin chapter 5 with further examination of the crossroads facing social democracy by exploring a second crisis that is arguably as great a challenge to traditional social democracy as so-called globalization. Indeed, the ecological crisis points to only one solution: confronting global capitalism head-on.

5

Facing the Ecological Crisis:
The Meaning of Green Politics

Each social democratic concession to neoliberal capitalism narrows the terrain of progressive social reform and places the burden of economic recovery squarely on the backs of working people. Social democratic leaders who pursue such a course do so with the promise that the short-term pain will revive the goose that laid the postwar golden egg: continued economic growth. The ecological crisis, however, suggests that the very goal of growth itself, in terms of increased material consumption, has reached its limits.

Environmental Warning Signs

Beginning his short economic history of the environment, John Bellamy Foster lays out the environmental wall that human society will hit this century. He writes:

> Human society has reached a critical threshold in its relations to the environment. The destruction of the planet, in the sense of making it unusable for human purposes, has grown to such an extent that it now threatens the continuation of much of nature, as well as the survival and development of society itself. The litany of ecological complaints plaguing the world today encompasses a long list of urgent problems. These include: overpopulation, destruction of the ozone layer, global warming, extinction of species, loss of genetic diversity, acid rain, nuclear contamination, tropical deforestation, the elimination of

climax forests, wetland destruction, soil erosion, desertification, floods, famine, the despoliation of lakes, streams and rivers, the drawing down and contamination of ground water, the pollution of coastal waters and estuaries, the destruction of coral reefs, oil spills, overfishing, expanding landfills, toxic wastes, the poisonous effects of pesticides and herbicides, exposures to hazards on the job, urban congestion, and the depletion of nonrenewable resources. According to the prestigious Worldwatch Institute, we have only four decades left in which to gain control over our major environmental problems if we are to avoid irreversible ecological decline.[1]

A few statistics will suffice to back up Foster's dire warning. While true that the earth has warmed and cooled over the course of its history, the current trend exceeds these natural patterns. Estimates for this century run from a 2°C to a 5°C increase in global temperatures—amounts equal to the earth's temperature change during the last ice age. The possibility of a twenty-six-inch rise in sea levels over this time by itself presents a major disaster. Add to this fluctuations in and increasing instability of weather patterns, already visible today, and the picture is one of steady "natural" disasters: drought, floods, hurricanes, and so forth. Ozone decreases over the course of the past two decades have averaged 3 percent. The subsequent increased exposure to UV-B radiation suppresses the immune system, leads to cataracts and skin cancer, damages plants and aquatic organisms, and reinforces the greenhouse effect. Eleven percent of the earth's vegetated surface has been moderately or severely degraded since 1945. With 5,000 to 150,000 species lost each year, at least one-quarter, and as much as one-third, of the planet's species are in danger of becoming extinct in the next two to three decades.[2]

The full gravity of the crisis is magnified by the fact that, although human beings have impacted the planet for millennia, the bulk of destruction has occurred this century, with most of it taking place since the end of World War II. For example, half of the world's forest loss over the course of human history occurred between 1950 and 1990.[3] The postwar revolution in human-made synthetics has vastly increased the toxicity and destructiveness of human production. Today there are around seventy thousand chemical preparations in use. Traces of four hundred of these have been found in human beings. Most of these preparations have never been tested for their toxic effect.[4] The growing need for people to resort to fertility drugs, in part, reflects a reality in which we are literally poisoning ourselves.

The basic problem of food production graphically illustrates the human catastrophe developing from environmental destruction. In 1985, 730 million people did not eat enough to lead fully productive working lives. Yet, each year the world loses 5 million hectares of cropland—due mainly to farming techniques and development patterns that favor large corporate interests over small producers, low-income consumers, and the health of the planet. Some 29 percent of the earth's land area currently suffers slight, moderate, or severe desertification. Each year the extent of desertification grows. The issue is clearly not the simplistic question of population sizes, but how the earth's productive capacity is used and maintained as well as how the produced wealth is distributed.[5]

The root cause behind today's accelerating environmental problems lies in the massive postwar increases in material consumption in the industrialized countries and the rise of consumer ideology worldwide. With roughly 15 percent of the world's population, the developed nations consume nearly three-quarters of the world's output.[6] Our society's faith in never-ending material consumption assumes an unlimited environmental capacity in what is proving a very finite world. Most businesspeople and financiers would consider foolhardy a person who, on inheriting millions of dollars, simply spends it away on extravagant excesses. Prudent business practice points toward investing the capital to preserve the wealth while allowing for continued future returns. Yet, every day these same economic managers use up the world's inheritance of natural capital at a staggering rate for what amounts to only a few decades of consumerist excess. Born in the era of triumphant material progress, traditional social democracy shares in the assumption of never-ending material growth. Indeed, a continually expanding material economic pie allowed social democratic policy makers to provide growing social benefits to working people while also allowing business to reap healthy rates of profit.

Driving Down the Road to Ruin

More so than any other single product, the automobile illustrates the interconnection between social strains and environmental destruction. It also demonstrates the impossibility of sustaining current economic practices. Personal motor transport has been, and continues to be, a symbol of capitalist and Western material progress. Despite the hype about the "service economy" of the future, the auto industry remains at the heart of Western economies. In the United States, for example, the work of one out of every six workers is directly or indirectly connected to the industry. It consumes three-quarters of all the rubber, three-quarters of the lead, three-fifths of the malleable iron, and one-fifth of all the aluminum used in the United States each year.[7] The experience and mythos surrounding the automobile has come to symbolize the supposed triumphs of material gain—speed, convenience, individual freedom, and technological progress. Yet, a growing body of literature now criticizes our society's near-total reliance on the personal automobile as a fundamental wrong turn in human development.[8]

The problems can be seen at several levels. The car's impact on the environment is well documented. Bradford Snell stated in a famous report to a U.S. Senate committee that "motor vehicle travel is possibly the most inefficient method of transportation devised by modern man."[9] A major consumer of non-renewable fossil fuels, only a small fraction of the energy consumed to power the personal automobile is actually used to propel the occupants.[10] Greater car use is a central factor in accounting for why the average American consumes three times the energy resources that their European counterpart does.[11] Automobile emissions are also a major source of greenhouse-effect-producing gases and other toxic emissions. Researchers at the Environment and Forecasting Institute in Heidelberg placed the carbon dioxide produced by a middle-class German car at fifteen tons in the manufacturing, forty-five tons in driving eighty-five thousand miles, and six tons in the disposal of it.[12] In the United States, reductions in pollution per vehicle have been wiped out by increases in vehicle use and miles driven. Automobiles also directly consume an ever-greater share of the earth's land. In American cities, one-third to one-half of all space is used to accommodate motor vehicles.[13]

These environmental costs alone suggest that the world has reached the physical limits of car production. Ironically, the mounting environmental problems are caused by an automobile market that is today stagnant. The industry experiences such sharp competition because the world market is stuck at roughly 50 million vehicles per year, while the industry has a capacity to produce 70 million units.[14] Under current conditions, further gains in productivity can serve only to increase this overcapacity, generate continued pressures for mergers and bankruptcies, and/or further shrink employment. Yet, even progressive, social democratic–style notions of redistribut-

ing the wealth do not offer a solution. With 5 percent of the world's population, the United States has 34 percent of the world's automobiles—with one car for every 1.3 Americans.[15] Yet, existing Western automobile use is already causing severe ecological damage. If the rest of the world acquired automobiles at even a fraction of the U.S. rate, the results would be an outright ecological catastrophe.

The destruction caused by automobile consumption, however, is not just environmental. In 1991, 43,500 Americans were killed and another 5 million injured in automobile accidents. Comparative statistics for other modes of transportation place the automobile as the least-safe alternative, not just for the occupants, but for everyone else. German statistics show that one-third of people killed in auto-related incidents were pedestrians and cyclists.[16] Also telling are the lives that are spiritually, emotionally, and even physically lost to automobile production. While much has changed since Henry Ford's day, scientific management and the moving assembly line still create a division of labor based around production jobs of alienating drudgery.

The automobile industry, however, builds far more than cars. It produces an entire way of life. In the United States especially, the mass promotion of personal automobiles accompanied the conversion of residential development from city and town neighborhoods to suburban patterns.[17] Critics of the suburban landscapes suggest that the automobile is linked to our society's epidemic sense of loneliness and alienation. For example, one study done in San Francisco found that people who lived in high-vehicle-density areas had one-third the friends and half the acquaintances as those who lived in areas with low levels of traffic.[18] In turn-of-the-century Germany, children could be independently active in an area up to three to four kilometers (over 2 miles) from home. Today, children are increasingly dependent on being driven to activities.[19] The auto-related social crisis is most visible in the United States where dominant patterns of suburban private development create an ever sterile "geography of nowhere." Ever-larger houses and shopping malls disperse living arrangements over an ever-greater car-dependent area. Open space, farmland, ecological balance, downtowns, and integrated neighborhoods are all being sacrificed to sell expensive suburban living units that offer only profound personal isolation. Automobile dependency also further magnifies social inequality. The poorest members of society cannot afford automobiles, and one-third of Americans (including many elderly and disabled as well as children) legally cannot drive. Vehicle transport is also at the center of our nation's urban blight as resources are taken out of the older urban areas to fund increasingly wasteful suburbs.

As one of capitalism's premier commodities, the automobile symbolizes how our economic system pushes ever-increasing and wasteful individual consumption at the expense of both the planet and society's well-being. Ironically, increased automobile use has even dismantled the very gains that the introduction of the car first promised. The media images of convenience, speed, and personal freedom have given way to realities of congestion, long commutes, and bland suburban uniformity. Far from using their automobiles as tools for wide-ranging travel, Americans spend two-thirds of their driving miles for local trips for shopping, personal socializing, and recreation.[20] A new four-lane highway requires roughly $7 million per mile. According to State of Michigan reports, estimates for the reconstruction of eleven miles of the six-lane I-94 cutting through inner-city Detroit run as high as $1.3 billion—$118 million per mile. By contrast, a possible one hundred-mile, thirty-station commuter rail system linking Detroit with outlying communities would cost $130 million—$700,000 per mile.[21] Yet, growing evidence suggests that massive outlays for more roads simply attract greater congestion. For example, a 1997 University of California study of thirty urban counties found that every 10 percent increase in road space generated a 9 percent rise in traffic.[22]

The automobile's rise belies the marketing images of an industry following popular demand. As has been well documented for both the United States and Europe, the auto, gas, and rubber industries pushed policy makers to develop national transportation policies that prioritized and promoted automobile dependency. In the United States, General Motors, in conjunction with Standard Oil and Firestone Tires, systematically bought up and dismantled many of the nation's streetcar lines. It also used its monopoly position in bus and locomotive production to undercut itself in urban transportation in order to expand profits from the production of personal automobiles.[23]

The economics of ever-increasing material growth provide no way out of the car society. In recent years, auto producers have attempted to wrap themselves in the mantle of sustainability and environmental responsibility. Due to government regulations and market cost incentives, they have devoted significant attention to reducing toxic outputs and reusing and recycling waste. The car producers have also unevenly made research and development investments in alternative-fuel-powered vehicles. Yet, regulatory and market-driven adjustments do not address the overall environmentally and socially unsustainable nature of society's reliance on the personal motor vehicle. Even when technological innovation can reduce pollution and raw material usage, the farmland destruction, congestion, alienation, poverty, and lost lives that come from automobile dependency remain. The problem is ultimately the product itself.

While the United States remains the world's most automobile-centered society, the ravages of the automobile society threaten Europe as well. Compared to the United States, Europe has done a far better job of maintaining tight urban development, preserving farmland and open space, and pursuing more balanced transportation options. Indeed, Americans can learn a great deal from past and present European land use and transportation policies. Nevertheless, the threats of automobile-induced sprawl, congestion, and environmental destruction have animated critics of the automobile just as impassioned as those found on this side of the Atlantic.

The real solution to the environmental and social consequences of automobile consumption lies in changing the product. Such an action means policies that mix and balance transportation options. Primarily human-powered methods (walking and biking) should be supplemented by streetcar, bus, and rail methods. Only once these other modes are given full weight can the personal automobile return to the picture. In the West, especially the United States, such a transformation requires wholesale restructuring of the purpose, products, and employment strategies of the vehicle industry. It also entails a complete redesign of land-use planning away from passive, market-driven mechanisms. Proactive local and regional public planning authorities need the capacity to design and implement community-based development plans that private construction then follows. Both restructuring an entire industry away from its primary product and shifting land-use decisions from private to public hands require actions and policy tools beyond the boundaries of traditional social democracy. Ultimately, such measures require social intervention into management decisions, thus breaking the postwar labor-management deal on which social democracy grew.

The Need to Subordinate Capitalism to a Higher Logic

The patterns seen in the case of the automobile apply to the economy as a whole. Recent progressive research has challenged the GDP measure used by governments worldwide, including those led by social democrats, to quantify society's progress. Under conventional economic wisdom, a GDP that does not grow fast enough is cause for concern, while a GDP that shrinks provides reason for panic. Yet, the GDP simply adds together activities that the capitalist marketplace assigns a monetary value. Thus, natural and human disasters, massive environmental destruction, wars, and so forth, all cause the GDP to increase as more resources are spent buying more commodities. Socially and environmentally valuable

activities—such as caring for children at home, volunteering in the community, or riding a bike to work—are either not counted or are seen to subtract from the GDP.

Progressive groups in both the United States and Europe have developed alternative measures that add in those positive human actions that the market does not value, and subtract socially and environmentally harmful activity. Thus, they attempt to measure overall quality of life, not just material consumption. The Genuine Progress Indicator (GPI) developed by Redefining Progress, for example, reflects the common picture that emerges from these alternative measures. Both the GPI and GDP increased in the United States during the postwar boom. However, for the past three decades, material commodity gains and social and ecological well-being have parted company. While the GDP continues to grow, the GPI has fallen dramatically. Seen from this measure, our society is working hard to outright digress, not progress, into the future.[24]

The social reality behind a falling GPI is readily apparent in many people's lives. Between the 1950s and today, the GDP, and hence the material consumption of the country, more than doubled. Yet, more Americans told pollsters that they were happier in the 1950s than today.[25] When asked to identify what gains are most important for a happy life, most Americans point to nonmaterial priorities: family life, friends, free time, a spiritual life, a sense of neighborhood and community, and so forth. Yet, capitalist reality offers people only bigger televisions, the Internet, DVD players, sport utility vehicles, bigger homes, and endless variations of snack foods. Not only are these material gains empty in their own right, they also pale in comparison to the quality of life improvements that capitalism offered during the first half of the twentieth century. The original consumer buying spree included running water, indoor toilets, showers, central heating, and refrigerators.[26] Today, people are offered greater material gains that provide far less of a meaningful transformation of everyday life. At the same time, continued emphasis on material consumption simply further erodes meaningful human interaction and environmental well-being.

As Harvard economist Juliet Schor documented, Americans are spending 163 more hours per year working than they did two decades ago. This time has been subtracted almost entirely from child rearing, family, and leisure activities.[27] The time spent at work seems to have become ever-more stressful as companies continuously attempt to do more with fewer people. Meanwhile, increasingly wasteful material consumption eats more time and creates even more strains. It is no secret that stress is an epidemic problem affecting all layers of our society. Authorities as diverse as medical researchers, spiritual practitioners, and political activists all argue that the paths out of the modern malaise lie in developing nonmaterial priorities. Since capitalism can only value that which creates a profit, society must subordinate the system's core mechanisms to democratic and public forces able to recognize the real sources of human happiness and ecological sanity.

Green Economics

The political sign that never-ending material growth no longer provided the basis for human advancement was signaled in 1983 when twenty-seven delegates of the newly formed German Green Party—dressed in bright shirts and dungarees and carrying potted plants—took their seats in the country's national legislature.[28] While not up to the vote levels of the SPD or the CDU, the Greens have nevertheless been able to capture election results ranging between 5 and 10 percent of the vote. Because of Germany's system of proportional representation, such returns have meant seats in local, state, and national legislatures. Greens have joined Social Democrat–led governments in the states of Hesse and Lower Saxony and the city-states of Berlin and Bremen. Nationally, such a red-green alliance formed the government in 1999. The German Greens have proved to be the flag bearers of what is today a global Green political move-

ment. Green parties are active throughout Europe, with varying degrees of success. For example, in recent European parliament elections, Green parties won as much as 10 percent of their national vote. A solid Green delegation exists within the parliament. Green mayors have also governed in such cities as Dublin and Rome.

The Greens are important because they fundamentally challenge both mainstream politics and social democracy. While environmental issues are central to Green policies, ecology provided the glue for uniting several diverse currents that made up the new left of the 1960s and 1970s. These elements include the peace movement, the women's movement, and the environmental movement. Operating outside parliamentary politics, sections within these so-called postmaterial movements had begun moving toward electoral activism by the 1980s. The Greens attempted to unite this grassroots, direct-action activism within a party of a new type.

The tensions between movement and party animated German Green debates throughout the 1980s and 1990s. Indeed, struggles within the Greens have threatened at times to paralyze the party. These differences on strategy and goals make a summary of Green beliefs a tricky matter. Nevertheless, all Greens share several core principles. They agree that environmental problems represent a fundamental crisis facing modern society. Greens question capitalism's faith in never-ending material growth and consumerism. They look toward a society based on qualitative improvement, rather than on quantitative expansion.

One of the early federal programs of the German Greens begins with a statement representative of how ecological concerns are linked to broad political principles:

> The Establishment parties in Bonn behave as if an infinite increase in industrial production were possible on the finite planet Earth. According to their own statements, they are leading us to a hopeless choice between the nuclear state and

nuclear war, between Harrisburg and Hiroshima. The worldwide ecological crisis worsens from day to day: natural resources become more scarce; chemical waste dumps are subjects of scandal after scandal; whole species of animals are exterminated; entire varieties of plants become extinct; rivers and oceans change slowly into sewers; and humans verge on spiritual and intellectual decay in the midst of a mature, industrial, consumer society. It is a dismal inheritance we are imposing on future generations. . . .

We represent a total concept, as opposed to the one-dimensional, still more production brand of politics. Our policies are guided by long-term visions for the future and are founded on four basic principles: ecology, social responsibility, grassroots democracy, and nonviolence.[29]

The Greens use their ecological understanding not simply to spotlight and counter environmental destruction, but also to develop a comprehensive vision that covers all aspects of life. Greens critique the authoritarianism and pressures for conformity and passivity found in the economic and political institutions of Western society. They see their role as progressively democratizing all aspects of life. They view the same hierarchical institutions that destroy the environment as also preying off of the poor, the working class, women, immigrants, and so forth. Thus, for example, they advocate for the full emancipation of women. This goal includes full equality between the sexes as well as fully valuing those realms of human activity traditionally assigned to women. The Greens firmly oppose the use of force in international affairs, calling for unilateral and complete disarmament. They are also committed to battling head-on the neoliberal logic of the world economy. The Greens point to solutions to global environmental problems that include ending exploitation of the south by the countries of the north. They have called for democratizing the IMF and World Bank, rewriting trade agreements to prioritize mutual development and high social and environmental standards, and canceling third world debt.

To build a new society, the Greens seek to move power away from depersonalized, bureaucratic authority and place decision making in the hands of grassroots democracy. Green thought has a heavy anarchist streak that rejects centralized authority in favor of people's direct participation in decisions that affect them. In addition to critiquing the hierarchies of capitalism, Greens also question the modern technocratic state, the traditional patriarchal family, and, for some, union and social democratic bureaucracies. Decentralization and grassroots participation is something that the Greens have tried to build in to the very structure of their party. For example, during their early years, the German Greens unsuccessfully tried a system of mandatory rotation for their officeholders.[30]

In short, the Green agenda makes clear that even within the boundaries of the "prosperous society," frustrations exist outside of what traditional social democracy is able to address. Most fundamentally, from a Green perspective, the social democratic parties have become part of the very establishment that they were originally founded to overthrow. While thus far the Greens do not threaten the major party predominance of the social democrats, they do capture a significant segment of the left vote, thus forcing social democratic leaders to confront environmental, social, and political issues.

The Green challenge, however, does not invalidate past social democratic gains. Indeed, in many ways, Green politics builds on this foundation. The immediate policy proposals found in German Green election platforms take a wealth of social democratic policy mechanisms in more radical directions. For example, the 1990 common election platform of The Greens/Alliance 90/Citizen Movements called for a thirty-five-hour workweek, the strengthening and extension of workplace representation and codetermination, a paid three-year child leave, equalizing part-time work to full-time standards, and a guaranteed basic income. The last of these would use the welfare state to provide minimum basic needs to all people not currently working in the market regardless of their individual circumstances or reasons.

Thus, if willing to live quite modestly, people would be free to pursue socially beneficial activities—such as child care, personal development, and community work—that the market fails to assign a monetary value. The Greens also aimed to uphold the country's national health care system by decentralizing it toward greater community control. Additionally, they proposed policies to use the health system's national scope to guide health care away from the one-dimensional logic of Western medicine (with its emphasis on drugs, surgery, and disease treatment) to more holistic and preventative conceptions of health.

While these proposals represent bolder versions of classic social democratic policies, the Green platform also went beyond this tradition. For example, it demanded a 50 percent reduction in carbon dioxide emissions by the year 2010 and the complete abandonment of fossil fuels by the end of the twenty-first century. The platform referred to automobiles as the "Number One environmental villain," calling for, among other things, a steady increase in the gas tax and a wholesale redirection of government spending toward public and pedestrian forms of transportation. Greens have also called for efforts to fundamentally alter one of Germany's chief industries: chemical production. They have looked toward increased regulations to dismantle the most dangerous chemical production and to convert the remaining industry toward more ecologically and human-friendly chemicals.

The common agenda also included such calls as the outright abolition of the Federal Defense Force and the complete redesign of land-use planning. It was quite open in its support for third world liberation. Among other policies, it advocated that the rich countries pay 1 percent of their GNP into an "international climate fund" to compensate poor countries for the economic costs of local measures to protect the global environment.

A Green Social Democracy?

The Green ability to build on traditional social democratic policies suggests that the ecological crisis does have a potential for radicalizing the social democratic agenda. Certainly, when detached from notions of unbounded material growth, many social democratic policies are compatible with sustainable development. For example, the sharing of resources inherent to practices of social citizenship is far more environmentally sound than the pursuit of personal consumption so trumpeted in the United States. Indeed, when social democracy has stood for collective problem solving, collective and public institutions, and human solidarity, it has helped steer European countries in directions that place them well ahead of the United States in experimenting with genuinely sustainable development.

For example, as mentioned above, while by no means free of the pressures of the car society, European land-use and transportation policies continue to be well ahead of American practices. Because of a combination of geography, land-use needs, and more planning-oriented government policies, the Netherlands enjoys a transportation pattern in which 40 percent of trips are done by bicycle, 30 percent by public transportation, and only another 30 percent by automobile.[31]

Americans are only just now discovering the concept of cohousing—an alternative to lonely and wasteful suburban developments. Cohousing began over a decade ago in Denmark and has spread to many parts of Europe. Cohousing communities combine modest traditional independent housing units with collective space designed by the residents themselves. Typically, cohousing neighborhoods place cars on the periphery and prioritize joint space and human interaction at the center. They include common buildings for shared meals and entertainment. Residents also share items such as lawn care equipment, laundry appliances, tools, and so forth. Cohousing reduces people's overall material consumption while enhancing their opportunities for community interaction. At the same time, it preserves the personal living space that has become the norm for Western societies.

It comes as no surprise that the boldest national

efforts at environmental planning come from nations with significant social democratic traditions. For example, the environmental pressures on the small, densely populated Netherlands have combined with political traditions not afraid to look beyond the logic of the capitalist market. Through its recent National Environmental Policy Plan (NEPP), the Dutch government has developed a comprehensive, long-term program for ecological regeneration for which it has allocated billions of guilders from state coffers.[32] The NEPP aims in one generation (twenty-five years) not only to stop environmental degradation, but to actively establish environmental recovery. Updated every four years, the plan sets clear goals for reducing environmental destruction. For example, by the year 2000, it called for the lowering of carbon dioxide emissions to 1990 (later 1995) levels. It also targeted 70 to 90 percent reductions in the overall waste stream. It aimed to improve energy efficiency 2 percent a year as well as double the overall life span of products. The plan aimed to outright stop the practice of exporting waste. It has also required automobile manufacturers, all of whom build outside the country, to take full responsibility for the disposal of the cars that they sell in the Netherlands.

In a classic application of the ideas of social partnership, the NEPP called for targeted sectoral agreements. The government would set overall goals and standards and then encourage the targeted industry sector to organize itself into associations that would implement the goals. Agreements are then signed between public and private authorities. The government routinely publishes environmental report cards accessing the nation's progress, and the NEPP is reviewed and updated every four years. While not achieving every goal, the nation has seen notable progress. Between 1988 and 1992, pesticide use dropped by 20 percent. By 1995, discharges of industrial waste into the Rhine had fallen to between 50 and 70 percent below 1985 levels. The government had also begun to flood farmland drained a century ago in order to restore 600,000 acres of wetlands. Between 1991 and 1994, 10 million tons of topsoil were treated for contamination. The total costs, shared by the government, industry, and users, are estimated to reach $7 billion by 2010.

Seen from the goal of moving from quantitative growth to qualitative improvement without material growth, the NEPP represents an important, yet only first, step along a longer path. Holding auto companies responsible for the disposal of their product and aiming to reduce carbon dioxide emissions is not the same thing as questioning fundamentally the concept of transportation centered around the personal automobile. Indeed, lower fuel prices and a subsequent upsurge in car purchases in the 1990s prevented the Dutch government from meeting its original carbon dioxide target. Nevertheless, the Dutch plan stands out for its official recognition of the gravity of the ecological problems and for making a national and comprehensive commitment to addressing the issues. With the government committing serious resources to raise environmental awareness, the NEPP has also shaped public discussions. And while it leaves private business plenty of room for maneuvering, the NEPP nevertheless dares to assert public intervention into the product and investment decisions carefully guarded by corporate managers.

Indeed, in their own ways, both the Green movement and the Dutch NEPP suggest that any serious, long-term effort to address the ecological crisis must involve establishing greater public controls over and participation in capitalist decision making. Replacing mindless material growth with sustainable quality-of-life improvements means interfering with capitalism's core operating features. Since neoliberal approaches simply clear the way for the most destructive and short-term of capitalist tendencies, they clearly offer only a prescription for ecological catastrophe. The question remains whether the organized left in Europe is willing and able to travel down the path of questioning management's fundamental prerogatives.

The difficulty of negotiating this question shows up even within a Green movement open to such anticapitalist commitments. From their beginning, the German Greens endured intense internal debates. Amid the many different Green currents, two major camps can be identified. On the one side, the "fundamentalists" focused on the life-threatening magnitude of the current ecological crisis and its source in the very organizing principles of Western civilization. They tended toward strategies that emphasized educating the populace to the need for fundamental social change. On the other side, the "realists," while sharing the same ecologically based concerns, sought to build toward fundamental change using immediate reforms that established concrete policy to build a broader movement.

Reflecting their basic disagreement, the fundamentalists tended to subordinate electoral work to nonelectoral movement building. In contrast, the realists tended to see parliamentary power as an end in its own right. When considering the possibilities for coalition governments, the fundamentalists were less willing to compromise their agenda. They tended to enter into coalitions on only Green terms. By sticking tightly to their principles, the fundamentalists hoped to push the Social Democrats to transform their agenda along Green lines. If this coalition strategy failed in this regard, the Greens would be in a position to highlight the differences between them and the now-revealed hopelessly proestablishment Social Democrats. By contrast, the realists emphasized a flexible approach that sought compromise in order to ally with left-wing social democrats. In doing so, they hoped to try to strengthen that group's influence within its party. At the same time, such coalitions would allow Greens to participate in governing.

The tensions between the realists and the fundamentalists were ultimately resolved when the former gained the upper hand within the German party and the latter subsequently split, with many of the more strident fundamentalist camp leaving the party. The Green Party that recently formed a nationally governing coalition was led by currents willing to seek common ground with social democrats through significantly reduced expectations about the possibilities of progressive change.

Social Democracy, Progressive Politics, and the Possibilities of Revolutionary Reform

In a general way, the strategy differences found within the Greens echo an equally fervent debate that took place almost a century ago within the working-class movement that produced social democracy. By reexamining these origins, we can further clarify the road that progressive economics needs to travel today.

The Historic Debate

Social democracy's roots began with revolution, not reform. As the political wing of an emerging European labor movement, most social democratic parties can trace their nineteenth-century origins to calls for public ownership and the outright abolition of capitalism. Given the steady proletarianization of the population and capitalism's worsening cycles of boom and bust, the possibilities for revolution seemed close at hand. Indeed, capitalism experienced three major crises early this century in two world wars and one global economic collapse. And these upheavals did lead to a revolution in Russia and brief parallel worker governments in Germany, Austria, and Hungary. However, these later revolutionary efforts in central Europe met with ultimate defeat. The Russian Revolution thus became isolated in a country that, as its own revolutionary leaders freely admitted, was ill prepared to pursue the kind of socialist agenda developed for the fully industrialized West. Amid these great upheavals, the European labor movement debated its future. Should the working-class movement build toward revolution or should it steer its efforts into securing immediate and concrete reforms to improve the lives of workers within the current system?

All sides agreed that capitalism had serious problems and was responsible for a good part of the misery experienced by large sections of the working population. Most also shared a vision of a future society in which capitalist competition was replaced by democratic control over economic resources and where the fruits of production were shared by all. The catch, which split the movement, was how to bring this new society into being. One camp, the reformers (or "revisionists" as their opponents labeled them), saw the seeds of a better society growing within capitalism. Their strategy was to use parliamentary power to reform society beyond a capitalist existence. In contrast, the other side saw capitalist society as heading not toward a better world, but toward continued immiseration and a growing economic crisis. These revolutionaries called for increasing confrontation with the established authorities in order to polarize society so that capitalism could be overthrown in a dramatic mass revolt.

The differences between reformist and revolutionary tendencies showed up around many specific questions such as whether the party should try to appeal to voters who were not working class; whether elected parliamentary delegations should enter into coalition governments; and whether campaign material should emphasize immediate issues or larger social transformation. For years, both tendencies coexisted within Europe's major left parties—each contributing to the growth of the movement. The final showdown came when World War I and the Russian Revolution forced clear decisions that compelled an organizational split.

In looking at the history of the early socialist movement, many on the American political left today tend to sympathize with the concerns of the revolutionaries. This is understandable. Historically, within most social democratic parties, the reformers eventually won the upper hand. They then embarked on a course that seems, in the eyes of those who hope for fundamental social change, to have sacrificed the movement's original anticapitalist goals. One of the great betrayals in this regard came at the start of World War I. In country after country, the "revision-

ist" majority voted to support their respective nation's war efforts—thereby sending their working class off to kill workers from other countries. Although the details differ, in country after country, the dominant left party eventually abandoned revolutionary ambitions to pursue a reform agenda.

Lessons for Americans

Today, the dominant forces within European social democracy do seem to have become a solid part of the establishment, having long abandoned any desire to question capitalism itself. This long historical trajectory lies heavy in the minds of many U.S. progressives. Social movement activists who may not even consider themselves socialist still look at social democracy and see the danger of building a political movement only to see the leadership turn into a bureaucratic part of the status quo.

While we share the desire not to construct a political movement only to see it absorbed into politics-as-usual, there is a danger of drawing the wrong conclusions from this experience. The question is why did social democracy become part of the status quo? One answer looks toward electoral politics. By focusing on winning votes and building coalition governments, the socialist parties engaged in a series of compromises that eventually led them to lose sight of their ideals and principles. Furthermore, as leaders won election to state power, they developed a vested interest in staying in office even if it meant going against the movement's overall goals and principles.

A related answer looks at the hazards of large organizations. In his famous "iron law of oligarchy," Roberto Michels pointed to the gradual bureaucratization and undemocratic maneuvering that developed within the social democratic parties as inevitable to any large organization.[33] Once developed, this socialist oligarchy, with its careerist and party professionals, was much more willing to compromise the movement in order to gain favor with the establishment.

Both of these explanations point to real dangers that progressives need to understand. However, unless qualified by a more complex picture, they can lead progressives to very dangerous conclusions. Activists might decide that electoral politics is simply a waste of time because it will inevitably compromise the movement. They might also develop a kind of blind, automatic distrust for any form of national organization, fearing an inevitable tyranny by bureaucrats. These explanations can also encourage a narrow sectarianism as activists refuse to work with any individual or group who does not pass the true "revolutionary" credentials and is instead labeled a sellout or naively "reformist."

Fortunately, the above explanations point to only one side of the experience and offer a very ahistoric interpretation of the tensions involved. Three aspects of the social democratic trajectory point toward a more complex understanding of this history. First, we will reconsider the historical context. Second, we examine the content of reformism. Third, we will look at how the very distinct global environment that we face today has changed the nature of a reformist agenda.

The sharp debate between reformers and revolutionaries did not break out simply because one side wanted to sell out the movement or the other was naively utopian in its revolutionary sentiments. Rather, the conflict reflected a concrete turning point faced by the socialist movement caused by two major developments. First, the movement had achieved notable success, with socialist parties gaining considerable support among the working population. Because of these gains, the movement faced the question of how to continue to grow into an outright majority by gaining new supporters. Second, the capitalism that socialists faced in the early parts of the twentieth century looked quite different from the capitalism of Karl Marx. The gradual victory of liberal democracy and limited social reforms on the one hand, and imperialism and colonialism on the other, confronted socialists with questions as to how to react to these new realities.

To fully understand the ensuing debate between reformers and revolutionaries, we have to realize that neither side had the full answer. Or to put it another way, both were right and both were wrong. The revisionists were right in their argument that in Europe, at that time, revolution was not on the agenda. Instead, capitalism was about to enter a major transformation in its operation. Although often quite reluctantly, the corporate class accommodated itself to such major reforms as the legalizing of unions and collective bargaining, the development of the welfare state, and the enhanced role of government intervention in macroeconomic decisions. Through such changes, capitalism was able to enter, at least in the short run, a period in which it delivered unparalleled material prosperity to much of the working population in the West for several decades. While the Great Depression brought mass misery, the majority of the population did not look to revolution, but to these potential reforms. In the 1930s and 1940s, such changes offered real improvements in people's lives and were far more within reach than the complete overthrow of the established system.

If the socialist movement had not taken up the reform agenda, it would have surrendered reform efforts to the corporate parties who would have enacted more limited reforms shaped by their political and economic interests. As we have discussed repeatedly in this book, genuine working-class reform, such as social citizenship, contrasts starkly with elite reforms, such as the liberal American welfare state. The differences are not just in terms of the material effects, but also in the way social democratic and liberal measures shape class organization and the balance of power. We must also recognize that social democratic reformism did not come simply from those at the top of the party, but it also reflected the desires of a large number of ordinary working people. Generally, calls to reform, not revolution, inspired the political loyalties of the majority of working people.

However, the revolutionaries proved accurate in several judgments. The reforms initiated by social democracy did not lead to further steps toward transforming capitalism, let alone establishing a creeping socialism. Indeed, the welfare state and Keynesian state economic intervention helped, at least in the short run, to rationalize and legitimize the capitalist order. The critics were also correct that the reformism promoted by the leadership did set the movement on a course through which it lost sight of its founding ideals. Social democratic parties have largely become part of the very establishment that they first set out to overthrow.

Ultimately, the clearest sign of social democracy's failure came not in the 1930s, when it first accepted reformism, but today. In the 1930s, social democratic parties could accurately lay claim that they were supporting and giving voice to the desires of their base. The same is not true now. In the face of neoliberal capitalism, the social democratic parties have failed to provide new ideas. Instead of serving as vehicles for a mass discussion of the new realities, and for a popular mobilization against them, many of the parties seem more like entrenched bureaucracies out of touch with their social movement origins. Such bureaucracies, when confronted with the growing obsolescence of their old programs and with little sense of mass mobilization, have often caved in to neoliberal calls for austerity as the seeming only path. At its worst, the impasse has given rise to neoliberalism in social democratic disguise. The so-called Third Way espoused by such figures as Tony Blair and Gerhard Schröder accepts the basic free-market rules of the global economy. Their policies focus on preparing citizens to best compete in this new world order.[34]

In short, the political and economic conditions of the early part of this century did not offer the socialist movement a clear way out. The compromises required to follow a reformist path involved serious dangers. Yet at the same time, the revolutionary alternative to reformism was not an obviously better solution. Simply opposing reforms and pointing to the need to overthrow the entire system may have further polarized society toward a revolutionary moment. However, mass misery and need could have also simply provided business with strike breakers

to crush unions, and right-wing politicians with an ideal climate for scapegoating and pitting people against each other. Alternatively, with the left offering no program for reform, the establishment parties may have simply won popular support by offering their own versions of limited change.

The lesson for progressives today is to avoid turning these historical splits into universal conclusions that apply to situations of completely differing times and conditions. The trade-offs between reformism and more fundamental change represent a tension that has to be negotiated by activists in terms of their particular historical situation, not separate positions from which one has to choose one or the other. A political movement has to recognize that in dealing with questions of tactics and strategy, because of the complexity of the issues involved, it will incorporate people with differing positions along this spectrum. By focusing on differing aspects of a complex reality, conflicting tendencies can highlight and correct the excess and limitations of each other's agenda. A movement needs a structure and internal culture that can best channel these differences into productive and creative strategies, rather than infighting and paralysis. Understanding how such tensions either enhanced or split movements in the past is certainly one necessary step for activists today.

The Social Democratic Legacy Lives On

We should reiterate again that the current social democratic impasse lies in a lack of innovation in the face of change, not the past social democratic achievements that we have described. Indeed, while under attack by those entranced by "American success," the basic concepts of social citizenship, codetermination, strong unions, social partnership, and public control still enjoy substantial support. For example, it is in the nations with the weakest and most liberal welfare states, the United States and Britain, that antigovernment spending movements have achieved their greatest influence. By contrast, spending cuts in countries such as Sweden point toward consolidating, rather than abandoning, social citizenship within the boundaries of balanced budgets.

In Sweden, government reforms in the 1990s did trim the nation's welfare state. However, the basic structure remains intact and is still light years ahead of the United States. For example, the basic rate for unemployment, sick pay, and parental leave dropped from 90 percent to 80 percent of full pay. While changes increased copayments in health care, the amounts are still far below what most insured Americans face. Reforms also reduced public-sector employment across the board, reorganized the ATP system, and initiated some deregulation. These changes, however, mark a commitment to adjust social citizenship to within the financial boundaries of the existing budget and economic growth, not a move to a fundamental dismantling of the system. Indeed, in 1999, a *New York Times* headline declared: "A New Swedish Prosperity Even With a Welfare State." In classic patronizing corporate style, the article admits that "this largely unreconstructed welfare state is one of Europe's most vibrant economies."[35]

Similarly, while European employers have pushed for greater decentralization in collective bargaining, they are still far from the dominant American behavior. To this day, European labor activists, even those who lived through such hard times as Thatcher's Britain, are shocked by stories of the common union-busting and fear campaigns that are typical of labor relations in the United States.

Throughout Europe, the popularity and attraction of the U.S. neoliberal model remains uneven even within the ranks of European business. One recent set of polls suggested that our nation's example is downright unpopular. In April, for example, over two-thirds of French surveyed said they were worried about America's status as a superpower. Less than a third said there was anything to admire across the Atlantic. Polls in Germany, Italy, and Britain showed similar concerns.[36]

Recent legislative actions, such as the adoption of sabbatical leaves in Norway and Denmark, suggest that the traditional social democratic agenda still

has life. Indeed, in the face of corporate downsizing, the European labor movement has succeeded in placing the reduction of work time on the political agenda. This has come through efforts to directly lower the workweek—such as the thirty-five hours negotiated through collective bargaining in Germany and Socialist national policy in France. It has also involved further extensions of mandatory paid vacation times, increased family and personal leave rights, and earlier retirement. While the ability of such reforms to solve the long-term problem of unemployment remains mixed (the French government predicted over one hundred thousand new jobs), at a social level it offers a tool for turning capitalist rationalization and modern technology into increased leisure and family time. It also suggests that productivity gains can be used for more than simply increased material consumption.[37]

European integration also points to multiple possibilities. Developments such as the Maastricht Treaty and the single currency clearly steer in neoliberal directions. Attempts to build a strong European social charter have thus far not achieved the desired success. However, strong currents within European social democracy continue to hold hopes for reconstituting social democracy at a European level. A strong European federation empowered to raise national standards toward the highest examples set by member states is certainly economically feasible. A single European currency, for example, could prove less vulnerable to the backlashes of international currency markets not happy with the domestic policies pursued by member states. Since 90 percent of trade by European countries occurs within the EU, a federated Europe would encompass much of the basic "global" economic forces. Ironically, by the year 2000, the European left had achieved an important precondition of a social democratic Europe with left parties coming to power in all the major nations. Unfortunately, many of these governments are dominated by Third Way social democrats committed to neoliberal economics.[38] The problem with the current unification process is not the ideal of a united

Europe, but a reality in which the process thus far is dominated by a business neoliberal agenda.

The issue, therefore, is not that the gains of the old agenda need to be abandoned. But rather, traditional social democracy by itself can no longer fully address the economic and ecological crisis facing the world today. Thus, it has largely failed to offer a vision of a new path to inspire popular hopes for the future. To regain momentum, the left must extend its traditions of collective institutions and collective solutions into more fundamental economic areas. Specifically, social democracy has to go beyond the postwar deal in which business agreed to discuss the distribution of the economic pie as long as management was allowed to decide how the pie was made. Neoliberalism breaks with this deal from the capitalist side as corporations now demand more of the pie. In the long run, the left's only viable path is to also break with the deal by demanding greater control over how the pie is made. Without such an agenda, social democratic governments run the continued risk of presiding over neoliberal policies for regaining economic growth—paths that inflict great pain and stress on social democracy's core supporters. Such reduced expectations only encourage a rampant public cynicism that cripples progressive thinking and often delivers disaster at the polls. Winning votes by providing the "lesser evil" does not provide a basis for long-term political strength. Even worse, failure to provide an alternative allows parties of the far right to drape themselves in the mantle of antiestablishmentism.

Structural Reformism

Initiatives such as the AES and the Swedish wage-earner funds point to a rival of an old idea lost in the historical polarization between reformist and revolutionary camps. Early in the twentieth century, the European movement did debate the possibilities of paths between the reefs of reform or revolution. In the 1920s, discussions took place within the Austrian labor movement that offer the best historical

formulations that attempted to combine the best of the reformist and revolutionary paths. These "Austro-Marxists" agreed that capitalism would not be overthrown in one revolutionary upsurge. But, they also foresaw that reforms that confined themselves to tampering with economic externals would be insufficient. Instead, they advocated what could be called "revolutionary reforms" (or structural reforms), which asserted a creeping public role in corporate decisions. Such reforms sought to deliver concrete results while establishing the ground for further extension of collective decision over economic matters. An agenda of structural reforms fundamentally challenges capitalism by mobilizing popular sentiment around notions that economic decisions should not be left in the hands of business specialists and the vaunted "invisible" hand of the market. Public policy and popular action then implement these ideals through an ongoing process of extending popular controls over corporate decisions. Both the AES and the Swedish wage-earner funds aimed at such structural changes.

The notion of structural reforms can certainly be applied to the United States. Indeed, such a transformation lies at the heart of the national reform agenda, which we will offer in chapter 12. Here, we will confine ourselves to a few specific applications. For example, any progressive agenda must have a plan for rebuilding the nation's inner cities. Any such plan must include massive public spending. The bulk of such government outlays, when directed by mainstream politicians, has traditionally taken the form of tax breaks for private business and elaborate downtown development benefiting suburbanites. Such traditional strategies have resulted in few resources finding their way into poor neighborhoods. Indeed, such policies often provide resources to the very same corporations whose profit-driven logic was the source of urban decay in the first place. However, progressives could redefine urban renewal efforts in ways directed at neighborhoods and driven by the residents themselves. At the local level, examples already exist of community-driven redevelopment.[39]

With the proper resources, such resident initiatives could easily include alternative, cooperative, and ecologically sound forms of economic enterprises such as worker- and community-owned businesses. Similarly, people could revitalize their housing and public space in a manner that establishes laws and norms of greater collective public control over land use. The good of the community would supersede the currently dominant rights of private developers. Successful socially minded banks, such as Shore Bank in Chicago, have demonstrated how alternative financial institutions can do well by making funds available to low-income residents. A progressive urban renewal effort could use public and private resources to support the development of such new financial institutions that are publicly controlled and socially oriented. By using such alternative means as a way of rebuilding our cities, progressives would not only address the crisis of urban blight, but also create inner cities that provide a living vision of a better society built around democratic public institutions.

Structural reforms could also take the form of measures designed to increase the ability of social movements to grow and develop. For example, today U.S. labor laws lean so heavily in favor of employers that major progressive reforms would offer much-needed help toward rebuilding the U.S. labor movement. Such reforms might include an easier process for workers to gain legal recognition of their union, far harsher penalties for employers who violate the law, and repeal of laws that ban certain kinds of worker solidarity. We can also envision even bolder changes. Labor laws could establish a legal framework for state-mandated sectoral bargaining. Through such a system, the government would recognize unionization not just by individual firms, but by entire industries. All employers within that sector would be legally bound to participate in one master collective bargaining agreement. Among other benefits, such a system would increase the ability of unions to organize in the service sector with its thousands of small, dispersed workplaces.

Today, we are experiencing a major debate over who will control the emerging high-tech forms of communication. Progressives could pass laws that not only prioritize public over private control of the new technologies (such as the Internet and new cable systems), but could also lead to a reconsideration of past laws that granted access over public airwaves to private television and radio networks. Establishing a truly public media in this country would clearly represent a major step toward altering the balance of power both in politics and in American culture. Similarly, the political reforms already being advanced by progressive groups around campaign finance reform and proportional representation would also structurally democratize our political system in ways that could open the door for further popular power.

Structural reformism allows activists to maintain their basic critique of our existing society. However, it also allows them to embrace democratizing reforms that reflect the current desires of the majority of the population. While such actions may encompass less-than-fundamental change, they also clearly enhance the ability of popular organizing to grow and develop. Such a strategy displays a basic faith that as ordinary people become more organized and involved in politics and their communities, they will seek more fundamental changes. Indeed, over time, the basic contradictions within our society and the resistance of "the powers that be" will play themselves out by pointing the way for further, more fundamental changes.

The Potential Today

So, if structural reformism offers such a wonderful way out of the current dilemma, why hasn't it happened? Existing social democratic practices have already demonstrated possibilities of structural reform. They have shown that greater public control does not necessarily mean more governmental bureaucracy. Governments can empower others to participate in economic decisions. They can also set the rules around which activity takes place. And economic activity can be placed directly in the hands of public institutions that are more efficient and more socially and economically rational than private enterprise. Indeed, when advanced by a social movement, traditional social democracy applied to the United States would provide the first steps of a structural reform agenda.

Historically, however, social democratic reforms have risen in a context of class compromise. The dominant social democratic parties rose to prominence around a postwar deal between labor and management. Management agreed to live with collective bargaining and social democratic reforms as long as neither dimensions challenged what management saw as its fundamental rights. Thus, while the growing welfare state, codetermination, nationalization, and social partnership all marked clear popular gains, they also established firm boundaries around management's "right to manage." After six decades of entrenched social democratic practices, today these boundaries are hard to cross, even when business has begun to consider other options.

The internal evolution of the major left parties during this time period also undercut the potential for wholesale structural reform. Over time, the major social democratic parties have lost much of their origins as movement organizations. Strictly electoral considerations have gained increasing predominance. During the postwar boom, such a focus could pay off as calls for traditional social democratic reforms were used to build electoral coalitions connecting the manual working class to middle-class voters. Today, however, the focus on winning the next election can easily imprison leaders within the confines of the policies of the present. When electoral platforms correspond to the findings of the most recent polls, party strategists are limiting their appeals around where public opinion currently lies. Yet, such public sentiment is shaped by the agenda presented in the media and by established political leadership. It will thus hardly reflect calls for radical economic change. However, even within these polls are expressions of significant dissatisfaction with the status quo. Structural reformism offers a path of mobilizing this discontent by replacing pacifying cynicism with powerful hopes for the future. Such appeals, however, are unlikely to win the next election. Structural reform instead provides a path of patient organizing that promises history-making political triumphs down the road.

The tools to unleash such long-term potential are quite different from the American-style media advertising that increasingly characterizes European politics. Developing popular support for ideas of fundamental reform means returning to the grassroots, movement-oriented organizing that first built the European left. As we will see in an American context in Part II, old-fashioned door-to-door, neighborhood-by-neighborhood mobilizing and community building still works even in an age of flashy corporate media. Such strategies, however, require progressive political parties organized quite differently than the centralized bureaucracies that predominate Europe's left.

The dominant social democratic leadership continues to cling to the old class compromise. Yet, the foundation of this historical labor-management deal came not from cooperation, but confrontation. At a certain level, business agreed to live social democratic reform only when faced with the prospect of far more radical and potentially revolutionary alternatives. The Great Depression and fascism had given capitalism such a black eye that corporate leaders needed to re-establish their credibility. Thus, even Christian democratic governments were willing to enact social democratic policies in the face of an opposition that continued to call for wholesale nationalization. Today, arguably, the left is not going to gain the cooperation of corporate leaders by simply confining its agenda to within the boundaries comfortable to neoliberal capitalism. Rather it must rebuild its grassroots base as a social movement capable of approaching corporate decision makers from a position of strength. The high-road path to economic success requires power sharing. To continue down the high road, the left today must reopen the debate about who makes the crucial economic decisions.

In short, having evolved around an environment of class compromise, social democracy today is ill equipped for the new period of social polarization and capitalist offensive. Nevertheless, as the slogan goes in union-organizing circles, "management policies are often the best union organizer." Neoliberal capitalism can solve neither the social nor the environmental problems growing in the world today. Indeed, it remains to be seen whether it can maintain itself even by its own narrow economic criterion.

Growing fault lines can be seen within traditional social democratic politics. Europe's unions are far more restricted than the Social Democratic Party leadership in their ability to go down a conformist, neoliberal road. Sitting on the front lines, unions are faced with economic restructuring and aggressive employer demands that they must resist at some level if they are to survive and retain any allegiance among their membership. Thus, in one way or another, the unions are being forced to look for alternative ways out. And as we have already discussed, Green politics represents a continuing challenge to the embrace of neoliberal solutions.

In 1995, events in France showed the level of popular frustrations with over a decade of promises, by both left and right, that with just a little more neoliberal sacrifice prosperity was right around the corner.[40] In October of that year, Jacques Chirac was elected president on promises to make the struggle against unemployment and the "social fracture" his top concern. A month later the government began announcing reforms that made clear that balancing the budget, not social concerns, was the number one priority. However, in addition to new taxes and budget cuts, the government also revealed plans to restructure control over the provision of key social services, such as health care and pensions, in ways that critics described as leading to an American-style two-tiered system. Over time, an increasingly impoverished public tier would lose out to enriched private companies enjoying increased control over social provisions.

With the help of the unions, a series of strikes and marches engulfed the country. These began on November 24, with events involving three-quarters of a million people, and peaked on December 12, with actions encompassing nearly 2 million. While the breadth of activity found throughout the provinces was particularly noteworthy, the most dramatic scenes came from Paris. A public transportation strike paralyzed the city and led other public servants to also walk off the job. The major drama, however, was not the strikes themselves, but the mass demonstrations that supported them. There is nothing potentially more unpopular than a transportation strike. Yet, according to polls, 60 percent of the population supported the strikers. Indeed, the atmosphere among the large crowds was particularly joyous and celebratory. The prostrike banners draped from the windows of a prison near one of the march routes symbolized the protests' popularity.

The nature of the "winter of discontent" was such that it was only a matter of time before the movement peaked and declined. Indeed, the government negotiated concessions with various groups while leaving its overall social budgeting commitments intact. However, the upheaval revealed the shape of a new era. In the inevitable comparisons to the famous protests of 1968, one clear contrast emerged. In 1968, students and workers protested the cracks of what was still the prosperous society. In 1995, people took to the streets driven by a bleak picture of persistent mass unemployment.

The winter of discontent, coupled with protest waves in Italy in 1994 and Germany in 1996, demonstrated that a substantial cross section of Europe's population was not happy with the neoliberal future it was being offered. Indeed, the 1990s saw the growth of an infant social movement of the marginalized—the unemployed, immigrants, the poor. This decentralized movement networks grassroots groups across the region. Through marches, occupations of social security and utility offices, collective not paying to ride public transportation, and demonstrations in front of grocery stores, people marginalized by corporate restructuring have demanded a different path. These groups have linked together across national borders. And they have joined with growing dissident currents within organized labor and other movements such as those against racism and for women's rights. A common agenda emerging from these protest currents includes the institution of basic European-wide rights to a guaranteed income, benefits, and pensions.

The ongoing task remains to develop a clear alternative. In the 1997 elections, the French Socialists took power, forming a government that included one Green and three Communist ministers. Yet, as elsewhere, left success owed as much to the bankruptcy of the opposition as it did the Socialists' ability to blaze a trail of innovative thinking. Indeed, the party's leader, Lionel Jospin, had been notable mainly for his active role in helping to "normalize" the party during the Mitterrand years. Beyond the adoption of a thirty-five-hour workweek, it re-mains to be seen what the Socialists will offer.

The message for American progressives is clear. Progressive change in this country is not only desirable, but economically feasible. In fighting for change, activists can draw support from proven and popular policies forged by the European labor movement over the course of the last century. These can help progressives overcome the "bogeyman" thrown up by champions of neoliberalism—namely that active government is futile and undesirable; only the individual pursuit of happiness provides a real path. U.S. progressives, however, cannot simply look to the past. They need to see themselves as part of a new generation of activist movements that combine the old with the new. Americans must use the examples of social citizenship, codetermination, social partnership, public ownership, and ecological and social sustainability to produce a new agenda that raises the call for economic democracy to new levels.

6

The Progressive Potential in the United States: Liberal Confinement and Radical Renewal

While American media and policy debates often act as if the United States is the center of the world and the model for others, as we have seen, our country is actually an outlier among the industrial world. The United States is unique in the degree to which its policies celebrate the market, promote individualism, drive mass consumption, and foster an advertising style of contentless politics. For decades this "American exceptionalism" fostered debates over why social democracy did not make as deep an inroads into American politics as it did in Europe. We begin by taking up this debate through identifying the major historical forces that limited social democratic change in America. At issue is the extent to which these forces continue to limit a progressive potential today. In the second part of this chapter, we will look at the flip side: the ways that current conditions favor progressive change. In certain respects, the prospects for progressive economic alternatives are particularly promising in the United States.

Why Less Social Democracy in the United States?

Cultural Explanations

Obviously, cultural differences exist between the United States and Europe. These contrasts are often used to explain why social democratic policies have proven weaker in this country. The United States is different from Europe, so the cultural explanations

go, because Americans are so different from Europeans. We have the American dream of individualized success. We look toward hard work and individual talent to get ahead. And this personalized success revolves around material wealth. No other society seems so obsessed with consumeristic gain as the United States. Similarly, in few other industrialized countries is the suspicion of government and the desire to have a "checks and balances" system stronger.

In the midst of today's official political atmosphere, it is easy to buy into the notion that this country does not have a strong sense of social solidarity because most Americans are simply too individualistic and too wrapped up in their personal prospects for gain. Yet, cultural explanations alone offer a dangerous path for anyone concerned with progressive economic change. Indeed, they point to conclusions that offer only a cynical passivity in the face of a static and all-pervasive "American culture."

Thankfully, rooting the weakness of American social democracy in cultural factors provides at best a weak explanation, for several reasons. First, defining "American culture" assumes a unity and coherence that hardly fits the complex reality. The nation's diversity along class, race, and ethnic background alone speaks against such conclusions. Furthermore, individual Americans generally are much more complicated than many cultural definitions allow. The same individuals who might express open hostility over their tax burden and "meddling government bureaucrats" might also be those who would vote for a national health care system if given a chance to select government that delivers clear results.

While individualism and consumerism certainly affect people in this society, we have to realize that the institutions that define our official culture are biased toward giving a favored place precisely to cultural aspects that fit most closely with the needs of corporations. Both through direct ownership and advertising, corporations control the major media. Similar patterns of corporate money, and more indirect forms of influence, shape official political debates and penetrate the education system. These dominant institutions, therefore, naturally reflect cultural norms most in line with capitalist values. Thus, the news, for example, highlights stories of individual success, yuppie buying patterns, antigovernment militias, and social friction. Local groups organizing to cross barriers between people, actions of worker solidarity, and stories of people rejecting the consumer society typically do not make the evening news. Nightly sitcoms revolve around formulas in which typically white, middle-class suburbanites display the self-centered individualism, materialism, and banal political and social cynicism that fits well with the ideological needs of corporations.

Real Americans are much more heterogeneous and complicated than the media images give them credit for. Progressives need to draw their conclusions as much from what the official organs of opinion do not cover as from what they do. That many Americans continue to express desire for various forms of collective problem solving and social solidarity in the face of an official corporate culture that continuously attempts to discredit such notions is a testament to the presence of strong cultural elements potentially supportive of progressive politics. Polls, for example, continue to reveal a public that continues to be big government spenders well after the official political leadership has long abandoned the New Deal. At the height of the Reagan years, one poll found that while 80 percent of respondents said they favored cuts in government spending, on the very next question, 68 percent said they also sup-

ported "government financing to create more jobs."[1] By 1996, 44 percent of American workers said they would join a union if given a choice. That figure is up from 30 percent in 1984.[2] Faced with growing economic strains that close options for individual success, a significant number of Americans are open to collective solutions despite the predominant practice among the media and official political leaders of treating unions and active government as obsolete special interests.

Second, cultural obstacles also provide cultural opportunities. For example, within so-called American individualism is a flip side in latent distrust of authority and official organs of power. This sentiment can have progressive potential. For example, a 1998 survey by the Economic Policy Institute found that a full 85 percent of respondents agreed that "corporations have too much power." In 1999, a Harris poll conducted for *Business Week* found that over two-thirds of respondents thought business was doing a poor job of raising living standards, and three-quarters thought the benefits of the new economy were too unevenly distributed. In the same poll, over half of the respondents sympathized with the Seattle WTO protestors, and over half felt trade agreements were unfair.[3] Despite decades of official portrayals of America as the classless society, such mass skepticism about corporations and the direction of our economy suggests continued possibilities for class-based politics. Certainly, so-called American beliefs in private entrepreneurship cannot be equated with a wholesale belief in American capitalism.

The student revolt of the 1960s provides clear historical evidence that the culture of suburban materialism also breeds its own contradiction. Indeed, today the growth of nonmainstream religion (from New Age spirituality and American Buddhism to religious fundamentalism) suggests that the isolation and loneliness of hyperconsumerism and individualism breeds a search for greater personal meaning and a broader identity. This yearning can be harnessed by both the left and the right.

Historically, the most culturally conservative part

of the country, the South, has also given rise to some of the most powerful social movements including the antislavery struggle and Reconstruction, the great Populist revolt of American farmers in the 1880s and 1890s, and the modern civil rights movement. Had historical battles produced different results, the South could have provided a beacon of progressive change, rather than a bulwark of reaction. Today, the very difficulties that unions face organizing in the South also mean that any significant success in this region will produce a labor movement that is multiracial, militant, and rooted in social alliances and a broad social agenda. Scholars of European history have similarly noted how traditional conservatism in countries such as Germany and Austria, with its mixture of critique of and qualified support for modern capitalism, both aided and shaped social democratic–style reforms.

Finally, people's understanding of the past shapes their sense of what is possible in the present. Yet, the predominant versions of U.S. history take the viewpoint of those in power. Thankfully, the historical profession has produced over the past couple of decades a now-rich library of research documenting the past through the eyes of ordinary Americans.[4] This material points to two conclusions. First, most of what progressives would consider as positive changes in this country have come from the collective struggles by ordinary Americans who often demanded broad and sweeping change. Second, many of the current policies that frustrate progressives, including the modesty of U.S. social programs and the predominance granted to market forces, were historically contested by popular groups. In other words, the weakness of social democracy in the United States is not because mass movements similar to those in Europe never battled for it. Rather, the limits grew from historic struggles in which these movements suffered different forms of victories, defeats, and compromises than their European counterparts. Our analysis thus moves from the supposed limitations of American culture to the rich, and all-too-easily forgotten, history of past social battles.

The Historic Confinement of American Social Democracy

An Australian Ph.D. candidate in American history once remarked, "you people have a really radical history." Indeed, every couple of decades, this country has witnessed a major upwelling of activism as ordinary people make history. Much of what we examined in Europe has been proposed and fought for in the United States. At its core, social democracy is a belief in the positive role of government to pursue social justice and economic health. Such a faith in government as the natural friend and ally of ordinary people has a long tradition in this country. We will restrict ourselves, however, to four moments that parallel events in Europe when social democracy became a potent political force. In each case, forces that led to social democracy in Europe suffered more limited victories in the United States. As a result, at an official policy level, American reformism developed a more limited conceptual framework of liberalism.

For a Cooperative Commonwealth

One of the most visible political differences between the United States and Europe is the absence in this country of a truly left-wing political party. In American politics, what are essentially two elite parties battle over different variations of a business-oriented agenda. Both the Republicans and the Democrats were founded by and for a wealthy ruling class. Despite occasional populist leanings, the Democrats were traditionally the party of slavery, states' rights, and the conservative South. Ironically, the Republicans have more progressive origins as a third party founded to oppose the extension of slavery. While the party included significant abolitionist currents, ultimately it served the interests of Northern capitalism. By contrast, whether they are called labour, social democrat, or socialist, the major left parties in Europe were all built by the powerful labor movements that emerged in the second half of the nineteenth century.

Interestingly, an observer comparing politics in

the late nineteenth century would have noticed little difference between the United States and Europe. Between 1880 and 1920, our nation experienced a political revolt that appeared as strong as any of the left party movements growing across the Atlantic. In this country, the efforts to break up the two-party system came in two phases: populism and socialism.[5] People's Party governors sat in office in several western states, while socialists governed cities such as Milwaukee, Wisconsin; Schenectady, New York; and Reading, Pennsylvania, sometimes for decades. In 1911, over twelve hundred socialists held office, mostly local, throughout a large part of the country. Most important, both parties fostered a vibrant grassroots life that opened the way for millions of ordinary people to participate in politics. Every year, thousands of farmers and workers, for example, would travel to huge Populist and Socialist encampments where music was always playing, kids would ride the Ferris wheel, and people would discuss the key political issues of their time. Routine local party meetings were family events. Thousands of dirt farmers learned to read and write at classes held during Populist meetings. Literally millions read the populist and socialist newspaper *Appeal to Reason*—making it one of the three founding organs of the modern national mass-circulation newspaper.

Both the Populist Party and the Socialist Party were social movements as much as political organizations. Their power lay in their grassroots strength, not the number of votes gained by their candidate for U.S. president—the criterion used in most history books to dismiss them. Both grew out of years of patient organizing. Both adapted to their political environment. While their platforms touched many issues, economic questions provided the bedrock of populist and socialist politics. Both movements sought to save the country from the ravages of corporate power. They both looked toward a "Cooperative Commonwealth" in which the fruits of labor were shared by all and the democratic ideals upheld in America were practiced in all spheres of human life. They both saw democratic government truly of and for the people as a central tool to achieve the just society. Indeed, both movements framed their activities as a great crusade to save the nation's democratic civic heritage from the chokehold of corporate power.

This grassroots energy had a lasting impact that spilled into the other social movements of the day. It also compelled the two major parties to implement many populist- and socialist-championed reforms such as child labor laws, universal education, direct election of the U.S. Senate, and the construction of adequate sewers and clean streets in working-class parts of town. The so-called Progressive Reform Era that took place early in the twentieth century did not happen by itself, but was, in part, a reaction to populism and socialism.

Ultimately, the Democrats and Republicans blocked the further growth of these movements through undemocratic and eventually illegal means. Their dirty tricks included jailing third-party activists (Socialist candidate Eugene Debs won over a million votes from jail in 1920), banning publications, arranging police raids of third-party headquarters, race-baiting, inciting vigilante violence, and outrightly stealing elections. Most important, both major parties conspired to demobilize roughly half of the American electorate. Electoral "reform" instituted registration procedures that discouraged voting among people of more modest means. Race and ethnicity were used to bar people from voting—be it Jim Crow laws in the South or anti-immigration laws throughout the country. Faced with a Populist and Socialist challenge, the two corporate parties also simply lost their enthusiasm for their grassroots armies that got out the vote. Instead, over time, both parties gravitated toward money-driven advertising forms of electioneering through which they competed for the loyalties of those who actually voted. Before the great purge of the electorate, Americans (males) voted at rates of 80 and 90 percent in all elections. In defeating populism and socialism, the major parties forced this portion down to the modern 50 percent during presidential years and even lower turnouts during other elections. Needless to say, the ranks of those who do not vote, then as now, are made up of those people who in Europe support left-wing parties.

While populism and socialism pushed issues into the public debate, for the establishment of social democracy, the ultimate victory of the two-party system has meant that popular movements have either had to seek an alliance with one of the elite parties, the Democrats, or reattempt the difficult task of building a truly social democratic and progressive party from scratch. As we will see, a reliance on the Democratic Party has proved a weaker base for launching social democratic change.

The Social Democratic Strengths and Weaknesses of the New Deal

While most official history recognizes the hard times of the Great Depression, it often fails to appreciate the level of class polarization and violent confrontation that the economic collapse produced. By 1932, one out of four American workers could not find a job. In industrial cities such as Detroit and Toledo, half the population or more was unemployed. That year, the intake records at Detroit's emergency-receiving hospital averaged four deaths per day from malnutrition! Nationally, wages for those who had work fell by 50 percent or more.

Such desperate needs fostered a simmering class war. Workers who did not have union recognition, for example, engaged in desperate and spontaneous strikes sparked by the fourth or fifth pay cut. Between 1930 and 1939, the National Guard was called out on forty different occasions to suppress striking workers. In 1932, Henry Ford's private security forces fired on a march of several thousand unemployed workers in Dearborn, Michigan. Sixty-five thousand people attended the funeral procession of the five workers killed by Ford's actions. In 1937, Chicago police shot into a crowd of striking Republican Steel workers, killing ten and wounding another forty. Facing court injunction, riot police, and

the Ohio National Guard, workers at the Toledo Auto Lite plant in 1934 forced the company to sign a union contract only after several workers had been killed and joint crowds of workers and the unemployed fought the forces of "law and order" in open pitched battles. In rural areas, armed groups of the poor broke into grocery stores. Facing farm foreclosure when crop prices collapsed in 1930 and 1931, armed farmers simply shut down local courts.[6]

The combination of the depth of the economic collapse, the desperate needs of millions, and the often callused and violent response by those in authority bred radical conclusions. A sign carried in a rally of the unemployed in downtown Detroit in 1932 captured the sentiments of many working people across the nation. Its plea—"Don't Starve in the Richest Land on Earth"—suggested that the real problem was not the economic collapse, but the hoarding by the few that caused the starving of the many.

The serious prospect that ordinary Americans were going to take matters into their own hands forced the newly elected Democrats—including the new president, Franklin Roosevelt—to act. The famous New Deal launched an alphabet soup of new programs aimed at restoring economic growth and saving American capitalism.[7] Most of these programs are still around today, including the Fair Labor Standards Act (FLSA) (forty-hour workweek, time and a half for overtime, the minimum wage, and a ban on child labor); the Social Security Act (social security pensions and unemployment insurance); the Federal Deposit Insurance Corporation (FDIC) (protecting personal savings); and the National Labor Relations Act (providing legal recognition for unions). After the worst of the Depression was over, corporate lobbyists succeeded in getting the direct government employment programs (the Works Progress Administration [WPA] and the Civilian Conservation Corps [CCC]) shut down and their potentially instructive memory forgotten.

The New Deal broke with the nation's century and a half of laissez-faire, minimal-government policy traditions and established the foundation for our modern federal government. Specifically, the federal government took on two new major roles. First, it established a minimal social safety net. This marked a recognition that under capitalism, hard-working people can still starve. It also signified the acknowledgment that the roots of the Great Depression lay in the extreme inequalities of wealth that had prevented many Americans from buying the goods that the nation produced. Facing limited consumer demand, companies had cut costs by laying off workers—thereby further shrinking demand in a steady downward spiral. Second, both through social spending and direct regulation, the federal government established a public role in steering the nation's economy. The Great Depression was only unique in its outright severity. The nineteenth century had witnessed a continuous cycle of ever-worsening booms and busts inherent to the capitalist system. Government policies to curtail the worst excesses and irrationalities of capitalism became necessary to preserve the system as a whole.

As historians have documented, the ideas of the New Deal had been developing within a liberal wing of the business community for a considerable length of time. These "enlightened" capitalists had begun to conclude that a modern and rational form of capitalism needed some government social and economic policy. It might also require some accommodation with what most top managers saw as their great class enemy: the American labor movement. Such sentiments, however, while influential within the Roosevelt administration, arguably represented only a minority opinion in overall corporate circles. Indeed, the great institutional champion of a conservative business order, the U.S. Supreme Court, declared the initial New Deal policies unconstitutional. Such action followed a long tradition created by court actions to strike down state laws enacting a minimum wage, a forty-hour workweek, bans on child labor, and any other progressive initiative that dared to restrict the unquestioned right of private ownership. Indeed, the corporate community as a whole met the 1935 passage of the National Labor

Relations Act with a constitutional challenge and a general refusal to respect the law. When workers mounted the great union-organizing wave of 1936–1937 they did so with the moral support of the law, but with no effective legal enforcement. When Roosevelt ran for reelection in 1936, the campaign became largely a referendum on the New Deal with nearly every corporate media outlet explaining to voters why Roosevelt needed to go.

The fact that FDR won reelection by the then largest landslide in the nation's history testifies to the New Deal's popularity and growing strength of a rejuvenating labor movement.[8] At the beginning of the Great Depression, few observers would have foreseen the great worker awakening that broke onto the national scene in 1936. Mass unemployment appeared to provide more of a tool for pitting working people against each other than a spark for mass solidarity. Less than 10 percent of U.S. workers were in unions by 1932. The major mass production industries were largely union free. And the main institutions of the American labor movement, the AFL and its affiliated unions, were firmly locked into conservative nineteenth-century methods. They avoided confrontations and restricted themselves largely to organizing skilled workers into separate, craft-style unions. The desperate battles of 1931 through 1935, however, fostered a new generation of union leadership that laid the seeds for a resurgent mass movement. In 1935, the Mineworkers walked out of the AFL to establish the institutional umbrella for this new labor movement: the CIO.

The 1936 sit-down strike by the infant UAW union against General Motors proved a turning point. Facing company spies and the continual prospect of losing their jobs, a relatively small group of committed UAW members successfully laid the groundwork for a six-week strike that forced the world's largest corporation to recognize the union. In the eighteen months following the victory, 3 million American workers organized themselves into unions.

This CIO-led labor activism of the 1930s and 1940s differed in several important respects from the union movement that evolved after the war. It gave organizational expression to a grassroots movement involving millions of Americans. The labor battles stand out for the degree to which they united workplace and community activism. CIO unions organized workers regardless of race, ethnicity, and gender. Faced with employers who used racial and ethnic divisions as a weapon against workers, these unions succeeded only by merging labor rights with civil rights.[9] With a vast network of cooperative stores, sports teams, social clubs, credit unions, and labor media, the union hall also became part of a broad community network encompassing an entire way of life.

This labor social movement emerged out of its founding battles with a broad and far-reaching agenda. CIO unions defined their mission not simply in terms of negotiating better wages and benefits for their membership, but as advancing the cause of working people. Specifically, they looked toward extending the New Deal's social policies into full-blown social citizenship and its tentative steps of economic intervention into full-scale economic planning.

This social democratic potential was both enhanced and weakened by the domestic experience during World War II. The government war effort recognized unions as a legitimate part of the economic process. In pursuit of labor-management peace, the National War Labor Board compelled companies to recognize union shops in which all new workers hired became union members. The war mobilization also imposed significant government controls over the economy—regulating wages, prices, and production. Not only did this leave the nation with a positive experience in large-scale governmental economic planning, but unions played a major role in the process through tripartite, corporatist mechanisms that brought together business, government, and labor representatives. The official war effort, however, also created friction within the ranks of labor. To support the war mobilization, labor leaders agreed to no-strike pledges and wage freezes. Such commitments took the focal point of union action out of the hands

of the workplace activist and into the halls of often ineffective government-sponsored grievance procedures. The wartime planning boards invited labor leaders to the table but gave little role to the labor movement's grassroots base. As company profits soared and worker grievances grew, union leaders found themselves stuck between official government channels on the one side and unauthorized wildcat strikes and rank-and-file protests on the other.

A substantial body of leadership within the CIO unions emerged from World War II looking to extend wartime planning models in clear social democratic directions. The CIO proposed an Industry Council Plan that would have given labor an ongoing voice in codetermining production, investment, and employment decisions in core industries. Most labor, business, and government leaders feared that the nation's economy would sink back into depression once it had lost the artificial wartime demand. For many of the nation's industrial unions, the solution was to raise demand through social democratic–style social programs, mechanisms of social partnership, and nationally oriented collective bargaining aimed at promoting wage solidarity.

Corporate opposition ultimately defeated this agenda by confining the progressive legacies of the 1930s and early 1940s. A business counteroffensive sought to reestablish management's controls both at the shop floor and in the boardroom. It also aimed to restrict government activity to limited intervention at the macroeconomic level—leaving the microeconomic decisions up to the corporate owners and managers. Labor's social democratic agenda did not go down without a fight, however. In towns and cities across the country, corporate leaders pushed an ideology of consumerism, anti-left patriotism, and free-market worship, while unions tried to build on the values of collective gain, social solidarity, and participatory democracy. The battlegrounds included the nation's schools, churches, media, and ultimately the halls of government. The eventual triumph of capitalist consumerism demonstrated both the relative strength of corporate America and weakness within the labor movement. Divided between rival AFL and CIO union federations, organized labor did not have the grassroots muscle to fully push the New Deal into full-blown social democracy.[10]

The limits of American social democracy were signified in several turning-point battles. In 1946, the UAW struck General Motors, demanding a 30 percent wage increase with no increase in the price of the product. With wages held down during the war, the company was willing to admit to some need for significant wage increases. However, General Motors management refused to recognize the UAW's assertion of a right to discuss the company's business decisions. Indeed, the union was attempting to place itself as a champion of working-class interests broadly defined. The headquartering of the community strike support committee in the offices of the National Association for the Advancement of Colored People (NAACP) reflected the potentially broad social movement connections of which the union was a part. General Motors refused to budge. The UAW eventually settled for significant wage gains, but at the cost of conceding management's right to run the company.[11]

The terms of this "Treaty of Detroit" would come to define the postwar peace deal between corporate America and organized labor. Companies agreed to routine and incremental collective bargaining that improved wages and benefits over time. In return, outside of what was explicitly specified in the contract, management exercised exclusive right to run the company. This narrowing of collective bargaining helped steer industrial unions from their roots as a social movement toward a status as "special interests." For unions that achieved national negotiations, the system of collective bargaining would also have other contradictory effects. When the major employers of an industry could be steered toward common pattern agreements, unions succeeded in taking wages, benefits, and working conditions out of the terms of competition between companies. However, such large-scale agreements also took the locus of union activism out of the realm of the rank-and-file activist.

The labor-management deal became fully established only after efforts by the labor movement to achieve broader social aims by political means suffered major defeats. Several turning points are notable.[12] In contrast to Franklin Roosevelt's, the presidency of Harry Truman offered far less opportunities to left-wing supporters of the New Deal. Over time, most of FDR's cabinet, including all the left New Dealers, left office. The limits of labor's political reach became clear shortly after the war when a bill that would have established a national health care system was defeated in Congress.

In 1946, the Democrats lost Congress for the first time since 1930. A coalition of Republicans and conservative Democrats then promptly passed, over Truman's veto, the Taft-Hartley Act. The law banned two major expressions of broad social-movement-style union solidarity: secondary boycotts and secondary strikes. Taft-Hartley also opened the door for states to pass the antiunion "right to work" laws.[13] It blocked foreman and supervisory workers from forming unions—thus undermining potential solidarity between hourly workers and management's front-line police. And it required anti-Communist affidavits—a tool used to eliminate or marginalize many of the labor movement's most active cadre of rank-and-file leaders. All of these provisions had been on the agenda of the National Association of Manufacturers since the late 1930s. This body chose not to directly challenge a union presence, which was too strong to defeat outright, but to confine unions within the narrow and safer boundaries of workplace-level collective bargaining.

The Cold War, and its embrace by the mainstream of the labor movement, proved disastrous for labor's broad social and political potential. While official histories often portray the McCarthy-era anticommunist witch hunts as irrational, the national campaign against "communism" served to disrupt forces pushing for a left-wing New Deal. McCarthyism is most famous for its persecution of left and liberal intellectuals, artists, and journalists. However, its main focus centered against organized labor.[14] Some of the most democratic and militant unions, such as the Longshoremen and the United Electrical Workers, were thrown out of the official house of labor for being "communist-dominated" and their membership raided by other, more "patriotic," unions. Internally, union leaders purged suspected "communists" whose only real sin might come from being an effective rank-and-file leader seen as threatening to the political position of the leadership slate in office. Such internal purges served only to further weaken workplace activism.

Anticommunism and the Cold War also helped tip the balance against labor's foray into third-party politics. Frustrations with Truman and the Democratic Party had led a significant number of union leaders to seriously consider the option of forming a third party. In 1946, C. Wright Mills found that among CIO national officers, 65 percent favored a labor party political initiative in ten years' time.[15] Ironically, the actual launching of a third party, the Progressive Party, signified an end to such thinking. In 1948, left New Dealer, and former vice president, Henry Wallace, ran as the Progressive Party's candidate for U.S. president. Wallace campaigned on a platform of extending the New Deal, détente with the Soviets, repeal of Taft-Hartley, and the advancement of civil rights. His agenda offered the possibilities of a dramatically different postwar history. Internal union records reveal how close many union leaders came to making the third-party leap.[16] However, in the end, the labor movement as a whole chose to remain loyal to the Democratic Party. In January 1948, the CIO executive council passed a resolution rejecting the Progressive Party. Deft maneuvering on the part of Truman also helped bring civil rights organizations within the Democratic camp. In the end, Wallace received only 3 percent of the vote. The Cold War and anticommunism would go unchallenged.

The New Deal's more social democratic potential was also held back by the nation's continued unwillingness to challenge Southern apartheid. The influence of the Democratic Party's conservative Southern wing shaped New Deal reform since its beginning. The Social Security Act, for example, excluded sharecroppers and domestic servants—the two major professions available to Southern blacks. The 1934 National Housing Act was also established in such a way as to allow redlining to exclude blacks from subsidized mortgages. The 1937 Housing Act led to ghettoized public housing. Any major form of social democracy directly threatened Southern segregation. Universal social programs defied racist rationality and promised to provide African Americans with greater means to escape economic slavery. The defection of the Southern Democrats from the New Deal coalition helped to ensure the failure of national health care and the passage of Taft-Hartley.

This Southern conservative influence did not go unchallenged. In 1949, the CIO launched "Operation Dixie" to unionize the low-wage South.[17] Had it succeeded, it could have eliminated the South as a source of cheap, nonunion labor. It would also have broken the political power of the conservative Southern Democrats and cemented the ties between the labor and civil rights movements. The effort, however, failed. Competing with a rival AFL effort to bring authentic "American" unionism, the CIO ran into a wall of resistance. Breaking the Deep South required a social movement that the CIO was not able to launch. Some of its most talented and most multiracially committed union organizers were lost in the anticommunist purges. At the same time, the New Deal's active promotion of mechanization in agriculture forced many farmers, both black and white, off the land. Eventually this would produce conditions favorable to the civil rights movement by proletarianizing many rural blacks and producing a great wave of African-American migration to Northern cities. In the short run, however, this social change provided a surplus of labor used by Southern business to pit workers against each other.

By the 1950s, the profile of the postwar era had been set. Even social democratic unions such as the UAW, having failed to achieve broad social and economic reform, would focus on winning company-specific wage and benefit gains at the bargaining table. These bargaining gains were not inconsequential. They created a large American "middle class" whose buying power staved off further economic collapse and fueled the material prosperity of the 1950s and 1960s. Labor as a social movement, however, had moved toward labor the interest group. National policy would promote a limited liberal version of the welfare state. At the same time, a bastard form of Keynesian economic policy reduced the government's role to limited regulations and narrow fiscal policy.[18] The market, not social partnership or public policy, would determine the fate of American postwar prosperity.

A Liberal, Not Social Democratic, Response to Civil Rights

Cold War politics and consumeristic individualism would not go unchallenged. The civil rights movement and the New Left of the 1960s forced major changes in the American political and social landscape. However, the narrow confines of postwar liberalism continued to confine social and economic reforms. While in Europe the social democratic seeds of the 1930s and 1940s would bloom, in the United States the foundations were laid for the conservative revolution of the 1980s.

The civil rights movement put the central economic and social contradictions of American society back onto the national stage.[19] As the buttresses of Southern apartheid began to fall, the economic barriers faced by much of black America became ever clearer. The civil rights movement would, in part, split over these economic questions. Having dismantled Jim Crow, would civil rights activism attempt to integrate within the boundaries of American liberal society, or would the movement challenge the very nature of that society, especially its gross economic inequalities? Before his death, for example, Martin Luther King Jr. was preparing to use the tactics of the civil rights struggle to launch a multiracial poor people's movement. Such calls would have forced the nation to confront the inter-

twined class and racial economic issues that lay at the foundation of American capitalism.

Pressures from the civil rights struggle and the ghetto revolts did force the Johnson administration to launch the Great Society programs and declare a War on Poverty. The latter encompassed several national measures, including the training, education, and job opportunity programs of the Job Corps, Neighborhood Youth Corps, Manpower Development Training Act, the Upward Bound college program, Head Start, and the Teacher Corps. The War on Poverty also led to food stamps, the school lunch program, Title I of the Education and Secondary Education Act, Medicaid, neighborhood health centers, Legal Services, the enhancement of Social Security, the Economic Opportunity Act, Model Cities, and Community Action. In the second half of the 1960s, total public expenditures on social insurance and income transfer assistance programs doubled to $61 billion—growing from 4.6 to 6.1 percent of the GNP. While cause and effect between government policies and end results is always a complicated matter, poverty among Americans did decline from nearly one out of five Americans at the beginning of the War on Poverty to one out of ten by 1973.

For all its flowing rhetoric, however, the Great Society and its War on Poverty remained within the liberal boundaries set by the narrowing of the New Deal. Government programs focused on removing obstacles and preparing people to effectively compete in the private market. The basic fundamentals of American capitalism and the limited reach of governmental social and economic policies went unchallenged. The intellectual effort behind the War on Poverty also included no small amount of research and rhetoric that blamed the victim by identifying supposed "social pathologies" and other "deficiencies" of the poor. Official debates sought the roots of poverty in an eclectic mixture of factors that sidestepped questions of corporate power.

Although the majority of poor people in this country were and continue to be white, debates over poverty cloaked this question primarily as an issue of race. Thus, the economic issues raised by the civil rights movement and the ghetto uprisings became "minority" questions outside the core of American "middle class" society. The separation of race and class was also reflected in the contradictory manner by which the American labor movement approached the great civil rights battles of the 1950s and 1960s. Individual unions did play a direct role. The UAW, for example, helped pull together the famous 1964 March on Washington. Prior to the action in the nation's capital, a multiracial support parade of over one hundred thousand marched through the streets of Detroit. The AFL-CIO teamed up with the NAACP to successfully lobby Congress to include fair employment practices in the famous 1964 Civil Rights Act. Originally, the legislation outlawed racial discrimination in public accommodations but said little about private workplaces. Yet, much of the house of labor stuck to the narrow confines of the postwar deal and sat on the sidelines. The AFL-CIO's lobbying efforts were not accompanied by a strong campaign to deal with racism within labor's own ranks. Indeed, from the perspective of the civil rights activists, some unions, such as in the building trades, were part of the problem of racial discrimination. For African-American critics of the mainstream civil rights movement, such as Malcolm X, even support from unions such as the UAW was part of a general problem in which the actions of white liberals ended up steering black activism down narrow paths. Certainly, the civil rights and labor movement never coalesced into a unified force for building a new and social democratic New Deal.

The Great Society and War on Poverty did offer some promise. The programs mobilized the capacity of the national government behind society's least-advantaged, and they did assert a positive role for government in fostering social and economic change. Furthermore, a new agency, the Office of Economic Opportunity, broke with the New Deal tradition of administering programs through local governments. To get around local defenders of Jim Crow, the agency placed funds directly in the hands of com-

munity activists through direct grants to public and private nonprofit organizations. Thus, federal funds went to support neighborhood health centers, emergency food and medical services, local job and literacy training, various counseling programs, and migrant workers' assistance.[20]

While this community action funding was embedded in the War on Poverty's various "culture of poverty" notions, it did place funds into the hands of people who had been powerless. While the Office of Economic Opportunity favored black moderates, funds also ended up in the hands of more left-leaning civil rights activists. In a significant number of cases, community action money helped provide local residents the resources to speak with their own voice. The political and economic establishments did not like what they heard. In Newark, New Jersey, for example, community-action-funded organizations provided a base for mobilizing poor people against the establishment's agenda of "urban renewal." The attempt to use Model City funds to clear 150 acres of ghetto housing for a medical and dental college was greeted by powerful grassroots resistance. In 1965, Congress caved in to the pressures of local political establishments by passing a series of amendments that removed the Office of Economic Opportunity's mandate to use "maximum feasible participation" in the implementation of its programs. In 1973, the Nixon administration abolished the Office of Economic Opportunity altogether.[21]

The reorientation and subsequent cancellation of programs such as community action stripped the War on Poverty of its most potentially progressive features. What remained was an increasingly bureaucratic system of patronizing and narrow social programs run by a "liberal elite" that conservatives would become so fond of caricaturing in the years to come.

Liberalism Survives the 1960s

The student revolt and social upheavals of the 1960s and early 1970s placed the dark sides of American society once again into public debate.[22] Indeed, it demonstrated that the very people who benefited most from material prosperity could reject the "affluent society" as oppressive and life destroying. The 1960s activism produced a series of changes. It furthered the battle against racism. It sparked a deep and ongoing revolution in gender roles and attitudes. It gave birth to the modern gay/lesbian/bisexual movement and the modern environmental movement. Furthermore, a new generation of workers questioned the postwar deal that had traded material prosperity for work that was often monotonous, dangerous, and alienating. A wave of wildcat strikes and new militant worker organizations raised issues of class, race, and gender within the working class. While the AFL-CIO supported the Vietnam War, individual unions such as the UAW did not. The general antiwar movement left American policy makers shackled by the "Vietnam Syndrome" of potential mass resistance to direct and prolonged U.S. military intervention abroad.

However, at a policy level, the reforms that came out of the 1960s and early 1970s remained confined within the boundaries of postwar liberalism. These limitations can be seen even in one of the boldest reform proposals of the period—Nixon's Family Assistance Plan (FAP). The plan offered a universally guaranteed minimum income through a negative income tax. Low-wage workers would receive a systematic public income to supplement their wages. The FAP would have largely equalized earnings at the bottom of the wage scale between blacks and whites, men and women, and low- and better-paid workers. The threat of further urban revolts helped spark the proposal. However, the FAP also fulfilled conservative ends. The Republican Party had just begun its Southern strategy to capture the white backlash to the civil rights movement. The FAP would have helped the party woo poor and working-class whites. It reinforced patriarchy by steering employment and training assistance to men. Indeed, the FAP was designed in part to counter the so-called "crisis of the black family." Patronizing researchers and policy makers had concluded that

the key to helping black America lay in restoring the male to his proper role as head of the household. The FAP also stretched, but ultimately fell within, the narrow confines of postwar liberalism. Not only did it not challenge low-wage employers, it would have actually subsidized their operations by having the public provide a portion of the wage. The FAP's demise before a mixture of opposition took down with it any hope for any further major extensions of the New Deal—such as a national day-care plan.[23]

During the 1960s, many activists challenged the very nature of society and called for revolutionary changes. However, actual policy campaigns operated largely within the boundaries of interest group politics. Thus, government reforms affirmed the capitalist marketplace by removing barriers to equal participation. Increases in spending to programs, such as Nixon's increases to Social Security and food stamps, and new programs, such as those for the disabled, did not push social spending past liberal boundaries. Targeted government regulations curbed the worst excesses of corporate behavior but did not question the right of the market and business, rather than conscious public action, to decide the economic fate of the country. The Occupational Safety and Health Act, for example, was a major political victory for organized labor. However, its enforcement mechanisms relied on government administration rather than empowering workers on the shop floor. Fundamental economic questions remained off the policy table. The New Deal Coalition remained a collection of specialized and fragmented interest groups.

The Historical Triumph of Liberalism

The preceding overview suggests that the weakness of social democracy in the United States does not come from a lack of interest. Indeed, we saw how the nation has produced powerful social movements that, under a different historical experience, could have secured broad social democratic–oriented policies and institutions. The policy limitations came from the ability of various elements within the

American power structure to direct this social energy into the more narrow boundaries of a reform-minded liberalism. The final outcomes, however, were ultimately the results of the historical battles within particular historical conditions.

These historical battles do point to several powerful forces that continue to evolve within American society to impede social change. These elements include the nation's ongoing struggle with racism and our unique two-party system. History also reveals that for all of the hoopla about the Bill of Rights and the rule of law, our nation has experienced a level of violence in defense of capitalism that stands out among the ranks of industrialized countries. This includes the military force used against the labor movement and the extensive covert policy operations made against the civil rights movement and the New Left. We can also identify the ongoing role of corporate liberalism as a tool for coopting and demobilizing mass unrest.

While these elements remain forces that progressives must grapple with today, they are not static and permanent roadblocks to progressive change. Many offer two sides. The level of violence seen in U.S. labor history, for example, testifies to the level of radicalism that American workers have displayed in the workplace. Indeed, historians have repeatedly grappled with ironic contradiction shown between American workplace militancy and political apathy. Similarly, while racism has served as a ball on the chain of many progressive movements, it has also sparked such great mass movements as abolitionism and civil rights. Furthermore, historical battles did make lasting inroads into the forces arrayed against progressive change. Open and legalized racism, for example, is today the exception not the rule. Today, institutional racism operates in much subtler and more hidden ways than in the past. In addition, centuries of struggle against racism within popular movements have clearly changed the contours of progressive activism. American progressives are not doomed to simply repeat past divisions and limitations around race. Finally, as we will see below, one

major obstacle, liberal reformism, today looks quite moribund, while the pillars of the two-party system rest no longer on active popular engagement but on mass cynicism and apathy.

The track record in the United States demonstrates that new mass movements will arise to press the battle further. Indeed, as Part II will demonstrate, America's grassroots today offer rich signs that our nation is heading toward a new wave of social awakening. As we will see below, current economic and political conditions hardly point to a mere repetition of past victories and defeats. Indeed, twenty years of corporate restructuring has stripped away much of the liberal reform order that proved so instrumental in containing social movement gains over the last century.

The Legacy of Liberal America

The triumph of liberal over social democratic reform has left an ongoing legacy in American politics and economic structures. This inheritance presents progressives today with both obstacles and opportunities.

The Rise of the New Right

While American liberalism proved an effective tool for limiting the boundaries of progressive reform, it also established fertile ground for the rebirth of conservative politics. Liberalism helped lay the groundwork for today's "conservative revolution" at five major levels.

First, it focused the welfare state around narrow means-tested programs and income transfers rather than universal services. As discussed in chapter 1, such a welfare state is vulnerable to the right-wing politics of division. Many Americans experience a sense that only a fraction of the money taken from their paycheck actually ever benefits them and their community. While this feeling may at times overstate the reality, in truth a huge amount of people's federal tax money, indeed a majority according to some counts, does go to military spending and corporate welfare. With American liberalism sharing in the Cold War and its general silence on "aid to dependent corporations," right-wing politicians can steer popular resentment at the rather modest liberal welfare programs that they tarnish with benefiting "those people."

Second, in the transition from New Deal to Great Society, the official axis of government reform moved from class to race. Even though most poor Americans are white, official debates over liberal reforms were often couched in racial terms. Ultimately, when constrained by liberal acceptance of the basic structures of society, such a focus does not lead to an effective discussion of racism, however. Effective explorations of race must be connected to issues of class and capitalism. Narrow liberal debates over race simply reduce social reform to matters of state supports for "minority" concerns. Thus, conservatives enjoyed an opportunity to split working-class whites away from working-class blacks, Latinos, and other people of color. The new right tapped white working-class frustrations with declining living standards by substituting race, and resentment against a mythical minority living off special privileges, for the real source of falling living standards: the corporate restructuring of the economy. The narrow confines of liberal reform helped play into right-wing images of the "limousine liberals" who lived high off public cash given to "those people."

Third, liberalism focused economic debates on the narrow single issues of interest group politics. Raising fundamental economic questions, by contrast, favors broad alliances as people unite across class, race, and gender to face the common problem of corporate power. By denying such broader questions and by taking the basic contours of American capitalism for granted, liberalism helped reduce debates over the economy to disconnected questions of interest rates, government spending, deficits, and taxes. The new right used the opportunity to step into the vacuum by raising issues that divide the New Deal Coalition: crime, abortion, gun control, welfare, school prayer, and homophobia.

Fourth, by failing to pursue any meaningful form of social partnership and by limiting and dismantling programs such as Community Action, liberalism helped reduce government policy to the bureaucratic administration that conservatives are so found of caricaturing. Indeed, as Francis Fox Piven and Richard Cloward argued in their famous 1971 work *Regulating the Poor*, the often paternalistic and top-down operation of many government poverty programs betrayed a purpose for controlling, as much as helping, the poor. The new right took people's general sense of disempowerment in a society dominated by concentrations of power and directed it narrowly at public employees. Having failed to question the legitimacy of exclusive corporate control over the economy, liberalism provided little material for countering with the more numerous examples of corporate inefficiencies and bureaucratic irrationality. As progressive economist David Gordon detailed in his book *Fat and Mean*, American corporations are saddled with an adversarial form of worker-company management that leaves them particularly top heavy. In the United States, 13 percent of the workforce is classified as managerial or administrative, compared with 3.9 percent in Germany, 4.2 in Japan, and 2.6 in Sweden. While some of the contrast may come from the different ways nations classify employees, the spectacular contrast in official figures nevertheless suggests that U.S. corporations are certainly vulnerable to charges of bureaucratic waste far more destructive than the worst examples of government ineptitude.[24] Furthermore, the most blatant examples of government waste are, arguably, the high amounts of public money that shamelessly go to bloated military contracts and other forms of corporate welfare—examples that liberalism is ill equipped to raise.

Finally, both liberalism and conservative politics rest on this nation's low voter turnout rates and depressed political participation. While the most direct legal restrictions used to defeat populism and socialism are no longer in operation, the overall discouragement of mass political participation remains.

The lack of a genuinely left-wing political party in American politics denies the majority of Americans access to political agendas best suited to inspire their participation. In turn, a demobilized electorate makes progressive political organizing a more involved undertaking than winning votes. Both major parties have consciously and unconsciously allowed their grassroots structures to decay. Indeed, at an organizational level, neither the Democrats nor the Republicans can be called political parties in the classic definition of the term. Legally they do not exist at a national level, their base organization being the state party. And from the state on down, the Democrat and Republican parties are generally loose, candidate-centered networks that come together during election time, rather than real organizations of mass political participation. Both parties favor a politics of media advertising that largely avoids serious discussion of comprehensive policy and that substitutes corporate money in place of grassroots enthusiasm. While a demobilized public serves elite interest generally, it particularly favors right-wing politics. As has been amply documented, the ranks of the minority of Americans who vote is clearly skewed toward the better off, while much of the voting base for a social democratic majority stays home. The 1994 "Republican Revolution" came from narrow margins among the 38 percent of Americans who bothered to go to the polls. Thus, less than one out of six Americans actively chose to have a Republican Congress.

Faced with an aggressive and ascendant new right, by the 1980s American liberalism proved a weak counterforce. Since actual conservative policies, especially its economic agenda, address the interests of only a tiny minority of Americans, conservative politics should be quite vulnerable. However, an effective counterattack requires going exactly where American liberalism refused to go. Right-wing government bashing and selfish individualism can be countered only with a full-scale, unapologetic advocacy of expanded public and collective spheres. Universal social citizenship is the best reply to government bashing. A half-hearted defense of welfare for the poor, for example, is not going to unleash the enthusiasm of the apathetic majority the same way that advocacy of a universal family allowance, paid parental leave, national health care, a living minimum wage, paid vacation time, a shorter workweek, and subsidized child care would. All of these social democratic reforms would both better address the needs of poor families and connect such interests to the material needs of the vast majority of Americans.

Capturing the political initiative from the right also requires mobilizing the vast majority of Americans. The largest political block in the United States is the party of nonvoters. As E. E. Schattschneider wrote three decades ago: "Anyone who finds out how to involve the forty million [nonvoters] in American politics will run the country for a generation."[25] Jesse Jackson's 1984 and 1988 presidential bids offered the Democratic Party a path to majority power by mobilizing this silent majority through social democratic–style reforms that would further distinguish the Democrats from their Republican opponents. The potential strength of this strategy was suggested in 1988 by the 7 million votes cast for Jackson in the Democratic primary despite the overwhelmingly negative coverage heaped on his campaign by the nation's media. Jackson won these votes through both his agenda and the efforts of thousands of grassroots activists to raise voter turnout among working-class voters. Instead, the Democrats chose the opposite route to power. As Clinton-style right-wing "centrism" became the party's national image, the Jackson camp was marginalized within the party. Centrist Democrats attempt to compete with the Republicans by stealing away the active swing voters. However, this continued competition between right-wing politics and right-wing-politics-with-a-human-face has produced further declines in voter turnout and guaranteed that official political debate ignores the major social and economic questions facing the nation. The fiasco of Albert Gore's 2000 presidential bid underlines the continued weakness of centrist politics—especially when forced to confront Republicans skilled at adopting a "moderate" image even when their policies are right wing.

The "Casino Economy"

The narrow confines of liberal reform have also helped encourage a distinctly American and short-sighted form of capitalism. Chapter 4 provided data suggesting that U.S. long-term postwar economic performance has proven inferior to that of the rest of the industrial world. The underlying weakness of the American economy has grown considerably as the nation's financial system separates further and further from on-the-ground social and economic health.

Our government's mild liberal interventions into the realms of finance have coupled with the explosive growth of private pensions (a result of limited Social Security pensions) to produce a financial system that even some corporate leaders complain is particularly shortsighted. While the majority of resources for business investment comes from internal profits, companies also need to secure capital outside their operations. The U.S. economy stands out by the degree to which our stock market, rather than banks or other forms of direct credit, fills this financial role. While companies gain from Wall Street investment, the U.S. stock market places investors in a dangerously powerful position. The financial resources that come from issuing new stock are a one-shot deal. The ownership and influence that this stock provides, however, is permanent.

Once a company issues stock, its management must compete in two markets: one for the product, the other for stock owners. If investors lose confidence in a firm's management, they can send the company into a financial crisis simply by selling off stock. While such investor control may sound like a healthy check against mismanagement, the stockholders' power over major U.S. corporations has become all the more ominous. Today, the majority of stocks in publicly traded American firms are held by institutional stockholders—insurance companies, mutual funds, brokerage firms, and so on. While, in

1950, institutional stockholders held only 8 percent of all stock, in 1990, this share had climbed to 60 percent.[26]

The private pensions that mushroomed during the postwar boom provided a major impetus behind the growth of these investment firms. Confined to negotiating private benefits for their membership through collective bargaining, unions successfully fought to get companies to set aside pension money into funds separate from company operations. Such advanced funding was critical to protecting the long-term pension safety. Without such steps, future company financial difficulties or bankruptcy could wipe out workers' retirement. Institutional investment companies grew tremendously out of the need to manage and invest these now-massive funds.

Institutional investors buy and sell huge amounts of stock aiming to increase the size of their overall portfolio. The timeline that governs their definitions of success, however, can be quite short. Many mutual funds, for example, report back to their customers in quarterly reports. On average, domestic stock funds turn over nearly two-thirds of their holdings each year.[27] Thus, American managers can face serious pressure to deliver in this short time horizon. This priority means pursuing the low road. Outsourcing or demanding wage concessions improves the quarterly report. High-road strategies such as worker training and product development simply use up resources in the short run.

Pressures for short-term performance can force U.S. managers to act against their better judgment. Reflecting on his experiences as chairman of Chrysler Corporation, for example, Lee Iacocca explained:

> We're short term in our outlook because most of our stock belongs to institutional investors who'll lose interest in it the minute that earnings statement turns sour.
>
> That's tough enough for a manager to deal with, but when the raiders get involved—people who buy huge chunks of stock to hold for a couple

of weeks or a couple of days looking for an over-night windfall—you've got even bigger problems. You're forced to do things that make no business sense at all just to stay alive.[28]

The raiders that Iacocca refers to represent the worst excess of American finance. Raiders grab control of a company by purchasing a controlling share of its stock. This is typically done by offering stock-holders a quite generous price and hence a quick profit. To finance the takeover, raiders go into serious debt. Once they are in control of the company, they then pursue the shortest of short-term strategies—often simply stripping companies of anything of value. Their goal is to have a pot of gold that they can walk away with once they have paid off the debt and left the company in ruin. Even the threat of stock-holder action can force U.S. companies to mortgage their long-term plans in the interests of short-term survival. For example, fearing a hostile takeover by stockholder Kirk Kerkorian in 1995, the Chrysler Corporation had to take resources slated for new product development and use them to buy back its own stock. This action raised the stock's value enough to persuade shareholders not sell to Kerkorian.[29] However, it compromised the company's long-term strategic plans.

The fate of U.S. Steel amply demonstrates how the stock market can take precedence over the product market. At the beginning of the 1980s, U.S. Steel had the most productive steel operations in the world—bringing in a 7 percent annual return, the best in the industry. However, as CEO David Roderick told the press: "We are in the business to make money not steel." The best steel mills in the nation could not compete in Roderick's mind with the much higher annual returns offered by oil, shopping malls, and other industries. In a telling move, the company changed its name to its stock market symbol, USX, and proceeded to use the profits of its steel operations to finance its move into these other sectors. The steel mills were allowed to atrophy. When the Japanese, Brazilians, and Germans flooded American steel markets,

USX's aging plants couldn't compete. Rather than blaming their deliberate disinvestment, however, upper management decided the problem was their so-called overpriced union workforce.

The influence of the stock market over American economic decisions, coupled with the lack of any pretense of public or government planning, suggests the scary conclusion that our nation's economic future is being driven without any long-term vision at all. Indeed, our economy suggests the image of a ship with no one at the helm while investor passengers scramble between themselves for the greatest spoils among first class. The free-market ideology shared by both American liberals and conservatives makes the situation worse as policy makers eat away at the safeguards put in place in response to the last great economic collapse.

Prosperity Blues

As a result of conservative resurgence and a Wall Street–driven capitalism, our nation sailed through the 1990s with an official prosperity that leaves the majority of the population in an alarmingly insecure position. A few statistics are enough to illustrate the point.[30] After a decade of economic boom, the buying power of wages for the majority of Americans remains below 1989 levels. Although many families spent the 1980s and 1990s sending both spouses out to work, overall family purchasing power has barely increased. On average, American families worked 129 more hours in 1997 than they did in 1987 but have little to show for the sacrifice. Indeed, during the longest boom in the nation's postwar history, more and more Americans can maintain their standard of living only by going further and further into debt. The U.S. savings rate was 2.3 percent in 1999, down from 10.6 percent in 1984. By the end of the 1990s, banks and credit institutions were lobbying the halls of government to rewrite the nation's personal bankruptcy laws in order to ensure that payments to them, not for items such as child support, get top priority.

The source of these disturbing statistics is not hard to find. The 1990s boom was built by transferring wealth from the many to the corporate few. The share of the nation's wealth owned by the richest 1 percent rose to 40.4 percent by 1997—putting the ratio nearly at the 44 percent high point reached in 1929, the year beginning the Great Depression. The fact that CEO pay at large corporations went from forty-two times the average factory worker's pay in 1980 to 419 times it in 1998 conveys a pretty good sense that American corporations have drastically increased their ability to extract an ever greater share of the economic pie out of working Americans.

As their lobbying behavior demonstrates, American credit card companies have certainly become aware of the possibilities for the future. If a decade-long boom has only strained the lives of most Americans without delivering real standard-of-living gains, what is going to happen when the economy inevitably runs out of steam? Twenty years of corporate offensive also demonstrates that American companies have, by and large, failed to find ways to compete other than extracting an ever larger share of wealth from their workforce and the community. For all the hype about the new high-tech economy, our nation's dominant service sector economy remains trapped in low-road methods. Although since the 1970s productivity growth has slowed throughout the industrialized world, the stagnating performance has been especially long lasting and severe in the United States. Poor productivity performance has been especially noticeable in the nation's nonmanufacturing sectors. While output per labor-hour in U.S. manufacturing rose by 2.6 percent between 1979 and 1990 and 3.4 percent between 1993 and 1996, it only increased by 1 percent and half a percent in all nonfarm business over the same period.[31] Firms that have attempted to compete through higher wages, training, and ecological sustainability are the exception, not the rule. And they must operate in an overall political and economic environment that hardly supports such high-road thinking.

Today's Progressive Opportunities

While the legacy of historical battles shapes current politics, new developments have also created new opportunities for organizing for fundamental economic change.

How the United States Is Not Different from Europe

While an important mixture of history separates the United States from Europe, in looking toward the possibilities of a more progressive future, we should note our common experience. Seen from the perspective of the long-term evolution of capitalism, the differences between the United States and Europe represent variations on a common theme. Both American liberalism and European social democracy rested on a postwar deal between business and the labor movement. Labor dropped its calls for abolishing capitalism and recognized the fundamental right of management to run the company. Thus, basic investment and other microeconomic decisions would not be subject to public debate or controls. In return, business agreed to accept the existence of unions and bargain over the distribution of the economic pie. Governments influenced the distribution of wealth through powers of taxation and spending. They could also influence investment decisions by shaping the macroeconomic contours within which business operated. However, neither unions, nor workers, nor governments interfered with the core rights of capitalist ownership.

The difference between the United States and Europe lay in the exact way in which social movements influenced the specific development of their nation's worker-management bargaining, macroeconomic policies, and governmental spending. As discussed in chapters 1 through 4, these institutional differences have a significant impact on the quality of life and economic vitality found within contrasting national versions of capitalism. However, today both American and European progressives face the same fundamental challenges presented by the global crisis of capitalism and its corporate solution. Both American and European activists need the same necessary remedy: far greater public control over capitalist activity. Whether in Europe or the United States, people must dare to question the fundamental prerogatives of management. For the past twenty years, to one degree or another, corporations have questioned the terms of the postwar deal. Thus far, however, the dominant political leaders of the major parties allied with labor in both the United States and Europe have proven unwilling to do the same. The task on both sides of the Atlantic is, therefore, to build a renewed social movement for economic democracy.

Backwardness Can Provide Advantages As Well As Obstacles

Past historical limitations and defeats, while shaping the present, do not predetermine the future. Indeed, seeming backwardness during one historical era can lead to a leading role in the next era. Ironically, European social democracy drew political advantage because of Europe's backwardness in electoral democracy relative to the United States. Universal suffrage among white men came one hundred years earlier in the United States than it did in most of Europe. While a hindrance, the battle for the right to vote also helped European social democratic parties grow as mass movements. When the right to vote was won, Europe's small elite parties had to play catch-up to left parties with an established grassroots. By contrast, when the corresponding populist and socialist revolts developed in the United States, they had to contend with an elite party tradition that had had a century of practice in finding grassroots ways to generate local political loyalties.

Similarly, historians have attributed both Japanese and German economic success, in part, to the active role their states played in promoting industrialization. Both nations entered the ranks of industrialized nations relatively late in the game. This relative backwardness required extensive governmental intervention for industrialization to proceed. Both Britain, the world economic power, and the rising star the United States could afford laissez-faire economic policies. Germany and Japan, by contrast, could not afford the luxury of leaving economic development to the dictates of the market. Over the long haul, this state planning left both nations with economies that enjoy certain long-term advantages over our system.

The final stage of the American rise to industrial predominance rose out of backwardness. The fact that an American, Henry Ford, first implemented the modern system of industrial mass production comes as no surprise. During the late nineteenth and early twentieth centuries, the United States suffered from a major shortage of skilled workers. The great waves of immigrants coming from such places as Europe did not include significant numbers of skilled automobile craftsmen. These highly valuable workers had a prosperous living where they lived in the home country. Supply drove wage rates. Thus, during the early years of the auto industry, American manufacturers operated with significantly higher labor costs than their European counterparts. This disadvantage pushed U.S. employers to innovate far sooner than in Europe. Henry Ford found a way to use the vast ranks of immigrant labor by standardizing work into hundreds of mind-numbing assembly-line jobs requiring little or no prior skill. By the end of the 1920s, the productive capacity of America's mass assembly lines was far ahead of Europe's.

At a certain level, the very excesses of America's particular brand of capitalism make the need for major public intervention all the more visible. The outright economic abandonment of so many American cities, a phenomenon without parallel in Europe, provides a screaming need that could offer a laboratory of progressive institutional change. Similarly, the continued lack of national investment in basic material and social economic infrastructure points to the need for a major reevaluation of the priorities of public spending. Our nation is also at the center of the ecological crisis. More so than any country in the world, our basic quality of life is being choked under the weight of rampant and unsustainable material consumption. Finally, the casino economy of our nation's financial system cannot but produce economic disasters that will further highlight the need for a far more rational, and potentially publicly controlled, system of economic investment. Imagine, for example, if the public bailout of the savings and loan industry had been conducted by extending greater public controls over the industry, rather than simply using taxpayer money to protect the assets of the private investors.

The End of Liberalism

There is a saying in union organizing circles that "management is often the best organizer." Sooner or later, the company will provide workers with plenty of reasons to want to form a union. The same can be said of the current political scene. While the conservative agenda has been painful, ugly, and threatening over the last two decades, it has also helped progressive activism by thoroughly discrediting mainstream liberalism. The establishment no longer has the liberal tools to coopt and narrow popular unrest the way it did in the postwar period. For the foreseeable future, no New Deal or Great Society is on the horizon. The terrain of significant social and economic reform has been left for progressive activism to occupy.

While liberal reform as a political agenda has been largely abandoned by the political establishment, this does not mean that the values espoused by both liberal and social democratic traditions have no continued resonance among the general public. Beliefs in fundamental fair play, nondiscrimination, equal opportunity, democracy and popular control, community, and human connection arguably remain deeply held social norms. Mainstream politicians realize the strengths of these values. Thus, President Clinton campaigned on rhetoric that made ample use of images that touched such beliefs. His actual neoliberal policies, however, offered only cynical and narrow adjustments to a menacing status quo. Today, progressive reform provides the only mechanism for translating people's basic values into concrete policy.

Taking the nation's history as a whole, one of the ongoing myths buttressing American politics has been an unquestioned belief in progress. As bad as things seemed, mainstream politics could always promise, if not always deliver, that conditions would improve as the nation marched down a path of ever-increasing prosperity. Today, however, mainstream politics has lost this collective vision. The belief that the next generation will live better than the current one is no longer taken for granted. Rather, mainstream American politics increasingly revolves around the cynical hope for hanging on to what people already have. The best way to a happy future is to shore up one's personal possessions and build the wall of private security. Dark apocalyptic visions saturate contemporary culture. Witness, for example, the often violent themes that pervade corporate movies and television, in which individuals struggle against an uncaring and hostile world.

A political system that appeals primarily to the fears of the minority of the population who actually vote is a fragile house of cards. Progressives have the opportunity to present the only agenda that offers people a believable hope for a brighter future. Progressive politics provides the only agenda with an unqualified belief in the positive nature of human beings and the promise of mobilizing that potential for wholesale social advancement. It places the roots of social problems in social institutions and power structures that human hands can change. Today, cynicism, the belief in the impossibility of change, is a major tool protecting establishment politics. The politics of hope offers a powerful antidote.

From Interest Groups to
Social Movements

In discrediting mild, market-oriented liberal reform, corporate politics and economic restructuring has rendered interest-group politics far less viable. The grassroots experiences that we will detail in Part II paint a picture of a diverse collection of progressive groups that have all reached the same conclusion:

Working in the old ways is no longer as effective as it was. Focusing on a single issue and mobilizing a distinct group of interest around that issue does not deliver the same success that it did when liberal politics dominated during the postwar boom. The neoliberal agenda is far less open to being pushed in a progressive direction than a liberalism that at least acknowledged a positive role for government in social and economic change.

Conservative politics and corporate economics cannot be defeated piecemeal. While issue activism will remain the bread and butter of progressive organizing, today groups must seek broader alliances. All of the examples that we will examine below share the common experience of local groups coming together in coalitions. Participants repeatedly describe these experiences as unique or noteworthy for their breadth and strength. More and more individual groups seem to be looking for more comprehensive solutions. Separate issues have become more visibly linked to the common problem of corporate power and the basic economic direction of the country.

When economics is broadly defined as the way people make their basic livelihood—be it production or reproduction—then what could be called the "economic question"—who controls the economy, how it is organized, and for what purpose—has been at the core of most of this country's great social movements from abolitionism to women's rights to labor organizing. Certainly, the "economic question" lay behind the three great social upheavals of the twentieth century—the union organizing of the 1930s and 1940s, the modern civil rights movement, and the social movements of the sixties. While certainly each period had significant overlap with the others, in both people and ideals, each major current occurred in historical succession, not as three legs of a common political force. Looking into the next century, progressives must consider the serious possibility that conservative politics and global corporate restructuring may have laid the material conditions to bring all major currents of social activism together. If properly conceived, the economic question as it is emerging today encompasses issues of class, race, gender, ecology, and community. It points toward a bold agenda of economic democracy and fundamental societal change.

In the Belly of the Beast

American progressives often bemoan the lack of democratic reforms relative to the social and economic achievement of social democracy in Europe. However, today and for the foreseeable future, we live in the one single country best positioned to influence the course of world history. The material preconditions already exist for the United States to chart a fundamentally different direction solely on our nation's own resources.

For example, the U.S. Congress already has control over funds that could be used for major steps toward establishing social citizenship. Total military spending—including the Department of Defense and all the other military-related items elsewhere in the budget—accounts for one-quarter of federal spending and half of all discretionary funds that Congress decides each year how to allocate. Military spending amounts to roughly $350 billion annually. This sum exceeds all social spending combined, excluding the Social Security trust fund. The Pentagon's official justification for this massive national commitment is the need to fight two wars the size of the Gulf War simultaneously in two different parts of the world—a need that arguably most Americans would find hard to justify, especially if you compare it to other possible uses. That mainstream politicians and media will not even raise the question of the level of military spending, offers an opportunity for progressive politics to break the silence.

In examining the pressures of so-called globalization, the United States is also the one nation most capable of defying the new world order. The United States has the largest internal consumer market in the world. Eighty percent of all our economic activity, and 90 percent below the Fortune 500 companies, is for domestic use. While the dollar no longer holds the status of a fixed world currency (as was the case during the postwar boom), it is still one of the world's central currencies. Our long-term negative trade balance means that Americans import far more than we export. Coupled with the vast size of the U.S. consumer market, this means that when regions of the world talk about exporting their way to economic prosperity, they are often talking about selling to Americans. Quite simply, if a progressive U.S. government were to enact popular controls over capital flows into and out of the country and to restrict imports to only goods produced under socially and environmentally sound conditions, there is not a great deal that the rest of the world could do about it. Furthermore, American multinationals cannot easily threaten to simply leave the country if they do not like government policy. While they can build abroad, they still have to sell their products back in the United States.

For decades, American officials have demonstrated their private awareness of the ability of this country to achieve unilateral action. Unilateral policy practice has been the general rule in American military affairs, despite the fig leaf of "coalition" campaigns. Furthermore, critiques of American foreign policy also point to our nation's long-standing policy tradition of using the nation's central position in the world economy to force our domestic economic problems onto the rest of the world through unilateral trade, currency, and interest-rate policies. Indeed, the neoliberal world order has developed only to the extent that our nation has succeeded in propelling it onto the rest of the world.[32]

Progressive change in the United States would arguably bring the entire process of corporate globalization to a screeching halt. While the WTO and the various free trade agreements establish clear guidelines for lowering public standards to the lowest levels, the world economy has yet to produce a global authority capable of enforcing "free trade." Ultimately, individual national governments have to enforce WTO rulings.[33] The United States is still the big economic powerhouse in this regard, in terms of both its own economic strength and the central role it plays in institutions such as the IMF and the World Bank. U.S.

policy makers have the power to decide which WTO rulings to pursue and which to ignore. When American authorities seem to bow down before a WTO decision against U.S. labor or environmental standards, they are displaying more their ties to corporate interests hostile to such standards in the first place, rather than surrendering to an all-powerful global force.

Furthermore, faced with half a century of opposition from revolutionary and nationalist movements throughout the developing world, global capitalism has maintained itself only through the strength of direct and indirect military intervention. The United States has served, and continues to serve, as capitalism's global policeman. The direct invasions of Vietnam, Grenada, Panama, and so on. have been amply supplemented with covert operations to overthrow and destabilize "questionable" governments and movements throughout the globe. Although nations such as Germany and Japan have begun to expand their quite limited military abilities, it is clear that for the foreseeable future, the American role as world policeman will remain intact. Thus, the simple progressive acts of cutting the U.S. military budget, restricting future foreign military interventions, and withdrawing all military support for foreign governments would have a decisive influence over the future of world history.

In short, we live in the country most responsible for today's economic order. Our nation's weak liberalism, its casino economy, and its relative autonomy and power meant that when world capitalism slowed down in the 1970s, the United States would give birth to the new corporate agenda. As the remaining world superpower, the United States is the driving force behind global free trade liberalization and economic restructuring. When European progressives organize against economic change, they are battling attempts to reorient their economies more like the United States. Living in the belly of the contemporary world capitalism, American progressives need to think big. Just as our version of capitalism is driving current change, so can progressive reform in the United States change the course of world history.

Part II

Organizing for the High Road at Home

7

The Living Wage Movement Sweeps the Nation!

If one had to pick a single sign to demonstrate the beginnings of a grassroots reawakening in America that sign would come from the mushrooming living wage movement. By mid-2001, sixty-eight communities had passed living wage ordinances. At least seventy other localities had active campaigns to do so (see Tables 7.1 and 7.2). Successful living wage efforts spanned from the nation's largest cities—New York, Chicago, and Los Angeles—to Ypsilanti, Michigan, population twenty-five thousand. While active living wage coalitions are found in areas of traditional progressive strength—the Northeast, the industrial Midwest, and the West Coast—today such campaigns also dot the South and the Southwest. In the past couple of years, living wage organizing has also broken out on American campuses—with nearly a dozen university campaigns now under way.

The effectiveness of the living wage concept lies in its ability to combine concrete practical efforts to impact local policy with deeper questions about the economic direction of our society. Living wage campaigns unite broad coalitions, take people out into the streets, place the reality of working poor into public debate, and point to fundamental questions concerning economic development, corporate responsibility, and governmental accountability. Their pervasive appeal makes them an ideal tool for movement building. Thus, by examining living wage efforts, we gain a window into the heart of today's grassroots resurgence. For greater details on the nuts

and bolts of both organizing these campaigns and the opposition's tactics, see our two-hundred-page handbook, *Living Wage Campaigns: An Activist's Guide to Building the Movement for Economic Justice*, published by the Association of Community Organizations for Reform Now (ACORN) and listed in the annotated bibliography.

Living Wage Basics

In December 1994, Baltimore's mayor signed into law Council Bill 716 requiring city contractors to pay service workers at least $6.10 an hour. The first of its kind in the nation, the new living wage ordinance followed a year-long, broad-based grassroots campaign organized by the American Federation of State, County and Municipal Employees (AFSCME) and a group of fifty multidenominational churches called Baltimoreans United in Leadership Development (BUILD).

The victory's impact spread far and wide. Before the win, Charles Riggs, a thirty-two-year-old who cleaned Oriole Park at Camden Yards, checked in at the local homeless shelter every night because his $4.25 an hour full-time wage couldn't support a rented room. Thanks to the new law, Riggs saw his wages increase by almost 50 percent immediately. Furthermore, he could look forward to additional raises to a legally guaranteed minimum of $7.70 an hour by 1999.

Table 7.1

Living Wage Policies As of April 2001

Municipality	Contracts		Other provisions
	Thresholds	Living wage	
Baltimore (1994)	All service contracts	Set by wage commission 1994 $6.10 in three steps to 1999 $7.70	
Milwaukee (1995)	Contractors at $5,000 or more	$6.05 adjusted annually for poverty line family of three	
Milwaukee School District (1996)	All schools and contractors to the schools	$7.70 an hour	
Milwaukee County (1997)	Janitorial, security, parking lot attendant	$6.25 indexed to wage increases of county employees	
New York (1996)	Security, temporary office service, cleaning, and food services	Prevailing wage for the industry as determined by city comptroller. Estimated $7.25–$11.25	
Portland, OR (1996)	Janitors, parking lot attendants, security, and temporary clerical	1996 $6.75 1997 $7.00 Indexed to wage increases of city employees	
Jersey City (1996)	Clerical, food, janitorial, and security	$7.50	• Require health care • Require vacations
New Haven (1997)	All city service contracts	Poverty line family of four in 1997 increasing to 125% of poverty line in 5 years	• First consideration hiring to referrals from community hiring halls
Durham (1998)	All service contracts	Wages at least equal to minimum city employee ($7.55 in 1998)	
Chicago (1998)	Security, parking, day laborers, home and health care, cashiers, elevator operators, custodial, and clerical	$7.60	
Cook County , IL (1998)	All contractors	$7.60	• Collective bargaining agreement may supersede
Pasadena (1998)	Contracts $25,000 or more	$7.25 with health benefits $8.50 without	• Earlier the coalition had gotten the same living wage for city employees
Multnomah County, WA (1998)	Janitorial, security, and food service; also seeking state funding to enable county to cover social service contracts	$9 wages and benefits	• New janitorial contracts must first interview workers employed on previous contract
Hudson County, NJ (1999)	Security, food service, janitorial, and clerical	$7.50/hr. + at least $2,000 a year of health care	• One week paid vacation

Table 7.1 *(continued)*

| | Contracts | | |
Municipality	Thresholds	Living wage	Other provisions
Haywood, CA (1999)	City employees over $25,000: automotive repair, building maintenance, janitorial, landscaping, laundry services, temporary personnel, pest control, security services, and social service agencies	$8 with health benefits $9.50 without	• 12 days paid vacation, 5 unpaid • Collective bargaining agreement may supersede
Miami-Dade County, FL (1999)	Service contracts $100,000+ for listed occupations; also applies to airport licensees	$8.56 $9.81 without health benefits	• Also applies to all county employees
Somerville, MA (1999)	$50,000 to decrease over four years to $10,000	Poverty level family of four	• Also applies to all full- and part-time city employees
Los Angeles County (1999)	Full-time employees on contracts $25,000 or more	$8.32 with health benefits $9.46 without	• Employee retention • Limits part-time work • Collective bargaining agreement may supersede • No county funds may be used to inhibit employee organization (unionization)
Buffalo (1999)	Contracts $50,000 or more; includes workfare workers	$6.22 in 2000; $8.08 in 2002 $1 more if no health benefits	• Prior to contract must submit hiring and wage goals; quarterly reports after receive contract
Tucson (1999)	Maintenance, refuse and re-cycling, custodial, landscape, security, moving, temporary employees, pest control	$8.00 with health care $9.00 without	• Must maintain a workforce of at least 60% city residents
Corvallis, OR (1999)	Prohibits city from entering into contracts of $5,000+ if not paying a living wage	$9.00/hr.	
Denver (2000)	$2,000 or more engaged in parking attendant, security, clerical support, or child care	Poverty family of four	
San Fernando, CA (2000)	Contracts or grants $25,000+ Includes employees of temp agencies	$7.25 with health benefits $8.50 if without	• 6 paid days off + 6 unpaid
Alexandria, VA (2000)	All service contractors	$9.84 indexed to poverty threshold	
San Francisco (2000)	Contracts, including non-profits, and leaseholders at airport	$9; $10 in 2001; 2.5% increase next three years Companion legislation requires one of three health insurance options	• 12 paid vacation days • 10 unpaid days for family emergencies
Eau Claire County, WI (2000)	Contracts over $100,000	$6.67 with health benefits or $7.40 without	

(continued)

Table 7.1 *(continued)*

Municipality	Thresholds	Living wage	Other provisions
Contracts			
Santa Cruz (2000)	Contractors, including non-profits Includes city employees	$11 with health benefits or $12 without	
Rochester, NY (2001)	Contracts at least $50,000	$8.52 with health benefits, $9.52 without; indexed to inflation	• Will cover subsidies at such time as county enacts a similar requirement
Ferndale, MI (2001)	Contracts at least $25,000	$8.50 with health benefits, $9.75 without; indexed annually	
Economic development			
Santa Clara County (1995)	New tax abatements	$10	• Require health care or suitable alternative • Must disclose how many jobs will be created, the wages and benefits, and other subsidies being sought
St. Paul (1997)	$100,000 Phase in to also cover contractors	110% poverty line family of four; 100% if provide health care	• Requires 60% new hiring from city residents
Minneapolis (1997)	$100,000 Phase in to also cover contractors	110% poverty line family of four; 100% if provide health care	• Goal of 60% new hiring from city residents • Ban privatization if result in lower wages • Preference to union-friendly businesses
San Antonio (1998)	70% of employees in new jobs created	$9.27 nondurable goods and service $10.13 durable goods	• Business may be available for more tax abatements if 25% new hires go to disadvantaged individuals • Retail facilities are deemed ineligible for tax abatements
Kankakee County, IL (1999)	Local enterprise zone tax breaks	$11.42 or 130% federal poverty level; provide at least 80% of health and dental for full-time employees, and offer pension and profit sharing	• Must repay all subsidies if relocate within 5 years or fail to maintain at least 50 new jobs • Prohibit hiring antiunion consultants • Prevailing wage on construction • Must participate in approved apprenticeship and training programs
Missoula, MT (2001)	City development assistance	At least the lowest full-time city employee (currently $7.95/hr.)	

(continued)

Table 7.1 *(continued)*

Contracts and economic development

Municipality	Thresholds	Living wage	Other provisions
Los Angeles (1997)	$25,000 contracts Leases on city property $1 million subsidy or $100,000 if on a continuing annual basis	$7.39 with health care or $8.64 without	• Require 12 paid vacation days and 10 unpaid sick days • Collective bargaining agreement may supersede • Antiretaliation and worker protections
Duluth (1997)	$5,000 contracts $25,000 financial assistance	$7.25 with health care or $6.25 without	• Work contracted out must pay a living wage
Boston (1997–98)	$25,000 contracts $100,000 financial assistance —modified to mandate only community hiring, not a living wage	Poverty level for a family of four	• Must use community-based hiring halls and/or job centers • As part of contract signing, contractor must report hiring, wage levels and training plans • Quarterly reporting required • Living wage advisory committee with labor and community representatives
Oakland (1998)	$25,000 contracts Leases on city property $100,000 subsidies	$8.00 with health care or $9.25 without	• Require 12 paid vacation days and 10 unpaid sick days • Collective bargaining agreement may supersede
Chicago (original proposal defeated)	$5,000 contracts $50,000 financial assistance	$7.60	• Community hiring hall • As part of application must report hiring, wage levels, and training plans • Quarterly reporting required
Detroit (1998)	$50,000 in contracts or financial assistance for the purposes of job growth or economic development	Poverty line family of four with health care or 125% if no health care	• Where possible prioritize city residents for hiring
San Jose (1998)	Contracts over $20,000 Direct financial grants over $100,000/year	$9.50 with health insurance $10.75 without	• Companies must ensure labor peace • Central labor council noticed when bids let out • New contractors hire existing workers
Madison, WI (1999)	Contacts $5,000+ Financial assistance $100,000 City employees	$7.91 By 2001, 110% poverty line family of four	• Collective bargaining agreement may supersede *(continued)*

Table 7.1 *(continued)*

Contracts and economic development

Municipality	Thresholds	Living wage	Other provisions
Ypsilanti Twp, MI (1999)	All contracts and financial assistance $10,000+	$8.50 with health care $10 without	• Collective bargaining agreement may supersede • Nonprofits unfairly harmed may be exempted
Ypsilanti, MI (1999)	All contracts and financial assistance $20,000+	$8.50 with health care $10 without	• Collective bargaining agreement may supersede • Nonprofits unfairly harmed may be exempted • City will also pay a living wage • Encourages local hiring and contractors • Annual recognition list of living wage employers
Dane County, WI (1999)	Contracts and development assistance $5,000+ County employees	Poverty line family of four Possible health care will be considered in July 1999	
Cambridge, MA (1999)	$10,000 contracts or assistance	$10 adjusted annually using CPI	• Also applies to all city employees • Annual city report and community advisory board
Hartford (1999)	Certain city contracts over $50,000 Development projects of $100,000+	110% poverty family of four health plan requiring employee contribution of no more than 3% of wages or must pay additional rate equal to the cost of health care	• Development projects allow workers to be represented by a union in exchange for "labor peace" (no-strike clause)
Warren, MI (2000)	Contracts or tax breaks $50,000+	100% poverty for family of four 125% without health care	
Omaha, NE (2000)	Contracts and other firms that benefit from at least $75,000 Includes city employees	Poverty level family of four with health care or 110% without	
Toledo (2000)	Contracts over $10,000 & 25+ employees; subsidies over $100,000 & 50+ employees; Tenants of properties that have benefited from city assistance	110% federal poverty level with health care or 130% without	
Cleveland (2000)	Contracts and subsidies $75,000+ Covers workers 30+ hour/wk Includes leaseholders or tenants of recipients of assistance	$8.20 in 2001; $9.20 in 2002 then indexed	• At least 40% of new hires must be city residents • Incentives to provide health care
St Louis, MO (2000)	Contracts $50,000+ Subsidies $100,000+	Lift family of three above eligibility for food stamps (in 2000, $8.84 with benefits, $10.23 without)	

Table 7.1 *(continued)*

Contracts and economic development			
Municipality	Thresholds	Living wage	Other provisions
Berkeley, CA (2000)	City contracts; financial assistance; city employees; and businesses that lease land from the city Amended to include all companies at the Berkeley Marina	$9.75 with health benefits or $11.37 without	
Ann Arbor, MI (2001)	$10,000 contracts, grants, or subsidies	$8.70 with health benefits; $10.20 without Indexed annually	• Also covered city employees—prior resolution
East Pointe, MI (2001)	$50,000 contracts or tax breaks	100% poverty with health benefits; 125% without	
Pittsfield Township, MI (2001)	$10,000 contracts, grants, or subsidies	$8.70 with health benefits; $10.20 without Indexed annually	

Source: ACORN Living Wage Resource Center. 2001. www.livingwagecampaign.org.

But the benefits went further. Local church soup kitchens and homeless shelters no longer had to feed and shelter workers such as Riggs. The AFSCME/BUILD coalition persuaded the mayor to take back, as government jobs paying a living wage, custodial services previously contracted out at thirty-six schools. As part of the campaign, activists also set up an organization of low-wage workers: the Solidarity Sponsoring Committee (SSC). With five hundred dues-paying members and an extensive network of contacts, the SSC continues to mobilize low-wage workers to fight for living wages, benefits, job security, and the right to organize.

Most important, Baltimore's example sparked a grassroots movement. Across the country, labor, community, and religious groups began teaming up to organize for living wages and economic justice. While the specifics have varied, all campaigns have followed the basic formula used in Baltimore by requiring companies receiving public money to pay a living wage and to fulfill other community-driven criteria. Table 7.1 summarizes the laws passed as of

early 2001. The differing specifics often depend on the strategic goals of local activists and their evaluation of the local balance of power.

The Ordinances

About half of all living wage laws follow Baltimore's model covering city contractors. With privatization all the rage among governmental leaders, municipal contracts have become ever more numerous. Whole categories of work typically end up as low-paying jobs, including: custodial, clerical, security, parking, day labor, home and health care, and cashiering.

In 1995, a second major focal point emerged when a labor-community coalition in Santa Clara County, California, successfully attached wage requirements to a particular local tax abatement program being used to subsidize poverty-wage-paying and antiunion retail chain stores. Such low-paying service employers were part of the reason why nearly half of all workers in the prosperous Silicon Valley economy did not earn enough to meet their minimum needs,

Table 7.2

Living Wage Campaigns Under Way As of April 2001

City and County Campaigns

Birmingham	AL	Albuquerque	NM
Little Rock	AR	Binghamton	NY
Sacramento	CA	Ithaca	NY
Santa Barbara	CA	Niagara County	NY
Marin County	CA	Rockland County	NY
Richmond	CA	Syracuse	NY
Santa Monica	CA	Rochester	NY
Sonoma Co/Santa Rosa	CA	New York City	NY
San Diego	CA	Westchester County	NY
San Mateo	CA	Albany	NY
Ventura County/Oxnard	CA	Reno	NV
Bridgeport	CT	Columbus	OH
New Britain	CT	Oklahoma City	OK
Grand Junction	CO	Salem	OR
Boulder	CO	Eugene	OR
Washington	DC	Medford	OR
Gainesville	FL	Philadelphia	PA
Davenport	IA	Pittsburgh/Allegheny	PA
Iowa City	IA	Providence	RI
Champaign-Urbana	IL	Charleston	SC
South Bend	IN	Knoxville	TN
Indianapolis	IN	Nashville	TN
Manhattan	KS	Dallas	TX
Wichita	KS	Austin	TX
Lawrence	KS	Salt Lake City	UT
Lexington	KY	Charlottesville	VA
Louisville	KY	Richmond	VA
New Orleans	LA	Burlington et al.	VT
Baton Rouge	LA	Racine	WI
Brookline	MA		
Montgomery County	MD		
Portland	ME		
Kalamazoo	MI		
Washtenaw County	MI		
Grand Rapids	MI		
Lansing	MI		
St. Louis County	MN		
Missoula	MT		
Bozeman	MT		
Greensboro	NC		
Portsmouth	NH		
Camden	NJ		

Campus Campaigns

Princeton University
University of Virginia
Harvard University
Johns Hopkins University
Brown University
Stanford University
University of Tennessee
Fairfield University, CT
Earlham College, IN
American University/Washington College of Law, DC
Agnes Scott College, GA
Swarthmore College, PA

Source: Information complied by ACORN Living Wage Resource Center. 2001. www.livingwagecampaign.org.

given the area's high cost of living. Two years later, the twin cities of St. Paul and Minneapolis broadened the concept by applying a living wage requirement to financial assistance generally. This category included all the mechanisms, of what is known as "corporate welfare," such as tax abatements, bond financing, tax increment financing, tax credits, and loans subsidized or given by local governments. Starting in Los Angeles, a growing number of campaigns have combined living wage coverage to span both contracts and financial assistance.

As the living wage movement has developed, campaigns have gotten even more aggressive in their reach. Many campaigns now push local governments to ensure that their own employees are paid a living wage—either as part of a living wage ordinance or as a separate action. Lessees and users of city-owned land can often house significant pockets of poverty-wage jobs. Los Angeles, Oakland, and San Francisco applied living wage and other provisions to companies operating at their large city airports and port authorities. Campaigns have also attached living wage requirements to the operations of special public redevelopment authorities. The campaigns in Berkeley and Santa Monica targeted their coastal zones where restaurants, hotels, and shops enjoy special public supports and restricted competition.

The actual amount defining a living wage has grown over time. Many campaigns set their living wage in terms of the official federal poverty line for a family of either three or four. For a family of four, this wage worked out to $8.83 an hour by 2001. The federal poverty formula, however, has received its fair share of criticism. The calculation is based on an estimated grocery bill that is then multiplied by three based on the assumption that families spend one-third of their total budget on food. While this may have been true in the 1950s, data from which the standard originated, it clearly is not the case today. Researchers have suggested that a more accurate measure would set a poverty threshold by multiplying the base estimate by a factor of five or six.

Reacting to local costs of living, many campaigns have raised their required wages. In 1998, San Jose made headlines with the highest living wage at that time: $9.50 an hour with health benefits or $10.75 without. A year later, Kankakee County, Illinois, went further with $11.42 an hour (130% of the federal poverty line for a family of four). In 2000, San Francisco joined the ranks of top contenders by requiring $10 an hour in 2001, a 2.5 percent increase during each of the next three years, and an additional $1.25 either given to the employee as cash or health insurance or made as a contribution to a public health insurance fund for such workers.

As the movement has developed, living wage laws have added additional requirements. Campaigns increasingly attempt to include health insurance—setting their living wage appreciably higher if such benefits are not provided. Since American labor law does not require paid vacation or sick days, many low-wage workers can toil for years without any break. To address this need, Los Angeles, Oakland, and San Francisco mandated twelve paid vacation days and ten unpaid sick days a year. Other provisions reflect the specific strategic goals of coalition partners. In Boston, for example, ACORN sought a requirement that covered employers must first use a community hiring hall in recruiting new workers. By getting one of their community programs officially designated as such a hiring hall, the local ACORN chapter has increased its opportunities to organize among low-income residents. Similarly, the Los Angeles law, and related legislation, contains specific provisions that aid union organizing and collective bargaining. Similarly, San Jose requires company actions to ensure that services will not be disrupted by labor unrest. Specifically, firms have to agree to remain neutral during union elections by not hiring antiunion consulting firms or terrorizing their employees. They also have to provide the union a list of workers and access to them. The living wage enforcement mechanisms have also gotten more sophisticated over time. They can include detailed reporting requirements, harsh financial penalties, public review boards, and the right of workers or their representatives to sue an employer.

The Living Wage Mobilization

The breadth and strength of a living wage campaign is not simply a question of the law's technical provisions, but the political struggle involved in putting it in place and enforcing it. Indeed, what makes the living wage movement significant is the broad spectrum of local groups that it brings together. The breadth of support is clear by the sample coalition list taken from Chicago (see Table 7.3). Chicago's coalition is reflective of patterns nationwide. While to some extent different groups may have worked together prior to the living wage, activists repeatedly describe the breadth of support and level of involvement of different groups in their living wage campaigns as something new and unique. Specifically, living wage campaigns have fostered true partnerships between labor, community, and religious organizations and individuals. Such cooperation raises local progressive activism to new levels.

Such broad coalitions are necessary to overcome opposition typically led by the local chamber of commerce and all too often aided by mayors. Today, anti–living wage forces have a national network. The Employment Policies Institute (not to be confused with the progressive Economic Policies Institute) provides a central clearinghouse for anti–living wage materials, including a slick manual published with the innocent-looking title "Living Wage Policy: The Basics."

The arguments used by living wage opponents have not changed much over the past seven years. They rely much on hysterics and very little on concrete facts. Opponents claim that living wage laws will drive up taxpayer costs, lead to job losses and reduced employment opportunities for low-wage workers, give the area a reputation for having a bad business climate, and crush innocent nonprofit organizations. A growing body of studies demonstrates that such claims are baseless.[1] The overall amounts

needed to pay living wages are quite modest. Furthermore, short-term wage costs can be offset by long-term savings from lower employee turnover and productivity gains from higher worker morale. Increased quality of services can also help contractors gain and retain contracts even when their bids are not necessarily the lowest. Similarly, cities that erode their tax base through tax breaks to poverty-wage-paying companies hardly create a positive business climate. Indeed, high-road employers typically shy away from communities unable to offer the public infrastructure and high quality of life necessary for their operations.

For several years now, the Employment Policy Institute has offered grants to researchers willing to question the living wage. Despite this effort, the institute has managed to produce only a shrill critique of an early pro–living wage Baltimore study—subsequent research has upheld the study—and a highly misleading survey of economists claiming support for opposition claims.[2]

A lack of facts, however, has not prevented the opposition from getting up in front of city council after city council and predicting all manner of dire consequences if this "municipal socialism" is allowed to become law. Working behind the scenes, it has sought mayoral vetoes and legal challenges. The opposition has attempted to obtain state laws rendering local living wage laws illegal. And when it has not been able to block legislation, it has tried to water it down into meaninglessness.

The most creative opposition came from Santa Monica, where several luxury hotels were so concerned about having to pay a living wage in the waterfront district, that they formed a group called "Santa Monicans for a Living Wage" and placed a "living wage" ordinance on the November 2000 ballot. The ordinance, however, applied only narrowly to city contractors and explicitly would have prevented the city from enacting any other form of wage legislation. As few as sixty-two workers would have been covered. The hotels spent nearly $1 million attempting to pass the ordinance. However, the real

Table 7.3

Chicago's 1997 Living Wage Coalition
78 Groups

ACORN
AFGE Local 1395
AFSCME Council 3
Amalgamated Transit Union Local 308
Americans for Democratic Action
Association House
Bakery, Confectionery and Tobacco Workers, Local 1
Bickerdike Redevelopment Corporation
Black Elected Officials of Illinois
Center for Economic Policy Analysis
Center for Neighborhood Technology
Chicago Coalition for the Homeless
Chicago Federation of Labor
Chicago Institute on Urban Poverty, Headland Alliance
Chicago Jobs Council
Chicago Jobs with Justice
Chicago New Party
Coalition of Labor Union Women
Committee for New Priorities
Community Renewal Society
Congressman Bobby Rush
Congressman Danny Davis
Congressman Jesse Jackson Jr.
Congressman Luis Gutierrez
Cook County Clerk David Orr
Council of Religious Leaders
Democratic Socialists of America
Eighth Day Center for Justice
Fireman and Oilers Local 7, SEIU
Homeless on the Move for Equality
Humbolt Park Empowerment Partnership
IBEW Local 134
IBEW Local 1031
Illinois Center for Youth Advocacy
Illinois Nurses Association
Illinois Public Action
Illinois State Council of Senior Citizens
Institute for Economic Justice
Interfaith Committee on Worker Issues

Italian American Labor Council
IVI-IPO
Jeffrey Manor Community Revitalization Court
Jewish Council on Urban Affairs
Jewish Labor Committee
Kenwood Oakland Community Organization
Labor Coalition on Public Utilities
Lawndale Christian Development Corporation
League of Women Voters
Logan Square Neighborhood Association
Midwest Center for Labor Research
Network 49
Northwest Neighborhood Federation
ONE
Our Lady Gate of Heaven Church
PSEU Local 45
Redmond People Full Gospel Church
Rogers Park Community Action Network
SEIU Local 1
SEIU Local 25
SEIU Local 73
SEIU Local 236
SEIU Local 880
St. Benedict Peace and Justice Committee
State Senator Alice Palmer
State Senator Jesus Garcia
Teamster Joint Council No. 25
Teamster Local 705
Teamster Local 726
Teamster Local 733
Teamster Local 743
UAW Region 4
UE District Council Number 11
UFCW Local 100A
UFCW Local 881
UNITE Chicago and Central State Joint Board
United Steelworkers Local 1010
UNITE Midwest Region
Uptown People's Development Corporation

living wage campaign defeated the measure—79 percent to 21 percent—through a massive voter turnout drive.

Despite the opposition, living wage campaigns have rarely proven failures. Part of the reason for their pervasive success lies in the fact that the business opposition comes from primarily ideological, not financial sources. As such living wage campaigns

prompt opposition, but not the kind of mass corporate mobilization that, for example, a minimum wage increase might encounter. Activists have to contend with testimony from chamber of commerce supporters and local businesspeople. They also have to overcome negative press coverage and the maneuverings of corporate-oriented politicians. However, they generally have not contended with multimillion-dollar war chests or the expressed opposition of large corporations. The flip side, however, is that the living wage is also a compelling and popular issue. That makes opposition difficult. Telling the public that it cannot set conditions on how tax money is used represents an uphill battle.

The strength of the living wage as an organizing tool has been demonstrated by the fact that even when campaigns have met with initial defeat, they have kept on organizing. For example, the St. Paul campaign lost an initiative vote early in the history of the national movement but went on to win a living wage law passed by the city council. Hard fought, but unsuccessful, minimum wage campaigns in Denver, Albuquerque, and St. Louis gave way to vigorous and successful living wage efforts. Similarly, as we will see, Chicago organizers developed such a spectacular effort that they won an ordinance in 1998 despite losing a council vote a year earlier.

The living wage has proven such a powerful organizing tool because it simultaneously taps specific group concerns while building a common project. Different groups are attracted to the living wage for a variety of reasons. Clearly, poverty wages are a major problem facing even the most prosperous communities. The buying power of the minimum wage has declined dramatically since its peak in 1968. This despite the fact that the economy is about 50 percent more productive now than in 1968. A minimum wage that has kept pace with productivity gains would be roughly $11.20 today. Instead, at $5.15 an hour, a full-time worker still earned $6,750 below the $17,050 poverty line for a family of four in 2000.

The reality of low-wage jobs recasts the image of poverty in this country. By 1992, nearly one out of six Americans, and almost one-quarter of all children, lived below the federal government's poverty line, a statistic that has remained nearly constant despite the long official 1990s boom. Nearly half of all families with children under eighteen maintained by women live in poverty. The fact that over one out of six workers earned below $6.15 an hour in 1997 suggests that poverty is a symptom of exploitation

at work. Poverty wages can be found even in the most prosperous communities. Alexandria, Virginia, for example, has one of the highest median income levels in the country. Yet, living wage organizers found that one out of five residents lives in poverty.

The issue of poverty wages has become even more pressing as welfare "reform" pushes more parents into low-wage jobs. Indeed, living wage campaigns speak directly to groups struggling with so-called welfare-to-work initiatives. The real solution for families on welfare is straightforward: decent jobs with family-supporting wages and benefits supported by a national commitment to universal child care, full education opportunities, and public transportation. Instead, while welfare-to-work programs give lip service to such supports, in reality they often force parents to work at jobs for rates at or below the minimum wage. States have even forced parents out of community colleges to work for their meager public assistance. In cities such as New York, "workfare" workers have been used directly to replace unionized employees.

The impact of taxpayer-funded poverty wages goes even further. In the name of cost cutting, communities across the country face ongoing battles against growing efforts by elected officials to hand public services over to private companies. Such privatization typically replaces well-paying unionized jobs with nonunionized employers who lower wage levels and cut employment. In the long run, once they have secured the contracts, these companies often end up raising their fees while delivering inferior services. [3] A government agency need only cover its costs, but a for-profit company must make money for its owners. By mandating a living wage, activists can discourage privatization by taking away a poverty-paying contractor's bidding edge.

The living wage directly challenges local "job at any cost" development policies. For the past two decades, business lobby groups have helped convince many local officials that the only way they can attract job investment is to offer businesses lucrative deals with few strings attached. Typically, questions of the wages paid and long-term job retention does not enter the picture. Yet, poverty jobs are not better than no job at all. They cost the community dearly in social services and run-down neighborhoods. And by sacrificing the local tax base to attract such low-road companies, governments spend money that could be invested in the local infrastructure, education, and other elements of high-road economics. Living wage campaigns implicitly assert a fundamental principle that both government and the community must become active players who steer business activity toward a better economic future.

The living wage also offers concrete opportunities for practical, on-the-ground organizing. The opportunities for door-to-door grassroots work offered by a campaign provide ways for local groups to mobilize their own membership and to talk with area residents. ACORN, the national organization most systematically involved in leading the living wage movement, has used the campaigns to build its organization within low-income communities. Similarly, campaigns in Baltimore, Los Angeles, San Jose, Oakland, and elsewhere have directly tied into union-related organizing as central labor councils and individual union locals have provided key living wage leadership.

The living wage also shakes up "politics as usual." For groups looking to organize for political change, a living wage campaign will put local politicians on the spot and open up opportunities for activists to run for local office. In Madison, Wisconsin, for example, the 1998 elections saw the media adopting the living wage as a key issue in covering local candidates. Local chapters of the New Party have used the living wage as a major organizing tool to elect people to office in places such as the Twin Cities, Little Rock, Chicago, and Montgomery County, Maryland. In Pine Bluff, Arkansas, ACORN made support for living wage a requirement for its congressional endorsement. Their pro–living wage Democratic candidate won the election in a previously Republican seat. In Little Rock, activists put the living wage on candidate lawn signs. For the 2001 New

York mayoral contest, three of the four contenders, including the front-runner, pledged to pass a living wage law within weeks of being elected into office.

In short, the living wage appeals to a broad array of groups along lines ranging from very specific daily concerns about the working poor, to worries about public job loss, to general questions of local economic development, to various organizing opportunities. In the past, these diverse concerns may have led groups to act alone or in small coalitions. This was especially the case since so many progressive battles over the past two decades have been defensive struggles. The living wage experience demonstrates how moving from defense to a proactive agenda fosters greater progressive unity. At the most general level, the living wage phenomenon demonstrates the possibilities outlined at the end of chapter 6. While the corporate restructuring and right-wing politics of the 1980s and 1990s may have brought a great deal of pain, they also have sparked a unifying grassroots reaction.

The Living Wage in Action

The full significance of living wage campaigns is best demonstrated by the details of actual campaigns. The first three sections draw from some of the most noteworthy living wage efforts in the country. The last case section shows how even more modest campaigns have had an impact.

Chicago

When leaders from Chicago ACORN and the Service Employees International Union (SEIU) Local 880 considered developing a living wage campaign, they knew they faced an uphill battle. Their city boasted the most famous of the last great political machines. Since Harold Washington's death, the machine had regained control of the mayor's office—placing the son of long-term boss Richard Daley in the same chair as his father. Some activists assumed that in such conditions, a living wage campaign could not win. However, a strong mobilization promised to shake up Chicago politics, restructure the terms of political debate, and plant seeds for further organizing. As the campaign unleashed an enormous upwelling of energy, many began to believe that even an outright victory was possible.

The campaign began in the summer of 1995 when ACORN pulled together a steering committee of key organizations. On the community side, ACORN was joined by the Chicago Coalition for the Homeless, an organization of neighborhood groups, and key religious networks. Labor leadership came from union locals that directly represented, or sought to organize, workers potentially impacted by a living wage law. These locals included SEIU, AFSCME, the Teamsters, and the United Food and Commercial Workers (UFCW).

The coalition's decision to push for an ordinance covering both city contracts and financial assistance meant that the campaign was raising questions about considerable sums of money. With financial assistance alone, the city was giving away half a billion dollars a year with very few strings attached. For example, Whole Foods, an organic food store chain, had received $10 million from the city in the name of job creation. Yet campaign researchers found that the company had both hired out of the city and paid poverty wages.

By the late fall, activists began to systematically contact all fifty members of the Chicago Board of Aldermen. In December, organizers exceeded their own goals when they packed a local Teamster hall with seven hundred fifty living wage supporters. At this energized kickoff rally, thirteen aldermen, including several key players, publicly signed on to the campaign. For the rest of the winter and into the spring, the campaign pushed hard to win further sponsors and to hold on to their existing supporters. In the end, twenty-six aldermen cosponsored the actual legislation, with another ten promising to vote for the law. It seemed that Chicago might actually win a living wage.

The biggest obstacle remained, however: Mayor Daley. For several months, the campaign's escalating mobilization attempted to convince the mayor not to oppose the living wage. Further rallies drew even larger crowds. Door knocking took the living wage into the community. Coalition members tried to pull strings. The leadership of most of the area's labor unions sent a letter to the mayor, unsuccessfully requesting a meeting. Cardinal Bernardin wrote to Daley, asking him to support the living wage. AFL-CIO president John Sweeney sat down with the mayor. SEIU delegates at their national convention staged a street parade supporting the campaign.

The Chicago Jobs and Living Wage Campaign also took up the cause of Vienna Beef—a company located in the city that employed 430 people at an average of $10.50 an hour. Thanks to bureaucratic red tape within the city administration, this living wage company was being compelled to leave Chicago. Highlighting the irony that the city was funding poverty employers while driving out more desirable employers, the campaign succeeded in pressuring Daley to intervene on Vienna Beef's behalf.

The campaign, however, never won Daley's support. In May, activists introduced their legislation in a council chamber packed with five hundred supporters. In June, campaign organizers planned a similar audience for ordinance hearings. They had lined up over fifty leaders of key organizations to testify on the proposed law's behalf. However, a few days before the hearings the mayor announced his opposition.

Daley claimed that he supported the concept of a living wage, but he argued that the city simply could not afford the costs. The administration and the Chicago-area chamber of commerce carted out a forty-page study predicting all kinds of dire consequences if a living wage law were enacted. On the surface, the mayor's numbers seemed impressive: an almost $36 million increase in yearly costs to the city and a loss of 1,337 jobs from among 9,807 workers affected by the living wage. A detailed examination, however, revealed that the numbers were misleading, to say the least. To arrive at their job-loss figures, for example, the authors simply froze the current payroll of all covered firms and then cut jobs until the now higher wages could be paid. Obviously, no company's payroll remains fixed. It certainly doesn't simply lay off people every time it gives a raise. Indeed, Chicago living wage activists could point to a statement signed by 101 of the nation's prominent economists, including three Nobel winners, stressing that "the minimum wage can be increased by a moderate amount without significantly jeopardizing employment opportunities." Even more dramatic, the opposition's generous estimate of a $19.8 to $36 million tax bill fell into insignificance when placed in proper relation to the city's $4.5 billion annual budget. Indeed, as economist Ron Baiman testified before the city council, Chicago was spending $27 million dollars to build a new lakeside park, yet supposedly could not afford to raise the wages of thousands of residents!

Given Chicago politics, the mayor's opposition meant that the living wage would not pass. However, the campaign kept the pressure on—forcing local political figures to go on record. On the Teamster building across from the 1996 Democratic Party National Convention, the campaign hung a huge sign trumpeting the living wage. Activists successfully sued to gain access to Navy Pier in order to picket the mayor as he welcomed Democratic delegates to the city. Delegates went on public "tours of shame" to visit low-wage-paying recipients of local corporate welfare. *Streetwise*, a paper sold on the streets by the city's homeless, ran a special living wage issue.

To forestall a public vote, Daley entered into protracted negotiations with the campaign. With these talks going nowhere, activists decided in the summer of 1997 to push for a vote. This action would bring closure to the campaign and place the city council on the spot. The maneuvering continued. The opposition even tried to hold public hearings without the campaign's knowledge. When activists found out, they packed hearings, and pro–living wage councilors did a fine job of defending the ordinance.

The final drama came on the day of the actual council vote. Building security illegally barred living wage supporters from the public meeting under the pretext that the chamber was already full. News photographs showing the half-empty hall revealed the lie. Meanwhile, the arrest of six prominent living wage supporters for attempting to enter the council chambers dramatized the scandal. In the end, however, the mayor's will held sway—thirty-one councilors voted against the living wage.

Despite losing the vote, the Chicago campaign had gained a great deal from two years of activism. Ironically, the very strength of the opposition helped to foster a mobilization on a scale that will have lasting effects on Chicago politics. The fact that a remarkable seventeen councilors defied their mayor to vote in favor of the living wage indicates the degree to which the campaign had thrown open "machine politics as usual." The living wage had become a hugely popular issue. Most important, the campaign brought together a solid core of organizations and made them familiar with working with each other. The over seventy organizations that formally joined the living wage coalition represented a combined membership of over 250,000 people. For those members of the coalition who saw the living wage campaign as part of broader project to reshape Chicago politics, the shameless flip-flop by city council members presented clear electoral possibilities. Indeed, activists began to organize ward-by-ward accountability sessions and to move petitions for living wage ballot resolutions. Because of his leadership role in the living wage campaign, Illinois ACORN president, Ted Thomas, went on to win election in the city's thirteenth council ward in 1998 despite having never held public office.

This electoral threat from a campaign that had demonstrated its ability to mobilize public sentiment eventually won the Chicago Jobs and Living Wage Campaign an actual living wage law. During the summer of 1998, the mayor and the city council prepared to enact for themselves a hefty salary increase. Yet, the mayor and council had voted down the living wage ordinance the year before under the pretext that the city could not afford it! When the groups involved in the living wage began demonstrations linking the salary vote increase to the living wage vote, the mayor backed down and the council passed a living wage law covering city contracts. While the law is not as strong as the original living wage ordinance, it is a start. Its passage after such determined opposition demonstrates that living wage organizers had made a clear and lasting impact on Chicago politics. The business-driven priorities of local government spending and economic development policy could no longer be taken for granted. Following right on the heels of the Chicago law, Cook County passed a living wage law. In 1999, neighboring Kankakee County followed suit with a strong subsidy accountability ordinance that includes a living wage requirement.

Los Angeles

From the beginning, organizers have linked the Los Angeles living wage campaign to a broader agenda of labor movement revival. The lead organization— the Los Angeles Alliance for a New Economy (LAANE)—was created in 1993 by the Hotel Employees and Restaurant Employees (HERE) Union Local 11 in order to foster a climate favorable to organizing low-wage workers in the tourism industry— the city's second-largest economic sector. Several environmental factors favored a community-oriented organizing approach. Unlike such cites as Detroit and New York, Los Angeles has traditionally not been known as a strong union town. Such relative weakness makes union go-it-alone strategies even less of an option. Furthermore, like Detroit and New York in the early part of the twentieth century, Los Angeles today has witnessed a massive influx of immigrant workers. According to census data in 1990, Los Angeles County had 45 percent of the foreign-born population in California. Forty percent of the county's population was Hispanic and 11 percent was Asian. In such immigrant communities, the line between community and workplace organizing is particularly thin. The predominant Catholic character of the Hispanic population also helped link faith-based concerns to labor issues. In addition to its model living wage effort, in recent years Los Angeles has been the scene of such stunning union victories such as Service Employees Union's 2000 janitors strike and its unionization of seventy-five thousand home care workers.

The Living Wage Campaign

The Los Angeles living wage effort's specific origins lay in the battle to defend the jobs of one thousand unionized workers at the city's main airport. Three hundred of these jobs were lost when the city brought in nonunion contractors, such as McDonald's. The remaining seven hundred jobs promised to suffer the same fate. Under LAANE's auspices, a core from the hotel workers and service employees unions joined with several community groups to map out a response. Their strategy involved passing three pieces of legislation connecting public funds to community standards. The first required companies receiving city contracts to retain the existing workforce. Activists won this legislation in the fall of 1995. The second was the living wage law. The third aimed to establish local legal protections for workers' right to organize. The link between public funds and private employers proved important not just at LAX, but also in the city's tourism industry with its intimate links to taxpayer money and government regulations.

The eighteen-month battle to win Los Angeles's living wage ordinance produced a broad alliance of labor and community groups. Indeed, the campaign's coalition grew to over one hundred endorsing organizations. Activists systematically targeted each city councilor with activities and inside pressure designed to move that particular individual. As with many other cities, Los Angeles's mayor opposed the living wage, compelling the campaign to build a veto-proof super majority on the city council. It also had to overcome a steady barrage of hysterics from the chamber of commerce and its allies. For example, the "Coalition to Keep LA Working," as it called itself, ran "fact sheets" used by the local media that claimed that: "ultimately, a business will have to cut jobs in order to deal with higher labor costs. There will be fewer entry level wage earners. This ordinance will hurt the very constituency it claims to serve." It also cried that "a socially responsible business will not be able to compete with a similar business not having to pay higher labor costs." The "fact sheet" did not explain how a poverty-wage-paying business was "socially responsible."

To keep the pressure on, activists organized a campaign to phone in to the city council. Organizations faxed letters of support. Over a thousand "New Years" cards flooded in from city residents. For two weeks, delegations visited the council twice a day, three days a week. Some actions become quite dramatic. For Thanksgiving, the campaign asked groups and individuals to mail counselors over a thousand decorated paper plates symbolizing the struggle to feed a family on poverty wages. For the winter holidays, one hundred clergy and others accompanied a volunteer actor playing the part of the ghost of Jacob Marley who went to city hall draped with chains to decry the mayor's Scrooge-like opposition to the living wage. Volunteers went caroling at city hall and nearby restaurants with lyrics modified for the living wage. The living wage coalition also sought support from high-road employers. Two top executives from Bell Industries and Pioneer Foods wrote an opinion piece published in the *Los Angeles Times* defending the living wage from the standpoint of their company's success in pursuing policies of higher wages. Thirty-three Hollywood film and television producers also sent a letter to the Los Angeles city council urging passage of the living wage ordinance.

Los Angeles labor activists self-consciously structured their effort to produce opportunities for union organizing. The living wage law, for example, contains a provision allowing a union contract to supersede the law's requirements. This gives some unions potential leverage with employers. In the hotel industry, for example, many workers receive a significant portion of their income from tips that do not count as wages for determining a living wage. The hotel workers union has tried to pressure owners to agree to neutrality over unionization and/or a first contract in return for flexibility over the living wage provisions.

Organizers deliberately recruited among workers affected by the ordinance to provide them a clear role in the campaign. At the airport, for example, workers organized a media event in which they took reporters and city hall staff on a tour highlighting the conditions under which they had to work. Low-wage workers also provided powerful human stories. Bobbi Murray, the campaign's media director, stated "Workers came to City Hall and testified about injuries that went untreated because there was no time off permitted for a doctor visit, and no insurance or way to pay for it anyway; families crowded into tiny one-bedroom apartments in dangerous areas of town just to make rent, and visits to food pantries to manage the groceries every month." The participation of affected workers not only strengthened the campaign for the living wage law, but also developed an activist nucleus among low-wage workers that could feed into union activity. The testimony of these workers also proved critical in gaining some positive media coverage. While the local press went with their usual probusiness slant, the best stories always provide a human-interest angle. And that angle came from the compelling stories of workers provided by the campaign.

The living wage campaign's work paid off big. In March 1997, the Los Angeles City Council unanimously passed the living wage. A month later they overrode Mayor Richard Riordan's veto.

The campaign also delivered other benefits. It fostered a lasting interfaith network that harks back to the religious support shown for union organizing during the 1930s and 1940s. Organized by leadership from Protestant, Catholic, and Jewish congregations, Clergy and Laity United for Economic Justice (CLUE) continues to mobilize strong religious support behind ongoing worker struggles. For example, HERE hit a wall of employer resistance when it campaigned at several downtown luxury hotels. The Westside Hotels balked at an agreement with the union to gradually raise housekeepers' wages from $8.15 to $11.05 an hour. While workers staged temporary walkouts, CLUE dispatched small teams in full ministerial garb to deliver brief sermons on workplace fairness while ordering coffee at several hotel dining rooms. On April 8, 1998, an interfaith procession of sixty ministers, priests, and rabbis marched through Beverly Hills. They deposited bitter herbs outside the Summit Hotel, which still had not signed the HERE agreement, and offered milk and honey to the two that had. Two months later, the Summit signed. CLUE has organized similar religious support for a campaign against a union-busting hotel in Santa Monica, an organizing drive at St. Francis Hospital, protests over the University of Southern California's decisions to contract out work to low-wage employers, and a successful living wage campaign in Pasadena.

The network has also called on churches to lead by their own examples. Along with the Southern California Ecumenical Council, CLUE has campaigned for religious institutions to pay their staff a living wage. Churches sometimes "make people feel they have a moral-religious obligation to do the work of the church without concern to how much money they make," Jeff Utter, president of the Valley Interfaith Council and United Church of Christ pastor, told the *Los Angeles Times*. "People should be paid the equivalent of what they would be paid in other segments of the economy. If a church employee wants to return part of that money as a church contribution, then they are free to do that." At the urgings of the Los Angeles diocesan leaders, the national Episcopal convention adopted a living wage recommendation at its July 1998 convention.

Combining Enforcement with Organizing

Enforcement has been one of the greatest challenges to the living wage movement. Even with the best legal details, the surest way for a living wage to be-

come reality has been for the coalition to establish ongoing enforcement work that continues the grassroots activism. LAANE has turned enforcement needs into an opportunity by using it to further build a climate for union organizing.

As a first step, the campaign negotiated with the city council to establish a program for educating affected workers on the living wage. All living wage ordinances should require employers to provide workers written details of their rights under the living wage law. However, Los Angeles organizers administer a program that trains city contract workers directly about the living wage. While the city prints the materials, obtains the training location, and does the advertising, the campaign designs the classes and provides the trainers. The workshops, which the campaign conducts twice a month, seek to reach an estimated five thousand to eight thousand low-wage workers covered through city contracts.

Organizers have also sought to bring affected workers into contact with the campaign by taking advantage of the living wage's health insurance provisions. The campaign found that most employers opted for the extra $1.25 an hour rather than provide insurance. In response, activists negotiated with UCLA Health Care to offer a decent family insurance package, with no major deductibles, for $1.25 an hour. The campaign has been working with the city and businesses to get employers to adopt the package.

LAANE developed its own database on city contracts and subsidies. LAANE knows when existing contracts and assistance come up for renewal and when the city considers new contracts and financial assistance packages. Combining this information with the data that firms are supposed to file with the city (which they may or may not actually do) allows the campaign to target specific employers both for enforcing the living wage and for possible union organizing. For example, the coalition offers support in applying for public money to employers who agree to pay living wages and play fair during unionization drives. Ideally, the campaign seeks to get employers to sign neutrality agreements allowing their employees an unmolested union vote free from professional union busters and terror tactics. Employers can also agree to recognize the union without an election once a majority of workers sign union cards. For companies who choose not to play fair, the living wage coalition can threaten to slow or block a company's application for contracts or financial assistance.

Such leverage enabled LAANE to gain a living wage and card check neutrality agreement at a large-scale entertainment and hotel development project in Hollywood in return for supporting approval of the project and tax breaks. LAANE has also negotiated similar agreements at other development projects such as the new Dreamworks studio, where a community partner, the Metro Alliance, also won a landmark victory around job access and training for low-income communities.

The living wage campaign has also directly tied into the union-organizing efforts at the Los Angeles Airport. Living wage implementation has given activists in the role of trainers more access to work sites than as union organizers (a sad commentary on the state of our nation's labor laws). And the coalition won protections from employer retaliation for workers who organize around the living wage— mechanisms more expedient than the all-too-often lengthy procedures followed under the National Labor Relations Act's protections for union activity. Because the living wage effort made a point of recruiting among affected low-wage workers, the campaign also established a leadership cadre among airport workers open to further organizing.

LAANE has used its ability to intervene in the public bidding process to provide organizing leverage. For example, two companies might bid on a contract to sell food at airport concessions. One employer proves cooperative and signed a card check neutrality agreement. The other decides to be uncooperative. In such cases, the living wage coalition has urged public authorities to go with the more worker-friendly company. The worker retention law

passed two years prior to the living wage has also proven an important tool. The law requires companies receiving a contract previously held by another firm to hire the employees already working on the contract. Without such job security, employers can threaten workers with a loss of contract, and hence their jobs, if they unionize or do not give in during bargaining. Furthermore, if workers do not remain on the job, any union can legally vanish as soon as a new company gets the contract. By stabilizing the workforce, the retention law opens more ground for lasting organizing work.

As the above overview suggests, the Los Angeles living wage campaign has not been a one-shot effort, but an ongoing political project linked to union organizing. In addition to its direct monitoring and enforcement work, LAANE has continued to push for legislative change. A year after the living wage ordinance went into effect, LAANE released a "report card" evaluating the record of different parts of the city administration in implementing the law. While specific departments had proven open to working with campaign organizers to develop their capacity to enforce the law, the actual city office charged with overseeing the living wage had proven uncooperative. Activists got the city council to place oversight in the hands of a new five-staff body dedicated to the living wage.

The coalition has also successfully lobbied the city council to strengthen and extend the ordinance. Some bones of contention have made headline news. In March 1998, for example, the campaign organized a march of seven hundred against United Airlines, whose airport lease was soon to run out. United was claiming that it was not covered by the ordinance. Revisions to the law have closed any possible loophole in this regard. By 2001, LAANE was developing efforts to win living wage and labor peace deals at large development projects linked to public funds. In addition to building the projects with family-supporting union construction workers, the campaign aims to put in place long-term stipulations that require all companies that move into the retail, entertainment, and office facilities to abide by public wage and employment criteria.

Community Benefits for Economic Development

LAANE has continued to develop its legislative agenda. Activists pulled together a successful living wage effort in Pasadena. LAANE also launched a strong living wage coalition in Santa Monica, called Santa Monicans Allied for Responsible Tourism (SMART), to pass living wage requirements for all employers in the city's coastal zone. Having defeated the phony living wage ballot initiative mentioned above, SMART passed a strong real living wage in 2001.

LAANE also looks toward further extending the living wage concept beyond contracts and employers who receive subsidies to require community standards in large development projects. What makes LAANE's goals distinct is that it does not simply seek to require projects to meet such community criteria as living wages, labor peace, and local hiring while they are being built. Rather, LAANE wants written into the project agreement a "Community Development Plan" that applies to all businesses that subsequently use the facility. Such provisions would include requirements for job training, local hiring, living wages, affordable child care, and transportation. Thus, for example, in a shopping mall built under such an agreement, all the chain stores that commonly frequent such facilities would have to pay their employees a living wage and meet the other requirements.

Such mandates aim to bring the community into the development process and help ensure that local neighborhoods really benefit from development. Currently, the San Fernando Valley faces a series of large-scale office, retail, and entertainment developments. These projects are pushed by wealthy developers who, despite their wealth, seek various public subsidies. Such large-scale developments are often sold as a way to address the problem of urban blight. Yet, when not steered by community input, they end up pushing low-income people out of the way, exploiting low wages rather than raising wage standards, and draining economic energy from the surrounding community. Teaming up with local social service agencies and residents, LAANE won a breakthrough project agreement with developers of the massive Los Angeles sports and entertainment district. The agreement calls for many community and job benefits including 20 percent affordable housing set-asides, 70 percent living wage jobs, open space subsidies, parking set-asides, and monetary assistance to a local nonprofit development corporation.

Through its many interconnected projects, LAANE seeks to reorient local economic development policy around public standards and community input. LAANE has accompanied its efforts to change public policy with research efforts to publicize the bankruptcy of current directions. In 2000, LAANE released a report detailing the magnitude of social and economic problems produced by the massive growth of low-wage jobs. A year before, LAANE unveiled studies of two major local economic development programs: the city's Commercial Redevelopment Agency and the mayor's Los Angeles Business Team. With access to millions of dollars in public subsidies and other incentive mechanisms, these two programs helped drive development in the city. Researchers found that job quality was not a criteria being used in either program. Public efforts were not targeted specifically toward underserved communities. Indeed, the city had no coherent strategy targeting key industry sectors, but rather focused its energy on attracting individual firms. The reports recommended far less emphasis on retail and much greater attention to smaller projects. The recommendations also looked toward living wage policies, labor peace compacts, greater attention to job creation and job quality, and far more public accountability. Together, these three reports show a glimpse into an organizing agenda that promises to energize local progressive politics for many years to come.

Founding a Long-Range Movement

While the organizers of most living wage campaigns look toward gaining more than simply a new piece of legislation, living wage organizers in Los Angeles stand out by the degree to which they framed their effort as part of a larger project. Other campaigns have also used the living wage as a way for systematically establishing the formal and informal building blocks of a long-term movement. LAANE's example of a nonprofit founded to support ongoing and long-range economic activism has been followed in several communities, including the northern California Bay Area and San Diego.

The East Bay Alliance for a Sustainable Economy (EBASE) brings together labor, community, and faith-based organizations to end low-wage poverty and create economic equality in the San Francisco East Bay area. Like LAANE, this nonprofit combines coalition building with economic research, leadership development, and legislative campaigns. In the first few years of its existence, EBASE helped launch the successful Berkeley Living Wage Coalition, the East Bay Interfaith Committee for Worker Justice, and the Coalition for an Accountable Port (CAP).

The latter of these groups has led a strong campaign to ensure that the multibillion-dollar redevelopment of Oakland's port facilities delivers living wage jobs available to local residents. The port employs eleven thousand workers directly and another eleven thousand indirectly. In 2000, CAP won a historic project labor agreement that not only required construction work to be done with union labor, but that at least half of the work hire local residents. It also required that at least one out of five jobs be apprenticeships—thus providing a path to a career beyond the immediate work. The labor agreement signified a noteworthy alliance between the high-wage building trade unions and low-income residents. Traditionally, these two groups had fought each other over access to construction jobs and the use of minority-owned nonunion firms.

EBASE has also organized to evaluate and strengthen Oakland's living wage ordinance. The coalition was also part of San Francisco's successful living wage campaign. In the end, the San Francisco effort had to threaten to place the matter before voters by collecting nineteen thousand signatures for a ballot initiative. This action pushed the city council past the Minimum Compensation Ordinance on August 21, 2000. The campaign also persuaded the San Francisco Airport Commission to adopt a quality standards program as part of the airport rules and regulations applying to private firms operating at the airport. For 2001, the program sets minimum hourly compensation at $10 an hour with benefits or $11.25 without for all covered workers. It also sets minimum hiring standards for covered positions, minimum training requirements, and public standards for all equipment used at the airport that impacts safety and security. Not surprisingly, research has found that the higher wages have led to noticeable improvements in the quality and effectiveness of airport security.

In contrast to the Bay Area, San Diego has a reputation as a conservative community with an antiunion political environment, a sparse field of community-based organizations, low levels of political participation and representation among the poor, and elected officials who have accepted the notion that a good business climate equals low taxes and little government regulation.[4] The border city also has a dramatic polarization of income with the gulf widening between the affluent Anglo population and Chicano, Mexican, and other communities of color. In 1997, progressive labor leaders created the Center on Policy Initiatives (CPI) as an institutional support for developing a growing labor-community movement.

The CPI has embarked on a systematic program to lay the groundwork necessary for launching a living wage campaign. This work includes academic research documenting the local economic strains, outreach to potential community and labor allies, and a media campaign to highlight the city's social disparities. CPI's first legislative effort follows the lead of the environmental movement by seeking "right to know" policies to bring private information about public contracts and subsidies into public debate. Indeed, such information will likely show that, under current policies, public expenditures contribute to the growth of poverty-wage jobs.

Like San Diego, but in an area with a much stronger labor tradition, the western Pennsylvania living wage campaign spent considerable time systematically laying the foundations for a long-term social movement for economic justice. Indeed, the campaign's original plan set two years simply for laying the groundwork prior to introducing a living wage. And its geographical focus covers a multicounty area in and around Pittsburgh.

In the coalition's statement of purpose, passing local living wage laws is only one of four goals. The other three are:

- Building an inclusive, broad-based movement of working people through their unions, religious institutions, and other community-based organizations.
- Supporting the rights of workers trying to organize; to preserve existing living wage jobs by fighting privatization and contracting out; and to sustain prevailing wage standards and other such struggles.
- Providing broad public education that explains economic change and regional economic development from the perspective of working people and their communities.

Concretely, these broad objectives have produced several projects related to, but separate from, the actual tasks of passing a living wage law. For example, with the county government changing to Republican control for the first time in forty years, activists organized a campaign to block the privatization of four nursing homes. The coalition also helped organize support for nursing home workers on strike at a company where three out of five workers made the minimum wage. The health and

human service sector presents important living wage issues. The local county governments are major funders of day care, mental health, and other human service providers. These sectors often pay notoriously low wages. The living wage coalition worked with other groups to update a 1989 statewide survey of conditions in these industries, highlighting the problem of poverty wages. After a year 2000 home-rule change went into effect, county voters gained the ability to pass a living wage law by ballot.

Similarly, the campaign has organized support for steelworkers who faced the loss of five hundred jobs at a local coke-processing plant and three hundred fifty Nabisco workers who faced a plant closing in violation of their collective bargaining agreement. As in Los Angeles, these efforts around worker justice have fostered an ongoing religious task force focused on economic justice issues. Long-range movement building was also behind the campaign's development of a popular economics workshop. Organizers trained volunteers in a basic half-hour curriculum that highlighted issues of national and local economic disparity. These volunteers then held gatherings among their fellow union members, church parishioners, neighbors, students, and so forth to discuss the economics facing working people and what to do about it. During its first year, the program trained over two hundred volunteers who met with over five thousand people.

The patient preparation work has helped the western Pennsylvania campaign flip around what has proven a thorny issue facing living wage activists: the question of nonprofit employers. By spreading misleading information and drawing on the more corporate-oriented of the nonprofit staff, living wage opponents have used nonprofit organizations as a fig leaf to hide the real sources of their opposition to a living wage ordinance. For example, a November 1998 article in the Detroit press exclaimed: "One Hundred Thousand Families Won't Receive Thanksgiving Turkeys Due to Living Wage." This alarm came from bogus claims made by the head of the local Salvation Army that the new Detroit living wage ordinance was going to cost the organization millions of dollars. Never mind that the actual impact on the organization's two Detroit facilities was minimal or that the working poor who cleaned and guarded city facilities were now going to get a hefty raise.

To avoid such hysterics, some living wage campaigns have restricted or waived coverage of nonprofit employers. However, such employers are often a chief source of publicly funded poverty-wage jobs. A survey by researchers at Wayne State University of nonprofit organizations covered by Detroit's living wage law found the claims of mass ruination inaccurate. A year and a half after the law's passage by voters, most nonprofits had been able to comply with the new law's $8.35 an hour wage with benefits or $10.44 without. However, a minority of such organizations had faced financial obstacles. While the overall cost of the wage increase was relatively small, some nonprofits dependent on outside grants had little room to maneuver. And a small handful had become dependent on paying a majority of their employees poverty wages. The report recommended policies to target additional funds to nonprofit employers most in need. The total estimated costs of such a program fell below 1 percent of the funds currently flowing to nonprofits through the city administration.[5]

While city-based living wage laws can cover nonprofits, generally speaking, the real streams of human-service-related funds typically flow through county governments. This distribution certainly proved true in Allegheny County. In seeking to pass a county living wage law that covered nonprofit employers, the western Pennsylvania living wage campaign set out to neutralize nonprofit ideological opponents and gain the nonprofit community as a whole as an ally. The key lay in advancing demands for greater funding. Through research and testimonials, the campaign documented the widespread awareness among nonprofit employers that low wages cost them dearly in terms of employee turnover and poor-quality work. Not only were poverty wages unfair to workers, but they jeopardized important public services in areas such as public health, child care, and elder care. In developing a county living wage ordinance, the campaign recognized the need to phase in nonprofit compliance in order to give these organizations time to obtain more funds. In the meantime, the campaign sought a county commitment to increase its portion of money going to support nonprofit programs and to lobby the state legislature to provide additional funds for use specifically in raising wages (the bulk of nonprofit funds flowing through the county originate from state coffers). With few nonprofit organizations prepared to publicly oppose an effort that would increase their funding and raise the quality of their employment practices, the living wage campaign silenced nonprofit critics and gained many nonprofit allies.

More Modest Living Wage Campaigns

The above examples draw from the ranks of the movement's most innovative and vibrant campaigns. At the opposite end of the living wage spectrum are campaigns whose activities and strategic horizons appear more limited. Such campaigns often grow out of the initiative of a handful of individuals or organizations. Their activities focus mainly on drafting an ordinance, developing a list of endorsing organizations, getting a good turnout at council hearings, and lobbying elected officials. These campaigns do not develop the kinds of elaborate and long-range organizing plans of the kind we profiled above. Nor do they found nonprofit organizations or other new institutions to support ongoing coalition building and movement activism.

The Toledo campaign, for example, grew out of the actions of one city councilor who came out of the UAW. By drafting and introducing a living wage law, he sparked local labor and community activists into action. The successful campaign also benefited from the controversy surrounding a massive public subsidy granted to Jeep for the construction of its new Toledo assembly plant. In building the new plant to replace an existing facility, the company did not pledge to create any new jobs, only to limit the loss of existing jobs.

In Detroit, the local AFL-CIO placed the living wage on the ballot primarily to help raise voter turnout for the 1998 November elections. The massive 80 percent vote in favor of the initiative came mainly by including living wage materials in the labor movement's existing get-out-the-vote coordinated campaign in the city. This strategy was complemented with an outreach effort to area churches. The outreach sparked living wage–related activity in about three dozen congregations. Similarly, in evaluating the character of the Miami-Dade County living wage effort, researcher and participant Bruce Nissen concluded that, from a social movement perspective, the campaign had a limited grassroots mobilization and little large-scale religious involvement.[6]

Yet, even these more modest campaigns still signify a clear change at America's grassroots. All of the above efforts successfully passed living wage laws. All had to do so in the face of concerted efforts by the chamber of commerce, and often the local mayor, to undermine the campaign. And while not as dramatic as such cases as Chicago or Los Angeles, all these campaigns signified a noticeable shift in local activism. For example, in pointing to the limits of the Miami experience, Nissen nevertheless stressed that the effort still marked the first time in many years that the local labor movement had engaged in such a coalition. Clearly, a network of progressive local labor and nonlabor leaders had learned to work together for a common cause.

The Detroit campaign also displayed results beyond the passage of an ordinance. The stunning ballot victory in the city inspired activists and the central labor council to develop legislative campaigns in surrounding suburban communities. In early 2000, the Detroit suburb of Warren, Michigan's third-largest city, passed a living wage ordinance. By 2001, active campaigns had developed in several other surrounding communities, and Ferndale and East Pointe had passed laws. And living wage activism spread

to other parts of the state, including Kalamazoo, Lansing, Grand Rapids, and Washtenaw County. By the summer of 2001, eight Michigan municipalities had passed living wage ordinances.

All of these are modest, yet significant, affairs. The Washtenaw County campaign, for example, has maintained its activism largely on the volunteer efforts of no more than a dozen core activists. Its grassroots efforts have been limited to successfully turning out supporters to public hearings. Its budget has never exceeded a couple of hundred dollars and no local organization has made the living wage a full-time project. Nevertheless, the campaign has enjoyed notable success and made a clear impact. Most of the core leaders and volunteers—who come from a mix of labor, community, and faith backgrounds—had never worked together before. The campaign marked the first time that the two main labor bodies in the county had worked together in coalition for more than a couple of months. The living wage effort drew clergy endorsements of religious leaders well beyond the "usual suspects" from activist churches. The campaign also linked up the militant antisweatshop student group at the University of Michigan with local labor and community activists. Most important, despite relying on volunteer energy, the living wage has proven a cause able to maintain activism over a long period of time, exceeding three years by 2001.

The Washtenaw campaign also developed enough momentum that local elected officials took it quite seriously. Following the passage of a living wage law in Ypsilanti Township, the small city of Ypsilanti passed a similar law. Although the mayor privately worked to get out opposition against the law, she publicly voted for it—a sign that she could not afford the political fallout from direct opposition. Ann Arbor's Republican mayor vetoed a living wage law only because she had chosen not to run for reelection. Indeed, in November 2000, a living wage champion on the city council was elected Ann Arbor's mayor and the Democrats established a super majority on the city council. In early 2001, Ann Arbor and Pittsfield Township passed living wage laws. Washtenaw County also became the first municipality in the country to pass a Road Commission living wage policy covering work, such as building maintenance, contracted through the commission.

The greatest sign in Michigan that local living wage campaigns had established something new and meaningful came from the state's legislature. With the maintenance of a Republican-dominated state government following the 2000 elections, the Michigan legislature attempted twice unsuccessfully to pass a law banning local government from requiring wages in excess of the state's minimum wage law. Apparently, the ability of grassroots coalitions to use public authority to regulate business employment decisions had proven simply too dangerous a precedent for the chamber of commerce and its Republican majority to allow. Such state prohibitions have been passed in Arizona, Virginia, Colorado, and Missouri. Thus far, they have not stopped living wage activism. Subsequent to the state law, Tucson, Alexandria, Denver, and St. Louis passed living wage ordinances—the first three by council action, the latter by ballot initiative. It has yet to become clear whether state laws banning wage regulations that conflict with a state's minimum wage can legally be applied to living wage laws concerned with the core local government powers to negotiate contracts and subsidy programs. Thus far, living wage opponents have not tried to enforce existing state laws but have sought new state actions that explicitly trample local home rule by telling municipalities that they cannot mandate wage levels in their contract and subsidy agreements. Yet, legislatures have proven unwilling to pass such draconian legislation. In 2001, while a court decision struck down the St. Louis living wage law because of some problematic wording, the judge nevertheless emphasized that the city did have the authority to pass a living wage ordinance despite a state law claiming otherwise. Living wage supporters are now pushing the city council to pass a cleaned-up ordinance. In Michigan, the stillborn actions of the legislature have fostered an even stronger living wage movement, as the backlash to the attempted legislation has made the living wage an even more public cause and allowed activists to establish an even broader statewide living wage network capable of fostering more local campaigns and potential statewide action.

A Sign of the Times

Taken as a whole, the living wage movement's greatest achievements have come at the political level. While real workers have seen real wage gains, the actual number of people lifted out of poverty by living wage laws has often been modest. Oakland's ordinance originally covered fewer than 500 workers; Boston's ordinance 1,000–1,500. The original estimates in Baltimore of 4,000 workers were revised closer to 1,500. Robert Pollin and his team estimated that between 3,924 and 7,626 workers would enjoy wage increases directly from the original Los Angeles living wage law. This does not include the up to 10,000 workers earning above, but close to, the living wage who might experience a ripple effect. Even adding these workers to the count, however, the figures are still modest when compared to an estimated 870,513 low-wage workers who would benefit from a citywide increase in the minimum wage to $6.50 an hour.[7] We should note that recent living wage efforts to cover large-scale public facilities, coastal zones, and major development projects does promise to increase the number of workers covered. Estimates of San Francisco's living wage law that includes the city airport leaseholders, for example, run up to 22,000 workers gaining from the ordinance. Activists also pushed through a separate Health Care Accountability Ordinance that requires contractors and lease users to either provide their employees $1.25 an hour in health benefits, pay $1.25 an hour into a city health pool to purchase benefits for the employees, or pay the same amount into a city health fund. The measure was estimated to cover 20,000 of the city's 130,000 uninsured workers.

The most important legacy of the living wage, however, is the process that it puts into motion. A successful campaign means that a diverse array of labor, community, and religious organizations have come together around the belief that through collective action they can organize for a better economic future. The basic grassroots ingredients assembled in the living wage efforts represent the beginning seeds capable of becoming the kind of movement for economic justice and democracy that can push wholesale economic change. While the number of workers directly benefiting may be modest, it is real—demonstrating that grassroots activism that pushes legislative reform can achieve real change. Indeed, it will come as no surprise as we continue through the rest of this book that living wage campaigns will continue to crop up as a component in today's boldest and most far-reaching efforts at economic change.

Before moving on to these other cases, we conclude by summarizing three main elements revealed by the living wage experience that are common to all of the currents of progressive grassroots organizing emerging today. These are:

1. Revival of Labor–Community Alliances

Living wage campaigns bridge past tensions and neglect to foster coalitions that have long historic precedent. During those times in which the labor movement has been at the center of societal change, two connections have been particularly relevant. First, unions connected to faith communities. Indeed, today's revival of faith-based worker justice networks harks back to such heydays as the mass union organizing waves in the late 1930s and 1940s. Under the postwar labor-management accord, however, such alliances atrophied. Today, they are being rebuilt. According to an August 28, 1998, article in the *Los Angeles Times*, between 1996 and 1998, the number of interfaith labor organizations around the country jumped from twelve to thirty-eight. "I think there's a widespread sense in the religious community that

social and economic inequalities are growing and that something has to be done about it," explained CLUE activist Reverend Dick Gillette. Frank Clark, the executive director of the Ecumenical Council of Pasadena Churches, agreed with this sentiment, adding that, "Ten years ago you wouldn't have seen evangelicals, Pentecostals, Catholics, Jews, struggling with these issues as much as now."[8]

Second, labor organizing intertwined with low-income and communities of color. Indeed, the great union surge of the 1930s would not have been possible without crossing the racial divide. In industries such as autos and textiles, multiracial union organizing successes translated into grassroots efforts to dismantle discrimination at work and segregation in the community. Unfortunately, these connections were also allowed to wither as the labor movement took an uneven approach to the civil rights movement. Some unions proved obstacles to racial justice. The leadership of many others simply did not place themselves at the forefront of the battle against racism. That living wage campaigns typically witness alliances between unions and such low-income neighborhood groups as the Association of Community Organizations for Reform Now promises well for the future. Indeed, historical periods in which labor-community-religious activism has become prevalent have been times of great social awakening.

The alliances built through living wage activism often carried into ongoing cooperation. The campaign to win a living wage ordinance in Boston, for example, forged an enduring partnership between the Association of Community Organizations for Reform Now and the Massachusetts AFL-CIO. Together the two groups have spearheaded coalitions behind two initiatives. The first increased the state's Earned Income Credit (EIC), a tax break that puts cash in the pockets of working families. Thus far, the coalition has successfully increased the EIC from 10 percent of the federal Earned Income Tax Credit to 15 percent. The second raised the state's minimum wage by $.50 to $6.75. The campaign now aims for additional legislation to index the minimum wage to increase automatically with inflation. In Little Rock, the local ACORN and the Central Labor Council have recently translated years of informal cooperation into a formal alliance—complete with its own logo on T-shirts and ball caps. One of the first projects of this new partnership is an active living wage campaign.

The living wage movement has also begun overlapping with the national antisweatshop movement. The textile workers union—United Needle and Industrial Textile Employees (UNITE)—has helped successfully push antisweatshop procurement legislation in over thirty municipalities. These ordinances require that when cities purchase apparel, they enter into contracts with only those manufacturers that adhere to international and U.S. labor, environmental, and human rights laws and that pay their workers a living wage. For example, in 1999, Newark, New Jersey, required companies producing city uniforms and other apparel to pay a living wage and disclose all factory sites so that conditions could be independently verified. On American campuses, a growing student antisweatshop movement has targeted the $2.5 billion collegiate licensing apparel industry. Through demonstrations, building takeovers, infiltration of university public events, and other organizing, students have pressured their administrations to adopt codes of conduct mandating public disclosure of factory sites, a guaranteed living wage for workers, and independent monitoring of factory conditions. With the assistance of UNITE, activism spread to two hundred campuses. By 2001, fifty-seven universities and colleges had adopted the codes of conduct developed by United Students Against Sweatshops and become members of the Workers Rights Consortium—an independent monitoring program established as an alternative to the industry-oriented Fair Labor Association.[9]

As dramatized by events at Harvard, this student movement has begun linking up with local living wage struggles. In April 2001, forty Harvard students occupied the president's and other offices in Massachusetts Hall. This was not the first living wage sit-in on a college campus; that honor goes to Johns Hopkins students. However, the twenty-day Harvard sit-in drew national media attention. The students demanded a living wage of at least $10.25 for the estimated four hundred mainly janitors, dining hall workers, and security guards currently paid below this amount. They also wanted the same policy applied to several hundred temporary workers subcontracted for below a living wage. The students built a broad coalition that included all of the unions on campus and the key union and community players behind the successful Boston, Cambridge, and Somerville living wage campaigns. The sit-in was endorsed by four hundred Harvard faculty members, Massachusetts's two U.S. senators, and both Massachusetts and national AFL-CIO leaders who visited the students. In the end, while not agreeing directly to a living wage, the university did change its no negotiation stance to agree to a committee of faculty members, workers, officials, and students that would reexamine the university's wage policies. Harvard also agreed to suspend outsourcing custodial and dining service work to subcontractors in order to await the committee's recommendations. Through the subcontracting, workers were maintaining the same jobs but receiving a pay cut when the official employer status changed. During the Harvard sit-in, students at the University of Connecticut occupied their president's office in support of university janitors.

2. Proactive Activism

While living wage campaigns represent a reaction to broad economic and political trends, they ultimately originate as proactive decisions by progressive organizers. By offering a forward-looking positive agenda, they place grassroots activism on the offensive. This character comes in stark contrast to the battles that most progressive groups have fought since the late 1970s. Be it fending off management union busting, assaults on the Clean Air Act, right-wing welfare "reform," attacks on a woman's right to choose, or various forms of "reverse Robin Hood" tax and fiscal policies, progressive groups have continuously found themselves reacting to a corporate offensive. Unfortunately, defensive battles can often narrow strategic horizons, divide potential allies against each other, and fail to address the cynicism that has become so prevalent in contemporary society.

By contrast, living wage campaigns offer a positive view of the future through practical reforms linked to a wide range of concerns. And as we have seen, the living wage concept naturally leads to continued economic justice organizing beyond the winning of any specific law. Most important, living wage campaigns demonstrate the right and ability of ordinary people to participate in the economic decisions that affect their lives. It is this principle that motivates chamber of commerce opposition. As we have mentioned, the research has shown that the financial burden to employers is generally modest while the potential gains of living wage employment practices are quite real. The opposition is not driven out of concern for direct financial costs, but by the political threat. Living wage opponents commonly talk about living wage laws as local across-the-board minimum wages. This characterization reflects not just a desire to overstate the supposed costs, but a recognition that successful living wage efforts produce active coalitions capable of pursuing further activism. Such a growing movement can produce even bolder economic measures such as increases in the minimum wage, further forms of business regulation, union organizing, and other "socialistic" practices.

3. The "Free Market" Isn't All That Free

Our nation's official debates have always treated the economy as a self-regulating system driven by the market's "invisible hand." The revival of neoliberal thinking and "globalization" over the past two decades has only further strengthened notions that the direction of the economy is well beyond the reach of deliberate public policy. Living wage campaigns throw into the light of day the hidden reality that government policy has been, and continues, intimately

shaping the "free market." Whether government action participates directly in economic decisions, such as through subsidies, or indirectly, by not requiring wage and job standards for those subsidies, public policy lies at the heart of our economy. Living wage campaigns open a can of worms that the chamber of commerce would rather leave sealed. As Part I demonstrated, once we accept that public policy can play a positive role in structuring the economy, most business practices that Americans today take for granted turn out not to be so inevitable. Indeed, when policy reforms are connected to growing grassroots activism, wholesale societal change moves from an abstract dream to a practical possibility.

A Sign of Things to Come

With more campaigns now under way than the sixty-eight communities that have already passed laws, the living wage movement continues to expand. As one of its next stages, this activism is beginning to spread to the state level. In Illinois, for example, the key players of the Chicago campaign have put together an effort to push the state legislature to increase funding for home health care providers—raising them to a living wage. In Minnesota, a similar effort has organized for state funds dedicated to raising wages among public-funded child care workers. In New Mexico, ACORN, the state AFL-CIO, Human Needs Coordinating Council, and others are fighting to raise the wages of direct state employees. As we will see, much of the organizing covered in the rest of this book has some kind of link to living wage campaigns.

In the remaining chapters we will further develop these possibilities by geographically and thematically broadening our focus beyond single local campaigns. In the next chapter, we will examine a model effort to develop a progressive regional economic agenda. In chapter 9 our focus will move from local to statewide reforms. The remaining chapters will then profile agendas and movements that provide further the evidence of a national awakening.

8

Building a High-Road Agenda:
Examples from Wisconsin

Living wage campaigns begin a progressive dialogue about economic priorities, business practices, and the role of public policy. Ultimately, such beginnings need to translate into more comprehensive agendas for economic change. In this chapter, we explore several interconnected examples from Wisconsin. Together they demonstrate how even at a local level progressives can begin a process of economic transformation.

In the past several years, Wisconsin has been home to several model community and labor initiatives to steer their local and regional economies toward the high road. Today, the state boasts one of the nation's premiere metropolitan-wide community economic planning initiatives—the Campaign for a Sustainable Milwaukee. The Wisconsin Regional Training Partnership (WRTP) is the largest sectoral training and modernization consortium in the country. And together CSM and the WRTP help run one of six pioneering urban jobs initiatives supported by the Annie E. Casey Foundation. These projects have brought together labor, community, government, nonprofit, and business groups to pave the way for a high-road future. Today, similar work has been pulled together in Dane County—home of Madison, the state capital. Together these examples show how people begin to take hold of their collective economic destiny.

The Economic Context

Urban Decay

A scan of the media headlines would suggest that the working people of Wisconsin had reasons to celebrate the 1990s. In business terms, the state's economic performance had exceeded the nation's in several categories. While family income grew annually at an average of 0.5 percent nationally, Wisconsin's rate showed 0.9 percent. Unemployment reached a twenty-five-year low of 2.8 percent in August 1995. In the early 1990s, Wisconsin was the only state in the nation ranking in the top ten in both its share of existing firms reporting increased employment and in the survival rate of an impressive number of new firms. Furthermore, following the national trend, productivity and profit rates had markedly improved.

However, as a yearly study done by the Center on Wisconsin Strategy makes clear, workers and their families have not reaped the full benefits of the business boom.[1] Indeed, business success was all too often bought at working people's expense. The long-term picture told a different story than the media headlines. While between 1970 and 1989 median family income in the United States increased 3.6 percent, in Wisconsin it actually fell by 1.7 percent. While average real hourly wages fell 3.2 percent in the nation as a whole between 1979 and 1993, in Wisconsin they dropped by 8.6 percent—almost three times as fast. Despite growth during the second half of the 1990s, real median wages were still below 1979 levels. When broken down by race, the statistics become even grimmer. Nationally from 1979 to 1993, black women's wages rose a modest 3 percent, yet in Wisconsin they fell 18.5 percent. The gap between white and black wages, while increasing nationwide, grew three to six times as fast in Wisconsin. The number of Wisconsin families living in poverty had increased at twice the national rate. By 1989, Wisconsin had the second-highest growth rate of black child poverty in America—a staggering 55.8 percent increase from a decade earlier. Researchers found that education did not insulate workers from these overall trends. In the best case of college-educated workers, their overall wages simply were holding constant. For the 80 percent majority with three years or less of post–high school education, the trends pointed to falling wages.

Equally revealing were the deeper patterns behind these grim income statistics. Poverty jobs, those paying full-time equivalents below the federal poverty line for a family of four, increased from one-quarter of all Wisconsin jobs in 1979 to over one-third by 1993. By this time, over half of all black men and nearly two-thirds of black women in Wisconsin worked at poverty-wage jobs. For all too many workers, poverty wages meant poverty careers. Over half of those who were paid below the poverty line in 1990 were still paid poverty wages in 1997. Meanwhile, 11 percent of those paid above the line in 1990 had fallen below by 1997. Researchers found that only a small proportion of falling wages could be attributed to the commonly cited employment shifts from manufacturing to service sector. While the share of employment in manufacturing had declined modestly, from 32 percent to 26 percent from 1979 to 1993, this was less than the national average. And in terms of actual number of workers, Wisconsin manufacturing employment was nearly the same as it had been twenty years before.

What became most noticeable to researchers was the drastic move of manufacturing out of the high-paying unionized localities that had been the economy's strength. The jobs had not gone overseas or down south, however. Employers were relocating down the freeway—taking work out of the cities to suburban and rural areas. And when employers moved the jobs, they left the unions behind. During the 1980s and 1990s, the heavily union areas of Milwaukee, Racine, and Kenosha lost ninety-six thousand manufacturing jobs. At the same time, the rest of the state gained seventy-eight thousand such jobs—often with the same employers. This shift had led to a $3,000 loss in average annual wages—for a total of $421 million in lost yearly worker income. In the state's private sector, unionization fell from 20 percent to 13 percent between 1983 and 1993 (although the public sector had climbed to 53 percent over this same period). Adding to this trend was a growing reliance by business on part-time, temporary, and self-employed workers. Government policies of deregulation and privatization had simply added mechanisms for manufacturers to pay less.

While economic strains hit working people throughout the state, Milwaukee and other urban industrial centers had been particularly hard hit. During the 1980s, the city lost a full one-third of its manufacturing jobs. Over forty thousand family-supporting jobs had left the city. Nationally, this fate has been shared by fifteen other cities that, together with Milwaukee, accounted for 70 percent of the 1.9 million manufacturing jobs lost that decade.[2]

As a result of this corporate disinvestment, Milwaukee needed at least fifty thousand new jobs to employ everyone looking for work. Yet, with some 30 percent of jobs paying under $6 an hour in 1994, the problem was not simply work, but family-supporting jobs. In 1994, Milwaukee ranked just behind Los Angeles and Miami as the city with the greatest level of low-wage job creation. This crisis has drastically widened the racial divisions in an already divided city. A three-year study done by the University of Wisconsin's Center for Economic Development put into numbers what black and Latino residents had long known. Of the tens of thousands of new jobs created in downtown Milwaukee during the 1980s, African Americans held fewer than 8 percent. Among those who got the new jobs created since 1982, a full 95 percent of blacks and Latinos earned under $20,000 a year. Half of the new jobs went to white suburbanites—four out of five of whom earned over $40,000.[3]

Urban Possibilities

While it may seem that the suburbs gained at the expense of the cities, Milwaukee's experience, along with that of other cities, suggests more complex conclusions. While the city lost 30 percent of its manufacturing jobs between 1978 and 1988, Milwaukee County, which includes the city, actually lost even more—a full 34 percent. And the inner-ring suburbs lost nearly one out of five such jobs during the 1980s. This suggests that when employers moved jobs out of the city, they went thirty miles or more in search of a "favorable investment climate." Indeed, according to one study of fifty-nine metropolitan areas, the share of suburban income attributable to the density and income of the central cities rose from 41 to 67 percent from 1979 to 1987. In dollar terms, that meant that every $1,000 gained or lost in per capita city income meant a $690 loss or gain for its suburbs.[4] The image these figures create is one of an ever-expanding geographical doughnut. As new investment moves farther away from the cities, it pulls the doughnut ever wider—leaving a growing hole of decay. Such an analysis has important political implications. While right-wing politics openly attempts to pit suburban voters against the cities, actual economic patterns suggest a progressive alliance joining the city with at least its inner-ring suburbs against corporate America.

Practitioners of conventional economic development policy view decaying cities as a source of problems and deficits that need to be filled from the outside. However, as we will see, organizers in Milwaukee offer a different vision. Far from being relics of a bygone past, the nation's cities offer a key platform for a high-road future. Indeed, for policy makers and activists hoping to develop high-road economics, cities hold several advantages. Unlike the suburbs, they were built to be communities. That means, for example, that many cities originally were designed around public transportation and walking. Residential areas cluster around business districts. The result, when properly maintained, is the infrastructure for an efficient, low-energy transportation system. The cities combine relatively low land use with a much greater feeling of neighborhood and community. This benefits both the environment and people.[5] Cities also hold a wealth of educational institutions clustered in a compact area.

None of the above can be said of the suburbs. The latest sprawl simply spreads out housing, business, and infrastructure in a mindless pursuit of cheap land, weak zoning, and the promise of happiness through isolation. In chapter 11 we will profile the enormous short- and long-term expenses of constructing ever more suburbs. As our nation devotes ever-greater energy to converting life-sustaining countryside into wasteful, high-consumption, alienated living and work units, our genuine community-building capacity, found in the cities and towns, languishes from lack of resources.

Revitalized, people-oriented cities have much to offer business, as well as the general community. Efficient transportation and education mean concrete cost benefits for high-road firms. These firms can also enjoy clear advantages of geographical concentration. As we will examine below, the most successful businesses are the ones that cross-fertilize with other firms. Clustering related companies in a single geographical area also offers each individual firm ready access to suppliers and customers. Furthermore, when integrated through public/private partnerships, clustering allows innovations in work design, technology, and worker training to filter from one firm to another.

Cities also offer special advantages to progressives

looking for economic change. They are still the strongholds of unionism. Their diverse populations include various communities whose daily lives illustrate dramatically the basic economic contradictions facing our nation and the true nature of its power structure. It comes as no surprise that in 70-percent black Detroit, over four out of five voters chose a living wage in 1998. Indeed, living wage campaigns are just one demonstration of the power of our cities' wealth in labor, religious, and community groups. In short, our nation's cities, especially when allied with their inner-ring suburbs, offer excellent ground for establishing models for the kinds of progressive economy we want to build and the people-oriented communities where we want to live.

COWS Promotes the High Road

All of the initiatives discussed below have one thing in common: the Center on Wisconsin Strategy (COWS). COWS is a "think and do" tank based at the University of Wisconsin-Madison. Its activities focus on fostering avenues for workers, unions, communities, governments, and businesses to pursue high-road economics through innovative partnerships and coalitions.

COWS's work encourages potential partners to rethink their strategies and practices. Business organizations, for example, must move beyond their traditional trade associations model toward more active and collective problem-solving bodies that facilitate high-road success. Unions need to move beyond traditional contract issues to play a more active role in management decisions by promoting high-road practices around skill development, high productivity work organization, labor-management cooperation, and industry coordination. Community organizations must link their particular set of issues to broader regional economic planning. They can help prepare workers for gainful employment and link job development to other aspects of community life such as housing, public safety, land use, and so forth. Finally, governments must abandon the prevailing market-led wisdom to assert a much-neglected role as the source of public economic standards. They can also foster nongovernmental bodies and networks that promote high-road development. By working with a broad range of groups, COWS aims to develop the regional infrastructures necessary for high-road economics.

COWS served as the incubator for the initiatives discussed below. In addition to research and technical assistance, COWS helped design the projects, bring in funds, and provide initial staff. Once the programs have passed from infancy into full independence, COWS continues to provide technical and research support as well as helping leverage resources from private foundations, government, business, and labor. In 1998, COWS ran on $800,000; and its spin-off projects had combined budgets on the order of $3 million.

Activist Economic Research

A visit to the COWS Web site reveals a wealth of research reports and media materials—all aimed at highlighting current problems and promoting high-road alternatives. In the early 1990s, COWS conducted a series of regional economic analyses for the Milwaukee area that is particularly instructive on how progressives can use research to build a strategic vision.[6]

In order to close off the low road and pave the high road, labor and community groups need to understand the operations of their area's economy. Which sectors and individual firms are creating new jobs? Which offer the greatest potential for decent wages and sustained careers? Which enhance the community and which tear it down? Most important, which firms and sectors hold the potential for the high road, if provided a push and support in this direction?

To capture the central interactions occurring among related firms, researchers focused on a regional level. By helping business compete through regional cooperation, unions, community groups, and local governments cannot only foster high-road jobs, but also insert their own voices as partners in the economic decision-making process. The research drew on the examples set in Europe by such regions as the so-called "Third Italy" (the provinces of Tuscany, Emilia-Romagna, and Veneto), West Jutland in Denmark, Mondragon in Spain, and Baden-Württemberg in Germany. In these areas, small to mid-sized firms produce specialized, high-value-added products using a skilled workforce and high-road business practices. These firms can successfully compete with large multinational corporations because cooperation with other firms and a dense network of community institutions allow them access to technology, training, credit, and markets well beyond their individual means. Research suggests that such networked firms have a flexibility often lacking in larger companies.[7] Most notably, all four regions are characterized by a highly organized society that includes high union densities and a long and influential left-wing political tradition.

The regional economic analysis used by COWS aimed to identify the possibilities for such high-road partnerships in Wisconsin. Successful regional economic specialization promised not the fragmented free market so championed by the chambers of commerce, but a powerful and dense institutional infrastructure to link business with community success. The research model involved more than a one-shot research report—an ongoing project whose main components spanned several years. The methodologies of analysis, testing, feedback, and reevaluation aimed not simply to develop ever more detailed and targeted data on the local economy, but in the process, develop relationships between the researching group and potential high-road businesses. The methodology broke down into three broad stages: quick gains, sectoral analysis, and cluster analysis. A brief summary of each stage provides a sense of how the research links to the projects that we will profile below.

The first stage aimed at quick success by identifying those firms that paid family-supporting wages and were hiring or likely to hire in the future. Using government data, researchers targeted particular areas of the economy. They then contacted specific firms to discuss their hiring practices and particular barriers and opportunities for employing residents from distressed areas. From this data, researchers and activists brainstormed ways to use existing community services to connect local residents with decent jobs in growing parts of the economy.

In stage two, researchers identified those economic sectors in which regional strategies could aid long-term, high-road growth. In which sectors are related firms particularly prospering as a group compared to other parts of the country? These are the targets of local strength that activists want to build on. By consulting trade publications and government authorities, and by conducting detailed interviews with selected firms, researchers traced the factors that influenced competition with these targeted sectors. The goal was to identify the opportunities for collective problem solving by collaboration among firms, unions, the community, and local government.

For the final phase, researchers further refined their targeting by identifying clusters of firms, in the same or related industries, that both depended directly on one another and that drew from the same collective pools of labor, technology, and markets. Such firms suffer or prosper together. Once again, researchers looked for opportunities for collective intervention to aid firms by promoting innovation, reducing transaction costs, stimulating supportive services, and enhancing market visibility. For example, firms in a cluster may share the same labor pool as workers change jobs and companies but stay in related work. Such firms can benefit by coordinating with each other to collectively enhance the skills and preparations of this workforce. At the same time, by aiding the process, unions and community groups can secure more stable career opportunities for workers and access to decent jobs for residents. Other areas of collective problem solving include missing links in their supply chains, difficulties in finding access to financing, and obstacles to technological innovation or effective research and development.

This kind of regional economic analysis supported and accompanied the founding and growth of the projects detailed below. Not only did COWS researchers develop the information necessary to define and target specific projects, but in the course of the research, COWS developed contacts and working relationships among many of the key players needed to pull such projects together.

The Campaign for a Sustainable Milwaukee

The Campaign for a Sustainable Milwaukee (CSM) is one of the nation's premiere efforts at metropolitanwide, community-based economic planning. The coalition began with the development of a detailed and comprehensive community plan for the future of the city. Today, it supports a wide range of activities that work to make the ideas of the plan a lived reality. Sustainable Milwaukee's impressive list of participating organizations includes nearly two hundred groups from among union, religious, community, educational, and governmental circles.

In addition to support from COWS, the AFL-CIO Milwaukee County Labor Council (MCLC) played a key founding role. Historically, Milwaukee has had a strong labor tradition. With four decades of socialist mayors during the first half of the twentieth century, the city boasted one of the strongest labor-socialist traditions in the country. At the time of its 1959 founding, the MCLC brought together unions representing 120,000 members. By 1996, that number had dropped to 85,000. Worse, union density in the area had fallen from 34 percent in 1984 to 18 percent a decade later. Like many central labor councils across the county, the MCLC found that the postwar strategies followed by the American labor movement had left it ill prepared to tackle the economic transformation of the area. Indeed, as unions focused on workplace bargaining, the kind of comprehensive intervention in the regional economy that was now needed proved well beyond the MCLC's past practices.

However, in 1993, MCLC leaders launched a new path when they sponsored a gathering of labor leaders, housing activists, environmentalists, community organizers, religious leaders, third-party activists, and government officials to develop a proactive economic program. "We knew what we were opposed to in this economy, but we weren't always sure what we were for. The Campaign is an attempt to answer that question," explained the then MCLC secretary-treasurer Bruce Colburn.[8] That from the beginning the MCLC brought a broad range of community leaders and activists in as equal partners in the process reflected a notable awareness of the need to build a coalition agenda beyond labor's internal efforts.

Pulling together such a broad coalition was no small accomplishment. Indeed, organizers convinced a diverse group that participating in a year-long planning process to draft a grassroots plan would not prove a waste of time, but an investment in new and lasting activism. Organizers tapped into growing feelings among local activists that they needed to do something new and different. For years, a vibrant array of labor, environmental, religious, and community organizations had fought battles over individual issues. They often launched innovative programs targeted at specific problems and formed coalitions around specific concerns. Now, however, they were faced with a right-wing agenda and an economic transformation that threatened to overwhelm these efforts. All too often their battles proved defensive. Traditional activism was not getting at the root economic and political forces. What they needed was a common plan that would address people's immediate needs while fundamentally changing the rules of the game. They needed an alternative model of community-driven economic development that would bring together progressives and the broader community into a proactive, visionary effort—one aimed at turning Milwaukee into a sustainable, vibrant, and life-affirming city.

For a year the coalition engaged in a two-pronged process. While creating decent-paying jobs was its central priority, the coalition defined its economic issues broadly. Thus, the group launched four task forces around the interconnected areas of jobs and training, credit, transportation and the environment, and education. Each task force went through a three-step process of analyzing the problems and highlighting the general principles relevant to addressing them, formulating an outline of proposed solutions, and, finally, developing a list of specific recommendations that could be taken to the community for greater feedback and discussion. While the task forces worked on their specific areas, the larger group also continued to meet. To encourage people to step out of their traditional areas of concern, at each step task forces reported back to the larger group so that the broader coalition could discuss each specific area.

Organizers strove to create an open and inviting process that would involve a diverse array of people. As the group's final document explains: "a community plan for economic reconstruction, we believe, should be authored by the community, not outside 'experts.' As a community, we know better than anyone else what ails us, and as much as anyone else about what can work to solve our problems." The task forces received important technical support from COWS. The final recommendations also incorporated many ideas and concrete projects that local groups had already pioneered, but that had not been connected to a more comprehensive plan.

CSM organizers deserve a great deal of credit for establishing a process that came across as serious enough for very busy people to want to give their time and energy to it. As the planning continued, the group grew. The four task forces involved almost ninety official participants including labor activists; teachers; elected officials; social service staff; religious activists; people from neighborhood organizations; members of African-American, Latino, and Native American groups; and environmentalists. Members and organizations involved in the process took the preliminary plan back to their boards, to their community groups, and to thousands of individual Milwaukee citizens. After a year of work, CSM unveiled its plan on October 22, 1994, at a six-hour "Community Congress" attended by almost three hundred representatives.

Entitled *Rebuilding Milwaukee from the Ground Up,* the plan offered a bold vision for Milwaukee's future. It combined broad analysis with a concrete sense of the power that local governments and community have to make real changes. With a length of sixty-four pages, the report contains many policy ideas that we cannot detail here. However, Table 8.1 provides a selective summary.

CSM's vision seeks to unite the city with its inner-ring suburbs. *Rebuilding Milwaukee from the Ground Up* also combined the powers available to local and state government with community mobilization. Many proposals were formulated in such a way as to develop what the report calls greater "community capacity"—developing skills and organization within the community so that ordinary people can speak and act on their own behalf. Finally, the plan not only offered concrete analysis and alternatives, but it also upheld basic social and moral values such as family-supporting jobs, healthy communities, racial and gender justice, responsible business practices, and democratic community participation. We live in an age in which the right appeals to people's sense of a loss of values, yet hypocritically engages in policies that undermine those very values. By contrast, CSM seeks to practice its values in economic and political life.

The time spent developing *Rebuilding Milwaukee from the Ground Up* paid off in a wealth of grassroots activity. We will cover four dimensions here. The Central City Workers Center, which is a major part of the campaign's work, will be covered later as part of the Milwaukee Jobs Initiative.

Spreading the Living Wage

Given the CSM process, it should come as no surprise that Milwaukee has been an early and ongoing living wage community. From the beginning, organizers embarked on a multilayer effort to secure living wage laws at all three levels of local government.

Table 8.1

Summary of *Rebuilding Milwaukee from the Ground Up*

Jobs and Training The report highlights how deindustrialization, racism, suburban sprawl, and government corporate giveaways combined to gut the city's economy. The authors estimated that the city needs at least 50,000 new jobs to employ everyone who wants work. To foster jobs that enhance workers, their families, and the community, the report's recommendations include:

- Local and state legislation to raise the minimum wage and establish minimum health, family leave, and child care standards.
- Steering tax abatements and other financial assistance away from general giveaways and toward targeted investment in community-sustaining jobs.
- Using public money to foster community-driven training programs and businesses as well as provide a framework for worker and community buyouts of local firms.
- Providing jobs directly by developing community-serving, public-service work.
- Community support for union organizing.
- Establishing a grassroots early warning system to detect signs of plant closings.

Credit Both Milwaukee residents and businesses have been starved for capital as financial institutions deny credit to entire areas of the city. To overcome this financial racism, the report points to:

- Concrete ways to strengthen, enforce, and expand government regulations that foster socially responsible banking.
- Alternative financing from state government deposits, socially targeted pension funds, and the creation of "public purpose" banks dedicated to community development.

Transportation and Environment Sustainable Milwaukee seeks to move beyond mainstream economic wisdom that pits the environment against jobs. The report links traditional environmental concerns for pollution and nature preservation with inner-city residents' battles over toxic dumping, workers' struggles for a safe workplace, and suburban residents' feelings of a loss of community. In the end, a vibrant urban community, rather than suburban sprawl, offers the best path toward an environmentally

sustainable future. Specifically, the plan encourages:

- Environmentally friendly jobs while also strengthening the ability of workers to identify and speak out against unsafe and toxic conditions.
- A shift of public transportation dollars away from highway construction and toward the development of light rail and an expanded bus system.
- New land use policies that encourage concentration and spatially diversified and integrated communities.
- Resources for housing reconstruction.
- Neighborhood-based environmental advocacy and enforcement efforts.
- Expanded governmental regulations against corporate pollution.

Education While defending public education from right-wing attacks, the education task force was, nevertheless, frank about the need for genuine public school reform. Schools must be made more accountable to the community and tied to broader efforts at community revitalization. Specifically, the report calls for:

- Equity in school funding.
- A curriculum that is multicultural and tied to students' reality.
- Reduced class size.
- More ethnically diverse teaching staff.
- Elimination of tracking.
- Increased administrative openness and accountability.
- Greater and more diverse parental and community involvement. The report suggests a reform of the state's Family Leave Act that would allow parents the equivalent of two days a year of paid leave from work to take part in school-related activities.
- Major changes in "school to work" programs to include topics such as workers' right to organize, the history of the labor movement, health and safety protections, racial and sexual harassment, family leave laws, and the value of community service.
- The rebirth of the area's historical experience with "lighted schoolhouses" in which schools become community centers open from early in the morning until late in the evening, providing both jobs and services for neighborhood residents.

They began with the city council—the body with the most favorable political balance. To impress on council members the seriousness of the cause, local organizers took to the streets. For example, organizers sent out teams of residents door knocking to ask people to sign cards in support of the living wage and to encourage turnout at city council hearings.

The campaign designed volunteer efforts to build grassroots organization. As volunteers talked to residents, they also actively recruited for the campaign. Starting with a very modest initial pool of several dozen volunteers, after one season the campaign had established a network of eighty-six precinct leaders and several hundred volunteers who had signed "activist contracts" committing themselves to regular work on electoral and issue campaigns. Such success allowed activists to spread their grassroots organizing to other parts of the city.

Grassroots organizing and a broad coalition paid off. Although the campaign had to compromise on the living wage amount and drop a health care requirement, it won the important basic principle in 1995 with a living wage for city contracts set to the federal poverty line for a family of three ($6.05/hour at that time). A year later the campaign won a minimum of $7.70 an hour for all workers employed by the public schools or contractors with the schools. Roughly thirty-eight hundred workers gained from this living wage—many jumping up from near the minimum wage. In 1997, the campaign secured a living wage of $6.25 at the county level for janitorial, security, and parking lot attendants. This wage was indexed to increases in county wages that come through collective bargaining. Organizers plan further activism to expand existing living wage laws and increase the wages and benefits.

Having passed ordinances at the city, school district, and county levels, CSM has also explored ways to take the living wage to employers not directly connected to local tax money. For example, the coalition brought together key decision makers from religious, labor, and community groups—as well as city, county, and state elected officials—to serve on Workers' Rights Boards. These boards use a combination of moral and public pressure to encourage fairness and equity at work. For example, in 1995 CSM drew attention to the plight of asbestos-removal workers by holding a public board hearing. With media and public officials in attendance, half a dozen workers and their union related story after story of how cutthroat competition was, pushing companies to shortcut on safety and pay low wages. Two years later, CSM joined a nationwide effort to highlight the destructive impact of welfare reform. At a Workers' Rights Board hearing, nine former welfare recipients and several social workers spoke to the reality of the state's W-2 reform. The hearing helped to end a practice by W-2 providers of arbitrarily classifying people as "job ready" and hence cutting off their public assistance. The hearing also pointed to the real solutions for welfare: access to living wage jobs, job training, child care, transportation, and education.

In the summer of 1998, CSM's living wage task force began stirring up life in the fast food industry. Research on area McDonalds revealed that inner-city franchises were paying wages significantly below their suburban counterparts, even when they charged more for the food! Volunteers, including a member of the city council, visited targeted locations, handing workers information sheets on the wage differences and leaving a phone number to call for information on unionizing.

CSM has also worked as a major partner in an ongoing wage/lien coalition dedicated to undoing changes in the state's bankruptcy laws. Concluding that an economic downturn was likely, by the end of the 1990s corporate financial institutions across the country had begun pressuring government officials to rewrite the bankruptcy codes in order to protect their financial interests at the expense of working families. In 1998, creditors such as First State Bank won changes to Wisconsin's bankruptcy laws that gave priority to the liens held by financial institutions over the wages owed to workers. As a result, laid-off workers at U.S. Leather tanneries and Steeltech Manufacturing Company were left holding an empty bag of owed wages while company assets were used to pay off creditors. In 2001, the grassroots coalition was pushing the legislature to restore protections for workers' wages. Volunteers from the living wage task force reached out to affected workers who lived in Milwaukee's north side to provide them basic information and to enlist them in the struggle.

By 2001 CSM was also back organizing around the living wage. The county's living wage law included a provision that automatically increased the living wage by the portion in which unionized county workers enjoyed yearly raises. That provision, however, was due to sunset after three years. Thus, the living wage task force had begun organizing both to maintain the annual wage adjustment and to add a provision guaranteeing that the living wage would also be at least one dollar above the federal minimum wage.

Fighting for Job Access

With its birth in 1995, the Job Access Task Force helped team up two groups with a history of battling each other—the civil rights organizations and the building trades unions. The historical battle lines centered around local hiring issues. Construction work is one of the industries in which unions can still legally serve as hiring halls—workers first must become union members in order to gain access to unionized jobs. Traditionally, craft-type unions, such as in construction, maintained their bargaining leverage by ensuring that the supply of skilled workers was tight and among the union membership. While the basic concept is not inherently discriminatory against people of color or women, the historical practice across the country offered numerous examples of blatant racism and patriarchy. Indeed, as late as 1955, some craft-type unions had provisions in their bylaws penalizing members from sharing skills with workers who were not white, male, and U.S. born. Such formal and informal practices had created a construction industry overwhelmingly

white and male. This pattern was continued by traditions—such as giving sons of existing members first access to union membership and apprenticeship training—that were not overtly discriminatory but that served to maintain the biased profile of the industry. It was these patterns that the civil rights movement ran into at full force. The result was often intense conflict between community groups and the building trades unions.

Times have changed, however, opening up new possibilities. Like the labor movement generally, today the building trade unions face a harsh anti-union climate that they need help to overcome. At the same time, by one course or another, some of these unions had begun to make serious commitments to diversifying their ranks. The civil rights organizations also were looking for allies. Large sums of public funds were going to support local construction projects, yet few local taxpayers were gaining access to the jobs. The terms of an alliance were clear. Team up the unions and the community to push for union construction jobs with employment opportunities for local residents.

The Jobs Access Task Force won its first victory in 1997 when it secured a state commitment for 25 percent minority and 5 percent female hiring at construction of the new Wisconsin Convention Center. The task force also successfully pushed for prevailing wages through agreements signed with the Milwaukee Building Trades Council. They also pushed to maximize the ratio of apprentices to journey persons (thus increasing access for workers to enter the skilled professions) and for first-source hiring through community-based organizations such as the Central City Workers Center. Task force coalition work secured a similar agreement for the construction of the new Milwaukee Brewers Stadium.

CSM won such agreements by having the ability to mobilize coalition partners to pressure local officials. This action included public support by prominent figures and organizations and taking to the streets. Such grassroots action has also proven necessary to ensure that agreement targets become actual reality. By the summer of 1998, for example, the task force was mobilizing to push the Brewers stadium advisory committee to take seriously the commitments for minority and female hiring. Hiring and apprenticeship goals were not optional targets, but serious mandates.

While in Milwaukee the partnership between the building trade unions and the community focused on publicly funded projects, similar coalitions elsewhere have gone after totally private undertakings. For example, neither community groups nor local unions were initially taken seriously by the organizers of the 1996 Atlanta Summer Olympic Games. As one of the most commercially driven games ever, the entire affair was being funded out of corporate coffers. With the game's weak reliance on public funds, the public seemingly had little grounds for leverage. Certainly neither the community nor the labor movement alone could have won its separate demands. Indeed, with Georgia a right-to-work state, the unions were operating in a particularly antilabor environment. Nevertheless, their vulnerability fostered cooperation. By teaming up to push for both union jobs and local hiring, a broad coalition of labor, community, and religious groups won significant concessions from Olympic organizers. Highlights of the five-year battle included a march of ten thousand and a takeover by one hundred activists of the Olympic Committee's office. In the end, the coalition won union wages and benefits as well as jobs and apprenticeships for community residents.

CSM entered 2001 organizing for a People's Economic Summit. The gathering would allow CSM to broaden its job access work to a more general platform around economic development, training, job creation, and basic human and civil rights.

Transportation Is a Living Wage Issue

While conventional wisdom suggested that transportation was a nonconcern, CSM unearthed a mountain of inner-city discontent. Indeed, because companies had moved many decent-paying jobs to the suburbs, effective public transportation was a living wage issue. Between 1991 and 1996, Milwaukee's Central City saw a job increase of only 2,481, while surrounding suburban communities added 64,329 new jobs.[9] Yet, according to a study by the Milwaukee Employment and Training Institute and the UWM Social Sciences Research Facility 64 percent of central city job seekers had no car.

This reality meant that a large proportion of inner-city residents needed a decent regional public transportation system to have access to gainful employment. Unfortunately, an inadequate city bus system only added to the broader area's failure to provide public transportation linking city residents to suburban jobs.

Testimony by local residents, mobilized by CSM, put a human face on the statistics. Henry Caldwell, for example, had been forced to leave two well-paying jobs simply because he didn't have a car. He was forced to quit the first job after the several-hour commute, which ended in a three-mile walk, proved too overwhelming. He lost the other job when repeatedly late bus service to Waukesha caused him to miss the only shuttle of the day to his place of employment. Gene Harris lived in Milwaukee but was employed at the Waukesha County airport. Due to inadequate public transportation, Harris resided at a homeless shelter in Waukesha during the week so that he was within biking distance of his work. Joanna Watkins had to rely on public transportation to attend classes at the technical college, conduct her job search, and transport her children to child care. The lack of reliable and efficient transportation had blocked her efforts to obtain successful job placements through temporary agencies.

A pot of $241 million in federal transportation funds provided an opportunity to begin to address these issues. The funds were dedicated to supporting a balanced transportation plan for the region. To gain access to the federal funds, all relevant levels of local government had to agree on a plan. The federal funds also required significant public participation. Yet, only a handful of mostly businesspeople were turning out for the poorly advertised hearings.

Teaming up with the Alliance for Future Transit (a coalition of mainly corporate and business members, but also including university, union, and community organizations), CSM helped develop a balanced transportation plan that included significant improvements to the region's bus system. It also proposed a new ten-mile city light rail line that would link up with a thirteen-mile commuter rail line going into suburban Waukesha. By rerouting buses to connect to the rail stations, the rail plan promised to significantly reduce commuter travel times and provide a central conduit for moving central city residents to suburban jobs. Furthermore, the plan's architects also envisioned using light rail stations as focal points for grassroots-driven urban revitalization.[10]

CSM's Central City Transit Task Force helped go into the community to build support for the public transit plan. Activists attended public meetings, met with local leaders, and knocked on doors. The ranks of supporters included a Catholic-run homeless advocacy and service organization called Repairers of the Breach, veterans' organizations, environmental groups, unions, neighborhood organizations, and business groups. Together they transformed the small, quiet transportation meetings into lively sessions packed with public transit supporters.

In 1996, the organizing paid off when the Public Policy Forum's Transportation Policy Committee, a panel of civic and business leaders, recommended a $2.47 billion plan that included $257 million to establish the light rail line, $60 million for the Waukesha commuter line, and at least $351 million to expand the area's bus system. Activists then helped get Milwaukee's mayor and the Milwaukee county government to endorse the plan. Strong grassroots lobbying even persuaded the Waukesha Board of Supervisors to come on board. Unfortunately, Waukesha County's chief executive, Daniel Finely, vetoed the board's resolution calling for a continued study of the transportation plan.

Suburban merchant George Watts openly ex-pressed the racism that undergirded the debate over the light rail proposals at one of the public hearings. Watts claimed that light rail would "bring in strangers who are not only a threat to your property, but to your children."[11] Apparently, car-driving white suburbanites were not the same kinds of strangers in Watts's mind. While opponents of light rail complained of its expense, the $317 million combined project paled in comparison to the $788 million to $1.79 billion being proposed to rebuild the city's part of I-94. With several dozen task-force members confronting Finely at a televised meeting, activists were able to get the chief executive to agree to support the bus parts of the plan.

The ongoing controversy, however, blocked the light rail. Focusing entirely on road construction, the state legislature voted to ban any study that even considered light rail. With the excuse that the $271 million in federal funds would be taken away if not used, Governor Thompson, in effect, pilfered the money. In 1998, in an eleventh-hour move, conservative Congressman Thompson Petri (from Fond du Lac) successfully amended the massive federal transportation bill to turn control of the $241 million over to Wisconsin's governor, who was dedicated to the interests of suburban road builders.

Despite the defeat, CSM continued to organize. The group proposed a $21.2 million bus expansion plan to begin addressing central city residents' transportation needs. In the summer of 1998, the Transit Task Force successfully brought Ronald Stroman, the director of the U.S. Department of Transportation's Civil Rights office, to Milwaukee to hear residents' grievances against the governor. They also organized to send a busload of local activists and residents to Chicago for a Conference on Transportation Equity. The group did join with the NAACP and others to launch a civil rights suit against the State of Wisconsin, the governor, and the state's Department of Transportation for long-standing and ongoing discrimination against African Americans. While the suit aimed to restore the light rail and bus money, the legal process became ever longer and more expensive. Eventually, CSM decided it needed to settle its part of the case out of court.

One thing is clear, however. Despite setbacks, the several years of activism has transformed regional transportation policy—once assumed to be the quiet preserve of local officials, developers, and suburban road builders—into a hotly debated topic. CSM had helped take an issue supposedly lacking in public interest and used it to mobilize significant activism in Milwaukee's central city neighborhoods. The coalition looks toward a future of revived activism around transportation concerns.

Union Organizing

As CSM continued to organize around family-supporting jobs, it also moved into the area of union organizing. According to Bureau of Labor Statistics data for 1997, union members made on average $162 more per week than their nonunion counterparts. This difference makes union organizing a major source for creating family-supporting jobs. With the local AFL-CIO leadership looking to implement the national call for greater attention to organizing, CSM developed its role as a community organizing partner.

Part of the effort has involved following the tracks of the living wage victories. In September 2000, labor and community activists convinced the Milwaukee County Board of Supervisors to pass a "labor peace" ordinance. The new law requires businesses providing social services or special transportation services under county contracts worth over $250,000 to sign agreements recognizing the right of their workers to organize. Such agreements prohibit employers from giving workers false or misleading information about unions, holding mandatory "captive-audience" meetings with their workers, or using other various forms of intimidation techniques. Employers must agree to provide lists of workers and allow organizers level-playing-field access to work sites. In exchange, unions must promise not to strike or picket during organizing campaigns.

CSM has also directly aided union organizing

efforts. Its staff has helped train union organizers and has identified workplaces suitable for community-supported organizing. CSM played a central role in organizing the Kramer International Foundry. In organizing the plant, the United Steel Workers faced a major challenge in reaching out to the foundry's largely Latino workforce. As a community-based organization with extensive connections to Milwaukee's Latino south side, CSM was able to help the union successfully organize using people from the community and by organizing public support. Having won a union contract, CSM and the Milwaukee Labor Council for Latin American Advancement continue to aid the Steelworkers by initiating bilingual training sessions, publishing a bilingual newsletter, and providing Spanish-speaking union representatives health and safety and other information. Sustainable Milwaukee has also assisted the Hotel and Restaurant Employees Union (HERE) in their efforts to unionize several downtown hotels.

This labor organizing among a Latino workforce has also linked CSM to two other projects. Employers often use immigration laws and the threat of a raid by the Immigration and Naturalization Service (INS) as a weapon against union organizing and solidarity among Latino workers. To break this employer stick, CSM has assisted in the development of the Wisconsin Coalition for a Just and General Amnesty that would move the focus from catching undocumented workers to enforcing the nation's labor laws among employers of such workers. CSM has also worked with other partners to establish a worker center for Milwaukee's south side. Such a facility would provide a focal point and resource pool to build activism among the community's workers.

The Future

The 1993 planning process and plan had led to seven years of new and inspiring grassroots activism. By 2001, CSM organizers saw the need and opportunity to reenter a planning process that would build a coalition and strategy for the new decade. Organizing in the past decade had raised a range of basic economic and social justice issues and demonstrated that an organized community could begin to tackle these issues. However, much more needed to be done. For example, a study on the state's welfare-to-work program found that in Milwaukee there were five job seekers for every job available. By contrast, the suburban communities had six jobs for every seeker!

Working with Women in Poverty, Esperanza Unida, 9 to 5, and the North Avenue Community Development Corporation, CSM had begun to organize for a People's Economic Summit. The gathering would bring together a diverse collection of grassroots groups and leaders to target four to six areas of economic concerns that were not being portrayed accurately by the official economic development forums. The issues included redefining economic development programs in terms of job quality and retention—rather than simply lucrative public subsidies. Organizers also looked toward further workforce training programs, the right to organize, amnesty and worker rights for undocumented workers, and the meeting of basic human needs such as heating, affordable housing, health care, and so on. By convening a new planning process, CSM also hoped to draw in many new groups to broaden further the scope of the active members of its coalition.

CSM also entered 2001 developing a new process for drawing inner-city residents involved in its campaigns and services into an active membership. Through house visits and meetings, organizers hoped to pull together these members into a forum for regularly discussing the issues facing their communities and then organizing concrete actions to bring about change.

The Wisconsin Regional Training Partnership (WRTP)

The WRTP was formally launched in 1992 as a consortium of unions and a dozen companies committed to building high-performance high-road workplaces. Today, it is one of the premier initiatives of its kind in the country. By 2001, it included one hundred firms employing over sixty-five thousand workers. Thirteen unions, representing most of these workers, are also members. The WRTP seeks to foster both competitive companies and healthy communities through joint labor-management problem solving within the firm and by linking related firms and unions to shared resources, knowledge, and experience.

Early initiative for the WRTP came from COWS, which held a series of conferences to pull together labor, business, and government leaders around research done on the state's manufacturing sector. This effort coincided with the 1991 development of recommendations by the governor's commission on education and training for incumbent employees, dislocated workers, and youth in manufacturing. In May 1992, business and labor leaders entered an agreement to form a consortium to promote workplace education, apprenticeships, and training. Wisconsin's governor, Milwaukee's mayor, and the county chief executive joined with state labor and business leaders to announce the launching of the WRTP in September.

The bulk of the WRTP's member firms came from the densely linked metalworking, machinery, plastics, and equipment industries. Despite the massive wave of plant closures and downsizing in the 1970s and 1980s, these industries remained a pillar for the greater Milwaukee economy. Most important, they offered a sector with clear opportunities for labor-community action to help management foster high-road employment growth. Increasingly fierce national and international competition confronted these firms with a clear set of choices. They could increase the short-term bottom line with low-road strategies of wage cuts, downsizing, and plant closures, or they could lay the groundwork for long-term industry leadership through the high-road path of high quality, internal flexibility, and state-of-the-art technology.

Most, although not all, of the companies participating in the WRTP are unionized. This connection is not accidental. The presence of a union increases the costs and risks of a low-road path. At the same time, an evolving local labor movement had begun to see the need for increased worker involvement in actual firm decisions. By cofounding the WRTP, unions offered management ways to address the major obstacles standing between them and a high performance future.

The WRTP is structured around joint labor-management participation. Far more companies participate in specific WRTP programs are formal members. An equal number of management and labor representatives sit on the WRTP's Board of Directors. Nonvoting, advisory members come from public sector partners such as the area's technical college. The WRTP activities are organized around three joint committees focusing on the major barriers to high-performance workplaces: current workforce training, developing the future workforce, and plant modernization.

Workplace Education

The WRTP began as a consortium focused on one of the greatest roadblocks facing its member firms. In an age in which successful high-road, global competition requires ever more skillful and adaptable workers, manufacturing companies found themselves with a workforce that was undertrained and underskilled. This challenge, and the WRTP solution, is well illustrated by the transformation of the Navistar Foundry. Indeed, the foundry's experience provided a model for WRTP programs.[12]

Located in suburban Waukesha, the foundry is a subsidiary of the Fortune 500 company Navistar International Transportation Corporation—an internationally prominent truck and diesel engine manufacturer. Now a very successful and expanding facility, in the 1980s the foundry looked like it was heading toward plant closure. The problems stretched back through three decades of poor strategic planning by the parent company. With little competition

in the 1950s, the then International Harvester followed a familiar American path as it sat back enjoying its success—assuming that predominance would always be a fact of life. As a result, management introduced new products only sporadically, did not make investments in productivity increases, and allowed plant equipment to age. By the 1970s, International Harvester had lost its lead in agricultural equipment to John Deere and its medium-truck sales to Ford. When the 1981 recession hit, the company's long-term decline made it particularly vulnerable. A costly six-month strike by the UAW in 1980 combined with obsolete factories and years of neglected product development to push the company to the edge of bankruptcy. By 1986, it had shed 85 percent of its employment and closed forty-two of its forty-eight plants. The newly renamed Navistar International continued along the low road, in particular by expanding its foreign-based capacity.

The crisis placed the United Steel Workers, who represented the workers at the Waukesha foundry, in a particularly bad situation. The foundry's existence depended entirely on supplying truck parts to other Navistar plants. By the mid-1980s, production had fallen dramatically and corporate executives were demanding wage and benefit cuts. Unless the plant found a way not only to continue to supply parts at competitive rates, but to also contribute to the overall financial health of the company, its future looked bleak.

Plant management, however, provided Steel Worker Local 3740 an opening. Unlike the typical low-road management response, the foundry team decided that more cost-cutting tactics would simply destroy what was left of worker and managerial morale and gut the facility. Instead, they chose a course of "continuous improvement"—promoting high product standards and service quality. While investing physically in the plant provided part of the solution, management realized that the key lay in "employee participation and unsurpassed product quality."[13] Management's plan aimed not only at returning to plant competitiveness, but also capturing an industry-leading share of target markets through superior labor relations and employee education, training, and development. The latter was especially critical for expanding the plant's capacity to diversify into producing machined parts and assemblies. That meant workers with new skills and a new capacity to adapt to ongoing change.

Realizing that major change was necessary to save the plant from closure, the union moved beyond the traditional American arms-length, "us versus them" relationship with management. The United Steel Workers envisioned a partnering role in designing and implementing the move toward high-performance manufacturing. This action put the union leadership at potential risk. If joint decisions either didn't work out or created problems on the job, members could accuse the union leadership of "being in bed with management."

Union participation, however, was critical for tackling the top barrier confronting management's plans. The training and education levels of the existing workers were woefully inadequate for a state-of-the-art workplace. An in-house survey showed that 65 percent of workers had no high school diploma and that critical math skills were very low. New technology and work methods required both technical and general skills that workers simply had not been given. To address these deficiencies, the union brought in a consultant from the Wisconsin AFL-CIO's Help in Re-Employment program who developed a worker-centered solution to the plant's training needs. Using pilot experiences as guides, the union pressed for an on-site workplace education center that would enable workers to shift into the new job classifications and machining positions that would grow out of management's upgrading plans. A joint steering committee found a site, secured state and company funds, and established a curriculum and instructors from the Waukesha County Technical College (WCTC).

The founding of the Employee Education Center stands out for the large degree to which it was based on worker input. Without the confidence that they were helping drive the process, workers would have had ample reason to fear change. The education program was tied to work reorganization and job reclassification. When done by management alone, such change can degrade skills, downsize the workforce, and increase job stress. Workers had to have confidence that the new ways by which they were to be evaluated and promoted were built around opportunities to improve their individual and collective status. The confidence fostered by the union's leadership meant that, for example, when WCTC vocational specialists talked to workers about how they did their jobs (including all the many ways they improved on and superseded official management directions), workers were willing to share such key information because they had the trust that it would be used to enhance, not degrade, their jobs.

Worker input provided the basis for the core principles that have proven key to the Employee Education Center's success. The curriculum is based on what workers say they need. In addition to basic reading, writing, math, and technical skills, the center also offers programming that allows workers to develop themselves broadly. All workers have equal access to the programming. Participation is voluntary and confidential. Workers can enter and leave programs at their own pace. All these aspects are critical for ensuring that the education process is genuinely driven by the workers. Otherwise, management could ration training opportunities and/or force worker participation. The commitment to worker development comes from both the company and the employee. Workers are paid half-time wages—one work hour for every two hours they spend at the center. The center also established a peer advisory network—originally of union stewards, now also of other rank-and-file union members. The network uses personal, one-on-one contact to promote the center in the workplace. It also provides a vehicle for workers to help redesign and fine-tune center activity.

During the center's first ten years, roughly 10 percent of the foundry's workforce was active in its programming at any given moment, with more participating in one-time, walk-in activities. The benefits of training are always hard to quantify. However, clearly the foundry could not have successfully restructured its operations without it. By 1998, it was no longer a captive plant. Half its floor space was being used for new machining operations and 60 percent of the plant's output went to companies other than Navistar. During a two-year period, the plant hired 180 new workers. The center provided these new hires a standardized orientation. It also helped the plant attract and hold scarce skilled workers who saw the training opportunities as an attractive point in the foundry's favor.

The center's activities have helped define workplace change as an opportunity for workers, rather than a threat. By supporting the center, management made a commitment to implement change by developing its workforce, rather than degrading and replacing it. For example, when more sophisticated computer-driven technology outpaced the skills of machine tool operators, the company faced a choice in attempting to reclassify the jobs. It could either downgrade the jobs so that the work became sophisticated button pushing or it could reskill the work to allow workers to fix minor problems and identify programming "glitches." The union was able to successfully push for the latter—a solution made possible by the existence of the Employee Education Center.

The center's broad training mandate has also helped support the reorganization of work toward more high-efficiency, high-quality work methods. Workers increasingly operate in largely self-directed teams that not only produce the product, but also interact with customers and suppliers. Such methods require skills in effective communication, group work, and a broad understanding of the business, in addition to the more technical skills. The ability to produce highly skilled, highly flexible workers can prove a critical competitive edge. Such plants adapt far more readily to change and increasing product complexity and diversity than more traditional firms.

Clearly, worker-driven training is a key component for pursuing high-road strategies. The clearest sign of the Navistar program's success has been its emulation. A little more than three years after the center was established, Navistar Foundry joined with twenty-one other firms to help establish the WRTP. Almost all WRTP member firms have visited Navistar. As one of its first projects, the WRTP began to promote similar Employee Education Centers in other firms. The WRTP has also helped smaller companies pool their resources to establish collective centers. All these centers follow Navistar's experience in joint labor-management planning. The WRTP's technical support includes providing model language for union contracts; linking firms, unions, and the technical schools; and helping to ensure that training curricula are the most up to date and based on cross-firm standards. To continuously improve and develop worker-training programs, a Workplace Education committee networks firms and unions to trade experiences and expertise in worker training. The WRTP also actively promotes peer advisory networks. To avoid burnout among existing union leadership, these networks actively recruit and train rank-and-file advisors. The WRTP develops these networks both at the level of individual firms and by bringing together representatives from each company to trade expertise and experiences.

Future Workforce Development

When unions and the community help firms to successfully compete on the high road, those companies will likely increase employment and begin to look for new workers. Yet, in sectors such as manufacturing, the skills of the newer generations do not fit the increasingly rigorous needs of employers. Indeed, WRTP organizers found that typical K-12 school-teachers had little appreciation of the opportunities offered by manufacturing work. Stereotypes of the crude and unsophisticated factory worker unfortunately have proven far too common. For many teachers, the path to a high-wage profession meant a college education for white-collar work. Yet, many skilled trade jobs pay wages at or higher than many white-collar jobs. And these can provide careers in professions in great demand by a wide array of companies.

In response to both company needs and federal mandates, the state of Wisconsin had established school-to-work programs designed to help students from kindergarten through high school develop the skills needed in today's workplaces. Program emphasis included both technical training and skills centering on effective communication, cooperation, and adaptability. Across the nation such educational initiatives have enjoyed a wide range of experiences from the most ineffective and token to the most successful.

The WRTP's Future Workforce Development Committee assists area schools in developing effective school-to-work programming. Traditionally, such initiatives bring together government and employers. The WRTP focused on including organized labor as a third and equal partner. Indeed, unions can make enormous contributions to the success of such programs. The WRTP works with unions to help educate teachers on the value and career opportunities offered by skilled industrial work. They also acquaint teachers with industrial unions. Even though the National Educators Association and the American Federation of Teachers together have well over three million members, many teachers do not identify with the broader labor movement despite enjoying the benefits of a union contract. Direct contact with unionized skilled workers also helps address many of the stereotypes that white-collar professionals hold about industrial workers. The WRTP has fostered such contact by developing plant tours for teachers and students, by involving workers in classroom activities, and by bringing together workers, managers, and teachers in joint forums. Out of such meetings, the WRTP helped bring employers and unions together for "Take a Teacher to Work" days in which teachers take in-service days to experience manufacturing work firsthand. During the program they shadow production workers as well as engineers, sales representatives, and other employees.

The WRTP has also brought unions, teachers, and firms together to work out curricula relevant to contemporary industry needs. This includes fostering an awareness of the role of unions and collective bargaining. Since manufacturers increasingly look for employees with postsecondary training, the WRTP has helped school-to-work programs develop certification standards that allow high school graduates to enter postsecondary institutions with advanced standing.

Wisconsin's school-to-work efforts also established youth apprenticeships. This program provides work-based learning opportunities that give students exposure to a wide array of occupations within manufacturing. The WRTP has helped recruit firms and unions to sponsor youth apprentices. It has then worked with them to create a valuable experience for students. If not properly developed, apprenticeships can become a source of cheap labor with little educational value. Sponsors must devote time and effort to provide students a quality experience. By involving unions in these programs, the WRTP adds another crucial voice. Indeed, union members have become student mentors—exposing them to skilled industrial work and union activities. Through collective bargaining, unions have pushed to include youth apprentices as dues-paying members under the contract. This has provided both better pay and quality work experiences. By being involved in the design of the youth apprenticeships, the unions also ensure that students are not used to replace incumbent workers. By fostering effective employer and union involvement, the WRTP looked toward helping move several hundred young people into youth apprenticeships by the turn of the century. While still modest by the standards of European apprenticeship programs, this effort far exceeds other programs elsewhere in the state.

Plant Modernization

New technology is one of the elements driving the need for increasingly skilled and flexible workers.

If not able to effectively pursue new technology and best work practices, inefficient companies become breeding grounds for low-road, cost-cutting strategies. Many small to medium-sized firms, however, need help to successfully adopt new technology and methods.

The WRTP helps firms follow the high road by aiding their modernization process. The WRTP works in partnership with the Wisconsin Manufacturing Extension Partnership (a public-private entity that assists small and medium-sized companies to adopt technology) to help firms improve their work processes, develop products, prevent pollution, and assure high quality. As with all WRTP activities, work starts by networking firms and unions to share their collective knowledge. In particular, those that have gone farther down the road in a given area can help other firms by highlighting successful practices. WRTP activities are premised on including unions as equal partners in the modernization process. This benefits workers by helping to ensure that technology is used to enhance their work experience, rather than degrade, intensify, or outright eliminate their jobs. At the same time, companies can benefit by the union's ability to maximize effective worker participation. Workers will fully share their knowledge and commit to the process only if they have the kind of basic security offered by a union contract and sense that their ideas and concerns are being fully represented.

Investments in new technology pay off best when companies also invest equally in worker development. Modernization requires constant review and adjustment in which knowledgeable worker participation is key. The WRTP's Plant Modernization Task Force helps member firms share information and experiences about effective workplace culture and process changes—such as self-directed work teams, Total Quality Management, continuous improvement, and so forth. While across the country these concepts have shown a potential to enhance the quality of work, they have also provided management with ways to intensify and/or deskill work. By

including unions as equal partners, the WRTP promotes a process that encourages worker-friendly practices.

The Overall Experience

In 1997, COWS surveyed the WRTP's member firms. The results proved generally consistent with the assumptions that went into programming and appeared to bode well for the future.[14] WRTP organizers had indeed picked an economic sector with the potential for high-road growth. Individual firms had increased their employment from an average of 952 employees in 1994 to 1,103 in 1997. Most said they would be hiring in the near future. The companies included a mixture of supplier firms and final product producers. A significant volume of the final production went for export. Wages averaged $14.60 per hour for production workers and $17.37 for skilled trades.

Nearly all the firms were unionized. Two-thirds reported that education and training had become an explicit subject of collective bargaining. All the unionized firms had developed significant efforts at labor-management governance centered on worker participation and problem solving. Half the firms were engaged in formal, wide-ranging modernization programs. The greatest obstacle facing such programs was "employee resistance to change." The majority of these firms reported significant investments in productivity-improving new equipment. Nearly all had increased and were continuing to increase resources for worker training. All needed existing workers with increased skills. All were experiencing significant problems in finding qualified entry-level workers. And when they hired new workers, the firms were averaging forty days of orientation and training—a commitment that was getting only longer.

In short, the WRTP's focus had indeed connected to the collective problems faced by the firms that had joined the consortium. The survey also revealed that firms saw WRTP programming as effective.

Three-quarters of respondents reported that they planned to expand the scope of their participation in the WRTP in the coming year. Only two firms outright were not interested in expanding their involvement. Twenty-one out of twenty-nine described clear gains from WRTP programs. Many cited direct help in developing workplace education programming, youth apprentices, and school-to-work programs. Several stated that the WRTP had helped them identify public and/or private resources available for a variety of modernization and education issues. Several firms also credited the WRTP with providing impetus for ongoing workplace planning efforts in suburban Ozaukee County.

By 2001 WRTP could point to even more impressive numbers. Over the past five years, manufacturing employers in the area had added six thousand new jobs. At the same time, six thousand workers participated in direct training each year. Top business leaders had embraced the project and even the former Republican governor described it as a model for the future.

COWS directors Laura Dresser and Joel Rogers summarized the WRTP experience as follows:

> The apparent results of the WRTP have been significant improvement in the skill level of the work force, stabilization of employment in this hard-hit and highly competitive industry, wage improvements for incumbent workers, clear markers for entry-level and incumbent workers regarding job expectations and career advancement, and considerable improvement in the general quality of labor-management relations in affected firms. While the work of the WRTP is often customized to meet specific firm needs, the consistent attention to training and modernization issues throughout the sector develops benchmarks on skill that improve workers' mobility across firms, not only within them.[15]

While the WRTP experience has focused on the metalworking industry, Dresser and Rogers pointed to comparable projects in other industries both in Wisconsin and across the country. We will cover activities in Madison later in this chapter. In chapter 10 we will bring in experiences from elsewhere in the country. By 2001, however, the WRTP had secured Department of Labor grants to develop new partnerships in construction, data networking, health care, hospitality, and transportation.

The Milwaukee Jobs Initiative

All of the elements described in the course of this chapter came together in launching the Milwaukee Jobs Initiative (MJI)—a collaboration aimed at dismantling the economic isolation of Milwaukee's central city. The MJI represents a partnership between the community CSM, labor MCLC, and business (Greater Milwaukee Committee—a group of 175 of the area's top corporate leaders). COWS provided crucial research, designs, and implementation assistance. Financially, it was spurred by the prospects of Milwaukee becoming one of six cities to receive a multimillion-dollar grant from the Annie E. Casey Foundation's job initiative program. Having worked to improve the lives of poor children for years, the foundation had concluded that to further this mission it needed to help connect parents to family-supporting jobs.

The economic distress that we earlier discussed for Milwaukee as a whole is simply magnified for the central city areas targeted by the MJI. While, in 1995, unemployment for the city was 4.8 percent, in the central city it was 21.5 percent. For many, the lack of access to jobs was a long-term problem. Among those without work, one out of five in the central city had never worked, while nearly another third had not worked in five years. The issue was not simply jobs, however, but access to a family-supporting income. For Milwaukee County, one-third of residents worked at jobs that paid poverty wages; for the central city, this figure climbed to 56 percent.[16]

As depressing as these statistics were, MJI organizers further realized that the reality also contained untapped opportunities. While residents needed decent jobs, employers were becoming increasingly worried about how to find new workers. A survey of three hundred area firms, direct discussions with businesspeople, and the work done by the WRTP all pointed to employers who were experiencing great difficulty finding workers with job-ready skills. A clear potential existed for linking residents with employers to the mutual benefit of both.

However, existing labor market mechanisms were not making these links. The barriers came at several levels. For employers, existing school and training programs were not providing workers with appropriate skills. Part of the problem lay in not providing "hard" technical training, including basic reading, writing, and math skills. However, of equal or even greater importance, employers wanted workers with a range of basic "soft" employment skills. These include basic people skills—the ability to communicate effectively and to work in groups. Employers also said they needed workers with habits that made them reliable: promptness, a work ethic, and so forth. While programs existed in the community to provide different needed elements, employers found little coordination among them and little opportunity to help steer this often piecemeal activity toward their direct needs. While individual employers had attempted to work with community organizations to hire local residents, the quality of these programs was so diverse that employers found difficulties sorting out the effective ones from those that were not. The end result was firms that had accumulated many bad experiences in trying to recruit new workers. Frustrated company managers could easily conclude that the opportunities were simply not available and adjust their company strategies accordingly. That could mean less emphasis on job expansion and more reliance on less-skilled, low-road jobs.

Central city residents also had their share of frustrations. Many job-training programs did not connect to actual employment. And if they did, the training did not necessarily lead to good or even lasting jobs. Indeed, residents continued to experience discrimination in hiring. And when they did get hired, they often experienced continued discrimination and hostility, which prevented further advancement or even long-term employment. Residents needed careers as well as jobs. Yet, the prospects of career-long employment through a single company have become ever more a thing of the past. Today's employment practices shrink the number of job classifications and develop more cross-functionally defined positions. These trends increase the gaps between different levels of work—producing more and more entry- and mid-level jobs that represent dead ends. Company decisions to outsource work also undermine career ladders as low-skill, entry-level jobs that used to provide access to and up the corporate ladder are now isolated in supplier firms and temporary agencies with few career opportunities. To succeed in this new world of work, workers need access to the kinds of certifiable skill development and job networking that allow them to advance in the industry as a whole, as well as with their specific employer.

Furthermore, a host of direct barriers separated residents from jobs. As we discussed above, because most job growth had gone to the suburbs, job access meant decent transportation. Workers with families needed affordable and quality child care, an issue made all the more important as Wisconsin's welfare reform pushed more single mothers into the workforce. While some, largely underfunded, services existed, they were not well connected to actual residents. Indeed, the economic isolation of the inner city meant that basic information about the availability of jobs was not getting to the residents who needed it most. The end result was a population of residents who had developed serious skepticism about both the prospects of decent employment and programs that promised such gains.

The MJI sought to build on existing potential by removing the barriers that keep high-road employers and residents from connecting. It looked toward two major avenues for intervention. The first aimed at establishing a consortium to bring together employers, unions, community groups, residents, and local nonprofit and governmental institutions to best coordinate their existing activities and needs. The MJI then looked to fill the remaining gaps between residents and jobs.

MJI activities are premised on several principles. Activities must involve the input and the full buy-in of all the major actors concerned. They must also be built around clear grassroots participation. Any training must connect to real employment or the strong promise of actual jobs. And the final goals must look toward careers, not simply initial employment. This means providing supports for workers once they achieve employment, dealing with the obstacles they encounter on the job, and developing clear channels for continued work and advancement beyond a specific employer.

To bring these elements together, the MJI chose to focus its efforts on particular sectors within the local economy. A common problem of existing job programs lay in their inability to meet the specific needs of particular sets of employers. By contrast, a sectoral approach allowed for specific sectoral consortia to address the particulars of that industry. In choosing sectors, organizers looked to the criteria pursued by the COWS regional economic analysis research discussed above. For its opening activities, the MJI settled on three sectors: construction, metalworking, and printing. In 1996, the Casey Foundation committed to providing the MJI $700,000 annually for up to eight years. The MJI has also successfully pursued local matching funds reaching nearly the same level.

Construction Jobs

With an estimated $2.6 billion of new construction projected over a five- to seven-year period of the late 1990s and early new century, the construction industry provided clear opportunities for job growth. Furthermore, a significant proportion of this work would be connected to public funds—be it for large-scale projects such as the Wisconsin Center and Brewer's Stadium or $90 to $150 million of public infrastructure improvements. When the MJI formed, the construction industry employed 27,100 workers—a figure estimated to climb to 30,100 by 2005. With this enormous demand for construction, employers faced serious problems finding new workers—especially those for the higher-paid positions. Even worse, while the amount of work was increasing, the average age of the workforce was going up as well—presenting both employers and the building trades unions with the prospect of growing retirements.

Despite the possible common ground between the needs of employers and residents, connections were not being made. Construction firms had only piecemeal efforts to recruit inner-city residents and a lack of technical and soft skills had created some bad experiences. At the same time, residents were not seeking construction jobs because of a lack of information and a history of discrimination within the industry. While the median wage of construction workers in the metropolitan area was $13.07/hour, for workers from the central city it was only $7.85. Isolation while on the job and a dearth of on-the-job supports had driven many newly hired central city residents out of the industry.

While several existing programs offered partial solutions, the industry's situation provided areas in which joint intervention promised to fill significant gaps and deliver clear results. Initiative organizers decided to build from the community side by establishing, within CSM, a Central City Worker's Center (CCWC). The CCWC provides a middle connection between employers and local residents. On the employer side, it offers a source of reliable entry-level, work-ready workers with the basic skills needed for construction. CCWC industry liaison staff reaches out to area contractors. By participating with the CCWC, firms gain a hand in developing the CCWC's curriculum. In return, employers agree to use the CCWC as a focused one-stop center in hiring new employees.

Within the community, CCWC staff actively publicizes and recruits in central city neighborhoods. Outreach coordinators go to community organizations, churches, block clubs, and other gatherings or networks within the central city. The CCWC then provides the transitional support needed to move residents into construction jobs. Interested individuals attend workshops explaining the jobs, what they need to obtain them, and the process they will go through. Center staff meets individually with each resident. Through testing and interviews, the staff identify qualified applicants and determine what more they need to become job ready. For some residents, the needs can be material. Access to transportation and child care represent two of the most common such barriers. Individuals may need skill basics such as a high school equivalency diploma. They may need a driver's license or help in recovering suspended licenses. Or they may need help for problems that could harm their job performance, such as alcohol or drug abuse. The CCWC addresses some of these needs by direct, on-site programming. For others, it links up people with existing services in the community. The key to the entire process is that each individual can come to one place and find help that is tailored to his or her particular situation.

Reflecting its grassroots origins, the CCWC is not simply a service organization. All residents participating in programming become members who support the CCWC by contributing time or money. This provides people a sense of ownership of the center. And the volunteer time is spent on activities with the CCWC and the CSM. Thus, membership brings area residents into direct experience with grassroots organizing. The volunteer work also helps people develop or enhance their soft skills around communication, punctuality, and working with others.

The CCWC's work does not end when a person is placed in an entry job. Center staff follow up with individuals to help them retain good permanent jobs or to move from one job to the next, as in the case of construction. Through one-on-one outreach, staff provide workers access to the support they need while on the job and to paths for further developing their skills. CCWC staff help residents prepare and qualify for apprenticeship training programs. Such apprenticeships can take five to six years. Feeling pressures to meet immediate cost needs, many employers are reluctant to sponsor such on-the-job training. While the CCWC works with residents to help them pass qualifying exams, CSM's job access work helps pressure employers to increase the ratio of apprentices to journeypeople.

The involvement of the building trades unions has been a key part of the CCWC's work. The bulk of the employers participating in the CCWC are unionized. Because of retirements, many of these unions face significant membership turnover. Some have already taken steps to try to recruit more women and people of color. However, due to obstacles similar to those encountered by employers, these efforts are often unsuccessful. The CCWC's programming aims to fill in the gaps so that more residents have genuine opportunities to learn a high-paying trade. In return, the unions develop community connections and a pool of new highly motivated members exposed to collective and grassroots action. A physical sign of the burgeoning union-community partnership is the CCWC's actual offices. All the renovation work was done by the building trade unions.

During its first start-up year, June 1997–1998, the CCWC successfully prepared and placed thirty-seven individuals in construction jobs. Their wages averaged over $13 an hour. By the end of 2000, the CCWC had placed 293 residents in jobs averaging $13.33/hour. Ultimately, the CCWC aims to increase its performance to over two hundred placements per year. At the same time, it hopes to add twelve new firms annually to its member employers.[17] With over one thousand residents passing through its doors for orientation and assessment, the CCWC has an excellent pool to meet its placement targets. By the end of the first year, it had developed outreach to all twenty-two skilled trade unions and developed an active and quite positive relationship with many key union leaders.

Metalworking Industry

The CCWC's activities also support the MJI's efforts in the metalworking industry. The WRTP had developed programs to aid employers in developing their existing workforce. However, as with construction, firms faced both growing needs for new workers and significant obstacles in recruiting them. Indeed, metalworking employers faced growing retirement and a tight labor market. The industry employed 100,000 residents—15 percent of the region's workforce, but only 11 percent of central city workers. And as in construction, past and present barriers and discrimination meant lower wages. While the industry's overall median was $14.58/hour, central city residents averaged only $10.86.

With the WRTP already in place and the CCWC being developed, the tools for linking residents to decent manufacturing jobs were readily available. By channeling funds to the WRTP, the MJI helped expand the partnership's activities to include working with employers to identify new job and training needs. The CCWC recruits and prepares the residents. The WRTP then links the residents to any further training and to placement in actual jobs. The WRTP's peer advisory network also helps support residents once on the job.

In their first year, the CCWC and the WRTP jointly placed sixty workers in manufacturing jobs paying on average more than $10.50/hour. By 2000, 567 workers had been placed in jobs.

Printing

The MJI also launched a successful prototype to explore the hiring potential of the printing industry. Printing offered an industry with local comparative strength. With 436 printing establishments, 14,000 workers, and $1.8 billion per year in goods and services, the metropolitanwide industry ranked seventh in total printing output in the nation. Once again the prospects of large-scale retirements were coupled with local industry growth. While starting wages came between $7 and $9/hour, the industry offered rapid advancement to positions in the $10 to $12 range. Highly skilled work typically paid $16 to $20/hour. As with the other sectors, printing firms were experiencing significant difficulties recruiting new workers.

The industry had an already established union-management partnership: the three-decade-old Milwaukee Graphic Arts Institute (MGAI). The MGAI had good connections with many employers and operated a sophisticated training facility used primarily to train incumbent workers. The MJI proposed to build on these existing assets. First, it expanded on the MGAI's employer connections by reaching out to medium and small firms, ascertaining from all employers their entry-level workforce needs, and securing hiring commitments. Second, the MJI helped expand the MGAI's training capacity to run more programs aimed at new workers. Once again, the CCWC recruited and prepared local residents. A significant portion of the printing industry's workforce comes from Milwaukee's Latino community. With partner organizations, CSM has helped address the specific needs of these workers by, for example, establishing a bilingual person to work on this part of the MJI.

By the end of its first year, the prototype had placed twenty-three central city residents in jobs averaging $7.80/hour. This success proved strong enough that the activity was upgraded into a full-blown project. By the end of 2000, 155 workers had been placed in jobs averaging $8.83/hour. As with the union organizing, the efforts in the printing industry have further strengthened the connection between CSM and the city's Latino community. By 2001 the CSM and the MJI were working to develop within the printing industry a model career track for nontraditional workers and limited English-speaking workers.

The Future

The three projects in construction, manufacturing, and printing have all delivered growing success. By 2001, close to one thousand inner-city residents had been placed in jobs that promised a future. In addition to higher wages, MJI jobs offer access to health benefits. By comparison, only a third of participants had enjoyed health coverage at their previous job. The overwhelming majority of participants have been people of color, with 83 percent African American, 10 percent Latino, and 2 percent Native American.

From the beginning, the MJI planned to expand its activities into other industries as well. By 2000, organizers had launched a new prototype that experiments with building cross-sectoral career ladders. Many employers with whom the MJI interacts had made clear that the biggest barrier that they saw to successful hiring of central city residents was not formal or technical knowledge, but the soft skills related to personality, attitude, and behavior. At the same time, central city residents complained that much of the work available to them was made up of "dead end" jobs with few or no career prospects.

A new hospitality industry prototype aims to address both concerns by building career paths that move individuals between categories of employers. MJI organizers had built relationships in the hospitality industry. These employers faced continuous recruitment needs as low wages and little prospect for advancement held few workers to the jobs. One hotel owner, for example, complained of a turnover rate exceeding 100 percent a year! The MJI explored the possibility of linking work in this industry to job opportunities in sectors that offered better wages and more advancement opportunities. The basic idea runs as follows. The MJI helps recruit and prepare residents for jobs in the hospitality industry. For six months, organizers help residents use experience in these jobs to build their soft skills, and any basic formal training, such as a GED. After six months, the employer either promotes the worker or the MJI helps him or her move to a job in another sector. By participating in the project, hospitality employers would get motivated workers likely to stay on the job for at least six months. Firms in other sectors that hire out of the program know that they are getting proven workers with the crucial soft skills. The

residents gain from the possibilities of transforming seemingly dead-end, low-paying jobs into first steps toward more lasting careers. Forty-four people had been placed in jobs by the end of 2000.

In 2001, the MJI had begun to pull together another new project in the automotive and trucking mechanics sector. The new program aims to create apprenticeship opportunities that provide inner-city residents with state-certified portable skills. As part of its funding, the Casey Foundation had required the MJI to develop a plan for achieving systematic sustainable reforms in the operation of the regional labor market. MJI's initial experience highlights several lessons. Workers need skills that can be certified beyond a specific employer. The public sector cannot create these standards. Rather, firms must be brought together with related unions in industry collaborations to establish such standards and develop collective plans for workforce development. In turn, effective programs require the equal participation of business, labor, community groups, and government officials.

Jobs with a Future

One sign of project success in Milwaukee has been its extension by other groups and localities. In 1995, the Dane County Board of Supervisors (home of Wisconsin's capital of Madison) constituted the Dane County Economic Summit Council—a blue-ribbon commission of local business, labor, nonprofit, and public leaders. The council worked to develop a strategic vision for economic and workforce development in the county. COWS research had revealed that local employers were finding shortages of qualified workers a significant constraint on their growth and expansion.

With the help of COWS, the council launched an industry-consortium-building project called Jobs with a Future. Drawing on its Milwaukee experience, COWS researched the local economy to target specific sectors and to reach out to specific highroad, or potentially high-road, employers. Following interviews with specific firms and a series of conferences, the project has pulled together consortia in three major industries: manufacturing, health care, and insurance and finance.

The issues facing local manufacturing firms were similar to those in Milwaukee: recruiting and retaining new workers, upgrading the skills of incumbent workers, and effectively developing new methods of work organization. The manufacturing consortium's first program focused on recruiting and preparing entry-level workers. Member firms specified the different types of entry positions and the skills required for them. The Dane County Job Center recruited among food stamp and medical assistance recipients. By 2000, the consortium had also launched a successful English as a second language course geared to the social and job needs of manufacturing workers. The consortium has also brought firms together to share information.

Research on health care revealed an industry whose work structure was to experience significant change due to the pressures of restructuring and cost containment. As a result, health care employers were experiencing increasing difficulties filling specific professional and paraprofessional positions. They also had serious problems retaining help in areas such as food service and housekeeping. The consortium's first actions targeted problems among certified nursing assistants (CNAs). A COWS study documented the serious problems that local health care providers faced due to CNA turnover. While Wisconsin annual CNA job turnover is already 54 percent for full-time workers and 78 percent for part-timers, in Dane County the numbers ran at 99 percent and 127 percent.

In insurance and finance, computer technology was transforming office work. Local employers reported great difficulties in finding qualified people to staff their information systems departments. At the same time, many clerical workers were facing either dead-end jobs or unemployment as new technology required people with significantly upgraded skills.

While the details varied, all three industries offered opportunities to address the obstacles to high-road business strategies by teaming up employers, unions, and the community to build collective training, recruitment, and career-advancement institutions. Unlike in Milwaukee, some of these sectors offer a greater share of nonunion employers. Building a consortium in these areas offers opportunities to mix union and nonunion workers in industry-based programs as well as a challenge in overcoming employer fears that such programs could serve as secret ways for unions to organize.

Lessons from Milwaukee

When added together, the CSM, the WRTP, and the MJI paint a picture of a community that has begun to take hold of its own destiny.

This is not to say that there have not been bumps along the way. For example, the job initiative was originally conceived of as a direct project of the CSM. And while organizers had the support of key business leaders and groups, such as the Greater Milwaukee Committee, they also drew fire from the local conservative Bradley Foundation. The foundation leaked confidential information to two staff members at the San Francisco–based Institute for Contemporary Studies—an organization that the foundation funds. These two right-wing writers then planted two articles—one a guest piece in the *Wall Street Journal*, the other in *Milwaukee* magazine, accusing Milwaukee business leaders of being duped into promising $2.6 million to match the Casey foundation's $5.1 million grant. Didn't local business leaders and elected officials know that the local agent for the grant was CSM—an antibusiness organization that had mounted such subversive activities as living wage campaigns? Even worse, at the time, CSM was housed in the building of the Peace Action Center, which the authors described as a "potpourri of self-styled 'progressive' groups," including one with "open communist sympathies." The authors went on to note that Bruce Colburn, a key leader behind CSM, was no less than the secretary-treasurer of the MCLC and a leading member of Progressive Milwaukee, a chapter of the national New Party. "Like a gullible spinster who loans a

Lothario her credit cards, the Milwaukee corporations appear to be doing it [opening their wallets] in order to be loved," the authors counseled.[18] Writers in several other business and local publications also picked up on the theme of the business community's questionable and potential socialist partner.

Fortunately, the CSM's business and governmental partners held to their support. Indeed, the executive director of the Greater Milwaukee Committee told the local press that "the headline is that Milwaukee business is gullible. I think a more accurate description is that the *Wall Street Journal* is gullible."[19] That this support continued in the face of redbaiting testifies to the degree to which top corporate leaders saw their own interests served by the MJI partnership. It also speaks to the skill that organizers had used in developing ties to high-road businesses. Business leaders did become nervous enough, however, that the MJI was established as an independent nonprofit organization with the Greater Milwaukee Committee and CSM as key partners.

We should also note that the immediate material gains from the CSM, the WRTP, and the MJI are still quite modest. After its first year, for example, the MJI scaled back its targets from 900 placements by the third year to 626. The job access and living wage campaigns aim at very targeted subsets of employers. And Governor Thompson and selected suburban opposition held up the broad light rail and bus improvement plans. Indeed, all of these activities represent experiments in the process of evolving and proving themselves.

Nevertheless, the gains that have been made are real. Thanks to collective action, thousands of workers have seen their wages increase, their skills improved, and their prospects for the future brighten. Most important, all these activities mark important new directions for local groups and for local progressive activism generally. The change can be seen at five different levels.

First, local unions and community activists have moved from reacting to problems to developing proactive plans for the future. Through these initiatives, they are fighting for the kind of society they want to build, not the latest corporate, right-wing rage against them.

Second, their strategic understanding has evolved. Participants may have started with various general understandings of the economic and social forces at work in society, coupled with specific knowledge on the issues within which they worked. However, through the progressive initiatives, new and collective layers of understanding have developed. This new knowledge links the general picture to specific problems by identifying the specific economic and social forces at work within the particular community. General forces have become specific sectors with particular issues and identifiable players.

Third, a proactive and more strategic thinking has proven a natural force to bring groups together. In particular, all of the activities have witnessed growing relationships between unions and community groups. For example, Richard Oulahan, the director of Esperanza Unida, an innovative job-training program based in the Latino community, has been involved in progressive activism in the city for over twenty years. He has seen something new. "I have witnessed many coalitions come and go, but CSM is different," he commented.

> The group's meeting continues to be packed, whereas with other coalitions attendance tends to drop off after a while. People want to be there. I think part of the reason is a sense of urgency that comes with economic decay. However, I also credit the group's leadership. While a lot of people talk, CSM has been committed to doing. I have been impressed by how well the group has moved from talk to action.

Fourth, local activists have developed a sophisticated response to business. Very often progressives tend to view business either as the enemy or as an alien force to whom they have very few ties. While any capitalism is still capitalism, with all the negative forces that it breeds, the Milwaukee experience demonstrates the importance of identifying variations within the business community—ones that can be used as entry points for tactical and strategic alliances. While unions and community groups may battle business leaders on one set of issues, at the same time they can also build real win-win relationships in other areas. Indeed, confrontation and cooperation provide the two sides of a potentially complex relationship.

At least two elements have made labor-community-business cooperation in Milwaukee work. Through the CSM and the work of COWS, labor and community activists were able to first come together to work out their own independent plans. Thus, they approached business from the perspective of being full and equal partners. Their experience suggests that cooptation can best be avoided by groups that have developed a strong and autonomous sense of their own goals, have tied their activities and decision making to grassroots participation, and have taken the initiative to approach business, rather than reacting to corporate actions. Furthermore, through concrete research and planning, Milwaukee organizers developed a strategic perspective that allowed room for both battling and cooperating with corporate leaders. By developing relationships with employers and understanding how their environment worked, local organizers were able to identify the problem areas experienced by managers where community and labor had vested interests in helping provide solutions. By doing so, not only did they gain mutual benefits, but they also helped steer firms away from more negative, low-road alternatives. At the same time, because they had their own autonomous agenda, labor and community groups could also organize to shut down the low road. By developing a sophisticated approach to business, activists not only gained tactical and strategic allies, but also greater access to the internal knowledge of several industries. Thus, rather than simply opposing or supporting corporate plans from the outside, labor and community groups have gained the ability to use the knowledge of an industry to transform that industry.

Finally, the Milwaukee experience demonstrates how large issues, such as capital flight and urban decay, can be broken up into manageable projects that promise feasible results and to maintain a perspective on the overall issues. In doing so, Milwaukee suggests a people-oriented alternative to the corporate reconstruction of American cities. U.S. capitalism has not completely abandoned the cities. Indeed, as examples such as Cleveland and Atlanta demonstrate, an "urban renewal" agenda does exist within corporate America. However, this agenda offers only a market- and profit-driven vision of the future. Much of the city is seen as a source of problems and emptiness needing to be filled by investments from the outside. Old decay is bulldozed to bring in the bright and shiny monuments of suburban progress—large-scale office buildings, upscale entertainment centers, casinos and stadiums, closed-in shopping malls, private condominiums, and lots of space devoted to the predominance of the automobile. When done on a large scale, such corporate redevelopment produces sterile downtowns and private neighborhoods built in the image of the suburbs. Gone are the rambling small shops and neighborly streets that once provided the character of vibrant urban communities. Such corporate development is oriented on the needs of large-scale business and wealthier suburbanites. Rarely do the poor residents actually living in the city enjoy the prosperity. At best, they often become the low-wage labor serving the shiny office towers.

Activists in Milwaukee have developed an alternative vision. Cities do not have only problems; they also have the resources of a rich cultural and economic heritage. The people living in the city offer some of its greatest assets. And the dense networks of urban labor, community, and governmental organizations provide the key allies in a collective revitalization of the entire city. By bringing together a broad spectrum of progressive groups, by building real and sophisticated relationships with local employers, and by delivering real gains to local residents, these Milwaukee experiments point to the possibilities of a progressive urban future as our nation's cities become models of economic democracy and social partnership.

9

State Campaigns for Economic Justice

The last two chapters profiled examples suggestive of the rich mixture of economic justice coalitions emerging today at the grassroots level. This chapter moves our focus to the state level where economic restructuring has fostered a growing number of broad coalitions. A long tradition exists in this country in which reforms that are now taken for granted at the national level (bans on child labor, the forty-hour workweek, the minimum wage) were first enacted by state governments. We will focus on three areas of organizing: corporate subsidy accountability, contingent work, and the minimum wage. As we will see, this state activism has close links to efforts at grassroots reform.

"No More Candy Store"—Making Job Subsidies Accountable

In connecting public wage standards to public monies, the living wage has drawn on the fact that today public funds play an increasingly significant role in economic development decisions. Indeed, while many business leaders decry living wage laws or other attempts to set standards for business behavior as destructive interference with the "natural efficiencies" of the "free market," they have few hesitations in demanding public subsidies to help fund their profit-making activities. Today, often very wealthy corporations receive literally millions upon millions of dollars in free public money, typically with few or no strings attached. When the federal government

debated so-called welfare reform in the mid-1990s, opponents of this reform often argued that while great public energy was going into placing the fiscally tiny AFDC under the microscope, the billions of dollars given as "aid to dependent corporations" was a forbidden topic. Recent estimates place federal "corporate welfare" subsidies at over $150 billion a year, while state and local governments give away an estimated $48.8 billion.[1]

Today, however, a growing movement of unions, community groups, corporate watchdog organizations, and elected officials is challenging the generous terms of corporate subsidies.

The Growth of Corporate Welfare

The growing debate over the usefulness and purpose of corporate financial incentive packages reflects an increasing reliance by local and state governments on such measures. In 1977, for example, only twenty-eight states had programs to grant businesses property tax abatements for machinery and equipment. By 1993, forty-one states had such programs. Only thirteen states provided subsidized loans for machinery and equipment in 1977; forty-two did by 1993. And over this sixteen-year period, state governments passed laws empowering local governments to provide businesses with public aid. Eight states allowed local governments to offer loans in 1977; forty-five did by 1993.[2]

This explosion in public financial incentives reflects several trends. With the shift in economic development work away from the federal government in the 1980s, state and local governments increasingly had to take on this role. Hit by the blows of massive job losses in manufacturing and general urban decay, many older cities and towns began to view financial incentives as a necessary tool to attract corporate reinvestment. After all, with all the problems of older urban areas, public officials needed some extra incentives to offer would-be investors—so the argument went. Even taking this argument at face value, the problem has become that public financial packages have become so common that they no longer provide special features unique to specific communities. Today, suburban and rural areas use financial incentives just as much as towns and cities. Adding to these efforts, most state governments and economic development agencies have also entered the incentive game.

This policy shift has produced an environment in which different governments compete against each other to lure corporate investment into their state or community. Some of these bidding wars have become quite infamous. In 1980, for example, the state of Tennessee offered an incentive package of $11,000 per job to convince Nissan to locate its new assembly plant in the state. Four years later, the state upped the ante to lure General Motors's new Saturn plant at a cost of $26,000 per job. At the time, these were considered quite generous public perks. However, in 1992, South Carolina spent $68,421 a job to support BMW's new assembly facility. The current record, however, was set by Alabama in 1993 when it offered Mercedes-Benz $253 million in public financial aid. The state and federal government bought the land for Mercedes and used the National Guard to clear it. The state then developed the site, built roads, enlarged the airport industrial park, exempted imported components from tariffs, pledged to buy twenty-five hundred cars produced by the plant, provided an educational facility to train managers and teach German families to speak English, and renamed a strip of highway between Birmingham and

the Mississippi state line the "Mercedes-Benz Highway." All told, the state spent $170,000 per assembly-line job. State officials admitted that they would never recoup this sum, but argued that bringing such a world-class company to Alabama would help support the state's overall economic development goals.[3]

The scandals over lucrative public financial incentives have gone beyond the sheer size of the giveaways. In an alarmingly high number of cases, it is not clear what the public gets in return for their investment. For example, Illinois gave Sears a suburban land package and bonuses worth $240 million just to keep their national headquarters in the state. Yet, in the years after receiving the aid, Sears announced massive layoffs throughout the country—including many of the supposedly "saved" jobs in Illinois. Minnesota approved an $828 million package to supposedly create fifteen hundred jobs at two new Northwest Airlines facilities. After accepting an immediate loan of $270 million, which was part of the deal, the company announced that the repair facilities and all the new jobs were "on hold." In 1992, the township of Ypsilanti, Michigan, sued General Motors, alleging that when the company accepted seventeen years of tax abatements worth $1.3 billion, it had pledged to keep operating its forty-five-hundred-worker plant in Willow Run. Instead, General Motors pitted the Willow Run plant against a similar plant in Arlington, Texas, by announcing that one of the two would close. Although the township won a nationally acclaimed ruling and injunction at the trial court level, the Michigan Court of Appeals overturned the ruling. Today, the massive Willow Run plant sits empty. A 2000 study of eighty subsidy deals in New York City found that thirty-nine of the companies announced layoffs, large-scale mergers (which typically result in job losses), or the sale of the company or facility shortly after benefiting from subsidized retention deals![4]

The accountability problem comes not just from corporations that renege on their promises. In most cases of public financial support, governments simply do not ask much or anything in return for taxpayer-funded generosity. Walk into the offices of your average local municipal government and ask for a list of local financial incentive deals. In all likelihood, you will be met by blank stares. If any records are kept on public incentive packages, they are usually stored in the files of each separate department or agency. Rarely do local governments maintain comprehensive files. Detroit, for example, is one of several cities selected for the national Empowerment zone program. Companies locating in the zone can apply for several state and federal tax breaks. Which companies actually use these programs and how much financial aid they receive, however, is a complete mystery. The application for the tax breaks is made individually by each business as part of its IRS tax returns. Even the local Empowerment zone office, charged with attracting companies to the Zone, has no access to this information! An examination of the city's Industrial Facilities Tax Exemption program reveals that every major Big Three auto facility and top supplier plant in the city has been granted this major tax break—typically under a promise to simply retain existing jobs, not expand them. The city has no mechanism for monitoring if indeed the job levels are maintained.

The monitoring situation is just as poor at the state level. Only nine of thirty-four states responding to a National Governors Association inquiry could identify any sort of reporting requirements for companies receiving public incentives. Only eight states told the association that job quality (and not just quantity) was one of several criteria used to determine which companies get aid. Two-thirds of the thirty-six states responding to a National Association of State Development Agencies study could not even say what percentage of their incentive dollars were going to various types of businesses. As Clara Oleson, a labor educator and subsidy activist at the University of Iowa, commented, "To apply for food stamps in Iowa you need to fill out a 25 page form and update it every 90 days. Yet, a corporation can receive tax increment financing with no application form at all."

In short, state and local financial incentives have become a kind of candy store that often quite wealthy companies feed on simply by knowing the right people and making the proper vague references to jobs and the local tax base. Indeed, activists continuously run up against local and state economic development authorities and elected officials that have been utterly convinced by the business community that if they do not offer up incentive packages, then investments will go elsewhere. Ironically, a wealth of studies published in business journals suggests that public incentives are not a priority for most business location decisions. As Larry Ledebur and Douglas Woodward argued in the *Economists Economic Development Quarterly*:

> Most studies show that incentives have little influence on location decisions. . . . It is not surprising. . . . Governments have little or no control over the fundamental determinants of a firm's demand and costs. . . . Recent evidence . . . suggests that incentive bidding tends to feed on itself, with more expensive items often added at the last minute in an attempt to keep ahead of the competition. These hastily-assembled packages act like economic steroids. . . .[5]

What are the other factors that guide corporate location decisions? They include: proximity to sales market, proximity to suppliers, availability of appropriately skilled labor, transportation networks, capacity and cost of utilities, cost of land and buildings, quality and price of public services, and the overall quality of life in the community. As we detailed in the last chapter, local and regional governments can be partners in increasing the benefits of these other factors. By contract, aggressive financial incentive programs can actually jeopardize these more high-road-oriented elements. Financial giveaways erode the local tax base and deprive governments of resources that could be invested in infrastructure, training and education, and quality-of-life factors. Generous financial incentive programs can even be a sign to high-road businesses that an area will not be able to support the kinds of community factors that support their business strategies. A glance at the routine lists of "top cities or states for business"— and other similar ratings done by *Fortune*, *Business Week*, and similar publications—reveals many areas among the top ranked that have higher-than-average wages and that place greater regulations and requirements on companies.

It is true, however, that corporations are increasingly footloose. According to *Site Selection* magazine, corporate migration has roughly doubled to over eleven thousand moves a year today—up from fifty-two hundred annually between 1980 and 1994.[6] Most notably, the wandering corporations are no longer mainly manufacturing firms, but also represent a wide range of service occupations.

In short, the massive amount of public funds given to corporations each year has produced a poor record of public return or benefit. Instead, financial incentives have become a game of bluff. Companies, who, in many cases, have already made the overall decisions on where and how to invest, go to local and state governments to see what kind of goodies they can get. All too frequently, at the mention of "jobs," public authorities are eager to agree. Few are the officials willing to risk a "poisoned business climate" by either not offering incentives or mandating requirements in return.

We should note that corporate welfare also comes in the form of general tax policy, not just specific company deals. Reflecting a "race-to-the-bottom" bidding war, states and local governments have lowered their effective corporate tax rates by from 40 percent of their 1980s levels. In pushing the tax burden from corporations to working people, states are following a federal lead. One report on the national taxes paid by the 250 largest American corporations between 1996 and 1998 found that, thanks to a wide range of special tax breaks, 133 paid less than half the basic profit tax rate of 35 percent.[7] Even more alarming, 41 not only paid no taxes, but actually received rebates from the public! The list for 1998 of such lucky corporations included such giants as

General Motors, Goodyear, PepsiCo, and Phillips Petroleum. Had all 250 corporations actually paid the 35 percent tax rate in 1998, the federal government would have enjoyed a $257 billion increase in income—an amount equal to roughly one sixth of all revenues. In 2000, National Semiconductor was caught in one of the worst forms of tax subsidy abuse, double dipping. While the company paid South Portland, Maine, $10.5 million in property taxes, it received a $5.3 million rebate from the city and another rebate of $9.9 million from the state. In other words, the taxpayers ended up giving National Semiconductor a net $4.6 million!

Corporate subsidies cost the community dearly in lost tax revenues. For example, one estimate in Louisiana placed the lost property taxes at over a billion a year. This translated into local school boards forgoing significant proportions of their revenue base. In some cases, over half of potential school funds were lost through corporate subsidies! State audits of their economic development programs often reveal alarmingly high rates of loan defaults and generally lax attention to any form of performance criteria.[8]

The Movement for Corporate Accountability

Fortunately a growing movement of both public authorities and labor and community groups has begun to challenge the way financial packages are used. When Greg LeRoy authored the first guide to this activism in 1997—*No More Candy Store: States and Cities Making Job Subsidies Accountable*—he was able to document six jurisdictions with job-quality standards attached to their subsidy programs. By the beginning of 2000, this number had increased to sixty-seven—including thirty-seven states with job-quality standards for at least one subsidy program. While sixteen of the sixty-seven were local living wage laws that included financial assistance in their coverage, the rest took a related but different focus. Today, Greg LeRoy heads up a national clearinghouse of information and research about corporate accountability called Good Jobs First.

Corporate accountability measures have focused on three major dimensions. First, laws have demanded public access to basic information. Before a subsidy is granted, a company can be required to provide basic information on its finances, labor and environmental record, and a detailed plan concerning the use of public funds. Once public money is given, the community should have access to routine reports on how a company is meetings its promises. Firms can also be required to provide adequate advanced notification of major policy changes, such as plant closings or layoffs. Even more basic, communities can pass laws to lift the veil of secrecy that often surrounds the very process of subsidy granting. Government officials should be required to hold public hearings before decisions are made. Upon consideration of a financial aid package, authorities should be required to conduct a detailed community impact study, somewhat similar to environmental impact research, in order to weigh the potential benefits against the costs.

Second, laws require companies to make specific and enforceable commitments in return for public dollars. Such agreements can include wage standards, monitored job creation or retention plans, targeted hiring to populations in particular need, and other binding community commitments. Tax money should also not be given to companies whose job "creation" comes down to simply moving jobs from one location to another—essentially playing communities against each other. Prohibitions against such practices are called antipiracy measures.

Finally, as with the living wage ordinances, legislators have imposed harsh penalties on firms that violate agreements. At a minimum, public officials should be entering into only those contracts that specifically allow them to take back all taxpayer dollars if the company does not fulfill its promises.

Campaigns to establish greater public accountability have begun to develop at both the local and the state levels. Minnesota provides a pioneering example of a statewide labor-community coalition around subsidy accountability and economic justice.

Minnesota's Campaign for Corporate Welfare Reform

The groundwork for current efforts developed during the 1980s when a growing alliance of peace activists and labor unions sought to pressure the state's major high-tech defense contractors to explore conversion to civilian production. Traditionally, companies tried to pit their unions against the peace movement through the old argument that defense cuts mean job losses. However, the state lost 29,500 defense jobs in the late 1980s, with many of the remaining 85,000 at risk. Such wholesale change highlighted the importance of plants developing strategies to convert to civilian uses. It also revealed management's lack of initiative and even active resistance to such options. By the end of the 1980s, peace groups had overcome past friction to forge an ongoing coalition with the unions representing defense workers. They had also picked up the support of religious and other community organizations. Together this coalition pushed companies to establish alternative use committees of management, labor, and community members. Activists introduced legislation at the state level to provide incentives to establish such committees. They also cosponsored shareholder resolutions favoring such a course.

The conversion activism encountered a wall of resistance from management unwilling to concede a role for labor and the community in what it saw as its core powers. However, the growing cooperation of a diverse collection of groups set the stage for the corporate responsibility organizing of the 1990s. In 1988, activists established the Minnesota Alliance for Progressive Action (MAPA) as a formal coalition and research/advocacy institution to influence state politics. Today, MAPA has twenty-seven member organizations (see Table 9.1) representing such constituencies as labor, environment, women, disabled, low-income, seniors, peace, and citizen ac-

Table 9.1

MAPA's Member Organizations

Advocating Change Together
Alliance of the Streets
Associated Federation of State, County, and Municipal Employees
Association of Community Organizations for Reform Now
Black Indian Hispanic Asian Women in Action
Clean Water Action Alliance
Community Action of Minneapolis
International Union of Electronic, Electrical, Salaried, Machine and Furniture Workers
Minnesota Americans for Democratic Action
Minnesota Association of Professional Employees
Minnesota Citizens Organized Acting Together
Minnesota Coalition for the Homeless
Minnesota Community Action Association
Minnesota Consumer Alliance
Minnesota National Organization of Women
Minnesota Senior Federation
National Lawyers Guild Minnesota
OutFront Minnesota
Service Employees International Union
Union of Needletrades, Industrial and Textile Employees
United Auto Workers
United Food and Commercial Workers
United Steel Workers of America
United Transportation Union
Urban Coalition
Women Against Military Madness

tion. It maintains two offices with eight staff. Since its founding, the alliance has worked on campaigns for hate crime legislation, adding sexual orientation to the state Human Rights Code, fighting severe cuts in human needs spending, making the state tax system more progressive, and opposing the siting of a high-level nuclear waste dump. MAPA works with communities of color to develop grassroots political capacity and to increase voter education, registration, and get-out-the-vote. It has also helped initiate long-term wealth creation strategies for low-income communities. For 2000, MAPA focused on twin efforts around passing a clean election system for state elections and defending and furthering its path-breaking corporate accountability laws.

During the early 1990s, MAPA organized and lobbied for a more progressive state tax system. By 1994, it became clear to organizers that they had been over-

looking a major element of tax injustice: the over $1 billion a year that state and local governments quietly gave to corporations through tax breaks and other financial aid. Instead of addressing these outlays, state political leaders were mounting an aggressive effort to curb welfare for poor single-parent families. Pointing to "corporate welfare," MAPA launched a campaign to highlight the hypocrisy of policy makers who demand "accountability" from low-income families but were silent on issues of subsidies to corporations. In 1995, MAPA released its first report detailing the $1 billion a year the state was giving away to companies. It contrasted these figures to the $143 million spent on AFDC and work-readiness programs. While the corporate subsidies were given in the name of job creation, companies that failed to create new jobs generally faced no penalties.

Using its research, MAPA developed corporate

accountability legislation requiring firms receiving state financial assistance to create a net increase in jobs and to agree to meet specific wage and job creation goals within two years of receiving public aid. The state could take back the assistance from companies that did not meet these mandates. The measure applied to all firms receiving tax increment financing or $25,000 or more in grants and loans, but exempted small business. The original draft also included a minimal wage level of at least $7.28 per hour, or above the federal poverty line for a family of four.

MAPA helped organize a strong and multilayered grassroots campaign. For example, MAPA staff developed a workshop on corporate accountability that used popular education methods to tap into people's own knowledge and experiences. The workshops ran across the state. They also published a Corporate Welfare Activist Handbook that is now in its third edition. And they organized inside and outside of the legislature to win the necessary votes. Realizing that full and open opposition to the popular accountability measures would place them in a weak position, the chamber-of-commerce-type opponents focused their public efforts on blocking the wage requirements. Instead of rather self-serving-looking businesspeople showing up at hearings, the campaign had to counter the voices of local economic development authorities who predicted all kinds of dire consequences if their "hands were tied" by the proposed legislation.

Through this hard-fought and very public effort, the coalition won the passage of its law in 1995, minus the wage requirements. A year later, the coalition mounted a strong campaign that got the legislature to pass the wage stipulations. However, a veto by the governor scuttled the measure.

The lack of the wage requirements and the rather innocuous job goals could have left activists feeling defeated. However, the new law's simple reporting requirements proved particularly groundbreaking. Minnesota became the first state to collect systematic and comprehensive data on which companies received significant public subsidies, how many people they employed, and what they paid those workers. In 1998, Greg LeRoy and Tyson Slocum of Good Jobs First went through the initial rounds of 1996 and 1997 data. The reality they uncovered was shocking.

The title of the final report encapsulated the findings: "Economic Development in Minnesota: High Subsidies, Low Wages, Absent Standards." Of the 553 filed economic development disclosure reports examined, in 123 of the deals corporations received more than $35,000 of assistance per projected new job. This figure was used by the U.S. Department of Housing and Urban Development as a limit on Community Development Block Program loans. Loans from the federal Small Business Administration 504 Program have a similar cap per new or retained job. Thirty-eight of the Minnesota deals involved more than $100,000 per job!

And what was the public getting in return for its substantial investment? Apparently, a large number of low-paying jobs. Four out of five subsidized jobs paid wages below the state's average of $13.88 in 1996. This finding was all the more disturbing since two-thirds of the subsidized jobs were in the high-wage manufacturing sector. The researchers found that nearly three-quarters of subsidized jobs were paying wages below the state average for their industry; fully half paid 20 percent or more below the state-industry wage. The classic business argument that the lower wages come from younger workers employed in entry-level positions could not be used to cover up the reality. A survey of recent job takers across the state found that over half were age thirty or older, almost three-quarters were age twenty-five or older.

In interviewing over one hundred local economic development officials, LeRoy and Slocum found a significant number either indifferent to or poorly informed about attaching basic standards to financial assistance deals. As one official, who had been involved in many such deals, commented, "wage levels are not a high criterion on our list." In comparing the official wage and employment goals first projected in the formal subsidy deals with their actual performance, LeRoy and Slocum found a widespread practice in which local authorities and the companies "low-balled" their projections—thus making it nearly impossible for companies not to meet the official wage and job targets within two years. This meant that public officials were approving deals despite having projected wages even worse than the actual practice! For example, more than three-quarters of the deals were approved despite projecting wages that would qualify a family of three for Medicaid! In a large number of approved cases, local officials had set job targets at one new job per firm.

The research also found that many of the so-called new jobs were new only to the particular community. While the subsidy war between states has gotten more media attention, the Minnesota research showed that the main competitor for local economic development officials was another community in Minnesota. In nearly all of the cases using the state's tax increment financing program, the public had ended up subsidizing the relocation of a company from one part of the state to another.

LeRoy and Slocum did find cities that bucked the trend. Burnsville, for example, had negotiated thirty-seven deals that showed up in the database. Twenty-eight had projected wages of over $12 an hour. The researchers also documented several cities, including some high-growth Twin Cities suburbs, that had conscious policies to provide few or no subsidies at all. Local officials in these cities expressed the opinion that their area had enough other features to attract business and/or that subsidy deals were not worth the cost.

MAPA took up as policy goals the report's recommended reforms. These included wage floors pegged to local market levels, a cap on the subsidy amount per job, a prohibition against using subsidies to relocate within the state, and technical improvements to enhance the reporting system. Since the researchers also found that local authorities were reluctant to go after companies even when they failed to meet the already low projected goals, LeRoy and Slocum recommended changing the state's ability to recapture the assistance to a calibrated sliding scale rather than the all-or-nothing provisions given in the 1995 law.

Two years later, Good Jobs First released another report that used further Minnesota data to demonstrate how state and local subsidies were being used to support sprawl. Entitled "Another Way Sprawl Happens: Economic Development Subsidies in a Twin Cities Suburb," the report profiled suburban Anoka's aggressive use of the state's tax increment financing program to offer free land to companies willing to locate in its three hundred-acre Enterprise Park. The program successfully attracted twenty-nine companies employing sixteen hundred workers to a community with a stagnant low tax base on land that was partially contaminated.

However, seen from a regional perspective, the results were a disaster. The move to Anoka had taken the companies out of either the core Minneapolis urban area or suburban areas closer to the city. This meant that public funds had been used to move jobs farther from communities with high concentrations of people of color and/or low-income residents. The companies had also generally moved from locations more accessible by public transportation to those more car dependent. Furthermore, the state had spent millions of dollars subsidizing free land with no net gain in economic activity. In terms of the state's perspective, without the free land the companies would still have expanded their operations somewhere in the state; they simply may not have done so in Anoka.

With concrete evidence on the use and abuse of public funds, MAPA organized to secure a 1997 legislative commission on Corporate Subsidy Reform. While commissions can be a way of burying an issue, activists succeeded in getting sympathetic officials on the commission. Grassroots organizing packed regional hearings with campaign supporters and compelling testimony. A year later, activists introduced a new law based on the commission's recommendations. While the bill died in the legislature that year, in 1999 the campaign won the passage of the Business Subsidy Reform law. This victory came despite a political balance that did not seem entirely favorable. While the Democrats had a sizable majority in the state Senate, the Republicans had a four-seat majority in the House. Through hard work, the campaign gained the votes of several very fiscally conservative Republicans who opposed all forms of welfare—for corporations and the poor alike.

The new law requires communities to develop public purpose criteria for business subsidies that flow through their local governments. The criteria must involve more than the traditional "expand the tax base" justifications and must include a policy for wages for all newly created jobs. Under recent changes, the wage policy must provide the formula setting a clear wage floor. All local deals must be approved by an elected body and those worth more than $100,000 must be subject to a public hearing. Companies receiving public subsidies must agree to continue operations at the subsidized site for at least five years. The new law also strengthened the reporting mechanisms, mandated more detailed wage data, and required information on health care to be provided. Under the new rules, companies that fall short of their two-year wage and job goals must pay back, with interest, a prorated amount of the subsidy based on how far they fell short of the targets. Companies that fail to pay back such subsidies are banned from new public assistance for five years. Although activists have still not been able to enact direct wage requirements, the new law has provided an opportunity for grassroots organizing since it requires clear local subsidy policies adopted through an open, public process.

In cities where no organized group exists such criteria may only reflect boilerpolate criteria and the minimal legal requirements. However, in areas with grassroots organizing—such as Minneapolis, St. Paul, Mankato, and Duluth—the law opened a mandatory public process allowing activists to make corporate subsidies a hotly debated issue. As a result of such activism, Duluth, for example, requires answers to a list of specific questions concerning the public purpose, an evaluation of the environmental and eco-

nomic impact, and full disclosure of any conflicts of interest. The city's criteria also included labor peace requirements for card check and neutrality language to be included in subsidy deals.

Corporate subsidy abuse continues to animate Minnesota state politics. The 2000 legislative sessions saw the chamber-of-commerce-oriented Economic Development Association of Minnesota leading an unsuccessful campaign to weaken the 1999 law by raising the coverage threshold from $25,000 to $100,000, exempting large nonprofit businesses, and eliminating the requirement to stay at the site for at least five years. Clearly, MAPA's efforts have hit a raw nerve. Corporate accountability promises to provide a continued focal point for progressive coalition building for years to come.

In organizing around corporate accountability and other issues, MAPA has developed increasing sophistication in the art of coalition building. One sign of this evolution is the organization's recently launched Policy Leadership Project. The initiative grew out of a desire to increase the participation of member organizations that came out of communities of color and to expand the ranks of such groups that joined MAPA. Through listening circles, activists inside and outside these organizations discussed the issues driving the groups, their activities, and the possible role that MAPA might play in aiding their work. Participants highlighted their perception that MAPA had a great deal of policy-related expertise that many of their groups did not possess. Under the Policy Leadership Project, a full-time MAPA staff person is working with these groups to develop a popular education workshop about the policy-making process. In addition to discussing the formal legislative process, the workshop also raises a racial analysis of the ways in which bills become a law.

Corporate Accountability Around the Country

Minnesota's experience offers a leading example now being replicated in subsidy reform battles mushrooming across the country. Indeed, the Maine Citizen Leadership Fund has competed with MAPA in enacting the nation's best state subsidy accountability laws. In 1998, the Maine legislature passed a law that required annual progress reports; public disclosure of financial assistance granted; some wage, benefit, and job creation standards; and an eleven-member commission to evaluate the state's corporate welfare programs and recommend reforms.

In late 1999, Good Jobs First released an examination of the initial required filings by 190 companies. Since several of Maine's economic development programs already had wage standards, the findings were not as alarming as in Minnesota. Nevertheless, one-quarter of workers at subsidized jobs were paid below the appropriate county-specific livable wage standard. The average wage paid by these 13,879 subsidized jobs was $19,700. Nearly two-thirds of the companies receiving public subsidies paid at least some workers these substandard wages. The contrast of priorities was often stark. Two state subsidy programs that had cost $25.6 million were found to produce only 95 new jobs. At the same time, the $1.5 million that the state had spent on job training had produced 644 new jobs. According to the state's Department of Environmental Protection, 32 companies in 1998 and 1999 that had received large tax subsidies had violated environmental, health and safety, and/or labor laws during the previous decade. While these companies had paid $3 million in fines for this law breaking, the state of Maine had provided them $15 million in subsidies in 1998 alone![9]

With such exposures in hand, the Maine activists continue to organize around subsidy reform. In 2000, the coalition successfully amended the 1997 law to mandate job creation and wage and benefit goals, institute strong monitoring and reporting measures, and impose harsher penalties against companies that do not file their mandatory subsidy information. The amendments also increased funding to the state's incentive commission. Activists also organized to pass a "living wage" bill requiring companies receiving more than $10,000 in subsidies to pay a wage

at least equal to two-thirds of the average wage for the county in which they operated. The bill passed both houses only to be vetoed by Governor King.

A snapshot of the news developments during the early months of 2000 reveals the growing activism and controversy surrounding corporate welfare. In March, for example, the state comptroller in New York issued a report criticizing the state's array of economic development programs for lacking adequate means to measure their effectiveness. Two months before this release, Good Jobs First teamed up with the Fiscal Policy Institute to launch Good Jobs New York. The new organization works to document the state's subsidy practices and highlight ways to make subsidized corporations more accountable. Also that month, an audit of the Texas Department of Economic Development resulted in a stinging account of "gross fiscal mismanagement" and a lack of oversight of the agency's $201 million job-training program. A few weeks later, Democratic Representative Garnet Coleman from Houston announced his plans to develop reporting and accountability legislation similar to the laws passed in Minnesota and Maine. Daily newspapers in San Antonio and Austin immediately ran editorials favoring subsidy accountability. In Toledo, an attorney filed suit on behalf of local residents and small businesses after the city pulled together a $281 million subsidy package for Daimler-Chrysler's Jeep plant. While the company agreed to keep the facility in Toledo, it predicted a reduction in jobs from the current level of fifty-six hundred to between forty-nine hundred and forty-two hundred. In January, a study by Associated Oregon Industries—a business organization—concluded that large tax cuts are not effective in luring big company headquarters. This finding came despite the organization's record of advocating broad tax cuts.

Overall, by 2001, thirty-seven states, twenty-five cities, and four county governments had enacted some form of subsidy disclosure/corporate accountability legislation. And more efforts continue to swell this list.

The Promise of the Future

As an issue with clear public support, corporate accountability campaigns face an opportune future. An example of this potential comes from a recent campaign in Connecticut seeking to connect public money to high-road corporate standards.

Citizens for Economic Opportunity (CEO) brings together unions, community, and religious groups to broaden debate on economic issues and to promote a progressive legislative agenda. CEO grew out of battles against large-scale downsizing within the state's key insurance industry. While grassroots efforts had not blocked either a job-destroying merger involving Aetna Insurance or the conversion of Connecticut Blue Cross to a for-profit subsidiary of Anthem, organizing did raise a serious public debate over the mostly nonunion insurance industry. These initial campaigns also led CEO to focus on the general issue of corporate responsibility. By 1998, the coalition had developed a legislative agenda targeting three sets of policies:

- Measures that deny tax breaks to irresponsible corporations and grant them only to those that can demonstrate a record of living wages and decent jobs.
- Requirements for corporations receiving state economic assistance or state and municipal contracts over $50,000 to provide good wages (at the median wage for the industry), provide health insurance or additional compensation to purchase such insurance, and to not pay their chief executive officers salaries fifty times greater than the hourly rate of the company's lowest-paid worker.
- Legislation to discourage the replacement of full-time workers with contingent labor by requiring the same hourly pay and benefits for temporary and part-time employees as are paid to regular employees.

After several years of building up its forces, by the end of 2000, CEO was ready to move its agenda

in the state legislature. In April 2001, a CEO-backed corporate accountability bill passed the legislature's finance committee by one vote. The bill would require companies that receive at least $500,000 in state assistance and that employ more than fifty workers to pay an "industry standard" wage, pay part-time workers the same rates as full timers, adhere to all safety and health laws, and create jobs or lose their aid. The measure passed with two Republicans voting with a majority of Democrats in its favor.

The Maine and Connecticut efforts are part of a regionwide subsidy accountability effort called the Northeast Corporate Accountability Project. The project is a joint effort by the Commonwealth Institute in Massachusetts and the regional Northeast Action.

As of the spring of 2001, corporate accountability bills were pending in the Washington and Texas legislatures. Also that spring, the Kentucky Economic Justice Alliance introduced an annual disclosure law. Unfortunately, with the Democratic governor strongly opposed to the measure, the bill was defeated in committee. With corporate accountability proving a compelling issue capable of drawing bipartisan support, the battle has clearly only just begun.

Tackling Contingent Work

The last provision in CEO's agenda points to a second area of emerging economic activism: contingent work. Quincy, Massachusetts, resident Thomas Sullivan contacted the Campaign on Contingent Work for legal help with his official employers, local temp agencies. Sullivan, who temp worked mostly in telephone-call centers, had a list of grievances. One agency had made clear that the client company did not want him because, in his mid-forties, he was too old. Following a layoff, another agency had tried to prevent him from collecting unemployment compensation by claiming that he had quit. More generally, Sullivan was tired of doing the same work as other employees but getting paid less simply because he worked for a different temp agency.[10] As contingent work continues to expand throughout our economy, Sullivan's story has become all too common. Fortunately, advocacy campaigns such as the Massachusetts Campaign on Contingent Work have begun to develop across the country.

The Problem

According to a recent study released by the Economic Policy Institute, nearly one-third of American workers are in some from of "nonstandard" employment arrangements. This amorphous category, which we will simply call contingent work, includes temps, contract employees, part-time workers, leased workers, and "independent contractors." One national survey of employers found that 78 percent made use of "flexible staffing arrangements" with nearly 50 percent employing the services of temp agencies and 44 percent hiring workers as "independent contractors."[11] Today, temp agency giants such as Kelly and Manpower vie with each other for the distinction of being the nation's largest employer. On any given day nearly three million Americans hold a temp job. With annual turnover at more than 450 percent, and an average length of employment at 9.6 weeks, some 8.5 million workers—6 percent of the workforce—spent at least part of 1998 temping.[12] The ranks of contingent workers are growing. Since 1990, the number of workers employed by temp agencies has grown from 1.2 million to 2.9 million. In October 1999, over one-sixth of all new jobs created that month were temporary jobs. That same year a survey by the American Management Association found that half of the firms surveyed had eliminated jobs. Seventy percent of these firms downsized for reasons other than product demand. Almost one out of five firms used temps to replace workers laid off. Seven out of ten replaced some regular workers with temps for routine tasks.[13]

Contingent employment cuts across all job categories. Only one-fifth of contingent workers fit the classic image of clerical or administrative support personnel. Another fifth work in professional specialty occupations such as doctors, lawyers, writers, editors, and so forth. The largest group in this category work in the postsecondary teaching profession. Indeed, in colleges and universities across the country, often a majority of classes are taught by temporary adjunct faculty—many of whom piece together a living by combining employment at several institutions. Often paid by the course at $2,500 or less each, the annual wages of these Ph.D.-educated instructors can easily fall below $20,000 a year with no benefits. Overall, roughly half of all new faculty hired on American campuses are contingent workers.

Manufacturing, once the home of stable, often unionized, and high-paying jobs, has also seen a shift to contingent employment. In one national survey, manufacturing firms averaged 13.6 percent of their workforce as contingent work. Nearly one-third of all temp jobs are in manufacturing. Temp workers staff assembly lines alongside permanent employees. Both sets of workers may be subject to the supervision of a "rent-a-boss" as firms hire more contract supervisors. These numbers suggest that a significant portion of the so-called loss in manufacturing jobs has simply been a shift to contingent employment. A 1999 Federal Reserve estimate suggested that while manufacturing officially generated 550,000 new jobs between 1992 and 1997, with the inclusion of temp workers, the industry actually added over a million new workers.[14]

By a small, but noticeable, margin, women are overrepresented in the contingent workforce, as are racial minorities. A full 30 percent of all contingent workers are between sixteen and twenty-five years of age—double the portion of this age group in the workforce as a whole.[15]

Why such an explosion in contingent work? In some cases, workers want to have flexible job arrangements. Temporary, contingent, and part-time work can allow them to balance jobs with other personal commitments. Contingent work can also provide exposure to many different work environments and allow employer and employee to size up each other. As many as one-third of contingent workers do not seek permanent jobs. However, the remainder want permanent jobs. While lasting jobs are often promised to temporary workers, few get them. In one study, only 13 percent of temporary workers obtained permanent positions within the same firm one year after being hired. Another 43 percent found permanent employment at different companies. Nearly one-quarter were still employed as temps.[16]

When surveyed, employers rarely point to cost savings to describe their rationale for using temps. Only one-quarter of firms contacted in one study rated payroll reduction "very important." Instead, they pointed to such concerns as "flexibility in staffing," "finding specialized talent," and "temporary replacement of regular workers." However, one out of five surveyed firms did confirm that it had realized payroll reductions in full or in part due to the use of contingent workers.[17]

Indeed, the massive growth of nontraditional employment reflects the clear rise of new employment strategies over the past two decades. While contingent work was common among the early industrial workforce in the nineteenth and early twentieth centuries, it faded to the backdrop with the rise of large vertically integrated corporations that needed a large stable workforce to drive their competitive power. Union seniority provisions further strengthened long-term stable career ladders. Stable employment among the core workforce began breaking up in the 1970s. In the past twenty years, contingent arrangements have spread through all economic sectors as the concept of the "lean company" began to replace the ideals of the large-scale integrated firm. The basic idea is simple. Companies externalize all but their core operating costs. Core workers receive the better wages, benefits, and promotion possibilities. The remainder of the workforce become part-timers, temps, or work as independent contractors. The work can also be shifted to supplier firms contracted to deliver goods and services. Such arrangements allow management to operate with maximum "flexibility"—expanding and contracting operations to fit the level of their immediate business. This way,

costs are kept as tight as possible and companies can respond to small changes in product demand.

Since temporary and outsourced work is usually nonunion, the lean company can also feed a management antiunion agenda. For example, when workers at a small New Balance plant in Massachusetts voted to form a union, management used temp employment to block a first contract and promote a decertification of the union. Equally alarming for the American labor movement, a national survey of 1,248 firms found nearly no difference between union and nonunion firms in their rates of using contingent work.

The lean corporation attempts to transfer responsibility for an employee's welfare onto temporary agencies or the employee him- or herself. Such employment magnifies all the negative trends experienced by working people over the last two decades. With an average income of $329 per week, contingent workers earn almost $100 a week less than noncontingent workers do. Only 7 percent receive health benefits and only 4 percent obtain a pension benefit.[18] Contingent workers typically receive less training than regular employees and are placed on dangerous jobs with far less protections for their health and safety.

Since much of the nation's labor laws are oriented around traditional full-time work, contingent employment provides firms ample opportunities to get around our nation's employment standards and non-discrimination laws. They can avoid, for example, overtime laws, the Family Medical Leave Act, minimum wage, unemployment insurance, antidiscrimination laws, safety standards, and federal pension law. Indeed, the current legal framework for contingent work is so inadequate that hiring of "permatemps" has become increasingly commonplace. Under this notorious practice, called payrolling, firms hire workers to perform normal full-time work under their complete supervision. The only difference comes on payday when the permatemp's wages come from the payroll of a temp agency. As Kelly Services described in their promotional materials: Do you have "a group of your current or former employees that you choose not to have on your payroll? The solution: put them on our payroll." In essence, payrolling allows a firm to hire employees but pay them lower wages and benefits and have no legal responsibility to them.

Temp agencies are especially bad employers. As for-profit institutions, they make their money off the labor of contingent workers. While a few firms take the high road by offering employers well-paid, skilled, and reliable workers, most take the low road. In addition to low wages and nonexistent benefits, temp agencies exploit workers in other ways. They try to avoid increased payroll costs through various schemes to cheat contingent workers out of unemployment compensation. The Carolina Alliance for Fair Employment, for example, paid some two dozen temps to detail the problems they encountered during a week of contingent work. The stories included temp agencies that placed them in jobs for which they were not trained and that did not provide training; those that would not give written notice of the employment wages; agencies that placed workers in unsafe working conditions; and firms that illegally assigned jobs based on race, sex, or age.[19]

A reporter in Lawrence, Massachusetts, exposed temp agencies caught hiring out Cambodian immigrants for under-the-table wages below the legal minimum wage. Contingent workers were also working up to sixty-two hours in a week with no overtime pay. At one large Hewlett-Packard plant, the temp agency was housed in the actual facility. Because of an internal rule that a person cannot be hired as a temp for more than two years, workers were hired for just short of this time, fired for three months, and then rehired again. Temp agencies have also provided a way for employers to quietly not pay Social Security payroll taxes.

Across the country, temp agencies are working hard to use welfare-to-work reform and job training funds as a source of additional low-paid contingent workers. Indeed, in several localities across the country, temp agencies have succeeded in getting themselves designated as the official job center administering federal job-training funds! In the first quarter of 1997, 30 percent of single parents hired who received AFDC were employed by temp agencies.[20]

The behavior of temp agencies does not always work for the corporate customer either. A 1999 survey by the American Management Association found that nearly twice as many firms (36 percent overall) experienced unexpected problems using temps as reported unexpected benefits. The top four complaints were that the agency sent a person with the wrong qualifications, workers were unreliable or absent, temp turnover, and workers with what the employer considered "poor values and attitudes."[21] Obviously, the low pay, high exploitation, and meager preparation provided by many temp agencies do not foster highly motivated and skilled temp employees.

The growing use of contingent workers has also seen the reintroduction of day labor—a practice all but wiped out in many parts of the country. For example, today Labor Ready—one of the top ten temp agencies in the country—specializes in blue-collar jobs in which workers are hired on a day-to-day basis. The company pays wages in the range of $6.15 to $8 an hour, with no benefits. For this meager sum it requires people to wait for hours every day for jobs that may or may not materialize. Labor Ready does not check work for dangerous health and/or safety conditions. It does, however, fire workers for even small infractions of its many disciplinary rules. Labor Ready has also made public its willingness to provide "replacement workers" to help companies break strikes.[22]

The exploitation of contingent workers has made it into the courts. Microsoft Corporation has repeatedly been caught using contingent employment to abuse its workers. In 1990, the company admitted that it had avoided paying benefits and deducting payroll taxes for thousands of its workers by labeling them independent contractors. Although Microsoft promised to pay the back taxes and to convert the workers to regular positions, few workers actually received permanent jobs. Instead, the company shifted workers to employment through payrolling agencies. These second-class permatemps included writers, editors, Web-page designers, software testers, and some that had supervisory responsibilities. In December 2000, Microsoft agreed to settle the eight-year-old class-action suit by paying $97 million to an estimated eight thousand to twelve thousand workers.[23] Companies such as Time Warner, several major grocery and drug store chains in New York City, and several city and county governments have also been taken to court in recent years over contingent work.

Professor George Gonos of the State University of New York at Potsdam has studied temp work for twenty years. In summing up the national pattern, he argued that "this is about a massive secondary labor market that has been created in every occupational group, producing a burgeoning group of second-class workers."[24] With companies able to convert a wide range of traditional full-time jobs to nonstandard work, contingent work provides management a powerful threat to workers who do not cooperate with the official plan. Both directly and indirectly, contingent work operates as an important backdrop to our nation's growing disparity in wealth and the fact that so many workers did not benefit from the official economic boom of the 1990s.

Fortunately, grassroots coalitions of labor, community, and religious groups have begun to form to improve the lives of our nation's growing contingent workforce. Indeed, living wage campaigns, for example, have at times deliberately included part-time workers in their coverage. Three efforts built specifically around contingent work are particularly noteworthy for their distinct approaches: the Massachusetts Campaign on Contingent Work, the northern New Jersey Temporary Workers Alliance, and the various efforts to organize temporary workers into unions. We will detail these three experiences below. A final experience—the innovative temp worker organizing project in Silicon Valley—will be covered in chapter 10, as it is part of a multipronged economic development strategy.

The Massachusetts Campaign on Contingent Work

As we will detail in Chapter 13, since the 1980s New England has been a center of innovative political organizing with labor, environmental, civil rights, neighborhood, and other progressive groups building strong electoral coalitions in several states. Over time, such cooperation has also opened the possibilities for developing broad and innovative reform agendas that cut across individual organizations' traditional concerns. Economic issues, broadly defined, have provided a common focal point for such agendas.

In Massachusetts, contingent work has offered a basis for coalition building around economic issues. With a quarter of the state's workforce (more than 800,00 workers) at part-time, temporary, or other forms of contingent work, the issue is certainly compelling. The wages, hiring, and employment practices experienced by the state's contingent workforce touch the core concerns of a wide range of progressive organizations. In 1998, one-fifth of Massachusetts's workforce earned below $7.60 an hour—thanks in no small part to contingent work. Part-time workers averaged 60 percent of what permanent workers made. Temp workers made 70 percent. Table 9.2 lists the forty-one organizations that came together for the 1997 founding of the Campaign on Contingent Work.

The campaign developed a two-pronged strategy. Locally, the campaign fosters grassroots activity among contingent workers. Statewide, the campaign aims to pass legislation that would redefine the overall rules of contingent employment.

Strong grassroots organizing efforts have developed in Boston and the Merrimack Valley. The Boston project centers on a modest Contingent Workers Center modeled after similar immigrant worker organizations. Located at a UAW hall in Kenmore Square, the center provides a safe place for workers to meet and organize. It also provides a hotline for legal help and a newsletter on contingent work–

Table 9.2

Founding Organizations for the Campaign on Contingent Work

ACORN	Massachusetts Employees Association
Carpenters Local 40	Massachusetts English Plus Coalition
Center of Labor Research, UMASS Boston	Massachusetts State AFL-CIO
Chinese Progressive Association/Workers Center	Merrimack Valley Project
Citizens for Participation and Political Action	Neighborhood Legal Services, Lynn
Committee on Economic Insecurity	9 to 5, NAWW
Commonwealth Coalition	Northeast Action
Dorchester Labor Committee	Progreso Latino
Greater Boston Legal Services	SEIU District 925
Greater Roxbury Workers Association	SEIU Local 285
Immigrant Workers Rights Committee	SEIU Local 509
Industrial Cooperative Association	Tax Equity Alliance of Massachusetts
Inquilinos Boricuas en Accion	Teamsters Local 504
Inter-Valley Project	UAW Local 2324
IUE Local 201	UAW Massachusetts Community Action Program
Jewish Labor Committee	UMASS Boston—Legal Center
Jobs with Justice	UMASS Lowell, Technology and Work Program
Jobs with Justice Worker Rights Board	United for a Fair Economy
The Labor Page	United Steel Workers Local 9267
Massachusetts Committee on Occupational Safety and Health	Women's Institute for Leadership Development
	Woolworth Workers Justice Committee

related activities throughout the area. The center aims not to be an office dispensing services, but a catalyst for more extensive organizing among contingent workers. Thus, its activities are geared toward identifying and developing contingent-worker activists and leaders.

The center distributes information on workers' basic rights. The state's welfare reform gave this educational effort a particular focus and urgency. Work requirements forced thousands of welfare recipients out into the low-wage labor market. Of the 15,000 subject to work requirements in 1998, 11,000 held jobs paying so little that they still qualified for benefits. Contingent work was a big part of the picture. The other 4,000 recipients were enrolled in workfare jobs dispersed among nonprofit agencies. This situation promised to get worse. Unlike other states that adopted longer time limits, the state of Massachusetts implemented its welfare reform by cutting off recipients after two years of total aid. In 1998, 35,000 families in the state faced the elimination of their benefits by the end of the year—send-

ing a ready new supply of vulnerable workers into temp agency offices. Either contingent organizing efforts had to reach out to this influx of welfare recipients, or employers were going to pit these same people against existing contingent workers.

The campaign and Workers Center developed a flyer informing workers of their basic rights as workers. The flyer included brief information on the state's $5.25 minimum wage, overtime regulations, prevailing wage, health and safety rights, family leave, unemployment, and antidiscrimination laws. The materials also armed workers against other ways in which they might be ripped off. They could not be charged for uniforms or meals that they did not want. The employer must pay them in full, on time, once every week or two weeks. If they worked 6 hours or more, they had the right to a 30-minute break. They also had the right to collective action and to form a union or similar organization. The flyer also explained some of the campaign's immediate legislative goals, including the elimination of the 24-month welfare cutoff, an increase in the minimum wage, and equal pay with noncontingent work. Teams of volunteers visited work sites to hand out the flyers. The information was also distributed through local unions and other organizations and local media.

The center also helped organize direct-action campaigns. For example, when two women workers with between twenty and thirty years' work experience at a Boston Woolworth found themselves summarily fired, the Workers Center and the Chinese Progressive Association helped organize a campaign that discovered similar age discrimination at the stores all around the city. Activists organized picketing, a one-hour boycott of the downtown store, and a lawsuit by nine former employees.

The center has also joined with the Coalition of Contingent Academic Labor, Jobs with Justice, the American Association of University Professors, the Center for Campus Organizing, and a number of local unions to launch an areawide University Organizing Project. In the long term, the project aims to organize university and college contingent workers—from students to office staff to professors—into unions. Its immediate goal aimed to pressure area educational institutions to sign on to a new Charter of University Worker Rights. This document includes the rights to a living wage, decent benefits, and steady work. The project has also established a campus-based workers center to organize the many students employed as contingent workers.

The Merrimack Valley Project (MVP) has similarly combined education with direct action. A regional organization of forty-six religious, labor, and community groups, the MVP was organized in 1989 to preserve and create quality jobs in the valley. The area's two major urban centers, Lawrence and Lowell, are famous for the historical union battles of textile workers early in the twentieth century. Today, Lawrence has a majority Latino population and is the poorest city in New England. Roughly half of Lowell's population consists of first- and second-generation immigrants from Asia and Latin America. At first, much of MVP's energy went into battles to retain family-supporting, unionized jobs and to block plant closings. In 1997, however, the coalition launched a Better Jobs campaign to reach out to and organize among the area's large contingent workforce. As in Boston, the first step was to provide workers, in their native tongue, basic information on their rights, the unemployment compensation system, and tips for choosing an employment agency.

The project has also tried to build activism among contingent workers. Since low-wage contingent workers move from job to job, the task is not easy. Activists have used local churches, bus stations, unemployment offices, and other established networks to try to reach temp workers. In June 2000, the campaign held an assembly of temporary workers to launch organizing efforts around a temp workers' bill of rights. The list includes the basic legal protections around wages, overtime, health and safety, and discrimination. It also includes honest and full disclosure of information about permanent job prospects as well as wages and the rates charged to the employers. The bill of rights also aims to protect workers against various fees used to cheat them out of their full wage. The campaign aimed to use grassroots action to pressure large employers and temp agencies to sign on to the bill of rights.

The Better Jobs campaign also sought to get local government involved in protecting contingent-worker rights. Without a special dispensation from the statehouse, local governments in Massachusetts cannot enact their own regulations on contingent work. However, the MVP continues to pressure Lawrence to establish an employment rights committee that would study the problems associated with temp work, investigate reported abuses, and work with the state attorney general to prosecute violations of the law.

Ultimately, public policy has to change the ground rules on which contingent work is based. Indeed, reform efforts in the late nineteenth and early twentieth centuries had put in place state laws regulating the temp industry. At the same time, the growth of large integrated firms employing hundred of thousands of workers helped develop full-time standard employment as the norm. In the 1960s and 1970s, however, the temp industry waged a quiet, yet all-out, campaign to rewrite state laws. The results are the massive loopholes found today that exempt contingent work from most regulations and public standards. The industry continues to lobby. Recently, Professional Employer Organizations (a coalition of employee leasing companies) attempted to attach to more general pension and employment legislation a measure that would have essentially legalized permatemping by allowing a firm to place as much as 85 percent of its workforce on the payroll of a staffing agency!

The Massachusetts Campaign on Contingent Work is one of several efforts to reregulate the industry. Activists have drafted two pieces of legislation, which were introduced into the state legislature. The Workplace Equity Act would require equal pay for workers regardless of employment status; prevent discrimination against contingent workers in insurance, pension, and other benefits; mandate pro-rated benefits for all workers in part-time jobs; and require maternity leave and strengthen unemployment insurance for part-time workers. It would also commit the state to developing part-time and contingent work standards for all companies that contract with the state government. By leveling the playing field between full-time regular jobs and contingent work, the law aims to close contingent work as an avenue for pursuing low-road, low-labor-cost business strategies. The act is deliberately structured to apply to all forms of contingent work. When legislation addresses only one form of contingent work, it risks employers' simply shifting to other forms.

The original bill would also commission a "job gap study" to determine the number, nature, and quality of job vacancies. This study was also formulated as a separate lead-off piece of legislation. In addition to job vacancies, the study would quantify the "gap" between the number of livable wage jobs and job seekers as well as documenting the number of part-time and other contingent jobs.

Although both bills were originally introduced into the 1998–1999 legislative cycle, activists realized that passing the legislature represented a long-term battle still ongoing today. However, the proposed Massachusetts laws come as the best example of an entire line of legislation emerging in many states. In Rhode Island, the United Campaign for Permanent Jobs and the United Workers Committee of Progreso Latino successfully passed the Temporary Employment Protection Act. The new law requires temp agencies to provide written notice to their employees that includes pay rate, job descriptions, and work schedules. The law also established a joint legislative commission to study employment practices in the temp industry. South Carolina has enacted similar "right to know" measures.

The Massachusetts Workplace Equity Act has proposed parallels in Pennsylvania and Connecticut. Maine offers a leading example of a state that has passed legislation to sharply regulate its own use of temporary and contingent work. Washington State has seen a series of proposed pieces of legislation that would establish a Contingent Workforce Task Force, limit the state's use of long-term temporary and leased employees, require staffing agencies to disclose their client billing rates, restore the right to overtime pay for high-tech workers employed on an hourly basis, and penalize employers who misclassify their workers to avoid paying benefits. Washington's workplace health and safety law already offers an example of how to cover workers labeled by their employers as independent contractors. California recently passed legislation that makes garment manufacturers more liable when their subcontractors violate employment laws. Laws in Alaska, Illinois, Pennsylvania, and Oregon make employers who contract out work responsible for providing worker's compensation if the workers are not otherwise covered. As in Massachusetts, bills proposed in California, Connecticut, Pennsylvania, and Rhode Island would prohibit wage discrimination against part-time workers.[25]

New Jersey's Temporary Workers Alliance

The Merrimack Valley Temp Workers Bill of Rights has parallels in several efforts to establish employer codes of conduct similar to those that the anti-sweatshop movement has pushed in the apparel industry. In the mid-1990s, a community group called the Carolina Alliance for Fair Employment attempted to implement a code of conduct among temp agencies but hit a wall of company resistance. The group continues to organize, however, by providing legal help and advocacy for legislative change. By 2000, it had built up a dues-paying membership of one thousand contingent workers.

The New Jersey Temp Workers Alliance, an initiative of the Bergen Employment Action Project, has taken up the code-of-conduct idea with more success. It drew up a list of 24 "Principles of Fair Conduct" that include nondiscrimination, adequate on-site training and orientation, written job and employment descriptions, and fair treatment when filing for unemployment. The endorsing agencies also agree not to charge employers special fees for those workers whom they convert to permanent positions. The alliance then sent invitations to all 500 temp agencies in the state to sign on to the code. The National Association of Temporary and Staffing Services, however, mounted a vigorous campaign against the principles. Despite these efforts, 32 agencies have endorsed the Principles of Fair Conduct. These companies represent small to mid-sized firms that want to distinguish themselves from their competition as high-practice agencies. Such a reputation allows them to attract valuable workers in a tight job market. It also allows them to appeal to companies as a temp agency that provides quality services free from the problems of high turnover, inadequate preparation, and low motivation that often plague high-exploitation agencies.

To further enhance the meaning of the distinction between high- and low-road temp agencies, the Temp Workers Alliance also publishes a Consumer Guide to "Best Practice" Temp Agencies. The guide lists the Principles of Fair Conduct and details the 32 temp firms that have signed on. It also includes tips for considering temp work, information on basic worker rights, and recommendations on how to handle specific problems while temping. The alliance also maintains a Black Book with reports on over 170 agencies and solicits from workers one-page evaluations of their temp experience.

As with all of these contingent-worker projects, the Temp Workers Alliance is quite new. The group's long-range strategy is to build organization among temp workers and to form strategic alliances with selected agencies as a way of raising overall standards in the industry. Such work with high-road temp employers has also led to legislative action. When the Puerto Rican Congress established a model temp agency that paid living wages and actively sought positions leading to full-time jobs, it found itself undercut by poverty-wage employment agencies who illegally avoid paying payroll taxes and worker's compensation by shipping in workers from neighboring states. In November 2000, the Republican chair of the New Jersey Assembly's Labor Committee had sponsored legislation making the contracting companies ultimately responsible for withholding payroll taxes.

Labor Organizing

Unions have provided the classic tool for workers to improve their conditions at work. Unfortunately, in a country in which no form of labor organizing is easy, organizing among contingent workers is particularly difficult. By the very nature of their employment, many temps move from job to job. The average turnover of temp workers runs at 400 percent. Even the permatemps employed for years at the same company face inherent job insecurity. The nature of contingent employment often scatters workers. Small, isolated pockets of contingent workers are all the harder to organize.

Our country's weak labor laws also make contingent-worker organizing difficult. Over the past half-century, the main vehicle for workers to unionize has been the National Labor Relations Act (or state and federal level public sector equivalents). The law, however, does not apply to all workers and contingent work is often placed outside the system. Thus, for example, a large portion of the teachers at our nation's colleges and universities are not allowed the legal process for unionization because current national rulings consider graduate student assistants and adjunct faculty "casual labor" without a long-term attachment to the workplace. This ruling came despite the fact that at many institutions such employees can do as much as a majority of the teaching. Graduate students and lecturers in states such as California, Massachusetts, Michigan, and New York have succeeded in forming unions only because, as employees at public institutions covered by state statute, they were able to win state-based rulings in their favor.

Despite these difficulties, contingent organizing can succeed. Indeed, the building trades unions were formed among a contingent workforce. Employment in the construction industry comes through work-specific contracts. The unionization of construction work occurred by forcing employers to agree to abide by master bargaining agreements and to employ workers with the union serving as the hiring hall. Today, current federal law bans such closed-shop hiring arrangements in most industries outside those such as construction. However, the basic idea of organizing to compel employers to sign on to broad master agreements remains quite relevant. The National Labor Relations Act system does not provide the only avenue for union recognition. For over one hundred years before the effective implementation of the National Labor Relations Act in 1939, workers organized unions by using their collective solidarity to force employers to recognize their organization and enter into formal agreements.

The same is true today.[26] In New Orleans, for example, SEIU Local 100 organized and won contracts for temp garbage-truck workers. When the city privatized its municipal garbage collection, all the laborers who threw garbage into the backs of the trucks became contract workers hired through a variety of temp agencies. Instantly, eight hundred long-time city "hoppers" became minimum-wage temps. These workers had leverage, however. As contingent employees, the workers had some control over whether they showed up for work. When, during a hot New Orleans summer, the hoppers stayed home, the companies were forced to the bargaining table amid a looming residents' uprising over piled-up garbage.[27]

One of the largest organizing victories in recent years came from the unionization of 75,000 low-paid home care workers in California. The wages for these mostly women of color came through a county-administered program. The women, however, were officially considered "independent contractors" with their official employer being each person to whom they provided care. The SEIU mounted a multiyear, many-pronged strategy that included legal, political, and organizing elements. In 1992, the campaign won a state law empowering counties to create local home care authorities with which workers could legally bargain as the employer. SEIU then launched an all-out effort in Los Angeles County to win union recognition for the area's 75,000 home care workers. In 2000, voters in Oregon passed a ballot initiative to create the Home Care Commission to serve as the employer of record of home care workers—thus establishing an avenue for collective bargaining.

Today, the building trades unions also must confront a growing contingent construction workforce that averages over 200,000 nonunion temp workers each day and is growing by 15 percent a year. Nationally, the unions have launched a "Temp Workers Deserve a Permanent Voice@Work" campaign to educate and mobilize existing union members to help organize temp workers into unions, organize contractors using temp firms, and level the playing field through legislation. The campaign has targeted Labor Ready, one of the largest providers of temp construction workers in the country. As a Labor Ready shareholder, the unions took their case to the company's 2000 shareholders meeting. Events at the meeting were supported by rallies and demonstrations across the country. The campaign has highlighted Labor Ready's unfair check-cashing fees and special fees for worker transportation as well as its underreporting of worker's compensation. The unions have filed several lawsuits over these practices. They have also drafted a model piece of state legislation to establish a Temporary Workers' Bill of Rights.

The controversy and organizing at Microsoft has helped produce a new type of union for Web designers, technical writers, and software engineers employed for years as contingent workers. Called the Washington Alliance of Technology Workers (WashTech), the recently formed organization has attracted worker organizing at fifty high-tech companies. Affiliated with the Communication Workers of America, the new group focuses on bargaining with the main employer, not the temp agency intermediaries. However, in Microsoft's case, neither it nor the four temp agencies it uses would recognize the collective-bargaining unit demanded by twenty of its contingent employees. Microsoft, however, did begin to quietly reclassify their jobs to more accurately reflect the skills involved. Working with the Washington State Federation of Labor and the Center for a Changing Workforce, WashTech has developed a Bill of Rights for Temporary Workers legislation that would begin to provide protective regulation for the state's 150,000 temp workers. As a traditional labor organization, WashTech seems modest, with a membership that numbers only in the low hundreds. However, as a social movement, the effort has gained broad support, allowing it to mobilize an impact far greater than its formal membership numbers.

In association with the Worker's Organizing Committee Worker's Center, day laborers in Portland, Oregon, have formed their own union and pledge not to accept jobs for less than $8 an hour. In cooperation with local religious leaders and labor organizations, they held a series of vigils and marches that forced the INS to stop raiding among day laborers as they wait for work.

In Illinois, the Chicago Coalition for the Homeless is helping a largely Latino and African-American population of 30,000–50,000 day laborers get organized. With three-quarters of the city's homeless-shelter residents working as mostly day laborers, the link for the coalition is natural. The coalition launched the Day Laborer Organizing Committee/Latino Task Force. In February 2000, workers fought back with loud street protests, public hearings, and a one-day strike against one of the employing agencies. With media coverage and the help of a city alderman, they shut down two agencies engaged in unlicensed and illegal behavior. In partnership with Jobs with Justice and the University of Illinois Center for Urban Economic Development, activists are conducting a citywide survey of day laborers to document conditions in the industry. The campaign has also won a model piece of state legislation that requires all day labor agencies to register with the state. This information is then available to help enforce the law's protections. The state provides a toll-free number for workers to file complaints and the state has the power to revoke the registration of any agency that fails to comply with the act. The task force is now working to establish day-laborer co-ops that can directly negotiate better pay and working conditions. As a first step, the group has begun to lobby the city to spend $1.9 million to finance eight workers centers where day laborers can wait for work in peace.

The Boston area also offers a leading example of academic organizing with the Coalition of Contingent Academic Labor, affiliated with the Massachusetts Educators Association. With 58 institutions of higher education within 10 miles of the city, this organizing is tackling a dominant economic institution. The coalition lobbied successfully for state reform, raising the per-semester-course pay for contingent faculty at the University of Massachusetts in Amherst and Boston to $4,000. The national norm is between $1,800 and $2,500. The state also granted benefits to half-time faculty. Contingent organizers have pressured the leadership of the full-time faculty unions to make improving contingent employment a bargaining issue. Part of this struggle can involve including adjunct faculty in the existing collective bargaining unit. However, solidarity from traditional faculty is something that has to be built as professors can view contingent workers as a threat to their status. At a community college, for example, part-time faculty workers each got only a one-quarter vote to elect the union's executive board even though they had to pay dues at the full-time rate. The union had 1,500 full-time and 4,000 part-time faculty members. In some cases, contingent faculty have sought new union structures that recognize them as a distinct group within the larger union. By contrast, organizing with student, community, and full-time faculty support, the coalition won an independent adjunct faculty union at Emerson College.

Toward a National Movement

As infant state and local contingent workers campaigns have gotten under way, they have networked with each other. In 2000, thirty-five groups formally launched the National Alliance For Fair Employment. The alliance includes twenty contingent-worker groups plus such national organizations as ACORN and the AFL-CIO. It aims to foster further grassroots organizing among contingent workers as well as promote local, state, and federal legislation to expand legal protections and rights for contingent workers. In early 2000, the group released poll results showing that two out of three Americans consider it unfair when contingent workers are paid wages lower than full-timers doing the same work at the same level. Three out of five respondents had either directly experienced involuntary contingent work or knew someone who had. Six out of ten said that they would be more likely to vote for a candidate who backs legislation to require companies to pay part-time, contract, or temporary employees the same rate of pay and benefits as regular employees.

Ultimately, the goal is not to eliminate contingent work, but to equalize its pay, benefits, working conditions, and status so that it becomes a tool for employers and employees to work out mutually beneficial work arrangements, rather than a weapon to drive down our nation's work standards.

How to achieve such a goal is not a mystery. In the summer of 2000, the Israeli parliament passed legislation requiring that all temporary workers must be paid the same wages and benefits as full-time workers. Employers must also convert temp workers to permanent positions after nine months. Employers have challenged the new law in court. However, the ball is rolling. A few months later, the United Kingdom enacted regulations requiring employers to provide the same pay, pensions, vacation, and training to part-time workers as they do for full-time employees. The new regulations come as part of the EU's Part-Time Work Directive. In July 2000, senators Edward Kennedy and Robert Andrews introduced federal legislation that, if passed, would outlaw permatemping. It would also require that employee benefit plans meet objective eligibility criteria based on the terms of employment rather than the label assigned by employers. Clearly, contingent work will provide a wealth of organizing opportunities for many years to come.

Raising the Minimum Wage

Our nation's abysmal minimum wage is a central policy encouraging low-road business strategies. The federal minimum was passed in 1938 as part of the Fair Labor Standards Act. Both it and the broader New Deal aimed to set basic wage and employment standards so that the population could afford to buy the goods that the country had the capacity to produce. Such steps aimed to address the central demand-side cause of the Great Depression. The act noticeably excluded agriculture, service workers, and those employed narrowly outside interstate commerce reach of the federal government. Such holes left the primary employment opportunities for African Americans and Mexican Americans in the southern half of the country outside of federal standards.[28] Unfortunately, the minimum wage was not indexed to increases in the cost of living. Rather, a raise in the minimum wage requires an act of Congress. From the 1940s through the 1960s, such actions did raise the value of the minimum wage. In 1968, it reached its effective all-time high with an overall buying power the equivalent of $6.92 in 1998 dollars. During the Reagan years, however, Congress allowed the minimum wage to stagnate. In early 2001, at $5.15 an hour, a full-time worker earned only $10,712 a year if paid the minimum wage—more than $3,000 below the poverty line for a family of three and $6,000 below for a family of four.[29]

Why a Low Minimum Wage Hurts Everyone

The nation's low minimum wage has several consequences. Obviously, it relegates millions of Americans to poverty wages. According to the Economic Policy Institute, 11.8 million workers (over 10 percent of the workforce) would directly gain from a $1 increase in the $5.15-an-hour minimum wage. Another 9.8 million who earn between $6.15 and $7.15 an hour would likely benefit. Contrary to the chamber-of-commerce rhetoric about teenagers and other workers not in need of family-supporting income, nearly three-quarters of those directly gaining from a $1 increase are adults aged twenty and over. Parents with children represent a third of the direct beneficiaries. Single mothers are overrepresented in this group. Even among the teenage workers who figure so prominently in business propaganda, half live in households with below-average incomes. The reality of working poverty in this country is harsh. A study by Second Harvest, a national network of food banks, found that 40 percent of households seeking emergency food aid in 1997 had at least one member working. An internal review by the Chicago homeless shelter association determined that no less than three-quarters of the

people staying in area shelter beds worked for a wage!

The impact of a low bottom-wage floor, however, has effects far broader than those workers forced to live in poverty. It allows employers paying poverty wages of $7, $8, and $9 an hour to see themselves paying "fair" wages above the minimum. Poverty wages encourage corporate practices of outsourcing, contingent work, and other ways of tapping the low-wage labor market. A subpoverty minimum wage hits women and minorities especially hard—as these groups are overrepresented among the working poor. The substandard minimum wage also undermines the high road. Training and skill development, worker decision making, unionization, and worker-friendly technology all have a proven record of raising productivity and increasing the bottom line. Yet, when management can pay $5.15 an hour—or even $7, $8, and $9 an hour—it can deliver healthy profits without having to raise productivity in ways that involve sharing power. Low wages often require families to seek public assistance. Thus, poverty wages allow companies to profit by pushing the true costs of their operations onto the public.

Substandard wages do not have to be a fact of life. Already by 1994, Denmark's minimum wage worked out to $14 an hour. In the United States, workers among the bottom 10 percent of wage earners receive only 45 percent of what similar workers take home in Germany and 62 percent in Japan. Business opposition to the minimum wage relies on the same arguments used against the living wage: wage increases will lead to job losses for low-wage workers as companies either cut employment or hire more qualified workers. However, recent studies of minimum wage increases in New Jersey, Oregon, and nationally have challenged this assumption. Researchers have found that increasing bottom wages delivers concrete benefits to a significant number of workers with little or no noticeable loss in employment. Indeed, research in Oregon found that one of the major beneficiaries of the state's recent minimum wage increase was welfare recipients—a population that policy makers have been so fond of calling on to "work for a living." Thanks to the state's minimum wage increase, these typically single parents experienced significant wage gains without any losses in employment.[30]

Placing the Minimum Wage on the Ballot

In 1999, Congress debated increasing the minimum wage to $6.15 an hour. Even with such an increase, the minimum wage would have still been 15 percent below its 1979 level. Yet, even this modest step proved too much for most lawmakers. The rejected Democratic plan would have made the increase in two years. The House of Representatives instead passed a Republican plan that stretched the increase over three years. This GOP bill, however, also included provisions to weaken work-hour regulations and to institute a massive tax cut for the wealthy. Estimates suggested that for $1 gained by low-wage workers, wealthy individuals would see $11 in tax cuts.

Historically, the existence of the federal minimum wage was predated by numerous state and local efforts to establish such standards. In the 1920s, the conservative U.S. Supreme Court deemed these efforts dangerous enough that it struck down several state laws as unconstitutional. This opposition was reversed only when the Court reluctantly upheld the New Deal in the 1930s. Today, local and state campaigns have also taken the lead. Some state minimum wage laws simply apply to workers not covered by federal law. For example, in Texas, state law sets the minimum wage for domestic servants and farm workers at a mere $3.15 an hour thanks to former Governor Bush's refusal to allow an increase. However, other states cover all workers by mandating across-the-board minimum wages higher than the federal level. These are the laws that we profile below.

In 1996, California voters approved a ballot initiative to increase the state's across-the-board minimum wage to $5.75 in 1998. That same year, Oregon voters approved an increase in their state minimum wage to $6.50 by 1999—the then-highest minimum wage in the country. This record, however, will be exceeded over time in Washington State. In 1998, voters approved—by a two-thirds margin—ballot initiative 688 raising the state's minimum wage to $6.50 in 2000. Equally important, the new law indexes the minimum wage to increase automatically at the rate of inflation.

All of these ballot wins came as the result of strong labor-community coalitions. The campaign in Washington State is a case in point. By the end of the 1980s, the Washington State AFL-CIO had begun to shift its political strategy from its traditional emphasis on raising money for Democratic candidates to a more issue-driven and coalition-building mobilization agenda. In alliance with the Washington Association of Churches, Washington Citizen Action, National Organization of Women, Fair Budget Action Coalition, and a host of other community groups, the state labor council formed the Livable Income Campaign, which used a ballot initiative to raise the state minimum wage from $2.30 to $4.25 an hour in 1988. Ten years later, these groups took to the ballot box again with initiative 688 to raise the minimum wage from $4.90 to $6.50. This effort defied official political wisdom by relying on grassroots volunteers, rather than paid canvassers, to collect the 280,000 signatures needed to get the measure on the ballot. Over one hundred organizations and elected officials endorsed 688. Papers such as the daily *Seattle Times*, however, editorialized against the initiative by raising false alarms over the impact of the wage increase on corporate America's favorite fig leaf: "small businesses." The ballot initiative not only passed, but the issue and the grassroots campaign contributed to progressive efforts to get out the vote for the November election. Indeed, Washington voters defied the national trend of voter apathy to deliver the highest turnout in a nonpresidential election year since 1982. As a result, the Democratic Party was able to break into the previously all Republican suburbs around Puget Sound. This swung the state's congressional delegation to a Democratic majority. In an even greater upset, the Democrats took control of the state Senate and shared control of the state House. Building on their success, progressive groups in 2000 launched a living wage movement aimed at passing a Minnesota-style Corporate Subsidy Disclosure law and developing local living wage campaigns in several communities.

Such political successes around the minimum wage and other economic issues prompted a business backlash. In 1998, a national coalition of corporate interest placed proposition 226 on the California ballot. Dubbed "Pay Check Protection," proponents claimed the measure would empower workers to have more say over their union's political activities and how their dues money was spent. In reality the measure aimed to eviscerate the labor movement's broad range of political activities. It would have required unions to get annual written permission individually from each member before using any union dues for political purposes. Under national and many state laws, unions cannot donate dues money to the campaigns of political candidates, but must seek voluntary contributions through political action committees. Proposition 226 did not aim at this activity, but at the broader issue education, get-out-the-vote, and lobbying efforts that unions pursue to mobilize their membership around such issues as the minimum wage. According to initial polls, labor did not have a political future in California. In February 1998, 71 percent of union members supported proposition 226. Political observers predicted that a win in California would spark aggressive corporate "paycheck protection" campaigns across the country. However, an unprecedented grassroots effort by unions to educate and mobilize their membership and to build community allies paid off in a modern political miracle. On June 2, 71 percent of union members and 53.5 percent of overall voters knocked down 226. Rather than weakening labor, the proposition 226 campaign served to strengthen California's labor movement.[31]

Ballot initiative campaigns, however, have not always delivered progressive wins. In 1996, a minimum wage law in Missouri went down to defeat after massive corporate spending. Money and legal maneuvers have also undermined many recent local minimum wage ballot efforts. Depending on state law, municipalities can have the authority to set a minimum wage above state and national standards. In 1996 and 1997, grassroots efforts in Houston, Denver, and Tucson went down to ballot defeat following massive business spending. In 1996, in Houston, ACORN and other progressive groups organized a rather modest effort to pass a $6.50 citywide minimum wage by placing the measure on the ballot. They succeeded in collecting the forty-seven thousand signatures in thirty days needed to place the minimum wage before voters. However, local employers opposed to the measure outspent the campaign by a margin of 5 to 1. With a $1.3 million war chest, the opposition blitzed the public with anti-minimum wage ads on television and radio. They also sent half a dozen mailings making all kinds of drastic predictions on how higher wages would destroy the local economy. No member of the city council or the mayor actively supported the measure. In the end, public support went from polls showing a majority in favor to a final vote of 23 percent for to 77 percent against in a special January 1997 election. Where the campaign had organized a grassroots effort, however, the initiative gained over 60 percent. It also won by 55 percent in predominantly African-American neighborhoods. Groups like ACORN, which organized the campaign, gained valuable coalition contacts and a reputation for having forced large employers to mount a serious countercampaign.

Indeed, the grassroots coalitions behind these failed local minimum wage campaigns continued to expand. In 1999 and 2000, they passed living wage laws in Denver and Tucson. In Albuquerque, opposition to the minimum wage was aided by the city clerk questionably disqualifying petition signatures of newly registered voters. Efforts in New Orleans to set their local minimum wage to $1 above the federal standard prompted a state law banning local wage-raising efforts. Led by ACORN and SEIU Local 100, the campaign challenged the constitutionality of the new law in court. In the summer of 2000, the court ruled that the state's prohibition involved enough shaky constitutional questions to allow the ballot initiative to go before the public. If passed, the courts would then have to rule on the new law's conflict with the questionable state statute. With living wage campaigns successfully building strong coalitions across the country, the potential for successful local minimum wage efforts appears increasingly more promising.

Vermont's Livable Wage Legislative Campaign

The ongoing Vermont Livable Wage Campaign stands out for the way in which activists were able to use the policy process to systematically develop a statewide movement over several years. The Peace and Justice Center, located in Burlington, helped to get the ball rolling between 1997 and 1999 through a five-phase release of reports documenting the wage difficulties experienced by workers in the state. The studies included a compilation of the basic cost of living, the gap between these needs and the jobs that were being provided, the social costs of this gap, and policy recommendations. In addition to its legislative and media uses, this information also provided the basis for a popular education workshop run across the state. Activists aimed to gain recognition of the basic problem first, before entering a controversy over the solutions.

The center also helped foster two institutional supports: the Vermont Faith Communities for a Just Economy and the Vermont Workers' Center. The latter worked to build cross-union solidarity, rapid response networks, a right to organize campaign, and workers rights boards. Including a part-time Livable Wage Campaign director, these organizations could offer half a dozen mostly part-time staff to help with the campaign.

In the state capital, the Vermont Livable Wage Campaign gradually built legislative momentum. In 1998, the campaign won a modest raise in the state's minimum wage by $.10 an hour to $5.25. A year later, the campaign won a $.50 raise (to $5.75) and a $60,000 appropriation for a summer legislative study. This Summer Study Committee on Livable Wages commissioned a research team to further document the wage issues in Vermont. Following a public hearing, the committee drafted legislation that was introduced and passed in May 2000.

This Act 119 not only raised the minimum wage to $6.25, but also offered a comprehensive series of steps to address the wage-job gap. It allocated $3.5 million to increase the state's Earned Income Tax Credit from 25 percent to 32 percent of the federal credit. Through the act, activists got the state to take over the calculation of a basic needs budget and a range of other wage and benefit information, including the costs and availability of health care. State authorities also committed to reviewing the regional development plans linked to federal and state workforce training funds. The state will also examine its tax code in terms of how it impacts low-wage workers. The act also offered a range of benefits to small business and nonprofit organizations. The state will consider the feasibility of allowing such employers to buy into the state's health care program for its employees and hence enjoy the benefits of a larger purchasing pool. A new Small Business Advisory Commission was established to find ways of assisting such small employers in their interactions with the state administration. Roughly 90 percent of Vermont businesses employ fifteen workers or less.

By raising a fundamental discussion about wage levels, the campaign also encouraged various state agencies to reexamine their own employment policies and to put livable wage goals into their work plans. Through collective bargaining that was supported by community allies, the state employees unions won a wage floor of $8.10—the livable wage amount for a single person.

The campaign has also fostered a wealth of local organizing. By mid 2000, three cities had passed livable wage ordinances covering eight hundred municipal employees. In five other communities, town meetings had passed resolutions calling on the legislature to do more to create livable wage jobs. The campaign has helped support successful battles against privatization, provide strike support, and aid union contract campaigns. The campaign has also trained volunteers throughout the state to hold local popular education workshops about livable wages. Activists also pulled together Vermont Business for Social Responsibility in order to help business attract and retain quality employees through livable wages. This business group has produced a ninety-page toolkit explaining the hidden costs of low-wage employment, the steps for creating livable wage jobs, and concrete ways of overcoming the obstacles to such a business strategy.

By 2001, the campaign looked ahead to strengthening and expanding the network of local livable wage groups, adding new organizations to its state coalition, and conducting more popular education. As a next focal point, organizers looked toward pushing for livable wage policies for state college support staff. If successful, the model could then be applied to campaigns for K-12 support and paraeducational employees.

Toward National Change

At the national level the struggle continues. The 1996–1997 increase in the federal minimum wage from $4.25 to $5.15 did not come from the enlightened initiative of the Republican-controlled Congress. Following their 1995 election, the new leadership of the national AFL-CIO launched the "America Needs a Raise" campaign. With town hall meetings in twenty-six cities, the labor federation hoped to raise public awareness about the economic pressures faced by working people and the right to join unions. The project also focused on building alliances with community groups. This campaign, and other efforts, helped convince President Clinton to defy the wisdom of his Democratic Leadership Council and come out in favor of a minimum wage increase in his 1996 State of the Union address. Television and radio ads sponsored by the AFL-CIO in thirty congressional districts, phone banks to 200,000 union members, and lobbying by labor and other progressive groups helped convince twenty-seven Republican Senators and an even a larger number of Republican House members to jump ranks and vote with the Democrats to pass the minimum wage increase. In the end, polls showed that no less than 84 percent of the American public supported the wage increase.[32]

Government action to foster jobs at a decent wage continues to enjoy overwhelming public support. In early 2000, Jobs for the Future released poll results showing that a whopping 94 percent of Americans agreed that people who work full time should be able to earn enough to keep their families out of poverty (80 percent strongly agreed). Over three-quarters felt that government should help people leaving welfare get good jobs that offer opportunities for advancement and the chance to remain self-sufficient. Only one-fifth of respondents believed that people should be moved into jobs as quickly as possible regardless of a job's potential. Asked how much a family of four needs to "make ends meet," 69 percent said at least $35,000 a year—more than twice the federal poverty level for such a household and over three times the minimum wage.

10

The New Labor Movement

While the examples discussed throughout this book involve many currents of social activism, unions have been a major, and often key, player in these undertakings. Indeed, the strength and direction of the respective labor movements provide a core explanation for why capitalism in the United States differs from that in Europe. The progressive campaigns discussed in Part II offer signs pointing to promising changes within the American labor movement. In this chapter we place these examples in the broader context of the national AFL-CIO's efforts to rebuild the labor movement as a central force in the battle for progressive change. The first half of this chapter provides a general introduction to the AFL-CIO's new agenda for readers not familiar with these changes. In the second half, we detail the more specific topic of how unions have attempted to become players in their industries outside of the normal channels of collective bargaining. We will explore the industry partnerships that unions have formed with their employers in several parts of the country. We will also detail the noteworthy efforts of the central labor council in Silicon Valley to systematically build activism and coalitions for intervening in the decisions shaping their regional economy.

The Crisis of American Organized Labor

Numbers are not everything, but in labor relations they reflect a basic balance of power. At the peak membership density of 1955, over one-third of American workers belonged to unions. In many manufacturing industries, organized labor had become a way of life. In automobile production, for example, the UAW compelled the Big Three and the major supplier companies to recognize collective bargaining. This industrywide union strength allowed the UAW to achieve a strategy of pattern bargaining common in Europe but rare in the United States. The union negotiates a contract with one of the Big Three and then pushes the other two automakers to agree to the same basic deal. In this way, basic standards were set for the industry—taking workers' wages, benefits, and working conditions as factors out of capitalist competition.

Today, however, no more than 14 percent of American workers are in unions. If the more highly organized sectors of government employees are removed from this figure, union density in private industry falls to roughly 10 percent of workers. Part of this decline comes from shrinking manufacturing employment, which struck at the heart of the industrial labor movement. The UAW, for example, fell from a 1979 peak of 1.5 million to less than 700,000 today. Unionization in the independent auto supplier sectors has fallen to one out of five workers. This now largely nonunion parts industry translates into union jobs being outsourced to nonunion companies. Even in sectors such as health care and government, where union density has increased, such organizing gains can be overwhelmed by the labor movement's overall loss in strength. The sprawling service sector continues to confront organized labor with a lack of union bargaining power. For example, despite doubling its membership in the 1980s and 1990s, the SEIU has rarely achieved national industry union densities beyond 10 to 12 percent. In only a few geographical markets has the union organized enough employers to set areawide wage and benefit standards.[1]

Declining union density reflects a general crisis of organized labor. Shrinking union numbers have meant shrinking union voters. Even worse, Ronald Reagan's election came from the votes of so-called "Reagan Democrats"—disenchanted voters who were all-too-often union members grown cynical about traditional political action. When Reagan fired the nation's striking air traffic controllers in 1980, he signified a new and aggressively antiunion era in American politics. For example, while the National Labor Relations Act protects workers from being fired for striking, during the 1980s, an old loophole was revived that allows companies to "permanently replace" workers striking over economic issues.[2] Despite helping elect a Democratic president and maintain a Democratic Congress until 1994, the labor movement was not able to get this loophole closed. The 1948 provision in the Taft-Hartley law allowing states to pass "right to work" laws has also come back to haunt labor. Today, twenty-one states, mostly in the South, have active right-to-work laws that prohibit collective bargaining agreements from requiring new employees to join or otherwise financially support the union. While this "free choice" to join or not join a union sounds fair, in reality unions are still required to represent everyone. Right-to-work laws thus allow individual workers to get all the benefits of the union without having to pay to support it.

The weaknesses, however, have not always come from external sources. The collective bargaining system that emerged from the 1930s and 1940s emphasized formal and complex contractual agreements. At one extreme, for example, UAW Big Three na-

tional agreements can encompass four volumes! Union contracts need to be detailed because the bargaining table is the only time when workers can formally negotiate the rules at work. As described in chapter 6, under the postwar deal between labor and employers, unions conceded to management the exclusive right to run the workplace in return for steady improvements around wages, benefits, and working conditions. While this formalized system of collective bargaining delivered concrete gains for millions of workers, it reduced the role for labor's grassroots militancy. Instead, it encouraged unions to operate as service organizations—providing ever-better contracts and benefits to their largely inactive membership. The postwar system required specialized professional staff and skilled negotiators rather than rank-and-file steward activists capable of maintaining union activism on the shop floor.

As a result, as organized labor found itself under increasing attack by the 1980s, its ability to mobilize its own membership remained limited. Nor did the labor movement have strong external alliances. The collective bargaining norms of the 1950s–1970s heyday had also allowed labor's deep connections to the community to atrophy. The suburban dispersal of working-class whites away from the dense social fabric of the nation's cities only further undermined labor as a community force.

Yet, the fate of many communities is tied to the fate of American unions. Overall, wages in this country have followed the path of union strength. The American middle class grew during the boom years as union-negotiated wages and benefits spread to nonunion sectors. As union density has declined, so have the wages for four out of five workers. Leo Gerard, secretary treasurer of the United Steel Workers, touched on a good deal of truth when he commented that "we [organized labor] are the one force which corporate planners see standing in the way of their complete fulfillment of free market capitalism."[3] Just as union strength accompanied strong social democracy in Europe, so has union weakness allowed attacks on our New Deal and the promotion of market freedom. Today, professional union busting is a multibillion-dollar industry with American employers investing heavily in trained antiunion consultants. Indeed, American employers are infamous among the industrial world for their hostility to unions. As one longtime British trade unionist, who lived through the dark years of Reagan's political "sister" Margaret Thatcher, commented in a conversation: "we just cannot get over how antiunion your employers are." Weak social citizenship and declining union strength have made union busting all too doable and too rewarding.

The New AFL-CIO

By the early 1990s, the failure of familiar and trusted union strategies to address the challenges of a new economic environment had created pressure for change that reached to the top of the American labor movement. The AFL-CIO provides an umbrella organization to which most of the nation's unions belong. Following President Clinton's successful campaign to pass NAFTA and the Republican takeover of Congress in 1994, a critical mass of unions within the AFL-CIO asked the federation's president, Lane Kirkland, to retire. A complicated process of back and forth produced the first contested election for the federation's top officers since its founding in 1953. By a close margin, the "new voices" slate led by John Sweeney won on calls to "put the movement back in the labor movement." The progressive president of the United Mine Workers, Richard Trumpka, became the federation's vice president, and Linda Chavez-Thompson the new position of secretary treasurer.

In his prior position as head of the SEIU, John Sweeney had hardly been a left-wing radical. Indeed, critics charged that his administration at SEIU had displayed a good dose of old-style autocratic leadership. However, Sweeney's leadership of SEIU had displayed two important characteristics that he would bring with him to the AFL-CIO. First, Sweeney's administration had a record of hiring committed pro-

gressive activists and giving them the room to formulate innovative organizing strategies. Second, under Sweeney, the union had used strategic planning and other tools to develop an organizational consensus around change. These two elements had combined to produce innovative organizing strategies that helped the SEIU grow to 1.3 million members.

Upon taking the helm at the AFL-CIO, the Sweeney administration began a process of reorganizing the federation's resources and convincing the broader labor movement of the need for change—the urgency for which was not always felt in many sections of organized labor. Within the AFL-CIO, for example, Sweeney established a new Corporate Responsibility Department to provide union affiliates strategic analysis of corporations and industries. The change reflected the new administration's desire to more directly aid unions in developing broad corporate campaigns that hit intransigent companies at all levels—from the workplace to the community to the customer to the boardroom. The new department also oversees the Working for America Institute, which we will profile below, and the Heartland Capital Initiative. The latter explores new ways unions can use worker pension funds to promote high-road business practices.

As we will examine further in chapter 13, the new administration has attempted to reevaluate union political activity—emphasizing greater grassroots mobilization around workers' issue concerns. The new leadership also repudiated the disastrous Cold War international politics of the previous administrations. From the 1950s onward, the AFL-CIO's American Institute for Free Labor Development (AIFLD) had openly cooperated with and received funds from the Central Intelligence Agency (CIA) to battle "communist dominated" union movements in Latin America. This often meant that AFL-CIO leaders helped undermine authentic worker struggles by fostering weak and compliant unions. AIFLD also participated in several CIA-backed coups. In Mexico, the federation worked actively with the official Confederation of Mexican Workers labor federation that operated as an arm of Mexico's longtime ruling party. Only since the passage of NAFTA and the clear integration of several key North American industries have American unions begun to change their relationships to the Mexican labor movement. The Sweeney administration closed down AIFLD and has openly acknowledged the mistakes of past policies. In early 2000, the AFL-CIO also officially reversed its disastrous policy on immigration by moving from an anti-immigrant focus on sanctions against employers who hired undocumented workers to upholding universal worker rights regardless of legal residency status.

Organize the Unorganized

While changes at the AFL-CIO have involved many dimensions, the number one call from the Sweeney administration has revolved around organizing. As hostile as employers and government policy has been toward unions, the fact remains that declining union density has also been self-inflicted. For understandable reasons workers want to join unions. On average, union members make over $160 more per week than their nonunion counterparts.[4] The wage gains and opportunities provided by unionization make all the more difference for workers most disadvantaged by our current economy. Indeed, research has shown that women and workers of color are particularly receptive to unionization. In 1996, polling suggested that 44 percent of the nation's 110 million nonunion workers would like to join a union. That number was up from 39 percent in 1990 and 30 percent in 1984.[5] If all these workers were able to organize unions, the sixteen-million-member-strong labor movement would grow to four times its current size.

As we will explain below, the weakness of our nation's labor laws and the hostility of employers makes union organizing a difficult road. However, as the new AFL-CIO leadership has argued, organizing new workers has not been a priority of the labor movement for many years. Adding together all of the resources of American unions, only about

3 percent goes into organizing new workers, according to AFL-CIO estimates. Most union locals, where the bulk of resources are located, do no organizing at all. During the 1950s and 1960s such a distribution of emphasis made sense as the unions had fought the bid organizing battles of the 1930s and 1940s. The task during the boom years was to enjoy the fruits of these sacrifices by bargaining for and enforcing ever-better contracts. Today, however, the labor movement must return to the tasks of building and not just administering power.

The Sweeney administration has called on the nation's unions to make aggressive organizing a top priority—signified by the goal of placing 30 percent of their budgets into organizing. Such a shift poses a major challenge as staff resources, which currently support the existing membership through servicing activities, are relocated into organizing work. Reviving aggressive union organizing, however, is not just a matter of financial outlays and strategic commitments. Organized labor has to develop new and innovative ways of supporting workers' right to choose a union. Officially, the right to form a union is protected by the National Labor Relations Act. Under the act, workers who collect signatures from at least 30 percent of their workforce may formally request a government-monitored union election. If 50 percent plus one of the voting workers choose the union, the union is granted legal recognition and management must attempt to bargain in good faith.

Today's reality, however, leaves many observers wondering if workers truly have a legally protected right to organize. Union busting is a billion-dollar industry. Every year, professional antiunion consulting firms hold seminars across the country explaining to managers how to keep their workplace union free. These consultants can literally check the public records at National Labor Relations Board (NLRB) offices to identify workplaces where workers have filed for an election. They then contact the firm's management to offer their services. Bogus legal challenges often delay union elections and allow management time to implement its campaign.

The classic antiunion effort consists of two elements. For the carrot, management will suddenly discover great concern for the welfare of its workforce. Raises and other bonuses are given for a job well done. Managers go through sensitivity training to become caring, sensitive bosses. New grievance mechanisms spring up. The employer may even establish various "employee representation" committees and "problem-solving" groups that often flirt with the law's prohibition against employer-dominated mechanisms of so-called worker representation. Management will also foster and often direct worker "Vote-No" committees.

Management's carrot, however, usually comes with a powerful stick. Supervisors call workers into their offices for one-on-one meetings. As part of the conversation, the supervisor might explain the possibility of the workplace being closed if a union is voted in. Indeed, in over half of all union elections, management will threaten to close the workplace. In 12 percent of cases, they actually carry out their threat.[6] Managers may reassign active prounion workers to the worst jobs. Rumors circulate that people don't want to be seen with these "trouble-makers." At one auto parts plant in Michigan, for example, management started rumors that female union supporters were giving away sexual favors in the parking lot as a way of getting people to sign union cards. Typically, workers are forced to sit through professionally done antiunion videos. Managers have laid out stacks of tens of thousands of $1 bills, telling workers: "That's what you mean to the union." Most alarming is the now-common practice in which employers selectively violate the law in order to scare workers away from the union. In half of all union elections, management illegally fires key union supporters. With management lawyers skilled at legal stalling tactics, the firing case will likely drag out for years. While the aggrieved workers might win individual restitution, the workers will have long been scared into voting the union down. In a throwback to the 1930s, several years ago the Teamsters caught Kmart illegally hiring detectives who posed as workers in order to spy on union activists—keeping detailed records of their lives outside work as well as on the job. Finally, if management loses the battle and workers vote for a union, many companies will try to win the war by stonewalling bargaining to prevent workers from ever gaining a first contract. Their hope is to demoralize workers into voting the union out through a company-prompted decertification election.

The ferocious commitment of many American employers to keeping themselves union free is without parallel within the industrial world. To counter employer opposition, the labor movement must go beyond hiring more organizers and fostering more organizing drives. In the 1930s, with the National Labor Relations Act held up in courts, the legal protections for organizing were even less of a reality than they are today. To force employers to bargain with them, workers had to mobilize committed grassroots activism within the workplace supported by alliances within the broader community. Such a twin focus is being revived today.

More and more organizing drives approach their goals from many levels. For example, in the mid-1990s the United Steel Workers fought a long battle against Landis Plastics in Schenectady, New York. The union helped workers document the many cases of illegal racial and gender discrimination as well as flagrant health and safety violations. Activists built alliances with religious leaders and other community groups. Local clergy, for example, held a prayer vigil outside the plant gates. The coalition also drew in state legislators embarrassed to learn that the union-busting company had been lured to the area by generous public assistance from the state. Such community alliances are becoming increasingly common as unions search for allies to fight their uphill battles.

Unions have also explored ways to involve their existing membership. Through a growing number of volunteer organizer programs, union members visit the homes of fellow nonunion workers involved in a unionization drive. Such volunteers provide an authentic and effective voice about what it means to form a union. The contact is all the more effective when the union member's company is a customer of the nonunion company. The Communication Workers of America (CWA) have added thousands of new members by mobilizing their existing members to support organizing drives among nonunion subsidiaries of the same or related companies. They have also led the nation in securing collective bargaining agreements that require nonunion subsidiary firms to not campaign against the union (called neutrality), and to recognize the union voluntarily once a majority of workers has signed union cards (called card-check recognition). Neutrality and card-check recognition help ensure that workers are free to decide to form a union without threats or intimidation.

Labor has also begun to look beyond single-union, workplace-by-workplace organizing efforts. In the 1930s and 1940s, unions swept across America, organizing whole industry by whole industry. Today, large-scale organizing drives are making a comeback. In Las Vegas, for example, unions such as the Hotel Workers and those from the building trades formed an alliance to organize the city's hospitality industry at a communitywide level. By organizing workers and building broad community support, the drive pressured employers to sign fair-play agreements. Today, Las Vegas is the most unionized city in the nation.

Such new organizing strategies redefine the meaning of union activism. The right to organize is no longer the concern of isolated groups of workers in particular workplaces, but rather a community issue of basic social justice. Indeed, the AFL-CIO's call to "change to organizing" is ultimately a call to rebuild the labor movement as a social force working at the focal point of societal change.

This inspiring social movement vision represents a long road down which organized labor has only begun to travel. While unions such as SEIU, UNITE, and CWA have significantly reorganized themselves around organizing, other unions have done little, and many are somewhere in between. The AFL-CIO has no organizational control over the nation's unions. It must foster change through its moral leadership and modest resources. Aggressive organizing involves a level of member mobilization, community alliances, and innovative tactics that goes far beyond how most labor organizations have operated for decades. Yet, progress is being made. In 1996, the AFL-CIO estimated that to stay even at 14 percent of the workforce, American unions had to organize 176,000 new members each year. To increase union density by 1 percent of the workforce, labor has to organize 1.2 million members. In 1999, union membership grew by a net 200,000. For the first time in four decades, the American labor movement's density did not shrink. The task before American labor is not simply to maintain this modest momentum, but to turn it into the steady growth of over a million members a year.

Revitalizing the AFL-CIO's State and Local Labor Bodies

Adding one million new members a year requires a change not only within individual unions, but also within labor's cross-union bodies. While reorganizing its own national activities, the new AFL-CIO administration has sought to revitalize its state and local organizations to transform them into focal points for change. Each state has its own AFL-CIO organization. Below this are the roughly six hundred central labor councils. In rural areas these local federations can encompass several counties. In large urban areas, they can span a major city and its suburbs. While most national unions, but not all, belong to the national AFL-CIO, union membership in state bodies may prove more varied, and participation in local central labor councils can be highly irregular. Indeed, the local affiliates of a central labor council may not even encompass a majority of union members in that area. While central labor councils in larger urban areas have full-time staff, most councils operate largely on volunteer energy.

The patchy participation of unions in these AFL-

CIO bodies reflects the narrow mission provided for them during the postwar boom. Traditionally, the state federations were primarily concerned with political action. The state federations lobby their state legislatures and helped coordinate union activity during election seasons. The traditional model of union political action largely revolved around candidate endorsements, candidate-centered fundraising, and get-out-the-vote drives. Even as the state federations were involved in this process, each union often maintained its own individual political effort. Within unions, narrow lobbying efforts and candidate-centered electoral work operated largely as the terrain of "political junkies" rather than inspiring masses of volunteers.

Most of the core economic tasks—including collective bargaining and organizing—have been the terrain of the individual unions. Central labor councils traditionally confined themselves to perfunctory calls for solidarity and organizing Labor Day parades. As Leslie Moody, the newly elected president of the Denver Central Labor Council and a local organizer for Jobs with Justice put it, "some likened membership in the Denver Central Labor Council to paying grandmother's nursing home bill. You feel obligated to pay without hoping to get anything in return."[7] For the crucial task of organizing not only did central labor bodies play little or no role, but many unions often jealously guarded their organizing efforts from other unions whom they saw as rivals for the same workers. Thus, in calling for state and local AFL-CIO bodies to play a leadership role in reorienting the labor movement toward organizing, the Sweeney administration faced a task that was hardly a straightforward undertaking. Indeed, because of their narrow missions, many central labor councils had tended to attract older and more traditional labor leaders who did not see their bodies as centers for mobilization.

This balance of power between weak AFL-CIO cross-union labor bodies and strong individual union structures worked during the boom years when the labor movement centered on collective bargaining and interest-group lobbying to improve the lives of working people. Today, however, the labor movement needs new abilities that these old structures cannot provide. Coalition building, broad coordinated organizing, and aggressive social movement–style political action all require cross-union labor bodies quite different from what exist now.

Soon after taking office, the Sweeney administration pulled together a labor council advisory committee that included activists from some of the country's most dynamic central labor councils, including: Milwaukee, Atlanta, Seattle, and San Jose. A series of discussions at the AFL-CIO's national 1996 convention in Denver further developed an agenda now known as Union Cities. This program consists of eight elements summarized in Table 10.1 below.

The Union Cities agenda set out to revitalize labor organizing and community activity by using the AFL-CIO's central labor councils as a catalyst for change. Ideally, the central labor councils would both encourage their local unions to adopt the above strategies and develop for themselves a central role in these activities. The eight points were seen not as a one-size-fits-all program, but as a mechanism for sparking discussions and planning among local labor leaders. Ultimately, the designers of Union Cities aimed to foster a culture shift within the AFL-CIO's state and local bodies to move them toward a more forward-looking and active direction.

The two years following the launch of Union Cities saw some notable successes. In the fall of 1997, for example, the Cincinnati Central Labor Council helped the Amalgamated Transit Union win an organizing campaign among the city's school bus drivers and mechanics. The local union did not have the resources to counter the fear and intimidation campaign used against the mostly African-American and female bus drivers. However, through efforts of the Central Labor Council, other local unions, the NAACP, religious leaders, and other community groups successfully campaigned on the union's behalf. In early 1998, the Los Angeles Central Labor

Table 10.1

The AFL-CIO's Union Cities Agenda

1. Make organizing the priority—by promoting organizing as the top goal and getting half of the local unions to sign up for the "Changing to Organizing, Organizing to Change" initiative.

2. Mobilize against antiunion employers—by recruiting 1 percent of union members as a cross-union rapid response solidarity team.

3. Build political power—by organizing grassroots lobbying and political action committees, building alliances with community, and supporting candidates committed to working families.

4. Promote economic growth and protect communities—by building labor- and community-driven economic development initiatives and policies.

5. Provide economic education—through the Common Sense Economics curriculum suitable for group discussion within unions and neighborhood groups.

6. Support the right to organize—calling on elected leaders to pass resolutions supporting workers' right to organize.

7. Promote diversity—work to make sure that all official central labor bodies are as diverse as the membership represented by affiliated unions.

8. Increase union membership—by encouraging and coordinating organizing among unions to increase their membership by the year 2000.

Council became the first in the country to create its own organizing department. The new department provides research and logistical support to aid union organizing efforts. The labor council helped win major victories within the construction. The labor council helped obtain not only union jobs to build fully or partially public-funded sites, but also mandatory card-check neutrality for all service and retail workers employed at the facilities. It has also been a central player in developing the city's model living wage campaigns. Across the country, the living wage movement has drawn in the participation and leadership of central labor councils looking for new strategies and alliances.

Overall, two years into the program, roughly 162 central labor councils signed on to Union Cities. The areas covered by these bodies were home to over 8.2 million union members—half the labor movement's strength. In July 1998, a survey done by the national AFL-CIO found that, of the one hundred central labor councils responding, 69 percent participated in Street Heat actions; 55 percent joined

in the June 24, 1998, Right to Organize Day; 56 percent had sponsored economics education; and 51 percent had held regional organizing conferences. In addition, nearly two-thirds said that they were devoting greater resources to organizing, and a full two-thirds had elected, developed, or recruited more officers, delegates, and activists of color.[8]

The above findings suggested promising changes. However, over four hundred central labor councils had not signed on to Union Cities. Indeed, many of these bodies may simply not have functioned at all. The 1998 survey suggested that roughly seventy-five to eighty central labor councils have been really active in shifting their local union culture. Generally, however, most central labor councils had not been able to achieve the direct and central role in union organizing that the creators of the Union Cities agenda envisioned.

Union Cities was intended to start a reorganization within the labor movement. Clearly, the bulk of the task remains to be done. Unions confront economic forces in which decisions take place at many levels: the company, industry, sector, and business organization. The economy also operates at many geographical levels: workplace, neighborhood, state, nation, and globe. The labor movement needs structures that can affect each of these dimensions in the most efficient and effective ways possible. While existing labor organizations work at some of these levels, at others they function only weakly or not at all.

In 2000, the AFL-CIO unveiled a new reorganizing project called New Alliance. Under this program, national AFL-CIO leaders and staff initiate a long-range planning process within a particular state's labor movement. The first round focused on New York, Maryland, Connecticut, North Carolina, Kentucky, Colorado, Ohio, and Oregon. In each state, the AFL-CIO brings together leadership from individual unions, the state federation, and the central labor councils to map out a vision for where their state and local labor movements want to be down the road. The process asks labor leaders to identify concretely what they want the labor movement to be able to do, lay out which bodies within the movement should do each task, and then develop a plan for putting the necessary resources into these bodies. Working committees within each state focus on six key decisions: determining programs, restructuring the organization of labor councils, investing resources, a plan to move to full union affiliation with each state and local AFL-CIO organization, fostering diversity, and the best governance structures. The statewide vision is then pulled together in a New Alliance conference and follow-up convocations.

Judging from preliminary discussions that have already taken place, the New Alliance process promises to establish new roles for cross-union bodies. Central labor councils, for example, are likely to take on more responsibilities for coalition building around union organizing, broad economic development issues, and political power. Having redefined the roles of cross-union labor bodies in a manner appropriate to the needs of the unions, New Alliance aims to then persuade unions to fully participate in these bodies and provides them the resources needed to

fulfill their new mission. If successful, this process promises to further expand the strategic horizon of the American labor movement—fostering labor as a leader in progressive economic change and opening the movement further to alliances with community groups. A statewide convention in May 2000 made New York the first state to launch its New Alliance plan.

Building High-Road Partnerships

As part of its internal reorganization, the new AFL-CIO administration redesigned its old Human Resources Development Institute (HRDI) to become the new Working for America Institute. The new organization combined the old HRDI's focus on worker training with broader concerns for economic development generally. The institute helps unions foster high-road business strategies through two major paths. First, unions can help retain, expand, and create good jobs by promoting worker training and education, promoting worker-friendly modernization and new technology, and expanding markets for high-road firms. Second, the unions can become players in the local economy and specific industry sectors by showing leadership in progressive economic development strategies and building alliances with a diverse array of community groups. The Working for America Institute promotes these twin paths by providing a clearinghouse for innovative ideas. It publishes a *Working for America Journal* filled with examples, sponsors a yearly conference, and holds workshops to train union activists in high-road strategies. The institute also offers direct technical support to labor organizations.

The AFL-CIO sees labor-management partnerships such as the model WRTP as central tools for promoting high-road practices. The labor movement clearly has a stake in making unionized firms the most effective in their industries. Unfortunately, our economy provides plentiful opportunities to pursue the low road. This means that either unionized firms lose ground to low-road competitors, or management at union shops, feeling the pressure of low-road competition, seeks concessions from workers. Such pressures can be offset when unions become a tool for addressing the fundamental industry difficulties for which low-road strategies offer no, or only partial, solutions.

As the example of the WRTP demonstrates, partnerships between labor and management and among related firms can improve several key competitive elements that traditional management go-it-alone practices fail to address. As we have already mentioned, American firms and government programs woefully undertrain and ill prepare whole segments of our working population. In addition, small to medium-sized firms have trouble modernizing through new technology and new work practices using their own resources. And firms rarely seek to solve common problems through joint cooperation and sharing of knowledge and experiences.

Today, the Working for America Institute can point to a rich set of examples of sectoral partnerships such as the WRTP. For instance, founded in 1984 on the initiative of the International Ladies' Garment Workers' Union, the Garment Industry Development Corporation (GIDC) is an autonomous nonprofit partnership of industry, unions, and the city of New York. The union established the partnership as a way of addressing the flight of jobs out of the city's garment industry. The GIDC offers technical assistance in workplace organization, technology, management, training, education, and marketing—all aimed at allowing the local industry to compete on the basis of quality rather than sweatshop labor. Today, the partnership covers hundreds of employers and over thirty thousand union members. Its business development programs have generated more than $35 million in new sales. In 1997, more than fourteen hundred workers utilized its training and job placement services.

Also in New York, the militant hospital workers union 1199 has established the Employment Training and Job Security Program in the hospital industry. As the largest medical market in the country, New York City's health system helps shape the industry nationwide. With half of the union's membership at area hospitals, these employers represent the most unionized section of New York's health care industry. However, massive restructuring due to government reforms, the growth of managed care, new technology, and a growing population of elderly has threatened this union stronghold. Hospitals face major pressures to streamline costs, join health care alliances, and restructure the breadth and conduct of their operations. The average length of patient stays in hospitals has fallen. Yet, the nation today faces a profound shortage of nursing staff.

These pressures promised to foster management decisions threatening to both workers and the union—including massive layoffs. The union needed to help provide an alternative path. Forming a partnership was not easy. Most hospital management, even at unionized facilities, saw a nonunion workplace as their most competitive option. However, 1199 was able to build on its bargaining relationship with the Hospital League of New York, an association of fifty private nonprofit hospitals, nursing homes, and mental health facilities. Back in 1969, the union and the league had established a joint training fund to upgrade the skills of health care workers. In reaching out to employers, the union also tapped its leading role in health care–related political action at the state level. The union joined with employers to lobby state and local governments for policies that benefit both the industry and the workers.

Within the workplace, 1199 and the Hospital League established the Employment, Training and Job Security Program. This labor-management partnership uses training and worker education as a way to facilitate the restructuring of the industry in ways that retain workers. A Job Security Fund assists laid-off union members with training and placement services, as well as health and unemployment benefits. A Planning and Placement Fund, negotiated in 1994, created the Employment Center to serve as a primary source of referral for employers and placement for workers. The center also tracks industry trends through a research component.

As with the Wisconsin experience, training curriculum is broader and instruction methods far more innovative than what management would have developed on its own. The program has helped several thousand workers whose old jobs were eliminated to retain employment by retraining them for new and often more skilled jobs. By early 1999, more than 7,000 workers had been trained through the job-to-job program. The union has also used the training opportunities to offer workers in often difficult, labor-intensive, and low-skilled jobs opportunities for career paths and advancement. The industry-level training partnership has also helped foster some labor-management partnerships at the local hospital level. These innovative interventions in industry restructuring have also strengthened the union internally. The leadership of 1199 has seen a clear increase in worker interest, activism, and membership in the union. Today, the union-driven programs serve more than 300 employers and 85,000 area health care workers.

In Massachusetts, the Cape Cod Hospital Career Ladders Program provides another example of a joint union-management training program in the medical industry. The program develops clear career paths within the hospital's mixture of work. It then offers training opportunities to provide workers increased access to skilled and higher-paying jobs. At the same time, management gains experienced, reliable workers with the necessary skills.[9] The San Francisco Hotels Partnership Project offers an example of a union-employer partnership in an industry known for low-road practices and labor-management confrontation. A 1994 Multi-Employer Group bargaining agreement with the large and multiethnic HERE Local 2 put $1.8 million into an existing training fund and formed a partnership covering nearly 5,000 workers in 11 class-A hotels. Through training, language instruction, and upgrade programs, workers have gained new skills and promotion opportunities, customer relations have improved, hotel prof-

its and efficiency have increased, and labor-management relations have taken a turn for the better. The partnership has become a model for HERE nationwide.

New York City offers another compelling example of high-road practice in the Consortium for Worker Education (CWE). Founded in 1985 by several area unions, today the institution is funded through public sources and has grown to 40 unions representing 800,000 workers. The CWE provides schooling, training, and employment services to workers across the city. Participating unions include the building trades, 1199, government employees, the autoworkers, textile, hotel, the Teamsters, and the Machinists. In 1998, 40,000 workers participated in CWE's classes. CWE operates one-stop centers in all of the city's five boroughs where people entering or reentering the workforce, or who are looking for new opportunities for career development, can tap into all the services they need at one location. In 1997–1998 nearly 30,000 participants went through CWE training programs. In 1997, over 12,000 workers utilized the center's dislocation assistance.

Recently, CWE has developed a model program to help former welfare recipients to achieve meaningful work. The CWE recruits welfare recipients to provide them with 420 hours of training and work experience as day care providers. It then helps these women gain certification and materials necessary to transform part of their home into an off-site child care classroom. New York City day care agencies visit the homes regularly and provide support. The new child care provider is a union member of AFSCME Council 1707 and receives a starting salary of $18,200 a year with full benefits. In a city facing a critical shortage of day care slots, the program provides promising jobs for welfare recipients, allows them to continue to care for their own children, and provides other parents access to quality day care.

CWE has also partnered with New York's State Education Department to support fourteen parent resource centers in school districts with high levels of public assistance recipients. Parents can go to their children's school and receive job preparation assistance, training in basic skills, and other help to assist them in reentering the workforce. In 1998–1999, over two thousand participants used these services. Each center is operated through a subcontract with a community-based organization and in partnership with the teachers union. CWE runs pre-apprenticeship training and placement programs with the building trades. It is also developing comprehensive programs to support workers once they get jobs through peer support networks, counseling, and opportunities for skill upgrades and advancement.

Partnerships that bring together unions and management are not easy. The postwar deal between management and labor drew clear lines between wages, benefits, and working conditions—which were subject to collective bargaining—and management's prerogative in exclusively running the firm. Unions under this deal did not concern themselves with how the company was run. As management began to experiment in the 1980s and 1990s with ways to better tap the knowledge and ideas of its workforce, company-initiated labor-management cooperation all too often ended up in either empty promises or subtle ways of undermining union solidarity. However, partnerships initiated by unions can deliver effective proworker results because they involve workers in the design and functioning of the programs. Trained in scientific management techniques that emphasize top-down control, managers can see partnerships as a direct threat to their authority and the freedom of the firm to pursue its own best course of action. For these reasons, favorable preconditions for partnerships include: industries that face significant changes, managers confronting grim alternatives, union strength that makes low-road options less attractive, and enlightened individuals on both sides willing to develop a relationship.

Sectoral partnerships do not always require large amounts of resources. While the WRTP and the CWE were founded in large, heavily unionized urban areas, the New Baldwin Corridor Coalition in the Pennsylvania state capital of Harrisburg developed in a largely rural area not known for union prevalence. Indeed, the three central labor councils that helped pull together the consortium had no full-time staff. The companies involved in the partnership averaged between 200–250 employees. The partnership has been developed largely on volunteer time and energy. An initial catalyst came when an unsuccessful battle to save 500 jobs at a local Bethlehem Steel plant helped bring together labor and community activists around issues of saving and expanding the industrial jobs along a 13-mile industrial corridor rife with abandoned industrial sites (brownfields). The New Baldwin Corridor Coalition now includes participants from labor, community groups, employers, and local government. It operates on a budget of $10,000 a year. Its Metalworking Consortia involves eight companies brought together around a common program that addresses training and technology needs.

The coalition has also formed a cooperative program with area schools that exposes students to industrial work and to labor unions. It has put together a transportation/job link project with 40 suburban, mostly nonunion, companies that face severe worker shortages. With union involvement, the project establishes reliable transportation links between low-income communities and the employers. The coalition also coordinated a multicommunity planning effort to develop a common economic development vision and appropriate land-use measures. By helping found the coalition, the local labor movement has built key alliances and established its role in regional economic decisions. The coalition has shown a willingness to back out of economic development projects that do not provide family-supporting jobs. It has also succeeded in fostering commitments to family-supporting jobs. For example, it won a private agreement that a particular parcel of brownfield land would be reserved for companies that pay at least $12 an hour.

Silicon Valley's Labor Movement Takes the Lead

Examples of reinvigorated and dynamic local labor movements are beginning to emerge across the country. We have covered the activities of many of these in the preceding chapters: Milwaukee, Los Angeles, Atlanta, and so forth. In chapter 12, we will discuss the innovative King County Central Labor Council's role in the 1999 mobilization against the WTO. Here, we close this chapter with the example set by the South Bay Labor Council, whose executive director, Amy Dean, chaired the AFL-CIO's labor council advisory committee. The rebuilding of the labor movement in Silicon Valley illustrates not simply the dynamic turnaround of a central labor body, but also many of the themes that we have examined throughout this book.

Like central labor bodies across the country, the council in Silicon Valley had a relatively low profile—operating with just a couple of staff and few resources. While the local labor movement had made few inroads into the area's high-tech industry, it had organized significant densities in construction, the public sector, health care, hotels, and certain retail sectors. Overall, with 100,000 union members in the area, unions represented over 10 percent of the workforce. In terms of union members, the local central labor council was potentially the fifteenth largest in the country. Furthermore, activism among neighborhood organizations, women's groups, environmentalists, and labor during the 1960s and 1970s had overturned the region's Republican "old guard" and elected Democrats to local, state, and federal offices.

These seeds were pulled together by Amy Dean following her election as the nation's youngest head of a central labor council. Dean realized that to advance in one of the strongholds of the "new economy," the Silicon Valley labor movement needed a sophisticated understanding of this economy's operations, broad alliances with other groups, and active campaigns to build worker political and economic power. Since her election in 1994, Dean has built up a committed staff of over two dozen individuals whose ethnic and gender diversity reflect the population of the South Bay area. Today, the central labor council assists affiliated union locals with organizing campaigns and manages labor's increasing role in regional politics.

One of the central new institutions established to support the council's expanding role is an innovative nonprofit organization called Working Partnerships USA (WPUSA). WPUSA provides a mechanism to research the region's economy, build coalitions, develop leadership, and foster economic education. As a nonprofit, the organization is also able to tap foundation grants that support much of its staff and activities. Both the organization and the central labor council aim to establish a broad progressive social movement in the valley whose goals and activities span beyond individual campaigns.[10]

Exposing the Dark Side of Silicon Valley

To formulate effective strategies, social movements need to know what they are up against. WPUSA, in partnership with the Economic Policy Institute, won national media attention in 1998 when it released a report detailing the dark side of Silicon Valley. For years, the media, businesspeople, politicians, and academics had held up the South Bay area as a shining example of the "prosperous" high-tech economy. Indeed, twenty of the world's one hundred largest electronic and software firms are headquartered in Silicon Valley, and the area boasts the largest export market in the nation.

However, as *Growing Together or Drifting Apart?* detailed, huge sections of the population were not enjoying the prosperity. Indeed, many had become its victims. The hourly wages of three-quarters of the valley's workers actually fell between 1989 and 1996. The much-trumpeted jobs for system analysts and electronic engineers were accompanied by mushrooming work as waitpersons, janitors, and cashiers. At the same time, the cost of living had increased dramatically. Researchers found rents for one bed-room apartments averaging $1,100 a month in 1997. The median purchase price of a home had increased nearly 20 percent in one year to $323,000. In short, a full 55 percent of Silicon Valley's jobs did not pay enough to support a family of four independent of public assistance. The sixty-eight-page report also detailed a growing crisis in public services and large-scale environmental damage and pollution.

Two years before *Growing Together or Drifting Apart*? WPUSA issued its first research report, "Shock Absorbers in the Flexible Economy," which exposed the rapid expansion of contingent employment in Silicon Valley. The report detailed the story described in chapter 8: low pay, no health insurance, no pensions, and often unreasonable administrative practices. In 1999, WPUSA released its most extensive report, *Walking the Lifelong Tightrope*, which expanded its analysis of the new economy to the entire state of California. As WPUSA policy director Bob Brownstein summarized:

> Amid the drama of IPOs and technological wizardry in California, the report discerned a work life characterized by extraordinary instability and insecurity. On a daily basis, working families confronted an economy in which median job tenure is three years, temporary employment is one of the fastest-growing industries, older workers are discarded as obsolete, and everything in major firms but the core occupations essential to product development is subject to outsourcing.[11]

Most important, the economic and social analysis done by WPUSA provided a framework for developing a progressive response.

Building Grassroots Leadership

The profile of the regional economy fed directly into WPUSA's pioneering Labor/Community Leadership Institute. Working in affiliation with San Jose State University, the institute designed a training program for union leaders, community activists, concerned clergy, and policy makers to develop, advocate, and implement policies benefiting working families. The eight session program includes such topics as: globalization and the regional economy, the regional political economy, the role of unions, privatization, and the role of government. It draws over one hundred participants a year, who are enrolled by invitation.

The curriculum seeks not simply an intellectual analysis. WPUSA actively recruits current and future labor, community, religious, and elected leaders. Participants not only meet in class, but team up to work on a concrete project (in the initial curriculum outline this project focused on different components for a living wage campaign). By combining analysis with action, the institute produces a pool of local leaders and activists familiar with each other, with each group's particular concerns, and with a common vision of progressive economic change. The curriculum also trains people in the role of local boards, commissions, and elected offices, with an eye toward preparing participants to assume positions of public power. Indeed, several participants have been elected to local office.

The course costs each participant $350 (with scholarships available) and includes continuing education credits. WPUSA actively recruits for each class—looking to bring together a diverse and representative collection of participants. Following feedback from the initial rounds, WPUSA has developed a Senior Fellows program that allows participants to maintain contact with each other and reconvene around campaigns and further education.

Grassroots Action

Together the central labor council and WPUSA have helped launch a series of aggressive grassroots campaigns. In 1995, research by WPUSA analyzed the types of controls used by other communities in their local tax subsidy programs. Using these ideas, the labor council organized a coalition that successfully won county policies requiring that tax rebate recipients provide jobs with health insurance. Employers who fail to generate the promised jobs must refund the subsidies. Over the objections of the Santa Clara County Manufacturing Group, the board of supervisors also adopted guidelines for allocating rebates that include consideration of a company's history of fair labor practices and adequate health and safety policies. Prior to these new policies, tax subsidies had been used by large chain retail stores, of the Super Kmart variety, which hardly deserve public aid. Following the tax rebate battle, the central labor council was able to call on its allies to join in a boycott of a new Super Kmart that had violated its promises to be both neutral in union organizing and to use union workers to build the store. The coalition persuaded the city council to pass a resolution in support of the boycott.

In 1998, the WPUSA and the labor council organized another coalition to campaign successfully for a San Jose living wage law with the then-highest required wage in the country—$9.50 with health insurance or $10.75 without. The law also required all contractors to assure the city basic labor peace by remaining neutral during a union election and bargaining fairly. On Labor Day that year, living wage advocates spoke from the pulpit of eighty churches and synagogues about the moral right of a fair wage. The campaign witnessed the local *San Jose Mercury* lamenting the "increasing influence" of labor on the mayor. The paper urged the city council not to be "stampeded" into a "perilous" act damaging the city's probusiness climate.

Coalition Building

In addition to fostering allies through specific campaigns, WPUSA has worked to build lasting institutions of cooperation. In 1997, WPUSA founded the Interfaith Council on Religion, Race, Economics, and Social Justice. The new network brought together over sixty community groups and congregations to organize around positive social change based on the

moral values of social compassion, economic justice, and personal responsibility. With members seen at the front of marches and rallies supporting fair treatment for janitors, farm workers, and others, the council has helped redefine worker struggles from a "narrow" battle between labor and business to one demanding that corporate and government practices reflect high moral values. The council has helped inspire such successful community campaigns for the inclusion of an additional $25 million in Redevelopment Agency funds for very low income housing, greater access to public benefits for immigrants, San Jose's living wage law, and a current campaign in support of a code of conduct for temporary workers.

Building on its pioneering research, WPUSA today is also facilitating labor-community focus groups to develop a community-centered, progressive policy framework for reforming local economic development. Hundreds of participants have come from minority chambers of commerce, unions, religious organizations, small businesses, neighborhood associations, schools, community-based organizations, environmental groups, health clinics, women's groups, and numerous other projects and causes. The policy proposals that will emerge out of this process focus on areas such as health care, housing, economic development, the environment, transportation, education, and neighborhood revitalization. Some specific ideas include a joint city-county commitment to provide health insurance to all children in San Jose, a light rail line to the city's economically disadvantaged East Side, and the application of inclusionary zoning for affordable housing to some of San Jose's urban reserves.

New Labor Organizations for a New Economy

To pave the high road, the South Bay labor leadership looks toward new models for labor representation. Silicon Valley's high-tech firms offer leading examples of the "virtual corporation." These companies invest less in large-scale plants and facilities and more in networks of suppliers and subcontractors. This produces a workforce that labors in smaller plants and whose jobs are more often contingent, temporary, and part time. The lean corporation also renders many traditional union bargaining goals—such as set work rules and detailed job classifications—less relevant. Protecting worker interests in the new workplace increasingly requires battling for direct worker voice in workplace decisions.

WPUSA has pioneered two innovative programs. It has secured funds for a large-scale, multifaceted temporary workers project. The project offers contingent workers a new form of labor organization, the Working Partnerships Membership Association, that offers low-cost health benefits, training opportunities, and the ability to advocate on their own behalf. Working with area employers, unions, and educators, the project also plans a skills certification program so that contingent workers can receive adequate and ongoing training and have their skills formally recognized and documented. In this way, workers can enjoy active career paths even though they may frequently change employers. Also as part of its temporary worker project, WPUSA has established Working Partnerships Staffing Services in the clerical field. With over four hundred workers enrolling by the end of 1999, the new organization aims to become a model temporary employment agency by providing workers wages above industry standards and operating in a worker-friendly manner. The project has also pulled together an effort to push for a code of conduct for temporary employment agencies similar to those discussed in chapter 8. Since the county has placed a substantial number of welfare-to-work clients in such agencies, the coalition has also pressed the county to specially investigate whether the temp companies are living up to the code. In 1999, the local Labor Day once again witnessed religious leaders speaking out on economic issues— this time the plight of contingent workers.

As its second foray into worker organization, WPUSA helps labor-management committees foster high-performance workplaces by increasing worker skills and participatory decision making. When pursued by management alone, such "employee participation" schemes frequently prove ineffective or, even worse, outright hostile to workers and unions. Yet, workers and unions clearly need proactive strategies to promote models that genuinely empower workers. WPUSA's first customers were local government administrations faced with the threat of privatization. Through effective labor-management cooperation, these offices sought to maintain high-paid union jobs while delivering efficient and quality services superior to those offered by low-road contractors. WPUSA's work reorganization project also looks toward aiding private industry in utilizing training and new technology to support the kinds of skilled, empowered workers key to high-performance workplaces. The organization serves as a contractor to the Northern California Manufacturer Extension Partnership.

Political Action

All of the above activities are linked in one way or another to public policies and political action. In the past few years, the central labor council has been able to reinvigorate its political action program. More funds have been allocated to the council's Political Action Committee. The endorsement process has become more demanding as labor and its allies develop clear standards for public policies. The council's election volunteer operations have become more systematized and attract growing ranks of grassroots activists. During the San Jose living wage campaign, the council mounted an equally elaborate and labor intensive effort to elect the council's political director, Cindy Chavez, to the city council against Tony West, a chamber-of-commerce-type, Harvard-educated federal prosecutor. Despite a last-minute flood of business-driven pro-West mailings, Chavez won the election by two hundred votes following one of the strongest labor-community get-out-the-vote drives in the city's history.

A year later, the central labor council's political

operations were in full swing again. This time it backed Manny Diaz—a city councilman who had strongly supported the living wage—for an open state assembly seat. The challenger was none other than Tony West—this time backed by San Francisco's mayor, the state attorney general, and a number of statewide business interests. Outspent two to one, labor relied on some ten thousand hours of volunteer time to produce a 53 percent victory for Diaz.

The Whole Is Greater Than the Parts

While each individual component of the South Bay Labor Council's activities is impressive, the full strength lies in the greater whole. Taken together, the activities are laying the foundations for a broad social movement for regional economic justice and democracy. The research and advocacy campaigns have uncovered a huge vacuum in public policy that can allow labor and its allies to tap the hopes and frustrations of broad sections of the community.

Local unions have begun to see the spillover benefits. For example, when SEIU Local 1877 entered tough negotiations for a new master contract in early 2000, it did so in a political environment in which the media have had to acknowledge the unacceptable gap between rich and poor. It also had the reassurance that if it had to fight, it would not struggle alone, but could tap into broad networks of clergy, elected officials, community groups, neighborhood leaders, and other unions grown familiar with coalition efforts on behalf of economic justice.

11

Melding Environmental and
Social Justice Activism:
The Emerging Battle Against Sprawl

Don't You See the Waves of Wealth
Washing Away the Soul from the Land
—Capercaille

We have seen how organizing to close the low road and open the high road brings together many strands of social justice activism. Such activism also has the potential to connect social justice concerns to the growing currents of environmental activism. The same low-road practices that destroy workers and communities and that perpetuate discrimination also wreak havoc on the environment. By contrast, a high-road future promotes economic activity that is both socially and environmentally just and sustainable. While the potential is great, the environmental and social justice movements remain generally separated. In this chapter, we focus on this dilemma and the possibilities for using the growing struggle against sprawl as a tool for connecting environmental and social activism.

Perils and the Promise

The history of the social justice movements and environmental activism in the United States includes many examples of groups colliding rather than cooperating. A suddenly discovered concern to "preserve" jobs is a common way corporations try to fend off environmental regulations. No matter that the same corporations typically pursue job-destroy-

ing strategies when they are not fending off environmental regulations.

The timber war of the 1980s and 1990s provides a classic example of the tension that arises when corporations attempt to pit jobs against the environment.[1] According to one estimate by the Wilderness Society, the United States has lost all but 10 percent of its original forests.[2] Much of the remaining old-growth forests are on public lands. The timber controversy in the Pacific Northwest grew out of the unsustainable logging practiced by the major timber corporations. Having overcut their private holdings, the companies then demanded increased access to public old growth forests. Through years of direct action and legal challenges, environmentalists brought the issue before the public and won a temporary injunction against old-growth logging in 1992. During the battle, the endangered northern spotted owl emerged as a benchmark indicator for protecting the broad ecosystem. Legal action succeeded in getting the owl placed on the endangered species list in 1990. The controversy continued, however. President Clinton's 1994 deal to permit regulated old growth harvesting was subject to separate unsuccessful legal challenges by both the Sierra Club and the timber companies.

The timber war saw logging workers, their communities, and their unions pitted against environmental activists. The friction centered on jobs. By the 1980s, company automation strategies and concession demands had already cut many timber jobs. Because the companies could not sustain their volume of logging on their private lands, further job losses were inevitable. Environmental groups estimated 31,600 to 45,900 jobs over twenty years would be lost if the old-growth forests were fully protected; the companies claimed over 100,000. Environmentalists, however, argued that more jobs would be sacrificed through company automation strategies than measures to protect the owl.

The timber war witnessed ugly confrontations between environmentalists and workers. Tree sitters were hurt when their trees were felled. Workers were injured when their saws hit spikes planted by environmental activists. Environmentalist Judi Bari had her pelvis shattered when a bomb exploded in her car. The problems came not simply from the difficult questions of balancing logging jobs and environmental protection. Cultural differences between working-class logging communities and middle-class urban environmentalists fostered a gulf of misinformation and stereotypes. Workers saw environmentalists as misguided fanatics who exaggerated the environmental problems. Environmentalists viewed the unions and workers as shortsighted and narrow-minded. A complex web of confrontation and cooperation with the various timber companies by both groups also served to further complicate dealings between workers and environmentalists.

Over time, workers and environmental activists have managed to build cooperation across the class divide. However, the history of the timber war highlights the importance of proactive efforts to raise broad questions of economic development before company policies pit workers against environmentalists. In the case of the logging controversy, both workers and environmentalists had an ultimate common interest in a timber industry built around sustainable logging practices. Such a long-term goal, however, required substantial public and worker intervention over the strategic planning of large timber corporations for whom a sustainable, long-term industry was not a central concern.

Even without full-blown confrontation, relations between the environmental and social justice communities rarely live up to their full potential. For example, while environmental justice was one of CSM's five original task forces, it proved the weakest and the shortest lived. With toxic waste sites concentrated in poor, minority neighborhoods, CSM was able to organize around issues of environmental racism. For example, it helped convene a town hall meeting at which State Senator Gwendolynne Moore pledged to introduce environmental justice legislation. Activists also helped sponsor an "EnviroFest" to educate residents about the need for cleaning brownfields, asbestos and lead paint removal in public buildings and older homes, and the disposal of hazardous waste. Despite these notable activities, however, the connection between social justice and environmental concerns never developed a sustained momentum. From the viewpoint of the CSM staff—who had to decide how to ration their scarce time—environmental justice did not offer the same level of urgency as the other projects. Living wages, transportation, job access, the CCWC—all of these projects directly addressed the central concern confronting inner-city residents: access to family-supporting jobs. While environmental work had the potential to link to this concern, the possibilities never developed into clear and immediate projects.

In Washtenaw County, Michigan, the lack of deep connection between environmental and social activism led to a major policy defeat. In 1998, the environmental community succeeded in getting on the ballot a county proposal to fund an open space protection program. While focusing on the purchase of development rights from farmers, which we will discuss below, the proposal also included funds for the direct acquisition of land and the redevelopment of abandoned industrial sites in poorer communities. A "Smart Growth" coalition of developers, however, raised money statewide to oppose the measure. Unfortunately, this front group succeeded in winning partial support from some of the building trades unions. While other unions, including the UAW, supported the environmental proposal, the campaign was not one of their top priorities. While a majority of voters in the college-town city of Ann Arbor voted for the proposal, the measure went down to defeat countywide. Noticeably, the measure failed in the older working class and unionized parts of the county that would have benefited the most from the redevelopment funds. Two years later, a religious-labor-community coalition campaigning for living wage laws faced a tough, although ultimately successful, battle in Ann Arbor. Although they received some sympathies from individual activists, the environmental community did not participate in the struggle.

Signs of Hope

Fortunately, the last decade has also witnessed hopeful signs of cooperation between environmental and social-justice groups. Washington State, a focal point for the timber war, has also been home to several noteworthy alliances.

For example, the state organization for the building trades has developed a growing relationship with the state's major environmental lobby group.[3] The momentum for cooperation began at the local level. Following the example of several building trades unions in California, IBEW Local 46 launched a new community outreach effort with a 1987 campaign against a change in Seattle's electrical code to allow polyvinyl chloride (PVC) pipe to be used in encasing wires. For employers, the PVC pipe was less expensive and required less skilled labor. PVC, however, gives off deadly fumes when it burns. While the union lost this particular policy fight, it gained valuable allies among community and environmental organizations not used to a union knocking at their doors. In 1988, the Seattle Building Trades Council founded Rebound—a new organization aimed at enforcing prevailing wage, safety, and other laws as well as eliminating unfair and illegal competition in the construction industry. The organizations brought together unions, community groups, and environmental organizations to campaign against owners and contractors that undercut community economic and environmental standards. None of this cooperation came easily. Different environmental groups were skeptical of working with unions. Some building trades unions refused to join Rebound or work with environmental organizations. Indeed, some of the labor leaders most active in promoting change were not reelected within their own unions.

Nevertheless, the seeds took root. By the early 1990s, the state-level Washington Building Trades overcame a history of conflict to forge an alliance with the Washington Environmental Council (WEC). In 1991, the WEC president testified at the state capital in defense of the state's prevailing wage law that supports union wage standards on publicly funded construction work. That same year, the Building Trades joined with the WEC to fight against a maneuver by the Association of Washington Business to undermine efforts to strengthen the state's Growth Management Act. In a media backlash, several editorials attacked environmentalists for cooperating with the building trades unions. In a joint press conference, the Building Trades and WEC explained their cooperation in terms of a common concern for the overall quality of life—concerns that encompass both safe, family-supporting jobs and sustainable and environmentally sound communities.

Recent years have also seen cooperation among the sides colliding in the timber war. In December 1999, a small flotilla of vessels from the environmental organization Earth First! blocked an Australian cargo ship carrying 650,000 tons of aluminum ore bound for the Kaiser aluminum-smelting plant. A banner forty feet by fifty feet that hung from the pier's conveyer read, "Hurwitz cuts jobs like he cuts trees." Charles Hurwitz was the CEO and principal shareholder of Maxxam Corporation, the owner of both Kaiser Aluminum and the Pacific Lumber Company. The Earth First! action came in support of thirty-one hundred striking members of the United Steelworkers. Maxxam gained control over Kaiser Aluminum, the second most profitable company in the state, through $1 billion in junk bonds. The corporation then proceeded to slash union jobs through a strategy of wholesale outsourcing and overseas production.

Earth First! was well acquainted with Maxxam's slash-and-burn business strategies. In 1985, the company had gained control over Pacific Lumber through a hostile takeover. In addition to raiding the employees' pension fund, Hurwitz liquidated much of the company's vast redwood holdings—thus prompting the massive clear-cutting that sparked the timber wars. The same year that environmentalists showed their support for striking steelworkers, the union organized its members to send over one thousand written comments to the U.S. Fish and Wildlife Service denouncing a deal struck between the Clinton administration and the timber company. In addition to addressing rallies in Oakland and Eureka, the steelworkers also lobbied state and federal authorities. The Clinton deal not only allowed Pacific Lumber greater logging access, but also committed the government to providing $480 million in compensation for portions of the Headwater Forest—money that Maxxam would likely use to outlast striking steelworkers.[4]

The labor-environmental cooperation against Maxxam has produced the Alliance for Sustainable Jobs and the Environment. In 1999, the network established the Houston Principles as a simple statement of common ground between social justice and environmental activism. The principles target corporate power and its threat to democracy as the common uniting threat. By early 2001, over two hundred activists from environmental and labor organizations had signed on to the principles. While most come from the Pacific Northwest, the endorsers also include activists from other parts of the country. On the labor side, the list includes leaders from the United Steelworkers, AFSCME, the Seattle/King County Building Trades Council, the Oregon AFL-CIO, and numerous local unions and central labor councils. On the environmental side, signers included officers and activists from such groups as Friends of the Earth, the Sierra Club, Global Exchange, Clean Water Action, Ozone Action, and various local environmental groups and coalitions.

While the above examples of cooperation reflect specific circumstances, they also point to deeper underlying changes affecting activism in the United States. The period from the end of World War II to the mid-1970s was a distinct period in U.S. history. The prosperity of the postwar boom years delivered material gains to millions of Americans. This seeming "middle class" society shrank the visible constituency for progressive change. At the same time, the boom years supported a system of interest-group liberalism that offered progressive movements distinct avenues for expanding the New Deal's mixture of government regulations and social spending. By working within the Democratic Party and/or protesting outside the electoral process, progressives won substantial, although not unproblematic, reforms. However, interest-group liberalism also encouraged progressive organizations to organize around specific issues and concerns while deemphasizing broad alliances around a more generalized vision of societal transformation.

The postwar economic boom, however, ran out by the mid-1970s, creating a new economic and political landscape. The complacent "middle class" society has been transformed into a more polarized and disillusioned population. For almost three decades, an economic restructuring that spans the globe has driven down the standard of living and quality of life for the majority of Americans. The new political economy has also altered progressive social movement activism. The rising predominance of conservative cost cutting and deregulation politics has steadily weakened interest-group liberalism. No longer can progressive activists simply mount separate single-issue campaigns and hope to win the same levels of reforms that they achieved during the boom years. They cannot defeat the dominant corporate agenda piecemeal. The growth of coalition efforts reflects the reality that more and more activists are concluding that they need allies and a more unified and comprehensive reply.

This general dynamic has particulars within specific social movements. For example, faced with declining union density, the American labor movement is gradually becoming more open to forging community alliances. Unions have never been entirely unconcerned with environmental issues. The UAW, for example, helped sponsor the first Earth Day. Issues of health and safety provide a wealth of opportunities to bring together workers and community activists around company policies that threaten both. However, the postwar peace settlement between organized labor and management encouraged unions to steer their energy toward workplace-centered collective bargaining. As we saw in the last chapter, today's corporate strategies are forcing unions to break out of this box to take up broad questions of economic development and corporate decision making. As labor begins to tackle broader economic issues, the opportunities for coalition building increase.

At the same time, the environmental movement has also traveled a path toward wider economic questions. Traditional environmental activism, dating back well into the nineteenth century, focused primarily on natural resource conservation and wilderness and wildlife preservation. The environmental activism of the 1960s and 1970s added concerns over pollution and general environmental degradation. For the mainstream of the movement, however, such new issues could be treated as specific environmental concerns. Yet, in the past twenty years, the movement has experienced a growing awareness that links environmental to social concerns. For example, explanations that blame environmental problems on population growth, while still used by some activists and intellectuals, have given way to more sophisticated approaches that highlight the vast differences in consumption between the industrialized and developing world. The worsening and deepening of the environmental crisis have also highlighted the need for broader economic changes. As a result, many environmentalists share a growing awareness that ecological issues can be fully tackled only by addressing the social issues with which they are enmeshed. In other words, society can fully address its exploitation of the environment only when it addresses the exploitation of people.

A major force helping to expand the horizons of mainstream environmentalism has been the environmental justice movement that emerged in the 1980s and 1990s. The mainstream movement had long assumed that communities of color had little interest in environmental issues. However, racism has helped ensure that the worst elements of capitalism's environmental destruction are often inflicted on people of color. For example, according to a 1987 study commissioned by the United Church of Christ Commission for Racial Justice, race proved to be the most significant variable associated with the location of commercial hazardous waste facilities. Communities with such facilities averaged twice the minority population of communities without them.[5]

The environmental justice movement emerged out of grassroots battles over industrial dumping, toxic landfills, waste incinerators, and other aspects of environmental racism. This activism stood out for its ability to link environmental concerns with social issues. Indeed, for communities of color, racism, social exploitation, and corporate power were the underlying problems regardless of whether they took an environmental or economic guise. As this growing environmental justice focus has gained strength, it has helped broaden the concerns of the environmental movement as a whole.

As activists from different progressive movements broaden their issues and seek more comprehensive solutions, their ability to find common ground increases. Thus, for example, the battle against free trade has brought together a wide range of social justice and environmental groups and activists as the same corporate forces undermine both living standards and environmental health. The broad coalitions that formed around NAFTA, the WTO, and the World Bank and IMF protests are relatively well known. We will touch on the organizing process behind them in the next chapter. Below, however, we detail another emerging activist axis that has the potential to unite a diverse array of groups around a fundamental issue of economic development: the war against sprawl.

The Growing War Against Sprawl

Sprawl can be defined as unplanned development driven by the individual needs of developers and corporations. Its hallmarks include low-density and single-use projects, a lack of transportation options, the separation of residential and nonresidential property, and a general lack of an integrating vision of community. Since the impact of sprawl includes wide-ranging social as well as environmental damage, a grassroots response to it can potentially unite a diverse range of progressive activism.

Sprawl As an Environmental Problem

Several major environmental groups, including the Sierra Club and the National Resources Defense Council, have taken up the banner of the battle against sprawl. In many states today, uncontrolled suburban development and farmland and open space destruction represent the top sources of environmental damage. As a new residential development or shopping mall paves over a former farm or woods, the signs of environmental damage are readily available to the naked eye. Years of research have confirmed that the visible destruction contributes to an underlying ecological disaster.

Airborne pollution is one example. On the positive side, public regulations have helped the nation implement significant reductions in such pollution as airborne lead, carbon monoxide, and ground-level ozone (urban smog). Unfortunately, this record is counterbalanced by increased pollution directly linked to suburban development. The United States, with under 5 percent of the world's population, accounts for over one-third all greenhouse-gas carbon dioxide emissions. The Department of Energy projects that overall U.S. carbon output will increase 1 percent a year—with transportation sources growing at a faster rate. In 1996, highway vehicles accounted for 29 percent of the nation's volatile organic compound emissions, 31 percent of the nitrogen oxide, 62 percent of the carbon monoxide, and 50 percent of the carcinogenic and toxic air pollutants such as benzene and formaldehyde. A 1998 EPA study estimated that traffic-related particulate pollution costs the nation $20 billion to $64 billion annually from the adverse health impact. Reflecting the poor quality of our nation's air, roughly one out of six emergency room visits is for asthma. All of this growth in pollution comes from the increased vehicle use generated by sprawl. While government regulations forced manufacturers to clean up auto emissions, most gains have been wiped out as people are compelled to drive increasingly more among living and work arrangements ever more spread out.[6]

With transportation consuming two-thirds of our nation's overall oil consumption, sprawl-induced traffic is also a major force behind our country's spectacular consumption of oil. The average U.S. citizen uses five times as much energy for transportation as the average Japanese, and three times that of the average European. Today, Americans consume one-third of all the world's transportation energy—with estimates predicting a steady increase in U.S. consumption over the next several decades.

News stories of record floods rarely highlight a common culprit: unplanned suburban development. As developers convert water-absorbing farmland and natural areas into side streets and large parking lots, rainwater has nowhere to go except to flood streams and rivers. This water carries with it all the street and lawn pollution typical of suburban lifestyles. The EPA has identified urban runoff ("non-point source" pollution) as the number one obstacle to cleaning up our nation's water. Having already lost half of the nation's original wetlands by the 1980s, we are in danger of losing more. Wetland destruction further strips nature of one of its primary flood control, water purification, and species-breeding mechanisms.

We are also in danger of losing a high portion of

our country's agricultural land as the most desirable locations for suburban development also have the best soils and climates. Over forty-five acres of prime farmland is lost every hour to suburban development. A study by the Farmland Trust found that within 127 highly productive farming regions across the United States, urban development had already consumed 32 percent of the region's prime and specialized farmland by 1997. The majority of our nation's fruit, vegetables, and dairy products come from counties with farmland directly threatened by development. Along with farmland goes habitats for a vast array of wildlife. By 1997, the U.S. Fish and Wildlife Service reported that 1,082 plant and animal species were listed as threatened or endangered—with another 119 likely to be added.[7]

Sprawl As a Quality-of-Life Problem

The environmental impact of sprawl is significant not simply due to the scale of the destruction. It also fundamentally redefines the nature of environmental issues. Often people think of environmental concerns as "out there"—the protection of a distant species or rainforest, or the pollution controls over the unseen plant miles down the road. However, sprawl literally brings the issues home—as the problems stem directly from people's daily way of life. Indeed, the broad coalition potential found in the battle against sprawl comes from the fact that as much as sprawl destroys the environment, it also undermines people's basic quality of life.

Stress is a rampant problem in our society. As roads become ever-more congested and people spend more time in their cars, studies have documented an increase in people's sense of stress. Americans now spend roughly one out of eight waking hours in their cars. Wasteful forced driving, therefore, has proven a major source of the often-heard complaint that people do not have enough time. The burden falls particularly hard on working parents who have to combine ever longer work commutes with efforts to shuttle children unable to walk or bike to school,

recreation, or any other meaningful location spread out in America's latest suburban communities.[8]

While the automobile once promised liberation from drab urban surroundings, Americans increasingly spend their time driving with little meaningful place to go. Today's developments offer a drab uniformity in which new housing in New England is scarcely different from suburban homes creeping into the Rockies. As national chains expand, new commercial strips and malls offer the exact same stores in the exact same format throughout the country. Yet, research suggests that people prefer older towns and genuinely rural areas. In a New Jersey survey, for example, 78 percent of respondents supported changes in development patterns in order to preserve farmland. Three-quarters said that they want to see development occur within existing cities and older suburbs, not on land currently in open space or rural areas.[9] In another study, citizens shown slide images gave the lowest ratings to new "cookie cutter" subdivisions, highway strip development, and shopping plazas with large parking lots. They responded favorably to pedestrian-oriented downtown areas and village-style housing on narrow lots with modest street setbacks.[10]

In poll after poll, Americans say that they want a sense of belonging, of community, and of place. Yet, today's sprawl development offers the opposite—isolation. Unable to provide the foundations of friendly neighborhoods, developers try to sell the "luxury" of larger lots and ever more distance from each neighbor. Unable to build housing with high-quality craftsmanship in pleasing community landscapes, developers instead simply "supersize" houses. One hundred years ago, luxury living meant expensive woodwork, creative designs, ample windows, and attractive entranceways. Today's high-cost "luxury" developments simply offer large lots and larger floor space in homes that are often rapidly constructed with no shortage of softwood and cheap plastic materials. Writer James Howard Kunstler apply entitled his 1993 critique of American landuse patterns the *Geography of Nowhere*.

Sprawl As a Public Fiscal Problem

Antisprawl efforts can also tap into people's tax frustrations since unplanned development is a major source of fiscal irresponsibility. Across the country, areas experiencing mushrooming development display common public problems: overcrowded schools, never-ending road construction, increasing utility rates, declining services, and increased taxes. The inefficiencies of suburban "convenience" are remarkable. Between 1980 and 1990, in Montgomery County, Maryland, taxpayers had to pay for seventy new schools even though overall enrollment had dropped by ten thousand pupils and school districts had closed sixty-eight schools over the same period! Across the country, governments continue to place far more money into new roads and infrastructure construction than in maintaining past investments. Yet, maintaining the existing infrastructure can be as or more expensive than adding new. The result: each year, our overall infrastructure and road network fall into further and further decay, while government policies expand the future costs.

In a study of forty communities in the Northeast and Midwest, the American Farmland Trust found that for every dollar in revenue generated by residential development, the public had to bear $1.11 in costs. By contrast, farmland, forests, and open space used only $.31 for every dollar they generated. The reason for the contrast is straightforward. As development spreads out, the costs for providing roads, sewers, police, schools, and other services increase far faster than the revenues. Rebuilding existing urban areas, by contrast, is a fiscal benefit. According to two University of Chicago researchers, each new middle-income household that moves to the outer suburbs costs taxpayers $900 to $1,500 per year, while a move to the inner city actually contributes a net $600 to $800.[11]

Sprawl As a Social Issue

Although many social justice activists and organizations are only just beginning to make the connections, sprawl affects the core issues of several key American social justice movements. The labor movement's future, for example, is an urban future. While older urban areas are known for a relative wealth in community institutions, suburban development patterns are ever-more inhospitable to these same institutions. Unions are one of these community institutions. The distribution of union density is generally higher in older cities and towns and lowest in the newest suburbs. Research pulled together by Good Jobs First for Chicago found that most union members worked in older urban areas. For manufacturing, union density in older Cook County, which includes Chicago, ran at 12 percent, while in the two sprawling northern counties, only 2 to 4 percent of manufacturing jobs were unionized. In the hospitality industry, of the area's forty-four unionized hotels, forty-one were in Cook County.[12] Indeed, while overseas investment is the most publicized corporate strategy of union avoidance, relocating facilities from urban areas to new suburbs and greenfield sites is actually the more common daily threat for unions facing plant closures, downsizing, and outsourcing.[13]

Sprawl affects unions also in less obvious ways. The high-road development strategies that unions are beginning to push today work best in an environment rich in the types of business clusters, efficient transportation and infrastructure, and community institutions provided by towns and cities. Sprawl undermines all of these elements—making go-it-alone low-road strategies all the more attractive. The increased fiscal strains caused by sprawl put enormous pressure on local governments to cut costs. This can mean difficult public sector contract bargaining and privatization to lower-paying, nonunion contractors. Ever-diminishing air quality can also cause problems for unions. The Chicago area, for example, is ranked by the EPA as one of the ten worst air quality sites in the nation. Over half of the problem emissions comes from traffic—a share that is increasing. The EPA designation, however, doesn't reduce traffic so much as drive up costs for factories and other industrial air-pollution sources. While these "single point" sources account for only a quarter of problem emissions, the companies either have to buy extra pollution credits to offset the increase in traffic emissions or they end up relocating or expanding elsewhere.[14]

Battling sprawl has also become key to fighting poverty and racism. When the suburbs were first built, the construction of the highway system that connected them to city jobs downtown often bulldozed through inner-city and predominantly African-American and Hispanic communities. In Detroit, Atlanta, Los Angeles, Nashville, the South Bronx, Durham, and many other large and medium cities, freeways destroyed the hearts of black communities—often by deliberate design. Suburban development extracted jobs, infrastructure resources, and the better-off portion of the white population from the cities, killing many downtowns and leaving many neighborhoods focal points of urban blight. In metropolitan areas such as Chicago, Cleveland, Detroit, Greensboro, and Louisville, the suburbs have accounted for 100 percent of recent metropolitan job growth. Yet, as the nation continues to underfund public transportation and the dollars that do exist go disproportionately into suburban communities, city residents are left with few options to reach suburban jobs. In short, racism cannot be solved without redirecting resources back into older urban communities and by designing land-use policies that combine social equity with environmental and social sustainability.

For both labor and many communities of color, continued sprawl means increasing political power for forces hostile to both groups. Across the country, older urban areas tend to be more Democratic, while newer suburbs are more Republican. In Chicago, for example, maps illustrating the record of state and federal elected officials in casting votes in the direction advocated by labor revealed a quite high proworker vote in Chicago and surrounding older urban areas, with this record declining to zero as the legislative districts move farther into latest sprawl.

For decades, the social justice issues related to urban decay often divided inner cities from their surrounding suburbs. Indeed, the suburbs of the 1950s through 1970s were the resource beneficiaries of disinvestment from cities. Today, however, these now inner-ring suburbs are experiencing similar sprawl-related disinvestment and decay. The potential common bond between city and its inner-ring has increased. As these older suburbs fail to provide a "promised land," developers and public policy offer only the same old solution: move even farther away from the city. Yet, while newer and cleaner, the new "exurbs" are even more alienating and stressful than the suburban experience that inspired the youth revolt of the sixties.

Why Now: How the Latest Sprawl Is Distinct

Sprawl is not a new phenomenon but dates back to development policies begun in the 1920s and that took off following World War II. However, today's sprawl is of a scale and reach that its coalition and movement building potential is far greater than the battles against earlier suburban expansion.

A few statistics highlight the acceleration in the problems caused by our nation's poor land-use policies. According to the Department of Agriculture's 1992 National Resources Inventory, nearly one-sixth of all the land developed over the course of the nation's history was claimed for development between 1982 and 1992. The Maryland Office of Planning projected that between 1995 and 2020, more land will be converted to housing in the region than in the past three and a half centuries. Metropolitan Detroit is currently developing land at a rate thirteen times the pace of population growth. Planners in Cleveland project that between 1995 and 2010, the area's population will decrease by 3 percent, while the development of residential land will grow by 30 percent. Atlanta's north-south reach went from 65 miles in 1990 to 110 miles only eight years later. Los Angeles tripled its geographical reach in the past two decades, while its population grew by only half.

These statistics point to a vast expansion in the dispersion and wastefulness of both residential and business development. The traditional suburban developments of the 1950s through 1970s at least aimed for some resemblance of community as individual developments straddled commercial strips. Today, however, the exurbs intersperse former farmland with oversized houses built on one- to five-acre lots isolated from commercial or community institutions. In many parts of the country, one acre or larger housing lots are the fastest-growing form of development. Business land use is also increasingly spread out. The so-called edge cities now hold two-thirds of all the nation's office space. The steady takeover of retail by large "big box" stores has similarly increased our nation's ratio of retail and parking lot space per person.[15]

All of this unplanned, dispersed development has increased car-related stress. Traffic doubled between 1970 and 1990, with current growth projections of 2.2 to 2.7 percent a year. The average American driver spends 443 hours per year—the equivalent of 55 eight-hour working days—behind the wheel. A typical family household living in the new suburbs owns 2.3 cars, takes 12 automobile trips a day, and drives 31,300 miles a year. During peak-hour travel times, 70 percent of the nation's urban interstate highways operate at more than 80 percent capacity. The average vehicle speed using Washington's Beltway declined from 47 mph in 1980 to 23 mph by 1990.[16]

In short, an increasing portion of our population is being drawn into living patterns that promise spacious luxury living and convenience while actually delivering excessive travel, congestion, increasing expenses, and an overall decline in the quality of life. Meanwhile, as the older suburbs run down, people lose what attracted them to these communities in the first place—instead, they are left with all of the sprawl-related problems.

Behind the mounting sprawl crisis lies a ticking time bomb within our nation's domestic food system. Dispersed development is possible because ag-

riculture no longer provides a living for many of our nation's farmers. Today, when adjusted for inflation, many crop prices are below the levels that prompted farmer protests in the late 1970s and early 1980s. Squeezed by corporate agribusiness and distribution channels, many farmers can work the entire growing season and make little or no actual money. To make any kind of living off the land, farmers must often operate with several thousand acres. Such large-scale farming makes chemical-intensive farming a necessity. As a nation, we are dependent on the ability of an ever-shrinking number of farms to force ever-larger yields from less and less land. As the better part of a generation of farmers now approach retirement as the last in their line to farm, the basic security of the nation's domestic food supply rests on shaky grounds.

Alternatives to Sprawl

Even a short trip to Europe makes clear that our nation's land-use experience is completely unnecessary. Throughout Europe, tightly packed cities and towns abruptly give way to open countryside. Generally speaking, the only housing and businesses operating in the European countryside are related to farming. So many parts of Europe are picturesque not because of something unique to the European physical landscape, but because development policies have maintained local building styles and a strong separation between town and country. By contrast, many Americans view attractive surroundings as something they vacation to, not have a right to live in. The average American has become conditioned to accepting a level of physical ugliness in their surroundings that few Europeans would tolerate. Metropolitan areas in Europe average three to four times the density of American cities. Even their outer suburbs have four times the density of those in America. The quality of life that so many Americans say they want—living and working in the same town, opportunities to walk to shopping and entertainment, ready access to parks and other public institutions—still forms the basis of many European land-use policies. While overdependence on car use and more spread out, less integrated development is an issue throughout Europe, the debates are on a level quite different from here. For example, European communities debate whether any American-style strip shopping should be allowed at the edge of town, not if and how the latest big-box stores should be regulated.

While sharing many of the same economic and social forces of the United States, Canada has also done a better job of controlling growth, preserving countryside, and maintaining intact downtowns and inner cities. Public transit in Canada claims 15 percent of all trips—compared to 3.6 percent in the United States. Toronto is 2.82 times as dense as the average American city. Residents of ten large U.S. metropolitan areas drive over twice the amount as do Canadians living in Toronto.[17]

Americans, however, do not have to venture beyond their borders to find alternatives. Since the 1970s, the population of the greater Portland, Oregon, area has grown by 50 percent to over one million. Yet, the area increased its land use by only 2 percent.[18] Today, Portland enjoys a thriving downtown, an excellent public transportation system, and a high quality of life. The area topped the real estate industry's 1997 list of smaller-market regions most attractive to investors.

Portland's relative success in managing sprawl comes from two forces.[19] First, the state of Oregon has aggressively sought to protect farmland and open space from runaway and unplanned development. In 1973, the state legislature passed Senate Bill 100, which changed the course of land use in the state. The new law required every local government to prepare a comprehensive land-use plan that had to be approved by the State Land Conservation and Development Commission (LCDC). In turn, local governments had to make land-use decisions consistent with their plan. The law empowered county governments to reconcile local plans. Most important, the law required each metropolitan area to establish ur-

ban growth boundaries to encircle a supply of land sufficient for twenty years of growth. Beyond the boundaries, the vast majority of land had to be zoned for "exclusive use" farming or forestry. Local governments had to demonstrate how their plans adequately met anticipated growth.

By itself, however, the institution of growth boundaries did not guarantee strong controls over sprawl. Indeed, unlike Portland, other Oregon metropolitan areas developed generous growth boundary areas that accommodated conventional suburban development. In Portland, however, the state's land-use actions coincided with the foundation and subsequent development of a regional governance structure, known as Metro. Because the Portland metropolitan area spans three counties, regional authorities were given control over the process of setting the growth boundary. The new regional authority also benefited from other state actions that placed authority and resources in its hands—giving local governments incentives to cooperate in a regional process. Furthermore, the city of Portland had the distinct advantage of not having a significantly sized suburban municipality or coordinating suburban body capable of competing for regional policy leadership. As a result, regional land-use and transportation policies have reflected priorities aimed at maintaining a vibrant inner city.

Initially developers and business leaders claimed that the Portland growth boundary and other policies would stifle growth. In practice, however, the policies have encouraged investment. Indeed, while restricting developers to where they can build, the regional policies have actually streamlined the approval process for development in designated areas. The area has become home to a significant electronic industry and several Fortune 500 headquarters.

Over the course of two and a half decades, Portland's regional policies have encouraged a distinct pattern of development. For example, in the 1970s, Portland's mayor embarked on a set of policies aimed at combining downtown redevelopment with livable neighborhoods. Mayor Goldsmith and the city council encouraged the growth of neighborhood associations, limited downtown parking spaces to encourage other methods of transit, developed a bus-only transit mall, and defended city neighborhoods from freeway construction. Beginning in 1975, the regional authority and the city of Portland launched an effort that successfully lobbied the state to substitute a light rail system in place of funding for a proposed freeway. Opened in 1986, the TriMet transit system saw an increase in the portion of the population that used transit at least twice a month from 17 to 31 percent. Voters approved a recent referendum to temporarily increase taxes to pay for additional spurs.

In the 1980s, regionwide coordination of housing development received a significant boost from the state LCDC when it issued the Metropolitan Housing Rule for the Portland area. Drawing on attempted regional plans, the new regulations required a mix of at least 50 percent multifamily or attached single-family housing within the region. It also required a minimum number of dwelling units per buildable acre—with ten units per acre for the largest municipalities and unincorporated areas. The measure aimed to encourage density and to insure that new development included significant affordable housing. As a result, each community within the area has had to accept its share of responsibility for providing affordable housing—including the more affluent suburbs. As of 1991, the zoning of all vacant land within the growth boundary allowed for 54 percent multifamily units. A study released jointly by the state's homebuilders and a principal land-use environmental group found that housing was two to three times more affordable in Portland than such comparable areas as San Diego, Sacramento, and Seattle.[20]

The present urban growth boundary encompasses 334 square miles. Environmental organizations opposed this limit as encompassing more than twenty years of growth. However, since the boundary's adoption, not one residential or commercial development has been allowed outside the boundary lines,

and local authorities have also resisted efforts to significantly expand the boundaries. Regional policies push communities to plan for housing and employment opportunities at equal levels. As a result, the area does not have the vast differences in employment locations and living units that force people into long commutes. Accessibility to downtown Portland has been increased without resort to the cars, freeways, and parking lots that destroy much of the historic character of American downtowns. Between 1960 and 1980, the central business district actually increased its share of metropolitan employment while its office space has tripled. While density in other urban areas has declined, in the greater Portland area it increased by nearly 10 percent between 1960 and 1990.[21]

The future poses challenges, however. While regional land-use policies promoted a balanced mixture of jobs, high-density apartments, and single-family homes, many of the traditional market-driven suburban patterns remain. While residents have short commutes to work and shopping, development patterns still have them using cars. The tight, fine-grained mixture of development required to support walking, biking, and public transit remains to be developed. However, in the 1990s, the regional transit authority ventured into the more recent suburbs by planning a west-side light rail line. The authority routed the new line along undeveloped lands within the growth boundary, hoping to encourage new, less car-oriented development. Indeed, suburban communities have zoned land along the route for a minimum of fifteen residential units per acre or thirty jobs per commercial acre.

Regional transportation policies have had notable success. Bus, rail, biking, and walking account for 40 percent of commutes to Portland's central business district. For the entire metro area, public transit accounts for 9.2 percent of work trips. On weekdays, roughly 200,000 people ride the TriMet rail system. Yet, plans to expand the system need to capture far more passengers. The car society's pressures are strong. Every day, the area's population engages in an estimated four million auto trips. In 1991, the state LCDC issued new regulations requiring that the metro area meet a 20 percent reduction in per capita vehicle miles traveled over the next thirty years.

While building a more inclusive housing market, regional planning also needs to make further inroads against the area's inequality. The small population of African Americans is extraordinarily segregated in Portland. Regional disparities in income and job growth, while not as bad as many American metro areas, are still noticeable issues.[22]

Despite the challenges, Portland's experience is notable for its success in bringing development issues into the public debate and resolving them at a regional level. The policies have withstood strong opposition and referendum attempts only because citizen groups have mobilized to defend them. In 1992, voters passed a referendum enhancing the powers of the regional Metro authority—providing it with permanent status and a tax levy of $12.5 million a year. The Metro council has launched an ongoing process that looks to where the area wants to be by 2040. In 1994, a diverse coalition of thirty-four environmental and social justice groups formed the Coalition for a Livable Future. The group aims include strengthening Oregon's land-use law, moving toward regional equity through revenue sharing, and fair housing.

Overall, according to the Sierra Club, Oregon has been able to preserve twenty-five million acres of farmlands and forests. Where the state once lost thirty thousand acres of agricultural land each year, today it loses only two thousand.[23] In the words of Don McClave, head of the Portland Chamber of Commerce, "far from being a detriment to economic growth, [the growth boundary] has turned out to be perhaps our strongest tool in the diversification and revitalization of Oregon's economy."

Policies to Fight Sprawl

The Portland experience points to many of the policy ingredients used today in the battle against sprawl.

What makes Portland distinct is its combination through regionwide planning that integrates land-use, transportation, and economic development policies. Unfortunately, the municipal fragmentation typical of suburbia makes such coordination difficult. Despite these limitations, however, a wide range of policy options exists to provide organizing tools for grassroots activism. And activists should keep in mind that controlling sprawl enjoys massive popular support. In one poll, for example, 78 percent thought their state should do more to manage and plan for new growth; 75 percent wanted to see more coordination among towns to plan for growth; 81 percent supported public low-interest loans and tax credits to revitalize older cities, towns, and suburbs; 66 percent agreed that new housing developments should be required to include housing for moderate and low-income families; and 83 percent supported zones off-limits to developers reserved for green space, farming, and forests.[24]

Growth Boundaries

Oregon and Portland are not the only governments to adopt growth boundaries. Recently, the city of San Jose, for example, adopted a growth boundary beyond which development cannot occur. Baltimore County, Maryland, has maintained a good portion of its rural feel, despite its closeness to a major city, by not providing increases in county services beyond clear growth areas. "The greatest conflict with an agricultural area is a house," explained the county's planning director Pat Keller. "So if you live in a rural area, we're not going to fix the roads, we're not going to fix the bridges, the police response time will be 20 minutes, not two. The fire department will be volunteer, and your house may well burn down. Take any service county government provides, and the way the county provides the services will be very different in an urban area versus a rural area."[25]

Maryland's governor Parris Glendening has taken a leading role in the battle against sprawl by his successful efforts to enact a package of legislation known as the Neighborhood Conservation and Smart Growth Initiative. In 1994, Glendening ran on a platform to steer development back into existing urban areas. At the centerpiece of the program is a 1997 law that prohibits state funds from going to any growth-related project outside "priority funding areas." These zones must exhibit a minimum density of at least 3.5 dwellings per acre and be within a ten-year water and sewer plan. Existing municipalities automatically qualify, including all areas within the Baltimore and Washington beltways and designated "rural villages." Each county is permitted to designate priority-funding areas, with the goal being to support and revitalize existing urban areas.

Essentially, the Smart Growth Initiative means that all state road, sewer, school, housing, and economic development funds will be evaluated based on whether they contribute to the revitalization of existing communities or foster further sprawl. Already, by executive order, the governor shifted state educational spending so that 80 percent goes to rebuild existing schools, with only 20 percent going to new school construction. The initiative also gives the state a role in local development and land-use policies— helping to foster regional planning rather than the fragmented localism that contributes to sprawl. In addition to the priority funding areas, a Rural Legacy Program allows counties to apply for state funds to purchase agricultural and undeveloped lands. A Job Creation Tax Credit provides an income tax benefit to employers who create at least twenty-five full-time jobs within priority funding areas. The Live Near Your Work project provides home-buying assistance to purchasers in targeted areas where participating employers provide matching resources. A brownfields program limits liability for those developing abandoned or underutilized industrial sites unless they increase contamination or create new pollution.

Environmentalists and antisprawl activists would like to see Maryland's initiative go further. The 3.5 dwelling minimum density is still low. A compromise on the legislation also allowed county governments openings to draw expansive priority funding areas beyond the spirit of the legislation. Some, for example, tried to stretch the designation to cover most of the developable land in their county. Others attempted to include proposed developments in the label "existing urban areas." Furthermore, local governments can still use local money to fund infrastructure improvements. Nevertheless, as in Portland, Maryland's new laws take development decisions out of the closet and make land-use planning a topic of public debate.

Zoning

While new laws are welcome, especially those that foster regional planning, local governments already possess strong land-use powers that typically are not properly used to preserve the existing community. In a nation whose official culture so idolizes the "free market," local zoning powers allow governments to tell private landholders what they can and cannot do with land. Unfortunately, current zoning practices actually encourage sprawl. First developed early in the twentieth century, zoning patterns aimed to keep polluting factories out of urban neighborhoods. However, over time, zoning practices also separated out apartments, shopping, and housing. As a result, most communities are legally divided into separate "monoculture" areas, with single-family homes of certain price ranges exclusive to certain areas, shopping segregated in other areas, and work opportunities nowhere near anything else. The end results are insulated, homogenized neighborhoods cut off from all other aspects of life. Indeed, the densely developed, integrated, mixed-use communities that were the norm until the 1940s are actually illegal to build in most parts of the country.[26] Yet as rising housing prices in many older urban areas suggest, this is exactly the lifestyle many Americans want.

Generally speaking, local planning boards have the power to change these patterns. Most, however, do not challenge the status quo. They either do not have the knowledge to use their powers in innovative ways, or they buy into the development industry's propaganda, or they simply become intimidated by developers who aggressively use legal action to punish boards that do not give in to unplanned development. They also listen far too much to traffic engineers and thus end up designing developments for automobiles rather than people. In other words, local land-use plans provide ample opportunity for grassroots activists to intervene in a process much in need of improvement.

Local land-use planning consists of two components. A comprehensive master plan should provide a vision for the community's future. Such plans provide legal support for the specific zoning regulations that apply to individual land parcels. Often, however, communities either don't have a comprehensive plan or the plan is not well designed. Master plans should aim to infill existing urban areas and preserve open space, farmland, and natural areas. Depending on state law, planning boards that have a solid master plan can often enact strict zoning regulations to protect the community's vision. Zoning measures, for example, can designate overall land use. While traditional zoning separates commercial and residential uses, mixed-use zoning systems can foster neighborhood commercial zones that encourage walking. Local zoning can also challenge the myopic wisdom of traffic engineers to narrow streets, place buildings nearer curb sides and mandate alleys, and prioritize pedestrian-friendly designs.[27] Local zoning can regulate building size, encourage multistory rather than sprawling one-story buildings, limit parking lots, and require detailed architectural review and impact analysis that place the fiscal, community, and environmental effects into public debate. Local laws can also require that any major changes to local zoning and land-use plans be subject to a popular vote.

State laws can help or hinder effective local land-use planning. When state law, for example, defines "agricultural" zoning in terms of five-or ten-acre minimum lot size, it simply encourages expensive "McMansion"-style housing that replaces rural areas with noncommunities of five-acre suburban mini-fiefdoms. When states tax farmland at its potential development value, rather than its farming value, they similarly undermine the fiscal viability of family farms located near sprawl.

By contract, state laws that require local communities to enact comprehensive land-use plans foster public debate and can require local plans to conform to state regional guidelines. Since 1970, Vermont's land-use regulation, Act 250, has helped empower local communities to decide their own destiny. The law has successfully withstood legal and constitutional challenges from developers. The act provided local authorities ten criteria for judging developments. For example, authorities can reject a subdivision or development if it will "have an undue adverse effect on the scenic or natural beauty of the area, aesthetics, historic sites or rare or irreplaceable natural areas."[28] The state's Environmental Board has included settled areas and farmland under the rubric of "scenic or natural beauty." It has also defined aesthetics to include visual harmony and "peace and quiet." Act 250 also mandated a regional impact analysis. Projects can be rejected that would place an unreasonable burden on the ability of local governments to provide municipal services. This applies not just to the community where the development is located, but also the fiscal impact on surrounding communities. Thus, authorities can reject sprawl development in one community that would cause deterioration and blight in an older urban area.

Tax and Spending

In chapter 9, we examined how local and state corporate welfare-type development policies can encourage sprawl. Both historic and current patterns of sprawl were fueled by such government spending as subsidized home loans, infrastructure investments, and road building. As much as business complains about how antisprawl policies interfere with "the market," in reality, sprawl happens as a partnership between business and the taxpayer. In the name of reducing congestion, new and wider roads simply replicate the problem by providing avenues for further sprawl. Yet, citizens can pressure state and local governments to redirect the public purse. Public funds can be used to preserve natural areas and redevelop older urban locations. The general public, for example, has been repeatedly willing to spend tax dollars to preserve undeveloped land. Maryland has allocated $140 million to protect open space. In 1998, Arizona voters approved $200 million for the same purpose, while New Jersey voters approved more than $1 billion over ten years. Communities or local land trusts can also directly acquire the development rights to lands, but not the land itself, either by conservation easement donations or by purchasing the development rights from the owners. Indeed, the purchase of development rights can allow farmers to get some of the dollar value out their land, while also preserving the land for farm use. Notwithstanding a population of 800,000 and a border with the nation's capital, Montgomery County, Maryland, for example, has legally protected over ninety-five thousand acres of farmland through such measures. Altogether the county aims to protect about one-third of its 317,000-acre base of agricultural land.[29] Lancaster County, Pennsylvania, has similarly used an aggressive purchase of development rights programs to protect its famous Amish countryside from rapacious development.

Alternative Housing

The planning and architectural community has a wealth of innovative ideas for better ways to build communities. Within development circles, the so-called "New Urbanism" concept aims to return to traditional integrated communities based on strong neighborhoods and walkability. The nation once built tight new towns and villages. It can again.

Indeed, authors Andres Duany, Elizabeth Plater-Zyberk, and Jeff Speck lay out in detail the basics of neighborhood-building in *Suburban Nation*. Their book draws on their direct experience in helping create over two hundred "new urbanist-style, developments," and urban revitalization plans.[30]

Furthermore, a promising cohousing movement has leapt across the Atlantic, to American soil. Cohousing developments are designed, usually with the input of future residents, to combine modest private living units with ample opportunities for community. Generous common space and footpaths foster human contact, while individual living units and small private backyards provide personal space. Collectively owned and operated buildings offer facilities for community meals and social gathering. Cohousing allows residents to share tools and machinery. Parents also enjoy access to a network of neighborhoods known to their children—allowing kids to roam and parents to work out cooperative child care arrangements. Cars and space for parking are typically relegated to the margins of the development—rather than the defining centerpiece of more typical construction. Today, cohousing is a growing movement with examples of cohousing neighborhoods in almost every state.

Urban Revitalization

Controlling sprawl ultimately means rebuilding existing urban areas. As the gentrification of former decayed neighborhoods in such diverse cities as Chicago, San Francisco, and Philadelphia demonstrate, many people are looking to live in revitalized urban areas. The challenge is to use public authority and resources to ensure urban renewal that is available to everyone, rather than "urban removal" by which lower-income people are displaced by the wealthy. All of the ideas discussed in this book would either directly or indirectly contribute to a genuine grassroots urban revitalization.

Connecting Social and Environmental Action Through Sprawl

Using the above tools, grassroots activists across the country have begun to organize against sprawl. These battles are often local and not publicized beyond their immediate area. Typically, they are led and organized by environmental organizations or new voices within the development community. However, many social justice groups, while not seeing themselves as battling sprawl, do already struggle with its component parts. Thus, for example, unions fight workplace relocation decisions. Low-income groups demand affordable housing and access to effective public transportation. Below we examine samples of self-conscious antisprawl campaigns that feature alliances between environmentalists and social justice groups.

Slam-Dunking Wal-Mart[31]

The past decade has witnessed the takeover of the U.S. retail sector by so-called "big box" retail stores of the Wal-Mart, Home Depot, and Super Kmart variety. A grassroots resistance movement has developed to prevent these stores from infiltrating into even more communities. At the center of this general struggle is the symbol of big box retailing: Wal-Mart.

America's second-largest corporation, Wal-Mart is such a mean, nasty company that a diverse array of activists can find reason to oppose it. As of early 1999, the company had 910,000 employees with 3,562 stores in seven countries. With its huge buildings and sprawling parking lots, usually built on formerly open space, Wal-Mart is an environmental disaster—damaging water drainage, creating toxic runoff, and destroying natural habitat. It is an engine of the car society. One estimate places the number of car trips per 150,000-square-foot big box store at 2,700 to 5,600 a day.[32] The company is viciously antiunion. When ten meat cutters at a Texas Wal-Mart won union recognition, the company closed its meat-cutting operations at this and 179 other locations throughout the South.[33] Wal-Mart defines a "full time" employee as one who works twenty-eight hours or more. Annual income estimates for such "full time" employees run from $9,000 to $11,000 a year. The company's "Personal Choice" health care

plan has such restrictive rules that a majority of employees are not covered and those that are pay nearly a third of the premiums. The roughly 219,000 "peak employees" who work under twenty-eight hours a week get no vacation time, no medical, and no other benefits.

While Wal-Mart has touted a policy of "Made in America," a 1998 in-store survey by the National Labor Committee (NLC) in a dozen states found that 85 percent of the stores' clothing items were made overseas. Wal-Mart imports more foreign goods than any other single American retailer in history. One recent NLC exposé found Wal-Mart buying Kathie Lee handbags from a factory in China where one thousand workers labored twelve to fourteen hours a day, seven days a week, for take-home pay running between ten cents and eight-tenths of a cent per hour![34] When it isn't encouraging sweatshops overseas, Wal-Mart promotes the low road at home. Not only does the company demand that manufacturers provide low prices, but Wal-Mart has been sued by its suppliers for sending back and demanding refunds on "defective" goods that were not defective, demanding further discounts on goods that did not sell, and for other breaches of contract. The influence of Wal-Mart's business practices can be felt far and wide. In 1998, for example, Fruit of the Loom announced plans to cut 2,909 jobs in the United States. The company explained its belt-tightening as necessary to remain "a low-cost provider of quality family apparel." Wal-Mart is one of Fruit of the Loom's largest customers. Thirteen years after Nike first accused Wal-Mart of selling sneakers under a fake Nike label, Wal-Mart was again caught in 1996 for the same trademark infringement—a practice that does not seem confined to footwear.

Wal-Mart's market-saturation strategy provides ample room for worry by both environmentalists and social justice advocates alike. As founder Sam Walton explained in his autobiography, the company aims to become "our own competition." When Wal-Mart comes to town, it does not seek to fill new shares of a growing market, but to take over that market outright by brute force. As Walton explained:

> We figured we had to build our stores so that our distribution centers could take care of them. . . . Each store had to be within a day's drive of a distribution center. . . . Then we could fill in the map of that territory, state by state, county seat by county seat, until we had saturated that market area.[35]

In an oversaturated market, many retailers will be driven out of business, with only Wal-Mart left surviving. What dies are smaller downtown businesses—7,326 according to a ten-year study of the impact of big box stores in Iowa.[36] Wal-Mart also causes the closure of existing suburban shopping centers. It thus destroys remaining open space in order to render already-built areas derelict. The chains that go under are often older unionized companies. The United States has four thousand abandoned shopping malls and ten times the shopping space per person than Britain. Indeed, we have more shopping centers than high schools. Yet, Wal-Mart and other big box stores keep adding to the inventory. However, once Wal-Mart has paved over a greenfield and wiped out the competition, there is no guarantee that it will stay. The company had 333 empty buildings in 1999.[37] And while Wal-Mart enters markets with the slogan "We sell for less," court proceedings have found that the company lifts its prices as the competition goes under.[38]

In short, Wal-Mart deserves a wall of resistance and that resistance is beginning to grow. As of 2000, citizens in nearly one hundred communities across the country had successfully blocked Wal-Mart from moving into their town. The list ranges from Santa Rosa, California, to Gilbert, Arizona, to St. Petersburg, Florida, to Plymouth, Massachusetts, to Lorain, Ohio. By exposing the impact of Wal-Mart and pressuring local officials to use their zoning authority, grassroots activists have successfully countered Wal-Mart's bag of dirty tricks. Sensing the growing opposition, the company typically now tries to sneak into town. Antisprawl activist Al Norman has identified ten major tactics the company uses, including the creation of bogus "citizens groups," hiring local attorneys and PR firms, releasing biased opinion surveys, distributing a "community resource guide" with endorsements of Wal-Mart, and attempting to foster "Wal-Mart Yes" postcard campaigns.

Diverse arrays of groups have countered Wal-Mart's strategies.[39] The United Food and Commercial Workers (UFCW) maintains an active anti-Wal-Mart effort including a Wal-Mart Watch Web site and an anti-Wal-Mart billboard campaign. With the company already the number six grocery chain in the country, Wal-Mart's spread threatens the unionized jobs at companies like Kroger. In December 1998, two thousand UFCW and other union members marched on the town square of Wal-Mart's home in Bentonville, Arkansas. At the rally, AFL-CIO president John Sweeney told supporters that he would direct all labor credit unions to stop distributing Sam's Club membership cards and urge all union joint employer benefit funds to stop using Wal-Mart pharmacies.

The first ballot defeat against Wal-Mart occurred in 1993 in the small Massachusetts town of Greenfield, population nineteen thousand. Wal-Mart had successfully maneuvered to have two ballot proposals placed before voters. The first measure would have rezoned sixty-three acres of land; the second would have allowed buildings larger than forty thousand square feet in the general commercial district. Although the company went to considerable lengths to convince town voters, a grassroots group called Citizens for Responsible Development actively campaigned against the ballot proposals. Raising $17,000 and with a committed core of volunteers, the group won. With a high voter turnout of over 60 percent and a close vote margin, the citizens of Greenfield voted to keep themselves Wal-Mart free. Today, one of the key activists in the campaign, Al Norman, travels the country to support anti-Wal-Mart efforts and maintains a Sprawl-Busters clearinghouse.

And Wal-Mart is not the only big box store to encounter resistance. When the two hundred senior citizen residents of the Journey's End Mobile Park in Santa Rosa, California, were told that they would have to move in order to make room for a 154,000-square-foot Home Depot, they decided to fight back. With a petition drive and threatened picketing, they prompted Home Depot to move their plans elsewhere. The company then failed in a second bid to build elsewhere in Santa Rosa. Unfortunately, the company won a closely fought referendum campaign, allowing it to build in a neighboring town. On the other side of the country, Home Depot found such intense opposition to its attempt to locate in the Cape Cod community of Yarmouth, Massachusetts, that it ended up spending $88,407 ($26 per vote) to win a nonbinding referendum. However, the citizen group opposed to the company uncovered the extent to which Home Depot had concealed this funding. This exposure, combined with the actions of local officials who questioned the store's potential negative impact on Cape Cod, convinced the company to withdraw its proposals.

In 1996, Teamsters Local 264 in Buffalo built an alliance with Friends of the Earth and other local groups to oppose the plans of the Dutch-owned Royal Ahold company to build a new megawarehouse. The owner of several supermarket chains, the company wanted the facility in order to implement a new just-in-time warehouse system known as cross-docking. The plan would have eliminated union jobs and put smaller independent, and often inner-city, grocers at a severe cost disadvantage. Needless to say, the new megawarehouses would have been located in undeveloped farmland. In a model campaign that brought together labor, environmental, inner-city neighborhood, religious, and civil rights groups, the campaign successfully pressured the Erie County legislature to pass a resolution against cross-docking. Royal Ahold was forced to sign a code of conduct requiring it to work with the Teamsters and Friends of the Earth. The company cancelled most of its cross-docking plans.[40]

Fostering Alternative Land-Use Policies

Campaigns against specific developments help build alliances between environmental and social justice groups. However, ultimately, the most far-reaching and potentially powerful alliances are those that tackle sprawl at the level of regional economic development. While such projects are only just beginning to emerge, several examples point to the future possibilities.

Little Rock, Arkansas

With developers relentlessly working to expand Little Rock to the west, the city has become a hot point for battling sprawl. In 1998, the Sierra Club named Little Rock the fifth worst city for sprawl in the country. The environmental and quality-of-life issues created by this sprawl sparked a grassroots reaction led by groups such as Citizens for Accountable Growth. As with most places in the country, this environmental activism involved mainly white middle-class residents. However, by 1999, Little Rock's antisprawl battle had developed a notable alliance between the environmental community and low-income neighborhoods.

Several ingredients helped facilitate the social justice connections. The birthplace of the national ACORN, Little Rock continues to support an active local chapter. By 1999, the local ACORN had translated years of cooperation with the area's central labor council into a formal alliance between the two groups. Also, during the 1990s, ACORN helped launch the national New Party (described in chapter 13). By 1999, the local New Party chapter had elected numerous activists to local office—including four on the city council. In Little Rock, as elsewhere in the country, New Party political organizing drew in the participation of activists from both the environmental community and low-income neighborhoods.

The Little Rock antisprawl organizing focused on the efforts of developers to get the city to annex surrounding land. Incorporating such properties within the city limits provided access to city-level services and infrastructure. Without the annexation homes on these properties would have minimal police and fire protection, gravel roads, and no sewers. The aim of developers was clear. They wanted access to cheap land, but wanted the residents of Little Rock to pay for the infrastructure and services. The issue came to a head in 1999 when developer Delta Timber Corporation petitioned the city to annex 1,230 acres of densely wooded land. Since 1989, the company had succeeded in having 3,507 annexed—encompassing twelve hundred new homes and six hundred commercial sites. Without intervention, Delta Timber would likely win further annexation.

In 1999, New Party city council member Paul Kelly introduced legislation to place a moratorium on annexations until 2003 and require impact studies for new developments. Through public forums, hearings, and direct action, activists organized to pass Kelly's legislation and to persuade the city council to renew funds for Little Rock's 1997 Smart Growth program. During a three-hour "tour of sprawl," residents and the media visited gleaming new superstores on the outskirts of town and vacant shopping centers in the older parts of town. A crowd of forty people also rallied at a busy highway junction in west Little Rock.

Organizers worked hard to draw the links to social justice and to pull in residents of low-income communities. While the annexations were often sold as increasing the city's taxable land, in practice, the end result transferred service and infrastructure resources out of poorer areas to pay for new construction. In the new residential areas, developers built high-priced upscale homes with expensive infrastructure needs. Inner-city residents also paid the price as national chain stores closed older urban stores to move to greenfield locations. "They're closing our schools, and abandoning our neighborhoods, to spend more money on fancy new developments," summarized New Party city council member Johnnie Pugh. "We need to direct city services back to the low-income neighborhoods that need them most."

The campaign aimed to translate these abstract links into a concrete understanding of how sprawl affects people's daily lives.

Despite a vigorous campaign, the developer interests entrenched deeply within local politics prevailed. Paul Kelly's ordinance was voted down. In the next election, developers went after the at-large city councilor. Outspent three to one, Kelly lost his seat.

Despite these setbacks, grassroots organizing had forged connections between environmentalists and low-income residents. Through hard work, activists had built a genuinely multiracial coalition and made sprawl a social justice concern. And the battle is not over as new proposed developments continue to seek city action. By early 2001, activists were gearing up for opposition to a new proposed "Mega Mall." The project offers the possibility of connecting low-income residents on the city's east side with middle-income westsiders. The proposed mall's location threatens to drive two existing malls—one on the east side and one on the west side—out of business.

In Sacramento, California, ACORN has also linked low-income concerns to sprawl. The local chapter put together a coalition to oppose a 46 percent increase in sewage fees. The increase reflected the growing expense of expanding city sewage capacity to cover poorly planned new development. Despite a protest rally and a flood of mail, the city council voted 5–4 to approve the increase, However, the council did agree to work with community leaders to develop a revised fee structure that doesn't force older neighborhoods to subsidize sprawl.

Chicago

With affiliated unions representing 500,000 members, the Chicago Federation of Labor has taken notable first steps in making sprawl a social justice issue seen as an explicit threat to working families. Federation president, Don Turner, believes that sprawl has become and will remain for at least the next twenty years the dominant issue for urban

America. Recently, he agreed to join the Board of Directors for Chicago 2020, a business civic association formed to promote smart growth policies. He then prevailed on this group to pay for the development and delivery of a curriculum about sprawl and unions.

Good Jobs First, the clearinghouse and advocacy group for campaigns around corporate subsidy reforms, developed the curriculum entitled "Smart Growth, Good Jobs." In April 2000, over one hundred labor leaders attended a six-hour conference. Participants came from the local Federation's entire membership, including teachers, Teamsters, food and commercial workers, building trades, public transit, health care, public sector, professional and stage employees, mailers, building services, and manufacturing.

At the conference, union leaders were exposed to the wide range of problems linked to sprawl. These issues included the area's affordable housing crisis, organized labor's distinct urban roots, hospital closures, traffic congestion, air quality, taxes, the hotel industry, privatization, retail, manufacturing, economic development subsidies, and political power. In addition to identifying how sprawl linked to labor's top concerns, the discussion also highlighted how unions can aid the battle for alternative policies. In particular, unions can help provide development issues with a human face. Often sprawl debates come across as either abstract environmental concerns or as complicated and confusing issues. Unions can personalize the debate by highlighting the impact that sprawl has on jobs, housing, and day-to-day quality-of-life issues. In other words, labor can help make sprawl a social justice concern.

Sustainable Development

The concept of sustainable development, which has emerged from the environmental community, offers a potentially powerful conceptual tool to unite environmental and social action. The World Commission on the Environment and Development defines sustainability as "meeting the needs of the present without compromising the ability of future generations to meet their own needs." While specific formulations vary, as used by activists, sustainability seeks to integrate social, economic, and ecological goals with the aim of creating high-quality human activity that can be replicated and sustained over the long span of future generations.

Across the country and throughout the world, organizations and networks have developed to promote the concept of sustainability. At a grassroots level, many of the people involved in this movement are potential partners and allies with social justice groups. The concept of sustainability also has its adherents in official policy and business circles. In 1999, for example, thousands of business leaders, government officials, and activists converged in Detroit for a large-scale meeting sponsored by the Clinton administration's "President's Council on Sustainable Development." The council's co-chairs are Jonathan Lash, president of the World Resources Institute, and Ray Anderson, CEO of Interface Inc. The latter's company revolutionized the carpet and floor-covering industry by recycling carpet provided to a customer once the customer was done with its use or wanted it replaced. Within the corporate world, a growing number of business leaders have become interested in the concept of sustainability. By rethinking their products and business practices, for example, companies have found that they can significantly cut waste and pollution, while increasing the bottom line. Environmental writer Paul Hawken has become a famous spokesperson for the idea that incentives within the capitalist market can lead companies toward more sustainable practices. At the Ford Motor Company, for example, William Clay Ford, has emerged as a champion for more environmentally sound and sustainable business practices. At his urging, Ford pulled out of the auto and fuel industry's consortium that lobbies against air quality and climate control legislation. William Ford has also pushed the company to see its long-term future in providing diverse and more environmentally responsible transportation products rather than the exclusive focus on the personal automobile.

Corporate participants in the sustainability movement can provide grassroots environmentalists and social justice groups with business allies for fostering high-road economic development strategies. The key for effective cooperation lies in the community having a clear and independent picture of what it wants. While sustainability has fostered some innovative business thinking, it also has been used as a fig to provide a green gloss to the same old unsustainable corporate actions. While timber companies, for example, may hail their "sustainable" tree farms, the reality is that a tree farm is not an ecologically balanced forest and clear-cutting of old-growth forests continues. Unions, environmentalists, and community groups can work with auto manufacturing companies to reduce the toxic outputs of their plants and to build alternative vehicles. However, they will likely part company with the majority of auto executives when discussions move toward ways to reduce our nation's overall dependence on the automobile.

The transformation of Chattanooga, Tennessee, provides a model example of sustainable development that combined productive business involvement with grassroots activism. By the 1970s, the city had won the dubious distinction as the most polluted city in the nation. One hundred years of industry had rendered the Tennessee River a dirty, foul-smelling waterway. Air quality was so bad that "people had to turn on their head lights during the middle of the day."[41] Two forces helped push change. In the 1970s, the city was hit by industrial disinvestment. At the same time, the EPA essentially told the city that it would not permit any new industry within the valley unless air quality was improved. By 1984, the efforts of citizens, environmentalists, government, and industry to clean up the air had produced momentum for a more far-reaching process of change. Using a small nonprofit called Chattanooga Venture, the city launched a broad planning process, Vision 2000, that attracted over seventeen hundred participants. Together they produced a list of forty goals that have guided the actions of broad sections of the community.

Vision 2000 combined environmental recovery with social needs. The city has used its takeover of abandoned riverfront land to bring people back to downtown. The conversion of the Walnut Street Bridge to pedestrian-only use connects both sides of a model system of riverfront community parks. A new freshwater aquarium teaches about the river's ecology and offered a large-scale redevelopment project to help draw people downtown. City planners oriented downtown recovery around small business shops and restaurants as well as theaters and other entertainment facilities. Unlike many corporate versions of downtown recovery—which aim to bring upscale suburbanites back to the city—Chattanooga's plans aimed to provide a meeting place for all of the city's residents. During the summer, the downtown riverfront system offers a wealth of open-air public culture. City residents enjoy free bus transportation throughout downtown offered by Advanced Vehicle Systems—a new company attracted to the city. The manufacturing of the innovative electric buses provides city jobs, while the free bus service allows the company to test its vehicles with real-life use.

Chattanooga's economic development strategy seeks to establish the area as a leading home for the environmental technologies of the future. A new waste reduction and recycling plant provides first-step jobs for the mentally challenged and a sensible waste disposal strategy for the area. Planning authorities have developed plans for a zero-emission industrial park that would use abandoned industrial sites in a way that would allow workers to walk to work from surrounding revitalized neighborhoods. Indeed, Chattanooga's plans stand out for the degree to which environmental and economic recovery has been linked to meeting the needs of low-income residents. One of the first concrete projects to come out of Vision 2000 was a shelter for victims of domestic violence. Low interest loans have allowed twenty-five hundred low-income families to rebuild their neighborhoods. The management of a decrepit 1960s-style public housing project was taken over by the residents who renamed it after Harriet Tubman. Across the city, community gardens, co-op stores, and over one thousand new trees have begun to change the physical quality of neighborhoods. The city has also embarked on a series of progressive educational reforms after city residents set raising expectations for public education as a top goal.

In 1993, the city renewed its strategic vision through another planning process. Revision 2000 involved twenty-six hundred residents whose profile matched the diversity of the city. Today, Chattanooga's ongoing transformation has allowed it to sell itself as one of the nation's premiere environmental cities. Certainly, walking along the river parks during a summer evening, one is struck by the vitality of the surroundings. A diverse crowd of people stroll through beautiful landscaping on their way to a lively downtown. It is an energy that is distinctly public and one that no corporate mall or suburban entertainment center can offer.

Chattanooga's experience demonstrates the partnerships that can be achieved when the interests of local business and the community overlap. Ultimately, however, corporate versions of sustainability revolve around fostering enlightened business practices that are voluntary. Yet, at a general level, high-road business strategies are often only as attractive as the degree to which low-road alternatives have been blocked or made more expensive. It took deindustrialization and the EPA to help convert Chattanooga business and political leaders to sustainability. For most communities, closing the low road ultimately means contesting for power and imposing on the market basic human values.

Social justice groups can help the grassroots sustainability movement foster bold visions of economic change. They can highlight the connection between environmental issues and people's daily lives. And they can provide a crucial focus on power. Fundamental economic change means pushing core capitalist forces in new directions. While tactical and strategic alliances with business are part of the process, the community must foster its own vision of change and build its own bases of power. Ultimately, the most reliable ways of converting business to sustainable economic practices are strong alliances within a community capable of pursuing a bold agenda for economic change.

12

Toward a National Movement

Taken together, the efforts profiled in the last five chapters present currents of progressive activism that have filtered throughout the country. To what extent can this patchwork of local and state organizing translate into the national quilt of a self-conscious movement for fundamental economic change? This chapter explores the possibilities for a national economic democracy movement at two levels. First, we examine some of the perils and promises of bringing together diverse currents that make up today's progressive activism. Second, we tease out the basic ideas common to much of the organizing discussed in this book in order to suggest the general outlines of a progressive agenda for economic change.

Progressive Pitfalls and Promise

In 1997, the Peace Development Fund initiated a National Listening Project to explore ways in which foundations could better foster progressive movement building. Through interviews and focus groups, researchers spoke with eighty-two grassroots leaders who represented the broad diversity of progressive activism throughout the country. Participants were asked if they felt a progressive movement currently exists, to identify the barriers to aggregating progressive political power, to offer ideas for increasing the impact of progressive work, and to sketch the best role for foundations in supporting this activism.[1]

While participants identified a broad spectrum of active progressive projects, most felt that this activity was currently too disconnected to be considered a "movement." They identified fragmentation as the single greatest factor limiting overall progressive power. This lack of unity had several dimensions including geographical isolation, conflicts in reconciling the needs of networking and national organization building with local commitments, and wedge issues that split people along dimensions of race, gender, sexual preference, and other oppressions. Progressives also lack a common strategic vision and often even the resources necessary for long-range strategic planning. While hoping for a movement toward more comprehensive change, activists said that their energy often got used up pursuing the basic survival needs of their organization—especially funding. Participants also pointed to the lack of a clear and unified political identity as both an outcome and contributing factor to progressive invisibility in the corporate mass media.

The fate of a promising new network, Sustainable America, illustrated the difficulties identified by the Listening Project. Begun in 1995, Sustainable America pulled together a network of over eighty organizations active around economic concerns. Its membership building was particularly noteworthy for bringing together social justice organizations with environmental groups. The network included many of the groups profiled in this book. Sustainable America aimed to facilitate progressive networking through a combination of concrete assistance to local groups while also fostering greater unity and sense of common vision. The organization sponsored two national gatherings to allow its diverse members to meet and learn from each other. It established a technical assistance bank through which groups could offer and receive assistance from other groups. Sustainable America also sponsored four study groups focused around welfare reform, human rights, environmentally friendly taxes, and rural development.

Sustainable America eventually succumbed, however, to the forces identified above. With only modest staff resources of its own, the organization had to rely on the efforts of a range of activists already overburdened by their particular groups' projects. While Sustainable America attempted to facilitate cross-issue dialogue, participants naturally gravitated toward the components most connected to their existing work. The topics of the four study groups, for example, replicated classic divisions within progressive activism between antipoverty work, environmentalism, and human rights activism. Sustainable America was never able to go beyond the sum of its different parts. While at a general level, activists shared a common desire for economic change, how to translate this sentiment into a common vision and unifying agenda that transcended the separate actions of each individual group proved a barrier that the organization was never able to cross. Five years after its founding, Sustainable America closed its doors.

The Listening Project did not simply identify problems, however. It also asked participants to brainstorm solutions. Participants discussed the possibilities for a single issue that might cross traditional boundaries and unify diverse groups. While not ruling out such a prospect, they were skeptical of a single cause proving compelling enough to transcend each organization's particular agendas. Instead, they pointed to the possibilities for developing common action around multi-issue work as common problems, such as corporate power, increasingly connected individual issues. In addition to joint actions, participants called for greater structural cooperation between organizations through joint development of

strategies and coordination of resources. Ultimately, activists hoped that common action and increased organizational cooperation would foster a greater common vision that would transcend each individual group's current concerns and understanding. Progressives need more "movement consciousness" to see themselves as part of a great national movement for fundamental change.

Realizing such hopes is today's challenge. Recent developments have offered some promising signs. The 1999 and 2000 showdowns in Seattle and Washington, DC, against corporate globalization demonstrated the inspiring possibilities of a progressive movement for economic change. For three days in November and December 1999, 40,000–60,000 protestors in Seattle forced the corporate media to cover grassroots dissatisfaction with the status quo and led to the failure of the WTO's meeting.[2] Six months later, a similar collection of groups descended on Washington, DC, to make life difficult for the World Bank and IMF. The vast sea of humanity included trade unions, environmental groups, religious leaders, antipoverty activists, youth groups, human rights advocates, and protest delegations from nations throughout the world.[3] While each group had its own specific concerns, they were united by a vision of a common enemy: runaway corporate power. The protestors also advanced demands that offered such common themes as rewriting trade agreements to reflect human and environmental priorities, reorienting the agendas of global economic institutions, and redirecting the way in which the developed world interacts with the developing world. Many participants also came away from the demonstrations with some sense of being part of a common worldwide struggle.

Both the Seattle and Washington mobilizations also revealed significant structural cooperation among different progressive groups. Over 700 organizations in the United States and abroad participated in the Seattle protests. The coordination work was often impressive. For example, in Seattle, a year before the November protests, the King County central labor federation initiated a regional education process that helped turn out huge crowds. By developing materials, training volunteers, and coordinating outreach, the project educated people through one-on-one conversations about the nature of the WTO and progressive demands for a new set of global rules. From the beginning, the labor council included its community allies in planning and implementing the project as a joint labor-community effort. Also, before the WTO arrived in town, the Direct Action Network prepared thousands of nonviolent protestors through a training process of inclusion, consensus decision making, and group initiative. During the Seattle events, organizers held workshops throughout the week allowing people from different parts of the progressive community to interact and strategize together. While the labor and direct action protest began as separate events, as the days progressed and police repression increased, union activists were increasingly drawn into the direct action battles and demonstrations against police violence. Unions such as the United Steelworkers were so impressed by the sophistication and achievements of the many youthful direct action groups that afterward they initiated steps to maintain and foster ongoing and concrete connections to student networks.

The Seattle and Washington protests were ultimately single events. Much of the work to translate the energy of these demonstrations into a sustained national movement remains ahead. However, while protestors returned back to their particular groups, new connections had been made and cross-organization networks established or strengthened. The protests highlighted how corporate restructuring of the world's economy has compelled diverse groups to move beyond just battling specific symptoms to also attack the underlying disease. Activists Kevin Danaher and Roger Burbach, for example, were struck by how protests against the WTO brought environmental and social justice movements together on an unprecedented scale.[4] Most important, for two separate weeks a vast sea of humanity came together

to offer a momentary glimpse into a potentially massive movement for economic change.

Much of the activism covered in previous chapters has produced some level of national coordination and networking. For example, the living wage has entered the halls of Congress. In March of 2001, Rep. Gutierrez (D-IL) and Senator Wellstone introduced the Federal Living Wage Responsibility Act, which would require firms holding federal service contracts worth at least $10,000 to pay employees above the federal poverty line. The bill also requires that all direct federal employees be paid at least a living wage. With a Republican-majority House and President Bush, the bill is obviously not going to be passed anytime soon. The debate around the bill, however, provides an opportunity to network the 120 local living wages around coordinated national action. On November 30, 2000, for example, ACORN organized a National Day of Action for a Federal Living Wage with participation from living wage activists in over 50 cities. The Day of Action coincided with the release of a report by the Economic Policy Institute estimating that close to 500,000 government employees and those employed on federal contracts were making less than a living wage.

The Federal Living Wage Campaign is being coordinated by ACORN as part of the National Campaign for Jobs and Income Support. The National Campaign is a newly formed consortium of more than 25 community organizations and networks with an aggregate membership of 300,000 families and affiliates in more than 40 states. The mission of the campaign is to elevate issues of poverty and inequality on the national agenda and amplify the voice of low-income communities in public policy. The campaign is coordinating action on a range of important issues including welfare reform, health care, living wage, job training, immigrant amnesty, and access to public benefits.

Other dimensions of economic activism also have developed national networks. As described in chapter 9, contingent-work organizing has the National Alliance for Fair Employment. Good Jobs First, based in Washington, DC, provides a clearinghouse and technical support to the corporate subsidy accountability movement. The sustainability movement is a world unto itself with national and international organizations. Battles against sprawl have pulled in national organizations such as the Sierra Club and fostered national networks such as Smart Growth America and Sprawlwatch. The National Interfaith Committee on Worker Justice, based in Chicago, networks over 40 local interfaith coalitions such as CLUE in Los Angeles. We described the national reform efforts of the AFL-CIO leadership in chapter 10. Organizations such as United for a Fair Economy and the Center for Popular Economics promote grassroots economics education throughout the country.

While none of these networks, organizations, and clearinghouses represents a comprehensive national economic justice movement, they are suggestive of the many parts that can evolve into a greater whole. While the exact profile of a self-conscious movement for national economic change will only emerge in the process of building it, the efforts covered in this book do suggest some shared themes and possibilities. Below, we use the material covered in both parts of this book to pull together several common ideas and underlying themes. While organizing around specific issues and reforms provides the bread and butter of progressive activism, taking a moment to sit back and consider the long-range possibilities helps add further meaning and relevancy to the day-to-day struggles.

Toward a National Agenda for Economic Change

While we will illustrate each dimension with examples of specific sample policies, our main goal below is to highlight three overarching concepts capable of undergirding any particular agenda for progressive change: public standards, public wealth, and economic democracy. These elements reflect the main theme of this book: close the low road and pave the high road.

Much of the organizing going on today, while dealing with new details, revolves around classic themes that have driven American progressive reform since the founding of the country. These ideas are reflected in the most progressive parts found in the last great national economic reform project: the New Deal of the 1930s and its expansion through the Civil Rights era and the 1960s protest movements. As discussed in chapter 6, at its best the New Deal liberal tradition focused on using governmental powers to set basic standards for economic activity and developing various forms of public wealth and social citizenship. While many Americans may understandably be frustrated that they do not get their full money's worth for their tax dollars, these New Deal ideals continue to enjoy significant public support. That government policy should play a major role in the nation's economic and social life is generally accepted at a grassroots level—outside the ranks of the most committed libertarians. The New Deal also included the uncultivated seeds of an agenda for economic democracy, which were cut short by the limitations placed on the New Deal and its spin-offs.

The activism that we have examined in this book does not reject this liberal reform tradition. Instead, it seeks to rejuvenate and extend it in more progressive directions. The concepts that we develop below suggest ways of reviving and aggressively furthering notions of public standards and social wealth while also bringing goals of economic democracy into the full light of day. We will draw on both the ideas raised by current organizing as well as the examples from Europe. To illustrate the possibilities of each dimension, we will offer policy examples that include both immediate demands and more long-term reforms for fundamental change.

Public Standards—Closing the Low Road

Currently, mainstream government policies display great concern for protecting the private property rights of corporations to pursue their interests with as much freedom as possible. A progressive response obviously moves in the opposite direction. By asserting a greater public role for setting standards for economic behavior, progressive reform can outlaw or discourage business strategies built around low-road goals. The campaigns around living wages, corporate accountability, contingent work, job access, and free trade all assert the right of the public to set basic rules for economic activity. These standards aim either to establish basic rights—such as around wages and working conditions—or to limit management actions—such as environmental regulations. Both dimensions are ripe with possibilities.

The campaigns in this book point to a list of basic human rights that should be enshrined in law: the right to a family-supporting wage; equal pay for equal work; open and honest employment policies; and equal treatment regardless of race, gender, sexual orientation, age, or employment status. From Europe, we can also identify other rights such as: paid vacations, paid parental leave, and training opportunities. Far greater public standards over work time are also long overdue in this country. They should include a shorter workweek, increased compensation for overtime, the right to overtime by all employees, access to flexible work schedules, and more options for the timing and manner of retirement.

Pursued aggressively, such public standards can reshape economic activity. They would certainly limit the availability of low-road management strategies by reducing the vast disparities in wages and working conditions found in our country today. As the growing protests against corporate globalization make clear, public standards must also form the basis of world trade. Since our government and U.S. corporations are the strongest international forces pushing global economic liberalization, Americans are in the unique position to help push a counteragenda of public standards around human and environmental rights.

The notion that corporations should be held accountable for their actions runs throughout the campaigns covered in this book. This country could be far more aggressive at developing and enforcing basic environmental and land-use laws. We could also take a page from Europe with regulations restricting management's ability to lay off employees and close work facilities. Many existing limitations on corporate actions need to be expanded and provided more enforcement teeth. A glaring example, in this regard, is our nation's labor laws. A protected right to form a union is simply a legal fiction in many workplaces. Current penalties for illegal employer behavior are negligible and the enforcement process so cumbersome that it drags on for years. A truly democratic system for worker organizing would recognize union organization as soon as a majority of workers (or even a substantial minority) express their desire for unionization. Penalties should be stiff and government authorities empowered to act quickly against employer lawbreaking.

In the long run, progressive public standards could expand notions of accountability to challenge the supposedly sacred, untouchable existence of the corporation. Corporations were created through laws that allowed owners legal protection against liability for the actions of the corporation. Thus, stockholders cannot, and only under special circumstances can managers, be held legally responsible for illegal activity carried out by a company. Under current U.S. law, corporations operate with rights of personhood. Thus, the Bill of Rights has been used to protect the rights of corporations to buy our political system through campaign contributions (deemed "freedom of speech") and to operate in secret (the "right to privacy").

At the same time, the actual behavior of this corporate "person" is given remarkable deference by the current legal system. For example, if I as an individual engaged in wanton behavior that resulted in the death of other people, I could be found criminally responsible and be thrown in jail. Yet, the worst ramifications that tobacco companies face for their decades of knowingly promoting a product known to kill people are financial damages. While the tobacco settlements have involved often impressive amounts of money, they still allow the corporations to exist and to continue to sell and promote a lethal product. The same story is true for major chemical companies who routinely produce products that they know, through their own internal research, to be harmful to both workers and the general public. Typically, such production is stopped only after activists have amassed the scientific research to prove the harm and have endured a lengthy legal battle. Currently, the public has to prove that a new chemical is harmful, rather than a corporation prove that it is safe. With eighty thousand chemicals created since the 1940s, public science has only been able to test a small fraction for their impact on human and environmental health.[5]

Yet, as some grassroots groups have begun to assert, corporations exist only at the pleasure of the law. Indeed, the early corporate charters included explicit language stating their social mission and linking their legal existence to the good of the community. Laws that create corporations can also disband them. In Europe, governments have seized corporate assets when such action has been in the greater public interest. In the United States, state and federal authorities do have the power to repeal a corporation's charter—thus dissolving it and allowing for its assets to be seized. There is historical precedent for such action. In 1815, for example, the state court in Massachusetts ruled that a private corporation that misused its franchise could have its charter revoked. Since most of a corporation's employees are not to blame for its wrongdoings, it makes sense that if a private company's charter is revoked, its assets should be placed in public hands so that meaningful employment can be maintained around socially and environmentally responsible business practices.

Today's corporate misbehavior provides a wealth of possible candidates. Tobacco companies for decades willfully designed deadly products, enhanced their addictive power, and marketed them to children. Such action should be clear grounds for trans-ferring their assets to public hands and using this wealth to convert dependent workers and farmers toward more socially responsible crops and production. Indeed, in 1998 the attorney general for New York State asked the court to revoke the charters of two tobacco industry "research" corporations—in essence instituting the "death penalty" for repeat corporate lawbreakers. An Alabama judge also filed a complaint in state court demanding the revoking of the charters of five tobacco corporations for violating dozens of laws.[6]

Once the sacred right of corporate property has been punctured, a range of possibilities opens up. For example, the nation has laws that make outright business monopolies illegal. However, the technology of certain products naturally suggests high levels of centralization. For example, software development is naturally easier when most computers use a similar underlying operating system. Yet, when the development of such a system takes place through the private marketplace, the result is a corporate monopoly. Under current law, the only government solution to Microsoft's monopoly power was to break up the company and encourage competition. A more obvious approach, however, would maintain the benefits of a common operating system, but break private economic power by placing the company into public hands.

Returning to more immediate steps, several campaigns have used the connections between public funds and private companies as an avenue for developing public standards. Few outside of the halls of the chamber of commerce can argue that the public should not be able to set basic terms for how its money is used. These standards can then be generalized into across-the-board rights and rules. The process can also start local and move toward the national. Indeed, historically, local and state victories often set the stage for today's national standards.

We should also keep in mind that state and federal government do have the authority to regulate the actions of U.S. corporations abroad. In 1977, for example, Congress passed the Foreign Corrupt Practices Act, which prohibits American companies from using outright bribery in overseas projects. Author William Greider offers several areas in which laws can extend regulations popular at home to corporate behavior abroad. These standards include basic safety regulations such as fire prevention, fundamental worker rights as enshrined in the International Labor Organization's core labor standards, and perhaps even the right to a "living wage." Greider emphasized how requiring corporate disclosure of their plants, subcontractors, wage levels, and pollution output would make public information crucial for organizing against corporate abuse worldwide. Such disclosures would also aid in an emerging practice in which foreign citizens have taken U.S. corporations before American courts—suing them for environmental and human rights abuses in their country. As this is a gray area of the law, state and federal legislation could more formally grant clear standing for foreign citizens to sue U.S. companies in U.S. courts.[7]

The notion of full-cost accounting, which comes from the environmental movement, offers a final dimension for thinking about greater public standards. Corporations pursue low-road strategies because they are profitable. The financial rewards, however, come because the company does not pay for the full costs of its actions. Outcomes—such as pollution, sprawl, low wages, layoffs, and personal and social economic insecurity—all have price tags that companies force on the public. Requiring businesses to pay for the full costs of their activities would obviously increase the attractiveness of the high road while making the low road less cost effective. The living wage, corporate accountability, and antisprawl campaigns have highlighted how government already uses tax policy to penalize and reward certain kinds of economic activity. A progressive reform agenda could turn these seeds into a full-blown public fiscal framework regulating private economic behavior. Activity that harms society—sprawl, layoffs, pollution, and excessive wealth—could be taxed on increasing scales. At the same time, tax policies could provide rewards to strategies that benefit society—such as the development and introduction of environmentally friendly technology, worker training, the rehabilitation of older urban areas, or the construction of affordable housing. Over the past twenty years, corporations secured major reductions to their share of the tax burden. Because of these tax breaks, average Americans have been forced to shoulder a greater share of the tax burden. Basic fairness dictates an extensive tax increase on private and corporate wealth. Such a clearly popular measure could include a wealth of opportunities to develop a tax structure that rewards the high road and penalizes the low road.

Public Wealth and Social Citizenship

As discussed throughout the book, closing the low road is not enough. Public policies must also establish and foster more positive ways of conducting economic activity. Establishing greater access to social citizenship through greater public wealth and expanding mechanisms for greater economic democracy provide the two main channels for building the high road.

Today, official debates and culture define success in individual terms. Indeed, the official "American dream" revolves around the personal accumulation of wealth. The problem with this individualized dream is that half the wealth of the country is owned by no more than one-fifth of the population. Close to half of all assets held by people under the age of fifty come from inheritance.[8] As European social democracy makes clear, public wealth can offer the average person far more opportunity than an exclusive pursuit of private gain. Yet, our nation's public wealth is woefully underdeveloped. This public poverty affects progressive collective movements as well as individuals. American unions, for example, endure far more aggressive antiunion employers than in Europe, in part because so many basic benefits such as pensions and health care come through each employer rather than universal public institutions.

Twenty years of conservative government bashing and the failure of mainstream liberals to defend the ideals of the New Deal have left many progressives shy about boldly asserting the desirability of "big government." While the American activism that we have examined draws on and extends government spending, it does not self-consciously seek to use government as a tool for the expanding public wealth. Yet, an enormous potential exists. In poll after poll, a majority of Americans support such big government universal programs as Social Security and public education. Despite years of conservative attacks on the "welfare queen," the public continues to support even targeted social spending such as Medicaid, and opposes measures to simply cut people off welfare with no further supports or preparation.

A fiscal pie for expanding social citizenship already exists in our nation's military budget. With "defense" spending consuming nearly half of all federal discretionary spending each year, a progressive budget could draw on no less that $350 billion annually. Half of the current four million federal employees (excluding the Post Office) work for the military—a colossal waste of human energy and creativity. At the same time, conservative estimates place the level of federal corporate welfare at $150 billion annually. Thus, without even touching the nation's unfair tax system, our federal government already has the funds for a massive public investment. In addition, calls for progressive reform should include revamping our tax system to restore basic fairness. Capital gains should be taxed as income (not below the top income rates as is now the case). The income tax on the upper brackets should go far beyond the year 2000 39 percent maximum.

Establishing a national health system is an obvious candidate for any first progressive effort to expand public wealth. As the only industrialized country not to have nationalized health, our nation is saddled with an expensive, inefficient, and misdirected health care system. The difficulty that federal policy makers have had in passing even band-aid measures, such as the Patients Bill of Rights, guarantees that the dire need for major health care re-

form will continue to fester well into the future. During the health care debate of Clinton's first term, progressive activists in states such as Vermont launched notable efforts to debate state-based single-payer plans. While they did not secure such systems, they did raise serious public debates. The potential for renewed state-level activism offers inspiring possibilities. We must remember that, in Canada, it was the success of progressive campaigns to establish single-payer systems in a single province that initially led to the creation of the national system so admired by American progressives.

As of this writing, the state of Maine has embarked on a major confrontation with the pharmaceutical industry. The spectacular rise in the costs of medication have made pharmaceuticals the most profitable industry in the nation. In May 2000, Maine enacted a law that uses the state's bulk purchasing power to force lower drug costs for uninsured state residents. In October, a federal judge ruled in favor of the Pharmaceutical Research and Manufacturers of America by declaring key components of the Maine law unconstitutional. While Maine officials considered their legal options, the state's governor began meeting with Vermont's and New Hampshire's governors to establish a three-state drug-buying pool that would combine their buying power into leverage to negotiate reduced prices for the uninsured. The Maine law had also instructed the state's human service commission to seek voluntary price reductions.

Existing areas of social citizenship also offer ready opportunities to steer resources from military spending and corporate welfare toward more socially beneficial undertakings. While not the sole answer to the public education debate, revamping the level and manner in which our nation funds its public schools could provide resources for innovation and ensure a truly equal education for all children. Similarly, public income supports for people who are disabled or otherwise unable to work remains patchy and inadequate. American public transportation remains a disgrace as billions of dollars are poured into yet more roads. And expanding and properly utilizing our public land continues to provide an important prong of environmental protection and people's quality of life.

An aggressive pursuit of public wealth could also carry into less conventional areas. The inadequacies and propaganda function of corporate-owned media continue to grow with each new media merger. Yet, much of the media exists only at the behest of public permission. The television and radio airwaves belong to the public and are licensed to private businesses. Cable systems similarly depend on local franchises. These enormous public resources continue to be given away to corporations with little or no compensation or responsibility to the public owners. Meanwhile, our so-called public broadcasting system has to beg for corporate sponsors. Year after year, the public bemoans the low quality and often violent nature of so much of the media's offerings. The obvious solution is take control over media production and distribution out of private hands concerned mainly with increasing their bottom line. Government policy should retain more public airwaves and franchise rights for public media, charge far more for private uses of these public resources, and then use the resulting funds to establish a resource-rich and diverse public media. Indeed, establishing far greater ownership of basic infrastructure—from media to electricity to telephones—would simply move the United States into the mainstream of the industrialized world.

The inability of most parents to find affordable quality child care cries out for a public solution. A wealth of models for combining public financing with local control to provide affordable and effective child care exist both in this country and overseas. Similarly, local experiments in publicly owned, but resident-run, housing offer ways for redefining "public housing." Among others, the city of Burlington, Vermont, for example, has experimented with public land ownership in which residents buy a house but not the land on which it sits. This arrangement lowers the cost of the home while providing the community with control over land beyond the life of the building.

Public ownership does not always have to entail government control. Local and regional nonprofit land conservancies are a classic example of independent grassroots institutions whose public work is supported through public funds. Today, in cities and towns across the country, public arts and culture display a wealth of examples with governmental-grassroots partnerships. As chapter 2 detailed, much of the German social welfare system operates through a mixture of governmental and nongovernmental public organizations.

Greater public wealth can also provide powerful examples of higher standards of employment and business activity. Public employers can be organized around high-road practices that offer models for high-wage, high-performance, unionized, and socially and environmentally responsible employers. Already government is the most highly unionized of the general sectors of our economy. It comes as no surprise that the huge public human service sector in Sweden displays far better pay, work conditions, and social commitments than our private equivalents. During the Great Depression, federal government jobs programs employed over ten million Americans through projects that contributed to the physical and cultural wealth of the nation. After the worst of the crisis had passed, the nation's corporations worked hard to get the programs shut down and their subversive example officially forgotten.

The goals of greater public wealth offer a new way to define our nation's tradition of "rugged individualism." For the vast majority of Americans, the maximum possible wealth that they can hope to individually accumulate cannot come close to their possible share of public wealth. No matter how big, for example, a person's private yard cannot come close to the size and benefits of public parks, squares, and natural areas. The most expensive home cannot buy friendly neighbors and a vibrant community life. For a majority of Americans, tax-supported and tuition-free public universities and colleges are a much better financial deal than personally accumulating tens of thousands of dollars per child. Establishing publicly sponsored training and skill development programs outside of a collage education provide other ways of expanding educational opportunities over the course of people's lives. Most firms in this country cannot hope to develop the level of worker skills offered by a comprehensive public training system.

The lack of public wealth in the United States seriously restricts people's lives. How many workers do not leave an unsatisfying job simply because they cannot afford to lose their health insurance? For how many Americans does a disability present not only a physical challenge, but a financial one as well? How many parents have to decide between time spent raising a family and time spent earning an income? Within our system of private wealth, people who wish to change careers or develop new skills typically have to take on the entire financial and time burden individually, even though all of society benefits when people can develop themselves over the course of their life.

In short, our nation's official celebration of liberty focuses only on narrow, negative forms of freedom. Corporate culture prizes protections from restrictions on individual actions. However, in practice, this freedom revolves mainly around protecting private property rights from governmental action. Public wealth, however, offers more positive forms of freedom. An individual is only truly free when he or she can pursue his or her goals with full access to the necessary resources. Greater social citizenship would increase most Americans' opportunities to pursue the life they wish to lead. In the end, true individual opportunity requires true public wealth.

Economic Democracy

An aggressive agenda for pursuing public standards and public wealth offers progressive activism much possibility. The pursuit of the high road, however, remains limited as long as the bulk of economic decisions remains the exclusive preserve of private managers. The notion of economic democracy, however, aims to shatter this core capitalist prerogative by open-

ing private economic decisions to public debate. It seeks to include the interests of the "stakeholders," and not just the shareholders, in business decisions. The full development of economic democracy is a radical idea since it ultimately places the very notion of private ownership of the economic means into question. A progressive reform agenda, however, can build from existing practices and examples.

We have seen seeds of economic democracy within the examples covered in this book. The growing array of local partnerships between labor, management, and the community around high-road practices provides instructive examples. Groups of firms are willing to enter into partnerships that involve some power sharing because such sharing provides opportunities to access training, technology, worker recruitment, work reorganization, and skill certification beyond the capacity of the individual firm. These partnerships allow unions and community groups access to information about an industry. They also establish decision-making tables where union members and residents can sit. Over time, such access can allow participants to use the knowledge of an industry to transform the practice of that industry. Because these partnerships are voluntary, they allow management to maintain their autonomy. However, over time, they also enmesh firms within a collective network that, if successful, makes companies increasingly reliant on cooperative problem solving and grassroots institutions.

Public policy and progressive action could do far more to foster genuine public-private partnerships. The overall culture of American firms remains rooted in notions of scientific management that view labor-community-business partnerships with a large degree of skepticism. However, the attractiveness of partnerships as a competitive strategy increases as low-road options are closed. Similarly, the establishment of greater public wealth provides a bigger carrot for firms to partner around the high road than exists now. Unfortunately, current government programs around business technology and modernization, workforce training, work reorganization, and market promotion follow, rather then lead, the private market. Generally speaking, these programs receive scant resources. And labor and community groups are rarely invited to the table, let alone made key players.

The new federal workforce investment system highlights the problems of existing policy. In 1998, Congress passed the Workforce Investment Act (WIA) to replace the older Job Training Partnership Act. According to its backers, the new law aims to reorganize federal, state, and local public training resources to ensure better coordination and a better fit with the needs of employers. WIA set up a multiyear planning process by new state and local WIA boards. At the local level, WIA mandated one-stop shops that supposedly bring access to all public training resources under one roof. In passing WIA, however, Congress chose to forgo genuine partnerships with labor or community groups. Indeed, the act specifies that at least 51 percent of the state and local boards must be made up of business executives. Labor and community activists have had to fight their way onto the boards, with varying degrees of success. Even when they get on the general board, for example, they often find themselves locked out of the key decision-making executive committees.

As a result of only allowing business and their allies a voice at the table, WIA is unlikely to move in the direction of meeting the training needs of today's workforce. A year 2000 interim report by the National People's Action and the National Campaign for Jobs and Income Supports painted a grim picture. Most state plans remained in a remarkable state of disarray. Little coordination was taking place between WIA and Temporary Assistant (TANF) agencies—the new work-oriented welfare system. Unlike the old system, WIA has no requirements that training funds go to low-income workers most in need. Many state plans reflected recent welfare reforms in emphasizing "work first" over extensive worker training. Legal mandates for local public hearings and oversight have been ignored. Many one-stop centers have been located in areas that many

low-income people cannot access. Many local WIA boards were stacked with low-wage employers. And many temp agencies were making explicit efforts to coopt the public funds—in many cases getting themselves designated as the one-stop center! In the face of these problems, the AFL-CIO mobilized unions and their allies to gain seats at the table and to steer local and state plans in more worker-friendly directions. However, even where they are successful, ultimately WIA marks a token effort. In 1980, the federal government spent over $6 billion on job training (the equivalent of $12 billion in 1998 dollars). Under the WIA, the federal government is spending only $3 billion. This is less than two-tenths of 1 percent of the overall budget and roughly a billion dollars less than the Navy spent in 1995 to purchase new combat aircraft!

The deplorable state of our national public training effort points to the enormous opportunities for promoting a genuine alternative. Indeed, the public selling points for WIA could be turned into a progressive agenda. Public training resources should be brought together around a single coherent system. A real planning process would involve labor, community, public, and business representatives in a genuine partnership. And a far larger commitment of resources would both promise real training opportunities and provide an incentive for business to come to the table.

The grassroots organizing against sprawl touches on another set of widely accepted examples of greater economic democracy. The entire system of zoning and growth boundaries asserts the public's right to participate in private decisions. As the antisprawl movement develops, calls for public landuse decisions can move in even more extensive directions. Historically, capitalism developed through the mass creation of private ownership over land. The destruction of communal land holding and rights denied access to this life-sustaining resource to the majority of the population. Public efforts to recapture this resource can go in many directions. For example, basic food security mandates that our nation reverse its increasing reliance on smaller numbers of ever-larger corporate farms. Restoring family agriculture and fostering organic and sustainable farming methods requires a combination of public standards, public wealth, and ultimately direct public planning to restructure the industry over the long term. We should keep in mind that the public expropriation of large land holdings has a long tradition in human history. Similarly, one hundred years ago, the several million-strong Farmers Alliance developed detailed plans to use cooperative and publicly funded marketing, processing, transportation, and distribution institutions to replace the private middlemen who gleaned off so much agricultural wealth.

Increasing economic democracy also involves using governmental resources and authority to foster and empower grassroots activism. For example, federal law already shapes one of our nation's major social movements through the legal framework for recognizing and defining membership in labor unions. The National Labor Relations Act, however, is in dire need of an overhaul. Allowing workers to gain legal recognition by signing union cards, mandating enforceable employer neutrality, and enacting real employer penalties for violating the law would provide three straightforward steps. Such measures are hardly unusual. Canadian law, for example, recognizes unionization when a majority of workers sign union cards. U.S. law could also be rewritten to recognize labor organizations involving less than a majority of workers. And it could promote and provide a legal framework for collective bargaining above the level of the individual firm. For example, all employers in a given industry and geographical area could be required to enter into collective bargaining when union membership in an industry reaches a certain density.

Public policy could legally empower other grassroots groups. Laws can and do require citizen participation. For example, land conservancy and other environmental groups could be granted the right to participate on local planning boards. Even more basic, simply requiring private business to publicly

disclose a range of internal information could offer basic tools for a wide variety of grassroots groups to raise democratic debate over economic decisions.

Sustaining effective grassroots organizing over a long time requires resources. Typically, the corporate institutions that oppose grassroots groups have people who work for their cause full time. Grassroots groups need the ability to fund staff. The pioneering coalitions such as CSM and WPUSA maintain their staff through funds provided by progressive foundations. Replicating grassroots projects such as these across the country would require billions of dollars beyond the coffers of such private sources. A progressive redirection of state and ultimately federal budgets could establish public social funds available to a wide range of grassroots-based organizations. Since the government already provides public grants for a variety of purposes, such social funds would be a logical extension of existing practices.

Ultimately, greater economic democracy also means building a much larger governmental role in economic planning. As we have seen in both Europe and Asia, the state can play a much larger role in economic planning than our government's current reach. Public economic planning requires the creation of new institutions. Such bodies must draw broad public participation, have access to generous public resources, and have the ability to set clear standards and rules. As German and Austrian codetermination suggests, bringing more voices to the management table does not always mean direct government control. The health and safety committees found in Quebec, Canada, further demonstrate how such legally mandated codetermination can be fostered on this side of the Atlantic.

In addition to national institutions, public planning would also require rethinking lower levels of government. Existing state and local governments do not always fit with the organization of economic activity. For example, actual economic development in most urban areas takes place at a regional level far larger than the political borders of each individual municipality's zoning board. While companies can undermine local living standards by moving overseas, they can also do similar damage by moving down the road to the next municipality. Similarly, most environmental issues play themselves out at a regional level. For years, activists involved in economic development and environmental issues have proposed various new regional public bodies capable of planning or influencing economic activity. The current political borders are not written in stone. In the late 1990s, the conservative government in Ontario, Canada, for example, pushed through an amalgamation in which the city of Toronto was joined with its surrounding suburbs to create one new municipality. Throughout the nineteenth and into the twentieth century, American cities grew by annexing surrounding communities. In this way, city boundaries often reflected the actual split between urban and rural areas. Another possibility lies in increasing the powers of county governments or establishing new regional forms of government, such as Portland's Metro authority. The proliferation of fragmented suburban municipalities that segregate people by income and race is a relatively recent phenomenon. Suburban America's political organization makes no sense in a larger economic picture.

Any progressive agenda for economic democracy has to tackle the major economic institution promoting low-road capitalism: American finance. As we have seen, few other industrialized countries are so dominated by its stock market. Our Wall Street's short time horizons institutionally promote low-road strategies with ever-increasing vigor and myopia. In addition to progressive taxation, a logical first place to start would be to give working people more control over the stock market resources that they already collectively own. Through their pension funds, American workers own more than $4 trillion in assets, including one-third of all corporate equities and 40 percent of corporate bonds. In 1992, pension funds became a larger source of finance than commercial banks.[9]

Currently, Americans are given no say over how their pension funds are used. Indeed, by law, pension funds must be treated as other market investments with fund managers seeking to maximize returns. However, for most Americans, having a high return for one's retirement income does not help if in the meantime one's employer is pushed to pursue low-road strategies. Labor organizations such as the Steelworkers and the AFL-CIO have begun to explore ways of providing workers more control over how their pension funds are used. For example, each year the AFL-CIO rates the investment advisors who manage and vote proxies for union pension funds. Already, the financial world includes progressive investment companies, such as Domini Social Funds, that not only screen the companies that they invest in, but engage in shareholder activism to promote environmental protection and social justice. National laws allowing workers to set criteria for their pension funds would not be much of a leap. Already state and local governments have experimented with ways of steering public employee pension funds in socially targeted directions. In addition to the social and environmental screens, pension investments could also be provided more options for pursuing alternative investment sources such as worker-owned companies and community-based development banks and microlending programs.

German history illustrates how deliberate government policy can build up a nation's banking sector at the expense of financial markets. And governments in Europe and Asia have shown how establishing greater public ownership over financial institutions can aid national economic planning. In many cases, private financial institutions were simply taken over by government policy. In the United States, a network of credit unions and socially oriented banks (such as Shore Bank) already exists. Public policy could protect and favor these institutions as well as place more assets at their disposal. At the same time, government regulations and tax policy could make financial speculation and short-term investment strategies far less profitable.

The nation also already has a diverse network of cooperatives and employee-owned companies. The fifteen-year-old Ohio Employee Ownership Center, for example, has helped more than 11,500 workers buy fifty-seven companies. The center offers training programs to educate workers in their responsibilities as co-owners. Building on the best of these examples, public policy could favor and encourage such innovations. Legal rights and access to resources, for example, could provide workers the right to assume control over workplaces and facilities closed or abandoned by their owners. At the same time, an expanding pool of government and public-controlled financial institutions could also consciously support such alternative businesses.

An Urban Future

The task of rebuilding America's cities provides a natural focal point for uniting the ideas discussed in this chapter. All of the economic activism that we have discussed in Part II is connected to our cities and towns. Revitalized urban areas are the natural home of strong grassroots institutions. They provide the physical base for enmeshing business operations in dense networks of cooperation and participation. They are also society's environmental future.

The fate of our cities is being decided now. Having abandoned many cities, corporation circles have recently developed renewed interest in an urban future. Unfortunately, such urban redevelopment comes in a corporate image. Large, sterile office buildings, upscale stores and homes, entertainment facilities to lure white suburbanites—these are the features of corporate-oriented cities. Little of this activity benefits low-income and working-class parts of town. Meanwhile, urban decay now eats away at the suburban inner ring.

The activism that we have profiled in this book raises a different urban possibility. Cities that unite with their working-class suburbs have the social movement forces and the voting strength to build a progressive movement for economic justice. The concepts of public standards, public wealth, and economic democracy can provide the building blocks of a new urban agenda. They point to an economy that reduces the realms of private business and establishes greater public authority and wealth. With a sustained progressive movement, our nation's towns and cities could become shining examples of vibrant communities built around public riches, broad partnerships, and the fulfillment of democratic ideals.

13
Progressive Electoral Politics

Ultimately economic change must link to political change. Indeed, it comes as no accident that examples of economic organizing that we examined often link to innovative progressive political action. For example, Massachusetts, Maine, Connecticut, and Minnesota not only boast active corporate accountability and contingent-worker efforts, but also model state-level electoral coalitions. While the new AFL-CIO leadership has identified organizing as its top priority, building effective political action comes a close second. Indeed, the dynamic central labor councils that have proven an engine behind the innovative economic organizing in Milwaukee and the South Bay area also provide examples of reinvigorated grassroots political action. The New Party played a central role in several living wage campaigns and Little Rock's antisprawl efforts. The rise of its spin-off—the Working Families Party of New York State—has fed directly into New York City's living wage campaign and efforts to raise the state's minimum wage. Vermont's Livable Wage Campaign similarly benefits from the political shifts brought about by the most successful state-level progressive independent politics in the country.

Europe's experience also highlights the connection between political action and economic change. During its heyday, social democracy both was an economic reform movement and political party. Indeed, the stark contrast between a more social democratic Europe and a free market–dominated United States ultimately lies in a political difference.

Europe's political system has strong left-wing parties formed out of labor and other movements: the United States does not. Similarly, Europe's current progressive impasse liess, in part, in the political crisis of the major left parties in losing a vision of fundamental progressive economic change.

In this final chapter, we profile the innovative electoral organizing that often accompanies progressive economic change. While the U.S. political system presents activists with an array of obstacles, a wealth of grassroots examples demonstrates how people can successfully organize for political change. Much of the material below is taken from our earlier book *Democracy Unbound: Progressive Challenges to the Two Party System*.[1]

The Obstacles: Why the U.S. Political Spectrum Tilts So Narrowly to the Right

Ask many pundits or mainstream political scientists why the United States is one of the few liberal democracies to have its politics monopolized by only two parties, and they will suggest that Americans are getting exactly what they want. The political priorities our middle-class society, we are told, revolves around are the "political center" on which both major parties orient their appeals. However, as we have seen throughout this book, issues such as living wages, corporate accountability, contingent work, sprawl, and so forth, have great appeal among the general public, yet are hardly embraced by the mainstream of either party. Indeed, a majority of Americans routinely express their lack of support for the current political system when they stay home on election day.

The truth is that, in comparison to other liberal democracies, the U.S. election system compromises the principles of representational democracy in several serious ways. Our country has some of the most restrictive ballot access laws in the world. Petition requirements vary considerably by state but can run into hundreds of thousands of needed signatures simply to qualify an individual candidacy. In order to bypass such time-consuming efforts, groups can achieve official party ballot status—thereby automatically having a ballot line for their candidates. However, the requirements are often set so high that fledgling parties can put all their energy into just meeting the requirements.[2] These hurdles offer a stark contrast to the often simple filing requirements common in many other countries.

American-style election campaigning is distinctly dominated by big money. Incumbents receive far more financial support than challengers, the major parties qualify for matching funds far easier than third parties, and wealthy individuals and corporations outspend progressive groups by wide margins. In 1992, fewer than 900,000 Americans gave a direct individual campaign contribution of $200 or more. Yet, that year, 81 percent of congressional campaign money came from these high amounts.[3] The power of money also translates into control of the media, through both direct corporate ownership and the media's reliance on advertising. Even when a progressive candidate is able to force the national media to acknowledge his or her campaign, the coverage will, at best, get out fragments of a progressive agenda. When Jesse Jackson ran for president in 1984 and 1988, the corporate media was unable to ignore him. However, the coverage largely ignored his agenda, instead informing voters day after day why he could not seriously win.[4] The United States is one of the few nations to rely on private funding and coverage of its elections. In Europe and Canada, for example, public financing and subsidized or free media time are standard features.

The single greatest structural obstacle to an independent progressive politics, however, comes from our country's winner-take-all, single-district elections. Rather than choosing our representatives by the kind of proportional systems that allow small, infant parties a voice in state and national legislatures, the United States is one of a handful of countries that breaks down representation into separate single-member districts. Be it for U.S. Congress, state legislatures, or local government, voters are represented only if their candidate wins. Thus, for example, the U.S. Greens cannot win office by winning 5 to 10 percent of the general vote. Instead, to actually elect anyone, they have to focus on specific geographical districts where they can win the largest block of voters. By contrast, the German Greens made world headlines in the early 1980s after they won over 5 percent of the country's voters, because this threshold qualified them for proportional seats in the national legislature. Not only has proportional representation provided the German Greens far greater public visibility, but also for years they have been part of coalition governments in several state-level parliaments. In 1998, the Social Democrats returned to national power with the Greens as part of their governing coalition.

Proportional representation is clearly a more democratic system than our winner-take-all methods. In the United States, the preferences of only those voters lucky enough to back the winning candidate are represented in our legislatures. This fact, when coupled with data showing that a majority of Americans do not vote, leads to alarming statistics revealing that only between 12 percent and 35 percent of those registered to vote actually chose the person who sat from their district in the 1994–1996 Congress.[5] With its inability to represent a minority of voters, the winner-take-all system is easily used to exclude blacks and other people of color. Despite decades of drawing election boundaries to marginalize such voters and ensure white majorities, the Supreme Court only recently discovered "racial gerrymandering" when it struck down North Carolina's new 21st district—one drawn explicitly to provide African-American voters greater representation in Congress. The shameful limitations of the winner-take-all system are clearly reflected by the fact that only two other countries, Jamaica and Canada, use it as the exclusive mechanism in their electoral systems.[6]

While proportional representation can also be used by the right, the experience of every major industrial country makes clear that such systems favor organized left parties. Indeed, a party whose origins come out of the labor movement is a central political player in all these countries. Furthermore, our two-party system is already oriented so far to the right that the left side represents the clear growth area. Indeed, years of research on voting in the United States consistently reveals a class and race bias among nonvoters that represents the left's natural constituency.

While winner-takes-all elections pose a major barrier, experience in other countries suggests that by themselves, they do not totally block independent success. In Canada, the lack of proportional representation did not stop the New Democratic Party from bringing greater social democracy to that country. Even without ever taking national power, the New Democrats used their grassroots organizing, provincial-level victories, and minority seats in the national legislature to help put in place progressive reforms such as a national health care system. While valuable lessons can be learned from the current crisis of the New Democrats, we should not forget their achievements. Similarly, the early Mitterrand government's ultimate abandonment of its radical platform in France should not obscure the fact that it came to power in 1981 on a strong left platform in a country that also did not have proportional representation at that time. The French Socialists were also able to build their electoral coalition despite having one of the structurally weakest labor movements in Europe—both numerically modest and

sharply divided into three competing federations. Obviously, the United States is not Canada or France. The point is that structural barriers alone cannot account for the seeming absence of a strong progressive voice in the official U.S. political spectrum. The contrast between Canada and the United States, for example, revolves more around the past relative willingness of each country's major unions to support or not support third-party organizing.

Strategies for Progressive Electoral Organizing Within an American Context

While the undemocratic mechanisms built into the current U.S. election system represent serious challenges, the greatest obstacle to a progressive success is not external but internal. Years of past frustration and a massive amount of two-party propaganda have convinced many grassroots activists and intellectuals that politics is simply a waste of time. At the same time, as a legacy of liberal interest-group politics, many progressive organizations traditionally have focused their electoral activism narrowly on political work within the Democratic Party—action restricted largely to fundraising and get-out-the-vote activities. Yet, clear strategies exist for successfully organizing within our existing political environment. These methods are the same regardless of whether progressives organize inside or outside the Democratic Party. The broad outlines of organizing contain six proven ingredients: movement politics, bottom-up organizing, long time horizons, coalition building, electoral flexibility, and popular economics.

Movement Politics

Political projects that simply copy the activities of the two major parties are doomed to failure. It is a great myth, however, that our current media-driven, advertising-style of campaigns represent the only way to conduct elections. The historical origins of current practices came not from technological innovations such as television, as it is often assumed, but from political struggles. Indeed, historians have traced the first modern forms of electioneering to the turn of the twentieth century—an era prior to television and radio. During this period, the two-party system battled powerful populist and socialist challenges. In addition to often violent and illegal actions, the two major parties defeated this challenge by reorienting political activity away from the grassroots and toward a more money-driven advertising brand of electoral action. Yet, the old grassroots techniques still work. In organizing for political change, progressives must look toward their own social movement traditions, rather than professional campaign managers, for long-range models. The basic staple of progressive activism generally—door-to-door, round the year, grassroots, issue-driven organizing—applies to electoral politics as well.

With a majority of Americans staying home on election day, the key to winning lasting political power in this country lies in remobilizing a demobilized electorate. The largest party in this country is literally neither the Democrats nor the Republicans, but the party of nonvoters. Nonvoting comes as the legacy of the defeat of populism and socialism when the two major parties deliberately purged roughly half of the electorate to remove the progressive voting base from the rolls. Today, both scholarly research and practical experience suggest that the advertising style of elections generally fails to inspire increased voter turnout. Indeed, the prevalence of negative campaign ads appears to simply foster cynicism and low voter participation. Having an inspiring, positive candidate, however, is not enough. In 1988, Jesse Jackson won over seven million votes not just because of his progressive message, but also because literally tens of thousands of volunteers organized in their communities to get people to the polls using classic-style door-to-door campaigning.[7] In nearly every case where progressive candidates win election, voter turnout has increased.

Build from the Ground Up

Ironically, today's most successful progressive political projects are the ones that receive the least attention because they are active in arenas other than the one focused on by the media's pundits. All too often, progressives follow the media's lead in looking to national politics as their focal point for political change. Yet, a long list of progressive reforms—from women's suffrage, to the minimum wage, to the abolition of slavery, to the two-day weekend—all began with victories at the local and state level. Right-wing groups such as the Christian Coalition have well realized the effectiveness of building from the ground up by fostering active local groups around targeted issue and election campaigns.

Local elections should provide the bread and butter of progressive activism. The vast majority of all these contests are nonpartisan. With no party label on the ballot, a candidacy can hardly be stigmatized as "hopeless" if it comes from a third party. Where a party line does appear on the ballot, the Democratic primary may prove to be the actual election, especially in Democratic urban strongholds. Local contests generally are the most readily open to grassroots organizing by fledgling groups. And these offices hold power over decisions in such areas as school curriculum, zoning, labor standards, civil rights, and economic development that have a major impact on people's lives. Winning even the most local of races or changing very local policies can allow new progressive projects to establish themselves as serious, winning political efforts that people want to join.

Long-term Strategy

"It has taken the Left a long time to get in the bad situation we are in today," explains Dan Cantor, staff person for the Working Families Party. "It is going to take a long time for us to organize out of it." While social movements may experience periods in which they appear to explode onto the scene, the historical details of such mass events as the great labor organizing wave of 1936–1937 or the mushrooming civil rights struggle of the 1950s and 1960s reveal many years of slow, often only partially successful, organizing—work that laid the seeds for the mass awakenings that followed. To remobilize the apathetic majority, a progressive political project must reestablish grassroots channels for people to experience politics. This bottom-up, movement-oriented political strategy requires patient step-by-step efforts aimed at fostering an ever-growing array of active local groups. Our winner-take-all election system helps ensure that most electoral expressions of progressive activism will come as periods of patient organizing followed by seemingly sudden breakthroughs once progressives cross the threshold into electoral pluralities.

A long-term strategy compels organizers to rethink their definitions of success. Conventional political wisdom does not take any political project seriously that does not contest for national political power. Yet, between where progressives are now and sitting in the Oval Office is an entire spectrum of potential political gains. As we have seen in Part II, local and state governments set policies that have a major impact on people's lives. They offer crucial paths to demonstrating progressive policy alternatives. Furthermore, a political project does not have to govern outright in order to impact public policy and debate. Electing a few people to a local or state legislative body may not establish a progressive majority, but it does give activists clear champions who can provide critical support to movement-style issue campaigns seeking to change public policy.

Coalition Building

To be seen as serious and to gain access to the resource levels needed to sustain ongoing grassroots organizing, progressive political projects must draw in a broad spectrum of local progressive groups. Most progressives are quite frustrated with the state of American electoral politics. The key to gaining their active support is offering believable projects that do not waste their time. Organizers must understand where different groups currently stand in their strategic understanding. A political project must in turn offer these groups a course of action that represents a next logical step in their political development.

Political Flexibility

The tasks of coalition building and patient, bottom-up organizing requires a level of political flexibility that has proven quite controversial. Many activists seek to declare their political independence first, draw up a detailed political platform next, and then go out to try to organize mass support. Very often such a straightforward approach fails, however, because it does not fit with local conditions. Electoral organizing must grow out of the local matrix of political opportunities and potential progressive coalition partners. Ultimately, the goal of progressive political change is best served by strategies that successfully promote active movement building, rather than those that dogmatically draw the clearest political battle lines.

Because of the distinct nature of the U.S. political system, progressive politics must have an evolving relationship with the Democratic Party—one that adapts to local situations. In some cases, the best course of action is to run candidates as independents or on a third-party ballot line. However, in most of the cases covered in this book, the Democratic Party has been the main channel for progressive electoral activism. The winner-take-all system may simply compel activists to capture the Democratic ballot line for situations in which blurred electoral success proves far more valuable than independent failure. Fledgling groups, for example, can benefit enormously from the experience of simply running a successful election campaign. Placing progressive champions in public office, regardless of the ballot line on which they ran, can also provide a crucial tool for pushing a grassroots issue agenda that receives public attention.

Furthermore, most politically active progressive

groups today remain committed to their traditional ties to the Democratic Party. Any political strategy, for example, that seeks to draw in organized labor must recognize most unions' firm commitment to the Democratic ballot line. Political organizers must have a strategy for interacting with those genuinely committed progressive individuals and groups who have operated within the Democratic Party for years simply because it traditionally has been the only game in town. Throwing down a one-dimensional "us or them" gauntlet will simply marginalize progressive organizers.

Popular Economics

While a progressive political agenda must span many issues, the problem of corporate power and the call for economic democracy provides the unifying rallying cry of progressive politics, just as it has rallied the campaigns covered in this book. It comes as no accident that both major parties have agreed to keep corporate power as the best-kept secret in the official national debate. They are clearly sitting on top of a potential volcano. With the standard of living of most Americans having stagnated or fallen in the past two decades, a majority of people repeatedly tell pollsters that economic issues top their concerns. Challenging corporate power offers the common issue for uniting a broad majority.

Progressive Politics Today

The above strategies can be illustrated through three dimensions of political organizing that various progressive groups are pursuing today: nonpartisan campaigns to change the political rules, organizing within the Democratic Party, and progressive third parties.

Changing the Rules

The structural obstacles that maintain the two-party system can also be used as organizing tools to build progressive activism. We should remember that the major left-wing parties in Europe originally organized in a context of fighting for the basic right to vote.

In New Zealand in the early 1990s, a coalition of small third parties helped win a public referendum that changed the nation's election system from winner take all to a German-style proportional representation model. In the United States, the Center for Voting and Democracy operates as a clearinghouse for progressive efforts to enact proportional representation reforms. The winner-take-all system is not part of the U.S. Constitution. Rather, voting systems are selected by federal and state law.

Certainly a wealth of different voting options exists. Among the world's countries, the party-list system is the most commonly used. Each party receives a number of seats in a legislature based on the proportion of votes received. The actual representatives sent by each party are selected in top-down order from a list that each party provides during the election season. Typically, parties have to cross a threshold of votes (such as 2 to 5 percent) in order to achieve seats. By contrast, instant runoff voting provides a method in which voters still elect an individual, not a party. Under this system, voters rank their choices from most desirable to least. If their top choice is not among the top contenders, the vote count drops this candidate and adds those voters' second choice to the totals. The process continues until one candidate has won a majority. Instant runoff voting allows voters to choose their genuine choice first and the "lesser evil" second. Another voting system would allow several representatives to be chosen by combining current electoral districts. By still allowing each voter to choose only one candidate, the several member delegations from the combined district would reflect the top preferences of several rather than one voting block.

Some of these systems are already in use. Cambridge, Massachusetts, uses instant runoff voting for all local elections. Not surprisingly, the community has experienced higher voter turnout than the similar neighboring communities of Somerville,

Medford, and Worcester, which do not use this system. Legal action has forced local communities to enact some form of proportional representation. In 1992, for example, the NAACP filed suit against Atlanta, Texas. The town's winner-take-all election had helped ensure that no African American had ever won a seat on the community's five-member school board—despite a black population of over 20 percent. In the final settlement, town authorities agreed to a form of proportional representation that allowed Veloria Nanze to win election in 1995. Today, over fifty Texas communities have adopted similar systems. Where political contests present close margins, interest in election reform has increased. If not passed by the legislature before then, in 2002 Alaskans will vote on a ballot initiative to bring instant runoff to all state elections. The measure is supported by Republicans concerned with splits in the conservative vote as well as progressive activists. Legislators in New Mexico, Vermont, Washington, and California will also consider instant runoff reforms in the near future. In 2000, California voters approved instant runoff charter reforms in Oakland and San Leandro.

In the past several years, state-level coalitions have scored several major victories to reform the funding of elections. In 1996, voters in Maine passed the nation's first law establishing public financing for state elections. Because the Supreme Court has equated money with "free speech," passing legislation to outright ban private campaign contributions risks constitutional challenge. By contrast, the Maine Clean Election law established a public alternative. Under the new system a candidate for state office who voluntarily agrees to not collect further private contributions has their election campaign financed by a public fund. The amounts are set by past candidate spending levels and are generally comparable to those of privately funded candidates. To qualify for the public financing, the candidate must first show that he or she is serious by collecting a modest number of contributions in small amounts (such as $25). The candidate also has to agree to public debates and other socially responsible criteria. The system not only helps progressive candidates fund their campaigns, but it also sets up a potentially interesting set of campaign issues between candidates funded by the public purse and those who are beholden to private contributors.

Progressives have taken up the Clean Election model in several other states. Since the Maine win, Public Campaign has coordinated efforts across the country to enact similar laws. In 1998, voters in Massachusetts and Arizona passed Clean Election laws. Soon thereafter Vermont's state legislature enacted a similar measure. Unfortunately, November 2000 delivered two setbacks when clean election ballot initiatives lost in Oregon and Missouri. However, 2000 also marked the first election in which Maine, Arizona, and Vermont's laws were in effect. In Maine, one-third of the new legislature will take office as candidates who ran on public, rather than private, funds. Maine's 2000 elections also saw a 40 percent increase in the number of contested primaries and a noticeable increase in the number of women running for office. In 2001, Paul Wellstone (MN) introduced a Clean Election law into the Senate—helping further build grassroots interest in Clean Election reforms. Massachusetts's law will take effect in 2002. Building on its success around corporate accountability, MAPA is now well into a multiyear campaign to pass a clean election law in Minnesota.

Building a Party with the Democratic Party

From a progressive standpoint, the problem with the two major parties is not just their corporate policies, but the fact that they do not function like political parties in the classic sense of the term. Mass parties should provide a vehicle for people to debate political issues, mobilize within their communities, cultivate candidates, develop concrete agendas, and hold their elected officials accountable to these agendas. As organizations, however, both major U.S. parties do little of this activity. Instead, the Republicans and

Democrats function as loose federations of candidate-centered networks. Their focus is on individual campaigns and the funding and media spin needs of an advertising brand of politics. While this model of political work is suited for elite parties, it is the bane of real people-centered grassroots politics.

Because mainstream election work revolves around candidates, it organizationally leaves both parties as hollow shells vulnerable to take over at a local level. The Christian Coalition saw the possibilities within the Republican Party. By building a genuine grassroots structure within Republican ranks, the coalition was able to take over local and state party organizations throughout the country. One 1994 estimate placed the Christian Coalition in control of Republican state committees in at least twelve states. Their strategy reflected a right-wing version of the elements outlined above: Start at the local level, build on core issues, tap movement organizations, and develop grassroots activists. The coalition also made extensive use of "stealth" candidates who hid their Christian Coalition connections.

The AFL-CIO's New Politics

Fortunately, progressive examples of organization building within the Democratic Party are even more prevalent. Nationally, the AFL-CIO has reoriented its political strategy over the last several years. Shortly after Sweeney's election, the federation commissioned a study on the political views and actions of union members. Through surveys and focus groups, researchers found that most union members were turned off to both their union's political work and, like most Americans, politics generally. Many members also resented their union telling them whom to vote for. Apathy, however, did not mean a lack of concern. The study also found that most union members had strong issue concerns that matched closely with their union's political priorities. The overall lesson was straightforward. To revive its electoral work, the labor movement needed to talk less about candidates and more about the issues. And unions needed to take the political conversation down into the workplace with members talking to other members.

Beginning in 1996, the AFL-CIO began to shift its electoral operations. Less money was given to candidates as more went into issue ads and grassroots organizers. Individual unions have also begun to reorient toward a more grassroots electoral action. In 2000, for example, he worked with District 2 of the Steelworkers to established a systematic worker-to-worker mobilization for the state of Michigan. In the spring, participating local unions surveyed their membership to identify their issue priorities and to ask members how they preferred to receive political information. Throughout the summer and fall, the district developed information flyers around the issues identified by members (Social Security, health care, taxes, education, etc.). To take this information one-on-one into the workplace, it trained a network of workplace leaders to build grassroots volunteer networks. As the election neared, the flyers compared candidates on the variety of issue concerns.

While the model is still only beginning to take hold among the nation's various unions, such issue-based, worker-to-worker politics already has shown early signs of results. Over the past several elections, union members have turned out to vote in numbers far above the national averages. As a result, the portion of voters who are union members grew from 14 percent in 1994 to 22 percent in 1998, according to AFL-CIO figures. More union voters means clear Democratic gains. Statistics compiled by the AFL-CIO for 1998 showed that while roughly 70 percent of nonunion white men voted for Republicans, the same portion of union white men voted Democratic. Picking apart the famous "gender gap" in which women lean more heavily toward the Democrats reveals that it is union women that account for the leaning. Union leaders have argued that the increased union turnouts over the last several elections were the central factor in the steady erosion of the Republican congressional majority. For example, thanks to the Michigan AFL-CIO and the individual unions who developed worker-to-worker programs, nearly half of the November 2000 voters in the state came from union households even though less than a quarter of the workforce is unionized. As a result, the closely contested state went for Gore, and Democrat Debbie Stabenow became a U.S. Senator.

Getting out the union vote for Democratic candidates, however, is not enough. Ultimately, labor needs candidates who will articulate an agenda that inspires its grassroots. In the 1980s, unions lost the political loyalties of a significant block of their members when the weak liberalism of the reigning Democrats did not provide a convincing alternative to Ronald Reagan's politics of division. Centrist Democrats of the Bill Clinton style hardly offer an improvement.

Part of the answer lies in the labor movement becoming more involved in recruiting and training of candidates. Rather than waiting to endorse the "lesser evil," unions can develop candidates from within their own ranks of people willing and able to run for office. The AFL-CIO set and achieved the goal of running 2000 union members for office by the year 2000. The bulk of these people launched their political careers by running for local offices that are both accessible and most open to newcomers. At the same time, the many grassroots issue campaigns covered in this book provide ample material for an electoral agenda.

State Progressive Electoral Coalitions

Changes with the national orientation of the AFL-CIO have their predecessor in several state-level coalitions in which labor and community groups united around political change. Indeed, several of the economic campaigns covered in this book are the action agenda counterparts of state progressive electoral coalitions. The corporate accountability efforts in Connecticut, Minnesota, and Maine have partner coalitions in the Legislative and Electoral Action Program (LEAP), Pro-Vote, and the Dirigo Alliance. The Massachusetts campaign around contingent work is linked to the Common Wealth Coalition. Of these electoral projects, the founding model coalition comes from Connecticut's LEAP.

By the early 1980s, many progressive activists in Connecticut were fed up with politics as usual. More and more of the candidates they were asked to endorse were not strong enough to win. Or even worse, if elected, they did not act much different than their conservative opponents did. With the key support of the UAW's region 1A and the Connecticut Citizen Action Group, organizers decided to build an alternative. By forming LEAP, these organizations created a formal coalition that actively recruited progressive candidates from among the ranks of member organizations to run in Democratic Party primaries for state offices. For those willing to become candidates, the LEAP office provided campaign training while the member organizations pooled their fund-raising and volunteer power.

The end result was the most successful state-level labor community in the country. By the mid-1990s, roughly a third of all the Democrats in the Connecticut legislature were LEAP candidates. They included such people as retired autoworkers, union organizers, and women's rights activists. LEAP also proved a key vehicle for politically empowering the state's Puerto Rican community. In 1994, the year of the so-called Republican Revolution, LEAP defied the pundits. Twenty-five out of thirty-five of their candidates for state office won. These victories included Miles Rappenport, former Connecticut Citizen Action Group director who became the Secretary of State running on a platform of fundamental campaign finance reform. Although LEAP activist William Curry lost in the general election, the coalition nevertheless scored a major upset earlier that year when he defeated the party establishment's candidate in the Democratic primary for governor.

LEAP's model spread throughout New England and to other parts of the country. In 1996, LEAP and its spin-off coalitions helped elect New Hampshire's first woman governor, oust five incumbent Republican members of Congress, and swing four state legislatures to Democratic control. Progressive candidates with activist support have proven more effective than the Democratic Leadership Council's "centrist" Democrats. New England's labor-community coalitions were the organizing force behind the Clean Election laws in Maine and Massachusetts. Minnesota Pro-Vote was founded as an electoral coalition vehicle to complement the legislative and policy actions of MAPA.

LEAP and its spin-offs operate as much as a lobbying arm as an electoral tool. Thus, for example, when the legislature debated a global warming bill, the assigned subcommittee not only found itself sitting across from the "usual suspects" among environmental organizations, but also groups like the UAW as well. This coalition lobbying has included "street heat" when, for example, the UAW marched in a demonstration for gay and lesbian civil rights. Cooperation has also extended well beyond the halls of the legislature. When one thousand members of UAW Local 376 struck Colt Firearms, they faced an uphill battle against a hostile, concession-demanding employer. However, through LEAP and related experiences, the union was able to pull together effective community support that proved critical to winning the strike. In short, participation in LEAP-style political work provides a wide array of progressive groups an important channel to further their own specific work as well as the work of building a stronger progressive movement generally.

The current evolution of New England's labor-community coalitions also reflects many of the elements that we outlined above. Today, activists point toward two dimensions for future growth. First, they need to move beyond political platforms that simply gather together each member group's concerns into a kind of "laundry" list of progressive issues. To counter right-wing politics, progressives need more comprehensive, proactive, and majority-seeking agendas. This agenda revolves around challenging corporate power. Hence the organizing around contingent work and a Corporate Code of Conduct directly links to electoral work.[8]

LEAP-style politics has operated as a coalition of organizations, not building a membership body in its own right. LEAP's track record shows that much can be achieved through such a structure in a relatively short period of time. However, LEAP's coalition of organizations must rely on each group to mobilize its own membership behind progressive campaigns. Within such campaigns, the experiences of many volunteers can remain within their own group. And LEAP has no direct mechanism of its own to involve the vast ranks of people not connected to any progressive organization. Facing these considerations, some New England activists have begun considering the development of a grassroots structure.

Local Applications

The party-within-a-party strategy also has application at the local level. Given the innovative economic initiatives covered in chapter 8, it comes as no surprise that the Milwaukee County Labor Council has developed an aggressive worker-to-worker election program, has begun to recruit worker candidates, and has developed a forward-looking legislative program. The same is true of the South Bay Central Labor Council for whom reenergized political action is seen as the complement of its economic activism. Indeed, the passage of San Jose's living wage law developed amid a successful campaign to hold on to a key city council seat. Labor and its allies mounted one of the strongest get-out-the-vote operations in District 3's history when the living wage become a central issue between the union-backed incumbent and the anti–living wage opponent. The incumbent won by two hundred votes. Two weeks after the election, the living wage ordinance passed by a strong 8–3 vote.

Building a New Progressive
Political Party

The party-within-a-party strategy is by far the more common model. It fits with the traditional Democratic politics practiced by a wide range of progressive organizations ever since the New Deal coalition of the 1930s. However, in an ideal world, progressives should be able to do what the labor movement accomplished in most major industrialized countries: form its own political parties. As we covered above, the U.S. political system presents serious structural obstacles to such an undertaking. However, the biggest barrier is internal. Simply put, most progressive organizations with the resources to develop a new party are unwilling to invest their energy in a break with the Democratic Party. Any would-be third-party project has to confront this reluctance head on. In the 1990s, three major national projects attempted to offer a solution.

The New Party

Launched in 1992 with the help of ACORN, the New Party sought to build progressive interest by blending third-party organizing with concrete, doable electoral and policy actions. By the end of 1998, the New Party had established a record of two hundred victories out of the first three hundred races entered. The party had active chapters in a dozen states including Arkansas; Illinois; Maryland; Massachusetts; Minnesota; Missouri; Montana; New Jersey; New York; Oregon; Washington, DC; and Wisconsin.

The New Party's activity was rooted in three key strategies. First, the New Party only mounted races and campaigns that it had a chance to win. Party activists rejected purely "educational" campaigns on the grounds that key progressive organizations would not place their energy into efforts perceived as a waste of time. Reflecting the electoral opportunities, most New Party campaigns focused on local, mostly nonpartisan, races.

Second, New Party chapters linked electoral campaigns to grassroots policy action. Indeed, early on, the New Party emerged as the national political organization most experienced in the then-emerging living wage movement. In Little Rock, the New Party was a key partner in activist campaigns around sprawl,

living wages, affordable housing, and so forth. In other parts of the country, New Party chapters played leading roles in battles over police accountability, campaign finance reform, local spending priorities, land use, and public school reform. Such issue campaigns allowed New Party activists to build relationships with other progressive groups and establish the local party chapter as more than simply a protest group. In Chicago, for example, the New Party scored a major victory in 1999 when its chair, Ted Thomas, won election to the city's Board of Aldermen. Several years of living wage activism had built relations with several unions and community organizations that proved key in mustering the people power necessary to defeat the powerful Democratic machine. Those same relationships had helped the New Party in 1998 elect Willie Delgado to the Illinois State Assembly and Michael Chandler as an alderman.

The most controversial aspect of New Party strategy, however, has been its willingness to use ballot line flexibility. While most New Party campaigns were for local nonpartisan offices, roughly one out of five candidacies came through partisan contests in which local chapters entered Democratic primaries. While using the Democratic ballot line blurred political distinctions, New Party organizers saw this tactic as necessary to mount candidacies that would be taken seriously by key progressive groups. For example, through its electoral flexibility, the New Party was able to go to local unions and ask them to support specific winnable candidacies, rather than make a wholesale break with their traditional Democratic political action work. As local New Party chapters gained success, they hoped to build stronger ties and credibility with local unions—becoming increasingly relevant vehicles for union political work. New Party leaders similarly saw electoral flexibility as key to building a multiracial organization that attracted people of color. A significant number of the New Party candidates elected as Democrats were people of color, such as Congressman Danny Davis. While Davis joined the New Party and agreed to promote it, he ran as a Democrat. In the one-party system of Chicago, challenging the machine-endorsed candidate in a Democratic primary was in itself a bold undertaking. Running independently at the current stage would have been altogether political suicide. By having the flexibility to go with the logic of the local situation, the New Party won a major upset in Chicago politics and furthered its grassroots organizing within the black community.

In seeking a flexible ballot line path to attract traditional core Democratic political players, the New Party hoped to revive the old tactic of fusion by which a candidate runs on two or more ballot lines. Such a tactic would allow a third party to endorse progressive Democrats. Voters could then both choose a winning candidate and show their third-party preferences by voting for that person on the third party's ballot line. Using fusion, a third party could also have its candidates win access to the Democratic ballot line. In the late nineteenth century, the Populists used fusion tactics to win control of legislatures in states such as Kansas. The tactic, however, was also part of populism's death knell when it led to the 1896 endorsement of Democrat William Jennings Bryan for U.S. president. In reaction to populism, most states outlawed fusion. New Party organizers hoped to revive fusion by means of a legal challenge. In 1997, the party won a lower court ruling declaring state bans on fusion illegal. Had the ruling held and fusion been reopened across the country, New Party organizers would have tried to translate the interest that they had won from unions and other progressive groups into concrete alliances. Hopes were dashed the following year, however, when the U.S. Supreme Court overturned the ruling, using arguments that nakedly defended the two-party system.

The year 1998 marked a high point in New Party activism. Party leaders split over the question of the extent to which organizing could further expand in the face of the Supreme Court defeat. Key leaders most tied to fusion tactics decided to turn their attention to build the Working Families Party in New York—one of a few states to allow fusion. While today New Party chapters remain active players in

communities where deep roots were sunk—such as Little Rock, Madison, Chicago, Montgomery County, and Missoula—its national growth and organization appear to have peaked.

The Labor Party

In 1991, the Oil, Chemical and Atomic Workers union formed Labor Party Advocates (LPA) to build support for a third party within the labor movement. In 1996, over fifteen hundred delegates assembled in Cleveland to formally launch the Labor Party. Unlike the New Party, both LPA and the Labor Party rejected any use of the Democratic ballot line and stressed third-party independence. To avoid forcing unions to choose between political allegiances, the Labor Party focused on nonelectoral work. Party leaders argued that they could not successfully ask unions to endorse Labor Party candidates until the party has sufficient grassroots strength to mount believable efforts. Not until 1998 did the party even have a mechanism for entering elections, and to date no candidate has run as a Labor Party candidate.

By avoiding actual election campaigns, the Labor Party was able to maintain a firm stance for independent political action and at the same time gain endorsements from significant sections of the labor movement. By May 1998, almost 250 local unions and regional labor bodies had endorsed the Labor Party. The list included the Oil, Chemical and Atomic Workers, the United Electrical Workers, the Longshoremen, the Brotherhood of Maintenance of Way Employees, the United Mine Workers, the American Federation of Government Employees, the Farm Labor Organizing Committee, the California State Nurses Association, the UNITE Midwest Regional Joint Board, several central labor councils, and several smaller national unions. Unions such as the SEIU had not formally endorsed the Labor Party, but lent financial and other support.

The inability of the national Labor Party to grow beyond these promising seeds highlights the dilemma between desiring to build a truly independent political party and the need to win over labor leaders who view third-party activism as a waste of time and a threat to their traditional Democratic work. Generally speaking, the Labor Party has not been able to develop nonelectoral projects capable of translating union interest into strong grassroots action and broad chapter building. Indeed, the national party has sponsored activities that have been largely educational. It has been noticeably absent from the currents of economic activism covered in this book. Between 1996 and 1998, for example, the Labor Party sponsored an educational campaign around an amendment to the U.S. Constitution recognizing a right to a job at a decent wage. The project, however, did not provide enough concrete appeal to foster strong grassroots action.

A subsequent Just Health Care campaign, however, has revealed more promise as local groups have used the project to some success. During the 2000 elections, for example, in one State Senatorial and two State Representative districts, the Massachusetts Labor Party won voter approval for a ballot question calling for a single-payer health insurance system for the state. The Massachusetts Party also won 2–1 voter approval in six State Representative districts for a referendum calling for an end to required high-stakes testing of high school students. Through these ballot activities, the Massachusetts Labor Party has become an active part of MassCare—a coalition that has led the fight for single payer. MassCare and senior citizen organizations took part in collecting the signatures to place the health care measure on the ballot and campaigning for its passage. A successful third party needs such issue-driven coalition politics as a foundation for successful growth.

The Greens

Like the Labor Party, the various Green groups have also focused on third-party independence. For a decade, Greens have run for office. In doing so, they have been able to draw on their connections to a worldwide Green movement. As mentioned in chap-

ter 5, Green parties have become a lasting part of the European landscape.

How to adapt Green politics to the U.S. political terrain animated activist discussions throughout the 1990s and fostered a certain fragmentation among the U.S. Greens. The issues included how to balance issue politics and election campaigns, what kinds of races Green candidates should enter, where to get the resources to sustain organizational momentum, and how to relate to the Democratic Party. Generally speaking, the most successful of the Green groups followed the elements we outlined above.

The California Greens, for example, have run slates that included electing activists to local office, built coalitions with progressive groups, fostered active local chapters, and planned for long-term organizing. They scored the first election of a third-party candidate to their state legislature since 1917 when Audie Bock won the 16th Assembly district. Following the election of a Green council majority in 1996, Arcata, California, became the first city in the nation to pass popular referenda on corporate power. The new law establishes two town meetings around the theme of "Can we have democracy when large corporations wield so much power and wealth under the law?" and mandates that the city council pursue mechanisms for increasing public control over corporate activity within the city.

Overall, the Greens have sent over one hundred activists to elected or appointed offices. In states such as Alaska and New Mexico, Green candidates have shown an ability to secure enough votes that they have compelled the Democrats to take an active interest in instant runoff elections. However, in many parts of the country, Green politics remains marginal as local Green groups run for offices for which they have no ability to win more than a small percentage of the vote. The new century, however, has brought promising signs. By 2000, the major competing currents of Green electoral activism had worked out many of their differences, and the movement appeared headed toward greater operational unity. Ralph Nader's 2000 presidential campaign brought a significant boost to Green organizing. Roughly 250,000 volunteers, especially young people, worked on his campaign. While he received under 3 percent of the vote, 2.7 million people did vote for Nader and polls suggest that another seven million saw him as their top choice but instead voted for the "lesser evil." The key to Nader's potential impact lies in the ability of the Greens to translate the grassroots interest shown in 2000 into active, ongoing Green organizations. In 2000, the Greens were able to add Massachusetts, Montana, Minnesota, Rhode Island, and Texas to their state organizations with official ballot status. Nader has also continued to campaign—using his popularity to bring together people in forums for building grassroots organization.

Vermont

Vermont illustrates how quickly the political balance can shift once the proper seeds have been planted and external conditions fall into place. Burlington, Vermont, had been a staunch Democratic town. In several districts, Republicans did not even bother to run challengers. Yet, in 1981, by a plurality of only ten votes, independent and socialist Bernie Sanders became Burlington's new mayor. A year later, the stonewalling tactics used by the Democratic and Republican city council members against Sanders backfired when voters kicked out all but one of the Democrats up for reelection and increased Sanders's independent supporters to five. Since then, the Progressive Coalition, as it is now called, has become the dominant force in city politics—electing the mayor and the largest block on the city council almost unbroken since that time. In 1990, Sanders moved on to Congress by defeating the incumbent Republican by a landslide margin of sixteen points. He remains there today despite concerted efforts by the Republicans to unseat him.

Progressive election wins came through volunteer-intensive, door-to-door grassroots politics that produced clear increases in voter turnout. And while the "hippie" activist Vermont may have contributed to campaign organizing, the progressive vote has come on the strength of solid class politics among Vermont's working-class voters. Progressive success also involved a long electoral evolution. Sanders spent four terms as a mayor of the state's largest city before winning national office. His statewide campaigns were also aided by the internal evolution of the Vermont Rainbow Coalition. By 1986, the organization had become disillusioned with two-party politics. When Sanders ran as an independent for governor that year, he lost the race but picked up the Rainbow Coalition as a cofounder of the statewide Progressive Coalition. Sanders's unsuccessful campaign for Congress in 1988 also helped pave the way for eventual victory by drawing in crucial labor and other progressive support. Although Sanders lost, he established his credentials as the only viable alternative to the Republicans—the Democrat received only 3 percent of the vote. In the next election voters sent Sanders to Congress where he remains today. Congressman Sanders has used his staff resources and notoriety to foster further coalition building among Vermont's fragmented progressive groups. He is also a founder of Congress's fifty-member Progressive Caucus.

The future prospects of the Progressive Coalition further underline the importance of movement building for the long term. To found an outright political party, Progressive organizers felt they needed to establish a clear block of Progressive representatives in the state legislature. The rapid electoral breakthroughs in Burlington in the early 1980s opened the way for Progressives to fill up to three legislative seats from that area. However, building a political base in other parts of the state has compelled the Progressive Coalition to return to patient, long-range base building as activists attempt to translate the statewide Sanders vote into active and lasting local chapters. In 2000, organizers finally launched the official Progressive Party of Vermont. Using public funds, provided by the state's Clean Election law, the party's candidate for governor, Anthony Pollina, gained 10 percent of the vote. More voters likely favored Pollina but chose the lesser evil. Pollina's vote included clear progressive gains among Republican voters. His campaign also established the Progressive Party as a legitimate player in official state politics. Also, not surprisingly, Vermont state legislators are now seriously considering instant runoff elections.

New York's Working Families Party

The recently formed Working Families Party illustrates what the New Party had hoped to revive nationwide with fusion. New York not only is one of a few states to allow fusion, but also has an active tradition of cross-endorsements and active minor parties. With key support from CWA, UAW, Teamsters, the Buffalo Teachers Federation, ACORN, and the New Party, the Working Families Party was founded in 1998 and won ballot status that same year when over fifty thousand voters selected the Democratic Party nominee for governor on the Working Families Party ballot line.

The Working Families Party aims to build up an organizational political voice for working people while avoiding asking its supporters to endorse spoiler candidates that allow Republicans to win. When Democrats are elected by margins that come from the Working Families Party ballot line, the party gains leverage. A progressive voice becomes even stronger when the joint candidates come from within the Working Families Party coalition's ranks. The Working Families Party also provides a framework for unions and other groups to engage in authentic and independent party work: developing an agenda, mobilizing the grassroots, and fostering candidates.

In 1999, the party cross-endorsed 226 candidates. In two New York City Council races, the Working Families Party received 10 and 12 percent of the vote, helping elect Eva Moskowitz and Christine Quinn. The Working Families Party also provided margins of victory in races in Hempstead, Woodstock, Nassau County, and Dutchess County. A third-party candidate ran on both the Working Families Party and Green Party ballot lines to gain 14 percent of the vote against an entrenched Democratic incumbent in Brooklyn. In the November 2000 elections, 103,094 voters chose the Working Families Party ballot line.

The party has also become a growing leader in issue organizing. In March 2001, the party held a one thousand–person candidate forum in New York City in which three of the four mayoral candidates, including the front-runner, pledged to introduce the Working Families Party–backed living wage ordinance within seven days of becoming mayor! The Working Families Party has also led a coalition to raise the state's minimum wage to $6.75 an hour. In March, the New York legislature enacted the raise into law.

Conclusion: Organizing for a Progressive Future

Taken as a whole, the above examples of grassroots activism hardly leave room for cynicism about political change. Indeed, activists across the country should be able to find within the above cases some combination of strategies for organizing in their community. And first successes can feed on each other. Placing some progressives in office helps establish champions for changing the political rules. Election reforms in turn provide greater opportunities for grassroots activists to run for office. Organizing to bring about wholesale political change is a step-by-step process.

The same general lessons apply to all of the material covered in this book. Whether it is living wages, contingent work, sprawl, or electoral change, activists have found their causes to have popular appeal. Indeed, the campaigns covered in this book provide concrete evidence of a vast untapped sea of progressive potential and down-to-earth decency found among a majority of Americans. Most Americans do not live up to this potential because they are bombarded by cynical messages that "nothing can be done," and they see no concrete way to act beyond the official individualized paths to happiness. Yet, when the campaigns described in this book have provided people a positive vision and something concrete to do, people have responded.

In looking at history, we must remember that great political awakenings, such as the labor organizing of the 1930s or the civil rights movement of the 1950s and 1960s, did not begin with mass demonstrations and organizing activity. They started in small, yet pervasive, efforts that established the seeds for the larger social explosions to follow. These pioneer activities created the possibilities of collective alternatives that spread like wildfire once other conditions fell into place. Until their climactic high points, however, the seeds of these movements appeared too fragmented and modest to challenge the seemingly overwhelming obstacles they faced. Even a few years before the great union organizing of 1936 and 1937, for example, the labor movement appeared flat on its back. A small proportion of workers were in unions, mass unemployment was an everyday fact of Depression life, the threats of firings and company spies proved the bane of union sympathizers, and an existing labor federation was locked into outdated strategies and structures. Only in retrospect can we fully acknowledge the opportunities that lay beneath a very threatening and seemingly hopeless landscape.

The same is true today. None of the groups covered in this book, when they have gone out into their communities, have had their ideas rejected. Indeed, as they have gained the volunteer energy, financial resources, and coalition support needed to get their message out, they have met with steady success. In other words, the conditions exist now for developing a movement for basic progressive economic and political change. While this activity may not elect the next president or enact an instant national health care system, it does establish the capacity for greater progressive possibilities. Since our nation is on an economic and ecological path that is not sustainable over the long run, the next few decades promise to be times of significant upheaval and change—one way or another. If we act now and help build on the activism already out there, then one day we may look back on the fledgling efforts at the turn of the new century as laying the seeds for the great political awakening to come.

Notes

Introduction. Paving the High Road; Closing the Low Road

1. Stephen Padgett and William Paterson, *A History of Social Democracy in Postwar Europe* (London: Longman, 1991); Donald Sasson, *One Hundred Years of Socialism* (New York: I.B. Tauris Publishers, 1996).

2. Robert Kuttner, *The Economic Illusion: False Choices Between Prosperity and Social Justice* (Philadelphia: University of Pennsylvania Press, 1991)—first published by Houghton Mifflin Company in 1984.

3. Jonas Pontusson, *The Limits of Social Democracy: Investment Politics in Sweden* (Ithaca, NY: Cornell University Press, 1992).

Chapter 1. Social Citizenship: Lessons from Sweden

1. Paulette Kurzer, *Business and Banking: Political Change and Economic Integration in Western Europe* (Ithaca, NY: Cornell University Press, 1993). Kurzer offers a detailed description of Swedish employers and their relationship to social democracy on pages 119–131.

2. "Social Democracy and the Trade Union Movement" in *Creating Social Democracy*, Klaus Misgeld, Karl Molin, and Klas Åmark (University Park: Penn State University Press, 1988).

3. Unless otherwise stated all statistical data on Swedish social insurance and labor market policies in the late 1990s comes from information provided by the Swedish Institute. We have used fact sheets from August 1997 and September 1999 as well as the booklet *Social Insurance in Sweden 1999*.

4. Gøsta Esping-Andersen, *The Three Worlds of Welfare Capitalism* (Princeton, NJ: Princeton University Press, 1990), p. 84.

5. Michael Yates, *Longer Hours, Fewer Jobs* (New York: Monthly Review, 1994), p. 78; Diane Sainsbury, *Gender, Equality, and Welfare States* (New York: Cambridge University Press, 1996), p. 140; Robert Kuttner, *The Economic Illusion* (Philadelphia: University of Pennsylvania Press, 1984), p. 248.

6. Thord Strömberg, "The Politicization of the Housing Market" in Misgeld, Molin, and Åmark, pp. 237–269.

7. Esping-Andersen, 1990, p. 154.

8. The drug coverage begins picking up a portion of costs at SEK 400 and covers all costs over SEK 3,800. The maximum a family can pay for prescription drugs is SEK 1,300 per year. Mid-level wages averaged between SEK 14,000 and SEK 19,000 per month. Thus, the average family is guaranteed not to pay more than 1 percent of its income for prescription drugs.

9. Sainsbury, pp. 99–100.

10. Ibid., p. 15.

11. Esping-Andersen, 1990, p. 202.

12. The housing allowance is progressively reduced for families whose annual income exceeds SEK 117,000.

13. Nancy Folbre and The Center for Popular Economics, *The New Field Guide to the U.S. Economy* (New York: New Press, 1995), chart 6.4.

14. Sainsbury, p. 85.

15. "The Making of a Social Democratic Welfare State" in Misgeld, Molin, and Åmark, p. 36.

16. Esping-Andersen, 1990, p. 158.

17. Ibid.

18. "European Distinctions" in *Boston Review*, XXII, no. 3–4 (Summer 1997): 10.

19. David Gordon, *Fat and Mean: The Corporate Squeeze of Working Americans and the Myth of Managerial "Downsizing"* (New York: New Press, 1996).

20. Figures from Nancy Folbre and The Center for Popular Economics, chapter 7.

21. Ibid.

22. Deborah Mitchell, *Income Transfers in Ten Welfare*

States (Aldershot: Avebury, 1991), pp. 123–127.

23. Esping-Andersen, 1990, p. 56.

24. Sainsbury, p. 76.

25. T. Smeeding, B. Torrey, and M. Rein, "The Patterns of Income and Poverty: The Economic Status of Children and the Elderly in Eight Countries" in *The Vulnerable*, J. Palmer, T. Smeeding, and B. Torrey eds. (Washington, DC: The Urban Institute Press, 1988).

26. Esping-Andersen, 1990, p. 57.

27. Stephen Herzenberg, John Alic, Howard Wial, *New Rules for a New Economy* (Ithaca, NY: Cornell University Press, 1998), pp. 52–55.

28. Sainsbury, p. 163.

29. Ibid., p. 105.

30. Esping-Andersen, 1990, p. 155.

31. Gunilla Fürst, *Sweden—The Equal Way* (Stockholm: The Swedish Institute, 1999), p. 39.

32. Sainsbury, p. 192.

33. Esping-Andersen, 1990, pp. 208–210.

34. Deborah Figart and Ellen Mutari, "It's About Time: Will Europe Solve the Work/Family Dilemma?" in *Dollars and Sense,* no. 215 (January/February 1998): 28.

35. Ibid., p. 29.

36. Anthony Atkins, Lee Rainwater, and Timothy Smeeding, *Income Distribution in OECD Countries: Evidence from the Luxembourg Income Study* (Organization for Economic Co-Operation and Development, 1995), p. 28. Unemployment figures can be slippery statistics that vary depending on what is actually being counted and how. This can make cross-country comparisons difficult. However, the basic contrasts between the United States and Sweden are clear, as is Sweden's well-documented postwar achievement of full employment.

37. For a short overview of Keynes's life and his economic theories see Robert Skidelsky, *Keynes* (New York: Oxford University Press, 1996). The last chapter provides a concise overview of the current controversy that surrounds Keynes's legacy for today.

38. An excellent overview of the basic macroeconomic mechanism available to governments and their link to social democratic Keynesianism is provided by Fritz Scharpf, *Crisis and Choice in European Social Democracy* (Ithaca, NY: Cornell University Press, 1987), chapter 2.

39. Scharpf, pp. 33–37. The wage-price spiral is also at the center of Andrew Glyn's examination of the crisis of social democracy in "Social Democracy and Full Employment" in *New Left Review* (1995): 33–54.

40. Klas Åmark op. cit., p. 77.

41. Gøsta Esping-Andersen, *Politics Against Markets* (Princeton, NJ: Princeton University Press, 1985), p. 237.

42. Jonas Pontusson, *The Limits of Social Democracy:*
Investment Politics in Sweden (Ithaca, NY: Cornell University Press, 1992), p. 76–77.

43. Ibid., p 78.

44. Folbre, p. 1–14.

45. Youssef M. Ibrahim, "Welfare's Snug Coat Cuts Norwegian Cold," *New York Times*, December 13, 1996.

46. Andreas Jørgensen, "Efficiency and Welfare Under Capitalism: Denmark vs. the United States" in *Monthly Review,* February 1997, vol. 49, no. 9, pp. 34–42.

47. Esping-Andersen (1985) provides a detailed comparison of Sweden, Norway, and Denmark. This work plus the country-specific articles found in *Mapping the West European Left*, Perry Andersen and Patrick Camiller eds. (New York: Verso, 1994) provide the basis for the discussion presented in this section.

48. John Logue documents this rise and impact of the Socialist People's Party in *Socialism and Abundance: Radical Socialism in the Danish Welfare State* (Minneapolis: University of Minnesota Press, 1982).

49. Lars Mjøset, Ådne Cappelen, Jan Fagerberg, and Bent Sofus Tranøy, "Norway: Changing the Model" in Andersen and Camiller, pp. 68–69.

50. Chuck Collins and Felice Yeskel, *Economic Apartheid in America* (New York: New Press, 2000), p. 57.

Chapter 2. Associative Democracy: Lessons from Europe's German Powerhouse

1. Charles Sabel, Archon Funn, and Bradely Kakkainen, "Beyond Backyard Environmentalism," *Boston Review* 24, no. 5 (October/November 1999) provides a critique of environmentalism in the context of an alternative framework. This *Boston Review* also provides ten responses to Sabel, Funn, and Kakkainen's ideas. For a brief critique of OSHA see Joshua Cohen and Joel Rogers, *Associations and Democracy* (New York: Verso Books, 1995), pp. 87–90.

2. Paul Hirst, *Associative Democracy: New Forms of Economic and Social Governance* (Amherst: University of Massachusetts Press, 1994); Cohen and Rogers (1995) includes both the main essay by Cohen and Rogers and reactions by eleven respondents.

3. Hirst, p. 22.

4. Our focus is on the institutions that developed in West Germany. While their transfer to the East has produced notable mutations, the overall process of reunification revolved around the incorporation of East Germany wholesale into the West German system.

5. Interestingly the great "revisionist" Bernstein held

to his pacifist convictions and voted against the war.

6. Michael Dobkowski and Isidor Wallimann eds., *Radical Perspectives on the Rise of Fascism in Germany, 1919–1945* (New York: Monthly Review Press, 1989).

7. Quoted in Maurice Glasman, *Unnecessary Suffering: Managing Market Utopia* (New York: Verso, 1996), p. 38.

8. Ibid., p. 35.

9. For example see Gabriel Kolko, *The Politics of War: The World and United States Foreign Policy 1943–45* (New York: Pantheon, 1990); Joyce and Gabriel Kolko, *The Limits of Powers: The World and United States Foreign Policy 1945–1951* (New York: Pantheon, 1972); and Walter LaFeber, *America, Russia and the Cold War 1945–1980* (New York: Wiley, 1980).

10. Wolfgang Friedmann, *The Allied Military Government of Germany* (London: Stevens, 1947), p. 138.

11. For American actions in Germany see Friedmann and Kolko op. cit. and also Alfred Grosser, *The Colossus Again* (New York: Praeger, 1955).

12. Helmut Böhne, *An Introduction to the Social and Economic History of Germany* (New York: St. Martin's Press, 1978), p. 129.

13. U.S. policies contrasted sharply with events in the British zone in northern Germany. Since back in Britain, the Labour Party was itself nationalizing key industries, British policy makers hardly felt threatened by social democratic dominance in their area of occupation. Indeed, British authorities actively cooperated with unions and artisan organizations in restructuring the industrial heartland of the country. The U.S. voices held out, however, through American financial support to British occupation costs and the eventual merger in 1947 of the two zones.

14. Linda Weiss, *The Myth of the Powerless State* (Ithaca, NY: Cornell University Press, 1998), chapter 5.

15. Joel Rogers, "United States; Lesson from Abroad and Home" in *Works Councils*, Joel Rogers and Wolfgang Streeck eds. (Chicago: University of Chicago Press, 1995), p. 384.

16. Figures from Kirsten Wever, *Negotiating Competitiveness: Employment Relations and Organizational Innovation in Germany and the United States* (Cambridge, MA: Harvard University Press, 1995), pp. 38–39.

17. Figures come from the excerpts of the Works Constitution Act of 1972 in Wolfgang Streeck, *Industrial Relations in West Germany: A Case Study of the Car Industry* (London: Heinemann Educational Books, 1984), in the appendix and from Müller-Jentsch, p. 58.

18. Streeck, p. 162.

19. Müller-Jentsch, p. 56.

20. Ibid., p. 53.

21. Ibid.

22. Joel Rogers and Wolfgang Streeck eds. *Works Councils* op. cit. provides a good introduction.

23. Graham Taylor and Andy Mathers, "Social Partner or Social Movement? European Integration and the Prospects for Trade Union Renewal in Europe," presented at the 2001 UALE conference, pp. 6–7.

24. Streeck.

25. Under the old system, the workers elected only one-third of the board. However, because VW was a partially public-owned company, several SPD-connected government officials sat on the board. Their votes could potentially provide workers a parity voting block.

26. Peter Auer, "Institutional Stability Pays: German Industrial Relations under Pressure" in *Negotiating the New Germany: Can Social Partnership Survive?* Lowell Turner ed. (Ithaca, NY: Cornell University Press, 1997), p. 18.

27. Cited in Lowell Turner, *Democracy at Work: Changing World Markets and the Future of Labor Unions* (Ithaca, NY: Cornell University Press, 1991), p. 33.

28. These included increases in supplemental unemployment benefits, a new guaranteed income stream, and various plant-specific counseling, job placement, and retraining programs.

29. Wolfgang Streeck, "Industrial Relations and Industrial Change; The Restructuring of the World Auto Industry in the 1970s and 1980s" in *Economic and Industrial Democracy,* no. 8 (1987): 437–462; and "Successful Adjustment to Turbulent Markets: The Automobile Industry" in *Industrial Policy in West Germany: Toward a Third Republic,* Peter Katzenstein ed. (Ithaca, NY: Cornell University Press, 1989), pp. 113–156.

30. Increased overtime is a controversial subject. With time-and-a-half pay, workers who put in overtime can see their paychecks increase significantly. The lifestyles of some can come to depend on overtime. However, the drastic amounts of overtime that are sometimes put in has led the union to try to put a brake on the practice. During the 1996–1997 round of contract talks, GM in particular experienced a series of strikes by UAW locals typically over demands to hire more workers.

31. For the general issue and the experiences at VW and Opel see Streeck 1984, chapter 7.

32. The cases are taken from Wever, pp. 78–89.

33. Ibid.

34. Ibid., p. 84.

35. See Wever, pp. 77–78, for a summary and references on the German literature.

36. Walther Müller-Jentsch, "Germany: From Collective Voice to Co-management" in Rogers and Streeck op. cit., pp. 59–60.

37. Ibid., p. 63. The 1990 election figures put the union

proportion at 79 percent (see Auer op. cit).

38. In this way workers cannot "free ride" by enjoying the benefits of the union contract but not contributing toward it. An increasing number of states, however, have passed so-called right to work laws banning such agreements and allowing individual workers to free ride.

39. Even in the best cases, such as the auto industry where the UAW coordinates pattern bargaining among the Big Three, the crucial parts industry is not covered by the pattern. Thus, the Big Three have ample incentives to outsource parts production to nonunion parts companies.

40. Employer efforts can be seen in the increasing levels of corporate money spent on antiunion consultants and the statistics on illegal firings and concession demands. In *The Decline of Organized Labor in the United States* (Chicago: University of Chicago Press, 1987), Michael Goldfield comprehensively explores the various explanations of union decline, concluding that employer hostility and changing class relations offer the major cause. See also Wever, p. 59, and Nancy Folbre, *The New Field Guide to the U.S. Economy* (New York: New Press, 1995), chart 2.15.

41. Wever, p. 55.

42. The union's system of workplace activists, the "Vertraunenleute," has in practice taken a second seat in priority to the role of the elected works councilors. See, for example, Streeck, 1984.

43. The information for this section comes from Kathleen Thelen, "The Politics of Flexibility in the German Metal Working Industries," in *Bargaining for Change: Union Politics in North America and Europe*, Miriam Golden and Jonas Pontusson eds. (Ithaca, NY: Cornell University Press, 1992), pp. 225–234. Thelen also offers a second case focusing on union–works council interactions in promoting worker-friendly changes in technology and skills. The material for her article is taken from her book-length examination *Union of Parts: Labor Politics in Postwar Germany* (Ithaca, NY: Cornell University Press, 1991).

44. Quoted in Müller-Jentsch, p. 67.

45. The economic/productivity benefits of unions have been well documented. For example, in his comparison of 841 Michigan manufacturing firms, William Cooke found that unionized workplaces had a rate of value added per employee of $52,000—21 percent higher than $43,000 per employee at traditional nonunion workplaces. Unionized workplaces with active employee involvement programs raised the value added to $58,000—35 percent above a traditional nonunion firm. See William Cooke, "Employee Participation Programs, Group-Based Incentives, and Company Performance: A Union-Nonunion Comparison" in *Industrial and Labor Relations Review* (July 1994): 594–609.

46. Wever, p. 194.

47. The contrast between German and U.S. worker training is taken from Wever chapter 4 and Lisa Lynch, "Payoffs to Alternative Training Strategies at Work" in *Working Under Different Rules,* Richard Freeman ed. (New York: Russell Sage Foundation, 1994), pp. 63–96, as well as the author's direct experience in worker education in the auto industry. Lynch's article is the summary of a joint research project on comparative training published under her editorship as *Training and the Private Sector* (Chicago: University of Chicago Press, 1994). See also Maurice Glasman, *Unnecessary Suffering*, chapter 3.

48. Lynch, pp. 81–84.

49. Glasman, pp. 70–79, provides a concise overview of Handwerk including the figures cited.

50. Wever, p. 63.

51. *Capitalism vs. Capitalism: How America's Obsession with Individual Achievement and Short-term Profit Has Led It to the Brink of Collapse* (New York: Four Walls Eight Windows, 1993), p. 106.

52. Jochen Clasen, "Social Security—The Core of the German Employment-Centered Social State" in Jochen Clasen and Richard Freeman, *Social Policy in Germany* (New York: Harvester Wheatsheaf, 1994), p. 64.

53. A concise and handy introduction to the German welfare state is provided by Clasen and Freeman op. cit. Each selection also provides a guide for further reading. As the book was published in Great Britain, the primary basis of comparison is to English social policy. For a direct contrast of Germany to the U.S. and Sweden see Esping-Andersen, *The Three Worlds of Welfare Capitalism* (Princeton: Princeton University Press, 1990).

54. Clasen and Freeman, p. 11.

55. Clasen and Freeman, p. 64.

56. Esping-Andersen, p. 204.

57. "Women and Social Policy" in Clasen and Freeman, pp. 173–199; figures from p. 175.

58. Wever, chapter 7.

59. For a range of contrasting optimistic and more pessimistic evaluations of the impact of reunification on German industrial relations see Lowell Turner, *Negotiating the New Germany: Can Social Partnership Survive?* (Ithaca, NY: Cornell University Press, 1997).

Chapter 3. Social Partnership and Social Ownership: Lessons from Austria

1. Donald Sassoon, *One Hundred Years of Socialism: The West European Left in the Twentieth Century* (New

York: I.B. Tauris Publishers, 1996), pp. 471–472; Leland Stauber, *A New Program for Democratic Socialism: Lessons from the Market-Planning Experience in Austria* (Carbondale, IL: Four Willows Press, 1987), chapter 2.

2. A quite detailed description of the chamber system and the legal fabric which surrounds it is offered by Austrian lawyers Theodor Tomandl and Karl Fuerboeck in their book *Social Partnership: The Austrian System of Industrial Relations and Social Insurance* (Ithaca, NY: ILR Press, 1986).

3. Randall Kindley, "The Evolution of Austria's Neo-Corporatist Institutions" in *Austro-Corporatism*, Gunter Bischof and Anton Pelinka eds. (New Brunswick, NJ: Transaction Publishers, 1996), p. 72.

4. Ferdinand Karlhofer, "The Present and Future State of Social Partnership" in Bischof and Pelinka, p. 124.

5. Austria's annual GDP increase per capita between 1960–1980, 3.6 percent, was identical to the European OECD countries (Alois Guger, "Corporatism: Success or Failure? Austrian Experiences" in *Social Corporatism: A Superior Economic System?* Jukka Pekkarinen, Matti Pohjola, and Bob Rowthorn eds. [Oxford: Clarendon Press, 1992], p. 341). Over the same period the country's real GDP annual increase of 4.2 percent compared with the United States' 3.5 percent. The average annual unemployment rates were 1.7 percent and 5.5 percent respectively.

6. For a general examination of the economic superiority of social partnership see Pekkarinen, Pohjola, and Rowthorn.

7. Karlhofer, p. 135.

8. Ibid., p. 136.

9. Guger, p. 349.

10. GNP growth was 2.2 percent in Austria, 1.4 percent in OECD Europe, and 1.5 percent in the United States. The unemployment rates were 3.6 percent, 9.3 percent, and 6.6 percent, respectively. Karlhofer, p. 137.

11. Peter Katzenstein, *Small States in World Markets* (Ithaca, NY: Cornell University Press, 1985). See also Pekkarinen, Pohjola, and Rowthorn.

12. Eric Shaw, *The Labour Party Since 1945* (Oxford: Blackwell Publishers, 1996); Katzenstein, pp. 131–132.

13. Figures are from Jeanne Kirk Laux and Maureen Appel Molot, *State Capitalism: Public Enterprise in Canada* (Ithaca, NY: Cornell University Press, 1988), pp. 13, 18, and John Freeman, *Democracy and Markets: The Politics of Mixed Economies* (Ithaca, NY: Cornell University Press, 1989), pp. 172–175. See also Stauber, Part II.

14. Stauber, Part III explains the organization of the nationalized sector in great detail.

15. Freeman, pp. 185–186.

16. Freeman, p. 179. See also Stauber, Part IV.

17. Ibid., pp. 178–179.

18. Ibid., pp. 182, 184, 191.

19. Karl Aiginger, "The Privatization Experiment in Austria" published in *Privatization in the European Union*, David Parker ed. (New York: Routledge, 1998).

20. Polls in 1983 found that 61 percent evaluated the management of state industries as bad or not especially good. At the same time, 49 percent thought that state industries provided an economic advantage (23 percent saw them as a disadvantage) and 37 percent were willing to provide unqualified financial support, which another 60 percent were willing to do either if the same support was offered private business or the support was used to close unviable firms while saving the rest. Ibid., pp. 195–198.

21. Laux and Molot, p. 11.

22. Proportions taken from Laux and Molot, p. 13. Their book focuses on public enterprise in Canada.

23. Ibid., pp. 29–31.

24. Ibid., p. 186.

25. The $70 billion figure was quoted in a PBS *Newshour* report on 3/30/00.

26. Citation given in Dan Sweeney, *Building the Bridge to the High Road*, a report by the Midwest Center for Labor Research in Chicago, chapter 3.

27. Ibid., also see the September/October 1998 *Dollars and Sense*, which has six articles devoted to the experience of cooperatives and employee stock ownership plans.

28. Nancy Folbre, *The New Field Guide to the U.S. Economy* (New York: New Press, 1995), p. 1.14.

Chapter 4. Confronting "Globalization" and the New Capitalist Agenda

1. Work done by the National Bureau of Economic Research illustrates this line of argument. In reaction to deteriorating U.S. economic performance, the bureau undertook a four-year project to compare the labor market in the United States to those in western Europe, Canada, Japan, and Australia. There, research was organized around four topics: changes in wages and wage differentials, training within the firms, employee representation, and social programs and the labor market. An edited volume was published on each area. In addition, a single summary volume was published as *Working Under Different Rules*, Richard Freeman ed. (New York: The Russell Sage Foundation, 1994).

2. This trajectory was anticipated by Jürgen Habermas, "The European Nation-State and the Pressures of Globalization" in *New Left Review*, no. 231 (May/June 1998).

3. "The Spectre of Unemployment" in *A European*

Recovery Program, Ken Coates and Michael Barratt Brown eds. (Nothingham, England: Spokesman, 1993), p. 1.

4. Allan Larsson MP, "Can Europe Afford to Work?" in ibid., p. 5.

5. Ken Coates, "Unemployed Europe and the Struggle for Alternatives" in *New Left Review,* no. 227 (January/February 1998).

6. *Economic Restructuring and Social Exclusion,* Phillip Brown and Rosemary Crompton eds. (London: UCL Press, 1994) examines these patterns including the dimensions of race, class, and gender.

7. Martin Lee, "Fascism in Europe Spurred by Globalization," 1999, originally published in the *Los Angeles Times,* based on his book *The Beast Reawakens.*

8. Gary Teemple, "Globalization and the Decline of Social Reform" (New Jersey: Humanities Press, 1995), p. 4.

9. Paulette Kurzer, *Business and Banking: Political Change and Economic Integration in Western Europe* (Ithaca, NY: Cornell University Press, 1993), p. 252.

10. Fritiz Scharpf, *Crisis and Choice in European Social Democracy* (Ithaca, NY: Cornell University Press, 1991), p. 274.

11. Hugo Radice offers a short summary of this debate in "Taking Globalization Seriously" in *Global Capitalism Versus Democracy—Socialist Register 1999,* Leo Panitch and Colin Leys eds. (London: The Merlin Press, 1999), pp. 1–28. *Monthly Review* has run an ongoing series of articles debating globalization from a left perspective. See especially, July-August 1996, February 1997, March 1997, June 1997, July-August 1997, and November 1997.

12. Linda Weiss, *The Myth of the Powerless State* (Ithaca, NY: Cornell University Press, 1998), p. 171,; William Tabb, "Globalization Is An Issue, the Power of Capital Is The Issue," *Monthly Review,* vol. 49, no. 2 (June 1997): 24.

13. Weiss, p. 171.

14. Ibid., p. 176.

15. Ellen Meikins Wood, "Globalization or Globaloney," *Monthly Review,* vol. 48, no. 9 (February 1997): 22; Tabb, p. 22.

16. "The Effects of Plant Closing or Threat of Plant Closing on the Right of Workers to Organize," report submitted to the North American Commission for Labor Cooperation, September 30, 1996.

17. Stephen Herzenberg, John Alic, and Howard Wial, *New Rules for a New Economy* (Ithaca, NY: Cornell University Press, 1998), pp. 1, 16.

18. Weiss, p. 177.

19. Ibid., p. 186; Meikins Wood, p. 25.

20. According to UAW research figures, unionization among independent parts suppliers has fallen from nearly half in the 1950s to roughly one out of five jobs today.

21. Greg LeRoy and Tyson Slocum, "Economic Development in Minnesota: High Subsidies, Low Wages, Absent Standards" (Washington, DC: Institute on Taxation and Economic Policy, 1999).

22. Linda Weiss, "Managed Openness: Beyond Neoliberal Globalism" in *New Left Review*, no. 238 (November/December 1998): 138.

23. Ibid.

24. Ibid., pp. 170–176, and Tabb, p. 24.

25. Tabb, p. 21.

26. Richard Du Boff and Edward Herman, "A Critique of Tabb on Globalization" in *Monthly Review,* vol. 49, no. 6 (November 1997): 32.

27. Scharpf, chapters 10–12.

28. Weiss, *The Myth of the Powerless State*, pp. 190–191.

29. Eric Helleiner, *States and the Reemergence of Global Finance* (Ithaca, NY: Cornell University Press, 1994).

30. "Labor, The State, and Class Struggle" in *Monthly Review,* vol. 49, no. 3 (July–August 1997): 12.

31. That the United States is driving neoliberal globalization as a way of attempting to maintain American capitalist dominance is the central argument of Peter Gowan's insightful *The Global Gamble: Washington's Faustian Bid for World Dominance* (New York: Verso, 1999).

32. Michael Yates, *Longer Hours, Fewer Jobs* (New York: Monthly Review Press, 1994), pp. 56–69.

33. BLS 1999 projections.

34. Robert Brenner, *The Economics of Global Turbulence: A Special Report on the World Economy 1950–98* published as a special issue of *New Left Review,* no. 229 (May/June 1998): 250.

35. Ibid., p. 246.

36. Robert Pollin, "Anatomy of Clintonomics," *New Left Review,* no. 3 (May/June 2000): 29, 34.

37. Brenner, p. 235.

38. Pollin, p. 34.

39. See Pollin; Brenner.

40. Michel Albert, *Capitalism vs. Capitalism.* (New York: Four Walls Eight Windows, 1993).

41. Weiss, *The Myth.*

42. William Tabb, *The Postwar Japanese System: Cultural Economy and Economic Transformation* (New York: Oxford University Press, 1995); Martin Hart-Landsberg, *The Rush to Development: Economic Change and Political Struggle in South Korea* (New York: Monthly Review Press 1993).

43. Gowan, especially chapter 6; Stephen Gill, "The Geopolitics of the Asian Crisis" in *Monthly Review,* vol. 50, no. 10 (March 1999), pp. 1–9.

44. Weiss, *The Myth*.

45. The adaptability of the postwar German system is also the central question of the collection edited by Lowell Turner, *Negotiating the New Germany: Can Social Partnership Survive?* (Ithaca, NY: Cornell University Press 1997). See also Maurice Glasman, "The Siege of the German Social Market" in *New Left Review,* no. 225 (September/October 1997).

46. Weiss, *The Myth*, p. 235.

47. See Brenner 1998 for a more detailed explanation.

48. Birgit Mahnkopf, "Between the Devil and the Deep Blue Sea: The 'German Model' Under the Pressure of Globalisation," *Global Capitalism Versus Democracy—Socialist Register 1999*, Leo Panitch and Colin Leys eds. (London: Merlin Press, 1999). See also Glasman.

49. Figures from UAW-GM research statistics.

50. Quoted in Robert Brenner, "The Boom and the Bubble" in *New Left Review,* no. 6 (November/December 2000), p. 39.

51. Brenner, 2000; Gill; Mitchell Bernard, "East Asia's Tumbling Dominoes: Financial Crises and the Myth of the Regional Model" in Panitch and Leys.

52. Gowan, chapters 9–11.

53. For example, see Artilio Boron, "State Decay and Democratic Decadence in Latin America" in Panitch and Leys.

54. Brenner, 2000, p. 236.

55. This account of the Mitterrand experience draws on Thomas Christofferson, *The French Socialists in Power 1981–1986* (Newark: University of Delaware Press, 1991); Anthony Daley, *The Mitterrand Era: Policy Alternatives and Political Mobilization in France* (New York: New York University Press, 1996); Daniel Singer, *Is Socialism Doomed?* (New York: Oxford University Press, 1998); *Socialism, the State and Public Policy in France*, Philip Cerny and Martin Schain eds. (London: Frances Pinter, 1985); Donald Sassoon, *One Hundred Years of Socialism* (New York: I.B. Tauris Publishers, 1996); and George Ross and Jane Jensen, "France: Triumph and Tragedy" in *Mapping the West European Left*, Perry Anderson and Patrick Camiller eds. (New York: Verso Books, 1994), pp. 158–188.

56. See Christofferson, pp. 50–59.

57. Ibid.

58. Singer, pp. 275–276.

59. Our account of the Labour Left draws on Leo Panitch and Colin Leys, *The End of Parliamentary Socialism* (New York: Verso, 1997); Eric Shaw, *The Labour Party Since 1945* (Cambridge, MA: Blackwell Publishers, 1996); Lewis Minkin, *The Contentious Alliance: Trade Unions and the Labour Party* (Edinburgh: Edinburgh University Press, 1992); and Donald Sassoon, *One Hundred Years of Social-*ism (New York: I.B. Tauris Publishers, 1996). We have also consulted directly documents such as the *Alternative Economic Strategy* and debates within publications of the British left such as *Capital and Class* and *New Left Review*.

60. Panitch and Leys, p. 84.

61. The *Alternative Economic Strategy: A Response by the Labour Movement to the Economic Crisis* (London: CSE Books, 1980).

62. Panitch and Leys, pp. 125–126.

63. Ibid., p. 126.

64. For the most detailed discussion of the postwar Swedish debates over corporate decision making, including a chapter on collective share ownership, see Jonas Pontusson, *The Limits of Social Democracy: Investment Politics in Sweden* (Ithaca, NY: Cornell University Press, 1992). We have also used Jonas Pontusson, "Sweden: After the Golden Age" in *Mapping the West European Left*, Perry Anderson and Patrick Camiller eds. (New York: Verso Books, 1994), pp. 23–54; Gøsta Esping-Andersen, *Politics Against Markets* (Princeton: Princeton University Press, 1985), Part III; and Donald Sassoon, *One Hundred Years of Socialism* (New York: I.B. Tauris Publishers, 1996), chapter 23.

65. Pontusson, 1992, p. 200.

Chapter 5. Facing the Ecological Crisis: The Meaning of Green Politics

1. John Bellamy Foster, *The Vulnerable Planet* (New York: Monthly Review Press, 1994), pp. 11–12.

2. World Commission on Environment and Development, *Our Common Future* (New York: Oxford University Press, 1987), chapters 1 and 6; Carl Sagan, *Billions and Billions: Thoughts on Life and Death at the Brink of the Millennium* (New York: Random House, 1997), chapters 10 and 11.

3. Foster, p. 24.

4. Ibid., p. 116.

5. World Commission on Environment and Development, chapter 5.

6. Nancy Folbre, *The New Field Guide to the U.S. Economy* (New York: New Press, 1995), pp. 10–11.

7. Dan Peters, UAW-GM Manual on the Auto Industry, 2000.

8. Jane Holtz Kay, *Asphalt Nation* (Berkeley: University of California Press, 1997); World Resources Institute, *Car Trouble* (Washington, DC: World Resources Institute, 1998); Winfried Wolf, *Car Mania* (Chicago: Pluto Press, 1996); Wolfgang Zuckermann, *End of the Road: The World Car Crisis and How We Can Solve It* (Post Mills, VT:

Chelsea Green Publishing Company, 1991).

9. Foster, p. 115.

10. Radio interview with Stephen Hawkins, 2000.

11. Wolf, p. 145.

12. Kay, pp. 92–93.

13. World Resources Institute, p. 6.

14. Peters.

15. World Resources Institute, p. 20; Foster, p. 116.

16. World Resources Institute, p. 6; Wolf, p. 201.

17. Kay, Part II.

18. Wolf, p. 155.

19. Ibid., p. 190.

20. Kay, p. 20.

21. Keith Scheider, "Roads to Ruin: Why Billions for More Pavement Is Poor Policy," *Metro Times*, September 22–28,1999.

22. Kay, chapter 1.

23. Foster, pp. 115–116; Kay, chapters 7–12; Wolf, chapter 6.

24. Marc Breslow, "Is the U.S. Making Progress?" in *Dollars and Sense* (March/April 1996), pp. 16–21; Herman Daly, *Beyond Growth* (Boston: Beacon Press, 1996).

25. Poll data cited in the PBS documentary *Affluenza*.

26. According to the 1940 Census one-third of dwellings had no running water or indoor toilet, two-thirds had no showers or bathtubs, two-fifths had no central heating, and one-quarter had no mechanical or ice refrigerator. Robert Zieger, *The CIO 1933–1955* (Chapel Hill: University of North Carolina Press, 1995), p. 115.

27. Juliet Schor, *The Overworked American* (New York: Basic Books, 1991).

28. Material on the Greens comes from: *The German Greens: Paradox Between Movement and Party*, Margit Mayer and John Ely eds. (Philadelphia: Temple University Press, 1998); Thomas Scharf, *The German Greens: Challenging the Consensus* (Providence, RI: Berg Publishers, 1994); Andrei Markovits and Philip Gorski, *The German Left: Red, Green, and Beyond* (New York: Oxford University Press, 1993). In addition to the Mayer and Ely volume, two other works offer direct, documented examples of Green thinking. See Mike Feinstein, *Sixteen Weeks with European Greens: Interviews, Impressions, Platforms, and Personalities* (San Pedro, CA: R&E Miles, 1992) and The Group of Green Economists, *Ecological Economics: A Practical Programme for Global Reform* (London: Zed Books, 1992).

29. Quoted in Charlene Spretnak and Fritjof Capra, *Green Politics* (Santa Fe, NM: Bear & Company, 1986), p. 30.

30. In practice the system proved difficult to implement as it undermined the continuity, experience, and seniority rights of the Green's parliamentary group as well as un-

dercut the development of publicly known political figures required by the media.

31. Report by Paul Marx, senior economist with the Federal Transit Administration, U.S. Department of Transportation.

32. This summary is based on chapter 4 in Huey Johnson, *Green Plans: Greenprint for Sustainability* (Lincoln: University of Nebraska Press, 1995).

33. Roberto Michels, *Political Parties* (New York: Collier, 1962).

34. For a summary of this line of thinking from one of its major intellectual spokespeople, see T. Giddens, "The Third Way" in *Polity*, 1998.

35. Edmund Andrews, 10/8/1999.

36. Suzanne Daley, "In Europe Unease with U.S. Power Evident" originally offered by the *New York Times*, published in the *Ann Arbor News*, April 9, 2000.

37. *Working Time in Transition: The Political Economy of Working Hours in Industrial Nations*, Karl Hinrichs, William Roche, and Carmen Sirianni eds. (Philadelphia: Temple University Press, 1991).

38. German Social Democratic chairman Oskar Lafontaine highlighted the social democratic possibilities of a united Europe in a major speech given in 1997. He called on the Social Democrats to stand as the party committed to saying no to the neoliberal world order. However, in the 1998 election, Gerhard Schröder, not Lafontaine, became the party's candidate for prime minister. See Oskar Lafontaine, "The Future of German Social Democracy" in *New Left Review,* no. 227, (January/February 1998). See also Coates op. cit.

39. For example, Peter Medhoff and Holly Sklar offer a detailed and engaging account of Boston's successful resident-run Dudely Street Neighborhood Initiative in *Streets of Hope* (Boston: South End Press, 1994).

40. The information for this account of the French events comes from Daniel Singer, *Whose Millennium: Theirs or Ours?* (New York: Monthly Review Press, 1999) and from personal accounts of several people who were in Paris at the time.

Chapter 6. The Progressive Potential in the United States: Liberal Confinement and Radical Renewal

1. Herbert Gans, *Middle American Individualism* (New York: Oxford Press, 1988), p. 23. Gans's work probes the complex contradictions of blue- and pink-collar working America.

2. Figures come from polls commissioned by the AFL-CIO.

3. Economic Policy Institute; *Business Week,* December 27, 1999.

4. Examples of synthesis works include Howard Zinn's classic *A People's History of the United States* (New York: Harper Collins, 1998), American Social History Project, *Who Built America?* 2 volumes (New York: Pantheon, 1992), *The New American History*, Eric Foner ed. (Philadelphia: Temple University Press, 1990).

5. For a more detailed explanation and full annotated references see David Reynolds, *Democracy Unbound: Progressive Challenges to the Two Party System* (Boston: South End Press, 1997), chapters 1 and 2.

6. For a social/labor history of the Great Depression, see Irving Bernstein, *The Lean Years: A History of the American Worker 1920–1933* (New York: Da Capo Publishing, 1960); Lizabeth Cohen, *Making a New Deal: Industrial Workers in Chicago 1919–1939* (New York: Cambridge University Press, 1990); Steve Babson, *Working Detroit* (Detroit, MI: Wayne State University Press, 1986), Part II.

7. For a great overview of many of the dimensions that we will discuss below, see *The Rise and Fall of the New Deal Order 1930–1980,* Steve Fraser and Gary Gerstle eds. (Princeton, NJ: Princeton University Press, 1989).

8. For labor's rebirth through the early postwar years see Steve Babson, *The Unfinished Struggle* (New York: Rowman & Littlefield Publishers, 1999); Robert Zieger, *The CIO: 1933–1955* (Chapel Hill: University of North Carolina Press, 1995); Paul Le Blanc, *A Short History of the U.S. Working Class* (New York: Humanity Books, 1999); and Michael Goldfield, *The Color of Politics* (New York: New Press, 1997); Elizabeth Faue, *Community of Suffering and Struggle: Women, Men and the Labor Movement in Minneapolis 1915–1945* (Chapel Hill: University of North Carolina Press, 1991).

9. For a specific focus on race and the labor movement during this period, see Goldfield as well as Babson, 1986.

10. Elizabeth Fones-Wolf examines this battle in detail in *Selling Free Enterprise: The Business Assault on Labor and Liberalism 1945–60* (Urbana: University of Illinois Press, 1994).

11. For a detailed examination of the UAW history, with an eye to the larger implications, see Nelson Lichtenstein and *Walter Reuther: The Most Dangerous Man in Detroit* (Urbana: University of Illinois Press, 1995).

12. Nelson Lichtenstein provides an excellent overview of these battles in "From Corporatism to Collective Bargaining: Organized Labor and the Eclipse of Social Democracy in the Postwar Era" in Fraser and Gerstle op. cit.

13. These laws prohibit union security clauses that require new workers to join or pay support to the union. While each worker is thus left to individually decide to join or not join the union, right-to-work laws still require the union to represent all workers. Hence, the law allows workers a "free ride." Right-to-work laws have been passed in roughly eighteen states—mostly in the South.

14. For a discussion of this period and other waves of antilabor repression see Patricia Cayo Sexton, *The War on Labor and the Left: Understanding America's Unique Conservatism* (Boulder, CO: Westview Press, 1991).

15. Lichtenstein, 1989, p. 138.

16. Predicting a Truman defeat, the UAW had developed plans to build a third party after the 1948 elections. Truman's surprise victory preempted this effort. See Lichtenstein 1995.

17. See especially Zieger; Babson 1999; Goldfield.

18. Lynn Turgeon, *Bastard Keynesianism* (Westport, CT: Greenwood Press, 1996).

19. Jack Bloom provides a revealing look at the intersection between politics and economics in sparking, framing and limiting the civil rights movement in *Class, Race, and the Civil Rights Movement* (Bloomington: Indiana University Press, 1987). See also Fred Powledge, *Free at Last?* (New York: Harper Perennial, 1991); James Cone, *Martin & Malcolm & America* (Maryknoll, NY: Orbis Books, 1991); *Women in the Civil Rights Movement,* Vicki Crawford, Jacquelyn Anne Rouse, and Barbara Woods eds. ((Bloomington: Indiana University Press, 1990); Clayborne Carson, *In Struggle: SNCC and the Black Awakening of the 1960s* (Cambridge, MA: Harvard University Press, 1981).

20. Jill Quadagno, *The Color of Welfare: How Racism Undermined the War on Poverty* (New York: Oxford University Press, 1994), p. 33.

21. Ibid., chapter 2.

22. See, for example, Edward Morgan, *The 60s Experience: Hard Lessons About Modern America* (Philadelphia: Temple University Press, 1991); Todd Gitlin, *The Sixties: Years of Hope, Days of Rage* (New York: Bantam Books, 1987); and *The 60s Without Apology*, Sohnya Sayes, Anders Stephanson, Stanley Aronowitz, and Frederic Jameson eds. (Minneapolis: University of Minnesota Press, 1984).

23. Quadagno, chapter 5.

24. David Gordon, *Fat and Mean: The Corporate Squeeze of Working Americans and the Myth of Managerial "Downsizing"* (New York: Free Press, 1996), chapter 2, figures from p. 132.

25. E. E. Schattschneider, *The Semi-Sovereign People*, (Holt, Rinehart, and Winston, 1960) pp. 101–102.

26. "Capital Disadvantage," *Harvard Business Review* (September–October 1992), pp. 68–69.

27. The average was 63 percent as of 9/30/2000 as re-

corded by Morningstar PrincipalPro. This experience contrasts markedly with the investment strategies of alternative funds that aim to include social and environmental criteria. The Domini Social Equity fund's turnover rate for 2000 was under 10 percent.

28. Quoted in the *Detroit News,* 1/27/87.

29. In the end, Kerkorian was unable to secure the finances for his takeover bid. The Chrysler story comes from a curriculum model developed by Steve Babson, Labor Studies Center at Wayne State University, for use in the GM-UAW Paid Education Leave program.

30. The statistics are largely taken from Chuck Collins and Felice Yeskel, *Economic Apartheid in America* (New York: New Press, 2000).

31. Stephen Herzenberg, John Alic, and Howard Wial, *New Rules for a New Economy: Employment and Opportunity in Postindustrial America* (Ithaca, NY: ILR Press, 1998), p. 181.

32. See Peter Gowan, *The Global Gamble: Washington's Faustian Bid for World Dominance* (New York: Verso, 1999); Eric Alterman argues that not only does American foreign policy often act unilaterally in the world, but that influence over U.S. foreign policy decisions has been steadily insulated from the American public. See *Who Speaks for America?* (Ithaca, NY: Cornell University Press, 1998).

33. Indeed, WTO rulings simply provide formal permission for other nations to impose trade sanctions.

Chapter 7. The Living Wage Movement Sweeps the Nation!

1. See chapters 6 and 7 in David Reynolds, *Living Wage Campaigns: An Activist's Guide to Building the Movement for Economic Justice* (Published by ACORN, 2001 Edition), 125-page text portion, minus 80 pages of sample documents, also available at *www.laborstudies.wayne.edu.*

2. For example, in evaluating the possible impact, the survey asked respondents to treat living wage ordinances as if they were across-the-board minimum wage laws.

3. For example, Mark Cassell from Kent State and Policy Matters Ohio found that school districts that contracted out bus transportation paid significantly higher costs per mile and per pupil than those districts that kept such services in-house. See "Taking Them for a Ride: An Assessment of the Privatization of School Transportation in Ohio's Public School Districts." Copies available at *www.afscme.org/wrplace/takerdtc.htm.*

4. The San Diego profile comes from Carol Zabin and Isaac Martin, "Living Wage Campaigns in the Economic Policy Arena: Four Case Studies from California," a report for the Phoenix Workers and Communities Fund at The New World Foundation, June 1999.

5. David Reynolds and Jean Vortkamp, "The Impact of Detroit's Living Wage Law on Non-Profit Organizations" (2000) available from the Economic Policies Institute or *www.laborstudies.wayne.edu.*

6. Bruce Nissen, "Living Wage Campaigns as Social Movements: The Miami-Dade Experience" in *Labor Studies Journal,* vol. 25, no. 3, 2000, pp. 29–50.

7. See Robert Pollin and Stephanie Luce, *The Living Wage: Building a Fair Economy* (New York: New Press, 1998), chapter 4.

8. *Los Angeles Times,* August 28, 1998, pp. E1, E8.

9. Christine Kelly, "No Sweat: Students, Labor & Global Economy" in *New Politics* (Winter 2001), pp. 118–121.

Chapter 8. Building a High-Road Agenda: Examples from Wisconsin

1. Statistics and analysis taken from: Laura Dresser, Joel Rogers, and Julie Whittaker, "The State of Working Wisconsin" Center on Wisconsin Strategy, University of Wisconsin-Madison, years 1995 and 2000.

2. The fifteen are: Chicago, Gary/Hammond, Detroit, Flint, Newark, Buffalo, New York, Cleveland, Toledo, Youngstown/Warren, Allentown/Bethlehem, Philadelphia, Pittsburgh, Houston, and Providence/Warwick. See Midwest Consortium for Economic Development Alternatives, *Metro Futures: A High-Wage, Low-Waste, Democratic Development Strategy for America's Cities and Inner Suburbs* (1994), p. 15. A version of this paper was published as "Metro Futures: Economic Strategies for Cities and Their Suburbs," Don Luria and Joel Rogers eds. (Boston: Beacon Press, 1999).

3. *Rebuilding Milwaukee from the Ground Up!* by the Campaign for a Sustainable Milwaukee (1994), p. 11.

4. *Rebuilding Milwaukee from the Ground Up!* p. 12, and *Metro Futures,* pp. 6–7.

5. The common presence of porches on old city streets and their near absence in today's housing construction provides one simple sign contrasting urban community with suburban isolation.

6. Regional Technology Strategies Inc., which included COWS's director Joel Rogers, pulled together for the Annie E. Casey Foundation a guidebook on this research methodology, entitled "Using Regional Economic Analysis in Urban Jobs Strategies."

7. Larger vertical and horizontally integrated firms often understand this advantage. For example, the desire

for such flexibility is part of the motivation behind the Big Three automakers' drive to shed their parts operations in favor of networks with independent suppliers. However, as the U.S. auto industry demonstrates, in the hands of individual firms, such "flexibility" can lead to low-road practices of corporate downsizing, speed up, union busting, and outsourcing to low-wage supplier firms. See *Industrial Districts and Local Economic Regeneration*, Frank Pyke and Werner Sengenberger eds. (Geneva: International Institute for Labour Studies, 1992); *Industrial Districts and Inter-Firm Co-operation in Italy*, Frank Pyke, Giacomo Becattini, and Werner Sengenberger eds. (Geneva: International Institute for Labour Studies, 1990).

8. Quoted in Stuart Elmer, "From 'Business Unionism' to 'Social Movement Unionism': The Case of the AFL-CIO Milwaukee County Labor Council" in *Labor Studies Journal,* vol. 24, no. 2 (Summer 1999): 73.

9. Numbers taken from the "Summary of Complaint to be Filed Charging Discrimination Against African Americans in Transportation Planning," Summer 1998.

10. John Anner, "Making Tracks for Justice," *Third Force,* vol. 5, no. 3.

11. Larry Sandler, "Opponents Say Light Rail Brings Strangers," *Milwaukee Journal Sentinel,* Thursday, December 12, 1996.

12. The material on Navistar comes from Bill Luker, "Workplace Learning and Workplace Transformation at Navistar Foundry," report from the Center on Wisconsin Strategy, 1998.

13. Ibid., p. 5.

14. Bill Lucker, Jeffrey Rickert, and Gary Layden, "Wisconsin Regional Training Partnership Benchmark Employer Survey," report from the Center on Wisconsin Strategy, April 1998.

15. Laura Dresser and Joel Rogers, "Rebuilding Job Access and Career Advancement Systems in the New Economy," Center on Wisconsin Strategy, December 1997, pp. 14–15.

16. Unless otherwise noted, all statistics are from *Milwaukee Jobs Initiative Strategic Investment Plan* submitted to the Annie E. Casey Foundation November 29, 1996.

17. *Milwaukee Jobs Initiative Strategic Investment Plan 1998 Update,* submitted to the Annie E. Casey Foundation April 1, 1998.

18. Daniel McGroarty and Cameron Humphries, "Milwaukee's Gullible Corporate Donors," *Wall Street Journal,* Tuesday, August, 1995.

19. Kathleen Gallagher, "GMC Fires Back at Attack on 'Gullible Execs,' " *Milwaukee Journal Sentinel,* August 24, 1995, Section D.

Chapter 9. State Campaigns for Economic Justice

1. Kenneth Thomas, *Competing for Capital: Europe and North America in a Global Era* (Washington, DC: Georgetown University Press, 2000).

2. Numbers from the clearinghouse: Good Jobs First.

3. Unless otherwise noted, examples come from Greg LeRoy, *No More Candy Store* (available from Good Jobs First), chapter 1; AFL-CIO Human Resources Development Institute, *Economic Development: A Union Guide to the High Road*, chapter 2; and Michael Moore, *Downsize This* (New York: Basic Books, 1996).

4 "Payoffs for Layoffs" by the Center for an Urban Future, 2000.

5. Quoted in LeRoy, p. 1.

6. Referenced in "Shifting Workplace" by Louis Uchitelle in *New York Times*, July 24, 2000.

7. Institute on Taxation and Economic Policy, October 19, 2000.

8. Greg LeRoy, "Minding the Candy Store: State Audits of Economic Development," available from Good Jobs First, 2000.

9. Marc Breslow, Op Ed in the *Bangor Daily News,* July 3, 2000.

10. Aaron Bernstein, "A Leg Up for the Lowly Temp" in *Business Week,* June 21, 1999.

11. Upjohn Institute for Employment Research surveyed 550 employers of various sizes. Another study by the American Management Association of 1,248 firms found that 93 percent used contingent workers. For half of such firms, the contingent workers were 5 percent or less of their total workforce.

12. Numbers from the National Association of Temporary and Staffing Services cited in Bernstein op. cit. And "What's Wrong With Contingent Work?" by the Massachusetts Campaign on Contingent Work, 1999.

13. Christopher Cook, "Temps Demand New Deal" in *The Nation*, March 27, 2000; National Alliance for Fair Employment, *Contingent Workers Fight for Fairness*, (Boston, MA), 2000.

14. Massachusetts Campaign on Contingent Work (Boston, MA), 1999, p. 12.

15. This national Bureau of Labor Statistics data was published in *Minnesota Economic Trends,* March 1999, published by the MDES.

16. Federal Reserve of Chicago Working Paper (WP-96–26) by Lewis Segal and Daniel Sullivan.

17. American Management Association.

18. *Minnesota Economic Trends* op. cit.

19. Bernstein op. cit.

20. National Alliance for Fair Employment op. cit.

21. American Management Association.

22. "Forward into the Past With Labor Ready" in *Contingent Update* Number 5 (Center on Contingent Work).

23. From an interview with David West, who works for the law firm that won the recent ruling against Microsoft, posted on the New Jersey Temp Worker Alliance Web site. The Microsoft case was also described by James Sharft of AON Consulting in a Web posting by the Society for Industrial and Organizational Psychology (2001).

24. Cook, p. 15.

25. Maurice Emsellem and Catherine Ruckelshaus, "Organizing for Workplace Equity: Model State Legislation for 'Nonstandard' Workers," National Employment Law Project, November 2000 edition.

26. A main source for information about organizing around contingent work is "Contingent Workers Fight for Fairness," a report regularly updated by the National Alliance for Fair Employment.

27. Ibid., p. 18.

28. Jill Quadagno, *The Color of Welfare* (New York: Oxford University Press, 1994), chapter 1.

29. Marc Jacobson, "The Minimum Wage," Coalition for Human Needs Issue Brief, 2000.

30. David Card and Alan B. Krueger, *Myth and Measurement: The New Economics of the Minimum Wage* (Princeton, NJ: Princeton University Press, 1995); Jeff Thompson, "Oregon's Increasing Minimum Wage," Oregon Center for Public Policy, June 1999; Jared Bernstein and John Schmitt, "Making Work Pay; The Impact of the 1996–97 Minimum Wage Increase," Economic Policy Institute, 1998.

31. Ken Grossinger, "How Labor Defeated California's Proposition 226" in *Working USA* (September/October 1998), pp. 84–90.

32. David Kusnet, "The New Labor Movement and the Politics of Living Standards," in *Working USA* (September/October 1998), pp. 26–35.

Chapter 10. The New Labor Movement

1. The UAW information comes from the union. The SEIU data is from Stephen Herzenberg, "Reinventing the U.S. Labor Movement, Inventing Postindustrial Prosperity: A Progress Report," Keystone Research Center, January 2000, p. 14.

2. Workers who strike because their employer violated the law (an unfair labor practice strike) cannot be permanently replaced.

3. Speech given at Linden Hall, June 21, 2000.

4. Bureau of Labor Statistics, 1997 figures.

5. Peter Hart Research, 1997.

6. Kate Bronfenbrenner, "The Effects of Plant Closing or Threat of Plant Closing on the Right of Workers to Organize," report submitted to the North American Commission for Labor Cooperation, September 30, 1996.

7. Immanuel Ness, "The Road to Union Cities," *Working USA* (November–December 1998), p. 85.

8. The survey results are from the AFL-CIO Field Mobilization Department. These figures and the examples and quotations were used by Immanuel Ness op. cit., pp. 78–87. The analysis also comes from interviews with and presentations made by AFL-CIO staff.

9. Ibid., pp. 9–10, 12–13.

10. The material on WPUSA and the central labor council comes from interviews with several staff, both organizations' written materials, and an article by the WPUSA's policy director Bob Brownstein, published as "Working Partnerships" in *Working USA* (Summer 2000), vol. 4, no. 1, pp. 35–48.

11. Brownstein, p. 43.

Chapter 11. Melding Environmental and Social Justice Activism: The Emerging Battle Against Sprawl

1. Unless otherwise stated, information on the timber wars comes from Fred Rose, *Coalition Across the Class Divide* (Ithaca, NY: Cornell University Press, 2000), chapter 3.

2. The Public Health Institute and The Labor Institute, *Jobs and the Environment* draft (1994), p. 62.

3. This story is taken from Rose, chapter 8.

4. Christine Keyser, "Common Ground: Steelworkers and Environmentalists Team Up to Fight Corporate Greed" in *In These Times,* February 21, 1999.

5. Charles Lee, "Beyond Toxic Waste and Race" in *Confronting Environmental Racism,* Robert Bullard ed. (Boston: South End Press, 1993), pp. 48–49.

6. All figures come from F. Kaid Benfield, Matthew Raimi, and Donald Chen, *Once There Were Greenfields* (New York: National Resources Defense Council, 1999), chapter 2.

7. Ibid.

8. Ibid., chapter 4.

9. Ibid., p. 25.

10. Ibid., p. 73.

11. All figures from ibid., chapter 3.

12. Cited in a curriculum developed by Good Jobs First

entitled *Smart Growth, Good Jobs*, Greg LeRoy and Sara Hinkley, April 2000.

13. Dan Luria and Joel Rogers, *Metro Futures: Economic Strategies for Cities and Their Suburbs* (Boston: Beacon Press, 1999).

14. LeRoy and Hinkley curriculum.

15. Benfield, Raimi, and Chen, chapter 1.

16. Ibid., pp. 29–40.

17. Ibid., p. 39.

18. Ibid., p. 153.

19. Our discussion draws on the explanation of the institutional and policy process behind Portland's experience provided by Paul Lewis in *Shaping Suburbia: How Political Institutions Organize Urban Development* (Pittsburgh: University of Pittsburgh Press, 1996).

20. Ibid., pp. 180–181.

21. Benfield, Raimi, and Chen, p. 153.

22. Myron Orfield, *Metro Politics* (Washington, DC: Brookings Institution Press, 1997), pp. 157–160.

23. Sierra Club, 1999 Sprawl Report.

24. National September 2000 survey commissioned by *Smart Growth America*.

25. Quoted in "The State vs. Sprawl" in *Governing* (January 1999).

26. The stupidity of current zoning practices and the common sense of neighborhood-based alternatives is explored in detail in *Suburban Nation*, Andres Duany, Elizabeth Plater-Zyberk, and Jeff Speck eds. (New York: North Point Press, 2000).

27. Studies have shown that narrower, pedestrian-friendly streets actually reduce traffic accidents by slowing traffic and encouraging drivers to pay more attention to possible hazards. See ibid., pp. 33–37 and 64–83.

28. Cited in Al Norman, *Slam-Dunking Wal-Mart! How You Can Stop Superstore Sprawl in Your Hometown* (Atlantic City, NJ: Raphel Marketing, 1999), p. 163.

29. Benfield, Raimi, and Chen, p. 147.

30. Op. cit.

31. *Slam-Dunking Wal-Mart!* is the title of a book by Al Norman op. cit. We also used Bill Quinn, *How Wal-Mart Is Destroying America: And What You Can Do About It* (Berkeley: Ten Speed Press, 1998).

32. Norman, p. 18.

33. *Washington Post,* Saturday, March 4, 2000.

34. See the National Labor Committee's Web site: *www.nlc.org.*

35. Quoted in Norman, p. 33.

36. Norman, p. 26; Quinn, p. 4.

37. Norman, pp. 24–26.

38. Quinn, pp. 67–68.

39. All specific campaign cases come from Norman.

40. Bureau of National Affairs, *Union Labor Report Number 35,* August 31, 2000.

41. Ted Bernard and Jora Young, *The Ecology of Hope: Communities Collaborate for Sustainability* (East Haven, CT: New Society Publishers, 1997), p. 62. Their chapter 4 is devoted to Chattanooga.

Chapter 12. Toward a National Movement

1. The study's results were published by the Peace Development Fund as "The Listening Project: A National Dialogue on Progressive Movement-Building," 1999.

2. The IMF-World Bank demonstrations in Washington also drew media attention. For example, the April 24 editions of both *Time* and *Newsweek* ran stories covering the protests and even published focus articles suggesting that activists' critique of free trade pointed to some real problems. For an overview of the events and issues involved in the WTO protests, see *Globalize This!* Kevin Danaher and Roger Burbach eds. (Monroe, ME: Common Courage Press, 2000).

3. The largely white profile of the American contingents highlights a challenge facing the U.S. movement against corporate globalization. For a discussion of why more people of color were not involved in the protests and ways to address these issues see Elizabeth Martinez, "Where Was the Color in Seattle?" in Danaher and Burbach.

4. Danaher and Burbach, p. 10.

5. The dark story of the chemical industry was told, using internal industry documents, in the PBS documentary *Trade Secrets.*

6. Chuck Collins and Felice Yeskel, *Economic Apartheid in America* (New York: New Press, 2000), pp. 167–169.

7. William Greider, "It's Time to Go on the Offensive: Here's How" in Danaher and Burbach.

8. Referred to in Roberto Unger, *Democracy Realized* (New York: Verso, 1998), p. 144.

9. Randy Barber and Teresa Ghilarducci, "Pension Funds, Capital Markets, and the Economic Future" in *Transforming the U.S. Financial System,* Gary Dymski, Gerald Epstein, and Robert Pollin eds. (New York: M.E. Sharpe, 1993), pp. 287–288.

Chapter 13. Progressive Electoral Politics

1. Published by South End Press in 1997.

2. Edited by Richard Winger, the newsletter *Ballot*

Access News is devoted to detailing these obstacles and profiling efforts by groups to overcome and change them. *Ballot Access News,* Box 470296, San Francisco, CA, 94147, 415–922–9779.

3. John Bonifaz, "Losing Our Vote in the Wealth Primary" in report by the Center for Voting and Democracy 1995, pp. 130–131.

4. Reynolds, *Democracy Unbound* pp. 114–119.

5. "Representation Index" for 1994 Election is compiled by the Center for Voting and Democracy, 6905 Fifth St., NW, Suite 200, Washington, DC, 20012.

6. In Great Britain, the delegation to the European Parliament and the Scottish legislative body are selected by proportional representation.

7. For documented evidence of how grassroots activity, and not simply Jackson's candidacy, raised voter turnout, see Reynolds, chapter 4.

8. Louise Simmons, "Labor and the LEAP: Political Coalition Experiences in Connecticut" in *Working USA,* vol. 4, no. 1 (Summer 2000), pp. 19–34.

Annotated Bibliography and Contacts

The below references are intended to provide next-step readings for a general reader who wishes to explore specific topics in greater detail. For each topic, we recommend a couple of works. The endnotes for each chapter provide a more detailed and full list of the works used in our research.

Part I

Background on the European Left

The single best source on the European left is Donald Sassoon's massive *One Hundred Years of Socialism: The West European Left in the Twentieth Century* (New York: I.B. Tauris Publishers, 1996). Those seeking a short summary history should try Stephen Padgett and William Paterson, *A History of Social Democracy in Postwar Europe* (London: Longman, 1991).

Cornell University Press (Ithaca, NY) has an extensive publishing series on Political Economy dedicated to state industrial policies. Many of the authors published by Cornell are sympathetic to social democracy. All focus on state action as a key component of economic health and change. Cornell publications are cited throughout the below references and in the chapter endnotes.

A taste of current debates within European left academic circles can be found in the pages of the British publication *New Left Review*.

Working Under Different Rules, Richard Freeman ed. (New York: Russell Sage Foundation, 1994), summarizes the results of a large collaborative research project to compare U.S. and European economic practices. French businessman Michel Albert rails against U.S. business practices and defends German capitalism in *Capitalism vs. Capitalism: How America's Obsession with Individual Achievement and Short-term Profit has Led It to the Brink of Collapse* (New York: Four Walls Eight Windows, 1993).

Scandinavian Social Democracy

The classic work on the politics of social democracy is Gøsta Esping-Andersen, *Politics Against Markets* (Princeton, NJ: Princeton University Press, 1985). Esping-Andersen came to appreciate social democracy from his background begun in the New Left of the 1960s. His later work *The Three Worlds of Welfare Capitalism* (Princeton, NJ: Princeton University Press, 1990) provides a good overall discussion of the welfare state in the industrialized world.

The Swedish Institute provides a wealth of free information about the country. We used several of their four-page fact sheets. Two booklets were also quite helpful. *Social Insurance in Sweden 1999* provided a wealth of data on much of the basic Swedish welfare state, including brief descriptions of the actual programs. Gunilla Fürst, *Sweden—The Equal Way* (Stockholm: The Swedish Institute, 1999), offers an excellent short overview of Swedish efforts around gender equality. In addition to trumpeting the country's achievements, Fürst also looks hard at the failures and roads that still need to be traveled. Material from The Swedish Institute can be ordered through the Swedish embassy's New York offices. See *www.si.se.*

For additional discussion of the link between the welfare state and gender see Diane Sainsbury, *Gender, Equality, and Welfare States* (New York: Cambridge University Press, 1996) and *Gender and Economics: A European Perspective,* A. Geske Dijkstra and Janneke Plantenga eds. (New York: Routledge, 1997).

The essays in *Creating Social Democracy,* Klaus Misgeld, Karl Molin, and Klas Åmark eds. (University Park: Pennsylvania State University Press, 1988), provide a handy historical background on Swedish economics and politics. For a look at an early left-wing challenge to social democracy see John Logue, *Socialism and Abundance: Radical Socialism in the Danish Welfare State* (Minneapolis: University of Minnesota Press, 1982).

Jonas Pontusson, *The Limits of Social Democracy: Investment Politics in Sweden* (Ithaca, NY: Cornell University Press, 1992), provides an insightful look at how Sweden has used its pension funds, investment reserve funds, and codetermination laws to try to steer capitalism from without. Pontusson also provides a detailed discussion of the Wage Earner Funds debate.

Germany and Associative Democracy

Paul Hirst provides a good overview of the idea of associative democracy in *Associative Democracy: New Forms of Economic and Social Governance* (Amherst: University of Massachusetts Press, 1994). See also Joshua Cohen and Joel Rogers, *Associations and Democracy* (New York: Verso Books, 1995).

A good short summary of Germany's social market is provided by Maurice Glasman, *Unnecessary Suffering: Managing Market Utopia* (New York: Verso, 1996). For differing opinions on the extent to which German institutions can successfully evolve into the twenty-first century see *Negotiating the New Germany: Can Social Partnership Survive?* Lowell Turner ed. (Ithaca, NY: Cornell University Press, 1997).

While dated, Wolfgang Streeck's *Industrial Relations in West Germany: A Case Study of the Car Industry* (London: Heinemann Educational Books, 1984) still provides good details on the basic structure of codetermination. Codetermination also figures prominently in Lowell Turner's comparative look at workplace change in the United States and Germany entitled *Democracy at Work: Changing World Markets and the Future of Labor Unions* (Ithaca, NY: Cornell University Press, 1991) and Kathleen Thelen, *Union of Parts: Labor Politics in Postwar Germany* (Ithaca, NY: Cornell University Press, 1991). For a comparative look at works councils in Europe and Canada see *Works Councils,* Joel Rogers and Wolfgang Streeck eds. (Chicago: University of Chicago Press, 1995).

Austria, Social Partnership, and Public Ownership

English sources on the Austrian political economy are not easy to find. While dated, Theodor Tomandl and Karl Fuerboeck provide a quite readable introduction to the basics in *Social Partnership: The Austrian System of Industrial Relations and Social Insurance* (Ithaca, NY: ILR Press, 1986). *Austro-Corporatism,* Gunter Bischof and Anton Pelinka eds. (New Brunswick, NJ: Transaction Publishers, 1996), provides a good discussion of Austrian history and recent developments. The literature on corporatism could easily fill a library. For a starting point, Peter Katzenstein's *Small States in World Markets* (Ithaca, NY: Cornell University Press, 1985) provides an insightful introduction focused on European experiences. A series of assessments of corporatism in Europe is provided by *Social Corporatism: A Superior Economic System?* Jukka Pekkarinen, Matti Pohjola, and Bob Rowthorn eds. (Oxford: Clarendon Press, 1992).

Leland Stauber, *A New Program for Democratic Socialism: Lessons from the Market-Planning Experience in Austria* (Carbondale, IL: Four Willows Press, 1987), provides a detailed examination of Austria's nationalized sector during its heyday. As the title suggests, Stauber aimed to draw out lessons for how to organize a market economy around public-owned means of production. The Austrian nationalized sector also figures prominently in John Freeman's comparison of Austria, Sweden, Britain, and Italy in *Democracy and Markets: The Politics of Mixed Economies* (Ithaca, NY: Cornell University Press, 1989). Jeanne Kirk Laux and Maureen Appel Molot's *State Capitalism: Public Enterprise in Canada* (Ithaca, NY: Cornell University Press, 1988) has a good introductory chapter on public ownership generally and then a detailed examination of the experience in Quebec.

The Crisis of Social Democracy

Fritz Scharpf's *Crisis and Choice in European Social Democracy* (Ithaca, NY: Cornell University Press, 1987) is a classic presentation of the economic and political crisis facing social democracy. For other works in the field of political economy that focus on the crisis see the endnotes for chapter 4.

For those wishing to explore the roads not taken, three works together provide a good overview for Britain, France, and Sweden respectively: Leo Panitch and Colin Leys, *The End of Parliamentary Socialism* (New York: Verso, 1997); Daniel Singer, *Is Socialism Doomed?* (New York: Oxford University Press, 1998); Jonas Pontusson, *The Limits of Social Democracy: Investment Politics in Sweden* (Ithaca, NY: Cornell University Press, 1992). The debate over the AES can be followed through old issues of the British journals *Capital and Class* and

New Left Review. A major research library is also likely to have the basic articulation of the strategy, entitled: *Alternative Economic Strategy: A Response by the Labour Movement to the Economic Crisis* (London: CSE Books, 1980). Those wishing to pursue each case further should see the endnotes for chapter 4.

Globalization

The American and British left have debated "globalization" for over a decade. Three sources to follow this debate are *New Left Review*, *Monthly Review*, and the annual *Socialist Register*. Linda Weiss, *The Myth of the Powerless State* (Ithaca, NY: Cornell University Press, 1998), provides a well-written response to the globalization hype written from the perspective of a comparative political economy.

Two works provide an accessible historical overview demonstrating how states have created the current global economy, including the central role played by the U.S. government. See Peter Gowan, *The Global Gamble: Washington's Faustian Bid for World Dominance* (New York: Verso, 1999), and Eric Helleiner, *States and the Reemergence of Global Finance* (Ithaca, NY: Cornell University Press, 1994).

Green Politics

While Green parties are active throughout Europe, the German Greens are the best studied with material available in English. A good starting point is *The German Greens: Paradox Between Movement and Party,* Margit Mayer and John Ely eds. (Philadelphia: Temple University Press, 1998). For an idea of Green economics applied at a global level see The Group of Green Economists, *Ecological Economics: A Practical Programme for Global Reform* (London: Zed Books, 1992). Herman Daly is one of several famous American articulators of ecological economics. As a former employee of the World Bank,

Daly is able to critique conventional capitalist economics using its own terms. See, for example, his *Beyond Growth* (Boston: Beacon Press, 1996).

Triumph of Liberal America

The history of American social movement can easily fill a library. The notes provided in chapter 6 offer an introduction into key periods using some of the classic historical studies. *The Rise and Fall of the New Deal Order 1930–1980,* Steve Fraser and Gary Gerstle eds. (Princeton, NJ: Princeton University Press, 1989) provides summary articles that cover three of the four periods summarized in chapter 6. Those looking for an overview of American history from a social movement perspective should start with the American Social History Project, *Who Built America?* 2 Volumes (New York: Pantheon, 1992). The volumes include ample references. Elizabeth Fones-Wolf provides an important reminder that the predominance of American individualism is not a natural cultural condition, but something that business and ordinary Americans have contested. See *Selling Free Enterprise: The Business Assault on Labor and Liberalism 1945–60* (Urbana: University of Illinois Press, 1994).

Part II

Relative to the topics covered in Part I, far less has been written about current economic justice organizing, especially in book-length form. Most of what does exist represents intellectual expressions of the ideas behind organizing or research data that support specific progressive policy ideas. Often the best sources of information are the Web sites maintained by the many activist groups. Contact information for the organizations covered in this book is provided below.

The High Road–Low Road Concept

Several authors offer well-written presentations of the contrast between low-road and high-road busi-

nesses strategies. See Dan Sweeney, "Building Bridges to the High Road" available from the Midwest Center for Labor Research, 3411 West Diversey Ave., Suite 10; Chicago, IL, 60647, *www.mclr.org;* Dan Luria and Joel Rogers, *Metro Futures: Economic Strategies for Cities and their Suburbs* (Boston: Beacon Press, 1999); *Economic Development: A Union Guide to the High Road,* available from the AFL-CIO's Working for America Institute, 1101 14th, N.W., Suite 320, Washington, DC 20005, 202–638–3912, *www.workingforamerica.org.*

Myron Orfield, *Metro Politics: A Regional Agenda for Community Stability* (Washington, DC: The Brookings Institution Press, 1997), details the research and activism surrounding the research used to rethink regional economic policies in the Twin Cities.

Living Wage Campaigns

David Reynolds, *Living Wage Campaigns: An Activist's Guide to Building the Movement for Economic Justice* (Published by ACORN, 2001 Edition), details campaigns across the country and explains in detail how to organize an effective campaign. The guide includes five pages of contact information for organizations involved in living wage campaigns and related written reports and other items. A 125-page text portion, minus 80 pages of sample documents, is also available at *www.laborstudies.wayne.edu.* Robert Pollin and Stephanie Luce, *The Living Wage: Building a Fair Economy* (New York: New Press, 1998) provides the research data and policy overview to support living wage laws. The authors created the basic research methodology used across the country to estimate the impact of a local living wage law.

ACORN's Living Wage Resource Center provides a national clearinghouse for living wage campaigns. Contact: Jen Kern, 739 8th St. S.E., Washington, DC 20003, 202–547–2500, *www.acorn.org, natacorn cam@acorn.org.* For a look at the opposition see the Employment Policies Institute. Their Web site, *www.livingwage.org,* is dedicated to opposing the living wage.

Wisconsin

The best-written material on Wisconsin comes out of the Center on Wisconsin Strategy. The COWS Web site is particularly rich in material. Go to *www.cows.org*. The COWS site also hosts material for Jobs with a Future. The high-road piece referenced above by Dan Luria and Joel Rogers also directly reflects the Wisconsin experience. The MJI has a Web site at *www.mji.org*; the WRTP is at *www.wrtp.org*.

Corporate Accountability

Good Jobs First provides a national clearinghouse on efforts at subsidy accountability, including the latest reports documenting abuse and on efforts to enact policy changes. Contact: Good Jobs First, 1311 L Street, N.W., Washington, DC 20005, 202–626–3780, *goodjobs@ctj.org*, *www.goodjobsfirst.org*. For Minnesota contact the Minnesota Alliance for Progressive Action, 1821 University Ave, Suite 5-307, St. Paul, MN 55104, 651-641–4053, *www.mapa-mn.org*. For an academic work that compares the exploding use of subsidies in the United States to the more modest practices in Europe see Kenneth Thomas, *Competing for Capital: Europe and America in a Global Era* (Baltimore: Georgetown University Press, 2000).

Contingent Work

The single-best source of information on both the state of the problem and the state of the movement for change is provided in "Contingent Workers Fight for Fairness," a report regularly updated by the National Alliance for Fair Employment. The alliance provides a clearinghouse for information about contingent-worker organizing. Contact NAFE, 33 Harrison Avenue, 4th floor, Boston, MA 02111, 617-338–9966, *www.fairjobs.org*. The Winter 2000–2001 issue (vol. 4, no. 3) of *Working USA* was dedicated to contingent workers and the labor movement. Academic works dedicated to contingent employment include *Nonstandard Work,* Franiose Carré et al., eds. (Ithaca, NY: Cornell University Press, 2000); *Contingent Work,* Kathleen Barker and Kathleen Christensen eds. (Ithaca, NY: Cornell University Press, 1998); Jackie Krasas, *Rogers Temps: The Many Faces of the Changing Workplace* (Ithaca, NY: Cornell University Press, 2000).

Raising the Minimum Wage

The Economic Policy Institute maintains a wealth of information about the need for and impact of raising the minimum wage. Contact Economic Policy Institute, 1660 L Street, NW, Suite 1200, Washington, DC 20036, 202–775–8810, *www.epinet.org*. The Vermont Livable Wage Campaign maintains a Web site at *www.vtlivablewage.org*. Also contact the campaign at the Peace and Justice Center, 21 Church St., Burlington, VT 05401, 802-863-2345.

The New Labor Movement

Since the revitalization of the American labor movement is very much a work in progress, the best sources for the latest information are often found in journals. *Working USA* and *New Labor Forum* offer two sources dedicated to covering the labor movement in transition. The AFL-CIO's Web site offers much information and many links at *www.aflcio.org*. The organization's magazine, *America@Work,* is aimed at activists and dedicated to covering the national leadership's reform agenda through stories of on-the-ground activism. Among its many publications, the AFL-CIO has also produced*Communities@Work*—a guide to building labor-community alliances around the right to organize. The manual includes an entire section dedicated to detailed examples. Steve Babson offers a short and helpful overview of how the labor movement has confronted change at key moments in its history in *The Unfinished Struggle* (New York: Rowman & Littlefield, 2000). The fourth period

Babson examines is the current crisis of organized labor.

High-Road Partnerships

The AFL-CIO's Working for America Institute provides a good clearinghouse for union-company partnerships around the high road. Contact the institute at 1101 14th, N.W., Suite 320, Washington, DC 20005, 202–638–3912, *www.working foramerica.org*. The Center on Wisconsin Strategy's Web site (see above) is also a good source of information.

Stephen Herzenberg, John Alic, and Howard Wial offer a timely vision of the problems and high-road possibilities of work in today's service-based economy in *New Rules for a New Economy* (Ithaca, NY: Cornell University Press, 1998). These proposed reforms include new work standards, multiemployee partnerships, and new labor market institutions.

WPUSA

The group's Web site offers a wealth of information. Contact Working Partnerships USA, 2102 Almaden Road, Suite 107, San Jose, CA 95125, 408-269–7872, *www.atwork.org*. Their political director, Bob Brownstein, wrote an article summarizing the group's political experience published in *Working USA* (Summer 2000).

Labor-Environmentalist Coalitions

Fred Rose, *Coalition Across the Class Divide* (Ithaca, NY: Cornell University Press, 2000) offers a detailed discussion of coalitions between unions and environmentalists and the peace movement. In addition to his research, Rose has been an active participant in coalition building. The Alliance for Sustainable Jobs and the Environment can be contacted at 1125 SE Madison St., Portland, OR 97214, 503-736–9777, or on the Web at *home. pacifier.com/~asje/*.

Sprawl

A mushrooming array of research pieces and books now look at issues of land use and alternatives to sprawl. In the field of architecture and urban planning, "New Urbanism" is a term used to describe works that deal with this subject. Planners Andres Duany, Elizabeth Plater-Zybeck, and Jeff Speck drew from their experiences in designing over two hundred new neighborhoods and community revitalization plans to write *Suburban Nations: The Rise of Sprawl and the Decline of the American Dream* (New York: North Point Press, 2000). This work offers an excellent step-by-step look at the idiocy of suburban development patterns, and the economic and social superiority of traditional town planning. The authors show how sustainable, vibrant mixed communities are not only possible, but simply common sense. The book by F. Kaid Benfield, Matthew Raimi, and Donald Chen, *Once There Were Greenfields* (New York: National Resources Defense Council, 1999), offers a handy compendium of the negative effects of sprawl. It also offers some material on alternatives. The Sierra Club has taken up sprawl as one of its central issues. The group's Web site, *www.sierraclub.org*, has a wealth of material.

A growing number of antisprawl groups have developed on the Web. The Sprawlwatch clearinghouse is a rich source of material. See *www.sprawl watch.org*. Smart Growth America also offers a variety of materials and contacts at *www.smart growth.org*.

Wal-Mart

Al Norman, *Slam-Dunking Wal-Mart! How You Can Stop Superstore Sprawl in Your Hometown* (Atlantic City, NJ: Raphel Marketing, 1999), explains both the company's strategies and how people have fought back. Norman maintains a Web site that provides a good clearinghouse for information at *www.sprawlb usters.org*. The UFCW also has an anti-Wal-Mart

Web site at *www.walmartwatch.com.* For another book detailing Wal-Mart see Bill Quinn, *How Wal-Mart Is Destroying America: And What You Can Do About It* (Berkeley: Ten Speed Press, 1998). Stacy Mitchell offers a practical guide to preserving small business downtowns against chain stores in *The Home Town Advantage: How to Defend Your Main Street Against Chain Stores* (Minneapolis: Institute for Local Self-Reliance, 2000).

The Sustainability Movement

As a global movement involving a wide range of people, sustainability has generated a mountain of material that encompasses many different perspectives. To get started try the following. Herman Daly argues for sustainability using business's own terms in *Beyond Growth* (Boston: Beacon Press, 1996). Paul Hawken has emerged as an environmental activist who has built a following among corporate leaders. His recent *Natural Capitalism* (New York: Little Brown, 1999) summarizes sustainability from a business perspective. For short community case studies, see *The Ecology of Hope: Communities Collaborating for Sustainability,* Ted Bernard and Jora Young eds. (New Haven, CT: New Society Publishers, 1997) and *Eco-city Dimensions,* Mark Roseland ed. (New Haven, CT: New Society Publishers, 1997). Huey Johnson explores the notion of public environmental recovering plans in *Green Plans* (Lincoln: University of Nebraska Press, 1995).

The Shape of Change is an excellent multimodule curriculum for adults and high school students that details the concept and practice of sustainability from both an environmental and social-justice perspective. Available from: Creative Change Educational Solutions, *www.creativechange.net, educhange @irg.org.*

Seattle WTO Protests

Several compendiums were published soon in the wake of the Seattle protests. See, for example, *Glo-balize This!* Kevin Danaher and Roger Burbach eds. (Monroe, ME: Common Courage Press, 2000) and "After Seattle" a special issue of *Monthly Review,* vol. 62, no. 3 (July/August 2000). Jeremy Brecher and Tim Costello have written two quite useful works summarizing the struggle against globalization. See *Globalization from Below* (Boston: South End Press, 2000) and *Global Village or Global Pillage* (Boston: South End Press, 1994).

A Progressive Agenda

Many progressive writers have offered ideas for policy reforms and fundamental economic change. Two theoretical works stand out. Roberto Unger, *Democracy Realized* (New York: Verso, 1998), is quite abstract but offers an excellent vision. Dan Luria and Joel Rogers offer more down-to-earth strategizing in *Metro Futures: Economic Strategies for Cities and Their Suburbs* (Boston: Beacon Press, 1999). Luria and Rogers were part of a series of policy debates over economic, social, and political issues that ran in the *Boston Review.* Many of these debates have been published in book form by Beacon Press as part of their New Democracy series. Two other notable alternative policy summaries are: Juliet Schor, *A Sustainable Economy for the 21st Century* (New York: Seven Stories Press, 1998), and Sheila Collins, Helen Lachs Ginsburg, and Gertrude Schaffner Goldberg, *Jobs for All: A Plan for the Revitalization of America* (New York: United Nations Apex Press, 1994).

The Institute for Local Self-Reliance is a nonprofit research and educational organization that promotes strong communities, healthy local economies, and environmental sustainability. Their New Rules project provides a clearinghouse of new on-the-ground reform ideas. A magazine publication, *New Rules,* offers an excellent summary of these ideas. Contact: Institute for Self-Reliance, 1313 5th Street SE, Minneapolis, MN 55414, 612–379–3815, *www.ilsr.org.*

Organizing for Political Change

Efforts to reform the political system are best explored through two major clearinghouses. The Center for Voting and Democracy (6930 Carroll Ave., Suite 901, Takoma Park, MD 20912, 301–270–4616, *www.fairvote.org*) focuses on voting systems and proportional representation. Public Campaign (1320 19th Street, NW, Suite M-1, Washington, DC 20036, 202–293–0222, *www.publicampaign.org*) promotes Clean Election reforms. For how unions are rethinking their political action see the Summer 2000 issue of *Working USA* (vol. 4, no.1), which is dedicated to "Labor Rethinks Politics." See also the sources cited above for the new labor movement. Herbert Asher, Eric Heberlig, Randall Ripley, and Karen Snyder offer an interesting academic evaluation of union political activity and how it is changing in *American Labor Unions in the Electoral Arena* (New York: Rowman & Littlefield, 2001).

David Reynolds provides a detailed examination of past and present efforts to build independent third parties, as well as LEAP, in *Democracy Unbound*: *Progressive Challenges to the Two Party System* (Boston: South End Press, 1997). Professor Louise Simmons has written about LEAP and labor-community coalitions in Connecticut for years as both a researcher and participant. The *Working USA* issue above includes one of her latest pieces. The Independent Progressive Politics Network provides a clearinghouse on progressive third-party efforts at IPPN, P.O. Box 1041, Bloomfield, NJ 07003, *www.ippn.org*. The group's Independent Politics News provides a wealth of information written by the activists doing the organizing.

Interview List

Stephanie Luce, Political Economy Research Institute

Kerry Miciotto, Solidarity Sponsoring Committee-BUILD

Jeff Ordower, St. Louis ACORN (Formerly Houston)

Jim Niland, Minneapolis City Councilor

Gyula Nagy, Northern Virginia Living Wage Campaign, Tenants and Workers Support Committee

Jim DuPont, HERE 2850, Oakland

Madeline Janis-Aparicio, Los Angeles Alliance for a New Economy

Eddy Inny, SEIU 1877, Los Angeles-LAX

Reverend Dick Gillette, CLUE, Los Angeles

Linda Lotz, formerly of CLUE, Los Angeles

Erika Zucker, Los Angeles Alliance for a New Economy

Bruce Nissen, Miami-Dade County Coalition for a Living Wage, Florida International University

Ann Sink, Durham Living Wage Campaign

Madeline Talbott, Illinois ACORN

Lisa Clauson, Massachusetts ACORN

Monica Halas, Greater Boston Legal Services

John Speier, Kalamazoo Living Wage Campaign

Lisa Donner, ACORN National Campaign Director (Brooklyn)

Steve Cagan, Cleveland Jobs with Justice

Charles Murray, Cleveland Catholic Diocese

Linda Wambaugh, Alliance for Progressive Action/ Western PA Living Wage Campaign

Greg LeRoy, Good Jobs First

Cynthia Ward, Citizen for Economic Opportunity, Northeast Action

Louise Simmons, University of Connecticut

Tim Costello, Massachusetts Contingent Worker Campaign

Laura Younger, Massachusetts Contingent Worker Campaign

John Leopold, Working Partnerships USA

Bob Brownstein, Working Partnerships USA

Bill Dempsey, Campaign for a Sustainable Milwaukee

Dee Reynolds, Campaign for a Sustainable Milwaukee

Joseph Pepe Oulahan, Campaign for a Sustainable Milwaukee

Bruce Colburn, ALF-CIO (Milwaukee, now AFL-CIO Field Mobilization)

Muleka Aljuwani, Community Assets (Milwaukee)

Don Richards, Alderman, Milwaukee

Joel Rogers, Center on Wisconsin Strategy

Laura Dresser, Center on Wisconsin Strategy

Rhandi Berth, Wisconsin Regional Training Partnership

Tammy Johnson, formerly of Progressive Milwaukee

John Golstein, President Milwaukee Central Labor Council

Dan Cantor, Working Families Party, formerly director of the New Party

Jim Lynch, Little Rock New Party

Neil Sealy, Little Rock ACORN

Zack Pollet, Little Rock ACORN

Erik Petersen, Duluth Living Wage Campaign and Minnesota Alliance for Progressive Action

Beth Fraser, Minnesota Alliance for Progressive Action

David Morris, Institute for Local Self-Reliance

Ehlen Kahler, Vermont Livable Wage Campaign

This book also draws on material obtained at the following conferences: ACORN National Living Wage Training Conference 1998, ACORN National Living Wage Training Conference 2000, National meeting of Living Wage Researchers 1999, Working for America Institute's 2000 Conference, United Association of Labor Educators/AFL-CIO Conferences 1998, 1999, 2000, 2001.

Index

About the Author

David B. Reynolds is an activist, educator, and researcher in the Labor Studies Center at Wayne State University. He is a leader in the living wage movement—both nationally and in Michigan. Working in partnership with the Association of Community Organizations for Reform Now (ACORN), he authored *Living Wage Campaigns: An Activist's Guide to Building the Movement for Economic Justice* (2001). He headed two teams that researched the impact of Detroit's living wage law. Mr. Reynolds sits on the steering committee of several local living wage campaigns and has consulted and been interviewed nationally about living wage activism. In addition to his expertise in labor-community coalitions, Mr. Reynolds has helped unions develop worker-to-worker political mobilization programs. His *Democracy Unbound: Progressive Challenges to the Two Party System* (1997) explores grassroots progressive political organizing.